Frommer's®
Cancún, Cozumel & the Yucatán

My Yucatán

by David Baird

THE YUCATAN PENINSULA, TOGETHER WITH TABASCO AND CHIAPAS, is only a modest section of Mexico, but it offers almost all that makes this country special: beautiful beaches, mysterious ruins, thick jungles, tall mountains, and thriving Indian cultures. As with any part of Mexico, it has its own regional culture and cuisine. A trip here is not a substitute for a trip to central Mexico; rather it's a great way to get acquainted with the country.

Once I've had enough beach time (but how much is enough?), what I most like to do is rent a car and drive the back roads of the peninsula. Scattered about the area are the small villages of the Yucatek Maya, ruins, colonial convents, and many of those strange natural features known as cenotes, natural wells where water from underground rivers rises up close to the surface. If I have more time, I take a break from the lowland heat and head for the cool mountains in the central highlands of Chiapas. Here, myriad Indian villages surround the colonial city of San Cristóbal de las Casas, and each boasts a different handicrafts specialty, whether it's weaving, pottery, or embroidery.

In these pages, you'll see photos that show the Yucatán at its best—from the jungle ruins of Palenque to the eco-friendly water park at Xel-Ha to the beachfront megaresorts of Cancún.

SNORKELING (left) is my favorite watersport, and I particularly love exploring the Yucatán coast. It has the second longest reef in the world and offers plenty of places to dive. For beginners, there are also numerous sheltered areas where swimmers are protected from the currents and the waves. Here you see a snorkeler in Chankanaab National Park.

The gorgeous, natural lagoon at **XEL-HA MARINE PARK (above)** is the park's main attraction. This ecological park was established to preserve the area's beauty and provide access to visitors. You can catch a ride on a miniature train up to the innermost part of the lagoon and then drift or paddle down with your snorkel gear to where it meets the sea. Along the way you'll see lots of fish and sea life, and caves and cenotes.

It's always fun to see kids dress up on holidays in the local garb. These children are dancing around a **MAYPOLE IN MERIDA (above)**.

Mexicans have a genius for working with their hands. When given the opportunity, many artisans shine, but more often they produce the everyday goods that demand dictates. I try to seek out the less commonplace work that arises from the need for personal expression. This **MAYA VENDOR IN SAN CRISTOBAL DE LAS CASAS (right)** is selling nontraditional garments to tourists. She may have other, more interesting pieces, but the highland Maya are often difficult to engage in conversation.

I always enjoy visiting **MARKETS** when I have the chance, even when I'm not buying anything. You see a variety of produce and foodstuffs in most of them that would put a supermarket to shame. They also serve as the place where friends and neighbors meet, eat, and chat with each other about things of interest, such as local events and the latest scandals.

Chiapas is wetter than the Yucatán peninsula, and the water mostly stays above ground. There are some beautiful spots not far from Palenque where you can go for a refreshing swim in lush surroundings. This one, known as **AGUA AZUL (left),** is one of them. I enjoy it most when 3 or 4 days have passed without rain and the water does actually get blue, as its name suggests.

Of the many cenotes I've seen, **CENOTE DZITNUP IN VALLADOLID (above)** is one of the most beautiful. It has retained its ceiling, as many do, and the roots of trees have penetrated the chamber and grown down to the water. The contrast between the bright, hot outside and the cool, dark chamber is almost otherworldly. It's no wonder that the Maya considered cenotes sacred places.

The megalithic **OLMEC HEADS (above)** are some of the most intriguing pre-Colombian artifacts. Most are in out-of-the-way places like Villahermosa and Xalapa, but this modern reproduction can be found at Chankanaab National Park on the island of Cozumel.

Like much of Chichén Itzá's art and architecture, this statue of **CHACMOOL (right)** at the Temple of the Warriors reflects a style that originated in the faraway central highlands of Mexico. That it displays little or no Maya influence has raised questions regarding the true rulers of the city.

There is no place in Mexico that fills me with more awe than Palenque, a breathtaking city of the classic Maya period. The jungle setting, the rich iconography, the elegant geometrical shape of the temple platforms—nowhere else even comes close.

This building, the **TEMPLE OF THE INSCRIPTIONS** is named for the great stone hieroglyphic panels that were found inside. It also houses the tomb of the 7th-century Maya king Pacal.

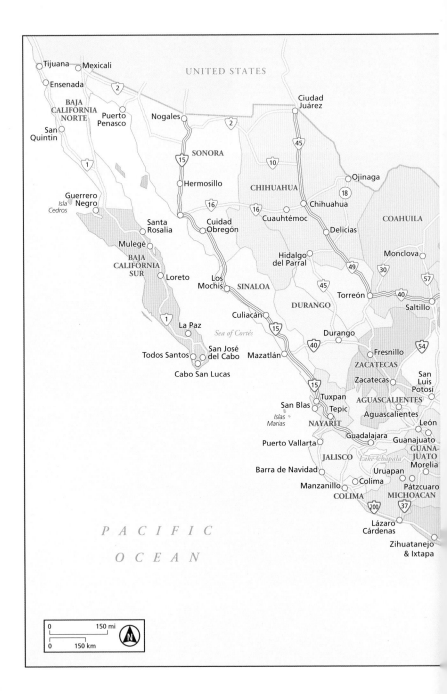

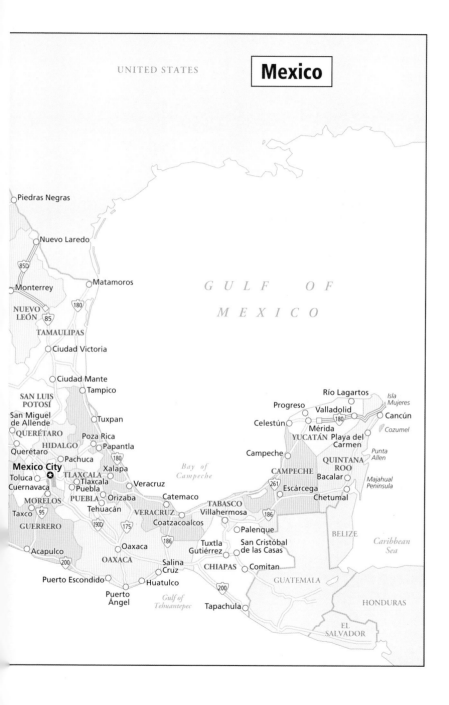

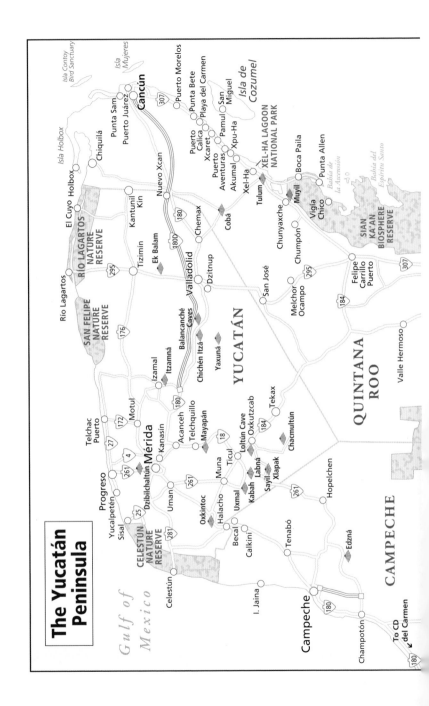

The Yucatán Peninsula

Gulf of Mexico

YUCATÁN

QUINTANA ROO

CAMPECHE

Isla Contoy Bird Sanctuary
Isla Mujeres
Isla Holbox

Bahía de la Ascensión
Bahía del Espíritu Santo

SIAN KA'AN BIOSPHERE RESERVE

RÍO LAGARTOS NATURE RESERVE
SAN FELIPE NATURE RESERVE
CELESTÚN NATURE RESERVE

Punta Sam
Cancún
Puerto Juárez
Puerto Morelos
Punta Bete
Playa del Carmen
San Miguel
Isla de Cozumel
Puerto Calica
Xcaret
Pamul
Xpu-Ha
Puerto Aventuras
Akumal
Xel-Ha
XEL-HA LAGOON NATIONAL PARK
Tulum
Boca Paila
Punta Allen
Chiquilá
El Cuyo
Holbox
Nuevo Xcan
307
Kantunil Kin
Muyil
Vigía Chico
Chumpón
Chunyaxche
Río Lagartos
Tizimín
Ek Balam
Chemax
180
Cobá
San José
Melchor Ocampo
Felipe Carrillo Puerto
295
184
307
295
Dzitnup
Valladolid
180D
176
Balancanché Caves
Chichén Itzá
Yaxuná
Izamal
Itzamná
Valle Hermoso
Telchac Puerto
Motul
172
27
Progreso
Dzibilchaltún
Mérida
Kanasín
Acanceh
Telchaquillo
Mayapán
180
Tekax
Yucalpetén
Sisal
267
4
Umán
Oxkintoc
Muna
Ticul
18
Loltún Cave
Oxkutzcab
184
Chacmultún
Halachó
Uxmal
Kabah
Sayil
Labná
Xlapak
Hopelchen
25
Dzibilchaltún
281
Becal
Calkiní
Tenabó
261
Edzná
I. Jaina
Celestún
Champotón
Campeche
180
To CD del Carmen
180

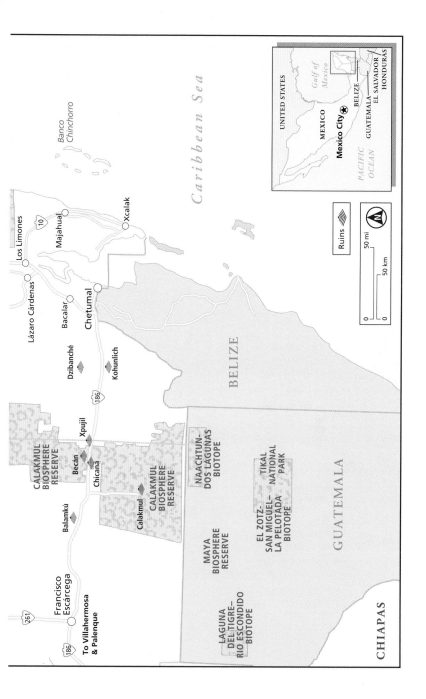

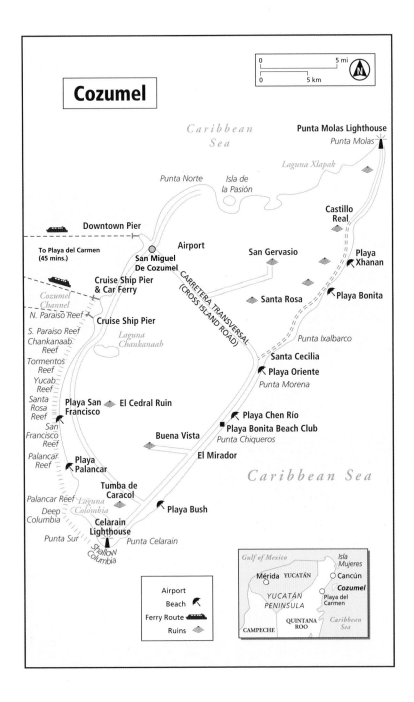

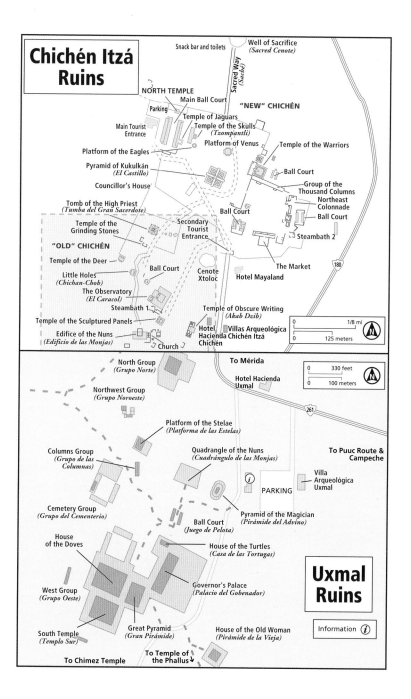

Chichén Itzá Ruins

Snack bar and toilets

Well of Sacrifice
(Sacred Cenote)

Sacred Way
(Sacbé)

NORTH TEMPLE

Main Ball Court

Parking

"NEW" CHICHÉN

Temple of Jaguars

Main Tourist Entrance

Temple of the Skulls
(Tzompantli)

Platform of Venus

Temple of the Warriors

Platform of the Eagles

Pyramid of Kukulkán
(El Castillo)

Ball Court

Councillor's House

Group of the
Thousand Columns

Tomb of the High Priest
(Tumba del Gran Sacerdote)

Northeast
Colonnade

Ball Court

Ball Court

Temple of the
Grinding Stones

Secondary
Tourist
Entrance

Steambath 2

"OLD" CHICHÉN

Temple of the Deer

Little Holes
(Chichan-Chob)

Ball Court

Cenote
Xtoloc

The Market

Hotel Mayaland

The Observatory
(El Caracol)

Steambath 1

Temple of the Sculptured Panels

Temple of Obscure Writing
(Akab Dzib)

Edifice of the Nuns
(Edificio de las Monjas)

Hotel
Hacienda Chichén
Chichén

Villas Arqueológica
Chichén Itzá

Church

180

| 0 | | 1/8 mi |
| 0 | 125 meters | |

To Mérida

| 0 | 330 feet |
| 0 | 100 meters |

North Group
(Grupo Norte)

Hotel Hacienda
Uxmal

Northwest Group
(Grupo Noroeste)

261

Platform of the Stelae
(Plataforma de las Estelas)

Columns Group
(Grupo de las
Columnas)

Quadrangle of the Nuns
(Cuadrángulo de las Monjas)

To Puuc Route &
Campeche

Villa
Arqueológica
Uxmal

PARKING

Cemetery Group
(Grupo del Cementerio)

Ball Court
(Juego de Pelota)

Pyramid of the Magician
(Pirámide del Advino)

House
of the Doves

House of the Turtles
(Casa de las Tortugas)

West Group
(Grupo Oeste)

Governor's Palace
(Palacio del Gobenador)

Uxmal Ruins

South Temple
(Templo Sur)

Great Pyramid
(Gran Pirámide)

House of the Old Woman
(Pirámide de la Vieja)

Information (i)

To Chimez Temple

To Temple of
the Phallus ↓

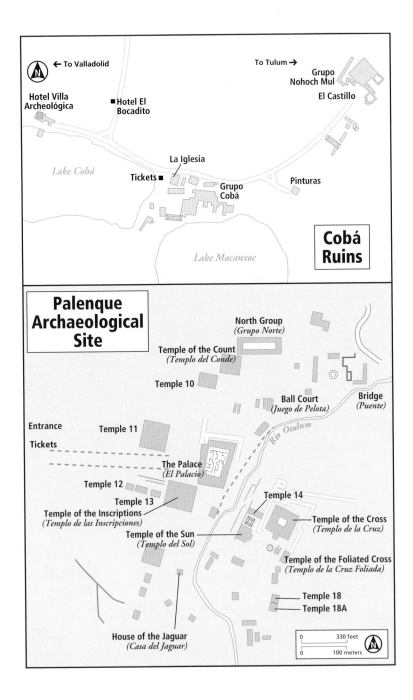

Cobá Ruins

← To Valladolid

To Tulum →

Grupo Nohoch Mul

El Castillo

Hotel Villa Archeológica

■ Hotel El Bocadito

Lake Cobá

La Iglesia

Tickets ■

Grupo Cobá

Pinturas

Lake Macanxoc

Palenque Archaeological Site

North Group *(Grupo Norte)*

Temple of the Count *(Templo del Conde)*

Temple 10

Ball Court *(Juego de Pelota)*

Bridge *(Puente)*

Entrance

Tickets

Temple 11

Río Otulum

The Palace *(El Palacio)*

Temple 12

Temple 14

Temple 13

Temple of the Cross *(Templo de la Cruz)*

Temple of the Inscriptions *(Templo de las Inscripciones)*

Temple of the Sun *(Templo del Sol)*

Temple of the Foliated Cross *(Templo de la Cruz Foliada)*

Temple 18

Temple 18A

House of the Jaguar *(Casa del Jaguar)*

0   330 feet
0   100 meters

Frommer's®

Cancún, Cozumel & the Yucatán

2009

by David Baird & Juan Cristiano

Here's what the critics say about Frommer's:

"Amazingly easy to use. Very portable, very complete."
—*Booklist*

"Detailed, accurate, and easy-to-read information for all price ranges."
—*Glamour Magazine*

"Hotel information is close to encyclopedic."
—*Des Moines Sunday Register*

"Frommer's Guides have a way of giving you a real feel for a place."
—*Knight Ridder Newspapers*

WILEY

Wiley Publishing, Inc.

About the Authors

A writer, editor, and translator, **David Baird** has lived several years in different parts of Mexico. Now based in Austin, Texas, he spends as much time in Mexico as possible. A former resident of Mexico City, Los Angeles native **Juan Cristiano** has written extensively about destinations in Mexico and Latin America, the United States, and Western Europe.

Published by:

Wiley Publishing, Inc.

111 River St.
Hoboken, NJ 07030-5774

ISBN 978-0-470-30628-4
Editor: Melinda Quintero
Production Editor: Jonathan Scott
Cartographer: Liz Puhl
Photo Editor: Richard Fox
Production by Wiley Indianapolis Composition Services

Front cover photo: Swimming beachside in Cancún.
Back cover photo: Maya god Chac Mool.

For information on our other products and services or to obtain technical support, please contact our Customer Care Department within the U.S. at 800/762-2974, outside the U.S. at 317/572-3993 or fax 317/572-4002.

Wiley also publishes its books in a variety of electronic formats. Some content that appears in print may not be available in electronic formats.

Manufactured in the United States of America

5 4 3 2 1

Contents

1 The Best of Cancún, Cozumel & the Yucatán   4

by David Baird & Juan Cristiano

2 The Yucatán, Tabasco & Chiapas in Depth   16

by David Baird

3 Planning Your Trip to the Yucatán, Tabasco & Chiapas   41

by Juan Cristiano

4   Suggested Yucatán Itineraries   79

by David Baird

5   Cancún   88

by Juan Cristiano

6   Isla Mujeres & Cozumel   118

by David Baird

7   The Caribbean Coast: The Riviera Maya, Including Playa del Carmen & the Costa Maya   149

by David Baird

8   Mérida, Chichén Itzá & the Maya Interior   193

by David Baird

9   Tabasco & Chiapas   250

by David Baird

Appendix A: Fast Facts, Toll-Free Numbers & Websites   285

Appendix B: Survival Spanish   293

Index   301

List of Maps

An Invitation to the Reader

In researching this book, we discovered many wonderful places—hotels, restaurants, shops, and more. We're sure you'll find others. Please tell us about them, so we can share the information with your fellow travelers in upcoming editions. If you were disappointed with a recommendation, we'd love to know that, too. Please write to:

Frommer's Cancún, Cozumel & the Yucatán 2009
Wiley Publishing, Inc. • 111 River St. • Hoboken, NJ 07030-5774

An Additional Note

Please be advised that travel information is subject to change at any time—and this is especially true of prices. We therefore suggest that you write or call ahead for confirmation when making your travel plans. The authors, editors, and publisher cannot be held responsible for the experiences of readers while traveling. Your safety is important to us, however, so we encourage you to stay alert and be aware of your surroundings. Keep a close eye on cameras, purses, and wallets, all favorite targets of thieves and pickpockets.

Other Great Guides for Your Trip:

Frommer's Cancún & the Yucatán Day by Day
Frommer's Portable Cancún
Frommer's Mexico 2009
Frommer's Spanish PhraseFinder & Dictionary
Pauline Frommer's Cancún & the Yucatán

Frommer's Star Ratings, Icons & Abbreviations

Every hotel, restaurant, and attraction listing in this guide has been ranked for quality, value, service, amenities, and special features using a **star-rating system.** In country, state, and regional guides, we also rate towns and regions to help you narrow down your choices and budget your time accordingly. Hotels and restaurants are rated on a scale of zero (recommended) to three stars (exceptional). Attractions, shopping, nightlife, towns, and regions are rated according to the following scale: zero stars (recommended), one star (highly recommended), two stars (very highly recommended), and three stars (must-see).

In addition to the star-rating system, we also use **eight feature icons** that point you to the great deals, in-the-know advice, and unique experiences that separate travelers from tourists. Throughout the book, look for:

Finds	Special finds—those places only insiders know about
Fun Fact	Fun facts—details that make travelers more informed and their trips more fun
Kids	Best bets for kids and advice for the whole family
Moments	Special moments—those experiences that memories are made of
Overrated	Places or experiences not worth your time or money
Tips	Insider tips—great ways to save time and money
Value	Great values—where to get the best deals
Warning	Warning—traveler's advisories are usually in effect

The following **abbreviations** are used for credit cards:

AE	American Express	DISC	Discover	V	Visa
DC	Diners Club	MC	MasterCard		

Frommers.com

Now that you have this guidebook to help you plan a great trip, visit our website at **www.frommers.com** for additional travel information on more than 4,000 destinations. We update features regularly to give you instant access to the most current trip-planning information available. At Frommers.com, you'll find scoops on the best airfares, lodging rates, and car rental bargains. You can even book your travel online through our reliable travel booking partners. Other popular features include:

- Online updates of our most popular guidebooks
- Vacation sweepstakes and contest giveaways
- Newsletters highlighting the hottest travel trends
- Podcasts, interactive maps, and up-to-the-minute events listings
- Opinionated blog entries by Arthur Frommer himself
- Online travel message boards with featured travel discussions

What's New in Cancún, Cozumel & the Yucatán

by David Baird & Juan Cristiano

The news out of Mexico isn't so bad these days. The economy is chugging along at a decent clip, inflation remains at historic lows, and the government continues to invest substantial amounts in the nation's infrastructure. The Yucatán continues to receive its share of this investment with several road improvements along the coast and in the interior. The regional economy is booming with lots of new construction and a proposed new airport for Tulum, though this remains a couple of years away.

For the American traveler, Mexico remains a budget destination, as the dollar continues steady against the peso even while it falls against other currencies. For Brits and Canadians, Mexico is an outright bargain. The Caribbean coast is more expensive than the rest of Mexico, but you can still find lodging and food bargains.

Public safety remains a challenge, with the government locked in combat against strong drug syndicates. But most of this conflict is occurring far from the Yucatán and shouldn't keep anyone from vacationing here.

Mexico is now home to one of the "New 7 Wonders of the World." The most famous Maya temple city, Chichén Itzá, received the designation in July 2007.

PLANNING YOUR TRIP TO MEXICO

New passport requirements are in effect for all travelers to and from the United States, which includes visitors who only have a layover in the U.S. Those traveling by **air** to the United States are required to present a passport or other valid travel document to enter or re-enter the United States. This goes for all U.S. citizens, as well. **For travel by land and sea:** U.S. citizens need to present either (a) a passport, passport card (available in spring 2008), or WHTI-compliant document; or (b) a government-issued photo I.D., such as a driver's license, along with proof of citizenship, such as a birth certificate. Beginning June 1, 2009, the U.S. government will implement the full requirements of the land and sea phase of WHTI. The proposed rules require most U.S. citizens entering the United States at sea or land ports of entry to have a passport, passport card, or WHTI-compliant document.

The Passport Card   U.S. citizens living in the border region can apply for a new, limited-use, wallet-size passport card. It will only be valid for land and sea travel between the U.S. and Canada, Mexico, the Caribbean region, and Bermuda. For more information, log on to http://travel.state.gov.

TAX REFUND   International tourists to Mexico can now make tax-free purchases while vacationing, thanks to a law passed by Mexico's Congress. The law grants international visitors a full refund of the tax added to purchases if the buyer adheres to certain criteria. The merchandise must be purchased in Mexico and verified by airport or seaport Customs, and be verified with a receipt presented at time of departure to be worth at least 1,200 Mexican pesos (approximately US$110/£61 at current exchange rates). Reimbursement to tourists will be contingent upon any added costs that a possible return may generate.

CANCUN   Cancún has been fully rehabilitated following the devastating Hurricane Wilma of 2005 and in many ways is better than before. But this region has not escaped continued run-ins with Mother Nature: 2007 was another busy hurricane season. Thankfully, the dangerous category 5 Hurricane Dean that people so feared passed south of Cancún and the Riviera Maya, avoiding a direct hit on the tourist resorts and leaving the region's infrastructure intact. However, there was some beach erosion to the south of Cancun, including in Playa del Carmen.

In light of Cancún's post-Hurricane Wilma face-lift, tourism officials are continuously working to make the resort more attractive to upscale travelers and soften its reputation as a wild spring break destination. Regulations—such as prohibiting more than four people sharing a room—have been put in place to restrict spring break and student tour groups. The majority of hotels damaged by the hurricane took the opportunity to upgrade their facilities and redecorate their rooms, helping to create a new and improved Cancún.

Aqua Cancún (© **800/343-7821;** www.fiestamericana.com) re-opened in time for the 2008 tourist season after it was completely destroyed by Hurricane Wilma in 2005. Water is the ever-present theme of this beautiful oceanfront resort, which offers eight extraordinary pools with chill-out music in the background and watersports activities at the beach. Located across from La Isla shopping center, the stylish resort also features an unforgettable spa, gourmet cuisine, and luxurious rooms and suites.

ISLA MUJERES   This small island remains a laid-back resort of small hotels, despite the recent construction of multistory condo towers on the north side of town. **Palace Resorts** (www.palace resorts.com) has opened up a small all-inclusive on the landward side about in the middle of the island. I wasn't able to visit because it hadn't opened yet, but I'm not sure about the reasoning behind putting an all-inclusive on this island. With inexpensive hotels and restaurants in town, within easy reach of the beach, what need is there for an all-inclusive?

COZUMEL   The town of San Miguel is busy at work doing some urban beautification projects, which had a couple of streets closed when I was last there. Word is that the town will continue to do this off and on during low seasons, repaving streets and adding trees and shrubs in the areas that see the most visitors.

The **Reef Club** all-inclusive resort is going to be converted into a Wyndham (www.wyndhamcozumel.com) property, though the ownership will remain local.

THE RIVIERA MAYA Mayakoba (www.mayakoba.com), the new golf course resort development between Playa and Puerto Morelos, continues with recent openings. The developers attracted a stellar lineup of resorts including The Fairmount, Rosewood, and Banyan Tree—all have spas and border a grand golf course designed by Greg Norman. The Fairmount has been open for a while. The Rosewood opened in 2008, and the other resorts are to open later in the year.

PLAYA DEL CARMEN   I'm sorry to say that the continued growth of condos in town has meant the demise of a few more hotels. One of my favorites, the Shangri-la Caribe, has closed, and so has the budget hotel Treetops. With all this new development, Playa has been having a hard time controlling growth and keeping the feel of an alternative resort.

AKUMAL   The project of widening the coastal highway (Hwy. 307) to four lanes all the way to Tulum continues making progress. The highway is now four lanes all the way to Akumal. Several of the turn-offs have been improved as well.

TULUM   Land ownership problems continue to plague the coast along Tulum. All the hotels I have listed in the book have secure property titles, but some hotels operating on this coast do not and might be closed in the future.

CHICHEN ITZA   The small chain of hotels Villas Arqueológicas, which was operated by Club Med and has properties at Chichén Itzá, Uxmal, and Cobá, was sold to a Mexican chain of resorts called Islander Collection. Some of the contact information changed. Check the website www.islandercollection.com for full details.

VILLAHERMOSA   This low-lying capital city of the state of Tabasco, situated on the Gulf coast between Oaxaca and Chiapas, had horrendous flooding in 2007 and, at the time of this writing, hasn't yet fully recovered. The Museo Regional de Antropología will most likely be closed until early 2009, but the Parque Museo La Venta—the park with the megalithic Olmec sculptures—has reopened.

1

The Best of Cancún, Cozumel & the Yucatán

by David Baird & Juan Cristiano

The Yucatán Peninsula welcomes more visitors than any other part of Mexico. Its tremendous variety attracts every kind of traveler with an unrivaled mix of sophisticated resorts, rustic inns, ancient Maya culture, exquisite beaches, and exhilarating adventures. Between the two of us, we've logged thousands of miles crisscrossing the peninsula, and these are our personal favorites—the best places to visit, the best hotels and restaurants, plus must-see, one-of-a-kind experiences.

1 The Best Beach Vacations

- **Cancún:** In terms of sheer beauty, Cancún has always been the site of Mexico's most alluring beaches. The powdery, white-sand beaches are complemented by water the color of a Technicolor dream; it's so clear that you can see through to the coral reefs below. It's also one of the world's most popular entertainment destinations. Cancún offers Mexico's widest selection of beachfront resorts, with more restaurants, nightlife, and activities than any other resort destination in the country. See chapter 5.

- **Isla Mujeres:** If laid-back is what you're after, this idyllic island affords peaceful, small-town beach life at its best. Most accommodations are small, inexpensive inns, with a few one-of-a-kind, luxury places tossed in. Bike—or take a golf cart—around the island to explore rocky coves and sandy beaches, or focus your tanning efforts on the wide beachfront of Playa Norte. Here you'll find calm waters and *palapa* restaurants, where you can have fresh-caught fish for lunch. If all that tranquillity starts to get to you, you're only a ferry ride away from the action in Cancún. See chapter 6.

- **Cozumel:** It may not have lots of big, sandy beaches, but Cozumel has something the mainland doesn't: the calm, flat waters of the sheltered western shore. It's so calm that it's like swimming in a pool, only this pool has lots of fish, so take your snorkeling mask even if you don't plan to do any diving. See chapter 6.

- **Playa del Carmen:** This is one of our absolute favorite Mexican beach vacations. Stylish and hip, Playa del Carmen has a beautiful beach and an eclectic assortment of small hotels, inns, and cabañas. The social scene focuses on the beach by day and the pedestrian-only Quinta Avenida (Fifth Avenue) by night, with its fun assortment of restaurants, clubs, sidewalk cafes, and shops. You're also close to the coast's major attractions, including nature parks, ruins, and cenotes (sinkholes or natural wells).

Enjoy it while it's still a manageable size. See chapter 7.

- **Tulum:** Fronting some of the best beaches on the entire coast, Tulum's small *palapa* hotels offer guests a little slice of paradise far from the crowds and megaresorts. The bustling town lies inland; at the coast, things are quiet and remain so because all these small hotels must generate their own electricity. If you can pull yourself away from the beach, there are ruins to marvel at and a vast nature preserve to explore. See chapter 7.

2 The Best Cultural Experiences

- **Exploring the Inland Yucatán Peninsula:** Travelers who venture only to the Yucatán's resorts and cities miss the rock-walled inland villages, where women wear colorful embroidered dresses and life seems to proceed as though the modern world (with the exception of highways) did not exist. The adventure of seeing newly uncovered ruins, deep in jungle settings, is not to be missed. See chapter 8.

- **Street & Park Entertainment** (Mérida): Few cities have so vibrant a street scene as Mérida. Throughout the week you can catch music and dance performances in plazas about town, but on Sunday, Mérida really gets going—streets are closed off, food stalls spring up everywhere, and you can enjoy a book fair, a flea market, comedy acts, band concerts, and dance groups. At night, the main plaza is the place to be, with people dancing to mambos and rumbas in the street in front of the town hall. See chapter 8.

- **San Cristóbal de las Casas:** The city of San Cristóbal is a living museum, with 16th-century colonial architecture and pre-Hispanic native influences. The highland Maya live in surrounding villages and arrive daily in town wearing colorful handmade clothing. A visit to the villages is a window into another world, giving visitors a glimpse of traditional Indian dress, religious customs, churches, and ceremonies. See chapter 9.

- **Regional Cuisine:** A trip to the Yucatán allows for a culinary tour of some of Mexico's finest foods. Don't miss specialties such as *pollo* or *cochinita pibil* (chicken or pork in savory *achiote* sauce), great seafood dishes, the many styles of *tamal* found throughout Chiapas and the Yucatán, and Caribbean-influenced staples such as fried bananas, black beans, and yucca root. For a glossary of popular regional dishes, see Appendix B.

3 The Best Archaeological Sites

- **Calakmul:** Of the many elegantly built Maya cities of the Río Bec area, in the lower Yucatán, Calakmul is the broadest in scope and design. It's also one of the hardest to reach—about 48km (30 miles) from the Guatemalan border and completely surrounded by jungle (actually, the Calakmul Biological Reserve). Calakmul is a walled city with the tallest pyramid in the Yucatán—a city whose primary inhabitants are the trees that populate the plazas. Go now, while it remains infrequently visited. See "Side Trips to Maya Ruins from Chetumal" in chapter 7.

Mexico

UNITED STATES

Tijuana Mexicali
Ensenada
BAJA
CALIFORNIA
NORTE   Puerto
Penasco   Nogales
San
Quintin

Ciudad
Juárez
Ojinaga

SONORA

CHIHUAHUA
Chihuahua
Hermosillo   Cuauhtémoc
Guaymas   Delicias

COAHUILA

Isla
Cedros   Guerrero
Negro   Ciudad
Obregón   Jiménez   Monclova
Santa
Rosalia   Hidalgo
Mulegé   del Parral
BAJA
CALIFORNIA   Los
SUR   Mochis   Torreón   Saltillo
Loreto   SINALOA
DURANGO
Culiacán
La Paz   Durango
Fresnillo

Todos Santos   San José   Mazatlán   ZACATECAS
del Cabo   Zacatecas   San
Cabo San Lucas   Luis
Potos

Tuxpan   AGUASCALIENTES
San Blas   Tepic   Aguascalientes   León
Islas   NAYARIT   Guanajuato
Marias   Guadalajara   GUANA
Puerto Vallarta   JUATO
JALISCO   Lake Chápala   Morelia
Barra de Navidad   Uruapan
Manzanillo   Colima   Pátzcuaro
COLIMA   MICHOACAN

Lázaro
Cárdenas
Zihuatanejo
& Ixtapa

PACIFIC
OCEAN

Gulf of California (Sea of Cortés)

0   150 mi
0   150 km

- **Tulum:** Some dismiss Tulum as less important than other ruins in the Yucatán Peninsula, but this seaside Maya fortress is still inspiring. The stark contrast of its crumbling stone walls against the clear turquoise ocean just beyond is an extraordinary sight. See "Tulum, Punta Allen & Sian Ka'an" in chapter 7.

- **Uxmal:** No matter how many times we see Uxmal, the splendor of its stone carvings remains awe-inspiring. A stone rattlesnake undulates across the facade of the Nunnery complex, and 103 masks of Chaac—the rain god—project from the Governor's Palace. See "The Ruins of Uxmal" in chapter 8.

- **Chichén Itzá:** Stand beside the giant serpent head at the foot of the El Castillo pyramid and marvel at the architects and astronomers who positioned the building so precisely that shadow and sunlight form a serpent's body slithering from peak to the earth at each equinox (Mar 21 and Sept 21). See "The Ruins of Chichén Itzá" in chapter 8.

- **Ek Balam:** In recent years, this is the site where some of Mexico's most astounding archaeological discoveries have been made. Ek Balam's main pyramid is taller than Chichén Itzá's, and it holds a sacred doorway bordered with elaborate stucco figures of priests and kings and rich iconography. See "Ek Balam: Dark Jaguar" in chapter 8.

- **Palenque:** The ancient builders of these structures carved histories in stone that scholars have only recently deciphered. Imagine the magnificent ceremony in A.D. 683 when King Pacal was buried deep inside his pyramid—his tomb unspoiled until its discovery in 1952. See "Palenque" in chapter 9.

4 The Best Active Vacations

- **Scuba Diving in Cozumel & Along the Yucatán's Caribbean Coast:** The coral reefs off the island, Mexico's premier diving destination, are among the top five dive spots in the world. The Yucatán's coastal reef, part of the planet's second-largest reef system, affords excellent diving all along the coast. Especially beautiful is the Chinchorro Reef, lying 32km (20 miles) offshore from Majahual or Xcalak. Diving from Isla Mujeres is also quite spectacular. See chapters 6 and 7.

- **Fly-Fishing off the Punta Allen & Majahual Peninsulas:** Serious anglers will enjoy the challenge of fly-fishing the saltwater flats and lagoons on the protected sides of these peninsulas. See "Tulum, Punta Allen & Sian Ka'an" and "Majahual, Xcalak & the Chinchorro Reef" in chapter 7.

- **Cenote Diving on the Yucatán Mainland:** Dive into the clear depths of the Yucatán's cenotes for an interesting twist on underwater exploration. The Maya considered the cenotes sacred—and their vivid colors do indeed seem otherworldly. Most are between Playa del Carmen and Tulum, and dive shops in these areas regularly run trips for experienced divers. For recommended dive shops, see "Cozumel" in chapter 6, and "Playa del Carmen" and "South of Playa del Carmen" in chapter 7.

- **Birding:** The Yucatán Peninsula, Tabasco, and Chiapas are ornithological paradises. Two very special places are Isla Contoy, with more than 70 species of birds as well as a host of marine and animal life (chapter 7), and the Huitepec Cloud Forest, with its flocks of migratory species (see p. 273).

- **An Excursion to Bonampak & Yax-chilán:** Bonampak and Yaxchilán—two remote, jungle-surrounded Maya sites along the Usumacinta River—are now accessible by car and motorboat. The experience could well be the highlight of any trip. See "Road Trips from San Cristóbal" in chapter 9.

5 The Best Places to Get Away from It All

- **Isla Mujeres:** If there's one island in Mexico that guarantees a respite from stress, it's Isla Mujeres. You'll find an ample selection of hotels and restaurants, and they're as laid-back as their patrons. Here life moves along in pure *mañana* mode, with little sign of the bustling commercialism that exists just across the bay. Visitors stretch out and doze beneath shady palms or languidly stroll about. In fact, Isla Mujeres feels worlds removed from Cancún, yet remains comfortably close for those who choose to reconnect. See "Isla Mujeres" in chapter 6.

- **The Yucatán's Riviera Maya:** Away from the busy resort of Cancún, a string of quiet getaways, including Paamul, Punta Bete, and a portion of Xpu-ha, offer tranquillity on beautiful beaches at low prices. See "North of Playa del Carmen" and "South of Playa del Carmen" in chapter 7.

- **Tulum:** Near the Tulum ruins, about two dozen beachside *palapa* inns offer some of the most peaceful getaways in the country. This stretch just might offer the best sandy beaches on the entire coast. Life here among the birds and coconut palms is decidedly unhurried. See "Tulum, Punta Allen & Sian Ka'an" in chapter 7.

- **Rancho Encantado Cottage Resort** (Lago Bacalar; ✆ **800/505-6292** in the U.S., or 983/101-3358; www.encantado.com): The attractive *casitas* are the best place to unwind at this resort, where hammocks stretch between trees. The hotel is on the shores of placid Lago (Lake) Bacalar, south of Cancún near Chetumal, and there's nothing around for miles. But if you want adventure, you can head out to the lake in a kayak, follow a birding trail, or take an excursion to Belize and the intriguing Maya ruins on the nearby Río Bec ruin route. See p. 183.

- **Hotel Eco Paraíso Xixim** (Celestún; ✆ **988/916-2100;** www.ecoparaiso.com): In these crowded times, space is a luxury that's getting harder to come by. Space is precisely what makes this place so great: Fifteen bungalows and 5km (3 miles) of beach bordering a coconut plantation. Throw in a good restaurant, a pool, and a couple of hammocks, and you have that rare combination of comfort and isolation. See p. 217.

- **Hacienda San José Cholul** (✆ **800/325-3589** in the U.S. and Canada; www.luxurycollection.com): Operated by Starwood Hotels, this hacienda is only an hour east of the bustling city of Mérida, toward Izamal, but it feels like another world. The quiet, unhurried manner of both guests and staff, and the beautiful tropical surroundings make it the perfect place to recoup some of the silence and slow time lost to the modern world. See "Haciendas & Hotels" on p. 210.

6 The Best Museums

- **Museo de la Cultura Maya** (Chetumal; ⓒ **983/832-6838**): This modern museum, one of the best in the country, explores Maya archaeology, architecture, history, and mythology. It has interactive exhibits and a glass floor that allows visitors to walk above replicas of Maya sites. See p. 185.
- **Museo Regional de Antropología** (Mérida; ⓒ **999/923-0557**): Housed in the Palacio Cantón, one of the most beautiful 19th-century mansions in the city, this museum showcases local archaeology and anthropological studies in handsome exhibits. See p. 205.
- **Museo Regional de Antropología Carlos Pellicer Cámara** (Villahermosa; ⓒ **993/312-6344**): This anthropology museum addresses Mexican history in the form of objects found at archaeological sites, with particular emphasis on the pre-Hispanic peoples of the Gulf coast region. See p. 252.
- **Parque–Museo La Venta** (Villahermosa; ⓒ **993/314-1652**): The Olmec, considered Mexico's mother culture, are the subject of this park/museum, which features the magnificent stone remains that were removed from the La Venta site not far away. Stroll through a jungle setting where tropical birds alight, and examine the giant carved stone heads of the mysterious Olmec. See p. 254.

7 The Best Shopping

Some tips on bargaining: Although haggling over prices in markets is expected and part of the fun, don't try to browbeat the vendor or bad-mouth the goods. Vendors won't bargain with people they consider disrespectful unless they are desperate to make a sale. Be insistent but friendly.

- **Resort Wear in Cancún:** Resort clothing—especially if you can find a sale—can be a bargain here. And the selection may be wider than what's available at home. Almost every mall on the island contains trendy boutiques that specialize in locally designed and imported clothing. The best is La Isla Shopping Center. See "Shopping" in chapter 5.
- **Duty-Free in Cancún:** If you're looking for European perfume, fine watches, or other imported goods, you'll find the prices in Cancún's duty-free shops (at the major malls on the island and in downtown Cancún) hard to beat. See "Shopping" in chapter 5.

- **Quinta Avenida, Playa del Carmen:** This pedestrian-only street offers leisurely shopping at its best—no cars, no hassle. Simply stroll down the street and let your eye pick out objects of interest. Expect a good bit of merchandise popular with counterculture types, such as batik clothing and fabric, Guatemalan textiles, and inventive jewelry and artwork. But you'll also find quality Mexican handicrafts, premium tequilas, and Cuban cigars. See "Playa del Carmen" in chapter 7.
- **Mérida:** This is *the* marketplace for the Yucatán—the best place to buy hammocks, *guayaberas,* Panama hats, and Yucatecan *huipiles.* See "Exploring Mérida" in chapter 8.
- **San Cristóbal de las Casas:** Deep in the heart of the Maya highlands, San Cristóbal has shops, open plazas, and markets that feature the distinctive waist-loomed wool and cotton textiles of the region, as well as leather shoes, handsome pottery, and Guatemalan

textiles. Highland Maya Indians sell direct to tourists from their armloads of textiles, dolls, and attractive miniature likenesses of Subcomandante Marcos—complete with ski masks. See "San Cristóbal de las Casas" in chapter 9.

8 The Hottest Nightlife

Although, as expected, Cancún is the source of much of the Yucatán's nightlife, that resort city isn't the only place to have a good time after dark. Along the Caribbean coast, beachside dance floors with live bands and extended happy hours in seaside bars dominate the nightlife. Here are some favorite hot spots, from live music in hotel lobby bars to hip techno dance clubs.

- **Cancún:** Longstanding Cancún favorites **Carlos 'n' Charlie's** and **Dady'O** offer potent drinks, hot music, and wild (if sometimes sloppy) dance floors. For a more subdued setting, **La Madonna** is a fashionable martini bar and restaurant in the La Isla Shopping Village, while **Bling,** with its outdoor terrace overlooking the lagoon, is the city's most chic cocktail venue. See chapter 5.

- **Forum by the Sea:** This seaside entertainment center in Cancún has it all: a dazzling array of dance clubs, sports bars, fast food, and fine dining, with shops open late as well. You'll find plenty of familiar names here, including the Hard Rock Cafe and Rainforest Cafe. It's also the home of Cancún's hottest club, **CoCo Bongo,** which regularly packs in up to 3,000 revelers. See p. 116.

- **The City:** One of Cancún's hottest nightclubs, the City is a raging day-and-night club, offering a Beach Club with a wave machine for simulated surfing, a water slide and beach cabañas, a Terrace bar serving food and drinks, and the sizzling Club, at which the world's top DJs have spun through the night until the sun once again rises over the turquoise waters. This is truly a City that never sleeps. See p. 115.

- **Mambo Cafe:** This is no cafe; it's a hot Caribbean dance club with live bands from Cuba, the Dominican Republic, Puerto Rico, and Columbia dominating the scene. Come here to swing your salsa and merengue in a sexy tropical ambience. See p. 116.

- **Quinta Avenida (Playa del Carmen):** Stroll along lively, pedestrian-only Fifth Avenue to find the bar that's right for you. With live-music venues, tequila bars, sports bars, and cafes, you're sure to find something to fit your mood. See p. 160.

- **San Cristóbal de las Casas:** This city, small though it may be, has a live-music scene that can't be beat for fun and atmosphere. The bars and clubs are all within walking distance, and they're a real bargain. See "San Cristóbal de las Casas" in chapter 9.

9 The Most Luxurious Hotels

- **Royal** (Cancún; ✆ **800/760-0944** in the U.S., or 998/881-7340; www.real resorts.com.mx): Opened in 2007, The Royal is a stunning all-inclusive, adults-only resort in which luxury abounds, from the sprawling infinity pools and gorgeous beach to the gourmet restaurants and sophisticated spa. The elegant marble lobby looks out one side to the Caribbean and the other to the lagoon, and the guest suites offer every conceivable amenity, including two-person Jacuzzis. Guests in the top-category suites have access to BMW Mini Coopers. The all-inclusive package includes gourmet meals, premium drinks, and evening entertainment. See p. 99.

- **JW Marriott** (Cancún; ⓒ **800/223-6388** in the U.S., or 998/848-9600; www.jwmarriottcancun.com): This gorgeous resort affords elegance without pretense, combining classic and Caribbean styling with warm Mexican service. The inviting free-form infinity pool extends to the white-sand beach, and families feel just as comfortable here as romance-seeking couples. The hotel includes a spectacular 3,250-sq.-m (35,000-square-foot) spa. See p. 98.

- **Ritz-Carlton Cancún** (Cancún; ⓒ **800/241-3333** in the U.S., or 998/881-0808; www.ritzcarlton.com): For years, thick carpets, sparkling glass and brass, and rich mahogany have surrounded guests at this hotel, the standard-bearer of luxury in Cancún. The service is impeccable, leaving guests with an overall sense of pampered relaxation. See p. 99.

- **Presidente InterContinental Cozumel** (Cozumel; ⓒ **800/327-0200** in the U.S., or 987/872-9500; www.intercontinentalcozumel.com): Surrounded by shady palms, this hotel also has the best beach on the island, right in front of Paraíso Reef. Favorite rooms are the deluxe beachside units with spacious patios and direct access to the beach—you can even order romantic in-room dining on the patios, complete with a trio to serenade you. See p. 144.

- **The Tides Riviera Maya** (north of Playa del Carmen; ⓒ **800/578-0281** in the U.S.; www.tidesrivieramaya.com): Small, secluded, and private, The Tides offers extraordinary personal service and spa treatments. Rooms are spread throughout the jungle, and there's a beautiful seaside pool and restaurant. See p. 155.

- **Maroma** (north of Playa del Carmen; ⓒ **866/454-9351** in the U.S.; www.maromahotel.com): You can't ask for a better setting for a resort than this beautiful stretch of Caribbean coast with palm trees and manicured gardens. You'll start to relax before you even take the first sip of your welcome cocktail. Service is very attentive, and the rooms are large and luxurious. See p. 155.

- **Paraíso de la Bonita** (north of Playa del Carmen; ⓒ **866/751-9175** in the U.S.; www.paraisodelabonita.com): Operated by InterContinental Hotels, this resort has a thalassotherapy spa, specializing in unique treatments that take their inspiration from the healing qualities of the ocean. The elaborate guest rooms are set among three pools and along an immaculately kept beach. See p. 155.

- **Hacienda Xcanatún** (outskirts of Mérida; ⓒ **888/883-3633** in the U.S.; www.xcanatun.com): With its large, boldly designed suites built with extravagance in mind, sprawling grounds, private spa, excellent restaurant, and ample staff, this hotel masters the difficult trick of being compact in size but expansive in offerings. See "Haciendas & Hotels" on p. 210.

10 The Best Inexpensive Inns

- **Rey del Caribe Hotel** (Cancún; ✆ **998/884-2028**; www.reycaribe. com): An inexpensive retreat in downtown Cancún, this hotel has considered every detail in its quest for an organic and environmentally friendly atmosphere. Set in a tropical garden, the Rey del Caribe provides sunny rooms, warm service, yoga and meditation classes, and healthful dining—all a welcome respite from party-hearty Cancún. See p. 102.
- **Hotel Colonial** (Campeche; ✆ **981/816-2222**): Okay, so it's not the most comfortable hotel in town, but it is by far the most endearing. It exudes character and a sense of timelessness that relaxes the spirit and transports

guests to an uncomplicated era. And for $25, it's a steal. See p. 236.
- **Casa San Juan Bed & Breakfast** (Mérida; ✆ **999/986-2937**; www. casasanjuan.com): This B&B, in a colonial house in Mérida's historic district, is the perfect combination of comfort and character at a great price. The guest rooms in the original building evoke an earlier time, while the modern rooms in back are quite large and border a lovely patio. See p. 212.
- **Hotel Real del Valle** (San Cristóbal; ✆ **967/678-0680**): In a city of inexpensive lodgings, this beats all the other bargain hotels for its combination of location, room size, and service. See p. 276.

11 The Best Unique Inns

- **Casa de los Sueños** (Isla Mujeres; ✆ **998/877-0651**; www.casadelos suenosresort.com): This B&B steeped in vibrant colors seems to descend into the cool Caribbean sea. Its small, but well-appointed, spa "Zenter," which is also accessible to nonguests, offers yoga classes, massages, and holistic spa treatments, which take place either outdoors or in a tranquil indoor space. See p. 126.
- **Hotel Villa Rolandi Gourmet & Beach Club** (Isla Mujeres; ✆ **998/877-0700**; www.villarolandi.com): In addition to being steps away from an exquisite private cove, a tranquil infinity pool, and Isla's finest restaurant, this intimate inn also pampers guests with every conceivable in-room amenity. Each unit even has a private Jacuzzi on the balcony and a shower that converts into a steam room. Guests are offered free transportation from Cancún via the hotel's private yacht. See p. 127.

- **Deseo Hotel + Lounge** (Playa del Carmen; ✆ **984/879-3620**; www. hoteldeseo.com): Perhaps it should be Hotel = Lounge. That might be an overstatement, but the lounge is at the center of everything, making Deseo the perfect fit for outgoing types who are into an alternative lodging experience. Enjoy a cocktail at the bar or on one of the large daybeds and chill to the modern, er, lounge music. See p. 161.
- **Casa Mexilio** (Mérida; ✆ **877/639-4546** in the U.S. and Canada, or 999/928-2505; www.casamexilio.com): An imaginative arrangement of rooms around a courtyard features a pool surrounded by a riot of tropical vegetation. The rooms are divided among different levels for privacy and are connected by stairs and catwalks. Breakfast here provides an extra incentive for getting out of bed. See p. 208.

- **Casa Na-Bolom** (San Cristóbal de las Casas; ✆ **967/678-1418;** www.nabolom.org): This unique house-museum is terrific for anthropology buffs. Built as a seminary in 1891, it was transformed into the headquarters of two anthropologists. The 12 guest rooms, named for surrounding villages, are decorated with local objects and textiles; all rooms have fireplaces and private bathrooms, and the room rate includes breakfast. See p. 270.

12 The Best Restaurants

Best doesn't necessarily mean most luxurious. Although some of the restaurants listed here are fancy affairs, others are simple places to get fine, authentic Yucatecan cuisine.

- **Gustino** (Cancún; ✆ **998/848-9600**): The JW Marriott's signature restaurant is a gourmand's paradise, with fresh seafood, steaks, and homemade pastas prepared in the open kitchen using classic Italian ingredients. The beautiful dining room makes this one of the city's most romantic places to dine. See p. 105.
- **Labná** (Ciudad Cancún; ✆ **998/892-3056**): Steep yourself in traditional Yucatecan culture at this downtown eatery, which showcases Maya cuisine and music. The Labná Special samples four of the region's best dishes, including baked suckling pig with guacamole. See p. 108.
- **Thai** (Cancún; ✆ **998/144-0364**): This enchanting Thai restaurant offers a handful of secluded tables in individual *palapas* over the lagoon. The waterfront setting provides a romantic backdrop to the classic and contemporary Thai cuisine. Plus, the restaurant's chill out lounge makes for a perfect before or after dinner drink. See p. 107.
- **100% Natural for *Licuados:*** This casual eatery serves terrific breakfasts and healthy snacks throughout the day. Come for one of the *licuados,* drinks made from fresh fruit mixed with water or milk. The chain offers a wide selection, including innovative mixtures such as the Cozumel (spinach, pineapple, and orange) and the Caligula (orange, pineapple, beet, celery, parsley, carrot, and lime juices)—a healthy indulgence. Cancún has several branches. See p. 108.
- **Casa Rolandi** (Isla Mujeres; ✆ **998/877-0700**): This exquisite restaurant attached to the Casa Rolandi boutique hotel serves the island's finest cuisine. The open-air establishment sits adjacent to the Caribbean and offers wonderful fresh fish, seafood, and pastas. See p. 129.
- **Cabaña del Pescador** (Cozumel; no phone): If you want an ideally seasoned, succulent lobster dinner, Cabaña del Pescador (Lobster House) is the place. If you want anything else, you're out of luck—lobster dinner, expertly prepared, is all it serves. When you've achieved perfection, why bother with anything else? See p. 145.
- **Prima** (Cozumel; ✆ **987/872-4242**): The Italian food here is fresh, fresh, fresh—from the hydroponically grown vegetables to the pasta and garlic bread. And it's all prepared after you walk in, most of it by owner Albert Domínguez, who concocts unforgettable shrimp fettuccine with pesto, crab ravioli with cream sauce, and crisp house salad in a chilled bowl. See p. 146.
- **Media Luna** (Playa del Carmen; ✆ **984/873-0526**): The inviting

atmosphere of this sidewalk cafe on Quinta Avenida is enough to lure you in. The expertly executed and innovative menu, together with great prices, makes it one of the top choices on the Caribbean coast. See p. 165.

- **Yaxché** (Playa del Carmen; *C* **984/ 873-2502**): No restaurant in the Yucatán explores the region's culinary traditions and use of local ingredients more than this one. Its menu presents several pleasant surprises and is a welcome relief from the standard offerings of most Yucatecan restaurants. See p. 163.

- **La Pigua** (Campeche; *C* **981/811-3365**): Campeche's regional specialty is seafood, and nowhere else will you find seafood like this. Mexican caviar, coconut-battered shrimp, and chiles stuffed with shark are just a few of the unique specialties. Thinking about La Pigua's pompano in a fine green herb sauce makes me want to start checking flight schedules. See p. 237.

2

The Yucatán, Tabasco & Chiapas in Depth

by David Baird

It's hard to believe that 35 years ago, the only people visiting the Yucatán were archeologists headed to the ruins and scuba divers going to Cozumel. All those miles of Caribbean coast just sat there alone, unappreciated and unvisited except for the occasional fisherman. The changes wrought by the creation and growth of Cancún on the Yucatán Peninsula and even distant Chiapas, all within the span of a single generation, have propelled the region from a forgotten backwater, to a major international holiday destination.

Tourism is now the big enchilada where before it was a mere afterthought. This change is most visible on the coast, where coconut plantations gave way to a long series of modern developments, one after the next, all the way south to Tulum and beyond. For the young Maya of the villages of the interior, this growth has meant new opportunities for work, the end of their isolation, and their first close contact with the modern world—and not just any aspect of the modern world, but specifically the modern world in vacation mode. What a culture shock it must have been to go from village society to vacation paradise!

Tourism has also moved inland, first to the major ruins—Chichén Itzá, Uxmal, and Palenque—and then, over time, to the ancient cities of the deep interior. These ruins are an intriguing wonder to behold, and it seems like every year more archeological discoveries are made. Some Maya ruins are just as newly discovered as some of the resorts on the coast are newly built.

Curiously, all this excavation and renovation has left small town life little changed. For those travelers that want to explore a place still largely left alone, you have only to drive inland from the coast or crossover into Chiapas, to find an older world, where the distinctive intonations of the Mayan language can be heard, and the old ways of living continue unimpeded by outside influences.

The turquoise waters and tropical climate of the peninsula may beckon you, but what will ultimately hold your attention is the unique character of this land and its people. There is simply no other place like it.

1 The Yucatán, Tabasco & Chiapas Now

In the five states that make up the Yucatán and southeastern Mexico great wealth lives alongside great poverty. Paradoxically, the indexes of both wealth and poverty in this region are higher than the national average. A lot of money is flowing into the area—in the case of Yucatán and Quintana Roo, from tourism; in the case of Campeche, Tabasco, and Chiapas, from the oil industry. But this money doesn't trickle down readily, and so many of the region's inhabitants have not benefited directly from the economic boom. These five states have a total population of almost 10 million, 10% of Mexico's population, but only account for about 6% of the economic activity.

Intensive development has been a two-edged sword. In some cases, it has increased the demand for the products and services of local workers such as fishermen and *palaperos,* the native roofers who create thatched roofs *(palapas)* that adorn many hotels—their services are in great demand every time a hurricane brushes the coast. At the same time, development has ruined the livelihood of other locals, such as the coastal coconut growers. When Cancún developers brought turf from Florida to build a golf course, they unwittingly introduced a disease that wiped out the original coconut palms. The consequences from the destruction of the mangroves, which play a vital role in the coastal food chain and protect the region from hurricanes, means diminished catches by fishermen and greater losses when a hurricane strikes.

The same give and take can be seen in the effects of oil production on the local economies of Tabasco and Chiapas. While oil increases resources for local governments, direct benefits tend to be confined to a minority of the population. However, oil wealth was unable to protect Tabasco and Chiapas from heavy flooding in late 2007, one of Mexico's worst natural disasters.

State governments have been slow to react to the region's recent economic prosperity. Much has been done to improve roads and other basic infrastructure, but no coherent policy for combating social ills has been formulated. The Zapatista revolt of the 1990s served to focus society's attention on the plight of Chiapas' rural poor, but ironically, this has had more of an effect on the national government than on the states and the region as a whole.

For most of the peasants and farmers and the rest of the rural populace who live outside the realm of the oil and tourism industries, life hasn't changed much during these boom years.

TODAY'S MAYA CULTURE & PEOPLE

As with lowlanders elsewhere in Mexico, Yucatecans are warm and friendly, and they show little reserve. Entering into conversation with them couldn't be easier. In the peninsula's interior, you might find people who are unexpectedly reticent, but most likely these are Maya Indians who aren't comfortable speaking Spanish. It may come as a surprise that you don't have to leave Cancún to meet the Maya; thousands come from the interior to work at hotels and restaurants in Cancún, and many can switch easily among Spanish, English, and Yukatek, the local Mayan language. More than 350,000 Maya living in the Yucatán's three states speak Yukatek, and most, especially men, speak Spanish, too.

Completely different are the estimated one million **Tabascan** and **Chiapan Maya,** who speak four different Mayan languages with dozens of dialects. The highland Maya communities around San Cristóbal de las Casas generally choose not to embrace outside cultures, preferring to live in small mountain hamlets and meeting only for ceremonies and market days. Their cloud-forest homeland in Chiapas is cold. They, too, live much as their ancestors did, but with beliefs distinct from their peninsular relatives.

In hindsight, the arrival of the Spaniards, in the early 1500s, seems almost apocalyptic. Military conquest and old-world diseases decimated the native population. A new social order predicated on a starkly different religion rose in place of the old one. Through all

The Yucatán, Tabasco & Chiapas in Depth

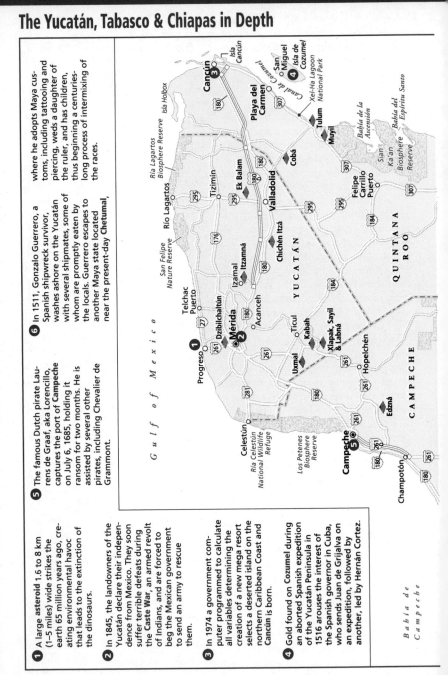

1 A large asteroid 1.6 to 8 km (1-5 miles) wide strikes the earth 65 million years ago, creating environmental havoc that leads to the extinction of the dinosaurs.

2 In 1845, the landowners of the Yucatán declare their independence from Mexico. They soon suffer terrible defeats during the **Caste War**, an armed revolt of Indians, and are forced to beg the Mexican government to send an army to rescue them.

3 In 1974 a government computer programmed to calculate all variables determining the creation of a new mega resort selects a deserted island on the northern Caribbean Coast and **Cancún** is born.

4 Gold found on Cozumel during an aborted Spanish expedition of the Yucatán Peninsula in 1516 arouses the interest of the Spanish governor in Cuba, who sends Juan de Grijalva on an expedition, followed by another, led by Hernán Cortez.

5 The famous Dutch pirate Laurens de Graaf, aka Lorencillo, captures the port of **Campeche** on July 6, 1685, holding it ransom for two months. He is assisted by several other pirates, including Chevalier de Grammont.

6 In 1511, Gonzalo Guerrero, a Spanish shipwreck survivor, washes ashore on the Yucatán with several shipmates, some of whom are promptly eaten by the locals. Guerrero escapes to another Maya state located near the present-day **Chetumal**, where he adopts Maya customs, including tattooing and piercing, weds a daughter of the ruler, and has children, thus beginning a centuries-long process of intermixing of the races.

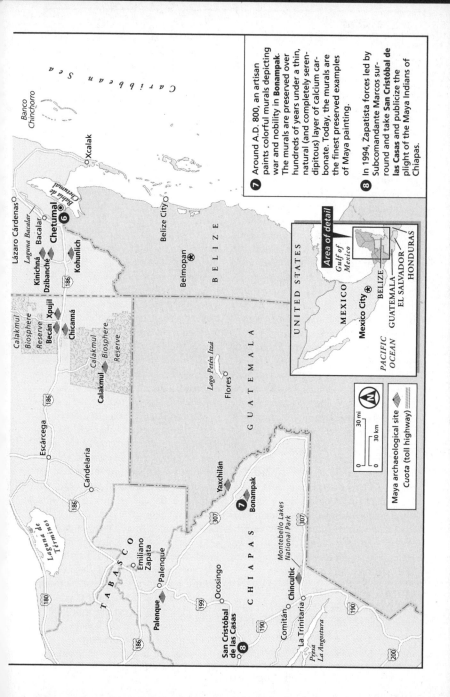

7 Around A.D. 800, an artisan paints colorful murals depicting war and nobility in **Bonampak**. The murals are preserved over hundreds of years under a thin, natural (and completely serendipitous) layer of calcium carbonate. Today, the murals are the finest preserved examples of Maya painting.

8 In 1994, Zapatista forces led by Subcomandante Marcos surround and take **San Cristóbal de las Casas** and publicize the plight of the Maya Indians of Chiapas.

Caribbean Sea

Banco Chinchorro

Xcalak

Lázaro Cárdenas
Laguna Bacalar
Bacalar
Chetumal **6**
Bahía de Chetumal

Kinichná
Dzibanché
Kohunlich
186

Belize City

BELIZE

Belmopan

Calakmul Biosphere Reserve
Becán Xpujil
Chicanná
Calakmul
Calakmul Biosphere Reserve
186

Escárcega
186

Candelaria

Lago Petén Itzá
Flores

GUATEMALA

Area of detail

UNITED STATES

Gulf of Mexico

MEXICO
Mexico City

BELIZE
GUATEMALA
HONDURAS
EL SALVADOR

PACIFIC OCEAN

N

0   30 mi
0   30 km

Maya archaeological site
Cuota (toll highway)

Laguna de Términos
180

TABASCO

Emiliano Zapata
Palenque
199

Ocosingo
307

Yaxchilán
Bonampak **7**

Palenque
186

San Cristóbal de las Casas **8**
190

Comitán
Chincultic
La Trinitaria
Montebello Lakes National Park
307

CHIAPAS

190

Presa La Angostura
200

Impressions

We both learned that the Maya are not just a people of the past. Today, they live in their millions in Mexico, Guatemala, Belize, and western Honduras, still speaking one of the 35 Mayan languages as their native tongue. They continue to cultivate their fields and commune with their living world in spite of the fact that they are encapsulated within a larger modern civilization whose vision of reality is often alien to their own.
—Linda Schele and David Freidel, *A Forest of Kings* (1990)

of this, the Maya held on to their language but lost most of the living memory of their pre-Hispanic ways. What they retained they cloaked in the language of myth and legend that was worked into a rough synthesis of old and new. They selectively appropriated elements of the new religion that could help make sense of the world, and this process continues today in the many Maya communities that have native churches, such as **San Juan Chamula** or **Zinacantán** outside of San Cristóbal de las Casas.

Those curious people, the Maya, are a fascinating and integral part of this land. The ancients left behind elegant and mysterious ruins that, despite all that we now know, seem to defy interpretation. Almost every year, archaeological excavation leads to the discovery of more ruins in this region, adding to a growing picture of an urban civilization that thrived in an area where only scantily populated jungle now exists. What can we make of such a civilization? What value do we accord the Maya among the other lost civilizations of the ancient world? Even this is unclear, but the art and architecture they left behind are stunning expressions of a rich and complex cosmological view.

LIVING WELL: THE BEST REVENGE

In the face of economic inequality, Mexican society remains amazingly resilient and cohesive—due in no small part to the way Mexicans live. They place a high value on family and friends, social gatherings, and living in the present; getting ahead and future uncertainties take a back seat. In Mexico, there is always time to meet with friends for a drink or a cup of coffee or attend a family get-together. The many spirited public celebrations that Mexico is famous for are simply another manifestation of this attitude.

American and English travelers have often observed that Mexicans have a different conception of time, that life in Mexico obeys slower rhythms. This is true, and yet few observers go on to explain what the consequences of this are for the visitor to Mexico. This is a shame, because an imperfect appreciation of the difference causes a good deal of misunderstanding between tourists and locals.

Mexican acquaintances have asked me why Americans grin all the time. At first, I wasn't sure what to make of the question, and only gradually came to appreciate what was at issue. As the pace of life for Americans, Canadians, and others has quickened, they have come to skip some of the niceties of social interaction. When walking into a store, many Americans simply smile at a clerk and launch right into a question or request. The smile, in effect, replaces the greeting. In Mexico, it doesn't work that way. Mexicans misinterpret this American manner of greeting. After all, a smile when there is no context can be ambiguous; it can convey amusement, smugness, or superiority.

One of the most important pieces of advice I can offer travelers is this: Always give a proper greeting when addressing Mexicans. Don't try to abbreviate social intercourse. Mexican culture places a higher value on proper social form than on saving time. A Mexican must at least say *"¡Buenos días!"* or its equivalent, even to total strangers—a show of proper respect. When an individual meets a group of people, he or she will greet each person separately, which can take quite a while. For us, the polite thing would be to keep our interruption to a minimum and give a general greeting to all.

Mexicans, like most people, will consciously or subconsciously make quick judgments about individuals they meet. Most divide the world into the well raised and cultured *(bien educado)* and the poorly raised *(mal educado)*. Unfortunately, many visitors are reluctant to try out their Spanish, preferring to keep exchanges to a minimum. Don't do this. To be categorized as a foreigner isn't a big deal. What's important in Mexico is to be categorized as one of the cultured foreigners and not one of the barbarians.

2 A Look at the Past

PRE-HISPANIC CIVILIZATIONS

The earliest "Mexicans" were perhaps Stone Age hunter-gatherers coming from the north, descendants of a race that had crossed the Bering Strait and reached North America around 12,000 B.C. This is the prevailing theory, but there is a growing body of evidence that points to an earlier crossing of peoples from Asia to the New World. What we know for certain is that Mexico was populated by 10,000 B.C. Sometime between 5200 and 1500 B.C., they began practicing agriculture and domesticating animals.

THE OLMECS & MAYA: THE PRE-CLASSIC PERIOD (1500 B.C.–A.D. 300)

Eventually, agriculture improved to the point that it could provide enough food to support large communities and enough surplus to free some of the population from agricultural work. A civilization emerged that we call the **Olmec**—an enigmatic people who settled the lower Gulf Coast in what is now Tabasco and Veracruz. Anthropologists regard them as the mother culture of Mesoamerica because they established a pattern for later civilizations in a wide area stretching from northern Mexico into Central America. The Olmec developed the basic calendar used throughout the region, established principles of urban layout and architecture, and originated the cult of the jaguar and the sacredness of jade. They may also have bequeathed the sacred ritual of "the ballgame"—a universal element of Mesoamerican culture.

One intriguing feature of the Olmec was the carving of colossal stone heads, several of which you can admire today in the Parque Museo La Venta in Villahermosa, Tabasco. We still don't know what purposes these heads served, but they were immense projects; the basalt from which they were sculpted was mined miles inland and transported to the coast, probably by river rafts. The heads share a rounded, baby-faced look, marked by a peculiar, high-arched lip—a "jaguar mouth"—that is an identifying mark of Olmec sculpture.

The **Maya** civilization began developing in the pre-Classic period, around 500 B.C. Our understanding of this period is only sketchy, but Olmec influences are apparent everywhere. The Maya perfected the Olmec calendar and, somewhere along the way, developed their ornate system of hieroglyphic writing and their early architecture. Two other civilizations also began their rise to prominence around this time: the people of Teotihuacán, just north of present-day Mexico City, and the Zapotec of Monte Albán, in the valley of Oaxaca.

It's Just a Game

The ancient Maya played a game with a solid rubber ball that held great importance for them. Go to any Maya city and you can view the ball courts where it was played (Bonampak being a rare exception). These are readily identifiable by their I-shaped layout with sloping walls in the center. The Maya weren't the only ones to play this game—ball courts have been found as far south as Nicaragua and as far north as Arizona.

We know little about the details of the game or its rules. What we do know comes from ancient depictions of the game, early accounts by the Spanish, and from the Maya epic, the Popol Vuh. We know that the ball was heavy and could inflict injury. The players wore thick cloth padding and protective gear. They played in teams of between 2 and 10 members, and the object was to get the ball to pass through a stone ring or other goal using mainly the hips.

We also know that the game was part sport and part religious ritual that, at times, involved human sacrifice, but we're not sure who was sacrificed—the winners, the losers, or perhaps prisoners of war who were allowed to play the game one last time before losing their heads. We know that the game was symbolically the affirmation of a cosmological belief system. In the Popol Vuh, the hero twins, Hunahpu and Xbalanque, challenge the lords of the underworld to a game, part of which they play with the head of one of the twins. Eventually the twins win the game and are allowed to return to the world of the living. Playing the game might have been one of the ways for cheating the underworld.

TEOTIHUACAN, MONTE ALBAN & PALENQUE: THE CLASSIC PERIOD (A.D. 300–900)

The rise and fall of these three city-states marks the boundaries of this period—the heyday of pre-Columbian Mesoamerican artistic and cultural achievements. These include the pyramids and palaces in Teotihuacán; the ceremonial center of Monte Albán; and the stelae and temples of Palenque, Bonampak, and Calakmul. Beyond their achievements in art and architecture, the Maya made significant discoveries in science, including the use of the zero in mathematics and a complex calendar with which the priests could predict eclipses and the movements of the stars for centuries to come.

The inhabitants of **Teotihuacán** (100 B.C.–A.D. 700—near present-day Mexico City) built a city that, at its zenith, is thought to have had 100,000 or more inhabitants covering 14 sq. km (5½ sq. miles). It was a well-organized city, built on a grid with streams channeled to follow the city's plan. Different social classes, such as artisans and merchants, were assigned to specific neighborhoods. Teotihuacán exerted tremendous influence as far away as Guatemala and the Yucatán Peninsula. Its feathered serpent god, later known as **Quetzalcoatl,** became part of the pantheon of many succeeding cultures, including the Toltecs, who brought the cult to the Yucatán where the god became known as Kukulkán. The ruling classes were industrious, literate, and cosmopolitan. The beautiful sculpture and ceramics of Teotihuacán display a highly stylized and refined aesthetic whose influences can be seen clearly in objects of Maya and Zapotec origin. Around the 7th century, the city was abandoned for unknown reasons. Who these people were and where they went remains a mystery.

TOLTECS & AZTEC INVASIONS: THE POST-CLASSIC PERIOD (A.D. 900–1521)

Warfare became more pervasive during this period. Social development was impressive but these latter civilizations were not as cosmopolitan as those in the classic period. In central Mexico, a people known as the **Toltec** established their capital at Tula in the 10th century. They were originally one of the barbarous hordes of Indians that periodically migrated from the north. At some stage in their development, the Toltec were influenced by remnants of Teotihuacán culture and adopted the feathered serpent Quetzalcoatl as their god. They also revered a god known as **Tezcatlipoca,** or "smoking mirror," who later became a god of the Aztecs. The Toltec maintained a large military class divided into orders symbolized by animals. At its height, Tula may have had 40,000 people, and it spread its influence across Mesoamerica. By the 13th century, however, the Toltec had exhausted themselves, probably in civil wars and in battles with the invaders from the north.

The Maya of the Yucatán, especially the Xiu and Itzáes, may have been something of an exception to the norm in that they seemed to have had broad trading networks and been the beneficiaries of multiple influences from the outside world. They built beautiful cities in and around the **Yucatán's Puuc hills,** which are not far south of Mérida. The regional architecture, called **Puuc style,** is characterized by elaborate exterior stonework appearing above door frames and extending to the roofline. Examples of this architecture, such as the Codz Poop at Kabah and the palaces at Uxmal, Sayil, and Labná, are beautiful and quite impressive. Associated with the cities of the Puuc region was Chichén Itzá, ruled by the Itzáes. This metropolis evidences strong Toltec influences in its architectural style as well as the cult of the plumed-serpent god, Kukulkán.

The precise nature of this Toltec influence is a subject of debate. But there is an intriguing myth in central Mexico that tells how Quetzalcoatl quarrels with Tezcatlipoca and through trickery is shamed by his rival into leaving Tula, the capital of the Toltec empire. He leaves heading eastward toward the morning star, vowing someday to return. In the language of myth, this could be a shorthand telling of an actual civil war between two factions in Tula, each led by the priesthood of a particular god. Could the losing faction have migrated to the Yucatán and formed the ruling class of Chichén Itzá? Perhaps. What we do know for certain is that this myth of the eventual return of Quetzalcoatl became, in the hands of the Spanish, a powerful weapon of conquest.

CORTEZ, MOCTEZUMA & THE SPANISH CONQUEST

In 1517, the first Spaniards arrived in Mexico and skirmished with Maya Indians off the coast of the Yucatán Peninsula. One of the fledgling expeditions ended in a shipwreck, leaving several Spaniards stranded as prisoners of the Maya. The Spanish sent out another expedition, under the command of **Hernán Cortez,** which landed on Cozumel in February 1519. Cortez inquired about the gold and riches of the interior, and the coastal Maya were happy to describe the wealth and splendor of the Aztec empire in central Mexico. Cortez promptly disobeyed all orders from his superior, the governor of Cuba, and sailed to the mainland.

He and his army arrived when the Aztec empire was at the height of its wealth and power. **Moctezuma II** ruled over the central and southern highlands and extracted tribute from lowland peoples. His greatest temples were literally plated with gold and encrusted with the blood of sacrificial captives. Moctezuma was a fool, a mystic, and something of a coward. Despite his wealth and military power, he dithered in his capital at Tenochtitlán, sending messengers with gifts and suggestions that Cortez leave. Meanwhile, Cortez blustered and negotiated his way into the highlands, always cloaking his real intentions. Moctezuma, terrified, convinced himself that Cortez was in fact the god Quetzalcoatl making his long-awaited return. By the time the Spaniards arrived in the Aztec capital, Cortez had gained some ascendancy over the lesser Indian states that were resentful tributaries to the Aztec. In November 1519, Cortez confronted Moctezuma and took him hostage in an effort to leverage control of the empire.

In the middle of Cortez's dangerous game of manipulation, another Spanish expedition arrived with orders to end Cortez's authority over the mission. Cortez hastened to meet the rival's force and persuade them to join his own. In the meantime, the Aztec chased the garrison out of Tenochtitlán, and either they or the Spaniards killed Moctezuma. For the next year and a half, Cortez laid siege to Tenochtitlán, with the help of rival Indians and a decimating epidemic of smallpox, to which the Indians had no resistance. In the end, the Aztec capital fell, and, when it did, all of central Mexico lay at the feet of the conquistadors.

Having begun as a pirate expedition by Cortez and his men without the authority of the Spanish crown or its governor in Cuba, the conquest of Mexico resulted in a vast expansion of the Spanish empire. The king legitimized Cortez following his victory over the Aztec and ordered the forced conversion to Christianity of this new colony, to be called **New Spain.** Guatemala and Honduras were explored and conquered, and by 1540, the territory of New Spain included possessions from Vancouver to Panama. In the 2 centuries that followed, Franciscan and Augustinian friars converted millions of Indians to Christianity, and the Spanish lords built huge feudal estates on which the Indian farmers were little more than serfs. The silver and gold that Cortez looted made Spain the richest country in Europe.

THE RISE OF MEXICO CITY & SPANISH COLONIALISM

Hernán Cortez set about building a new city upon the ruins of the old Aztec capital. To do this, he collected from the Indians the tributes once paid to the Aztec emperor, many of them rendered in labor. This arrangement, in one form or another, became the basis for the construction of the new colony. But diseases brought by the Spaniards devastated the native population over the next century and drastically reduced the labor pool.

Over the 3 centuries of the colonial period, Spain became rich from New World gold and silver, chiseled out by Indian labor. The colonial elite built lavish homes in Mexico City and in the countryside. They filled their homes with ornate furniture, had many servants, and adorned themselves in imported velvets, satins, and jewels.

A new class system developed. Those born in Spain considered themselves superior to the *criollos* (Spaniards born in Mexico). Those of other races and the *castas* (mixtures of Spanish and Indian, Spanish and African, or Indian and African) occupied the bottom rungs of society. It took great cunning to stay a step ahead of the avaricious Crown, which demanded increasing taxes and

A Sticky Habit

Cigar smoking and gum chewing are two pleasures that we have the Maya to thank for, and, of the two, the latter is the more innocuous. Gum comes from the sap of a species of zapote tree that grows in the Yucatán and Guatemala. Chewing causes it to release natural sugars and a mild, agreeable taste. From the Maya, the habit of chewing gum spread to other cultures and eventually to the non-Indian population. In the second half of the 19th century, a Mexican (said to have been General Santa Anna) introduced gum to the American Thomas Adams, who realized that it could be sweetened further and given other flavors. He brought the idea to the U.S. and marketed chewing gum with great success. Chemists have since figured out how to synthesize the gum, but the sap is still collected in parts of the Yucatán and Guatemala for making natural chewing gum. *Chicle* is the Spanish word originally from the Náhuatl (Aztec) *tzictli,* and those who live in the forest and collect the sap are called *chicleros.* Because the tree takes so long to produce more sap, there is no way to cultivate the tree commercially, so it is still collected in the wild.

contributions from its fabled foreign conquests. Still, wealthy colonists prospered enough to develop an extravagant society.

However, discontent with the mother country simmered for years. In 1808, Napoleon invaded Spain and crowned his brother Joseph king, in place of Charles IV. To many in Mexico, allegiance to France was out of the question; discontent reached the level of revolt.

HIDALGO, JUAREZ & MEXICO'S INDEPENDENCE

The rebellion began in 1810, when **Father Miguel Hidalgo** gave the *grito,* a cry for independence, from his church in the town of Dolores, Guanajuato. The uprising soon became a full-fledged revolution, as Hidalgo and Ignacio Allende gathered an "army" of citizens and threatened Mexico City. Although Hidalgo ultimately failed and was executed, he is honored as "the Father of Mexican Independence." Another priest, José María Morelos, kept the revolt alive with several successful campaigns through 1815, when he, too, was captured and executed.

After the death of Morelos, prospects for independence were rather dim until the Spanish king who replaced Joseph Bonaparte decided to make social reforms in the colonies. This convinced the conservative powers in Mexico that they didn't need Spain after all. With their tacit approval, Agustín de Iturbide, then commander of royalist forces, changed sides and declared Mexico independent and himself emperor. Before long, however, internal dissension brought about the fall of the emperor, and Mexico was proclaimed a republic.

Political instability engulfed the young republic, which ran through a dizzying succession of presidents and dictators as struggles between federalists and centralists, and conservatives and liberals, divided the country. Moreover, Mexico waged a disastrous war with the United States, which resulted in the loss of half its territory. A central figure was **Antonio López de Santa Anna,** who assumed the leadership of his country no fewer than 11 times. He probably holds the record for frequency of exile; by 1855 he was finally left without a political comeback and lived out his final days in Venezuela.

Political instability persisted, and the conservative forces, with some encouragement from Napoleon III, hit upon the idea of inviting in a Habsburg to regain control. They found a willing volunteer in Archduke Maximilian of Austria, who accepted the position of Mexican emperor with the support of French troops. The ragtag Mexican forces defeated the modern, well-equipped French force in a battle near Puebla (now celebrated annually as **Cinco de Mayo**). A second attempt was more successful, and Ferdinand Maximilian Joseph of Habsburg became emperor. After 3 years of civil war, the French were finally induced to abandon the emperor's cause; Maximilian was captured and executed by a firing squad near Querétaro in 1867. His adversary and successor (as president of Mexico) was **Benito Juárez,** a Zapotec Indian lawyer and one of the great heroes of Mexican history. Juárez did his best to unify and strengthen his country before dying of a heart attack in 1872; his impact on Mexico's future was profound, and his plans and visions bore fruit for decades.

YUCATECAN INDEPENDENCE & THE CASTE WAR

In 1845, with Mexico unable to establish a stable form of government, the Yucatán's landed oligarchy decided to separate from Mexico and declare the Yucatán independent. To defend the territory from invasion they armed the populace, including the Indians who had toiled for their entire lives on the haciendas. The Indians, unhappy with their status as serfs, realized that it wasn't so important to them whether their oppressors lived in Mexico City or Mérida, and, with arms in hand, they rose up against the landowners. Thus began the War of the Castes.

Far outnumbering the oligarchy and its constabulary forces, the peasants quickly gained control of most of the countryside. They were able to capture several towns and even the city of Valladolid. Mérida, too, might have been taken, but a strange thing happened. Planting season arrived, and, rather than press their advantage and take the capital, the Maya put down their weapons to return to their corn fields. This gave the non-Indians time to regroup, swear fealty to Mexico, and call for an army from the Mexican government. Eventually the Maya rebels were driven back into what is now Quintana Roo, where they were largely left on their own, virtually a nation within a nation, until a Mexican army with modern weaponry finally penetrated the region at the turn of the twentieth century.

DIAZ, ZAPATA, PANCHO VILLA & THE MEXICAN REVOLUTION

A few years after Juárez's death, one of his generals, **Porfirio Díaz,** assumed power in a coup. He ruled Mexico from 1877 to 1911, a period now called the "Porfiriato." He stayed in power through repressive measures and by courting the favor of powerful nations. Generous in his dealings with foreign investors, Díaz became, in the eyes of most Mexicans, the archetypal *entreguista* (one who sells out his country for private gain). With foreign investment came the concentration of great wealth in few hands, and social conditions worsened.

In 1910, Francisco Madero called for an armed rebellion that became the **Mexican revolution** ("La Revolución" in Mexico; the revolution against Spain is the "Guerra de Independencia"). Díaz was sent into exile; while in London, he became a celebrity at the age of 81, when he jumped into the Thames to save a drowning boy. He is buried in Paris. Madero became president, but **Victoriano Huerta** promptly betrayed and executed him.

Those who had answered Madero's call responded again—the great peasant hero **Emiliano Zapata** in the south, and the seemingly invincible **Pancho Villa** in the central north, flanked by Alvaro Obregón and Venustiano Carranza. They eventually put Huerta to flight and began hashing out a new constitution.

For the next few years, the revolutionaries Carranza, Obregón, and Villa fought among themselves; Zapata did not seek national power, though he fought tenaciously for land for the peasants. Carranza, who was president at the time, betrayed and assassinated Zapata. Obregón finally consolidated power and probably had Carranza assassinated. He, in turn, was assassinated when he tried to break one of the tenets of the revolution—no reelection. His successor, Plutarco Elias Calles, installed one puppet president after another, until **Lázaro Cárdenas** severed the puppeteer's strings and banished him to exile.

Until Cárdenas's election in 1934, the eventual outcome of the Revolution remained in doubt. There had been some land redistribution, but other measures took a back seat to political expediency. Cárdenas changed all that. He implemented a massive redistribution of land and nationalized the oil industry. He instituted many reforms and gave shape to the ruling political party (now the **Partido Revolucionario Institucional,** or PRI) by bringing under its banner a broad representation of Mexican society and establishing the mechanisms for consensus building. Cárdenas is practically canonized by most Mexicans.

MODERN MEXICO

The presidents who followed were more noted for graft than leadership. The party's base narrowed as many of the reform-minded elements were marginalized or chased out of the party. In 1968, the government violently repressed a democratic student movement during a demonstration in the **Tlatelolco** section of Mexico City. An unknown number of people died, and though the PRI maintained its grip on power, it lost its image as a progressive party.

Economic progress, much of it in the form of large development projects, became the PRI's sole basis for legitimacy. In 1974 the government decided to construct a completely new megaresort somewhere on Mexico's coast. To find the ideal location for this resort, the planners fed all the different variables into a computer, and out popped Cancún. The rest, as they say, is history that has forever changed Mexico's economy.

In putting together these kinds of projects, the government weathered several periods of social unrest caused by periodic devaluations of the peso. But in 1985, Mexico City suffered a devastating **earthquake** that brought down many of the government's new, supposedly earthquake-proof buildings, exposing shoddy construction and the widespread government corruption that fostered it. There was much criticism, too, for how the government handled the relief efforts.

Throughout these years the opposition parties were growing. The two largest ones were the **PRD** (Partido de la Revolución Democrática) on the left and the **PAN** (Partido Acción National) on the right. During the presidential elections of 1988 the government had to commit massive fraud to ensure that its candidate, Carlos Salinas de Gortari, was declared the winner over the PRD's, **Cuauhtémoc Cárdenas,** formerly of the PRI and son of former President Lázaro Cárdenas. The fraud was barely disguised; the PRI unplugged the election computers and claimed that it was a system failure.

Under pressure at home and abroad, the government moved to demonstrate a new commitment to democracy and even began to concede electoral defeats for state governorships and legislative seats. These policies led to divisions within the party between factions of reformists and hardliners. A power struggle ensued, resulting in several political assassinations including most famously the assassination of the PRI's next presidential candidate, **Luis Colosio.** After that assassination and the crippling economic crisis that came in 1994, soon after Salinas de Gortari stepped down, nothing could be the same. The replacement president, **Ernesto Zedillo,** spent his 6 years in office trying to stabilize the economy and bring transparency to government.

In 2000 he shepherded the first true elections in 70 years of one-party rule. The winner was the PAN's candidate, **Vicente Fox,** a former businessman who ran on a platform of economic liberalization and anti-corruption. Many Mexicans voted for him, not from support for his conservative views, but just to see if the PRI would let go of power. It did, and Fox ran the show for the next 6 years. He didn't prove to be the master politician that was necessary for a situation that required making political alliances in a divided legislature. His efforts to build a coalition with segments of the PRI failed to work, and little was accomplished during his last 3 years in office. The Mexican electorate felt widespread disappointment with his administration, especially regarding the efforts to combat corruption. But they also felt that the government had become more transparent.

The presidential election of 2006 proved a real test for Mexico's nascent pluralism because it was extremely close, and the results were bitterly disputed by the losing party, the PRD. The final ruling of the elections tribunal was unpopular. It declared Felipe Calderón the winner while denying the PRD's request for a recount. The losing candidate was Andrés Manuel López Obrador, with Madrazo, the PRI candidate, coming in a distant third. López Obrador did not take defeat gracefully and provoked a constitutional crisis, which only time has managed to heal. President Calderón, seeing how the PRD's campaign resonated with the poor, has tried to steal his opponent's thunder by announcing programs to boost employment, alleviate poverty, and stabilize the skyrocketing price of tortillas. Time will tell how well he handles the political situation, but in the first year of his presidency he has shown himself to be a more capable politician than his predecessor.

MODERN YUCATAN, TABASCO & CHIAPAS

Cancún was the scene of an ugly national scandal that broke in 2005 that continues to send shock waves through Mexican society. Journalist Lydia Cacho wrote an exposé about a large prostitution and pedophilia ring operating in the resort, implicating some of the region's most powerful businessmen. Two of those named were Kamel Nacif, from the state of Puebla, and Jean Succar Kuri, a local hotel owner. Nacif used his influence with the governor of Puebla, Mario Marín, to arrest Cacho in Cancún for defamation and transport her back to Puebla—Puebla is 1,609km (1,000 miles) from Cancún, and the little matter of jurisdiction gets lost in the case. On the long ride back, Cacho says that she was repeatedly threatened and had the barrel of a pistol stuck in her mouth. The officers deny it.

Several human rights organizations acted fast to get Cacho released and evidently foiled the governor's plans to have her tortured in prison. Cacho brought suit against Governor Marín, alleging that he violated her human rights. An immense amount of damning evidence made the case appear clear cut, but late in 2007, in a shocker, the nation's supreme court ruled against Cacho, stating that her rights weren't violated. The court's investigation found plenty of evidence to support a guilty verdict, but there was a late change of heart by two justices. To many observers, this case demonstrates that if one person's rights cannot be upheld in Mexican law, then the human rights of all Mexicans are at risk. An onslaught of criticism has ensued and continues to pour out of the media.

In Chiapas the main issue has been to gain some degree of local control over the state's gas and oil. This has been the main plank of the **Zapatistas,** who have gradually morphed from armed combatants to broad political movement. In 1994, the Zapatistas' political/military uprising in Chiapas focused world attention on Mexico's great social problems. A new political force, the Zapatista National Liberation Army (EZLN for Ejército Zapatista de Liberación Nacional), skillfully publicized the plight of the peasant in today's Mexico. The government was forced into negotiations with the EZLN, a position that brought it little if any political capital. Its tactic was to make some easy concessions and to stall on other demands. The EZLN continues to seek to improve the situation of the state's many rural poor, but they have to some degree changed their tactics, now favoring change through political movement, instead of armed insurrection.

3 Eating & Drinking

Authentic Mexican food differs quite dramatically from what is frequently served under that name in the United States. There's quite a bit of regional variety, as is the case in the Yucatán. But despite these differences, some generalizations can be made. Mexican food usually isn't spicy-hot or piquant when it arrives at the table (though many dishes must have a certain amount of piquancy, and some home cooking can be very spicy, depending on a family's or chef's tastes). The *picante* flavor is added with chiles and salsas after the food is served; you'll never see a table in Mexico without one or both of these condiments. Mexicans don't drown their cooking in cheese and sour cream, a la Tex-Mex, and they use a greater variety of ingredients than most people expect. But the basis of Mexican food is simple—tortillas, beans, chiles, squash, and tomatoes—the same as it was centuries ago before the arrival of the Europeans.

THE STAPLES

TORTILLAS Traditional tortillas are made from corn that's been cooked in water and lime, then ground into *masa* (a grainy dough), patted and pressed into thin cakes, and cooked on a hot griddle known as a *comal.* In many households, the tortilla takes the place of fork and spoon; Mexicans merely tear them into wedge-shaped pieces, which they use to scoop up their food. Restaurants often serve bread rather than tortillas because it's easier, but you can always ask for tortillas. A more recent invention from northern Mexico is the flour tortilla.

ENCHILADAS The tortilla is the basis of several Mexican dishes, but the most famous of these is the enchilada. The original name for this dish would have been *tortilla enchilada,* which means a tortilla dipped in a chile sauce. In like manner, there's the *entomatada* (tortilla dipped in a tomato sauce) and the *enfrijolada* (in a

People of the Corn

According to Maya text, the Popol Vuh, the gods made man out of corn.

Tequila 101

In the past 15 years, both the quality and the popularity of tequila have sky-rocketed. The makers of tequila are, with one exception, still all based in the state of Jalisco. They have formed an association to establish standards for labeling and denomination. The best tequilas are invariably 100% agave, which means that they were made with a set minimum of sugar to prime the fermentation process. These tequilas come in three categories based on how they were stored: blanco, reposado, and añejo. Blanco is white tequila aged very little, usually in steel vats. Reposado (reposed) is aged in wooded casks for between 2 months and a year. And añejo (aged) has been stored in oak barrels for at least a year.

bean sauce). The enchilada began as a very simple dish: A tortilla is dipped in very hot oil and then into chile sauce (usually with ancho chile), then quickly folded or rolled on a plate and sprinkled with chopped onions and a little *queso cotija* (crumbly white cheese) and served with a little fried potatoes and carrots. You can get this basic enchilada in food stands across the country. I love them, and if you come across them in your travels, give them a try. In restaurants you get the more elaborate enchilada, with different fillings of cheese, chicken, pork, or even seafood, and sometimes prepared as a casserole.

TACOS   A taco is anything folded or rolled into a tortilla, and sometimes a double tortilla. The tortilla can be served either soft or fried. *Flautas* and quesadillas (except in Mexico City, where they are something quite different) are species of tacos. For Mexicans, the taco is the quintessential fast food, and the taco stand *(taquería)* a ubiquitous sight.

FRIJOLES   In private households, pink or black beans are served at least once a day, and among the working class and peasantry, with every meal if the family can afford it. Mexicans almost always prepare beans with a minimum of condiments, usually just a little onion and garlic and a pinch of herbs. Beans are meant to be a contrast to the heavily spiced foods in a meal. Sometimes they are served at the end of a meal with a little Mexican-style sour cream.

Mexicans often fry leftover beans and serve them on the side as *frijoles refritos. Refritos* is often translated as "refried," but this is a misnomer—the beans are fried only once. The prefix *re* means "well" (as in "thoroughly"), so a proper translation would be "well-fried beans."

TAMALES   To make a *tamal,* you mix corn masa with a little lard, beat the batter, add one of several fillings—meats flavored with chiles—then wrap it in a corn husk or in the leaf of a banana or other plant, and steam it. Every region in Mexico has its own traditional way of making tamales. In some places, a single tamal can be big enough to feed a family; while in others, they are barely three inches long and only about an inch thick.

CHILES   There are many kinds of hot peppers, and Mexicans call each of them by one name when they're fresh and another when they're dried. Some are blazing hot with little flavor; some are mild but have a rich, complex flavor. They can be pickled, smoked, stuffed, or stewed.

DRINKS

All over Mexico, you'll find shops selling *licuados*—excellent and refreshing juices and smoothies made from several kinds of tropical fruit. You'll also come across *aguas frescas*—water flavored with hibiscus, melon, tamarind, or lime. Soft drinks come in more flavors than in any other country I know. Pepsi and Coca-Cola taste the way they did in the United States years ago, before the makers started adding corn syrup.

The coffee is generally good, and **hot chocolate** is a traditional drink, as is *atole*—a hot, corn-based beverage that can be sweet or bitter.

Of course, Mexico has a proud and lucrative **beer**-brewing tradition. A less-known brewed beverage is *pulque,* a pre-Hispanic drink made of the fermented juice of a few species of maguey or agave. Mostly you find it for sale in *pulquerías* in central Mexico. It is an acquired taste, and not every gringo acquires it. **Mescal** and **tequila** also come from the agave. Tequila is a variety of mescal produced from the *A. tequilana* species of agave in and around the area of Tequila, in the state of Jalisco. Mescal comes from various parts of Mexico and from different varieties of agave. The distilling process is usually much less sophisticated than that of tequila, and, with its stronger smell and taste, mescal is much more easily detected on the drinker's breath. In some places like Oaxaca it comes with a worm in the bottle; you are supposed to eat the worm after polishing off the mescal. But for those teetotalers out there who are interested in just the worm, I have good news—you can find these worms for sale in Mexican markets when in season. *¡Salud!*

REGIONAL SPECIALTIES

As in Mexico as a whole, cooking in the Yucatán is based on corn, beans, tomatoes, and chiles. What principally distinguishes this regional cooking is the use of several ingredients acquired from other lands, such as achiote or annatto and bitter orange, from the Caribbean Islands, peas, which probably came from interacting with the English, and Edam cheese through historical trade with the Dutch. You will even see a strong Middle Eastern influence thanks to recent immigrants living in the larger cities.

To start your day in the Yucatán, try *huevos moluleños*—fried eggs over sliced plantains, beans, and fried tortillas and topped with a dusting of salty cheese, some tomato sauce, and peas—but only if you're ravenous. Another morning dish is the well-known *cochinita pibil* (pork marinated in achiote and bitter orange and baked in a pit). The best place to have the former is in any reputable restaurant; the best place to have the latter would be a market such as **el Mercado de Santa Ana** in Mérida.

Original dishes for the afternoon meal include *relleno negro,* turkey cooked with a paste of charred chiles and vegetables with bits of hard boiled eggs; *escabeche blanco,* chicken or turkey cooked in a vinegar-based sauce; or *queso relleno,* mild Edam cheese stuffed with seasoned ground beef. For something lighter you can order grilled fish that has been lightly marinated

Food Hygiene

Many travelers to Mexico ask about the safety of beverages with ice. The truth is that most restaurants and bars buy ice made from purified water. This ice is made by the same kind of machinery all across Mexico. It produces ice cubes that have a rough cylindrical shape with a hollow center. They're easy to spot in your glass and are a sign that the ice is hygienic. Plain block ice carries no such guarantee. Likewise, almost all restaurants that cater to middle-class Mexicans use filtered water and disinfect vegetables, but street vendors and market stalls may not. I do eat in the market and in the street, but I'm careful to find places and pick foods that are relatively safe.

Dining Service Tips

- For the main meal of the day, many restaurants offer a multicourse blue-plate special called *comida corrida* or *menú del día.* This is the most inexpensive way to get a full dinner.
- In Mexico you need to **ask for your check;** it is considered inhospitable to present a check to someone who hasn't requested it. If you're in a hurry, ask for the check when your food arrives.
- Tips are about the same as in the U.S. You'll sometimes find a 15% value-added tax on restaurant meals, which shows up on the bill as "IVA." This is effectively the tip—a boon to arithmetically challenged tippers.
- To **summon the waiter,** wave or raise your hand, but don't motion with your index finger, which is a demeaning gesture that may even cause the waiter to ignore you. Or if it's the check you want, you can motion to the waiter from across the room using the universal pretend-like-you're-writing gesture.

in an achiote-based paste—it's called Tikinxic, or some variant of this. All of these dishes are served in restaurants for the afternoon meal, but in restaurants in Cancún and on the coast, they will also appear on the evening menu.

Evening foods traditionally are based on turkey and include different finger foods such as *salbutes* and *panuchos,* two dishes of masa cakes with various toppings, such as *frijoles* and shredded turkey or chicken.

Beyond the Yucatán, one enters into more familiar culinary terrain, with more of the same dishes that are available across Mexico. When I'm in Villahermosa, Tabasco, I generally look for some kind of seafood. They have a fish in Tabasco

called the *pejelagarto,* which has a delicious mild nutty taste. **La Jangada** in Villahermosa is my favorite place for this type of fish. Otherwise, I try to limit myself to simple dishes as neither Tabasco nor Chiapas have strong culinary traditions. Chiapas's cooking is similar to that of neighboring Guatemala—they use a lot of beef either grilled or in a stew. Either of these options is usually a safe bet. Chiapan tamales can be good; they are heavier and larger than central Mexican tamales and flavored differently, often with the leaf of a variety of pepper tree called *hoja santa.*

Be sure to read the food glossary in "Appendix B: Survival Spanish," to learn more about regional dishes.

4 Art & Architecture 101

Mexico's artistic and architectural legacy stretches back more than 3,000 years. Until the conquest of Mexico in A.D. 1521, art, architecture, politics, and religion were intertwined. Although the European conquest influenced the style and subject of Mexican art, this continuity remained throughout the colonial period.

PRE-HISPANIC FORMS

Mexico's **pyramids** were truncated platforms crowned with a temple. Many sites have circular buildings, such as El Caracol at Chichén Itzá, usually called the Observatory and dedicated to the god of the wind. El Castillo at Chichén Itzá has 365 steps—one for every day of the year. The

Temple of the Magicians at Uxmal has beautifully rounded and sloping sides. Evidence of building one pyramidal structure on top of another, a widely accepted practice, has been found throughout Mesoamerica.

Architects of many Toltec, Aztec, and Teotihuacán edifices alternated sloping panels *(talud)* with vertical panels *(tablero)*. Elements of this style occasionally show up in the Yucatán. Dzibanché, a newly excavated site near Lago Bacalar, in southern Quintana Roo state, has at least one temple with this characteristic. The true arch was unknown in Mesoamerica, but the Maya made use of the corbeled arch—a method of stacking stones that allows each successive stone to be cantilevered out a little farther than the one below it, until the two sides meet at the top, forming an inverted V.

The Olmec, considered the parent culture of Mesoamerica, built pyramids of earth. Unfortunately, little remains to tell us what their buildings looked like. The Olmec, however, left an enormous sculptural legacy, from small, intricately carved pieces of jade to 40-ton carved basalt rock heads.

Throughout Mexico, carved stone and mural art on pyramids served a religious and historical function rather than an ornamental one. **Hieroglyphs,** picture symbols etched on stone or painted on walls or pottery, functioned as the written language of the ancient peoples, particularly the Maya. By deciphering the glyphs, scholars allow the ancients to speak again, providing us with specific names to attach to rulers and their families, and demystifying the great dynastic histories of the Maya. For more on this, read *A Forest of Kings* (1990), by Linda Schele and David Freidel, and *Blood of Kings* (1986), by Linda Schele and Mary Ellen Miller. Good hieroglyphic examples appear in the site museum at Palenque.

Carving important historical figures on free-standing stone slabs, or **stelae,** was a common Maya commemorative device. Several are in place at Cobá; Calakmul has the most, and good examples are on display in the Museum of Anthropology in Mexico City and the archaeology museum in Villahermosa. **Pottery** played an important role, and different indigenous groups are distinguished by their different use of color and style. The Maya painted pottery with scenes from daily and historical life.

Pre-Hispanic cultures left a number of fantastic painted **murals,** some of which are remarkably preserved, such as those at Bonampak. Amazing stone murals or mosaics, using thousands of pieces of fitted stone to form figures of warriors, snakes, or geometric designs, decorate the pyramid facades at Uxmal and Chichén Itzá.

SPANISH INFLUENCE

With the arrival of the Spaniards, new forms of architecture came to Mexico. Many sites that were occupied by indigenous groups at the time of the conquest were razed, and in their place appeared Catholic churches, public buildings, and palaces for conquerors and the king's bureaucrats. In the Yucatán, churches at Izamal, Tecoh, Santa Elena, and Muná rest atop former pyramidal structures. Indian artisans, who formerly worked on pyramidal structures, were recruited to build the new buildings, often guided by drawings of European buildings. Frequently left on their own, the indigenous artisans implanted traditional symbolism in the new buildings: a plaster angel swaddled in feathers, reminiscent of the god Quetzalcoatl, and the face of an ancient god surrounded by corn leaves. They used pre-Hispanic calendar counts—the 13 steps to heaven or the nine levels of the underworld—to determine how many florets to carve around the church doorway.

To convert the native populations, New World Spanish priests and architects altered their normal ways of teaching and building. Often before the church was built, an open-air atrium was constructed to accommodate large numbers of parishioners for services. *Posas* (shelters) at the four corners of churchyards were another architectural technique unique to Mexico, again to accommodate crowds. Because of the language barrier between the Spanish and the natives, church adornment became more explicit. Biblical tales came to life in frescoes splashed across church walls. Christian symbolism in stone supplanted that of pre-Hispanic ideas as the natives tried to make sense of it all.

Almost every village in the Yucatán Peninsula has the remains of **missions, monasteries, convents,** and **parish churches.** Many were built in the 16th century following the early arrival of Franciscan friars. Examples include the Mission of San Bernardino de Sisal in Valladolid; the fine altarpiece at Teabo; the folk-art *retablo* (altarpiece) at Tecoh; the large church and convent at Maní with its *retablos* and limestone crucifix; the facade, altar, and central *retablo* of the church at Oxkutzcab; the 16-bell belfry at Ytholin; the baroque facade and altarpiece at Maxcanú; the cathedral at Mérida; the vast atrium and church at Izamal; and the baroque *retablo* and murals at Tabi.

When Porfirio Díaz became president in the late 19th century, the nation's art and architecture experienced another infusion of European sensibility. Díaz idolized Europe, and he commissioned a number of striking European-style public buildings, including many opera houses. He provided European scholarships to promising young artists who later returned to Mexico to produce Mexican subject paintings using techniques learned abroad.

THE ADVENT OF MEXICAN MURALISM

As the Mexican revolution ripped the country apart between 1911 and 1917, a new social and cultural Mexico was born. In 1923, Minister of Education José Vasconcelos was charged with educating the illiterate masses. As one means of reaching people, he invited **Diego Rivera** and several other budding artists to paint Mexican history on the walls of the Ministry of Education building and the National Preparatory School in Mexico City. Thus began the tradition of painting murals in public buildings, which you will find in towns and cities throughout Mexico and the Yucatán.

5 Religion, Myth & Folklore

Mexico is predominantly Roman Catholic, a religion introduced by the Spaniards during the Conquest of Mexico. Despite its preponderance, the Catholic faith in many places in Mexico (Chiapas and Oaxaca, for example) has pre-Hispanic undercurrents. You need only visit the *curandero* section of a Mexican market (where you can purchase copal, an incense agreeable to the gods; rustic beeswax candles, a traditional offering; the native species of tobacco used to ward off evil; and so on), or attend a village festivity featuring pre-Hispanic dancers, to understand that supernatural beliefs often run parallel with Christian ones.

Mexico's complicated mythological heritage from pre-Hispanic religion is full of images derived from nature—the wind, jaguars, eagles, snakes, flowers, and more—all intertwined with elaborate mythological stories to explain the universe, climate, seasons, and geography. Most groups believed in an underworld (not a hell), usually containing nine levels,

Gods & Goddesses

Each of the ancient cultures had its gods and goddesses, and while the names might not have crossed cultures, their characteristics or purposes often did. Chaac, the hook-nosed rain god of the Maya, was Tlaloc, the squat rain god of the Aztecs; Quetzalcoatl, the plumed-serpent god/man of the Toltecs, became Kukulkán of the Maya. The tales of the powers and creation of these deities make up Mexico's rich mythology. Sorting out the pre-Hispanic pantheon and beliefs in ancient Mexico can become an all-consuming study (the Maya alone had 166 deities), so here's a list of some of the most important gods:

Chaac   Maya rain god.

Ehécatl   Wind god whose temple is usually round.

Itzamná   Maya god important in creation myths, who invented corn, cacao, and writing and reading.

Ixchel   Maya goddess of water, weaving, and childbirth.

Kukulkán   Quetzalcoatl's name in the Yucatán.

Ometeotl   God/goddess, all-powerful creator of the universe, and ruler of heaven, earth, and the underworld.

Quetzalcoatl   A mortal who took on legendary characteristics as a god (or vice versa). When he left Tula in shame after a night of succumbing to temptations, he promised to return. He reappeared in the Yucatán. He is also symbolized as Venus, the morning star.

and a heaven of 13 levels—which is why the numbers 9 and 13 are so mythologically significant. The solar calendar count of 365 days and the ceremonial calendar of 260 days are significant as well. How one died determined one's resting place after death: in the underworld (*Xibalba* to the Maya), in heaven, or at one of the four cardinal points. For example, men who died in battle or women who died in childbirth went straight to the sun. Everyone else first had to make a journey through the underworld.

6 The Lay of the Land

The Yucatán Peninsula covers almost 134,400 sq. km (51,892 sq. miles), with nearly 1,600km (1,000 miles) of shoreline and has a unique geology found nowhere else on Earth. The entire peninsula is a flat slab of limestone that millions of years ago absorbed the force of a giant meteor—the same meteor thought to have extinguished the dinosaurs. The impact sent shock waves through the brittle limestone, fracturing it throughout, creating an immense network of fissures that drain all rainwater away from the surface. In fact, most of the Yucatán has no surface water; instead, rainwater runs into underground rivers. When driving through northern and central Yucatán, you'll notice no bridges, no rivers, lakes, or watercourses. The land has a surprising uniformity on the surface; most terrain is layered with a thin soil supporting a primarily low, scrubby jungle. A vast subterranean basin,

Underwater Wonders

Cozumel's reefs are amazing underwater mountain ranges—steep walls of coral, rock, and sponge that drop into an abyss, with colors and coral textures that rival the fall foliage of New England, in the United States. After a Jacques Cousteau film in 1961 publicized the reef system, Cozumel became one of the top dive destinations in the world.

which stretches for miles across the peninsula, holds nearly all the fresh water on the peninsula. **Cenotes,** sinkholes or natural wells that exist nowhere else on Earth, are perfectly round vertical shafts that provide a peek into this underground world. A fantastic example is the **Grand Cenote at Chichén Itzá.** Some cenotes even retain a partial roof, often perforated by tree roots. Quiet, dark, and cool, they are the opposite of the warm, brightly lit outside world. To the Maya, they were passageways to the underworld.

The only sense of height comes from the hills along the western shores of Campeche, rising inland to the border with Yucatán state. These are the Puuc Hills, less than 300m (984 ft.) high at their peak. The highways undulate a bit as you go inland, and south of Ticul there's a rise in the highway that provides a marvelous view of the "valley" and the misty Puuc hills lining the horizon.

As you move south, the soils get deeper, and the forest canopy grows taller.

A few surface lakes can be found along the southeastern shore of the peninsula, and wildlife and plant life become more varied.

Moving down from the peninsula to the isthmus, you reach Tabasco and Chiapas, which have a different geology all together. Tabasco is a low-lying state bordering the Gulf of Mexico at its most southern extreme. The capital, Villahermosa, lies in a shallow basin about an hour from the coast at the confluence of two rivers. Small lakes break up the city landscape, especially in the modern parts of the city. Parts of Tabasco are completely covered in a thick rainforest, which extends through Chiapas. Chiapas is a much larger state that extends from Tabasco all the way to the Pacific on one side and Guatemala on the other. In the center is a tall and dramatic mountain range which is the homeland of the highland Maya and the city of San Cristóbal.

7 Books, Film & Music

Studying up on Mexico can be one of the most fun bits of "research" you'll ever do. If you'd like to learn more about this fascinating country before you go—which I encourage—these books, movies, and musicians are an enjoyable way to do it.

BOOKS

HISTORY & CULTURE For an overview of pre-Hispanic cultures, pick up a copy of Michael D. Coe's *Mexico: From the Olmecs to the Aztecs* (Thames & Hudson) or Nigel Davies's *Ancient Kingdoms of Mexico* (Penguin). Richard Townsend's *The Aztecs* (Thames & Hudson) is a thorough, well-researched examination of the Aztec and the Spanish conquest. For the Maya, Michael Coe's *The Maya* (Thames & Hudson) is probably the best general account. For a survey of Mexican history through modern times, *A Short History of Mexico* by J. Patrick McHenry (Doubleday) provides a complete, yet concise account.

John L. Stephens's *Incidents of Travel in the Yucatán, Vol. I and II* (Dover Publications) are considered among the great books of archaeological discovery, as well as being travel classics. The two volumes chart the course of Stephens's discoveries of the Yucatán, beginning in 1841. Before his expeditions, little was known of the region, and the Maya culture had not been discovered. During his travels, Stephens found and described 44 Maya sites, and his account of these remains the most authoritative in existence.

For contemporary culture, start with Octavio Paz's classic, *The Labyrinth of Solitude* (Grove Press), which still generates controversy among Mexicans because of some of the generalizations Paz makes about them. For a recent collection of writings by Subcomandante Marcos, leader of the Zapatista movement, try *Our Word Is Our Weapon* (Seven Stories Press). Another source is *Basta! Land and the Zapatista Rebellion* (Food First) by George Collier, et al. For those already familiar with Mexico and its culture, Guillermo Bonfil's *Mexico Profundo: Reclaiming a Civilization* (University of Texas Press) is a rare bottom-up view of Mexico today.

Lesley Byrd Simpson's *Many Mexicos* (University of California Press) provides comprehensive account of Mexican history with a cultural context. A classic on understanding the culture of this country is *Distant Neighbors*, by Alan Riding (Vintage).

ART & ARCHITECTURE

Art and Time in Mexico: From the Conquest to the Revolution, by Elizabeth Wilder Weismann (Harper & Row), covers religious, public, and private architecture. *Casa Mexicana Style*, by Tim Street-Porter and Annie Kelly (Stewart, Tabori, and Chang), documents the interiors of some of Mexico's finest public buildings, and private houses.

Maya Art and Architecture, by Mary Ellen Miller (Thames and Hudson) showcases the best of the artistic expression of this culture, with interpretations into its meanings.

NATURE

A Naturalist's Mexico, by Roland H. Wauer (Texas A&M University Press), is becoming difficult to find, but *A Hiker's Guide to Mexico's Natural History,* by Jim Conrad (Mountaineers Books) is a good alternative. *Peterson Field Guides: Mexican Birds,* by Roger Tory Peterson and Edward L. Chalif (Houghton Mifflin), is an excellent guide.

LITERATURE

My favorite writer remains **Jorge Ibargüengoitia.** Although he died in 1983, he remains popular in Mexico. You can occasionally find his works in translation. His novel *Estas ruinas que ves (These Ruins You See)* gently pokes fun at Mexico's provincial life. His *The Dead Girls* is a fictionalized telling of a famous crime that happened in Mexico in the '70s. He has several personal narratives, too. All his works display a deft touch at characterization and an insightful and ironic view of life in Mexico.

Novelist **Carlos Fuentes** is Mexico's preeminent living writer. His earlier novels, such as **The Death of Artemio Cruz,** are easier to read than his most recent works, which are heavily post-structural and demand a great deal of effort from the reader. Angeles Mastretta's **Arráncame la vida (Tear Up My Life),** a well-written, straight forward narrative about life in Puebla, brimming with political gossip, is a delightful read. Another good novel covering roughly the same period, but with fewer social observations and more magical realism is **Like Water for Chocolate** by Laura Esquivel. This book and the movie of the same title did much to popularize Mexican food abroad.

Hasta No Verte by Elena Poniatowska is worth a read, as is anything by **Luis**

Alberto Urrea, the master of heart-wrenching works about third-world realities.

Guillermo Arriaga, the screenwriter for *Amores Perros,* is a brilliant writer of *literatura,* too. If you can read Spanish, pick up these books on your trip: *Retorno 201* was the name of the street Arriaga grew up on, and the book is filled with his impressions of Mexico City back then; *El Bufalo de la Noche* is a novel about a young man reeling from his best friend's suicide. Both books are due to be published in the U.S. by Atria, so keep an eye out for the English versions soon.

MEXICAN CINEMA
GOLDEN AGE & CLASSICS

Mexico's "Golden Age of Cinema" refers to a period in the 1940s when the country's film studios dropped their attempts at mimicking Hollywood and started producing black and white films that were Mexican to the core. The stars of the day are now icons of Mexican culture. **Mario Moreno,** aka Cantinflas, was the comedic genius that personalized the cultural archetype of *el pelado*—a poor, picaresque, slightly naughty character looking to get ahead by his wits alone, which, in fact, don't get him very far. His speech is a torrent of free association and digressions and innuendo that gives the comedy a madcap quality. **Dolores del Río** was the Mexican beauty who was later shipped off to Hollywood to fill the role of steamy Latin babe. **Pedro Infante** expressed the ideal of Mexican manhood, and was also Mexico's singing cowboy.

For some takes on old-school Mexico, check out Elia Kazan's 1952 classic, *Viva Zapata!,* written by John Steinbeck and starring Marlon Brando as the Mexican revolutionary Emiliano Zapata. Then there's Orson Welles's *Touch of Evil,* about drugs and corruption in Tijuana (preposterously starring Charlton Heston as a Mexican). Or rent the HBO flick

And Starring Pancho Villa as Himself with Antonio Banderas, a true story about how revolutionaries allowed a Hollywood film company to tape Pancho Villa in actual battle.

Luis Buñuel's dark 1950 film *Los Olvidados* explores the life of young hoodlums living in the slums of Mexico City. It was filmed partially in the Plaza de La Romita, a charming, somewhat hidden section of Colonia Roma.

THE NEW CINEMA

After the 1940s, Mexico's film industry entered a long period of unoriginal endeavors until a new generation of filmmakers came along who've had success both in Mexico and abroad. This new age is being dubbed *El Nuevo Cine Mexicano* (The New Cinema).

The first film to become a big hit outside Mexico was *Like Water for Chocolate* (1992), which was directed by Alfonso Arau, author Laura Esquivel's husband at the time. He continues to make films, mainly in Mexico.

Filmmaker **Alfonso Cuarón** had scored a critical and commercial success in Mexico with his debut film *Sólo con tu pareja* (1991), a mordant social satire that any film buff interested in Mexico should see. His *Y Tu Mamá También* (2001) follows a pair of teenage boys who end up on an impromptu road trip to a fictional beach with a sexy older woman they meet at a wedding. The film touches on the hypocrisy of the country's governing classes, and issues of social inequality, all with an ironic slant.

In search of larger budgets, Cuarón has since directed major international productions, including *Harry Potter and the Prisoner of Azkaban* and the science fiction thriller *Children of Men.*

In *Amores Perros* (2000), the director of *21 Grams* and *Babel* (Alejandro González Iñárritu) presents three connected stories about different ways of life in Mexico City that become intertwined at the site of a car accident. Taken together, the stories offer a keen glimpse into contemporary Mexican society. González Iñárritu's Academy Award–nominated *Babel* is another tour de force; its Mexican border scene is realistic, exhilarating, and frightening all at once.

Guillermo del Toro has also had parallel success. His debut film, ***Cronos*** (1993), was a dark, atmospheric piece that garnered critical acclaim in Mexico. From there, he moved on to the international scene and has directed several films with similar moods, including *Hellboy* and *Pan's Labyrinth.*

Julie Taymor's ***Frida*** (2002), produced and acted by Mexican national Salma Hayek, is a wonderful biopic about Frida Kahlo. Watch it and you'll learn everything you need to know about Kahlo's life and work, from her devastating accident to her relationships with Diego Rivera and Leon Trotsky. The exquisite cinematography captures Mexico's inherent spirit of magic realism, evinced in Kahlo's work.

Director Robert Rodriguez's breakout film, ***El Mariachi*** (1992) is set in a small central Mexican town. Made on a shoe-string budget, this somewhat cheesy action flick is at least highly entertaining. His ***Once Upon a Time in Mexico*** (2003) isn't as great but it's fun to see scenes of San Miguel Allende, where it was filmed. Ditto for the Brad Pitt and Julia Roberts' ***The Mexican*** (2001).

Man on Fire (2004) stars Denzel Washington and Dakota Fanning, as a bodyguard in Mexico City and the little girl he is hired to protect. There are some great scenes shot around the city, even though the plot is pretty depressing.

Sexo, Pudor y Lágrimas (1999), by director Antonio Serrano is a gritty, unflinching look at the battle of the sexes in Mexico City in the '90s. It was the second film to emerge from the new era of Mexican cinema, after *Like Water for Chocolate.*

Tijuana Makes Me Happy (2005), directed by Dylan Verrechia with music by Pepe Mogt from Nortec Collective, shows a thankfully bright and realistic picture of Tijuana. The film's goal is "to break down the preconceived notion of Tijuana as a city of sin by showing the humanity of its people: their struggle, the strength of character, and the love of life that flourishes within." Something must be working—the film has won Latin film awards and was screened in 2007 at the Slamdance festival.

If you want more info on what's happening now in border towns, rent Stephen Soderberg's Academy Award–winning ***Traffic*** (2000), starring Benicio del Toro. It includes some powerful scenes focusing on the drug war at the Tijuana border. Or get a hold of the documentary ***Tijuana Remix*** (2002), which celebrates the city's culturally unique and idiosyncratic qualities. You can also get a great "tourist guide" online via a short film called ***Tijuana es Addiccion*** made by local Jacinto Astiazaran.

MUSIC
MARIMBA & SON

Marimba music can be heard in many parts of southern and central Mexico, but it is considered a traditional music in only two places: the state of Chiapas, and the port city of Veracruz. From here, many bands travel to places like Oaxaca and Mexico City, where they play in clubs and restaurants. Marimba is played nightly for free in **Parque de las Marimba,** in Tuxtla Gutierrez, Chiapas.

Son is a native art form from many parts of Mexico. It is played with a variety of string instruments. One of the most famous forms is *Son Jarocho,* which often is fast paced and has a lot of strumming and fancy string picking. Dancing to this form of music requires a lot of fast rhythmic pounding with the heels of the feet *(zapateado)*. It comes from the southern part of the state of Veracruz. One of its traditional songs, "La Bamba," was popularized by Ritchie Valens in the '50s.

DANZON & BOLERO

Both of these musical forms came from Cuba in the late 19th century and gained great popularity here. *Danzón* is orchestra music, which combines a Latin flavor with a stateliness absent from later Latin music. Its popularity is greatest in Veracruz and Mexico City. *Bolero* (or *trova*) is the music mainly of guitar trios such as Los Panchos. It's soft, romantic, and often a touch melancholy.

MARIACHI & RANCHERA

Mariachi is the music most readily identified with Mexico, and *mariachis,* with their distinctive costume—big sombreros, waist-length jackets and tight pants—easily standout. The music originated from a style of *son* played in the state of Jalisco. It was rearranged to be played with guitars, violins, a string bass, and trumpets. Now you hear it across Mexico and much of the American southwest, but Jalisco and its capital, Guadalajara, are still considered the best place to hear mariachis.

Ranchera music is closely associated with mariachi music and is performed with the same instruments. It's defined by its expression of national pride, strong individualism, and lots of sentiment; hence its favored status as drinking music. The most famous composer is José Alfredo Jiménez, whose songs many Mexicans know by heart.

NORTEÑA, GRUPERA & BANDA

Norteña owes its origins to *tejano* music, coming out of Texas. Mexicans in south central Texas came in contact with musicians from the immigrant Czech and German communities of the Texas Hill Country and picked up a taste for polkas and the accordion. Gradually the music became popular further south. *Norteña* music tweaked the polka for many of its popular songs and later borrowed from the *cumbia,* slowing the tempo a bit and adding a strong down beat. It also incorporated a native form of song known as the *corrido,* which is a type of ballad that was popularized during the Mexican revolution (1910–17). *Norteña* became hugely popular in rural northern Mexico though the 1970s and later generated spin-offs, which are known as *grupera* or *banda,* a style of *norteña* from the area of Sinaloa, which replaces the accordion with electric keyboards. **Los Tigres del Norte,** with their catchy melodies backed by hopped up accordion and bass guitars, are probably the most famous practitioners of *norteña* music.

ROCK EN ESPAÑOL

Mexican rock gained its identity in the 1980s and exploded in popularity during the 1990s with bands such as Los Jaguares, Maná, and Molotov. Named for the old (1920s) cafe in the capital's Centro Histórico, **Café Tacuba** has been together since 1989. Their music is influenced by indigenous Mexican music as much as folk, punk, bolero, and hip-hop.

3

Planning Your Trip to the Yucatán, Tabasco & Chiapas

by Juan Cristiano

Unless you intend to stick to the well-serviced beaches of the Caribbean, a trip to Mexico's Yucatán Peninsula or the southern states of Tabasco and Chiapas will require planning, patience, and flexibility. Quintana Roo is by far the most advanced tourist state in this region, playing host to about half of all tourism to Mexico. It's easy to travel between Cancún and the beaches of the Riviera Maya, where tourist infrastructure is well developed. You can either plan on resort hopping along the Caribbean coast in a rental car, or taking buses to visit the Maya ruins in the Yucatán peninsula. Getting to and around Chiapas requires a little more ingenuity, and traveling in Tabasco has been complicated by the significant flooding of 2007. Be prepared and willing to deal with everything.

Travelers to Mexico should be aware of security concerns in certain parts of the country and take precautions to maximize their safety. For the most part, Mexico is safe for travelers who steer clear of drugs and those who sell them, but visitors should still exercise caution in unfamiliar areas and remain aware of their surroundings at all times. See "Safety," below, for more details; and visit the U.S. State Department's website, www.travel.state.gov, for up-to-date information on travel to Mexico.

For additional resources in planning your trip and for more resources in Mexico, see p. 285 in Appendix A, "Fast Facts, Toll-Free Numbers & Websites."

1 Visitor Information

TOURIST INFORMATION

The **Mexico Tourism Board** (© 800/446-3942; www.visitmexico.com) is an excellent source for general information; you can request brochures and get answers to the most common questions from the exceptionally well-trained, knowledgeable staff

More information (15,000 pages' worth) about Mexico is available on the official site of Mexico's Tourism Board, **www.visitmexico.com**.

The **Mexican Government Tourist Board's** main office is in Mexico City (© 55/5278-4200). Satellite offices are in the U.S., Canada, and the UK. In the **United States:** Chicago (© 312/228-0517), Houston (© 713/772-2581), Los Angeles (© 310/282-9112), Miami (© 786/621-2909), and New York (© 212/308-2110).

In **Canada:** Toronto (© 416/925-0704). In the **United Kingdom:** London (© 020/7488-9392).

STATE TOURISM BOARDS

The **Chiapas Tourism Board** is at Blvd. Belisario Dominguez 950, CP29060 Tuxtla Gutiérrez, Chiapas (© 961/613-9396). The **Quintana Roo Tourist Board** is at Carr. a. Calderitas 622, CP77010 Chetumal, Quintana Roo, (© 983/835-0860). The Tabasco Tourism Board is at Av. Los Rios s/n, Tabasco 2000, CP86035 Villahermosa, Tabasco (© 961/613-9396). The Yucatán Tourism Board is at Calle 59 No. 514, Centro, CP97000 Mérida, Yucatán (© 999/924-9389).

MEXICAN EMBASSIES

The Mexican Embassy in the United States is at 1911 Pennsylvania Ave. NW, Washington, D.C. 20006 (© 202/728-1750 or -1600).

The Mexican Embassy in Canada is at 055 Rue Peel, Suite 1000, Montreal, QUE, H3A 1V4 (© 514/288-2502); Commerce Court West, 199 Bay St., Suite 4440, Toronto, ON, M5L 1E9 (© 416/925-0704); 710 West Hastings St., Suite 1177, Vancouver, BC V6E 2K3 (© 604/684-1859); 1500-45 O'Connor St., Ottawa, ON, K1P 1A4 (© 613/233-8988; fax 613/235-9123.

The Mexican Embassy (Consular Section) in the United Kingdom is at 8 Halkin St., London SW1X 7DW (© 020/7235-6393).

2 Entry Requirements

PASSPORTS

All travelers to Mexico are required to present photo identification and proof of citizenship, such as a valid passport, naturalization papers, or an original birth certificate with a raised seal, along with a driver's license or official ID, such as a state or military-issued ID. Note that driver's licenses and permits, voter registration cards, affidavits, and similar documents are not sufficient to prove citizenship for readmission into the United States. If the last name on the birth certificate is different from your current name, bring a photo identification card *and* legal proof of the name change, such as the original marriage license or certificate. *Note:* Photocopies are *not* acceptable.

New regulations issued by the Department of Homeland Security now require virtually every air traveler entering the U.S. to show a passport. As of January 23, 2007, all persons, including U.S. citizens, traveling by air between the United States and Canada, Mexico, Central and South America, the Caribbean, and Bermuda are required to present a valid passport or other valid travel document. Effective January 31, 2008, U.S. and Canadian citizens traveling between the United States and Mexico by land or sea

will need to present either a WHTI-compliant document (see below), or a government-issued photo ID, such as a driver's license, plus proof of citizenship, such as a birth certificate. The Department of Homeland Security (DHS) also proposes to begin alternative procedures for U.S. and Canadian children at that time.

Other valid travel documents (known as WHTI-compliant documents; visit www.travel.state.gov for more information) for travel by land or sea include the new Passport Card and SENTRI, NEXUS, FAST, and the U.S. Coast Guard Mariner Document. Members of the U.S. Armed Forces on active duty traveling on orders are exempt from the passport requirement. U.S. citizens living in the border region can apply for the new, limited-use, wallet-size Passport Card which is designed to be a cheaper and easier form of international identification. The cards are valid only for land and sea travel between the U.S. and Canada, Mexico, the Caribbean region, and Bermuda.

From our perspective, it's easiest just to travel with a valid passport. Safeguard your passport in an inconspicuous, inaccessible place like a money belt, and keep a copy of the critical pages with your passport number in a separate place. If you lose your passport, visit the nearest consulate of your native country as soon as possible for a replacement.

For information on how to get a passport, see p. 288 ("Passports," in Appendix A, "Fast Facts, Toll-Free Numbers & Websites"). The websites listed provide downloadable passport applications and current fees for processing passport applications. For information on entry requirements for Mexico, see the Entry/Exit Requirements section in the Country Specific Information for Mexico at **http://travel.state.gov/travel/cis_pa_tw/cis/cis_970.html**. You may also contact the U.S. embassy or consulate of Mexico for further information.

VISAS

For detailed information regarding visas to Mexico, visit the Mexican Ministry of External Relations (SRE) at www.sre.gob.mx/english/services/visasforeigners.htm.

U.S. citizens do not require a visa or a tourist card for tourist stays of 72 hours or less within "the border zone," defined as an area from 20 to 30km (12–19 miles) of the U.S. border, depending on the location.

A visa is required, however, if you are going to stay in Mexico more than 72 hours and venture beyond the border tourist zone.

U.S. citizens traveling as tourists beyond the border zone or entering Mexico by air must pay a fee to obtain a **tourist card (FMT),** available from Mexican consulates, Mexican border crossing points, Mexican tourism offices, airports within the border zone, and most airlines serving Mexico. The fee for the tourist card is generally included in the price of a plane ticket for travelers arriving by air. For visitors arriving by other means, it's about $21. Airlines generally provide the necessary forms aboard your flight to Mexico. The FMT is more important

than a passport, so guard it carefully. If you lose it, you may not be allowed to leave until you replace it—a bureaucratic hassle that can take anywhere from a few hours to a week.

The FMT can be issued for up to 180 days. Sometimes officials don't ask but just stamp a time limit, so be sure to say "6 months," or at least twice as long as you intend to stay. If you decide to extend your stay, you may request that additional time be added to your FMT by an official immigration office in Mexico.

In **Baja California,** immigration laws have changed; they allow FMTs for a maximum of 180 days per year, with a maximum of 30 days per visit. This is to encourage regular visitors, or those who spend longer periods in Mexico, to obtain documents that denote partial residency.

For travelers entering Mexico by car at the border of Baja California, note that FMTs are issued only in Tijuana, Tecate, and Mexicali, as well as in Ensenada and Guerrero Negro. If you travel anywhere beyond the frontier zone without the FMT, you will be fined $40 (£20).

Note on travel of minors: Mexican law requires that any non-Mexican citizen under the age of 18 departing Mexico must carry notarized written permission from a parent or guardian who is not traveling with the child to or from Mexico. This permission must include the name of the parent, the name of the child, the name of anyone traveling with the child, and the notarized signature(s) of the absent parent(s). The U.S. State Department recommends that permission include travel dates, destinations, airlines, and a brief summary of the circumstances surrounding the travel. The child must be carrying the original letter (not a facsimile or scanned copy), as well as proof of the parent/child relationship (usually a birth certificate or court document) and an original custody decree, if applicable. Travelers should contact the

Cut to the Front of the Airport Security Line as a Registered Traveler

In 2003, the **Transportation Security Administration (TSA;** www.tsa.gov) approved a pilot program to help ease the wait time for airport security screenings. In exchange for information and a fee, persons can be pre-screened as **registered travelers,** granting them a spot at the front of the line when they fly. The program is run through private firms—the largest and most well-known is Steven Brill's **Clear** (www.flyclear.com), and it works like this: Travelers complete an online application providing specific points of personal information including name, addresses for the previous five years, birth date, social security number, driver's license number, and a valid credit card (you're not charged the **$99 fee** until your application is approved). Print out the completed form and bring it with you, along with proper ID, to an "enrollment station" (found in more than 20 participating airports and in a growing number of American Express offices around the U.S., for example). At this point, the process gets a little sci-fi: At the enrollment station, a Clear representative will record your biometrics, necessary for clearance, and digitally record your fingerprints and irises.

Once your application has been screened against no-fly lists, outstanding warrants, and other security measures, you'll be issued a clear plastic card that holds a chip containing your information. Each time you fly through participating airports (and the numbers are steadily growing), go to the Clear Pass station located next to the standard TSA screening line. Here you'll insert your card into a slot and place your finger on a scanner to read your print—when the information matches up, you're cleared to cut to the front of the security line. You'll still have to follow all the procedures of the day—such as removing your shoes and walking through the X-ray machine—but Clear promises to cut 30 minutes off your wait time at the airport.

On a personal note: Each time I've used my Clear Pass, my travel companions are still waiting to go through security while I'm already sitting down, reading the paper, and sipping my overpriced smoothie. Granted, registered traveler programs are not for the infrequent traveler, but for those of us who fly on a regular basis, it's a perk worth paying for.

—*David A. Lytle, Frommers.com*

Mexican Embassy or closest Mexican Consulate for current information.

MEDICAL REQUIREMENTS

No special vaccinations are required for entry into Mexico. For other medical requirements and health-related recommendations, see "Health," p. 59.

CUSTOMS

Mexican Customs inspection has been streamlined. At most points of entry, tourists are requested to press a button in front of what looks like a traffic signal, which alternates on touch between red and green. Green light and you go through without inspection; red light and your luggage or car may be inspected. If

Tax Refund

In June 2008, the government of Mexico began a tax refund program for foreign visitors. The Value-Added Tax (VAT or IVA in Spanish) can now be refunded at select Mexican airports (including Cancún and Mexico City). Visitors must prove that they have spent more than 1,200 pesos (approximately US$116/£61) in participating stores to receive a refund of up to 50% of the VAT (about 15% of the total value of an item). After filling out the appropriate paperwork, you will receive the refund either in cash or as a credit to your bank account. The refund is not applicable to hotels, restaurants, and services. Because this is a new initiative in 2008, expect a few kinks and delays in the system.

you have an unusual amount of luggage or an oversized piece, you may be subject to inspection anyway.

WHAT YOU CAN BRING INTO MEXICO

When you enter Mexico, Customs officials will be tolerant if you are not carrying illegal drugs or firearms. Tourists are allowed to bring in their personal effects duty-free. A laptop computer, camera equipment, and sports equipment that could feasibly be used during your stay are also allowed. The underlying guideline is: Don't bring anything that looks as if it's meant to be resold in Mexico. **U.S. citizens** entering Mexico by the land border can bring in gifts worth up to $50 duty-free, except for alcohol and tobacco products. Those entering Mexico by air or sea can bring in gifts worth a value of up to $300 duty-free. The **website for Mexican Customs** ("Aduanas") is www.aduanas.sat.gob.mx/webadunet/body.htm.

WHAT YOU CAN TAKE HOME FROM MEXICO

U.S. Citizens: Returning U.S. citizens who have been away for at least 48 hours are allowed to bring back, once every 30 days, $800 worth of merchandise duty-free. You'll pay a flat rate of duty on the next $1,000 worth of purchases. Any dollar amount beyond that is subject to duties at whatever rates apply. On mailed gifts, the duty-free limit is $200. Be sure to keep your receipts for purchases accessible to expedite the declaration process. *Note:* If you owe duty, you are required to pay on your arrival in the United States—either by cash, personal check, government or traveler's check, or money order (and, in some locations, a Visa or MasterCard).

To avoid paying duty on foreign-made personal items you owned before your trip, bring along a bill of sale, insurance policy, jeweler's appraisal, or receipts of purchase. Or before you leave, you can register with Customs items that can be readily identified by a permanently affixed serial number or marking—think laptop computers and cameras. Take the items to the nearest Customs office or register them with Customs at the airport from which you're departing. You'll receive, at no cost, a Certificate of Registration, which allows duty-free entry for the life of the item.

For specifics on what you can bring back and the corresponding fees, download the invaluable free pamphlet *Know Before You Go* online at **www.cbp.gov** (click on "Travel," and then click on "Know Before You Go! Online Brochure"). Or contact the **U.S. Customs & Border Protection (CBP),** 1300 Pennsylvania Ave. NW, Washington, D.C. 20229 (© **877/287-8667**) and request the pamphlet.

Canadian Citizens: For a clear summary of Canadian rules, write for the booklet *I Declare,* issued by the **Canada Border Services Agency** (*©* **800/461-9999** in Canada, or 204/983-3500; www.cbsa-asfc.gc.ca).

U.K. Citizens: For information, contact **HM Revenue & Customs** at *©* **0845/010-9000** (from outside the U.K., 020/8929-0152), or consult their website at www.hmrc.gov.uk.

Australian Citizens: A helpful brochure available from Australian consulates or Customs offices is *Know Before You Go.* For more information, call the **Australian Customs Service** at *©* **1300/363-263,** or log on to www.customs.gov.au.

New Zealand Citizens: Most questions are answered in a free pamphlet available at New Zealand consulates and Customs offices: *New Zealand Customs Guide for Travellers, Notice no. 4.* For more information, contact **New Zealand Customs Service,** The Customhouse, 17–21 Whitmore St., Box 2218, Wellington (*©* **04/473-6099** or 0800/428-786; www.customs.govt.nz).

3 When to Go

High season in the Yucatán begins around December 20 and continues to Easter. This is the best time for calm, warm weather; snorkeling, diving, and fishing (the calmer weather means clearer and more predictable seas); and for visiting the ruins that dot the interior of the peninsula. Book well in advance if you plan to be in Cancún around the holidays.

Low season begins the day after Easter and continues to mid-December; during low season, prices may drop 20% to 50%. However, in Cancún and along the Riviera Maya, demand by European visitors is creating a summer high season, with hotel rates approaching those charged in the winter months.

Generally speaking, Mexico's **dry season** runs from November to April, with the **rainy season** stretching from May to October. It isn't a problem if you're staying close to the beaches, but for those bent on road-tripping to Chichén Itzá, Uxmal, or other sites, temperatures and humidity in the interior can be downright stifling from May to July. Later in the rainy season, the frequency of **tropical storms** and **hurricanes** increases; such storms, of course, can put a crimp in your vacation. But they can lower temperatures, making climbing ruins a real joy, accompanied by cool air and a slight wind. November is especially ideal for Yucatán travels. Cancún, Cozumel, and Isla Mujeres also have a rainy season from November to January, when northern storms hit. This usually means diving visibility is diminished—and conditions may prevent boats from even going out.

Villahermosa is sultry and humid all the time. San Cristóbal de las Casas, at an elevation of 2,152m (7,059 ft.), is much cooler than the lowlands and is downright cold in winter.

Cancun's Average Temperatures

	Jan	Feb	Mar	Apr	May	June	July	Aug	Sept	Oct	Nov	Dec
Avg. High (°F)	81	82	84	85	88	89	90	90	89	87	84	82
Avg. High (°C)	27	27	28	29	31	31	32	32	31	30	28	27
Avg. Low (°F)	67	68	71	73	77	78	78	77	76	74	72	69
Avg. Low (°C)	19	20	21	22	25	25	25	25	24	23	22	20

CALENDAR OF EVENTS

Religious and secular festivals are a part of life in Mexico. Every town, city, and state holds its own specific festivals throughout the year commemorating religious and historic figures. Indeed, in certain parts of the country it sometimes feels like the festivities never die down, and the Yucatán, Tabasco, and Chiapas are no exception.

January

Año Nuevo (New Year's Day), nationwide. This national holiday is perhaps the quietest day in all of Mexico. Most people stay home or attend church. All businesses are closed. In traditional indigenous communities, new tribal leaders are inaugurated with colorful ceremonies rooted in the pre-Hispanic past. January 1.

Día de los Reyes (Three Kings' Day), nationwide. This day commemorates the Three Kings' presenting gifts to the Christ Child. On this day, children receive presents, much like they do at Christmas in the United States. Friends and families gather to share the Rosca de Reyes, a special cake. Inside the cake is a small doll representing the Christ Child; whoever receives the doll must host a tamales-and-*atole* (a warm drink made of masa) party on February 2. January 6.

February

Día de la Candelaria (Candlemas), nationwide. Music, dances, processions, food, and other festivities lead up to a blessing of seed and candles in a ceremony that mixes pre-Hispanic and European traditions marking the end of winter. Those who attended the Three Kings celebration reunite to share *atole* and tamales at a party hosted by the recipient of the doll found in the Rosca. February 2.

Día de la Constitución (Constitution Day), nationwide. This national holiday is in honor of the current Mexican constitution, signed in 1917 as a result of the revolutionary war of 1910. It's celebrated through small parades. February 5.

Carnaval, nationwide. Carnaval takes place the 3 days preceding Ash Wednesday and the beginning of Lent. In Cozumel, the celebration resembles New Orleans's Mardi Gras, with a festive atmosphere and parades. In Chamula, the event harks back to pre-Hispanic times, with ritualistic running on flaming branches. Cancún also celebrates with parade floats and street parties.

Ash Wednesday, nationwide. The start of Lent and time of abstinence, this is a day of reverence nationwide; some towns honor it with folk dancing and fairs.

March

Benito Juárez's Birthday, nationwide. This national holiday celebrating one of Mexico's most beloved leaders is observed through small hometown celebrations, especially in Juárez's birthplace, Guelatao, Oaxaca. March 21.

Spring Equinox, Chichén Itzá. On the first day of spring, the Temple of Kukulkán—Chichén Itzá's main pyramid—aligns with the sun, and the shadow of the plumed serpent moves slowly from the top of the building down. When the shadow reaches the bottom, the body joins the carved stone snake's head at the base of the pyramid. According to ancient legend, at the moment that the serpent is whole, the earth is fertilized. Visitors come from around the world to marvel at this sight, so advance arrangements are advisable. Elsewhere, equinox festivals and celebrations welcome spring, in the custom of the ancient Mexicans, with dances and prayers to the elements and the four cardinal points. It's customary to wear white with a red ribbon. March 21 (the shadow appears Mar 19–23).

April

Semana Santa (Holy Week), nationwide. Mexico celebrates the last week in the life of Christ, from Palm Sunday to Easter Sunday, with somber religious processions, spoofing of Judas, and reenactments of biblical events, plus food and craft fairs. Some businesses close during this traditional week of Mexican national vacations, and almost all close on Good Thursday, Friday, Saturday, and Easter Sunday.

If you plan to travel to Mexico during Holy Week, make your reservations early. Airline seats into Cancún in particular will be reserved months in advance. Planes and buses to towns across the Yucatán and to almost anywhere else in Mexico will be full, so try arriving on the Wednesday or Thursday before Good Friday. Easter Sunday is quiet, and the week following is a traditional vacation period. Early April.

May

Labor Day, nationwide. Workers' parades countrywide; everything closes. May 1.

Cinco de Mayo. nationwide. This holiday celebrates the defeat of the French at the Battle of Puebla, although it (ironically) tends to be a bigger celebration in the United States than in Mexico. May 5.

Feast of San Isidro. The patron saint of farmers is honored with a blessing of seeds and work animals. May 15.

Cancún Jazz Festival. For dates and schedule information, check ✆ **800/ 44-MEXICO** or www.cancun.travel.

International Gay Festival. This 5-day event in Cancún kicks off with a welcome fiesta of food, drinks, and mariachi music. Additional festivities include a tequila party, tour of Cancún, sunset Caribbean cruise, bar and beach parties, and a final champagne breakfast. For schedule information, check www.cancun.eventguide.com.

June

Navy Day (Día de la Marina). All coastal towns celebrate with naval parades and fireworks. June 1.

Corpus Christi, nationwide. The day honors the Body of Christ (the Eucharist) with religious processions, Masses, and food. Dates vary.

Día de San Pedro (St. Peter and St. Paul's Day), nationwide. Celebrated wherever St. Peter is the patron saint, this holiday honors anyone named Pedro or Peter. June 26.

August

Assumption of the Virgin Mary, nationwide. This is celebrated throughout the country with special Masses and in some places with processions. August 15 to August 17.

September

Independence Day, nationwide. This day of parades, picnics, and family reunions throughout the country celebrates Mexico's independence from Spain. At 11pm on September 15, the president of Mexico gives the famous independence *grito* (shout) from the National Palace in Mexico City, and local mayors do the same in every town and municipality all over Mexico. On September 16, every city and town conducts a parade in which both government and civilians display their pride in being Mexican. For these celebrations, all important government buildings are draped in the national colors—red, green, and white—and the towns blaze with lights. September 15 and 16; September 16 is a national holiday.

Fall Equinox, Chichén Itzá. The same shadow play that occurs during the spring equinox repeats at the fall equinox. September 21 to September 22.

What's Biting When?

It's fishing season year-round along the Caribbean coast. Here's a general breakdown of what to look for during your trip.

- **Blue Marlin:** June, July, and August.
- **White Marlin:** April through June.
- **Sailfish:** March through July.
- **Grouper:** October through December.
- **Wahoo:** November through January, April through June.
- **Amberjack:** September through December.
- **Dolphin Fish, Blackfin Tuna:** April through May.
- **Bonita:** April through August.
- **Barracuda, Kingfish:** October through December.

October

"Ethnicity Day" or Columbus Day (Día de la Raza), nationwide. This commemorates the fusion of the Spanish and Mexican peoples. October 12.

November

Day of the Dead (Día de los Muertos), nationwide. What's commonly called the Day of the Dead is actually 2 days: All Saints' Day, honoring saints and deceased children, and All Souls' Day, honoring deceased adults. Relatives gather at cemeteries countrywide, carrying candles and food to create an altar, and sometimes spend the night beside the graves of loved ones. Weeks before, bakers begin producing bread (called *pan de muerto*) formed in the shape of mummies or round loaves decorated with bread "bones." Decorated sugar skulls emblazoned with glittery names are sold everywhere. Many days ahead, homes and churches erect special altars laden with Day of the Dead bread, fruit, flowers, candles, favorite foods, and photographs of saints and of the deceased. On the 2 nights, children dress in costumes and masks, often carrying through the streets mock coffins and pumpkin lanterns, into which they

expect money to be dropped. November 1 and 2; November 1 is a national holiday.

Revolution Day. Nationwide. This commemorates the start of the Mexican Revolution in 1910 with parades, speeches, rodeos, and patriotic events. November 20.

Annual Yucatán Bird Festival (Festival de las Aves de Yucatán), Mérida, Yucatán. Bird-watching sessions, workshops, and exhibits are the highlights of this festival, designed to illustrate the special role birds play in our environment and in the Yucatán territory. Call © **800/44-MEXICO** or check out www.yucatanbirds.org.mx for details. Mid-November.

December

Feast of the Virgin of Guadalupe, nationwide. Throughout the country, religious processions, street fairs, dancing, fireworks, and Masses honor the patroness of Mexico. This is one of Mexico's most moving and beautiful displays of traditional culture. The Virgin of Guadalupe appeared to a young man, Juan Diego, in December 1531, on a hill near Mexico City. He convinced the bishop that he had seen the

What's on When?

For an exhaustive list of events beyond those listed here, check **http://events. frommers.com,** with its searchable, up-to-the-minute roster of events in cities all over the world.

apparition by revealing his cloak, upon which the Virgin was emblazoned. It's customary for children to dress up as Juan Diego, wearing mustaches and red bandannas. One of the most famous and elaborate celebrations takes place at the Basílica of Guadalupe, north of Mexico City, where the Virgin appeared. Every village celebrates this day, though, often with processions of children carrying banners of the Virgin and with *charreadas* (rodeos), bicycle races, dancing, and fireworks. December 12.

Christmas Posadas, nationwide. On each of the 9 nights before Christmas, it's customary to reenact the Holy Family's search for an inn, with door-to-door candlelit processions in cities and villages nationwide. These are also hosted by most businesses and community organizations, taking the place of the northern tradition of a Christmas party. December 15 to December 24.

Christmas. Mexicans extend this celebration and often leave their jobs beginning 2 weeks before Christmas all the way through New Year's Day. Many businesses close, and resorts and hotels fill up. Significant celebrations take place on December 24.

New Year's Eve. As in the rest of the world, New Year's Eve in Mexico is celebrated with parties, fireworks, and plenty of noise. December 31.

4 Getting There & Getting Around

GETTING TO MEXICO
BY PLANE

Mexico has dozens of international and domestic airports. Among the airports in the Yucatán region are Cancún (CUN), Cozumel (CZM), and Mérida (MID). The major airport in Chiapas is in Tuxtla Gutierrez (NTR) and in Tabasco, Villahermosa (VSA). For a list of the major international airlines with service to Mexico, turn to "Appendix A: Fast Facts, Toll-Free Numbers & Websites," p. 290.

The main departure points in North America for international airlines are Atlanta, Chicago, Dallas/Fort Worth, Denver, Houston, Las Vegas, Los Angeles, Miami, New York, Orlando, Philadelphia, Phoenix, Raleigh/Durham, San Antonio, San Francisco, Seattle, Toronto, and Washington, D.C.

Arriving at the Airport

Immigration and customs clearance at Mexican airports is generally efficient. Expect longer lines during peak seasons, but you can usually clear immigration and customs within an hour. For more on what to expect when passing through Mexican customs, see "Customs," p. 44.

LONG-HAUL FLIGHTS: HOW TO STAY COMFORTABLE

• Your choice of airline and airplane will definitely affect your leg room. Find more details about U.S. airlines at **www.seatguru.com.** For international airlines, the research firm Skytrax has posted a list of average seat pitches at **www.airlinequality.com.**
• Emergency exit seats and bulkhead seats typically have the most legroom.

Emergency exit seats are usually left unassigned until the day of a flight (to ensure that someone able-bodied fills the seats); it's worth checking in online at home (if the airline offers that option) or getting to the ticket counter early to snag one of these spots for a long flight. Many passengers find that bulkhead seating offers more legroom, but keep in mind that bulkhead seats have no storage space on the floor in front of you.

- To have two seats for yourself in a three-seat row, try for an aisle seat in a center section toward the back of coach. If you're traveling with a companion, book an aisle and a window seat. Middle seats are usually booked last, so chances are good you'll end up with three seats to yourselves. And in the event that a third passenger is assigned the middle seat, he or she will probably be more than happy to trade for a window or an aisle.

- To sleep, avoid the last row of any section or the row in front of an emergency exit, as these seats are the least likely to recline. Avoid seats near highly trafficked toilet areas. Avoid seats in the back of many jets—these can be narrower than those in the rest of coach. Or reserve a window seat so you can rest your head and avoid being bumped in the aisle.

- Get up, walk around, and stretch every 60 to 90 minutes to keep your blood flowing. This helps avoid **deep vein thrombosis,** or "economy-class syndrome." See the box "Avoiding 'Economy Class Syndrome,'" p. 60.

- Drink water before, during, and after your flight to combat the lack of humidity in airplane cabins. Avoid caffeine and alcohol, which dehydrate you.

BY CAR

Driving is not the cheapest way to get to Mexico, and it is definitely not the easiest way to get to the Yucatán peninsula. While driving is a convenient way to see the country, you may think twice about taking your own car south of the border once you've pondered the bureaucracy involved. One option is to rent a car once you arrive and tour around a specific region. The Yucatán peninsula is a great place to do this. Rental cars in Mexico generally are clean and well maintained, although they are often smaller than rentals in the U.S., may have manual rather than automatic transmission, and are comparatively expensive due to pricey mandatory insurance. Discounts are often available for rentals of a week or longer, especially when you make arrangements in advance online or from the United States. Be careful about

---

ⓘ Tips Carrying Car Documents

You must carry your temporary car-importation permit, tourist permit (see "Entry Requirements," earlier in this chapter), and, if you purchased it, your proof of Mexican car insurance (see below) in the car at all times. The temporary car-importation permit papers are valid for 6 months to a year, while the tourist permit is usually issued for 30 days. It's a good idea to overestimate the time you'll spend in Mexico so if you have to (or want to) stay longer, you'll avoid the hassle of getting your papers extended. Whatever you do, don't overstay either permit. Doing so invites heavy fines, confiscation of your vehicle (which will not be returned), or both. Also remember that 6 months does not necessarily equal 180 days—be sure that you return before the earlier expiration date.

estimated online rates, which often fail to include the price of the mandatory insurance. (See "Car Rentals," later in this chapter, for more details.)

If, after reading the section that follows, you have additional questions or you want to confirm the current rules, call your nearest Mexican consulate or the Mexican Government Tourist Office. Although travel insurance companies generally are helpful, they may not have the most accurate information. To check on road conditions or to get help with any travel emergency while in Mexico, call ✆ **01-800/482-9832,** or 55/5089-7500 in Mexico City. English-speaking operators staff both numbers.

In addition, check with the **U.S. Department of State** (see "Safety," later in this chapter) for warnings about dangerous driving areas.

Car Documents

To drive your car into Mexico, you'll need a **temporary car-importation permit,** which is granted after you provide a required list of documents (see below). The permit can be obtained through Banco del Ejército (Banjercito) officials at the *aduana* (Mexican Customs) building after you cross the border into Mexico.

The following requirements for border crossing were accurate at press time:

- **A valid driver's license,** issued outside of Mexico.
- **Current, original car registration and a copy of the original car title.** If the registration or title is in more than one name and not all the named people are traveling with you, a notarized letter from the absent person(s) authorizing use of the vehicle for the trip is required; have it ready. The registration and your credit card (see below) must be in the same name.
- **Original immigration documentation.** This is either your tourist permit (FMT) or the original immigration

booklet, FM2 or FM3, if you hold more permanent status.
- **Processing fee and posting of a bond.** With a credit card, you are required to pay a $27 (£14) car-importation fee. The credit card must be in the same name as the car registration. Mexican law also requires the posting of a bond at a Banjercito office to guarantee the export of the car from Mexico within a time period determined at the time of the application. For this purpose, American Express, Visa, or MasterCard credit card holders will be asked to provide credit card information; others will need to make a cash deposit of $200 to $400 (£100–£200), depending on the make/model/year of the vehicle. In order to recover this bond or avoid credit card charges, travelers must go to any Mexican Customs office immediately before leaving Mexico.

If you receive your documentation at the border, Mexican officials will make two copies of everything and charge you for the copies. For up-to-the-minute information, a great source is the Customs office in Nuevo Laredo, or *Módulo de Importación Temporal de Automóviles, Aduana Nuevo Laredo* (✆ **867/712-2071**).

Important reminder: Someone else may drive, but the person (or relative of the person) whose name appears on the car-importation permit must *always* be in the car. (If stopped by police, a nonregistered family member driving without the registered driver must be prepared to prove familial relationship to the registered driver—no joke.) Violation of this rule subjects the car to impoundment and the driver to imprisonment, a fine, or both. You can drive a car with foreign license plates only if you have a foreign (non-Mexican) driver's license.

Mexican Auto Insurance

Liability auto insurance is legally required in Mexico. U.S. insurance is invalid; to be insured in Mexico, you must purchase Mexican insurance. Any party involved in an accident who has no insurance may be sent to jail and have his or her car impounded until all claims are settled. This is true even if you just drive across the border to spend the day. U.S. companies that broker Mexican insurance are commonly found at the border crossing, and several quote daily rates.

You can also buy car insurance through **Sanborn's Mexico Insurance,** P.O. Box 52840, 2009 S. 10th, McAllen, TX (© **800/222-0158;** fax 800/222-0158 or 956/686-0732; www.sanbornsinsurance. com). The company has offices at all U.S. border crossings. Its policies cost the same as the competition's do, but you get legal coverage (attorney and bail bonds if needed) and a detailed mile-by-mile guide for your proposed route. Most of the Sanborn's border offices are open Monday through Friday; a few are staffed on Saturday and Sunday. **AAA** auto club (www.aaa.com) also sells insurance.

Returning to the U.S. with Your Car

You *must* return the car documents you obtained when you entered Mexico when you cross back with your car, or within 180 days of your return. (You can cross as many times as you wish within the 180 days.) If the documents aren't returned, heavy fines are imposed ($250 for each 15 days you're late), your car may be impounded and confiscated, or you may be jailed if you return to Mexico. You can only return the car documents to a Banjercito official on duty at the Mexican *aduana* building *before* you cross back into the United States. Some border cities have Banjercito officials on duty 24 hours a day, but others do not; some do not have Sunday hours.

BY SHIP

Numerous cruise lines serve Mexico. Some (such as Carnival and Royal Caribbean) cruise from Houston or Miami to the Caribbean (which often includes stops in Cancún, Playa del Carmen, and Cozumel). Several cruise-tour specialists sometimes offer last-minute discounts on unsold cabins. One such company is **CruisesOnly** (© **800/278-4373;** www.cruisesonly.com).

BY BUS

Greyhound-Trailways (or its affiliates) offers service from around the United States to the Mexican border, where passengers disembark, cross the border, and buy a ticket for travel into Mexico. Many border crossings have scheduled buses from the U.S. bus station to the Mexican bus station.

More than likely, if you travel to the Yucatán by bus from the northern border you will pass through Mexico City, the country's capitol and main transportation hub. Expect a trip from the border to last several grueling days of all day (and/or all night) travel on roads of varying quality.

In each applicable section in this book, we've listed bus arrival information.

GETTING AROUND
BY PLANE

Mexico has two large private national carriers: **Mexicana** (© **800/531-7921;** www. mexicana.com) and **AeroMéxico** (© **800/237-6639;** www.aeromexico.com), in addition to several up-and-coming low-cost carriers. Mexicana and AeroMéxico offer extensive connections to the United States as well as within Mexico.

Up-and-coming low-cost carriers are listed in "Appendix A: Fast Facts, Toll-Free Numbers & Websites," p. 291. These regional carriers aren't always the bargain they make themselves out to be, but they go to difficult-to-reach places. In each applicable section of this book, we've mentioned regional carriers with all pertinent telephone numbers.

Because major airlines may book some regional carriers, check your ticket to see if your connecting flight is on one of these smaller carriers—they may use a different airport or a different counter.

AIRPORT TAXES   Mexico charges an airport tax on all departures. Passengers leaving the country on international flights pay about $24 (£12) or the peso equivalent. It has become a common practice to include this departure tax in your ticket price, but double-check to make sure so you're not caught by surprise at the airport. Taxes on each domestic departure within Mexico are around $17 (£8.50), unless you're on a connecting flight and have already paid at the start of the flight.

Mexico charges an $18 (£9) "tourism tax," the proceeds of which go into a tourism promotional fund. Your ticket price may not include it, so be sure to have enough money to pay it at the airport upon departure.

RECONFIRMING FLIGHTS   Although Mexican airlines say it's not necessary to reconfirm a flight, it's still a good idea. To avoid getting bumped on popular, possibly overbooked flights, check in for an international flight 1½ hours in advance of travel.

BY CAR

Most Mexican roads are not up to U.S. standards of smoothness, hardness, width of curve, grade of hill, or safety markings. Driving at night is dangerous—the roads are rarely lit; trucks, carts, pedestrians, and bicycles usually have no lights; and you can hit potholes, animals, rocks, dead ends, or uncrossable bridges without warning.

The spirited style of Mexican driving sometimes requires keen vision and reflexes. Be prepared for new customs, as when a truck driver flips on his left turn signal when there's not a crossroad for miles. He's probably telling you the road's clear ahead for you to pass. Another custom that's very important to respect is

turning left. Never turn left by stopping in the middle of a highway with your left-turn signal on. Instead, pull onto the right shoulder, wait for traffic to clear, then proceed across the road. Be prepared for plenty of *topes,* speed bumps, on local roads, especially those that cut through small towns and villages.

GASOLINE   There's one government-owned brand of gas and one gasoline station name throughout the country— **Pemex** (Petroleras Mexicanas). There are two types of gas in Mexico: *magna,* 87-octane unleaded gas, and *premio* 93 octane. In Mexico, fuel and oil are sold by the liter, which is slightly more than a quart (1 gallon equals about 3.8 liters). Many franchise Pemex stations have bathroom facilities and convenience stores—a great improvement over the old ones. Gas stations accept both credit and debit cards for gas purchases.

TOLL ROADS   Mexico charges some of the highest tolls in the world for its network of new toll roads; as a result, they are rarely used. Generally speaking, though, using toll roads cuts travel time. Older toll-free roads are generally in good condition, but travel times tend to be longer.

BREAKDOWNS   If your car breaks down on the road, help might already be on the way. Radio-equipped green repair trucks, run by uniformed English-speaking officers, patrol major highways during daylight hours. These **"Green Angels"** perform minor repairs and adjustments free, but you pay for parts and materials.

Your best guide to repair shops is the Yellow Pages. For repairs, look under *Automóviles y Camiones: Talleres de Reparación y Servicio;* auto-parts stores are under *Refacciones y Accesorios para Automóviles.* To find a mechanic on the road, look for a sign that says TALLER MECÁNICO.

Places called *vulcanizadora* or *llantera* repair flat tires, and it is common to find them open 24 hours a day on the most traveled highways.

DRIVING RULES In Mexico, seat belts are mandatory for all vehicle occupants and drivers must obey the posted speed limits. Speed bumps (called *topes*) are an effective if sometimes overused way to slow traffic down in this region. Roads are well paved and marked along most of the Riviera Maya, but less developed in Chiapas, Tabasco, and parts of the Yucatán.

MINOR ACCIDENTS When possible, many Mexicans drive away from minor accidents, or try to make an immediate settlement, to avoid involving the police. If the police arrive while the involved persons are still at the scene, everyone may be locked in jail until blame is assessed. In any case, you have to settle up immediately, which may take days. Foreigners who don't speak fluent Spanish are at a distinct disadvantage when trying to explain their version of the event. Three steps may help the foreigner who doesn't wish to do as the Mexicans do: If you were in your own car, notify your Mexican insurance company, whose job it is to intervene on your behalf. If you were in a rental car, notify the rental company immediately and ask how to contact the nearest adjuster. (You did buy insurance with the rental, right?) Finally, if all else fails, ask to contact the nearest Green Angel, who may be able to explain to officials that you are covered by insurance. See also "Mexican Auto Insurance" in "Getting There," earlier in this chapter.

CAR RENTALS You'll get the best price if you reserve a car at least a week in advance in the United States. American and some local firms have offices in Mexico City and most other large Mexican cities. You'll find rental desks at airports, all major hotels, and many travel agencies. See Appendix A, "Fast Facts, Toll-Free Numbers & Websites," p. 291 for a list of car-rental firms with offices in Mexico.

Cars are easy to rent if you are 25 or older and have a major credit card, valid driver's license, and passport with you. Without a credit card, you must leave a cash deposit, usually a big one. One-way rentals are usually simple to arrange, but they are more costly.

Car-rental costs are high in Mexico because cars are more expensive. The condition of rental cars has improved greatly over the years, and clean new cars are the norm. You will pay the least for a manual car without air-conditioning. Prices may be considerably higher if you rent around a major holiday. Also double-check charges for insurance—some companies will increase the insurance rate after several days. Always ask for detailed information about all charges you will be responsible for.

Car-rental companies usually write credit card charges in U.S. dollars.

Deductibles Be careful—these vary greatly; some are as high as $2,500 (£1,250), which comes out of your pocket immediately in case of damage. On a compact car, Hertz's deductible is roughly $1,000 (£500) and Avis's is $500 (£250).

Insurance Car insurance (*seguros de auto*) is offered in two parts: **Collision and damage** insurance covers your car and others if the accident is your fault, and **personal accident** insurance covers you and anyone in your car. Read the fine print on the back of your rental agreement and note that insurance may be invalid if you have an accident while driving on an unpaved road.

Damage Always inspect your car carefully and note every damaged or missing item, no matter how minute, on your rental agreement, or you may be charged.

Warning **Bus Hijackings**

The U.S. Department of State notes that bandits target long-distance buses traveling at night, but there have been daylight robberies as well. First-class buses on toll roads have a markedly lower rate of incidents than buses (second- and third-class) that travel the less secure "free" highways.

BY TAXI

Taxis are the preferred way to get around almost all of Mexico's resort areas. Fares for short trips within towns are generally preset by zone, and are quite reasonable compared with U.S. rates. For longer trips or excursions to nearby cities, taxis can generally be hired for around $15 to $20 (£7.50–£10) per hour, or for a nego- tiated daily rate. A negotiated one-way price is usually much less than the cost of a rental car for a day, and a taxi travels much faster than a bus. For anyone who is uncomfortable driving in Mexico, this is a convenient, comfortable alternative. A bonus is that you have a Spanish-speak- ing person with you in case you run into trouble. Many taxi drivers speak at least some English. Your hotel can assist you with the arrangements.

BY BUS

Most Mexican buses run frequently, are readily accessible, and can transport you almost anywhere you want to go. Taking the bus is much more common in Mex- ico than in the U.S., and the executive and first class coaches can be as comfort- able as business class on an airline. Buses are often the only way to get from large cities to other nearby cities and small villages. Don't hesitate to ask questions if you're confused about anything, but note that little English is spoken in bus stations.

Dozens of Mexican companies operate large, air-conditioned, Greyhound-type buses between most cities. Classes are *segunda* (second), *primera* (first), and *ejec- utiva* (deluxe), which goes by a variety of names. Deluxe buses often have fewer seats than regular buses, show video movies, are air-conditioned, and make few stops. Many run express from point to point. They are well worth the few dol- lars more. In rural areas, buses are often of the school-bus variety, with lots of local color.

The major long-haul bus companies in Mexico are: **ADO** (www.ado.com.mx), **Cristóbal Colon Omnibuses de Mexico** (www.odm.com.mx), and **Primera Plus.** To purchase tickets for any of these bus lines, passengers can call © **800/702- 8000** in Mexico or click on www.ticket bus.com.mx.

Whenever possible, it's best to buy your reserved-seat ticket, often using a computerized system, a day in advance on long-distance routes and especially before holidays.

5 Money & Costs

Overall, Mexico is considerably cheaper than most U.S. and European destina- tions, although prices vary significantly depending on the specific location. The most expensive destinations are those with the largest number of foreign visi- tors, such as Cancún. The least expensive are those off the beaten path and in small rural villages, particularly in the poorer states of Tabasco and Chiapas. In the major cities, prices vary greatly depend- ing on the neighborhood. As you might imagine, tourist zones tend to be much more expensive than local areas.

Money Matters

The **universal currency sign ($)** is used to indicate pesos in Mexico. The use of this symbol in this book, however, denotes U.S. currency.

The currency in Mexico is the **peso.** Paper currency comes in denominations of 20, 50, 100, 200, and 500 pesos. Coins come in denominations of 1, 2, 5, 10, and 20 pesos, and 20 and 50 **centavos** (100 centavos = 1 peso). The current exchange rate for the U.S. dollar, and the one used in this book, is 11 pesos; at that rate, an item that costs 11 pesos would be equivalent to $1 (50p). The exchange rate for the British pound is 22 pesos.

Getting **change** is a problem. Small-denomination bills and coins are hard to come by, so start collecting them early in your trip. Shopkeepers and taxi drivers everywhere always seem to be out of change and small bills; that's doubly true in markets. There seems to be an expectation that the customer should provide appropriate change, rather than the other way around.

Many establishments that deal with tourists, especially in coastal resort areas, quote prices in U.S. dollars. To avoid confusion, they use the abbreviations "Dlls." for dollars and "M.N." (*moneda nacional,* or national currency) for pesos.

Don't forget to have enough pesos to carry you over a weekend or Mexican holiday, when banks are closed. In general, avoid carrying the U.S. $100 bill, the bill most commonly counterfeited in Mexico and therefore the most difficult to exchange, especially in smaller towns. Because small bills and coins in pesos are hard to come by in Mexico, the $1 bill is very useful for tipping. ***Note:*** A tip of U.S. coins, which cannot be exchanged into Mexican currency, is of no value to the service provider.

Casas de cambio (exchange houses) are generally more convenient than banks for money exchange because they have more locations and longer hours; the rate of exchange may be the same as at a bank or slightly lower. Before leaving a bank or exchange-house window, count your change in front of the teller before the next client steps up.

Large airports have currency-exchange counters that often stay open whenever flights are operating. Though convenient, they generally do not offer the most favorable rates.

A hotel's exchange desk commonly pays less favorable rates than banks; however, when the currency is in a state of flux, higher-priced hotels are known to pay higher rates than banks, in an effort to attract dollars. ***Note:*** In almost all cases, you receive a better rate by changing money first, then paying.

The bottom line on exchanging money: Ask first, and shop around. Banks generally pay the top rates.

You'll avoid lines at airport ATMs by exchanging at least some money—just enough to cover airport incidentals and transportation to your hotel—before you leave home (though don't expect the exchange rate to be ideal). You can exchange money at your local American Express or Thomas Cook office or at your bank. American Express also dispenses traveler's checks and foreign currency via www.americanexpress.com or © **800/ 673-3782,** but they'll charge a $15 (£7.50) order fee and additional shipping and handling costs.

Banks in Mexico are rapidly expanding and improving services. They tend to be open weekdays from 9am until 5pm, and often for at least a half day on Saturday. In larger resorts and cities, they can generally accommodate the exchange of

Tips A Few Words About Prices

Prices in this book have been converted to U.S. dollars and British pounds at 11 pesos to the dollar and 22 pesos to the pound. Most hotels in Mexico—except places that receive little foreign tourism—quote prices in U.S. dollars. Thus, currency fluctuations are unlikely to affect the prices most hotels charge.

Mexico has a **value-added tax** of 15% (*Impuesto de Valor Agregado,* or IVA; pronounced "ee-bah") on most everything, including restaurant meals, bus tickets, and souvenirs. (Exceptions are Cancún, Cozumel, and Los Cabos, where the IVA is 10%; as ports of entry, they receive a break on taxes.) Hotels charge the usual 15% IVA, plus a locally administered bed tax of 2% (in most areas), for a total of 17%. In Cancún, Los Cabos, and Cozumel, hotels charge the 10% IVA plus 2% room tax. The prices quoted by hotels and restaurants do not necessarily include IVA. You may find that upper-end properties (three or more stars) quote prices without IVA included, while lower-priced hotels include IVA. Ask to see a printed price sheet and ask if the tax is included.

dollars (which used to stop at noon) anytime during business hours. Some, but not all, banks charge a 1% fee to exchange traveler's checks. But you can pay for most purchases directly with traveler's checks at the establishment's stated exchange rate. Don't even bother with personal checks drawn on a U.S. bank— the bank will wait for your check to clear, which can take weeks, before giving you your money.

Travelers to Mexico can easily withdraw money from **ATMs** in most major cities and resort areas. The U.S. Department of State recommends caution when you're using ATMs in Mexico, stating that they should only be used during business hours and in large protected facilities, but this pertains primarily to Mexico City, where crime remains a significant problem. In most resorts in Mexico, the use of ATMs is perfectly safe—just use the same precautions you would at any ATM. Universal bank cards (such as the Cirrus and PLUS systems) can be used. This is a convenient way to withdraw money and avoid carrying too much with you at any time. The exchange rate is generally more favorable than at *casas de cambio.* Most machines

offer Spanish/English menus and dispense pesos, but some offer the option of withdrawing dollars.

The **Cirrus** (© 800/424-7787; www. mastercard.com) and **PLUS** (© 800/ 843-7587; www.visa.com) networks span the globe. Go to your bank card's website to find ATM locations at your destination. Be sure you know your daily withdrawal limit before you depart. *Note:* Many banks impose a fee every time you use a card at another bank's ATM, and that fee can be higher for international transactions (although seldom more than $2 in Mexico) than for domestic ones. In addition, the bank from which you withdraw cash may charge its own fee. For international withdrawal fees, ask your bank.

Credit cards are another safe way to carry money. They also provide a convenient record of all your expenses, and they generally offer relatively good exchange rates. You can withdraw cash advances from your credit cards at banks or ATMs, but high fees make credit-card cash advances a pricey way to get cash. Keep in mind that you'll pay interest from the moment of your withdrawal, even if you pay your monthly bills on time. Also, note that many banks now assess a 1% to 3% "transaction fee" on **all** charges you incur abroad (whether you're using the local currency or your native currency).

In Mexico, Visa, MasterCard, and American Express are the most accepted cards. You'll be able to charge most hotel, restaurant, and store purchases, as well as almost all airline tickets, on your credit card. Pemex gas stations have begun to accept credit card purchases for gasoline, though this option may not be available everywhere and often not at night— check before you pump. You can get cash advances of several hundred dollars on your card, but there may be a wait of 20 minutes to 2 hours. Charges will be made in pesos, then converted into dollars by the bank issuing the credit card. Generally you receive the favorable bank rate when paying by credit card. However, be aware that some establishments in Mexico add a 5% to 7% surcharge when you pay with a credit card. This is especially true when using American Express. Many times, advertised discounts will not apply if you pay with a credit card.

For tips and telephone numbers to call if your **wallet is stolen or lost,** go to "Lost & Found" in the "Fast Facts" section of this chapter.

6 Health

GENERAL AVAILABILITY OF HEALTH CARE

In most of Mexico's resort destinations, you can usually find health care that meets U.S. standards. Care in more remote areas is limited. Standards of medical training, patient care, and business practices vary greatly among medical facilities in beach resorts throughout Mexico. Cancún has first-rate hospitals, for example, but other cities along the Caribbean coast do not. In recent years, some U.S. citizens have complained that certain health-care facilities in beach resorts have taken advantage of them by overcharging or providing unnecessary medical care. Only rudimentary health care is generally available in much of Chiapas, Tabasco, and the Yucatán.

Prescription medicine is broadly available at Mexico pharmacies; however, be aware that you may need a copy of your prescription or to obtain a prescription from a local doctor. This is especially true in the border towns, such as in Tijuana, where many Americans have been crossing into Mexico specifically for the purpose of purchasing lower-priced prescription medicines.

Contact the **International Association for Medical Assistance to Travellers (IAMAT;** © 716/754-4883 or, in Canada, 416/652-0137; www.iamat.org) for tips on travel and health concerns in the countries you're visiting and for lists of local, English-speaking doctors. The United States **Centers for Disease Control and Prevention** (© 800/311-3435; www.cdc.gov) provides up-to-date information on health hazards by region or country, and offers tips on food safety. For travelers to Mexico and Central America, the number (with recorded messages) is © 877/394-8747. The U.S. Department of State's website (www. travel.state.gov) also offers medical information for Americans traveling abroad and a list of air ambulance services.

Travel Health Online (www.tripprep. com), sponsored by a consortium of travel medicine practitioners, may also offer helpful advice on traveling abroad. You can find listings of reliable medical clinics overseas at the **International Society of Travel Medicine** (www.istm.org).

COMMON AILMENTS

SUN EXPOSURE Mexico is synonymous with sunshine; most of the country

Avoiding "Economy Class Syndrome"

Deep vein thrombosis—or as it's known in the world of flying, "economy-class syndrome"—is a blood clot that develops in a deep vein. It's a potentially deadly condition that can result from sitting too long in cramped conditions such as an airplane cabin. During a flight (especially a long-haul flight), get up, walk around, and stretch your legs every 60 to 90 minutes to keep your blood flowing. Other preventative measures: Frequently flex your legs while sitting, drink lots of water, and avoid alcohol and sleeping pills. If you have a history of deep vein thrombosis, heart disease, or another condition that puts you at high risk, some experts recommend wearing compression stockings or taking anticoagulants when you fly; always ask your physician about the best course for you. Symptoms of deep vein thrombosis include leg pain or swelling, or even shortness of breath.

is bathed in intense sunshine for much of the year. Avoid excessive exposure, especially in the tropics where UV rays are more dangerous. The hottest months in Mexico's south are April and May, but the sun is intense most of the year.

DIETARY RED FLAGS Travelers' diarrhea (locally known as *turista,* the Spanish word for "tourist")—persistent diarrhea, often accompanied by fever, nausea, and vomiting—used to attack many travelers to Mexico. (Some in the U.S. call this "Montezuma's revenge," but you won't hear it called that in Mexico.) Widespread improvements in infrastructure, sanitation, and education have greatly diminished this ailment, especially in well-developed resort areas. Most travelers make a habit of drinking only bottled water, which also helps to protect against unfamiliar bacteria. In resort areas, and generally throughout Mexico, only purified ice is used. If you do come down with this ailment, nothing beats Pepto Bismol, readily available in Mexico. Imodium is also available in Mexico and is used by many travelers for a quick fix. A good high-potency (or "therapeutic") vitamin supplement and even extra vitamin C can help; yogurt is good for healthy digestion.

Since dehydration can quickly become life-threatening, be careful to replace fluids and electrolytes (potassium, sodium, and the like) during a bout of diarrhea. Drink Pedialyte, a rehydration solution available at most Mexican pharmacies, or natural fruit juice, such as guava or apple (stay away from orange juice, which has laxative properties), with a pinch of salt added.

The U.S. Public Health Service recommends the following measures for preventing travelers' diarrhea: **Drink only purified water** (boiled water, canned or bottled beverages, beer, or wine). **Choose food carefully.** In general, avoid salads (except in first-class restaurants), uncooked vegetables, undercooked protein, and unpasteurized milk or milk products, including cheese. Choose food that is freshly cooked and still hot. Avoid eating food prepared by street vendors. In addition, something as simple as **clean hands** can go a long way toward preventing *turista.*

BUGS, BITES & OTHER WILDLIFE CONCERNS **Mosquitoes** and **gnats** are prevalent along the coast and in the Yucatán lowlands. *Repelente contra insectos* (insect repellent) is a must, and it's not always available in Mexico. If you'll be in these areas and are prone to bites, bring along a repellent that contains the active ingredient DEET. Avon's Skin So Soft also works extremely well. Another good remedy to keep the mosquitoes away is to mix citronella essential oil with basil, clove, and lavender essential oils. If you're sensitive to bites, pick up some antihistamine cream from a drugstore at home.

TROPICAL ILLNESSES   You should not be overly concerned about tropical diseases if you stay on the normal tourist routes and don't eat street food. However, both dengue fever and cholera have appeared in Mexico in recent years. Talk to your doctor or to a medical specialist in tropical diseases about precautions you should take. You can also get medical bulletins from the U.S. Department of State and the Centers for Disease Control and Prevention (see "General Availability of Health Care," earlier in this section). You can protect yourself by taking some simple precautions: Watch what you eat and drink; don't swim in stagnant water (ponds, slow-moving rivers, or wells); and avoid mosquito bites by covering up, using repellent, and sleeping under netting. The most dangerous areas seem to be on Mexico's west coast, away from the big resorts.

On occasion, coastal waters from the Gulf of Mexico can become contaminated with rapid growth in algae (phytoplankton), leading to a phenomenon known as harmful algal bloom or a "red tide." The algal release of neurotoxins threatens marine life and can cause rashes and even flu-like symptoms in exposed humans. Although red tides happen infrequently, you should not enter the water if you notice a reddish-brown color or are told there is a red tide.

WHAT TO DO IF YOU GET SICK AWAY FROM HOME

Any English-speaking embassy or consulate staff in Mexico can provide a list of area doctors who speak English. The U.S. Embassy's consular section, for example, keeps a list of reliable English-speaking doctors. If you get sick in Mexico, consider asking your hotel concierge to recommend a local doctor—even his or her own. You can also try the emergency room at a local hospital or urgent care facility. Many hospitals also have walk-in clinics for emergency cases that are not life-threatening; you may not get immediate attention, but you won't pay the high price of an emergency room visit.

For travel to Mexico, you may have to pay all medical costs up front and be reimbursed later. Medicare and Medicaid do not provide coverage for medical costs outside the U.S. (that means neither Medicare nor Medicaid reimburses for emergency health care in Mexico, either). Before leaving home, find out what medical services your health insurance covers. To protect yourself, consider buying medical travel insurance (see "Insurance," in "Appendix A: Fast Facts, Toll-Free Numbers & Websites.").

Very few health insurance plans pay for medical evacuation back to the U.S. (which can cost $10,000 and more). A number of companies offer global medical evacuation services. If you're ever hospitalized more than 150 miles from

---

Tips **Over-the-Counter Drugs in Mexico**

Antibiotics and other drugs that you'd need a prescription to buy in the States are often available over the counter in Mexican pharmacies. Mexican pharmacies also carry a limited selection of common over-the-counter cold, sinus, and allergy remedies.

Tips Smoke-Free Mexico?

In early 2008, the Mexican Congress approved legislation banning smoking in workplaces, public buildings, and public transportation across Mexico. Under this ground-breaking law, private business would only be permitted to allow public smoking in enclosed ventilated areas. Violators would face stiff fines, and smokers refusing to comply could receive up to 36-hour jail sentences. At press time, the legislation awaited signature by the president and, following the law's enactment, businesses would have up to 6 months to create the ventilated smoking areas. It is too early to know how strictly authorities will enforce the law, and its application is likely to be uneven across the country. Before you light up, be sure to ask about the application of local laws in Mexican public places and businesses you visit.

home, **MedjetAssist** (© **800/527-7478;** www.medjetassist.com) will pick you up and fly you to the hospital of your choice, virtually anywhere, in a medically equipped and staffed aircraft—24 hours a day, 7 days a week. Annual memberships are $225 (£113) individual, $350 (£175) family; you can also purchase short-term memberships.

It is generally less expensive and more reliable to contract a U.S.-based company for a medical evacuation from Mexico to the U.S. than to contract a Mexican-based company. Contact the consular affairs section of the U.S. Embassy in Mexico City or nearest consulate for suggestions.

We list **additional emergency numbers** in the "Fast Facts" appendix, p. 286.

7 Safety

STAYING SAFE

Crime in Mexico, especially in Mexico City, in selected cities along the U.S. border, and in some states affected by drug violence, has received attention in the North American press over the past several years. Many feel this unfairly exaggerates the real dangers, but it should be noted that crime rates, including taxi robberies, kidnappings, and highway carjackings, have continued in recent years, and violence related to narco-trafficking and organized crime has been noteworthy, especially in the extreme northwest along the border and parts of the Pacific Coast. However, the areas covered by this book have generally not been affected by these problems.

The **U.S. Department of State** (© **888/407-4747** or 202/501-4444; fax 202/647-1488; www.travel.state.gov) consistently updates its **Consular Information Sheet** on Mexico. It's loaded with safety, medical, driving, and general travel information, gleaned from reports by the Mexico offices. The U.S. Department of State Country Specific Information (and any applicable travel alerts) for Mexico are available at www.travel.state.gov.

Travelers should always leave valuables and irreplaceable items in a safe place, or not bring them at all. There are a significant number of pickpocket, purse snatching, and hotel-room theft incidents. Use hotel safes when available. Public transportation is a popular place for pickpockets. Precautions are necessary, but travelers should be realistic. You can generally trust a person whom you approach for help or directions, but be wary of anyone who approaches you offering the same. The more insistent the person is, the more cautious you should be.

So-called "express kidnappings"—an attempt to get quick cash in exchange for the release of an individual—have occurred in almost all the large cities in Mexico and appear to target not only the wealthy, but the middle class. Car theft and carjackings are also a common occurrence.

Travelers should also exercise caution in traveling Mexico's highways, avoiding travel at night, and using toll *(cuota)* roads rather than the less secure "free" *(libre)* roads whenever possible. It is also advised that you should not hike alone in backcountry areas nor walk alone on less-frequented beaches, ruins, or trails.

There have been a number of rapes reported in Cancún and other resort areas, usually at night or in the early morning. Armed street crime is a serious problem in all the major cities. Some bars and nightclubs, especially in resort cities such as Cancún, can be havens for drug dealers and petty criminals.

All bus travel should be during daylight hours and on first-class conveyances. Although there have been several reports of bus hijackings and robberies on toll roads, buses on toll roads have a markedly lower rate of incidents than buses (second and third class) that travel the less secure "free" highways.

8 Specialized Travel Resources

TRAVELERS WITH DISABILITIES

Mexico may seem like one giant obstacle course to travelers in wheelchairs or on crutches. At airports, you may encounter steep stairs before finding a well-hidden elevator or escalator—if one exists. Airlines will often arrange wheelchair assistance to the baggage area. Porters are generally available to help with luggage at airports and large bus stations, once you've cleared baggage claim.

Mexican airports are upgrading their services, but it is not uncommon to board from a remote position, meaning you either descend stairs to a bus that ferries you to the plane, which you board by climbing stairs, or you walk across the tarmac to your plane and ascend the stairs. Deplaning presents the same problem in reverse.

Escalators (and there aren't many in the country) are often out of order. Stairs without handrails abound. Few restrooms are equipped for travelers with disabilities; when one is available, access to it may be through a narrow passage that won't accommodate a wheelchair or a person on crutches. Many deluxe hotels (the most expensive) now have rooms with bathrooms designed for people with disabilities. Those traveling on a budget should stick with one-story hotels or hotels with elevators. Even so, there will probably still be obstacles somewhere. Generally speaking, no matter where you are, someone will lend a hand, although you may have to ask for it.

Most disabilities shouldn't stop anyone from traveling. There are more options and resources out there than ever before.

Organizations that offer a vast range of resources and assistance to disabled travelers include **MossRehab** (© 800/CALL-MOSS; www.mossresourcenet.org); the **American Foundation for the Blind** (AFB; © 800/232-5463; www.afb.org); and **SATH** (**Society for Accessible Travel & Hospitality;** © 212/447-7284; www.sath.org). **AirAmbulanceCard.com** is now partnered with SATH and allows you to pre-select top-notch hospitals in case of an emergency.

Access-Able Travel Source, www. access-able.com, offers a comprehensive database on travel agents from around the world with experience in accessible travel; destination-specific access information; and links to such resources as service animals, equipment rentals, and access guides.

Many travel agencies offer customized tours and itineraries for travelers with disabilities. Among them are **Flying Wheels Travel** (© 507/451-5005; www.flying wheelstravel.com); and **Accessible Journeys** (© 800/846-4537 or 610/521-0339; www.disabilitytravel.com).

Flying with Disability (www.flying-with-disability.org) is a comprehensive information source on airplane travel. **Avis Rent a Car** (© 888/879-4273) has an "Avis Access" program that offers services for customers with special travel needs. These include specially outfitted vehicles with swivel seats, spinner knobs, and hand controls; mobility scooter rentals; and accessible bus service. Be sure to reserve well in advance.

Also check out the quarterly magazine *Emerging Horizons* (www.emerging horizons.com), available by subscription ($16.95/£8.50 year in the U.S.; $21.95/ £11 outside the U.S.).

The "Accessible Travel" link at **Mobility-Advisor.com** (www.mobilityadvisor.com) offers a variety of travel resources to disabled persons.

British travelers should contact **Holiday Care** (© 0845-124-9971 in the U.K. only; www.holidaycare.org.uk) to access a wide range of travel information and resources for disabled and elderly people.

For more on organizations that offer resources to disabled travelers, go to **www.frommers.com/planning**.

GAY & LESBIAN TRAVELERS

Mexico is a conservative country, with deeply rooted Catholic religious traditions.

Public displays of same-sex affection are rare and still considered shocking for men, especially outside of urban or resort areas. Women in Mexico frequently walk hand in hand, but anything more would cross the boundary of acceptability. However, gay and lesbian travelers are generally treated with respect and should not experience harassment, assuming they give the appropriate regard to local customs.

While much of Mexico is socially conservative, Cancún and Playa del Carmen are not. Popular with many gay travelers, both coastal resorts offer gay-friendly accommodations, bars, and activities. For more information, visit **MexGay Vacations** at www.mexgay.com. Information about gay-friendly accommodations in Mérida, Yucatán is available at www.gay places2stay.com.

The International Gay and Lesbian Travel Association (IGLTA; © 800/448-8550 or 954/776-2626; www.iglta.org) is the trade association for the gay and lesbian travel industry, and offers an online directory of gay- and lesbian-friendly travel businesses and tour operators.

Many agencies offer tours and travel itineraries specifically for gay and lesbian travelers. Among them are **Above and Beyond Tours** (© 800/397-2681; www. abovebeyondtours.com); **Now, Voyager** (© 800/255-6951; www.nowvoyager. com); and **Olivia Cruises & Resorts** (© 800/631-6277; www.olivia.com).

Gay.com Travel (© 415/834-6500; www.gay.com/travel or www.outand about.com) is an excellent online successor to the popular *Out & About* print magazine. It provides regularly updated information about gay-owned, gay-oriented, and gay-friendly lodging, dining, sightseeing, nightlife, and shopping establishments in every important destination worldwide. British travelers should click on the "Travel" link at **www.uk. gay.com** for advice and gay-friendly trip ideas.

The Canadian website **Gay Traveler** (www.gaytraveler.ca) offers ideas and advice for gay travel all over the world.

The following travel guides are available at many bookstores, or you can order them from any online bookseller: *Spartacus International Gay Guide, 35th Edition* (Bruno Gmünder Verlag; www.spartacusworld.com/gayguide), and the *Damron* guides (www.damron.com), with separate, annual books for gay men and lesbians.

For more gay and lesbian travel resources, see **www.frommers.com/planning**.

SENIOR TRAVEL

Mexico is a popular country for retirees. For decades, North Americans have been living indefinitely in Mexico by returning to the border and recrossing with a new tourist permit every 6 months. Mexican immigration officials have caught on, and now limit the maximum time in the country to 6 months within any year. This is to encourage even partial residents to acquire proper documentation.

AIM-Adventures in Mexico, Apartado Postal 31–70, 45050 Guadalajara, Jalisco, is a well-written, informative newsletter for prospective retirees. Issues have evaluated retirement in Aguascalientes, Puebla, San Cristóbal de las Casas, Puerto Angel, Puerto Escondido and Huatulco, Oaxaca, Taxco, Tepic, Manzanillo, Melaque, and Barra de Navidad. Subscriptions are $29 (£15) to the United States.

Sanborn Tours, 2015 S. 10th St., P.O. Drawer 519, McAllen, TX 78505-0519 (© **800/395-8482;** www.sanborns.com), offers a "Retire in Mexico" orientation tour.

Mention the fact that you're a senior citizen when you make your travel reservations. Although all the major U.S. airlines have canceled their senior discount and coupon book programs, many hotels still offer lower rates for seniors. In most cities, people older than 60 qualify for reduced admission to theaters, museums, and other attractions, and discounted fares on public transportation.

Members of **AARP,** 601 E St. NW, Washington, D.C. 20049 (© **888/687-2277;** www.aarp.org), get discounts on hotels, airfares, and car rentals. AARP offers members a wide range of benefits, including *AARP: The Magazine* (www.aarpmagazine.org) and a monthly newsletter. Anyone over 50 can join.

Many reliable agencies and organizations target the 50-plus market. **Elderhostel** (© **800/454-5768;** www.elderhostel.org) arranges study programs for those ages 55 and older. **ElderTreks** (© **800/741-7956;** www.eldertreks.com) offers small-group tours to off-the-beaten-path or adventure-travel locations, restricted to travelers 50 and older.

Recommended publications offering travel resources and discounts for seniors include: the quarterly magazine *Travel 50 & Beyond* (www.travel50andbeyond.com) and the bestselling paperback *Unbelievably Good Deals and Great Adventures That You Absolutely Can't Get Unless You're Over 50 2005–2006, 16th Edition* (McGraw-Hill), by Joan Rattner Heilman.

For more information and resources on travel for seniors, see **www.frommers.com/planning**.

FAMILY TRAVEL

If you have enough trouble getting your kids out of the house in the morning, dragging them thousands of miles away may seem like an insurmountable challenge. But family travel can be immensely rewarding, giving you the chance to see the world through the eyes of children.

Children are considered the national treasure of Mexico, and Mexicans will warmly welcome and cater to your children. Many parents were reluctant to bring young children into Mexico in the past, primarily due to health concerns, but I can't think of a better place to introduce children to the exciting adventure of

Tips Advice for Female Travelers

Mexicans in general, and men in particular, are nosy about single travelers, especially women. If a taxi driver or anyone else with whom you don't want to become friendly asks about your marital status, family, and so forth, my advice is to make up a set of answers (regardless of the truth): "I'm married, traveling with friends, and I have three children." Saying you are single and traveling alone may send the wrong message. U.S. television—widely viewed now in Mexico—has given many Mexican men the image of American single women as being sexually promiscuous. Check out the award-winning website **Journey-woman** (www.journeywoman.com), a "real-life" women's travel information network where you can sign up for a free e-mail newsletter and get advice on everything from etiquette and dress to safety; or the travel guide *Safety and Security for Women Who Travel* by Sheila Swan and Peter Laufer (Travelers' Tales, Inc.), offering common-sense tips on safe travel.

exploring a different culture. Some of the best destinations include Puerto Vallarta, Cancún, and La Paz. Hotels can often arrange for a babysitter.

Before leaving, ask your doctor which medications to take along. Disposable diapers cost about the same in Mexico but are of poorer quality. You can get Huggies Supreme and Pampers identical to the ones sold in the United States, but at a higher price. Many stores sell Gerber's baby foods. Dry cereals, powdered formulas, baby bottles, and purified water are easily available in midsize and large cities or resorts.

Cribs may present a problem; only the largest and most luxurious hotels provide them. However, rollaway beds are often available. Child seats or high chairs at restaurants are common.

Consider bringing your own car seat; they are not readily available for rent in Mexico.

Every country's regulations differ, but in general children traveling abroad should have plenty of documentation on hand, particularly if they're traveling with someone other than their own parents (in which case a notarized form letter from a parent is often required). For details on entry requirements for children traveling abroad, turn to p. 42 and go to the U.S. Department of State website (www.travel.state.gov); click on "International Travel," "Travel Brochures," and "Foreign Entry Requirements."

To locate accommodations, restaurants, and attractions that are particularly kid-friendly, refer to the "Kids" icon throughout this guide.

Recommended family travel websites include **Family Travel Forum** (www.familytravelforum.com), a comprehensive site that offers customized trip planning; **Family Travel Network** (www.familytravelnetwork.com), an online magazine providing travel tips; and **Travel WithYourKids.com** (www.travelwithyourkids.com), a comprehensive site written by parents for parents offering sound advice for long-distance and international travel with children.

For a list of more family-friendly travel resources, visit **www.frommers.com/planning**.

STUDENT TRAVEL

Because Mexicans consider higher education a luxury rather than a birthright, there is no formal network of student discounts and programs. Most Mexican students travel with their families rather than with other students, so student discount cards are not commonly recognized.

However, more hostels have entered the student travel scene. **Hostelling International México** (② 55/5518-1726; www.hostellingmexico.com) offers a list of hostels that meet international standards in Guadalajara, Guanajuato, Mérida, Mexico City, Oaxaca, and Puebla. Hostels.com offers a list of hostels in Acapulco, Cancún, Guadalajara, Mexico City, Oaxaca, Playa del Carmen, Puerto Escondido, Puebla, and Zacatecas.

9 Sustainable Tourism

Sustainable tourism is conscientious travel. It means being careful with the environments you explore, and respecting the communities you visit. Two overlapping components of sustainable travel are **ecotourism** and **ethical tourism.** The **International Ecotourism Society** (TIES) defines ecotourism as responsible travel to natural areas that conserves the environment and improves the well-being of local people. TIES suggests that ecotourists follow these principles:

• Minimize environmental impact.
• Build environmental and cultural awareness and respect.
• Provide positive experiences for both visitors and hosts.
• Provide direct financial benefits for conservation and for local people.
• Raise sensitivity to host countries' political, environmental, and social climates.
• Support international human rights and labor agreements.

You can find some eco-friendly travel tips and statistics, as well as touring companies and associations—listed by destination under "Travel Choice"—at the **TIES** website, www.ecotourism.org. Also check out **Ecotravel.com**, which lets you search for sustainable touring companies in several categories (water-based, land-based, spiritually oriented, and so on).

While much of the focus of ecotourism is about reducing impacts on the natural environment, ethical tourism concentrates on ways to preserve and enhance local economies and communities, regardless of location. You can embrace ethical tourism by staying at a locally owned hotel or shopping at a store that employs local workers and sells locally produced goods.

Responsible Travel (www.responsibletravel.com) is a great source of sustainable travel ideas; the site is run by a spokesperson for ethical tourism in the travel industry. **Sustainable Travel International** (www.sustainabletravelinternational.org) promotes ethical tourism practices, and manages an extensive directory of sustainable properties and tour operators around the world.

In the U.K., **Tourism Concern** (www.tourismconcern.org.uk) works to reduce social and environmental problems connected to tourism. The **Association of Independent Tour Operators** (AITO; www.aito.co.uk) is a group of specialist operators leading the field in making holidays sustainable.

Volunteer travel has become increasingly popular among those who want to venture beyond the standard group-tour experience to learn languages, interact with locals, and make a positive difference while on vacation. Volunteer travel usually doesn't require special skills—just a willingness to work hard—and programs vary in length from a few days to a number of weeks. Some programs provide free housing and food, but many require volunteers to pay for travel expenses, which can add up fast.

Before you commit to a volunteer program, it's important to make sure any money you're giving is truly going back to the local community, and that the work you'll be doing will be a good fit for you. **Volunteer International** (www.volunteer international.org) has a helpful list of questions to ask to determine the intentions and the nature of a volunteer program.

For general information on volunteer travel, visit **www.volunteerabroad.org** and **www.idealist.org**.

SUSTAINABLE TOURISM IN THE YUCATAN, TABASCO & CHIAPAS

Mexico is a huge country with a varied terrain and wildlife. Some of the country's most pristine ecosystems lie in the south, a consequence of the region's lack of large-scale development, except along the Caribbean coast. The Mexican Caribbean supports the Great Mesoamerican Barrier Reef, the second largest reef in the world, which extends down to Central America. This reef and other marine ecosystems face increasing pressure from sedimentation, pollution, overfishing, and exploitative recreational activities, all newly associated with growing regional tourism. The **Coral Reef Alliance** (www.coralreefalliance.org) is an example of an organization that, by teaming up with the **World Wildlife Fund** (WWF; www.wwf.org) and **United Nations Environmental Program** (UNEP; www.unep.org) has been working to address threats to the Mesoamerican Barrier Reef and improve environmental sustainability throughout the region. One of the best contributions a diver can make to support a healthy reef while diving is to avoid physical contact with the reef. Talk to your scuba outfitter about proper buoyancy control and body position to avoid damaging these fragile ecosystems.

The Yucatán peninsula has several natural protected areas, which are off-limits to development and are typically administered by local agencies or managed by local tourism cooperatives. You can read about these protected areas on p. 82.

Cancún was rapidly developed from a rural outpost to an international resort destination and the disappearance of coconut palms is a major ecological concern that has cropped up in the process. When the resort's golf courses were constructed, developers imported turf from Florida, thus introducing a disease that wiped out these trees. The region's mangroves, vital to protecting the land from hurricanes and as a key habitat for native species, have been decimated by the disease.

Tabasco suffered severe flooding in 2007 which devastated much of the land and brought widespread suffering to the population, which is among Mexico's poorest. The floods also affected Chiapas, though to a lesser extent. Tabasco's sinking land, and the extraction of oil and gas, land erosion, and deforestation all contributed to the state's vulnerability to flooding. As of spring 2008, the tourism infrastructure was up and running again.

Ecotourism opportunities abound in **Chiapas,** where a growing number of small, local tourism cooperatives have organized to take tourists on guided hikes, treks, and even kayak expeditions into the state's isolated jungles and nature reserves. **SendaSur** (© 967/678-3909; info@sendasur.com; http://www.aventura chiapas.gob.mx) is the umbrella organization which can help arrange trips to these difficult to reach places. Two private companies that run ecotours throughout Chiapas are **Ecochiapas** (Primero de Marzo 30, San Cristóbal de las Casas; © 967/ 674-6660; www.ecochiapas.com) and **Latitud 16** (Calle Real de Guadalupe 23, San Cristóbal de las Casas; © 967/674-6915; www.latitud16.com).

The **Mesoamerican Ecotourism Alliance** (© 800/682-0584 in the US; www.travelwithmea.org) offers award winning ecotours recognized by *National Geographic* to the Yucatán and Chiapas.

Tips It's Easy Being Green

Here are a few ways you can help conserve fuel and energy when you travel:

- Each time you take a flight or drive a car, greenhouse gases release into the atmosphere. You can help neutralize this danger to the planet through "carbon offsetting"—paying someone to invest your money in programs that reduce your greenhouse gas emissions by the same amount you've added. Before buying carbon offset credits, just make sure that you're using a reputable company, one with a proven program that invests in renewable energy. Reliable carbon offset companies include **Carbonfund** (www.carbonfund.org), **TerraPass** (www.terrapass.org), and **Carbon Neutral** (www.carbonneutral.org).

- Whenever possible, choose nonstop flights; they generally require less fuel than indirect flights that stop and take off again. Try to fly during the day—some scientists estimate that nighttime flights are twice as harmful to the environment. And pack light—each 15 pounds of luggage on a 5,000-mile flight adds up to 50 pounds of carbon dioxide emitted.

- Where you stay during your travels can have a major environmental impact. To determine the green credentials of a property, ask about trash disposal and recycling, water conservation, and energy use; also question if sustainable materials were used in the construction of the property. The website **www.greenhotels.com** recommends green-rated member hotels around the world that fulfill the company's stringent environmental requirements. Also consult **www.environmentallyfriendlyhotels.com** for more green accommodation ratings.

- At hotels, request that your sheets and towels not be changed daily. (Many hotels already have programs like this in place.) Turn off the lights and air-conditioner (or heater) when you leave your room.

- Use public transport where possible—trains, buses and even taxis are more energy-efficient forms of transport than driving. Even better is to walk or cycle; you'll produce zero emissions and stay fit and healthy on your travels.

- Eat at locally owned and operated restaurants that use produce grown in the area. This contributes to the local economy and cuts down on greenhouse gas emissions by supporting restaurants where the food is not flown or trucked in across long distances.

- For sustainable travel information about Mexico, visit the Global Journal of Practical Ecotourism (www.planeta.com), GloCal Mexico (www.glocaltravel.net), or Go Nomad (www.gonomad.com).

ANIMAL-RIGHTS ISSUES

The Yucatán presents many opportunities to swim with dolphins. The capture of wild dolphins was outlawed in Mexico in 2002. The only dolphins added to the country's dolphin swim programs since then were born in captivity. This law may have eased concerns about the death and implications of capturing wild dolphins, but the controversy is not over. Local

Frommers.com: The Complete Travel Resource

Planning a trip or just returned? Head to **Frommers.com,** voted Best Travel Site by *PC Magazine.* We think you'll find our site indispensable before, during and after your travels—with expert advice and tips; independent reviews of hotels, restaurants, attractions, and preferred shopping and nightlife venues; vacation giveaways; and an online booking tool. We publish the complete contents of over 135 travel guides in our **Destinations** section, covering over 4,000 places worldwide. Each weekday, we publish original articles that report on **Deals and News** via our free **Frommers.com Newsletters.** What's more, **Arthur Frommer** himself blogs 5 days a week, with cutting opinions about the state of travel in the modern world. We're betting you'll find our **Events** listings an invaluable resource; it's an up-to-the-minute roster of what's happening in cities everywhere—including concerts, festivals, lectures, and more. We've also added weekly **podcasts, interactive maps,** and hundreds of new images across the site. Finally, don't forget to visit our **Message Boards,** where you can join in conversations with thousands of fellow Frommer's travelers and post your trip report once you return.

organizations have been known to staple notes to Dolphin Discovery ads in magazines distributed in Cancún hotels. Marine biologists who run the dolphin swim programs say the mammals are thriving and that the programs provide a forum for research, conservation, education, and rescue operations. Animal rights advocates maintain that keeping these intelligent mammals in captivity is nothing more than exploitation. Their argument is that these private dolphin programs don't qualify as "public display" under the Marine Mammal Protection Act because the entry fees bar most of the public from participating.

Visit the website of the **Whale and Dolphin Conservation Society** at www. wdcs.org or the **American Cetacean Society,** www.acsonline.org, for further discussion on the topic.

Bullfighting is considered an important part of Latin culture, but you should know, before you attend a *correo,* that the bulls (at least 4) will ultimately be killed in a gory spectacle. This is not the case in some countries, such as France and Portugal, but the Mexicans follow the Spanish model. That said, a bullfight is a portal into understanding Mexico's Spanish colonial past, although nowadays bullfights are more of a tourist attraction, especially in tourist laden Cancún. To read more about the implications of attending a bullfight, visit **www.peta.org,** the website of People for the Ethical Treatment of Animals (PETA).

For information on animal-friendly issues throughout the world, visit **Tread Lightly** (www.treadlightly.org).

10 Packages for the Independent Traveler

Package tours are simply a way to buy the airfare, accommodations, and other elements of your trip (such as car rentals, airport transfers, and sometimes even activities) at the same time and often at discounted prices.

One good source of package deals is the airlines themselves. Most major airlines offer air/land packages, including **American Airlines Vacations** (☎ 800/321-2121; www.aavacations.com), **Continental Airlines Vacations** (☎ 800/301-3800; www.covacations.com), and **United Vacations** (☎ 888/854-3899; www.unitedvacations.com). Several big online travel agencies—**Expedia, Travelocity, Orbitz, Site59,** and **Lastminute.com**—also do a brisk business in packages.

Travel packages are also listed in the travel section of your local Sunday newspaper. Or check ads in the national travel magazines such as *Arthur Frommer's Budget Travel Magazine, Travel + Leisure, National Geographic Traveler,* and *Condé Nast Traveler.*

RECOMMENDED PACKAGERS

- **AeroMéxico Vacations** (☎ 800/245-8585; www.aeromexico.com) offers year-round packages to almost every destination it serves, including Acapulco, Cancún, Cozumel, Ixtapa/Zihuatanejo, Los Cabos, and Puerto Vallarta. AeroMéxico has a large selection (more than 100) of resorts in these destinations and more, in a variety of price ranges. The best deals are from Houston, Dallas, San Diego, Los Angeles, Miami, and New York, in that order.

- **American Airlines Vacations** (☎ 800/321-2121; www.aavacations.com) has year-round deals to Acapulco, Cancún, the Riviera Maya, Guadalajara, Los Cabos, Mexico City, and Puerto Vallarta. You don't have to fly with American if you can get a better deal on another airline; land-only packages include hotel, hotel tax, and airport transfers. American's hubs to Mexico are Dallas/Fort Worth, Chicago, and Miami. The website offers unpublished discounts that are not available through the operators.

- **US Airways Vacations** (☎ 800/235-9298; www.usairwaysvacations.com) has deals to Acapulco, Cancún, Cozumel, Guadalajara, Ixtapa, Los Cabos, Manzanillo, Mexico City, and Puerto Vallarta. Many packages to Los Cabos include car rentals. The website offers discounted featured specials that are not available through the operators. You can also book hotels without air by calling the toll-free number.

- **Apple Vacations** (☎ 800/365-2775; www.applevacations.com) offers inclusive packages to all the beach resorts, and has the largest choice of hotels in Acapulco, Cancún, Cozumel, Huatulco, Ixtapa, Loreto, Los Cabos, Manzanillo, Mazatlán, Puerto Vallarta, and the Riviera Maya. Scheduled carriers for the air portion include American, United, Mexicana, Delta, US Airways, Alaska Airlines, and AeroMéxico. Apple perks include baggage handling and the services of a company representative at major hotels.

- **Classic Vacations** (☎ 800/635-1333; www.classicvacations.com) specializes in package vacations to Mexico's finest luxury resorts. It combines discounted first-class and economy airfare on American, Continental, Mexicana, Alaska, America West, and Delta with stays at the most exclusive hotels in Cancún, the Riviera Maya, Mérida, Oaxaca, Guadalajara, Mexico City, Puerto Vallarta, Mazatlán, Costa Alegre, Manzanillo, Ixtapa/Zihuatanejo, Acapulco, Huatulco,

Choosing an Air & Hotel Package

Searching for air and hotel packages to any destination can be a daunting task thanks to the sheer number of options. Finding a satisfying deal takes time and research. Here are a few hints on making the most of your time to save you money in the long run:

- Be clear on the bottom line. With so many different packagers, be sure to make an "apples to apples" comparison: Go all the way through the online checkout (but don't hit the "Buy Now!" button) to see what taxes, fees, and costs are tacked on to each package.
- Avoid changing the package too much. The packages are set up to generate prices for certain criteria, such as certain flights or a certain class of room. If you change too many things, you might find that the deal evaporates.
- Read all the fine print and take note of all inclusions and exclusions. Does the package include airport transfers? What about breakfast? Travel insurance? If you want certain extras, take into account if you have to pay for them on top of the package deal. If you don't want extras, be sure to opt out of them.
- Know a good deal when it comes up. Because of changes in airfares or hotel occupancy, you could see a different price for the same package if you go back to the same site an hour later; the price might even be updated while you are looking at it. A package can disappear altogether if the hotel has filled up. Once you're satisfied with an offer, go for it.

and Los Cabos. The prices are not for bargain hunters but for those who seek luxury, nicely packaged.

- **Continental Vacations** (© 800/301-3800; www.covacations.com) has year-round packages to Acapulco, Cancún, Cozumel, Guadalajara, Huatulco, Ixtapa, Los Cabos, Mazatlán, Mexico City, and Puerto Vallarta. The best deals are from Houston; Newark, NJ; and Cleveland, OH. You must fly Continental. The Internet deals offer savings not available elsewhere.
- **Delta Vacations** (© 800/654-6559; www.deltavacations.com) has year-round packages to Acapulco, Cancún, Cozumel, Guadalajara, Ixtapa/Zihuatanejo, Los Cabos, Mazatlán, Mérida, and Puerto Vallarta. Atlanta is the hub, so expect the best prices from there.

- **Funjet Vacations** (© 888/558-6654; www.funjet.com) is one of the largest vacation packagers in the United States. Funjet has packages to Acapulco, Cancún, Cozumel, the Riviera Maya, Los Cabos, Mazatlán, Ixtapa, and Puerto Vallarta. You can choose a charter or fly on American, Continental, Delta, AeroMéxico, US Airways, Alaska Air, or United.
- **GOGO Worldwide Vacations** (© 888/636-3942; www.gogowwv.com) has trips to all the major beach resorts, including Acapulco, Cancún, Mazatlán, Puerto Vallarta, and Los Cabos. It offers several exclusive deals from higher-end hotels. Book through any travel agent.
- **Mexicana Vacations,** or MexSeaSun Vacations (© 800/531-7921; www.mexicana.com) offers getaways to all

the resorts. Mexicana operates daily direct flights from Los Angeles to Los Cabos, Mazatlán, Cancún, Puerto Vallarta, Manzanillo, and Ixtapa/Zihuatanejo.

- **Mexico Travel Net** (© 800/511-4848 or 619/474-0100; www.mexicotravelnet.com) offers most of the well-known travel packages to Mexico beach resorts, plus last minute specials.
- **Pleasant Holidays** (© 800/742-9244; www.pleasantholidays.com) is one of the largest vacation packagers in the United States, with hotels in Acapulco, Cancún, Cozumel, Huatulco, Ixtapa/Zihuatanejo, Los Cabos, Mazatlán, Mérida, Mexico City, Oaxaca, and Puerto Vallarta.

REGIONAL U.S. PACKAGERS

From the East Coast: Liberty Travel (© 888/271-1584; www.libertytravel.com), one of the biggest packagers in the Northeast, often runs a full-page ad in the Sunday papers, with frequent Mexico specials. You won't get much in the way of service, but you will get a good deal.

From the West: SunTrips (© 800/514-5194 for departures within 14 days; www.suntrips.com) is one of the largest West Coast packagers for Mexico, with departures from San Francisco and Denver; regular charters to Cancún, Cozumel, Los Cabos, and Puerto Vallarta; and a large selection of hotels.

From the Southwest: Town and Country (book through travel agents) packages regular deals to Los Cabos, Mazatlán, Puerto Vallarta, Ixtapa, Manzanillo, Cancún, Cozumel, and Acapulco with America West from the airline's Phoenix and Las Vegas gateways.

For more information on Package Tours and for tips on booking your trip, see **www.frommers.com**.

ONLINE PACKAGERS

Several websites sell packages to destinations around the world, and are often travelers' first stop when consulting prices. The following have some of the best listings for Cancún and the Riviera Maya:

BestDay.com (© 800/593-6259; www.bestday.com); **BookIt.com** (© 888/782-9722; www.bookit.com) offers a wide range of choices for all-inclusive resorts; **Orbitz** (© 800/504-3248; www.orbitz.com), occasionally includes its own special offers, such as 25% early-booking discounts or 10% to 20% off food and beverages; and **Vacation Travel Mart** (© 800/288-1435; www.vacmart.com) has the option of placing a 24-hour hold on a reservation before paying.

11 Special-Interest Trips

ACADEMIC TRIPS & LANGUAGE CLASSES

For Spanish-language instruction, **IMAC** (© 866/306-5040; www.spanish-school.com.mx) offers programs in Guadalajara and Playa del Carmen. The **Spanish Institute** (© 800/539-9710; www.spanishtoday.com) is affiliated with intensive Spanish language schools in Puebla and Mérida.

To explore your inner Frida or Diego while in Mexico, look into **Mexico Art Tours,** 1233 E. Baker Dr., Tempe, AZ 85282 (© 888/783-1331 or 480/730-1764; www.mexicanarttours.com). Typically led by Jean Grimm, a specialist in the arts and cultures of Mexico, these unique tours feature compelling speakers who are themselves respected scholars and artists. Itineraries include visits to Chiapas, Guadalajara, Guanajuato, Puebla, Puerto Vallarta, Mexico City, San Miguel de Allende, and Veracruz. Special tours involve archaeology, architecture, interior design, and culture—such as a Day of the Dead tour.

The **Archaeological Conservancy,** 5301 Central Ave. NE, Suite 402, Albuquerque, NM 87108 (© **505/266-1540;** www.americanarchaeology.com), presents various trips each year led by an expert, usually an archaeologist. The trips change from year to year and space is limited; make reservations early.

ATC Tours and Travel, Av. 16 de Septiembre 16, 29200 San Cristóbal de las Casas, Chis. (© **967/678-2550** or -2557; fax 967/678-3145; www.atctours.com), a Mexico-based tour operator with an excellent reputation, offers specialist-led trips, primarily in southern Mexico. In addition to trips to the ruins of Palenque and Yaxchilán (extending into Belize and Guatemala by river, plane, and bus if desired), ATC runs horseback tours to Chamula or Zinacantán, and day trips to the ruins of Toniná around San Cristóbal de las Casas; birding in the rainforests of Chiapas and Guatemala (including in the El Triunfo Reserve of Chiapas); hikes to the shops and homes of textile artists of the Chiapas highlands; and walks from the Lagos de Montebello in the Montes Azules Biosphere Reserve, with camping and canoeing. The company can also prepare custom itineraries.

ADVENTURE & WELLNESS TRIPS

AMTAVE (Asociación Mexicana de Turismo de Aventura y Ecoturismo, A.C.) is an active association of ecotourism and adventure tour operators. It publishes an annual catalog of participating firms and their offerings, all of which must meet certain criteria for security, quality, and training of the guides, as well as for sustainability of natural and cultural environments. For more information, contact AMTAVE (© **55/5688-3883;** www.amtave.org).

The California Native, 6701 W. 87th Place, Los Angeles, CA 90045 (© **800/** 926-1140 or 310/642-1140; www.calnative.com), offers small-group deluxe 7-, 8-, 9-, 11-, and 14-day escorted tours through the Copper Canyon. Many trips visit the towns of Batopilas, Urique, and Tejeban as well as the customary destinations of Creel, El Fuerte, Divisadero, Chihuahua, and Cerocahui. The guides are known throughout the area for their work with the Tarahumara Indians. They also cover Chiapas, the Yucatán, and Baja California.

Mexico Travel Link Ltd., 300-3665 Kingsway, Vancouver, BC V5R 5W2 Canada (© **604/454-9044;** fax 604/454-9088; www.mexicotravel.net), runs adventure, cultural, and sports tours to Mexico City and surrounding areas, Baja, Veracruz, the Copper Canyon, the Maya Route, and other destinations.

Trek America, P.O. Box 189, Rockaway, NJ 07866 (© **800/873-5872;** www. trekamerica.com), organizes lengthy, active trips that combine trekking, hiking, van transportation, and camping in the Yucatán, Chiapas, Oaxaca, the Copper Canyon, and Mexico's Pacific coast, and a trip that covers Mexico City, Teotihuacán, Taxco, Guadalajara, Puerto Vallarta, and Acapulco.

FOOD & WINE TRIPS

If you're looking to eat your way through Mexico, sign up with **Culinary Adventures,** 6023 Reid Dr. NW, Gig Harbor, WA 98335 (© **253/851-7676;** fax 253/851-9532; www.marilyntausend.com). It specializes in a short but select list of cooking tours in Mexico. Culinary Adventures features well-known cooks, with travel to regions known for excellent cuisine. The owner, Marilyn Tausend, is the author of *Cocinas de la Familia* (Family Kitchens), *Savoring Mexico* (Williams-Sonoma), and *Mexican* (Williams-Sonoma), and co-author of *Mexico the Beautiful Cookbook* (Palazuelos).

VOLUNTEER & WORKING TRIPS

For numerous links to volunteer and internship programs throughout Mexico involving teaching, caring for children, providing health care, feeding the homeless, and doing other community and public service, visit **www.volunteer abroad.com**.

12 Staying Connected

TELEPHONES

Mexico's telephone system is slowly but surely catching up with modern times. Most telephone numbers have 10 digits. Every city and town that has telephone access has a two-digit (Mexico City, Monterrey, and Guadalajara) or three-digit (everywhere else) area code. In Mexico City, Monterrey, and Guadalajara, local numbers have eight digits; elsewhere, local numbers have seven digits. To place a local call, you do not need to dial the area code. Many fax numbers are also regular phone numbers; ask whoever answers for the fax tone *("me da tono de fax, por favor")*.

The **country code** for Mexico is **52**.
To call Mexico:

1. Dial the international access code: 011 from the U.S. and Canada; 00 from the U.K., Ireland, or New Zealand; or 0011 from Australia.
2. Dial the country code: 52.
3. Dial the two- or three-digit area code, then the eight- or seven-digit number. For example, if you wanted to call the U.S. consulate in Acapulco, the entire number would be 011-52-744-469-0556. If you wanted to dial the U.S. embassy in Mexico City, the entire number would be 011-52-55-5209-9100.

To make international calls: To make international calls from Mexico, first dial 00, then the country code (U.S. or Canada 1, U.K. 44, Ireland 353, Australia 61, New Zealand 64). Next, dial the area code and number. For example, to call the British Embassy in Washington, you would dial 00-1-202-588-7800.

For directory assistance: Dial ✆ 040 if you're looking for a number inside Mexico. *Note:* Listings usually appear under the owner's name, not the name of the business, and your chances to find an English-speaking operator are slim.

For operator assistance: If you need operator assistance in making a call, dial ✆ 090 to make an international call, and ✆ 020 to call a number in Mexico.

Toll-free numbers: Numbers beginning with 800 within Mexico are toll-free, but calling a U.S. toll-free number from Mexico costs the same as an overseas call. To call an 800 number in the U.S., dial 001-880 and the last seven digits of the toll-free number. To call an 888 number in the U.S., dial 001-881 and the last seven digits of the toll-free number. For a number with an 887 prefix, dial 882; for 866, dial 883.

CELLPHONES

Telcel is Mexico's expensive, primary cell phone provider. It has upgraded its systems to GSM and offers good coverage in much of the country, including the major cities and resorts. Most Mexicans buy their cell phones without a specific coverage plan and then pay as they go or purchase pre-paid cards with set amounts of air-time credit. These cell phone cards with scratch-off pin numbers can be purchased in Telcel stores as well as many newspaper stands and convenience stores.

Many U.S. and European cell phone companies offer networks with roaming coverage in Mexico. Rates can be very high, so check with your provider before committing to making calls this way. An increasing number of Mexicans,

Online Traveler's Toolbox

Veteran travelers usually carry some essential items to make their trips easier. Following is a selection of handy online tools to bookmark and use.

- **Regional Travel** (www.travelyucatan.com; www.yucatantoday.com)
- **Expat Life on the Peninsula** (www.yucatanliving.com)
- **Yucatán Tourism Board** (www.mayayucatan.com.mx)
- **Local Government** (www.yucatan.gob.mx)
- **Airplane Food** (www.airlinemeals.net)
- **Airplane Seating** (www.seatguru.com; and www.airlinequality.com)
- **Foreign Languages for Travelers** (www.travlang.com)
- **Maps** (www.mapquest.com)
- **Time and Date** (www.timeanddate.com)
- **Travel Warnings** (http://travel.state.gov, www.fco.gov.uk/travel, www.voyage.gc.ca, www.smartraveller.gov.au)
- **Universal Currency Converter** (www.oanda.com)
- **Weather** (www.intellicast.com; and www.weather.com)

particularly among the younger generation, prefer the less expensive rates of **Nextel** (www.nextel.com.mx), which features push-to-talk service. **Cellular Abroad** (www.cellularabroad.com) offers cell phone rentals and purchases as well as SIM cards for travel abroad. Whether you rent or purchase the cell phone, you need to purchase a SIM card that is specific for Mexico.

To call a Mexican cellular number in the same area code, dial 044 and then the number. To dial the cellular phone from anywhere else in Mexico, first dial 01, and then the three-digit area code and the seven-digit number. To dial it from the U.S., dial 011-52, plus the three-digit area code and the seven-digit number.

VOICE-OVER INTERNET PROTOCOL (VOIP)

If you have Web access while traveling, consider a broadband-based telephone service (in technical terms, **Voice over Internet protocol,** or **VoIP**) such as Skype (www.skype.com) or Vonage

(www.vonage.com), which allow you to make free international calls from your laptop or in a cybercafe. Neither service requires the people you're calling to have that service (though fees apply if they do not). Check the websites for details.

INTERNET & E-MAIL WITH YOUR OWN COMPUTER

Wi-Fi access is increasingly common in Mexico's major cities and resorts, including Cancún. However, do not expect to find wireless Internet in many areas of Chiapas, Tabasco, or the Yucatán. Mexico's largest airports offer Wi-Fi access provided for a fee by Telcel's Prodigy Internet service. Most five-star hotels now offer Wi-Fi in the guest rooms, although you will need to check in advance whether this service is free or for a fee. Hotel lobbies often have Wi-Fi, as well. To find public Wi-Fi hotspots in Mexico, go to **www.jiwire.com**; its Hotspot Finder holds the world's largest directory of public wireless hotspots.

WITHOUT YOUR OWN COMPUTER

Many large Mexican airports have **Internet kiosks,** and quality Mexican hotels usually have business centers with Internet access. You can also check out copy stores like **FedEx Kinko's** or **OfficeMax,** which offer computer stations with fully loaded software (as well as Wi-Fi).

13 Tips on Accommodations

MEXICO'S HOTEL RATING SYSTEM

The hotel rating system in Mexico is called "Stars and Diamonds." Hotels may qualify to earn one to five stars or diamonds. Many hotels that have excellent standards are not certified, but all rated hotels adhere to strict standards. The guidelines relate to service, facilities, and hygiene more than to prices.

Five-diamond hotels meet the highest requirements for rating: The beds are comfortable, bathrooms are in excellent working order, all facilities are renovated regularly, infrastructure is top-tier, and services and hygiene meet the highest international standards.

Five-star hotels usually offer similar quality, but with lower levels of service and detail in the rooms. For example, a five-star hotel may have less luxurious linens or, perhaps, room service during limited hours rather than 24 hours.

Four-star hotels are less expensive and more basic, but they still guarantee cleanliness and basic services such as hot water and purified drinking water. Three, two-, and one-star hotels are at least working to adhere to certain standards: Bathrooms are cleaned and linens are washed daily, and you can expect a minimum standard of service. Two- and one-star hotels generally provide bottled water rather than purified water.

The nonprofit organization Calidad Mexicana Certificada, A.C., known as **Calmecac** (www.calmecac.com.mx), is responsible for hotel ratings; visit their website for additional details about the rating system.

HOTEL CHAINS

In addition to the major international chains, you'll run across a number of less-familiar brands as you plan your trip to Mexico. They include:

- **Brisas Hotels & Resorts** (www. brisas.com.mx). These were the hotels that originally attracted jet-set travelers to Mexico. Spectacular in a retro way, these properties offer the laid-back luxury that makes a Mexican vacation so unique.

- **Fiesta Americana** and **Fiesta Inn** (www.posadas.com). Part of the Mexican-owned Grupo Posadas company, these hotels set the country's midrange standard for facilities and services. They generally offer comfortable, spacious rooms and traditional Mexican hospitality. Fiesta Americana hotels offer excellent beach-resort packages. Fiesta Inn hotels are usually more business oriented. Grupo Posadas also owns the more luxurious Caesar Park hotels and the eco-oriented Explorean hotels.

- **Hoteles Camino Real** (© 800/901-2300 in Mexico; www.caminoreal. com). Once known as the premier Mexican hotel chain, Camino Real still maintains a high standard of service at its properties, although the company was sold in 2005, and many of the hotels that once formed a part of it have been sold off or have become independent. Its beach hotels are traditionally located on the best beaches in the area. This chain also focuses on the business market. The

---

Finds **Boutique Lodgings**

Mexico lends itself beautifully to the concept of small, private hotels in idyllic settings. They vary in style from grandiose estate to palm-thatched bungalow. **Mexico Boutique Hotels** (www.mexicoboutiquehotels.com) specializes in smaller places to stay with a high level of personal attention and service. Most options have less than 50 rooms, and the accommodations consist of entire villas, *casitas,* bungalows, or a combination. The Yucatán is especially noted for the luxury haciendas throughout the peninsula.

---

hotels are famous for their vivid and contrasting colors.

- **NH Hotels** (© 800/232-9860 in the U.S. and Canada; www.nh-hotels. com). The NH hotels are noted for their family-friendly facilities and quality standards. The beach properties' signature feature is a pool, framed by columns, overlooking the sea.

- **Quinta Real Grand Class Hotels and Resorts** (© 866/621-9288 in U.S. and Canada; © 800/500-4000 in Mexico; www.quintareal.com). These hotels, owned by Summit Hotels and Resorts, are noted for architectural and cultural details that reflect their individual regions. At these luxury properties, attention to detail and excellent service are the rule. Quinta Real is the top line Mexican hotel brand.

HOUSE RENTALS & SWAPS

House and villa rentals and swaps are becoming more common in Mexico, but no single recognized agency or business provides this service exclusively for Mexico. In the chapters that follow, we've provided information on independent services that we've found to be reputable.

Your best bet will be to look for home exchanges in and around Cancún. Although home-exchange opportunities in Cancún are a fraction of what's available in other parts of the world, a few networks do have Cancún listings, mostly for condos. Florida-based **HomeExchange.com** (© 386/238-3633; www.homeexchange. com) has the greatest number and includes some downtown family homes as well as beach condos. Other possibilities are the British agency **Home Xchange Vacation** (© 44-7736/810-974; www.homexchange vacation.com), **Exchange Homes.com** (© 903/454-7755; www.exchangehomes. com); and **U-Exchange** (© 877/586-619; www.u-exchange.com).

With regard to general online services with properties in other Yucatecan cities and towns, the most extensive inventory of homes is found at **Vacation Rentals by Owner** (VRBO; www.vrbo.com). They have over 33,000 homes and condominiums worldwide, including a large selection in Mexico. Another good option is **VacationSpot** (© 888/903-7768; www. vacationspot.com), owned by Expedia and a part of its sister company Hotels. com. It has fewer choices, but the company's criteria for adding inventory is much more selective and often includes on-site inspections. They also offer toll-free phone support.

For tips on surfing for hotel deals online, visit **www.frommers.com**.

4

Suggested Yucatán Itineraries

by David Baird

The following itineraries assume you're flying in and out of Cancún, by far the most common port of entry for the Yucatán. The airport is south of town in the direction of the Riviera Maya, so if you rent a car to drive down the coast, you won't have to deal with city traffic. For traveling around the Yucatán, rental cars work well. The roads are all easy to figure out, and there's not much traffic when you move inland. Finding your way around Mérida is a little tricky, but Cancún and the other cities of the peninsula are easy.

These itineraries are merely suggestions; you should tweak them to your specific tastes and interests. However, I recommend against being too ambitious with your vacation time. The heat and humidity bring about a lethargy that can be enjoyable if you're not preoccupied with a timetable. Keep in mind as well that it gets dark early here, and it's not a good idea to do much night driving.

1 The Regions in Brief

Travelers to the peninsula have an opportunity to see pre-Hispanic ruins—such as **Chichén Itzá, Uxmal,** and **Tulum**—and the living descendants of the cultures that built them, as well as the ultimate in resort Mexico: **Cancún.** The Yucatán peninsula borders the aquamarine Gulf of Mexico on the west and north, and the clear blue Caribbean Sea on the east. It covers almost 197,600 sq. km (76,294 sq. miles), with nearly 1,600km (1,000 miles) of shoreline. Underground rivers and natural wells, called cenotes, are a peculiar feature of this region.

Lovely rock-walled Maya villages and crumbling henequén haciendas dot the interior of the peninsula. The placid interior contrasts with the hubbub of the Caribbean coast. From Cancún south to **Chetumal,** the jungle coastline is spotted with all kinds of development, from posh to budget. This swath has been dubbed the **Riviera Maya,** and boasts an enormous array of wildlife, including hundreds of species of birds. The Gulf Coast beaches, while good enough, don't compare to those on the Caribbean. National parks near **Celestún** and **Río Lagartos** on the Gulf Coast are home to amazing flocks of flamingos.

To present the Maya world in its entirety, this book also covers the states of **Tabasco** and **Chiapas.** The Gulf Coast state of Tabasco was once home to the Olmec, the mother culture of Mesoamerica. At Villahermosa's Parque–Museo La Venta, you can see the impressive 40-ton carved rock heads that the Olmec left behind.

San Cristóbal de las Casas, in Chiapas, inhabits cooler, greener mountains, and is more in the mold of a provincial colonial town. Approaching San Cristóbal from any direction, you see small plots of corn tended by colorfully clad Maya. The surrounding villages are home to many craftspeople, from woodcarvers to potters to weavers.

The Yucatán Peninsula

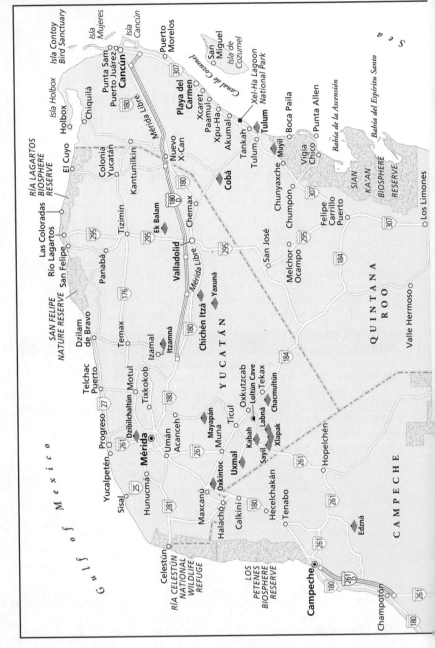

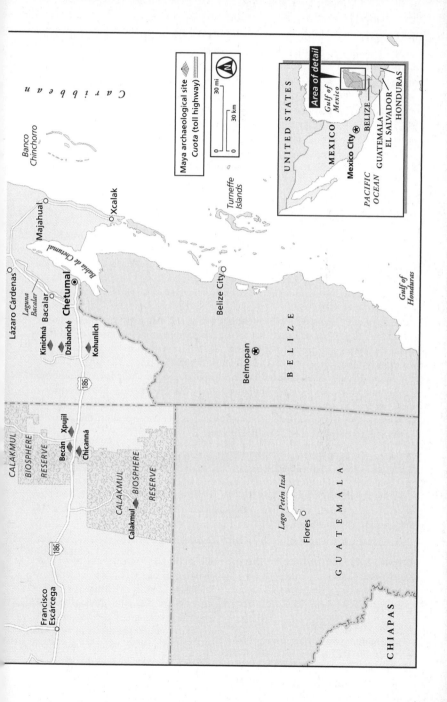

Caribbean

Banco
Chinchorro

Turneffe
Islands

Gulf of
Honduras

Xcalak

Majahual

Bahía de Chetumal

Belize City

Lázaro Cárdenas

Laguna
Bacalar

Bacalar

Chetumal

Kinichná

Dzibanché

Kohunlich

186

BELIZE

Belmopan

Becán   Xpujil

Chicanná

CALAKMUL
BIOSPHERE
RESERVE

CALAKMUL   BIOSPHERE
RESERVE

Calakmul

186

Francisco
Escárcega

Lago Petén Itzá

Flores

GUATEMALA

CHIAPAS

Maya archaeological site
Cuota (toll highway)

N

30 mi
0
0
30 km

UNITED STATES

Gulf of
Mexico

Area of detail

MEXICO

Mexico City

BELIZE

GUATEMALA

EL SALVADOR

HONDURAS

PACIFIC
OCEAN

In the eastern lowland jungles of Chiapas lie the classic Maya ruins of **Palenque.** Deeper into the interior, for those willing to make the trek, are the ruins of **Yaxchilán** and **Bonampak.**

NATURAL LIFE & PROTECTED AREAS   The Yucatán state's nature preserves include the 47,200-hectare (116,584-acre) **Río Lagartos Wildlife Refuge** north of Valladolid—where you'll find North America's largest flock of nesting flamingos—and the 5,600-plus-hectare (13,832-acre) **Celestún Wildlife Refuge,** which harbors most of the flamingos during non-nesting season. The state also has incorporated nature trails into the archaeological site of **Dzibilchaltún,** north of Mérida.

In 1989, Campeche state set aside 71,480 hectares (176,556 acres) in the **Calakmul Biosphere Reserve** that it shares with Guatemala. The area includes the ruins of Calakmul, as well as acres of thick jungle.

Quintana Roo's protected areas are some of the region's most beautiful, wild, and important. In 1986, the state ambitiously set aside the 520,000-hectare (1.3-million-acre) **Sian Ka'an Biosphere Reserve,** conserving a significant part of the coast in the face of development south of Tulum. **Isla Contoy,** also in Quintana Roo, off the coast of Isla Mujeres and Cancún, is a beautiful island refuge for hundreds of birds, turtles, plants, and other wildlife. Cozumel's Chankanaab Lagoon gives visitors an idea of the biological importance of Yucatán's lengthy shoreline: Four of Mexico's eight marine turtle species—loggerhead, green, hawksbill, and leatherback—nest on Quintana Roo's shores, and more than 600 species of birds, reptiles, and mammals have been counted.

Tabasco, though a small state, has set aside a vast preserve of wetlands called **Pantanos de Centla,** just northeast of Villahermosa. Three reserves in Chiapas encompass jungles and lakes, and some of Mexico's most bio-diverse lands. The largest by far is the nature preserve called **Montes Azules,** the old homeland of the Lacandon Indians in the extreme eastern lowlands bordering Guatemala. Not far from San Cristóbal de las Casas is also a small preserve of high cloud forest habitat called **Huitepec.** A good distance west of Tuxtla Gutiérrez, the state capital, is an extensive nature preserve containing upland forests called **Selva del Ocote.**

2 Northern Yucatán in a Week

You could extend this itinerary to 10 days, even 2 weeks—it all depends on how much time you want to spend on the beach. Once you've spent a little time in that clear blue water, it's hard to pull yourself away to move inland. But you'll probably find something in this trip to entice you.

Days ❶ & ❷: Somewhere on the Caribbean Coast
Spend a few days relaxing on the beach. See chapter 7 for more details.

Day ❸: Chichén Itzá ✸✸✸
Have a morning swim before driving to the ruins of **Ek Balam** (p. 247), which lie north of the colonial city of Valladolid. If you're coming from Cancún or the northern Riviera Maya, you can take the modern

toll highway and save a lot of travel time, though the toll of $22 is a bit pricey. If you're in Playa del Carmen or farther south, you're better off driving south to Tulum and taking the highway to Cobá. You can stop and see the ruins of **Cobá** (p. 178) if you allow enough time. When you get to Valladolid, head north on Highway 295 to the turnoff for Ek Balam. After climbing the main pyramid and inspecting the beautifully worked sacred

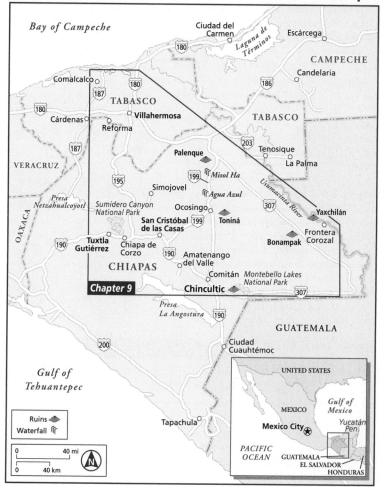

Bay of Campeche

Ciudad del Carmen

Escárcega

Laguna de Términos

CAMPECHE

Candelaria

Comalcalco

TABASCO

Villahermosa

TABASCO

Cárdenas

Reforma

VERACRUZ

Palenque

Misol Ha

Tenosique

La Palma

Usumacinta River

Presa Netzahualcoyotl

Simojovel

Agua Azul

Sumidero Canyon National Park

Ocosingo

Yaxchilán

OAXACA

San Cristóbal de las Casas

Toniná

Frontera Corozal

Bonampak

Tuxtla Gutiérrez

Chiapa de Corzo

Amatenango del Valle

CHIAPAS

Comitán

Montebello Lakes National Park

Chapter 9

Chincultic

Presa La Angostura

GUATEMALA

Gulf of Tehuantepec

Ciudad Cuauhtémoc

Ruins

Waterfall

0   40 mi
0   40 km

Tapachula

UNITED STATES

MEXICO

Gulf of Mexico

Mexico City

Yucatán Pen.

PACIFIC OCEAN

GUATEMALA

EL SALVADOR

HONDURAS

doorway, head back to Valladolid for a late lunch. Drive to Chichén Itzá via the old highway. Shortly after leaving town, stop to enjoy **Cenote Dzitnup** (p. 247). Continue on to **Chichén Itzá** (p. 237) and check into a hotel in the area. In the evening, see the sound-and-light show, and then visit the ruins the next morning.

Days ❹ & ❺: Mérida & Environs ★★
Drive to **Mérida** (p. 195) and enjoy an evening in this bustling tropical city. The next day, you can explore the town, or perhaps do some shopping. Or, as a third option, enjoy Mérida in the evening and take side trips during the day. Choices include the **Celestún National Wildlife Refuge** (p. 217), where you can take a boat ride and see some pink flamingos, or **Dzibilchaltún** (p. 218), to see the ruins and site museum. You might also consider visiting **Progreso** and **Xcambó** (for details on both routes, see p. 218), for another good chance of seeing flamingos.

Northern Yucatán in a Week

Day ❻: The Ruins of Uxmal ✦✦✦

No matter whether you take the short way or the long way (for details on both routes, see p. 222), try to get to **Uxmal** by late afternoon, so that you can rest and cool off before seeing the sound-and-light show. Uxmal's **Pyramid of the Magician** is one of the most dramatic structures in the Maya world and it becomes even more intriguing when lit at night. The next morning, you can explore the ruins in more detail. See p. 223.

Day ❼: Cancún

This last day will necessarily include a good bit of driving. Take the short route back via Umán, then use the loop or *periférico* to avoid entering Mérida. After about 45 minutes, you'll see signs for the highway to Cancún. See chapter 5.

3 An Eco-Adventure for the Entire Family

If you've got your own mask and snorkel (and fins, too) bring them for this trip; you can always get rentals, but you're better off with gear that fits well.

Day ❶: Arrive at Cancún Airport

For this itinerary, it's best to stay in the lower Riviera Maya, at a hotel or condo in the **Xpu-Ha–Akumal–Tulum** area. That puts you close to most of the places you'll be going. The drive from the airport to this part of the coast is at most 2 hours. See p. 169, 169, and 173.

Day ❷: Xel-Ha & the Ruins of Tulum ✦✦✦

Start by enjoying a nice swim at **Xel-Ha's** lovely lagoon (p. 171), go snorkeling, or simply enjoy the parklands encircling the water. You can stay here the entire day or combine this with a trip to see the ruins in **Tulum** (which you should do in the morning, when the air is cooler). See p. 173.

Day ❸: Hidden Worlds ✦✦✦ & Aktun Chen ✦

Between Akumal and Tulum are two attractions, each interesting in their own way. At **Hidden Worlds** (p. 172), you can snorkel in a couple of different cenotes (sinkholes or wellsprings) and subterranean rivers for which the Yucatán is famous. The water is cold, but wet suits are provided, as well as snorkel gear if you don't bring your own. **Aktun Chen** (p. 171) is a cavern that you can hike through and see lots of rock formations. The small zoo houses local species such as spider monkeys and tropical birds, including a toucan.

Day ❹: Alltournative

Consider spending today with **Alltourna-tive,** an adventure tour agency based in Playa del Carmen. Its day trips combine

An Eco-Adventure for the Entire Family

adventure with nature and interactions with contemporary Maya in one of their own villages. The tour company will pick you up at almost any hotel in the Riviera Maya. You can fly out over the jungle on a zip line, try your hand at rappelling, and have a Maya-style meal all in the same day. See p. 153.

Day ⑤: Sian Ka'an Biosphere Reserve ⋆

Explore the largest wildlife preserve in the Yucatán; snorkel down canals built by the Maya, visit the large, pristine lagoon at the center of the park, and observe various forms of wildlife as you get an up-close-and-personal view of the peninsula's natural habitat. Tour agencies do full-day tours. See p. 173.

Day ⑥: Chichén Itzá ⋆⋆⋆

Start the day snorkeling, then drive to **Chichén Itzá** in the afternoon. Check into a hotel, and in the evening you can enjoy the sound-and-light show at the ruins. Return the next morning to get a closer look in daylight. See p. 237.

Day ⑦: Cenote Dzitnup ⋆, Ek Balam ⋆⋆⋆ & Río Lagartos Nature Reserve ⋆

After seeing the ruins, head east on the old federal highway until you get to

Cenote Dzitnup, shortly before the town of Valladolid. You'll find a dark cenote with a beautiful pool of water illuminated by a column of sunlight that penetrates the roof. Nearby is a second cenote. After a quick dip, continue into **Valladolid** (p. 245) for lunch. After you're nourished, head north on Highway 295 to the turnoff for the recently excavated ruins of **Ek Balam** (p. 247), noted for a beautifully sculpted sacred doorway on the tallest pyramid in northern Yucatán. Continue north, past the town of Tizimín, until you get to the coastal village of **Río Lagartos.** Here you can get a room at one of the economical hotels fronting the water and arrange for an early-morning boat tour of the wildlife sanctuary. Not only will you see those eye-catching natural wonders—pink flamingos—but you'll see a host of other species as well, and enjoy a boat ride through mangrove and saltwater estuaries. See p. 248.

Day ⑧: Cancún

After your visit with pink flamingos, it's time to get back to Cancún and civilization. See chapter 5.

4 La Ruta Maya

This route, which connects the major Maya sites in Mexico, could be done quickly in 2 weeks, or more slowly in a month or perhaps broken up into two trips. I've kept the trip to the minimum by avoiding the city of Mérida, but you may want to visit it. There's a risk of overdosing on ruins by seeing too many in too short a time. I give you the fast-track approach here, but that doesn't mean that I'm encouraging you to move through this area that quickly. The best mode of travel would be a rental car: The highways have little traffic and are, for the most part, in good shape.

Day ❶: Arrive in Cancún

After you arrive, enjoy the rest of the day with a swim in the Caribbean or an afternoon by the pool. See chapter 5.

Day ❷: Ek Balam 𝕮𝕮𝕮 & Chichén Itzá 𝕮𝕮𝕮

Get on the modern toll highway that heads toward Mérida and take the exit for Valladolid. Head north, away from the town, to visit the ruins of Ek Balam (p. 247). Highlights include a sacred doorway richly decorated with vivid figures of gods and men. Then head back to the town of Valladolid for lunch before driving the short distance to Chichén Itzá (p. 237) on the old federal highway. Just outside of town, stop to see the cenotes of Dzitnup and Sammulá (for both, see p. 247). Further on is the Balankanché Cave (p. 244). When you get to Chichén, check into your hotel, and then go to the ruins later in the evening for the sound-and-light show. See p. 238.

Day ❸: Continuing to Uxmal 𝕮𝕮𝕮

Spend more time at the ruins of Chichén Itzá in the morning, then continue west on the toll highway toward Mérida, and turn off at Ticopó. Head south toward the town of Acanceh (p. 220) and Highway 18. Stop to see the small but interesting ruins in the middle of town, and then proceed down Highway 18 to the ruins of Mayapán (p. 221). Afterward, continue through Ticul to Santa Elena and Uxmal. Experience the sound-and-light show. See p. 223.

Day ❹: Edzná

Visit Uxmal (p. 222) in the morning, then drive back toward Santa Elena and take Highway 261 south to Hopelchén and on to the impressive ruins of Edzná (p. 228). Nearby is a fancy hacienda-turned-hotel, called Uayamón (p. 211; reservations can be made through Starwood hotels), where you can overnight, or drive into the town of Campeche and stay at more modest digs.

Days ❺ & ❻: Palenque 𝕮𝕮, Bonampak & Yaxchilán

Stay on Highway 261 to Escárcega, then head west on Highway 186 toward Villahermosa, then south on Highway 199 to the town of Palenque (p. 257) with its magnificent ruins. The next day go to the ruins of Bonampak and Yaxchilán (p. 263), using one of the local tour operators.

Days ❼ & ❽: San Cristóbal de las Casas 𝕮𝕮

Keep south on Highway 199 toward San Cristóbal (p. 265). On the way, take a swimming break at Misol Ha (p. 264), and visit the ruins of Toniná outside of the town of Ocosingo. From San Cristóbal, go with one of the local guides to see the present-day Maya communities of Chamula and Zinacantán (p. 272). Spend some time enjoying the towns.

Day ❾: Calakmul 𝕮𝕮𝕮

Retrace your steps to Escárcega and continue east on Highway 186. If you have time, visit the fascinating sculptures of

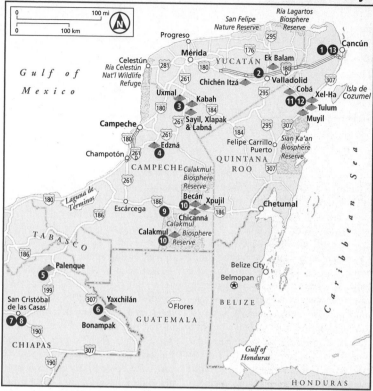

Balamkú (p. 192). Spend the night at one of the hotels in the vicinity of the turnoff for **Calakmul,** one of the prime city-states of the Classic age of the Maya, and not often visited.

Day ⑩: Calakmul & Becán ✦✦✦

Get to **Calakmul** (p. 190) early. Keep your eyes open for wildlife as you drive along a narrow jungle road. All the area surrounding the city is a **wildlife preserve.** For most of the city's history, Calakmul was the main rival to the city of Tikal, which is present-day Guatemala. It eventually defeated Tikal and subjugated it for 100 years. Calakmul's **Structure 2** is the highest Maya pyramid in Mexico. Afterward, continue east on Highway 186 to see the ruins of **Becán,** a large

ceremonial center with tall temples. Also in the vicinity are **Xpujil** and **Chicanná.** Spend the night on the shores of **Lake Bacalar,** where you can cool off in its blue waters. See p. 182.

Days ⑪ & ⑫: Tulum

Drive north on Highway 307 to **Tulum** and settle into one of the small beach hotels there. In the morning, walk through the ruins and enjoy the lovely view of the coast. See p. 173.

Day ⑬: Back to Cancún

Drive back to Cancún. Depending on your schedule, you can enjoy some more beach time, or head straight to the airport (25 min. south of Cancún) and depart. See chapter 5.

5

Cancún

by Juan Cristiano

It may be commercialized and more American than Mexican in spirit, but Cancún is still one of the finest beach destinations in the world—with enough pleasure-pursuits to make even the most unrelenting hedonists blush.

Due to its ideal mix of elements—its transparent turquoise sea, powdery white beaches, and immense potential for growth—a group of Mexican government computer analysts targeted the town for tourism development in 1974, transforming it from a deserted beach to a five-star resort in little more than 3 decades. Since then, Cancún sustained the devastations of Hurricane Wilma and other powerful tropical storms, only to emerge stronger and more irresistible. In the wake of Hurricane Wilma, which tore through the Yucatán peninsula in 2005, wreckage rapidly gave way to exacting renovations, luxurious upgrades, and brand-new destinations.

The secret of Cancún's allure hasn't changed much over the decades—it's still all about the Caribbean beach. The city limits of Cancún (which means "golden snake" in Mayan), stretch from the old city east to a 24km (15-mile) sliver of land that runs southwest, rimmed by white-sand beaches, connected to the mainland by two bridges. The land creates a ring around the expansive Nichupté lagoon, a lush reminder of Cancún's jungle past between the old and the new.

In addition to its spectacular coastline, Cancún also affords visitors the highest quality accommodations; easy access by air; an unrivaled range of shopping, world-class dining, and nightlife; and endless outdoor activities. And it's a gateway to the nearby ruins of Tulum, Chichén Itzá, and Cobá.

Cancún embodies Caribbean splendor and the exotic joys of Mexico, but even a traveler feeling apprehensive about visiting foreign soil will feel completely at ease here. English is spoken and dollars accepted; roads are well-paved and lawns manicured. Some travelers are surprised to find that Cancún is more like a U.S. beach resort than a part of Mexico. Indeed, signs of Americanism are rampant. U.S. college students continue to descend in droves during Spring Break—which, depending on your perspective, may be reason to rush headlong into the party or stay far, far away during this season. One astonishing statistic suggests that more Americans travel to Cancún than to any other foreign destination in the world. Indeed, almost three million people visit annually—most of them on their first trip to Mexico.

Yet Cancún is a convenient distance from the more traditional Mexican resorts of Isla Mujeres and the coastal zone now known as the Riviera Maya—extending down from Cancún, through Playa del Carmen, to the Maya ruins at Tulum, Cozumel, Chichén Itzá, and Cobá. All make for an easy day trip.

You will likely run out of vacation days, however, before you run out of things to do in Cancún proper. Snorkeling, dolphin swims, jungle tours, and visits to ancient Maya ruins and modern ecological theme parks are among the most popular diversions. A dozen malls sell name-brand and duty-free goods (with European imports for less than in the U.S.). With tens of thousands of hotel rooms and more than 350 restaurants and nightclubs, there's something for every taste and budget.

A day here might begin with a jet-ski tour of the nearby jungles or a visit to Maya ruins, followed by an afternoon of watersports or lounging poolside. After soaking up the sun, you could browse through a Mexican *mercado* (market) in search of bargains or visit upscale stores for duty-free deals. Then dine at one of several five-diamond-rated restaurants before heading out to a rocking bar or dance club filled with others who cannot bear to go to bed until dawn.

Cancún's luxury hotels have pools so spectacular that you may find it tempting to remain poolside—but don't. Set aside some time to simply gaze into the ocean and wriggle your toes in the fine, brilliant white sand. It is, after all, what put Cancún on the map—and no tempest of nature has been able to sweep it away.

1 Orientation

GETTING THERE

BY PLANE   If this is not your first trip to Cancún, you'll notice that the airport's facilities and services continue to expand. **AeroMéxico** (© **800/237-6639** in the U.S., or 01/800-021-4000 in Mexico; www.aeromexico.com) operates connecting service to Cancún through Mexico City. **Mexicana** (© **800/531-7921** in the U.S., 01/800-366-5400 in Mexico, or 998/881-9090; www.mexicana.com.mx) runs connecting flights to Cancún through Miami or Mexico City. In addition to these carriers, many **charter** companies—such as Apple Vacations and Funjet—travel to Cancún; these package tours make up as much as 60% of arrivals by U.S. visitors (see "Packages for the Independent Traveler," in chapter 3).

Regional carrier **Click Mexicana,** a Mexicana affiliate (© **01-800/112-5425** toll-free in Mexico; www.click.com.mx), flies from Cozumel, Havana, Mexico City, Mérida, Chetumal, and other points within Mexico. You'll want to confirm departure times for flights to the U.S. **Aviacsa** (© **01-800/711-6733** toll-free in Mexico; www.aviacsa.com); **Interjet** (© **01-800/01-12345** toll-free in Mexico; www.interjet.com.mx); and **Volaris** (© **01-800/7865-2747;** www.volaris.com.mx) are three other regional carriers that fly to Cancún from Mexico City.

Here are the U.S. numbers of major international carriers serving Cancún: **Alaska** (© 800/426-0333; www.alaskaair.com), **American** (© 800/433-7300; www.aa.com), **Continental** (© 800/231-0856; www.continental.com), **Delta** (© 800/221-1212; www.delta.com), **Frontier** (© 800/432-1359; www.frontierairlines.com), **Northwest** (© 800/225-2525; www.nwa.com), **United** (© 800/241-6522; www.ual.com), and **US Airways** (© 800/428-4322; www.usairways.com).

Most major car-rental firms have outlets at the airport, so if you're renting a car, consider picking it up and dropping it off at the airport to save on airport-transportation costs. Another way to save money is to arrange for the rental before you leave home. If you wait until you arrive, the daily cost will be around $50 to $75 (£25–£38) for a compact vehicle. Major agencies include **Alamo** (© 800/462-5266; www.alamo.com); **Avis** (© 800/331-1212 in the U.S., or 998/886-0221; www.avis.com); **Budget** (© 800/527-0700 in the U.S., or 998/886-0417; fax

998/884-4812; www.budget.com); **Dollar** (© 800/800-3665 in the U.S., or 998/886-2300; www.dollar.com); **National** (© 800/227-7368 in the U.S., or 998/886-0153; www.nationalcar.com); **Hertz** (© 800/654-3131 in the U.S. and Canada, or 998/884-1326; www.hertz.com); and **Thrifty** (© 800/847-4389; www.thrifty.com). If you're looking for an exotic car rental (such as a Porsche or Mercedes convertible) and don't mind paying a small fortune for it, try **Platinum** (© 998/883-5555; www.platinumcarrental.com), with an office inside the JW Marriott hotel. The Zona Hotelera (Hotel Zone) lies 10km (6¼ miles)—a 20-minute drive—from the airport along wide, well-paved roads.

The rate for a **private taxi** from the airport is $53 (£27) to Ciudad Cancún (downtown) or the Hotel Zone. The return trip with an airport taxi is discounted by 50%. *Colectivos* (vans) run from the airport into town. Buy tickets, which cost about $12 (£6), from the booth to the far right as you exit the airport terminal. There's **bus** transportation ($3.50/£1.75) from the airport to Ciudad Cancún. From there, you can take another bus for less than a dollar to Puerto Juárez, where passenger ferries leave to Isla Mujeres regularly. There is no *colectivo* service returning to the airport from Ciudad Cancún or the Hotel Zone, so you'll have to take a taxi, but the rate will be much less than for the trip from the airport. (Only federally chartered taxis may take fares *from* the airport, but any taxi may bring passengers *to* the airport.) Ask at your hotel what the fare should be, but expect to pay about half what you paid from the airport to your hotel.

BY CAR   From Mérida or Campeche, take **Highway 180** east to Cancún. This is mostly a winding, two-lane road that branches off into the express **toll road 180D** between Izamal and Nuevo Xcan. Nuevo Xcan is approximately 40km (25 miles) from Cancún. Mérida is about 320km (199 miles) away.

BY BUS   Cancún's **ADO bus terminal** (© **998/884-4352** or 01800/702-8000) is in downtown Ciudad Cancún at the intersection of avenidas Tulum and Uxmal. All out-of-town buses arrive here. Buses run to Playa del Carmen, Tulum, Chichén Itzá, other nearby beach and archaeological zones, and other points within Mexico.

VISITOR INFORMATION

The **State Tourism Office (SEDETUR),** Av. Yaxchilán Lote 6 SM 17, downtown across from Costco (© **998/881-9000;** www.qroo.gob.mx), is open Monday to Friday from 9am to 8pm. The **Cancún Municipal Tourism Office** is downtown at the Palacio Municipal (City Hall) on Avenida Tulum between Avenidas Uxmal and Cobá (© **998/887-3379**). It's open Monday through Friday from 9am to 7pm. Each office lists hotels and their rates, as well as ferry schedules. For information prior to your arrival in Cancún, visit the Convention Bureau's website, **www.cancun.travel**.

Pick up copies of the free monthly booklet, *Cancún Tips* (www.cancuntips.com.mx), and a seasonal tabloid of the same name.

CITY LAYOUT

There are really two Cancúns: **Ciudad Cancún (Cancún City)** and **Isla Cancún (Cancún Island).** The former, on the mainland, has restaurants, shops, and less expensive hotels, as well as pharmacies, dentists, automotive shops, banks, travel and airline agencies, and car-rental firms—all within an area about 9 square blocks. The city's main thoroughfare is **Avenida Tulum.** Heading south, Avenida Tulum becomes the highway to the airport and to Tulum and Chetumal; heading north, it intersects the highway to Mérida and the road to Puerto Juárez and the Isla Mujeres ferries.

> ## (Tips) The Best Websites for Cancún
>
> - **All About Cancún: www.cancunmx.com**   This site is a good place to start planning. Their database, called "The Online Experts," answers many of the most common questions. It's slow but current, with input from lots of recent travelers to the region.
> - **Cancún Convention & Visitors Bureau: www.cancun.travel**   The official site of the Cancún Convention & Visitors Bureau lists excellent information on events and attractions. Its hotel guide is one of the most complete available, and it has an active message board of recent visitors to Cancún.
> - **Cancún Online: www.cancun.com**   This comprehensive guide has lots of information about things to do and see in Cancún, though most details come from paying advertisers. The site lets you reserve package trips, accommodations, and tee times, or even plan a wedding online.
> - **Cancún Travel Guide: www.go2cancun.com**   These online information specialists are also an excellent resource for Cancún rentals, hotels, and attractions. Note that this site also lists only paying advertisers, which means you'll find most of the major players here.

The latter is a sandy strip 22km (14 miles) long, shaped like a "7." It's home to the famed **Zona Hotelera,** or Hotel Zone (also called the Zona Turística, or Tourist Zone), which stretches out along Isla Cancún, connected to the mainland by the Playa Linda Bridge at the north end and the Punta Nizuc Bridge at the southern end. Between the two areas lies Laguna Nichupté. Avenida Cobá from Cancún City becomes Bulevar Kukulkán, the island's main traffic artery. Cancún's international airport is just inland from the south end of the island.

FINDING AN ADDRESS   Cancún's street-numbering system is a holdover from its early days. Addresses are still given by the number of the building lot and by the *manzana* (block) or *supermanzana* (group of blocks). The city is relatively compact, and the downtown commercial section is easy to cover on foot.

On the island, addresses are given by kilometer number on Bulevar Kukulkán or by reference to some well-known location. In Cancún, streets are named after famous Maya cities. Boulevards are named for nearby archaeological sites, Chichén Itzá, Tulum, and Uxmal.

GETTING AROUND

BY TAXI   Taxi prices in Cancún are clearly set by zone, although keeping track of what's in which zone can take some doing. The minimum fare within the Hotel Zone is $6 (£3) per ride, making it one of the most expensive taxi areas in Mexico. In addition, taxis operating in the Hotel Zone feel perfectly justified in having a discriminatory pricing structure: Local residents pay about half of what tourists pay, and prices for guests at higher-priced hotels are about double those for budget hotel guests—these are all established by the taxi union. Rates should be posted outside your hotel; if you have a question, all drivers are required to have an official rate card in their taxis, though it's generally in Spanish.

Within the downtown area, the cost is about $2 (£1) per cab ride (not per person); within any other zone, it's $6 (£3). Traveling between two zones will also cost $6 (£3), and if you cross two zones, that'll cost $8 (£4). Settle on a price in advance, or check at your hotel. Trips to the airport from most zones cost $15 (£7.50). Taxis can also be rented for $20 (£10) per hour for travel around the city and Hotel Zone, but this rate can generally be negotiated down to about $15 (£7.50). If you want to hire a taxi to take you to Chichén Itzá or along the Riviera Maya, expect to pay about $30 (£15) per hour—many taxi drivers feel that they are also providing guide services.

BY BUS   Bus travel within Cancún continues to improve and is increasingly popular. In town, almost everything lies within walking distance. **Ruta 1** and **Ruta 2** (HOTELES) city buses travel frequently from the mainland to the beaches along Avenida Tulum (the main street) and all the way to Punta Nizuc at the far end of the Hotel Zone on Isla Cancún. **Ruta 8** buses go to Puerto Juárez/Punta Sam for ferries to Isla Mujeres. They stop on the east side of Avenida Tulum. All these city buses run between 6am and 10pm daily. Beware of private buses along the same route; they charge far more than the public ones. Public buses have the fare painted on the front; at press time, the fare was 60¢ (30p).

BY MOPED   Mopeds are a convenient but dangerous way to cruise through the very congested traffic. Rentals start at about $35 (£18) for a day, and a credit card voucher is required as security. You should receive a crash helmet (it's the law) and instructions on how to lock the wheels when you park. Read the fine print on the back of the rental agreement regarding liability for repairs or replacement in case of accident, theft, or vandalism.

FAST FACTS: Cancún

American Express The local office is at La Isla Shopping Center in the hotel zone (© **998/883-3918**; www.americanexpress.com/mexico), and there's another branch inside the airport. It's open Monday through Friday from 9am to 6pm, Saturday from 9am to 1pm.

Area Code The telephone area code is **998**.

Climate It's hot but not overwhelmingly humid. The rainy season is May through October. August through October is hurricane season, which brings erratic weather. November through February is generally sunny but can also be cloudy, windy, somewhat rainy, and even cool.

Consulates The **U.S. Consular Agent** is in the Plaza Caracol 2, Bulevar Kukulkán Km 8.5, 3rd level, 320–323 (© **998/883-0272**). The office is open Monday through Friday from 9am to 2pm. The **Canadian Consulate** is in the Plaza Caracol, 3rd level, Loc. 330 (© **998/883-3360**). The office is open Monday through Friday from 9am to 3:30pm. The **United Kingdom** has a consular office at the Royal Sands Hotel in Cancún (© **998/881-0100**, ext. 65898; fax 998/848-8662; information@britishconsulateCancun.com). The office is open Monday through Friday from 9am to 5pm. Irish, Australian, and New Zealand citizens should contact their embassies in Mexico City.

Crime Car break-ins are just about the only frequent crime here. They happen frequently, especially around the shopping centers in the Hotel Zone. Rapes have also been reported in Cancún. Most have taken place at night or in the early morning.

Currency Exchange Most banks sit downtown along Avenida Tulum and are usually open Monday through Friday from 9am to 2pm, although some are open later and even half the day on Saturday. Many have automated teller machines for after-hours cash withdrawals. In the Hotel Zone, you'll find banks in the Kukulcán Plaza and next to the convention center. There are also many *casas de cambio* (exchange houses). Downtown merchants are eager to change cash dollars, but island stores don't offer very good exchange rates. Avoid changing money at the airport as you arrive, especially at the first exchange booth you see—its rates are less favorable than those of any in town or others farther inside the airport concourse. Dollars are widely accepted throughout Cancún.

Drugstores Across the street from Señor Frog's in the Hotel Zone, at Bulevar Kukulcán Km 9.5, **Farmacías del Ahorro** (© 998/892-7291) offers 24-hour service and free delivery. Plenty of drugstores are in the major shopping malls in the Hotel Zone, and are open until 10pm. In downtown Cancún, **Farmacía Cancún** is located at Av. Tulum 17 (© 998/884-1283). It's open Monday to Saturday from 9am to 10pm and Sunday from 10am to 10pm. You can stock up on over-the-counter and many prescription drugs without a prescription.

Emergencies To report an emergency, dial © **060**, which is supposed to be similar to 911 emergency service in the United States. For first aid, the **Cruz Roja,** or Red Cross (© **065** or 998/884-1616; fax 998/883-9218), is open 24 hours on Av. Yaxchilán between avenidas Xcaret and Labná, next to the Telmex building. **Galenia Hospital** is one of the city's most modern, offering full emergency and other services with excellent care, at Av. Tulum, SM 12, at Nizuc (© **998/891-5200;** www.hospitalgalenia.com). **AMAT**, Av, Nader 13, SM 2, at Av. Uxmal (© **998/887-4422**), is a small emergency hospital with some English-speaking doctors. It's open 24 hours. Desk staff may have limited command of English. **Air Ambulance** (Global Ambulance) service is available by calling © **01-800/305-9400** in Mexico. It is usually easier and less expensive to arrange medical air evacuation services through a U.S. rather than Mexican company.

Internet Access **Häagen-Dazs** on the bottom floor of Kukulcán Plaza, Bulevar Kukulcán Km 13, has a free hotspot for wireless Internet access. Most hotels now have Internet access, and five star hotels have business centers.

Luggage Storage & Lockers Hotels will generally tag and store luggage while you travel elsewhere.

Newspapers & Magazines Most hotel gift shops and newsstands carry English-language magazines and English-language Mexican newspapers, such as the *Miami Herald.*

Police Cancún has a fleet of English-speaking tourist police to help travelers. Dial © **998/885-2277**. The **Procuraduría Federal del Consumidor (consumer protection agency),** Av. Cobá 9–11 (© **998/884-2634**), is opposite the Social Security Hospital and upstairs from the Fenix drugstore. It's open Monday through Friday from 9am to 3pm.

Post Office The main *correo* lies at the intersection of avenidas Sunyaxchen and Xel-Ha (© 998/884-1418). It's open Monday through Friday from 9am to 4pm, and Saturday from 9am to noon for the purchase of stamps only.

Seasons Technically, high season runs from December 15 to April; low season extends from May to December 15, when prices drop 10% to 30%. Some hotels are starting to charge high-season rates during June and July, when Mexican, European, and school-holiday visitors often travel, although rates may still be lower than in winter months.

2 Where to Stay

Island hotels—almost all of them offering modern facilities and English-speaking staffs—line the beach like concrete dominoes. Extravagance is the byword in the newer hotels. Some hotels, while exclusive, affect a more relaxed attitude. The water on the upper end of the island facing Bahía de Mujeres is placid, while beaches lining the long side of the island facing the Caribbean are subject to choppier water and crashing waves on windy days. (For more information on swimming safety, see "Beaches, Watersports & Boat Tours," later in this chapter.) Be aware that the farther south you go on the island, the longer it takes (20–30 min. in traffic) to get back to the "action spots," which are primarily between the Plaza Flamingo and Punta Cancún on the island and along Avenida Tulum on the mainland.

Following Hurricane Wilma's devastation, the news item that received the most coverage was the destruction of Cancún's famed white-sand beaches. Immediately following the storm, literally all of the sand was washed away from the northern border of Isla Cancún, and from Punta Cancún. However, thanks to Mother Nature and a $20-million effort by Mexico's government to pump the dislocated sand back to the beach, this is no longer an issue. The southern beaches of Isla Cancún actually benefited from the storm, and now they have especially wide beachfronts.

Almost all major hotel chains have real estate on Cancún Island. The reality is that Cancún is so popular as a package destination from the U.S. that prices and special deals are often the deciding factor for consumers rather than loyalty to any one hotel brand (see "Packages for the Independent Traveler," in chapter 3). Ciudad Cancún offers independently owned, smaller, less-expensive lodging, all a 5 to 10 minute cab

---

Tips Deciphering Hotel Prices

In all price categories, Cancún's hotels generally set their rates in dollars, so they are immune to variations in the peso. Travel agents and wholesalers always have air/hotel packages available, and Sunday papers often advertise inventory-clearing packages at prices much lower than the rates listed here. Cancún also has numerous all-inclusive properties, which allow you to take a fixed-cost vacation. Note that the price quoted when you call a hotel's reservation number from the United States may not include Cancún's 12% tax (a 10% federal tax and 2% state lodging tax). Prices can vary considerably throughout the year, so it pays to consult a travel agent or shop around.

Isla Cancún (Zona Hotelera)

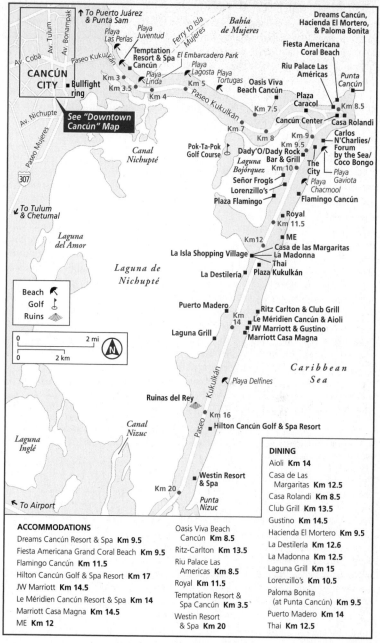

To Puerto Juárez & Punta Sam

Av. Cobá
Av. Tulum
Av. Bonampak

Playa Las Perlas

Playa Juventud

Paseo Kukulkán

Ferry to Isla Mujeres

Bahía de Mujeres

Dreams Cancún, Hacienda El Mortero, & Paloma Bonita

Temptation Resort & Spa Cancún

El Embarcadero Park

Fiesta Americana Coral Beach

CANCÚN CITY

Bullfight ring

Km 3

Km 3.5

Km 4

Playa Linda

Playa Lagosta

Playa Tortugas

Playa

Km 5

Riu Palace Las Américas

Punta Cancún

Oasis Viva Beach Cancún

Plaza Caracol

Km 8.5

Av. Nichupté

Paseo Kukulkán

See "Downtown Cancún" Map

Km 7.5

Cancún Center

Casa Rolandi

Km 7

Km 8

Km 9

Carlos N'Charlies/ Forum by the Sea/ Coco Bongo

Paseo Mujeres

Canal Nichupté

Pok-Ta-Pok Golf Course

Dady'O/Dady Rock Bar & Grill

Km 9.5

The City

307

Laguna Bojórquez

Km 10

Playa Chacmool

Playa Gaviota

Señor Frog's

To Tulum & Chetumal

Lorenzillo's

Plaza Flamingo

Flamingo Cancún

Royal

Km 11.5

Laguna del Amor

Km12

ME

Casa de las Margaritas

La Madonna

La Isla Shopping Village

Thai

Laguna de Nichupté

La Destilería

Plaza Kukulkán

Beach
Golf
Ruins

Puerto Madero

Ritz Carlton & Club Grill

Le Méridien Cancún & Aioli

0   2 mi

0   2 km

Km 14

JW Marriott & Gustino

Laguna Grill

Marriott Casa Magna

N

Caribbean Sea

Playa Delfines

Ruinas del Rey

Canal Nizuc

Paseo Kukulkán

Km 16

Hilton Cancún Golf & Spa Resort

Laguna Inglé

To Airport

Km 20

Westin Resort & Spa

Punta Nizuc

ride from the beach; prices are lower here off season (May to early Dec). For condo, home, and villa rentals, check with **Cancún Hideaways** (© 817/522-4466; fax 817/557-3483; www.cancun-hideaways.com), a company specializing in luxury properties, downtown apartments, and condos—many at prices much lower than comparable hotel stays. Owner Maggie Rodriguez, a former resident of Cancún, has made this niche market her specialty.

The hotel listings in this chapter begin on Cancún Island and finish in Cancún City (the real downtown), where bargain lodgings are available. Unless otherwise indicated, parking is free at Cancún's hotels.

CANCUN ISLAND
VERY EXPENSIVE

Fiesta Americana Grand Coral Beach ★★ *Kids*   This spectacular resort sits on one of the best locations in Cancún, with 300m (984 ft.) of prime beachfront and proximity to the main shopping and entertainment centers. The all-suites hotel includes junior suites with sunken sitting areas, whitewashed furniture, marble bathrooms, and soothing California colors, although some could use an upgrade. Guests staying in Grand Club suites have access to a private rooftop lounge, exclusive check-in, continental breakfast, hors d'oeuvres, and beverages. Service throughout this five-diamond property is gracious and attentive, and the expansive lobby is embellished with elegant dark-green granite and fresh flowers. The hotel's idyllic Punta Cancún location has the advantage of facing the beach to the north where the surf is calm and perfect for swimming, although you may feel tempted not to leave the magnificent pool area. Families will appreciate the *Fiesta Kids Activities*, which include nonstop games, contests, and shows for the little ones. There are daylong sports and social activities planned for adults, as well. The resort's international clientele includes many European, Japanese, Mexican, and American visitors.

Bulevar Kukulkán Km 9.5, 77500 Cancún, Q. Roo. © 800/343-7821 in the U.S., or 998/881-3200. Fax 998/881-3288. www.fiestamericana.com. 602 units. High season $514 (£257) and up double, $671 (£336) and up club-floor double; low season $339 (£170) and up double, $459 (£230) and up club-floor double. Parking $10 (£5). AE, MC, V. **Amenities:** 5 restaurants; 4 bars; outdoor pool w/swim-up bars; 3 indoor tennis courts; boutique spa; fitness center; sauna; watersports equipment/rentals; Kids' Club; multilingual concierge staff; travel agency; car-rental desk; business center; salon; room service; massage; babysitting; laundry service; concierge floor. *In room:* A/C, TV, CD player, Wi-Fi, minibar, hair dryer, coffeemaker, iron, safe.

Hilton Cancún Golf & Spa Resort ★★ *Kids*   Full of energy, this is a grand resort in every sense of the word. The Hilton Cancún sits on 100 hectares (247 acres) of prime beachside property, which means every room has a sea view (some have both sea and lagoon views). And there's an 18-hole par-72 golf course across the street. Like the sprawling resort, guest rooms are spacious and decorated in minimalist style. The Beach Club villas are the largest and best-located rooms, and come with continental breakfast and an evening cocktail hour. This Hilton is a kid-friendly hotel, with one of the island's best children's activity programs, children's pool, and babysitting. The spectacular multi-section swimming pool stretches out to the gorgeous beach. The Hilton is especially appealing to golfers because it's one of only two in Cancún with an on-site course (the other is the Meliá). Greens fees for guests during high season are $99 (£50) for 9 holes, $149 (£75) for 18 holes (low season discounts offered), and comes with use of a cart. The Wellness Spa includes oceanfront massage cabañas, yoga, and aromatherapy. This Hilton has a friendly vibe and boasts excellent service.

Downtown Cancún

Area of detail

Cancún City

Isla Cancún (Zona Hotelera)

(i) Information
✉ Post office
SM Supermanzana (Superblock)

To Punta Sam & Puerto Juárez

Avenida Chichén Itzá
Avenida García de la Torre
Avenida Bonampak

SM 1

SM 23

Chaca

Avenida Uxmal
Laurel
Pino

Bus Station

SM 2
SM 2-A

Avenida Tulum
Avenida J.C. Nader

Allen
Rosas
Rosas
SM 24
Valpich
Soliman
Yoquen
Conoco
Nicchehabi

Av. Yaxchilán
Margaritas
Margaritas

Azucenas
Azucenas

Avenida Uxmal
Toronjil
Lima
Rubia
Barracuda

SM 3

Jazmines
Jazmines
SM 22
Tulipanes
Tulipanes

Rubía
Mero
Mero

Barracuda
Cazon
Cazon

SM 28
✉
Mercado 28

Av. Sunyaxchen
Saramullo
Tauch

Gladiolas
Gladiolas
Marañon
Parque Palapas

Huachinango
Huachinango

Pargo
Pargo

(i)

Grosella
Grosella
Nancen
Av. Yax Av.

Chiabal
Coco
Chiabal
Piña

Orquideas
Orquideas

Claveles
Claveles
Crisantemas

SM 5

Cherna
Cherna

SM 25

Alcatraces
Alcatraces

Mojarra

Robalo
Juriel
Robalo
Sierra

Guaya
Guaya
Ciruela
Anona
Avenida Tankah
Guanabana
Calmito
Calmito
Guanabana

Avenida Cobá

Avenida Tulum

SM 35
Av. Yaxchilán
SM 52

Avenida Xcaret
Reno
Venado
Jaleb

Avenida Cobá

Briga
Nube
Sierra

Avenida Xcaret

Jaleb

Boulevard Kukulcán

To Hotel Zone (Cancún Island)

Tejon
Tejon

Lluvia
Lluvia

SM 4
Nube

Venado
Alce
Alce
Antilope
Avenida Antilope

SM 20

Pecari
Pecari
Liebre
Liebre
Jabali

Agua
Agua
Viento
Viento

Cielo
Cielo
Tierra
Tierra

SM 4-A

Avenida Bonampak

Avenida Labná
Gacela
Gacela

Mar

Fuego

SM 18

Bullfight ring

Fuego
Mar

Avenida Sayil

Av. Copán

SM 15
SM 15-A

To Plaza Las Americas

SM 7

PUERTO CANCÚN
Avenida Bonampak

0   200 yds
0   200 m

ACCOMMODATIONS ■
Hotel Hacienda **10**
Radisson Hacienda Cancun **2**
Rey del Caribe Hotel **3**
Xbalamque **7**

DINING ◆
La Habichuela **6**
Labná **5**
100% Natural **9**
Périco's **8**
Pizza Rolandi **1**
Roots **4**

Bulevar Kukulkán Km 17, Retorno Lacandones, 77500 Cancún, Q. Roo. © **800/228-3000** in the U.S., or 998/881-8000. Fax 998/881-8080. www.hiltoncancun.com. 426 units. High season $249 (£125) and up double, $309 (£155) and up villa room, $409 (£205) and up suite; low season $159 (£80) and up double, $199 (£100) and up villa room, $279 (£140) and up suite. AE, DC, MC, V. **Amenities:** 4 restaurants; 2 bars; 7 interconnected outdoor pools w/swim-up bar; golf course across the street; golf clinic; 2 lighted tennis courts; Wellness Spa and fully equipped gym; 2 whirlpools; watersports center; Kids' Club; concierge; tour desk; car-rental desk; salon; room service; babysitting; laundry service. *In room:* A/C, TV, Wi-Fi, minibar, coffeemaker, hair dryer, iron, safe, bathrobes.

JW Marriott 🐦🐦🐦   One of Cancún's most upscale and appealing properties, the JW Marriott offers elegance without pretense. From the expansive marble and flower-filled lobby to the luxurious oceanview guest rooms, the hotel combines classic and Caribbean styling with warm Mexican service. Guest rooms feature beautiful marble bathrooms with separate tub and shower, private balconies, flatscreen TVs, bathrobes and slippers, and twice-daily maid service. The inviting free-form infinity pool extends to the white-sand beach, and families feel as comfortable here as romance-seeking couples. A spectacular 3,252-sq.-m (35,000-sq.-ft.) spa includes an indoor pool and Jacuzzi, high-tech fitness center, and full range of massages, body scrubs and polishes, facials, and healing water treatments. **Gustino** is an outstanding Italian restaurant seated off the lobby (see "Where to Dine" later in this chapter), and after-noon tea with a musical trio is offered in the lobby lounge. Guests here also enjoy access to the adjacent Marriott Casa Magna.

Bulevar Kukulkán Km 14.5, 77500 Cancún, Q. Roo. © **800/223-6388** in the U.S., or 998/848-9600. Fax 998/848-9601. www.jwmarriottcancun.com. 448 units. High season $449 (£225) and up double; low season $300 (£150) and up double. AE, DC, MC, V. Small pets allowed with prior reservation. **Amenities:** 3 restaurants; deli; lobby bar and pool bar; expansive outdoor pool; indoor pool; full-service spa; 3 whirlpools; sauna; steam room; access to Kids' Club at Marriott Casa Magna; concierge; travel agency; car rental; business center; shopping arcade; gift shop; salon; room service; medical services; laundry service; club floor w/special amenities and complimentary cocktails. *In room:* A/C, flatscreen TV, Wi-Fi, minibar, hair dryer, iron, safe.

Le Méridien Cancún Resort & Spa 🐦🐦   Le Méridien is among Cancún's most inviting luxury options, with a refined yet welcoming sense of personal service. From the intimate lobby and reception area to the best concierge service in Cancún, guests feel immediately pampered. The relatively small establishment is more of an elegant boutique hotel than an immense resort—a welcome relief. The decor throughout the rooms and common areas is classy and comforting, not overdone. Rooms are gener-ous in size with small balconies overlooking the pool; due to the hotel's design, rooms do not have ocean views. Each has a large marble bathroom with a separate tub and glassed-in shower. The hotel attracts many Europeans as well as younger, sophisticated travelers, and it is ideal for a second honeymoon.

A highlight of—or even a reason for—staying here is the **Spa del Mar,** one of Mex-ico's most complete European spa facilities, with more than 4,570 sq. m (49,190 sq. ft.) of services dedicated to your body and soul. A complete fitness center with exten-sive cardio and weight machines sits on the upper level. The spa consists of a health snack bar, a full-service salon, and 14 treatment rooms, as well as men's and women's steam rooms, saunas, whirlpools, cold plunge pool, inhalation rooms, tranquillity rooms, lockers, and changing areas. **Aioli** is a splendid fine-dining restaurant (see "Where to Dine," later in this chapter).

Retorno del Rey Km 14, Zona Hotelera, 77500 Cancún, Q. Roo. © **800/543-4300** in the U.S., or 998/881-2200. Fax 998/881-2201. www.meridiencancun.com.mx. 213 units. High season $593 (£297) double, $680 (£340) suite; low season $430 (£215) double, $519 (£260) suite. Ask about special spa packages. AE, DC, MC, V. Small dogs accepted with prior reservation. **Amenities:** 2 restaurants; lobby bar; 3 cascading outdoor pools; 2 lighted championship tennis courts; whirlpool; watersports equipment/rentals; supervised children's program w/clubhouse, play equipment, wading pool; concierge; tour desk; car rental; business center; small shopping arcade; room service; massage *palapa* on the beach; babysitting; laundry service. *In room:* A/C, TV, CD player, Wi-Fi, minibar, hair dryer, iron, safe.

Ritz-Carlton Cancún *(Kids)* The exclusive Ritz-Carlton fronts a 366m (1,200-ft.) white-sand beach, and all guest rooms overlook the ocean and pools. Rooms and public areas have the low-key elegance that's a hallmark of the Ritz chain—think plush carpets, chandeliers, fresh flowers, and rooms with marble baths, fluffy featherbeds, and 400-count bed linens. Several new features will enhance your stay, including a culinary center that schedules daily Mexican and Maya cooking classes, as well as wine and tequila tastings. A group of specially designed "Itzy Bitzy Ritz Kids" guest rooms offer baby-friendly amenities and conveniences. In addition to the daytime Kids Camp, the Ritz offers a "Kids' Night Out" program that allows parents to steal away for the evening. The beachfront Kayantá Spa bases many of its treatments on traditional Maya rituals and therapies. The resort's oceanfront restaurant, **Casitas,** is the only beachside dining spot in Cancún, where you can dine on steakhouse fare in 1 of 16 candlelit cabañas. The hotel's primary restaurant, **Club Grill,** is reviewed in the "Where to Dine" section, below. The resort itself as well as Club Grill and Fantino, another Ritz-Carlton restaurant, have received AAA five diamonds.

Retorno del Rey 36, off Bulevar Kukulkán Km 13.5, 77500 Cancún, Q. Roo. ☎ **800/241-3333** in the U.S. and Canada, or 998/881-0808. Fax 998/881-0815. www.ritzcarlton.com. 365 units. May 1–Dec 19 $309–$409 (£154–£205) double, $509–$4,000 (£255–£2,000) club floor and suites; Dec 21–Jan 6 $869–$1,099 (£435–£550) double, $1,679–$5,500 (£840–£2,750) club floor and suites; Jan 7–Apr 30 $579–$679 (£290–£340) double, $799–$4,000 (£400–£2,000) club floor and suites. Ask about golf, spa, and weekend packages. AE, MC, V. **Amenities:** 6 restaurants; lounge w/ceviche bar; 2 outdoor pools (heated in winter); 3 lighted tennis courts; fully equipped fitness center; Kayantá Spa; culinary center; Kids Camp program; concierge; travel agency; business center; shopping arcade; salon; room service; babysitting; laundry service; dry cleaning; club floors. *In room:* A/C, TV, CD player, Wi-Fi, minibar, hair dryer, iron, safe.

Riu Palace Las Américas The all-inclusive Riu Palace is part of a family of Riu resorts in Cancún known for their grand, opulent style. This one is the smallest of the three, and the most over-the-top, steeped in pearl-white Greco style. The location is prime—near the central shopping, dining, and nightlife centers, and just a 5-minute walk to the Convention Center. All rooms are spacious junior suites with ocean or lagoon views, a separate seating area with sofa or sofa bed, and a balcony or terrace. Eight also feature a Jacuzzi. Two beautiful central pools overlook the ocean and a wide stretch of beach; one is heated during winter months. The hotel offers guests virtually 24 hours of all-inclusive snacks, meals, and beverages. Activities include water sports, daytime entertainment for adults and kids, live music and shows at night, and access to other Riu hotels in Cancún. The hotel's European opulence stands in contrast to the mostly informal North American guests.

Bulevar Kukulkán Km 8.5, Lote 4, 77500 Cancún, Q. Roo. ☎ **888/666-8816** in the U.S., or 998/891-4300. www.riu.com. 372 units. High season $412 (£206) and up double; low season $322 (£161) and up double. Rates are all-inclusive, and 2-night stay may be required. AE, MC, V. **Amenities:** 5 restaurants; 5 bars including disco; 2 outdoor pools; access to golf and tennis; fitness center; spa (extra charges apply); solarium; room service; sports program; nonmotorized watersports including windsurfing, canoeing, snorkeling, and introductory scuba lessons. *In room:* A/C, TV, hair dryer, iron, safe.

Royal Opened in early 2007, this adults-only luxury hotel sits at the pinnacle of Cancún's all-inclusive establishments, offering a level of services and amenities unmatched almost anywhere. From the stunning infinity pools and gorgeous beach to the gourmet restaurants and sophisticated spa, the owners have spared no expense

making this Cancún's Bellagio. The elegant marble lobby looks out one side to the Caribbean and the other to the lagoon. All of the innovative suites feature flatscreen TVs with CD/DVD players, marble bathrooms with rain showers, two-person Jacuzzis, and oceanview balconies with hammocks. Swim-up master suites have private plunge pools facing the resort's pool and beach; guests in the top-category suites have access to BMW Mini Coopers. The Maya-inspired oceanview spa includes a massage room, Jacuzzi, sauna, traditional *temazcal* steam bath, massage waterfall, and state-of-the-art fitness center. Actually, the range of services is almost hard to believe, except that you will be paying top dollar for it. The all-inclusive package includes gourmet meals, premium drinks, and evening entertainment.

Bulevar Kukulkán Km 11.5, 77500 Cancún, Q. Roo. ⓒ 800/760-0944 in the U.S., or 998/881-7340. www.realresorts.com.mx. 285 units. $444–$804 (£222–£402) double suite. AE, DC, MC, V. No children younger than 16. **Amenities:** 6 restaurants; 8 bars; expansive outdoor pool; tennis court; well-equipped fitness center; full-service-spa; sauna; steam room; concierge; travel agency; car rental; business center; salon; room service; laundry service; club floor w/special amenities and complimentary cocktails. *In room:* A/C, flatscreen TV, Wi-Fi, minibar, hair dryer, iron, safe.

EXPENSIVE

Dreams Cancún Resort & Spa ⚐ *Kids*   Formerly the Camino Real Cancún, the all-inclusive Dreams Resort has one of the island's most idyllic locations—29 hectares (71 acres) at the tip of Punta Cancún. The setting is casual, and the hotel welcomes children. The architecture of Dreams is contemporary and sleek, with bright colors and strategic angles. Rooms in the newer 17-story club section afford ocean views and extra services and amenities. Lower-priced rooms have lagoon views. The all-inclusive concept here includes gourmet meals, 24-hour room service, and premium brand drinks, as well as the use of all resort amenities, nonmotorized watersports, theme-night entertainment, and tips. Use of the spa costs extra. Unfortunately, service at the resort is inconsistent, perhaps owing to the all-inclusive concept.

Bulevar Kukulkán, 77500 Punta Cancún (Apdo. Postal 14), Cancún, Q. Roo. ⓒ 866/237-3267 in the U.S., or 998/848-7000. Fax 998/848-7001. www.dreamscancun.com. 379 units. High season $500 (£250) double, $560 (£280) club double; low season $370 (£185) double, $430 (£215) club double. AE, DC, MC, V. **Amenities:** 4 restaurants; nightclub; 2 outdoor pools; private saltwater lagoon w/dolphins and tropical fish; lighted tennis court; fitness center w/steam bath; watersports; kayaks; paddleboats; Catamarans; beach volleyball; biking; archery; yoga; dance lessons; Kids' Club; travel agency; car rental; business center; salon; room service; massage; babysitting (w/advance notice). *In room:* A/C, TV w/DVD player, minibar, hair dryer, iron, safe.

Marriott Casa Magna ⚐⚐ *Kids*   This sprawling Marriott resort is one of the most enticing family destinations in Cancún. Entering through a half-circle of Roman columns, you pass through a domed foyer to a wide, lavishly marbled lobby filled with plants and shallow pools. It looks out to the sparkling pool and Jacuzzi at the edge of the beach. Guest rooms are decorated with Mexican-Caribbean furnishings and tiled floors; most have oceanview balconies. The hotel caters to family travelers with specially priced packages (up to two children stay free with parent) and the Kids' Club Amigos supervised children's program. Among the many places to dine here, the *teppanyaki*-style (cook-at-your-table) Mikado Japanese restaurant is the best.

Bulevar Kukulkán Km 14.5, 77500 Cancún, Q. Roo ⓒ 800/228-9290 in the U.S., or 998/881-2000. Fax 998/881-2085. www.marriott.com. 452 units. $249–$309 (£125–£155) double; $454 (£227) and up suite. Ask about packages. AE, MC, V. **Amenities:** 4 restaurants; lobby bar w/live music; outdoor pool and whirlpool; 2 lighted tennis courts; spa; health club w/saunas, aerobics, and juice bar; concierge; business center; travel agency; car rental; spa; salon w/massage and facials; room service; babysitting; laundry service. *In room:* A/C, TV, minibar, coffeemaker, hair dryer, iron, safe.

ME (☆) The Spanish ME hotel by Meliá brings to Cancún a new level of minimalist chic with an atmosphere befitting a trendy nightclub more so than a beach resort. Bathed in hues of beige and mauve, with polished marble, onyx lamps, and modern artwork, the hotel creates its own fashion statement—and the hip clientele reflects it. The modern lobby feels a bit like an urban cocktail lounge, with designer bars, sensual artwork, and chill-out music filling the space. Guest rooms have distinctive contemporary furnishings, plasma TVs, CD players, and marble bathrooms with rain showers and Aveda bath products; half look to the Caribbean Sea and the other half to the lagoon. The super-stylish Yhi Spa overlooks the ocean and offers body glows and exfoliations, aromatherapy massages, body masks, and wraps. This is a place to indulge yourself until you're entirely rejuvenated.

Bulevar Kukulkán Km 12, 77500 Cancún, Q. Roo. (✆) **866/436-3542** in the U.S., or 998/881-2500. Fax 998/881-2501. www.mecancun.travel. 448 units. $239 (£120) and up double. AE, MC, V. **Amenities:** 3 restaurants; Internet cafe; 2 bars; 3 outdoor pools; beach club; fitness center; full-service luxury spa; whirlpool; salon; concierge; boutique; art gallery; concierge floor. *In room:* A/C, plasma TV, Wi-Fi, minibar, hair dryer, safe.

The Westin Resort & Spa Cancún

The strikingly austere architecture of The Westin Resort, impressive with its elegant use of stone and marble, is the stamp of leading Latin American architect Ricardo Legorreta. The hotel consists of two sections, the main building and the more exclusive six-story Royal Beach Club. Guest rooms offer contemporary white furnishings and, while spacious, can feel a bit cold. Those on the sixth floor have balconies, and first-floor rooms include terraces. Rooms in the tower boast ocean or lagoon views, furniture with Olinalá lacquer accents, Berber area rugs, oak tables and chairs, and terraces with lounge chairs. It's important to note that this hotel is a 15- to 20-minute ride from the liveliest section of the Hotel Zone, making it a preferred choice for those who want a little more seclusion than Cancún typically offers. However, it's easy to join the action—buses stop in front, and taxis are readily available.

Bulevar Kukulkán Km 20, 77500 Cancún, Q. Roo. (✆) **800/228-3000** in the U.S., 01-800/215-7000 in Mexico, or 998/848-7400. Fax 998/885-0666. www.starwoodhotels.com/westin. 379 units. High season $249 (£125) and up double; low season $159 (£80) and up double. AE, DC, MC, V. **Amenities:** 3 restaurants; 3 bars; 8 outdoor pools; 2 lighted tennis courts; gym w/Stairmaster, bicycle, weights, and aerobics; sauna; *temazcal* (sweat lodge); kids' club; pet service; concierge; travel agency; car rental; pharmacy/gift shop; salon; room service; massage; babysitting; laundry service. *In room:* A/C, TV, Wi-Fi, minibar, coffeemaker, hair dryer, iron, safe.

MODERATE

Flamingo Cancún (*Kids*) The all-inclusive Flamingo seems to have been inspired by the dramatic, slope-sided architecture of the Dreams Cancún, but the Flamingo is considerably smaller and less expensive (guests can opt out of the all-inclusive package, which includes three meals and domestic drinks). With two pools and a casual vibe, it's also a friendly, accommodating choice for families. The brightly colored blue and yellow guest rooms—all with balconies—border a courtyard facing the interior swimming pool and *palapa* pool-bar. The Flamingo lies in the heart of the island hotel district, opposite the Flamingo Shopping Center and close to other hotels, shopping centers, and restaurants.

Bulevar Kukulkán Km 11.5, 77500 Cancún, Q. Roo. (✆) **998/848-8870.** Fax 998/883-1029. www.flamingocancun.com. 260 units. High season $199 (£100) double, low season $126 (£113) double; all-inclusive plan high season $400 (£200) double, low season $210 (£105) double. AE, MC, V. **Amenities:** 2 restaurants; 2 bars; 2 pools; fitness center; kids' club; travel agency; car rental; room service; safe. *In room:* A/C, TV, hair dryer, minibar.

Oasis Viva Beach Cancún From the street, this all-inclusive hotel may not be much to look at, but on the ocean side, you'll find a small but pretty patio garden and Cancún's best beach for safe swimming. The location is ideal, close to all the shops and restaurants near Punta Cancún and the Cancún Center. Rooms overlook the lagoon or the ocean, and all were remodeled post–Hurricane Wilma. They are large, with simple decor, marble floors, and either two double beds or a king-size bed. Several studios have kitchenettes. There is wheelchair access within the hotel's public areas.

Bulevar Kukulkán Km 8.5, 77500 Cancún, Q. Roo. © **998/883-0800**. Fax 998/883-2087. www.oasishotels.com. 216 units. High season $232 (£116) and up double; low season $152 (£76) and up double. Rates are all-inclusive. Discounted rate for children. AE, MC, V. **Amenities:** 4 restaurants; 5 bars; 2 outdoor pools (1 for adults, 1 for children); marina. *In room:* A/C, TV.

Temptation Resort & Spa Cancún ⋆ This adults-only (21 and over) getaway is a spirited, sexy all-inclusive resort favored by people looking for significant social interaction. By day, pool time is all about flirting, seducing, and getting a little wacky with adult games (the main pools are top-optional). Come night, theme dinners, shows, and other live entertainment keep the party going. Note that tops are also optional on the beaches of Blue Bay, which has calm waters for swimming. The comfortable, modern rooms are housed in two sections with garden views. Surrounded by acres of tropical gardens, this moderate hotel is ideally located at the northern end of the Hotel Zone, close to the major shopping plazas, restaurants, and nightlife.

Bulevar Kukulkán Km 3.5, 77500 Cancún, Q. Roo. © **877/485-8367** in the U.S., or 998/848-7900. Fax 998/848-7994. www.temptationresort.com. 384 units. High season $179 (£119) per person per night double occupancy; low season $139 (£76) per person per night double occupancy. Rates include food, beverages, and activities. AE, MC, V. Guests must be at least 21 years old. **Amenities:** 6 restaurants; 5 bars; 3 outdoor pools; 7 whirlpools; spa w/services for fee; exercise room w/daily classes; nonmotorized watersports equipment; snorkeling and scuba lessons; marina; game room w/pool and Ping-Pong tables; limited room service; laundry. *In room:* A/C, TV, hair dryer.

CANCUN CITY
MODERATE

Radisson Hacienda Cancún ⋆ *(value)* This is the top hotel in downtown Cancún, and one of the best values in the area. The Radisson offers all the expected comforts of a chain, yet in an atmosphere of Mexican hospitality. Resembling a hacienda, the business-friendly hotel has rooms surrounding a large rotunda-style lobby with a cool onyx bar, as well as lush gardens and an inviting pool area. All have brightly colored fabric accents; views of the garden, the pool, or the street; and a small sitting area and balcony. The hotel lies within walking distance of downtown Cancún dining and shopping.

Av. Nader 1, SM2, Centro, 77500 Cancún, Q. Roo. © **800/333-3333** in the U.S., or 998/881-6500. Fax 998/884-7954. www.radissoncancun.com. 248 units. $100 (£50) and up double; $120 (£60) and up junior suite. AE, MC, V. **Amenities:** 2 restaurants; lively lobby bar; outdoor pool w/adjoining bar and separate wading area for children; lighted tennis courts; small gym; sauna; business center; travel agency; car rental; salon; limited room service (until 1am); free Wi-Fi in lobby. *In room:* A/C, TV, coffeemaker, hair dryer, iron, safe.

Rey del Caribe Hotel ⋆⋆ *(finds)* This ecological hotel is a unique oasis where every detail works toward establishing harmony with the environment. You might easily forget you're in the midst of downtown Cancún in the tropical garden setting, with blooming orchids and other flowering plants. The lovely grounds include statues of Maya deities, hammocks, and a tiled swimming pool. There's a regularly changing schedule of yoga, Tai Chi, and meditation sessions, as well as special classes on astrology, tarot, and other subjects. The on-site spa offers facial and body treatments. Rooms are large and sunny, with a kitchenette and your choice of one king-size or two full-size beds; some have a terrace. The extent of ecological sensitivity is impressive—ranging from the use of collected rainwater to waste composting. Recycling is encouraged, and solar power is used wherever possible.

Av. Uxmal SM 2A (corner of Nader), 77500 Cancún, Q. Roo. © **998/884-2028.** Fax 988/884-9857. www.reycaribe.com. 31 units. High season $92 (£46) double; low season $65 (£33) double. Rates include breakfast. MC, V. **Amenities:** Outdoor pool; spa; massages; classes. *In room:* A/C, TV, kitchenette.

INEXPENSIVE

Hotel Hacienda *Value*   This simple little hotel is a great value. The facade has been remodeled to look like a hacienda. At press time, it was being expanded to include a restaurant and larger lobby with an Internet kiosk. Guest rooms are very basic; all have dark wood furnishings, whitewashed walls, small tiled bathrooms, and two double beds—but no views. There's a nice small pool and cafe under a shaded *palapa* in the back. You can easily walk to any point downtown from here.

Sunyaxchen 39–40, 77500 Cancún, Q. Roo. © **998/884-3672.** Fax 998/884-1208. www.berny.com.mx. 36 units. High season $60 (£30) double; low season $55 (£28) double. Street parking. From Av. Yaxchilán, turn west on Sunyaxchen; it's on the right next to the Hotel Caribe International, opposite 100% Natural. **Amenities:** Outdoor pool. *In room:* A/C, TV, fan.

Xbalamqué   Creatively designed to resemble a Maya temple, this downtown hotel features a full-service spa, lovely pool and waterfall, and an authentic Mexican cantina. Live music plays evenings in the bookstore/cafe adjacent to the lobby. Guest rooms and 10 junior suites have rustic furnishings with regional touches, colorful tile-work, and small bathrooms with showers. Ask for a room overlooking the ivy-filled courtyard. A tour desk is available to help you plan your vacation activities, and the spa offers some of the best rates of any hotel in Cancún. A small *tamaleria* serving delicious regional tamales has opened adjacent to the lobby.

Av. Yaxchilán 31, Sm. 22, Mza. 18, 77500 Cancún, Q. Roo. © **998/884-9690.** Fax 998/884-9690. www.xbalamque.com. 99 units. High season $95 (£48) double; low season $75 (£38) double. AE, MC, V. **Amenities:** Restaurant; cafe; Internet café; cantina; lobby bar; outdoor pool; spa; travel agency. *In room:* A/C, TV.

3 Where to Dine

More than 300 restaurants spanning North American, European, and Asian cuisines have opened across Cancún. They have come to supplement the many U.S.-based franchise chains that have long dominated the Cancún restaurant scene. These include Hard Rock Cafe, Rainforest Cafe, Tony Roma's, T.G.I. Friday's, Ruth's Chris Steak House, and the gamut of fast-food burger places. The establishments listed here are typically locally owned, one-of-a-kind restaurants or exceptional selections at area hotels. Many schedule live music. Unless otherwise indicated, parking is free.

One unique way to combine dinner with sightseeing is aboard the **Lobster Dinner Cruise** (© **998/849-4748;** www.thelobsterdinner.com). Cruising around the tranquil, turquoise waters of the lagoon, passengers feast on lobster dinners accompanied by wine. Cost is $74 (£37) per person. There are two daily departures from the Aquatours Marina (Bulevar Kukulkán 6.5). A sunset cruise leaves at 5pm during the winter and 5:30pm during the summer; a moonlight cruise leaves at 8pm winter, 8:30pm summer. Another—albeit livelier—lobster dinner option is the **Captain Hook Lobster Dinner Cruise** (© **998/849-4451**), which is similar, but with the added attraction of a pirate show, making this the choice for families. It costs $86 (£43) per person, departs at 7pm from El Embarcadero, and returns at 10:30pm.

CANCUN ISLAND
VERY EXPENSIVE

Aioli ✶✶ FRENCH   The quality and originality of the cuisine and excellence of service make this a top choice for fine-dining in Cancún. The Provençal—but definitely not provincial—Aioli offers exquisite French and Mediterranean gourmet specialties in a warm and cozy country French setting. Though it serves perhaps the best breakfast buffet in Cancún (for $24/£12), most diners from outside the hotel come here in the evening, when low lighting and superb service promise a romantic experience. Delectable starters include foie gras and risotto with wild mushrooms; among the best main courses are pan-seared jumbo shrimp in lobster sauce, roasted lamb with a tarragon crust, and breast of duck. Desserts are decadent, especially the signature "Fifth Element," rich with chocolate.

In Le Méridien Cancún Resort & Spa, Retorno del Rey Km 14. ✆ 998/881-2200. Reservations recommended. No sandals or tennis shoes; men must wear long pants. Main courses $26–$37 (£13–£19). AE, MC, V. Daily 6:30am–11pm.

Club Grill ✶✶✶ INTERNATIONAL   The five-diamond Club Grill is the place for that special night out. Cancún's most acclaimed dining room is also among its most delicious. Even rival restaurateurs give it an envious thumbs up. The gracious service starts as you enter the anteroom, with its elegant seating and superb selection of cocktails and wines. It continues in the candlelit dining room with shimmering silver and crystal. Sophisticated plates of peppered scallops, truffles, and potatoes in tequila sauce; grilled lamb; or mixed grill arrive at a leisurely pace. The restaurant is exclusively nonsmoking, and service is impeccable. A band plays romantic music for dancing from 7:30pm on.

In the Ritz-Carlton Cancún, Retorno del Rey, 36 Bulevar Kukulkán Km 13.5. ✆ 998/881-0808. Reservations required. No sandals or tennis shoes; men must wear long pants and collared shirts. Main courses $39–$59 (£20–£30). AE, DC, MC, V. Tues–Sun 7–11pm.

Lorenzillo's ✶✶ (Kids) SEAFOOD   This longtime Cancún favorite hasn't changed much over the years. Lobster remains the star, and part of the appeal is selecting your dinner out of the giant lobster tank set in the lagoon (Lorenzillo's sits right on the lagoon under a giant *palapa* roof). A dock leads down to the main dining area, and when that's packed (which is often), a wharf-side bar handles the overflow. To start, I recommend *El Botin,* which consists of two soft shell crabs breaded and fried to perfection. Good bets for the entree include lobster (which comes prepared in any of 20 different ways), shrimp stuffed with cheese and wrapped in bacon, the *Pescador* (Caribbean grouper prepared to taste), and seafood-stuffed calamari. Desserts include the tempting "Martinique": warm apples, raisins, and walnuts caramelized with rum and wrapped in a pastry with vanilla ice cream. Lorenzillo's is as popular with families as it is with couples looking for lagoon-side romance.

Bulevar Kukulkán Km 10.5. ✆ 998/883-1254. www.lorenzillos.com.mx. Reservations recommended. Main courses $19–$44 (£20–£22). AE, MC, V. Daily 1pm–midnight.

EXPENSIVE

Casa de las Margaritas ✶ MEXICAN   La Casa de las Margaritas is a celebration of the flavors and *¡fiesta!* spirit of Mexico. With a decor as vibrant as a *piñata,* waiters dressed in regional costumes, and a soundtrack of background music that ranges from mariachi to *marimba,* the experience here is a crash course in the buoyant spirit of this colorful country. On the menu, best bets include the Margarita shrimp, flambéed in brandy, white wine, and chipotle chili sauce; chicken breast served with homemade mole; or traditional chicken enchiladas topped with tomato-and-sun-dried-pepper sauce with lettuce, avocado slices, and white cheese from Oaxaca. Inside La Isla shopping center, Casa de las Margaritas also serves a spectacular Sunday brunch buffet. Live music is offered nightly from 8 to 9pm.

Paseo Kukulkán Km 12.5, La Isla Shopping Mall, Loc. E-17. © 998/883-3222 or -3054. www.lacasadelasmargaritas. com. Reservations recommended. Main courses $13–$45 (£6.50–£23), Sun brunch $17 (£8.50). AE, MC, V. Mon–Sat 1–9:30pm; Sun brunch noon–5pm.

Casa Rolandi ★★★ SWISS/ITALIAN   Like its sister location on Isla Mujeres, Casa Rolandi blends sophisticated Swiss-Italian cuisine with fresh Caribbean fish and Mexican produce. Famous personalities, from international actors to American presidents, have dined here. The casually elegant restaurant offers white linen tables with roses and candles at night, yet welcomes informal dress. Among the sophisticated selections are homemade ravioli stuffed with wild mushrooms over a creamy Alba truffle sauce; tagliolini with sautéed shrimp and ginger doused with sparkling wine; fresh fish (usually snapper or sea bass) baked in salt and accompanied by fresh vegetables and seasoned mashed potatoes; and grilled 18-ounce rib-eye served sizzling. Finish with the sublime tiramisu served with chocolate and rum cream. Service is personalized and friendly.

Bulevar Kukulkán Km 8.5, in Plaza Caracol. © 998/883-2557. www.rolandi.com. Reservations recommended. Main courses $17–$38 (£8.50–£19). AE, MC, V. Sun–Thurs 1–11:30pm; Fri–Sat 1pm–2am.

Gustino ★★ ITALIAN   JW Marriott's signature restaurant Gustino offers romantic Italian dining unsurpassed in Cancún. The refined dining room includes a gorgeous centerpiece candle display, floor-to-ceiling windows looking out to a lazy man-made lagoon and the beach beyond, and live saxophone. Among the rich selection of *antipasti,* the black shell mussels, minestrone, and *Festival dei Frutti de Mare* for two are the best. For a main course, consider homemade pasta, the veal scaloppine, or filet of beef tenderloin in a red-wine sauce served with fresh vegetables. There's also a wide selection of fresh fish and seafood. Gustino boasts an open kitchen and wine cellar with an excellent variety of international grapes. Service is outstanding.

In the JW Marriott, Bulevar Kukulkán Km 14.5. © 998/848-9600. Reservations required. Main courses $14–$27 (£7–£14). AE, DC, MC, V. Daily 6–11pm.

Hacienda El Mortero ★ *Kids* MEXICAN   There's no escaping the fact that this traditional Mexican restaurant, which replicates an early–17th century hacienda in the northern state of Durango, looks out of place next to a row of discotheques in history-free Cancún. But if you're spending your entire trip in town, this may be your first opportunity to see what a Spanish colonial hacienda is supposed to look like. Popular with families and large groups, this festive restaurant serves authentic Mexican cuisine representing several regions. One popular option is the mixed *parillada* for two, which combines meat, seafood, and chicken with enough calories to feed a small village. I recommend the flavorful fish tacos, shrimp *pastor* with grilled pineapple, or filet mignon prepared with four chilies. A number of fish and meat dishes are prepared tableside, and the tortillas are homemade. Vegetarian tacos with a cilantro sauce are also available. The restaurant offers 100 types of tequila and mariachi music nightly.

At entrance to Punta Cancún, Bulevar Kukulkán Km 9.5. © 998/848-9800. www.elmorterocancun.com. Reservations recommended. Main courses $18–$50 (£9–£25). AE, MC, V. Daily 6–11pm.

Laguna Grill ⓒⓒ FUSION   Laguna Grill offers diners a contemporary culinary experience in a picturesque setting overlooking the lagoon. A tropical garden welcomes you at the entrance, while a small creek traverses the restaurant set with tables made from the trunks of tropical trees. As magical as the decor is, the real star here is the kitchen, with its selection of Pacific Rim cuisine fused with regional flavors. Starters include martini *gyoza* (steamed dumplings), filled with shrimp and vegetables, or seafood ceviche in sesame oil and curry. Fish and seafood dominate the menu, in preparations that combine Asian and Mexican flavors such as ginger, cilantro, garlic, and hoisin sauce. Grilled shrimp are marinated in rum, mint, and lime; surf-and-turf fusion dishes may include grilled lobster, beef, and shrimp skewers. For beef-lovers, the rib-eye served with mashed potatoes and black olives is excellent. For dessert, I recommend the crème brûlée served with a touch of Bailey's. If you're an early diner, request a table on the outside deck for a spectacular sunset view. An impressive selection of wines is available.

Bulevar Kukulkán Km 16.5. ⓒ **998/885-0267**. www.lagunagrill.com.mx. Reservations recommended. Main courses $16–$47 (£8–£24). AE, MC, V. Daily 4pm–midnight.

Paloma Bonita ⓒ ⓚⓘⓓⓢ REGIONAL   In a stylish setting overlooking the water, Paloma Bonita captures the essence of Mexico through its music and food. Since Paloma Bonita lies in a hotel (Dreams Cancún), prices are higher than at traditional Mexican restaurants in Ciudad Cancún, but this is a good choice for the Hotel Zone. There are three sections: La Cantina Jalisco, with an open kitchen and tequila bar; the Salón Michoacán, which features that state's cuisine; and the Patio Oaxaca. Mariachis serenade you while you dine in any of these areas. The menu encompasses the best of Mexico's other cuisines, with a few international dishes. A traditional starter is the *nopalitos* (cactus) salad with a vinaigrette dressing. For a main course, I recommend the stuffed chili La Doña—a mildly hot poblano pepper filled with lobster and *huitlacoche* (a type of mushroom that grows on corn) in a cream sauce.

In the Hotel Dreams, Punta Cancún (enter from the street). ⓒ **998/848-7082**. Reservations recommended. Main courses $11–$52 (£5.50–£26). AE, DC, MC, V. Daily 6–11:30pm.

Puerto Madero ⓒⓒ ARGENTINE/STEAKS/SEAFOOD   As a tribute to the famed Puerto Madero of Buenos Aires, this trendy restaurant has quickly earned a reputation for its authentic Argentine cuisine and buzzing atmosphere. Overlooking the Nichupté Lagoon, the decor re-creates a 20th-century dock warehouse, with elegant touches of modern architecture. Puerto Madero offers an extensive selection of prime quality beef cuts, pastas, grilled fish (my favorite here is swordfish), and shellfish, meticulously prepared with Buenos Aires gusto. In addition to the classic *carpaccio,* the tuna tartar and halibut steak are favorites, but the real standouts here are the tender grilled steaks (particularly the rib-eye), served in ample portions. Enjoy a cocktail or glass of wine from the extensive selection, while viewing the sunset from the lagoon-side deck. Service is excellent.

Marina Barracuda, Bulevar Kukulkán Km 14. ⓒ **998/885-2829** or -2830. www.puertomaderocancun.com. Reservations recommended. Main courses $14–$52 (£7–£26). AE, MC, V. Daily 1pm–1am.

MODERATE

La Destilería MEXICAN   To experience Mexico's favorite export on an enticing terrace overlooking the lagoon, this is your place (keep an eye out for Tequila, the lagoon crocodile who often comes to visit). La Destilería is more than a tequila-inspired restaurant; it's a minimuseum honoring the "spirit" of Mexico. It serves over 150 brands of tequila, including some treasures that never find their way across the country's northern border. No surprise, the margaritas are among the island's best. When you decide to order food with your tequila, you'll find an authentic Mexican menu, with everything from quesadillas with squash blossom flowers to fresh tuna with jalapeños or *arrachera* beef fajitas. The breaded fish tacos served with guacamole are amazing.

Bulevar Kukulcán Km 12.65, across from Kukulcán Plaza. © 998/885-1086 or -1087. www.cmr.ws. Main courses $12–$28 (£6–£14). AE, MC, V. Daily 1pm–midnight.

Thai ★★★ *(Moments* THAI   This sensual restaurant and lounge feels like it should be in Southeast Asia rather than the edge of a Mexican shopping plaza. The stunning outdoor setting includes thick foliage and plenty of bamboo, with individual *palapas* (each with its own table and sofa) constructed like tiny islands over the expansive lagoon. Unobtrusive service, soft red and blue lighting, and Asian chill and lounge music contribute to the ambience. Classic Thai specialties such as spicy chicken soup, Thai salad, chicken satay, and chicken and shrimp curries are served alongside exotic cocktails to the beautiful crowd. A DJ works the stylish lounge on weekends. Thai opens at sunset.

La Isla Shopping Center, Loc. B-4. © 998/144-0364. Reservations recommended during high season. Main courses $13–$31 (£6.50–£16). AE, MC, V. Daily 6pm–1am.

CANCUN CITY
EXPENSIVE

La Habichuela ★★★ *(Moments* SEAFOOD   In a musically accented garden setting with flowering white-lit hibiscus trees, this downtown Caribbean seafood restaurant is ideal for a romantic evening. For an all-out culinary adventure, try *habichuela* (string bean) soup; shrimp in any number of sauces, including Jamaican tamarind, tequila, or ginger and mushroom; and Maya coffee with Xtabentun (a strong, sweet, anise-based liqueur). Grilled seafood and steaks are excellent, and the menu includes luscious ceviches, Caribbean lobsters, an inventive seafood "parade," and shish kabob flambé. For something divine, try *cocobichuela,* lobster and shrimp in curry served in a coconut shell and topped with fruit. Top it off with one of the boozy butterscotch crepes. Service here is fabulous.

Margaritas 25. © 998/884-3158. www.lahabichuela.com. Reservations recommended in high season. Main courses $15–$46 (£7.50–£23). AE, MC, V. Daily noon–midnight.

Périco's ★★ *(Finds* MEXICAN/SEAFOOD/STEAKS   Périco's is a joyous parade of performance, play, and brightly colored tourist hilarity. The unique restaurant features entertaining waiters dressed in a variety of festive costumes, murals that seem to dance off the walls, a bar area with saddles for barstools, and leather tables and chairs. Its extensive menu offers well-prepared steak, seafood, and traditional Mexican dishes for reasonable rates (except for lobster and surf and turf). This is a place not only to eat and drink, but also to let loose and join in the fun, so don't be surprised if diners drop their forks and don sombreros to shimmy and shake in a conga line around the dining room. The entertainment kicks off at 7:30pm.

Yaxchilán 61. © 998/884-3152. www.pericos.com.mx. Reservations recommended. Main courses $14–$41 (£7–£21). AE, MC, V. Daily noon–1am.

MODERATE

Labná ★★ YUCATECAN   To steep yourself in Yucatecan cuisine and music, head directly to this showcase of Maya moods and regional foods. Specialties include a sublime lime soup, *poc chuc* (marinated, barbecue-style pork), chicken or pork *pibil* (sweet and spicy barbecue sauce served over shredded meat wrapped in banana leaves), and appetizers such as *papadzules* (tortillas stuffed with boiled eggs in a pumpkin seed sauce). The Labná Special is a sampler of four typically Yucatecan main courses, including *poc chuc,* while another specialty of the house is baked suckling pig, served with guacamole. The refreshing Yucatecan beverage, *agua de chaya*—a blend of sweetened water and the leaf of the *chaya* plant, abundant in the area, to which sweet Xtabentun liquor (a type of anise) can be added for an extra kick—is also served here. The vaulted ceiling dining room is decorated with black-and-white photographs of the region dating from the 1900s. A local trio plays weekend afternoons.

Margaritas 29, next to City Hall and the Habichuela restaurant. ☎ **998/892-3056.** Main courses $7–$20 (£3.50–£10). AE, MC, V. Daily noon–10pm.

INEXPENSIVE

100% Natural ★ VEGETARIAN/MEXICAN   If you want a healthy reprieve from an overindulgent night—or just like your meals as fresh and natural as possible—this is your oasis. No matter what your dining preference, you owe it to yourself to try a Mexican tradition, the fresh-fruit *licuado.* These smoothie-like drinks combine fresh fruit, ice, and water or milk. More creative combinations may mix in yogurt, granola, or other goodies. 100% Natural serves more than just meal-quality drinks—there's a bountiful selection of simple Mexican fare and terrific sandwiches served on wholegrain bread, with options for vegetarians. Breakfast is delightful, and there's an attached bakery featuring all-natural baked goods such as chocolate croissants and apple cinnamon muffins. There are several 100% Natural locations in town, including branches at Playa Chac-Mool, in front of Señor Frog's, and downtown.

Av. Sunyaxchen 63. ☎ **998/884-0102.** www.100natural.com.mx. Reservations not accepted. Main courses $5–$16 (£2.50–£8). AE, MC, V. Daily 7am–11pm.

Pizza Rolandi ★ (Kids) ITALIAN   At this shaded patio restaurant known for dependably tasty Italian delights, you can choose from an enticing selection of spaghetti, calzones, and Italian-style chicken and beef, as well as from almost two dozen delicious, if greasy, wood-oven pizzas (individual size). Why not try the deliciously spicy "Fiesta Mexicana" pizza with tomato, cheese, Mexican pepperoni, and jalapeños? A Cancún institution, Pizza Rolandi has a duplicate branch on Isla Mujeres (see chapter 15). It's as popular with locals as with tourists.

Cobá 12. ☎ **998/884-4047.** Fax 998/884-4047. www.rolandi.com. Pasta $9–$12 (£4.50–£6); pizza and main courses $7–$14 (£3.50–£7). AE, MC, V. Daily 12:30pm–12:30am.

Roots INTERNATIONAL   This popular hangout for local residents is also a fun spot for visitors to Cancún. Located in the heart of downtown, this dimly-lit restaurant and jazz club offers a smooth cosmopolitan ambience. The Caribbean-themed menu offers a range of casual dining choices, including salads, pastas, and fresh fish and steaks grilled on the *parilla.* It's accompanied by live music, including flamenco, jazz, and fusion. Decking the walls are original works of art by local painters. The music starts at 10:30pm, and Roots seldom fills up before 9:30pm.

Tulipanes 26, SM 22. ☎ **998/884-2437.** Main courses $6–$17 (£3–£8.50). MC, V. Tues–Sat 6pm–1am.

4 Beaches, Watersports & Boat Tours

THE BEACHES Big hotels dominate the best stretches of beach. All of Mexico's beaches are public property, so you can use the beach of any hotel by walking through the lobby or directly onto the sand. Be especially careful on beaches fronting the open Caribbean, where the undertow can be quite strong. By contrast, the waters of **Bahía de Mujeres** (Mujeres Bay), at the north end of the island, are usually calm and ideal for swimming. Get to know Cancún's water-safety pennant system, and make sure to check the flag at any beach or hotel before entering the water. Here's how it goes:

White	Excellent
Green	Normal conditions (safe)
Yellow	Changeable, uncertain (use caution)
Black or **red**	Unsafe—use the swimming pool instead!

In the Caribbean, storms can arrive and conditions can change from safe to unsafe in a matter of minutes, so be alert: If you see dark clouds heading your way, make for the shore and wait until the storm passes.

Playa Tortuga (Turtle Beach), Playa Langosta (Lobster Beach), Playa Linda (Pretty Beach), and Playa Las Perlas (Beach of the Pearls) are some of the public beaches. At most beaches, you can rent a sailboard and take lessons, ride a parasail, or partake in a variety of watersports. There's a small but beautiful portion of public beach on **Playa Caracol,** by the Xcaret Terminal. It faces the calm waters of Bahía de Mujeres and, for that reason, is preferable to those facing the Caribbean.

WATERSPORTS Many beachside hotels offer watersports concessions that rent rubber rafts, kayaks, and snorkeling equipment. On the calm Nichupté lagoon are outlets for renting **sailboats, jet skis, sailboards,** and **water skis.** Prices vary and are often negotiable, so check around.

DEEP-SEA FISHING You can arrange a shared or private deep-sea fishing charter at one of the numerous piers or travel agencies, and prices fluctuate widely depending on the length of the excursion (there's usually a four hour minimum), number of people, and quality of the boat. Marinas will sometimes assist in putting together a group. Charters include a captain, a first mate, bait, gear, and beverages. Rates are lower if you depart from Isla Mujeres or from Cozumel—and frankly, the fishing is better closer to those departure points.

SCUBA & SNORKELING Known for its shallow reefs, dazzling color, and diversity of life, Cancún is one of the best places in the world for beginning scuba diving. Punta Nizuc is the northern tip of the **Gran Arrecife Maya (Great Mesoamerican Reef),** the largest reef in the Western Hemisphere and one of the largest in the world. In addition to the sea life along this reef system, several sunken boats add a variety of dive options. Inland, a series of caverns and cenotes (wellsprings) are fascinating venues for the more experienced diver. Drift diving is the norm here, with popular dives going to the reefs at **El Garrafón** and the **Cave of the Sleeping Sharks**—although be aware that the famed "sleeping sharks" have departed, driven off by too many people watching them snooze.

A variety of hotels offer resort courses that teach the basics of diving—enough to make shallow dives and slowly ease your way into this underwater world of unimaginable beauty. One preferred dive operator is **Scuba Cancún,** Bulevar Kukulkán Km 5 (© **998/849-4736;** www.scubacancun.com.mx), on the lagoon side. Full open water PADI certification takes 3 days and costs $410 (£205). A half-day resort course for beginners with theory, pool practice, and a one tank dive at a reef costs $88 (£44). Scuba Cancún is open daily from 7am to 8pm. For certified divers, Scuba Cancún also offers PADI specialty courses and diving trips in good weather to 18 nearby reefs, as well as to Cenotes Caverns (9m/30 ft.) and Cozumel. The average dive is around 11m (36 ft.), while advanced divers descend farther (up to 18m/60 ft). Two-tank dives to reefs around Cancún cost $68 (£34); those to farther destinations cost $140 (£70). Discounts apply if you bring your own gear. Dives usually start around 9:30am and return by 1:30pm. Snorkeling trips cost $29 (£15) and leave daily at 1:30pm and 4pm for shallow reefs about a 20-minute boat ride away.

The largest dive operator is **Aquaworld,** across from the Meliá Cancún at Bulevar Kukulkán Km 15.2 (© **998/848-8327;** www.aquaworld.com.mx). It offers resort courses and diving at a reef barrier, as well as snorkeling, parasailing, jet-ski "jungle tours," fishing, day trips to Isla Mujeres and Cozumel, and other watersports activities. Single tank dives cost $60 (£30); two-tank dives $65 (£33). Aquaworld has the **Sub See Explorer,** a boat with picture windows that hang beneath the surface. The boat doesn't submerge—it's an updated version of a glass-bottom boat—but it does provide nondivers with a worthwhile peek at life beneath the sea.

Besides snorkeling at **El Garrafón Natural Park** (see "Boating Excursions," below), travel agencies offer an all-day excursion to the natural wildlife habitat of **Isla Contoy,** which usually includes time for snorkeling. The island, 90 minutes past Isla Mujeres, is a major nesting area for birds and a treat for nature lovers. You can call any travel agent or see any hotel tour desk to get a selection of boat tours to Isla Contoy. Prices range from $45 to $75 (£23–£38), depending on the length of the trip, and generally include drinks and snorkeling equipment.

The Great Mesoamerican Reef also offers exceptional snorkeling opportunities. In Puerto Morelos, 37km (23 miles) south of Cancún, the reef hugs the coastline for 15km (9⅓ miles). The reef is so close to the shore (about 460m/1,509 ft.) that it forms a natural barrier for the village and keeps the waters calm on the inside of the reef. The water here is shallow, from 1.5 to 9m (5–30 ft.), resulting in ideal conditions for snorkeling. Stringent environmental regulations implemented by the local community have kept the reef here unspoiled. Only a select few companies are allowed to offer snorkel trips, and they must adhere to guidelines that will ensure the reef's preservation. **Cancún Mermaid** (© **998/843-6517;** www.cancunmermaid.com) is considered the best—it's a family-run ecotour company that has operated in the area since the 1970s. It's known for highly personalized service. The tour typically takes snorkelers to two sections of the reef, spending about an hour in each area. When conditions allow, the boat drops off snorkelers and then follows them along with the current—an activity known as "drift snorkeling," which enables snorkelers to see as much of the reef as possible. The trip costs $50 (£25) for adults, $35 (£18) for children, and includes boat, snorkeling gear, life jackets, a light lunch, bottled water, sodas, and beer, plus round-trip transportation to and from Puerto Morelos from Cancún hotels. Departures are Monday through Saturday at 9am. For snorkelers who just can't get enough, a combo tour for $30 (£15) more adds a bicycle tour to additional snorkeling destinations. Reservations are required at least 1 day in advance; MasterCard and Visa are accepted.

JET-SKI/FAST BOAT TOURS   Several companies offer the thrilling **Jungle Cruise,** in which you drive your own small speed boat (called a *lancha*) or WaveRunner rapidly through Cancún's lagoon and mangrove estuaries out into the Caribbean Sea and a shallow reef. The excursion lasts about 2½ hours and costs $55 to $60 (£28–£30), including snorkeling equipment. Many people prefer the companies offering two-person boats rather than WaveRunners, since they can sit side by side rather than one behind the other.

Jungle cruise operators and names offering excursions change often. To find out what's available, check with a local travel agent or hotel tour desk. The popular **Aqua-world,** Bulevar Kukulkán Km 15.2 (© **998/848-8327**), calls its trip the Jungle Tour and charges $60 (£30) for the 2½-hour excursion, which includes 45 minutes of snorkeling time. It even gives you a free snorkel, but has the less desirable one-behind-the-other seating configuration. Departures are daily at 9am, noon, and 2:30pm. If you'd prefer a side-by-side boat, try **Blue Ray,** Bulevar Kukulkán Km 13.5, next to Mambo Café (© **998/885-1108**), which charges $55 (£28) with departures every hour between 9am and 3pm. Expect to get wet, and wear plenty of sunscreen.

BOATING EXCURSIONS

ISLA MUJERES   The island of **Isla Mujeres,** just 13km (8 miles) offshore, is one of the most pleasant day trips from Cancún. At one end is **El Garrafón Natural Park,** which is good for snorkeling. At the other end is a captivating village with small shops, restaurants, and hotels, and **Playa Norte,** the island's best beach. If you're looking for relaxation and can spare the time, it's worth several days. For complete information about the island, see chapter 6.

There are four ways to get there: **public ferry** from Puerto Juárez, which takes between 15 and 20 minutes; **shuttle boat** from Playa Linda or Playa Tortuga—an hour-long ride, with irregular service; **water taxi** (more expensive, but faster), next to the Xcaret Terminal; and daylong **pleasure-boat trips,** most of which leave from the Playa Linda pier.

The inexpensive but fast Puerto Juárez **public ferries** ⏱ lie just a few kilometers from downtown Cancún. From Cancún City, take the Ruta 8 bus on Avenida Tulum to Puerto Juárez. The air-conditioned *Caribbean Express* and *Ultramar* boats (15–20 min.) cost $4 (£2) per person. Departures are every half-hour from 6 to 8:30am and then every 15 minutes until 8:30pm. The slower *Caribbean Savage* (45–60 min.) costs about $3.50 (£1.75). It departs every 2 hours, or less frequently depending on demand. Upon arrival, the ferry docks in downtown Isla Mujeres near all the shops, restaurants, hotels, and Norte beach. You'll need a taxi to get to El Garrafón park at the other end of the island. You can stay as long as you like on the island and return by ferry, but be sure to confirm the time of the last returning ferry.

Pleasure-boat cruises to Isla Mujeres are a favorite pastime. Modern motor yachts, catamarans, trimarans, and even old-time sloops—more than 25 boats a day—take swimmers, sun lovers, snorkelers, and shoppers out on the translucent waters. Some tours include a snorkeling stop at El Garrafón, lunch on the beach, and a short time for shopping in downtown Isla Mujeres. Most leave at 9:30 or 10am, last about 5 or 6 hours, and include continental breakfast, lunch, and rental of snorkel gear. Others, particularly sunset and night cruises, go to beaches away from town for pseudo-pirate shows and include a lobster dinner or Mexican buffet (p. 103). If you want to actually see Isla Mujeres, go on a morning cruise, or travel on your own using the public ferry from Puerto Juárez. Prices for the day cruises run around $56 (£28) per person. Reservations aren't necessary.

An all-inclusive entrance fee of $65 (£33), $49 (£25) for children to **Garrafón Natural Reef Park** *((((℃ 998/849-4748;** www.garrafon.com) includes transportation from Cancún, meals, open bar with domestic drinks, access to the reef, as well as use of snorkel gear, kayaks, inner tubes, life vests, the pool, hammocks, and public facilities and showers (but not towels, so bring your own). There are also nature trails and several on-site restaurants.

Other excursions go to the **reefs** in glass-bottom boats, so you can have a near-scuba-diving experience and see many colorful fish. However, the reefs are some distance from the shore and are impossible to reach on windy days with choppy seas. They've also suffered from over-visitation, and their condition is far from pristine. Nautibus's **Atlantis Submarine** (℃ **987/872-5671;** www.atlantisadventures.com) takes you close to the aquatic action. Departures vary, depending on weather conditions. Prices are $79 (£40) for adults, $45 (£23) for children ages 4 to 12. The submarine descends to a depth of 30m (98 ft.). Atlantis Submarine departs daily at 9am, 11am, and noon; the tour lasts about 40 minutes. The submarine departs from Cozumel, so you either need to take a ferry to get there or purchase a package that includes round-trip transportation from your hotel in Cancún ($103/£52 adults, $76/£38 children 4–12). Reservations are recommended.

5 Outdoor Activities & Attractions

OUTDOOR ACTIVITIES

DOLPHIN SWIMS   On Isla Mujeres, you have the opportunity to swim with dolphins at **Dolphin Discovery** *((((℃ 998/877-0207** or 849-4757; www.dolphindiscovery.com). Groups of eight people swim with two dolphins and one trainer. Swimmers view an educational video and spend time in the water with the trainer and the dolphins before enjoying 15 minutes of free swimming time with them. Reservations are recommended (you can book online), and you must arrive an hour before your assigned swimming time, at 10:30am, noon, 2pm, or 3:30pm. The cost is $139 (£70) per person for the Dolphin Royal Swim. There are less expensive programs that allow you to learn about, touch, and hold the dolphins (but not swim with them) starting at $79 (£40). Ferry transfers from Playa Langosta in Cancún are available.

La Isla Shopping Center, Bulevar Kukulkán Km 12.5, has an impressive **Interactive Aquarium** (℃ **998/883-0411,** -0436, or -0413; www.aquariumcancun.com.mx), with dolphin swims and shows and the chance to feed a shark while immersed in the water in an acrylic cage. Guides inside the main tank use underwater microphones to point out the sea life, and even answer your questions. Open exhibition tanks enable visitors to touch a variety of marine life, including sea stars and manta rays. The educational dolphin program costs $65 (£33), while the dolphin swim is $135 (£68) and the shark-feeding experience runs $65 (£33). The entrance fee to the aquarium is $13 (£6.50) for adults, $9 (£4.50) for children under 11, and it's open daily from 9am to 6pm.

GOLF & TENNIS   The 18-hole **Pok-Ta-Pok Club,** or Club de Golf Cancún (℃ **998/883-0871**), is a Robert Trent Jones, Sr., design on the northern leg of the island. Greens fees run $135 (£68) for 18 holes including breakfast or lunch and golf cart (discounted twilight fees), with clubs renting for $40 (£20). A caddy costs $25 (£13). The club is open daily from 6:30am to 5pm and accepts American Express, MasterCard, and Visa.

Tips **An All-Terrain Tour**

Cancún Mermaid (© 998/843-6517; www.cancunmermaid.com) offers all-terrain-vehicle (ATV) jungle tours for $49 (£25) per person if riding double or $66 (£33) if riding single. The ATV tours travel through the jungles of Cancún and emerge on the beaches of the Riviera Maya. The 5-hour tour (including transportation time from your hotel to the destination) includes gear, instruction, the services of a tour guide, lunch, and bottled water; it departs Monday through Saturday at 8am and 1:30pm. Reservations are required.

The **Hilton Cancún Golf & Spa Resort** (© 998-881-8016) has a championship 18-hole, par-72 course around the Ruinas Del Rey. Greens fees during high season for the public are typically $199 (£100) for 18 holes and $149 (£75) for 9 holes; Hilton Cancún guests pay discounted rates of $149 (£75) for 18 holes, or $99 (£50) for 9 holes, which includes a golf cart. Low season and twilight discounts are available. Golf clubs and shoes are available for rent. The club is open daily from 6am to 6pm and accepts American Express, MasterCard, and Visa. The **Gran Meliá Cancún** (© 998/881-1100) has a 9-hole executive course; the fee is $30 (£15). The club is open daily from 7am to 3pm and accepts American Express, MasterCard, and Visa.

The first Jack Nicklaus Signature Golf Course in the Cancún area has opened at the **Moon Palace Spa & Golf Club** (© 998-881-6000; www.palaceresorts.com), along the Riviera Maya. The $260 (£130) greens fee includes cart, snacks, and drinks.

HORSEBACK RIDING   Cancún Mermaid (© 998/843-6517; www.cancunmermaid.com), about 30 minutes south of town at the Rancho Loma Bonita, is a popular option for horseback riding. Five-hour packages include 2 hours of riding through the mangrove swamp to the beach, where you have time to swim and relax. The tour costs $66 (£33) for adults and $60 (£30) for children under 13. The ranch also offers a four-wheel ATV ride on the same route as the horseback tour. It costs $66 (£33) if you want to ride on your own, and $49 (£25) per person if you double up. Prices for both tours include transportation to the ranch, riding, soft drinks, and lunch, plus a guide and insurance. Only cash or traveler's checks are accepted.

ATTRACTIONS

BULLFIGHTS   Cancún has a small bullring, **Plaza de Toros** (© 998/884-8372), near the northern (town) end of Bulevar Kukulkán at Av. Bonampak and Sayil. Bullfights take place every Wednesday at 3:30pm during the winter tourist season. A sport introduced to Mexico by the Spanish viceroys, bullfighting is now as much a part of Mexican culture as tequila. The bullfights usually include four bulls, and the spectacle begins with a folkloric dance exhibition, followed by a performance by the *charros* (Mexico's sombrero-wearing cowboys). You're not likely to see Mexico's best bullfights in Cancún—the real stars are in Mexico City. Keep in mind that if you go to a bullfight, *you're going to see a bullfight,* so stay away if you're an animal lover or you can't bear the sight of blood. Buy tickets, which cost $40 (£20) for adults and are free for children under 6, at the Plaza ticket counter the day of the event or in advance from a travel agent; seating is by general admission. American Express, MasterCard, and Visa are accepted

6 Shopping

Despite the surrounding natural splendor, shopping has become a favorite activity. Cancún is known throughout Mexico for its diverse shops and festive malls catering to international tourists. Visitors from the United States may find apparel more expensive in Cancún, but the selection is much broader than at other Mexican resorts. Numerous duty-free shops offer excellent value on European goods. The largest is **Ultrafemme,** Avenida Tulum, Supermanzana 25 (© **998/884-1402**), specializing in imported cosmetics, perfumes, and fine jewelry and watches. The downtown Cancún location offers slightly lower prices than branches in Plaza Caracol, La Isla, and Kukulcán Plaza. It's open Monday to Saturday from 9:30am to 9pm and Sunday from 2 to 9pm.

Handicrafts are more limited and more expensive in Cancún than in other regions of Mexico because they are not produced here. They are available, though; several **open-air crafts markets** are on Avenida Tulum in Cancún City and near the convention center in the Hotel Zone. One of the biggest is **Coral Negro,** Bulevar Kukulkán Km 9.5, next to Plaza Dady'O, open daily from 7am to 11pm. **Plaza La Fiesta,** next to the Cancún Center (© **998/883-4519**), is a large Mexican outlet store selling handicrafts, jewelry, tequila, leather, and accessories. It's open daily from 7am to midnight.

Cancún's main venues are the **malls**—not quite as grand as their U.S. counterparts, but close. All are air-conditioned, sleek, and sophisticated. Most are on Bulevar Kukulkán between Km 7 and Km 12. They offer everything from fine crystal and silver to designer clothing and decorative objects, along with numerous restaurants and clubs. Stores are generally open daily from 10am to 10pm.

The **Kukulcán Plaza** (© **998/885-2200;** www.kukulcanplaza.com) houses more than 300 shops, restaurants, and entertainment. There's a bank; a bowling alley; several crafts stores; a Play City with gambling machines; a liquor and tobacco store; several bathing-suit specialty stores; music stores; a leather goods shop (including shoes and sandals); and a store specializing in silver from Taxco. U.S. franchise eateries include Häagen-Dazs and Ruth's Chris Steak House. The adjacent Luxury Avenue complex features designer labels such as Cartier, Louis Vuitton, Pineda Covalin, Salvatore Ferragamo, and Ultrafemme. The mall is open daily from 10am to 10pm, until 11pm during high season. Assistance for those with disabilities is available upon request, and wheelchairs, strollers, and lockers are available at the information desk.

The long-standing **Plaza Caracol** (© **998/883-1038;** www.caracolplaza.com) was being renovated at press time and holds, among other things, Cartier jewelry, Señor Frog's clothing, Samsonite luggage, and La Fisheria and Casa Rolandi restaurants. It's just before you reach the convention center as you come from downtown Cancún.

The entertainment-oriented **Forum by the Sea,** Bulevar Kukulkán Km 9 (© **998/883-4425;** www.forumbythesea.com.mx), received a complete face-lift after Hurricane Wilma. Most people come here for the food and fun, choosing from Hard Rock Cafe, Carlos 'n' Charlie's, Rainforest Cafe, and CoCo Bongo, plus an extensive food court. Shops include Diesel, Harley Davidson, Señor Frog's, Sunglass Island, and Zingara Beachwear and Swimwear. The mall is open daily from 10am to midnight (bars remain open later).

One of Mexico's most appealing malls is the **La Isla Shopping Village,** Bulevar Kukulkán Km 12.5 (© **998/883-5025;** www.laislacancun.com.mx), a wonderful open-air complex that borders the lagoon. Walkways lined with quality shops and restaurants cross little canals (boat rides are even offered through the canals), and there's a boardwalk along the lagoon itself, as well as an interactive aquarium and dolphin swim facility (p. 112). Shops include Bulgari, Diesel, DKNY, Guess, Nautica, Nine West, Tommy Hilfiger, Ultrafemme, and Zara, as well a large Mexican handicrafts store called Casa Bonita. Among the dining choices are Johnny Rockets, Chili's, Italianni's, Planet Hollywood, the fun-filled Mexican restaurant La Casa de las Margaritas (p. 104), and the romantic Thai restaurant (p. 107). You will also find a movie theater, video arcade, and several bars, including La Madonna (p. 116).

7 Cancún After Dark

One of Cancún's main draws is its active nightlife. While the partying often begins by day at the beach, the cool crowd heads at happy hour to the many bars located along the Hotel Zone, which often serve two-for-one drinks at sunset. Hotels play in the happy hour scene, with special drink prices to entice visitors and guests from other resorts. Come night, the hottest centers of action are also along Kukulkán, and include **Plaza Dady'O, Forum by the Sea,** and **La Isla Shopping Village.** These places transform into spring break madness for most of March and April.

THE CLUB & MUSIC SCENE

Clubbing in Cancún is a favorite part of the vacation experience and can go on each night until the sun rises over that incredibly blue sea. Several big hotels have nightclubs or schedule live music in their lobby bars. At the clubs, expect to stand in long lines on weekends, pay a cover charge of about $40 (£20) with open bar, or $15 to $25 (£7.50–£13) without open bar and then pay $8 to $10 (£4–£5) for a drink. Some of the higher-priced clubs include live entertainment. The places listed in this section are air-conditioned and accept American Express, MasterCard, and Visa.

A great idea to get you started is the **Bar Hopper Tour** 𝒢𝒢 with tickets available at Señor Frog's, most hotels, or various travel agencies around town. For $65 (£33), it takes you by bus to the Congo Bar, Señor Frog's, and CoCo Bongo, where you bypass any lines and spend about an hour at each establishment. The price includes entry to the bars, one welcome drink at each, and transportation by air-conditioned bus, allowing you to get a great sampling of the best of Cancún's nightlife. The tour runs from 8pm into the wee hours, with the meeting point at the Congo Bar.

Numerous restaurants, such as **Carlos 'n' Charlie's, Hard Rock Cafe, Señor Frog's,** and **T.G.I. Friday's,** double as nighttime party spots, offering wildish fun at a fraction of the price of more costly clubs.

Bling 𝒢𝒢𝒢   This is one of the coolest nightspots in Cancún, featuring a chic outdoor terrace overlooking the lagoon. A fashionable 30-something crowd congregates amid sofas under the stars, a killer sound system, and flowing cocktails. A sushi and sashimi bar and some Mediterranean dishes are also offered. This upscale lounge is considerably more sophisticated than Cancún's typical frat-style bars, and it's open daily from 6pm to 4am. Bulevar Kukulkán, Km 13.5. ℭ **998/840-6014.**

The City 𝒢𝒢   One of Cancún's hottest and largest nightclubs, The City features progressive electronic music spun by some of the world's top DJs (the DJ station looks like an airport control tower). This is where Paris Hilton parties when she comes to town. With visiting DJs from New York, L.A., and Mexico City, the music is sizzling.

You actually need never leave, as The City is a day-and-night club. The City Beach Club opens at 10am and features a pool with a wave machine for surfing and boogie-boarding, a tower-high waterslide, food and bar service, plus beach cabañas. The Terrace Bar, overlooking the action on Bulevar Kukulkán, serves food and drinks all day long. For a relaxing evening vibe, the Lounge features comfy couches, chill music, and an extensive menu of martinis, snacks, and desserts. Open at 10:30pm, the 2,500-sq.-m (26,910-sq.-ft.) nightclub features nine bars, stunning light shows, and several VIP areas. Bulevar Kukulkán, Km 9.5. ✆ 998/848-8380. www.thecitycancun.com. Cover $25 (£13); $45 (£23) with open bar.

CoCo Bongo ✿✿✿ Continuing its reputation as the hottest party venue in town, CoCo Bongo's appeal is that it combines an enormous dance club with extravagant theme shows. It has no formal dance floor, so you can dance anywhere—and that includes on the tables, on the bar, or even on the stage with the occasional live band. This place can—and regularly does—pack in as many as 3,000 people. You have to experience it to believe it. Despite its capacity, lines are long on weekends and in high season. The music alternates between Caribbean, salsa, house, hip-hop, techno, and classics from the 1970s, '80s, and '90s. Open from 10:30pm to 3:30am, CoCo Bongo draws a hip young crowd. Forum by the Sea, Bulevar Kukulkán Km 9.5. ✆ 998/883-5061. www.cocobongo.com.mx. Cover $45 (£23) with open bar.

Dady'O This is a popular rave among the young and brave with frequent long lines. MTV, Playboy, Fashion TV, and E Entertainment have all hosted events here. It opens nightly at 10pm and has a giant dance floor and awesome light system. Bulevar Kukulkán Km 9.5. ✆ 998/883-3333. www.dadyo.com.mx. Cover $20 (£10); $45 (£23) with open bar.

Dady Rock Bar and Club The offspring of Dady'O, it opens at 8pm and goes as long as any other nightspot, offering a combination of live rock bands and DJs spinning grooves, along with an open bar, full meals, a buffet, and dancing. Bulevar Kukulkán Km 9.5. ✆ 998/883-1626. Cover $16 (£8); $35 (£18) with open bar.

La Madonna This architecturally dazzling martini bar and restaurant emerges unexpectedly from La Isla shopping center like an Italian Renaissance showroom along the canal. With more than 180 creative martini selections accompanied by relaxing lounge music, La Madonna also offers authentic Italian and Swiss cuisine. Enjoy your red mandarin, lychee, or vanilla peach martini elbow to elbow with Cancún's beautiful people on the expansive outdoor patio or upstairs terrace. Inside, the dining room resembles one of the mystical Buddha Bars, with an enormous replica of the Mona Lisa looking over the dazzled clientele. It's open daily from 1pm to 1am. La Isla Shopping Village, Bulevar Kukulkán Km 12.5. ✆ 998/883-2222.

The Lobby Lounge ✿ The most refined of Cancún's nightly gathering spots, with a terrace overlooking the lagoon, a special martini collection, and a list of more than 80 premium tequilas for tasting or sipping. There's also a sushi and seafood bar, as well as a humidor collection of Cuban cigars. It's open daily from 5pm to 1am, with live music Thursday through Sunday. Ritz-Carlton Cancún, Retorno del Rey 36, off Bulevar Kukulkán Km 13.5. ✆ 998/881-0808.

Mambo Cafe ✿✿ If you're looking for a hot Latin night out, Mambo Café is your place. The tropical rhythm club features a live Cuban band nightly, starting at 11:30pm, when sexy salsa dancers hit the floor with fervor. Every night has a drinking theme, whether it's two-for-one Tuesday, $3 (£1.50) Wednesday, or ladies-drink-free Thursday. Mambo Café is open nightly from 10pm to 4am, and salsa dance classes are Thursday at 9:30pm. Bulevar Kukulkán, Km 13.5. © **998/840-6498**. www.mambo-cafe.com.mx. Cover $10 (£5); $30 (£15) with open bar.

THE PERFORMING ARTS

Several hotels host **Mexican fiesta nights,** including a buffet dinner and a folkloric dance show; admission, including dinner, ranges from $35 to $50 (£18–£25), unless you're at an all-inclusive resort that includes this as part of the package. Check out the **Fiesta Americana Coral Beach**'s (© **998/881-3200**) a la carte dining show four times a week.

6

Isla Mujeres & Cozumel

by David Baird

Mexico's two main Caribbean islands are idyllic escapes from the hustle and bustle of Cancún and the Riviera Maya. Neither Isla Mujeres nor Cozumel is particularly large, and they have that island feel—with small roads that don't go very far, lots of mopeds, few if any trucks, and a sense of remoteness from the rest of the world. Yet they're just a short ferry ride from the mainland. Both offer a variety of lodging options, ample outdoor activities, and a laid-back atmosphere that contrasts with much of the mainland experience.

Isla Mujeres is a fish-shaped island 13km (8 miles) northeast of Cancún, which makes it a quick boat ride away. One of the most popular excursions from Cancún is a day trip to Isla Mujeres on a party boat. But if you want to do more than wander the streets, shop, or lie on the beach, it's best to stay overnight. Hotels range from rustic to regal.

Passenger ferries travel to Isla Mujeres from Puerto Juárez, and car ferries leave from Punta Sam, both near Cancún. More expensive passenger ferries, with fewer departures, leave from the Playa Linda pier on Cancún Island.

Larger than Isla Mujeres and farther from the mainland (19km/12 miles off the coast from Playa del Carmen), **Cozumel** has its own international airport. Life here revolves around two major activities: scuba diving and cruise ships making a port of call. Cozumel is far and away the most popular destination along this coast for both activities.

Despite the cruise-ship traffic and all the stores spawned by it, life on the island moves at a relaxed pace. There is just one town, San Miguel de Cozumel. North and south of town are resorts. The rest of the shore is deserted and predominantly rocky, with a scattering of small sandy coves that you can have practically all to yourself.

1 Isla Mujeres ★★★

13km (8 miles) N of Cancún

Isla Mujeres (Island of Women) is a casual, laid-back refuge from the heady tempo of Cancún. It lies not far off the coast and is visible from the resort. As Caribbean islands go, Isla is a bargain and a good fit for anyone who prefers simplicity and ease over variety and action. The island's only town is right next to North Beach, the best beach on the island. With beach towel in hand, you can leisurely stroll there from any hotel in town; there's no need for transportation. Don't think that Isla is an escape from commercialism—it isn't, though commercialism is writ small here, which is characteristic of the place. The island is small, the town is small, the hotels (with a couple of exceptions) are small, the restaurants, the bars, the excursion boats—small, small, small. There are several inexpensive hotels, mostly in town, and a smattering of luxury boutique hotels spread out to other parts of the island.

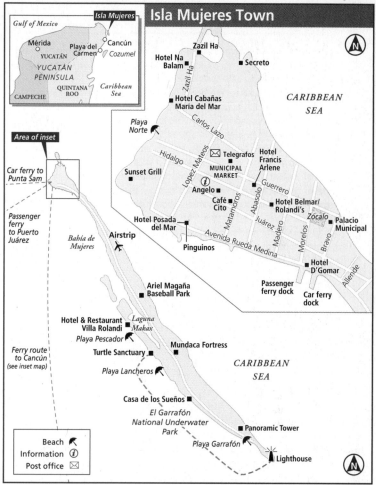

Isla Mujeres Town

Gulf of Mexico
Isla Mujeres
Mérida
Playa del Carmen
Cancún
Cozumel
YUCATÁN
YUCATÁN PENINSULA
CAMPECHE
QUINTANA ROO
Caribbean Sea

Area of inset

Car ferry to Punta Sam

Passenger ferry to Puerto Juárez

Ferry route to Cancún (see inset map)

Beach
Information
Post office

Zazil Ha
Hotel Na Balam
Secreto
Zazil Ha
Hotel Cabañas Maria del Mar
CARIBBEAN SEA
Playa Norte
Carlos Lazo
Hidalgo
Lopez Mateos
Telegrafos
MUNICIPAL MARKET
Hotel Francis Arlene
Sunset Grill
Angelo
Café Cito
Guerrero
Abasolo
Hotel Belmar/ Rolandi's
Zócalo
Palacio Municipal
Hotel Posada del Mar
Matamoros
Juárez
Madero
Morelos
Bravo
Allende
Airstrip
Bahía de Mujeres
Pinguinos
Avenida Rueda Medina
Hotel D'Gomar
Passenger ferry dock
Car ferry dock
Ariel Magaña Baseball Park
Hotel & Restaurant Villa Rolandi
Laguna Makax
Playa Pescador
Mundaca Fortress
Turtle Sanctuary
Playa Lancheros
CARIBBEAN SEA
Casa de los Sueños
El Garrafón National Underwater Park
Panoramic Tower
Playa Garrafón
Lighthouse

The scale of the island heightens the contrast between high season and low season, making the crowds and bustle much more noticeable at peak travel times. At midday, suntanned visitors from the Cancún tour boats hang out in open-air cafes and stroll the pedestrian streets lined with zealous souvenir vendors calling attention to their wares. The scene takes on a carnivalesque hue during the hours when the tour-boat traffic is at its peak. Then, later in the afternoon, things settle down.

Trips to the Isla Contoy bird sanctuary are popular, as are the diving, snorkeling, and fishing jaunts. In 1998, the island's coral coast became part of Mexico's Marine National Park system. The reef suffered substantial hurricane damage in 2005, but it's rebounding. The water clarity illuminates the wonderful array of coral and tropical fish living here. The underwater life you are likely to see includes French angelfish, longspine squirrelfish, trumpet fish, four-eye butterfly fish, green angelfish, stoplight parrotfish, southern stingrays, sharp-nose puffer fish, blue tang, and great barracuda.

Tips **The Best Websites for Isla Mujeres & Cozumel**

- **Isla Mujeres Tourist Information: www.isla-mujeres.net**   The official site of the Isla Mujeres Tourism Board provides complete information on Isla, from getting there to where to stay.
- **My Isla Mujeres: www.myislamujeres.com**   Get a local's view of the island; the active chat room and message boards are especially good.
- **Cozumel.net: www.cozumel.net**   This site is a cut above the typical dining/lodging/activities sites. Click on "About Cozumel" to find schedules for ferries and island-hop flights, and to check the latest news. There's also a comprehensive listing of B&Bs and vacation-home rentals.
- **Cozumel Travel Planner: www.go2cozumel.com**   This is a well-done guide to area businesses and attractions, by an online Mexico specialist.
- **Cozumel Hotel Association: www.islacozumel.com.mx**   Operated by the tourism-promotion arm of the hotel association, this site gives more than just listings of the member hotels. There's info on packages and specials, plus brief descriptions of most of the island's attractions, restaurants, and recreational activities.

The island and several of its hotels attract regular gatherings of yoga practitioners. In the evening, most people find the slow, casual pace one of the island's biggest draws. The cool night breeze is a perfect accompaniment to casual open-air dining and drinking in small street-side restaurants.

ESSENTIALS

GETTING THERE & DEPARTING   Puerto Juárez, just north of Cancún, is the **dock** (© **998/877-0382**) for passenger ferries to Isla Mujeres. *Ultramar* (© **998/ 843-2011;** www.granpuerto.com.mx) has fast boats leaving every half-hour from "Gran Puerto" in Puerto Juárez, making the trip in 15 minutes. There is storage space for luggage and the fare is about $4 (£2) each way. These boats operate daily, starting at 6am and usually ending at 10:30pm (check beforehand for latest schedules). They might leave early if they're full, so arrive ahead of schedule. Pay at the ticket office or, if the ferry is about to leave, aboard.

Note: Upon arrival by taxi or bus in Puerto Juárez, be wary of pirate "guides" who tell you either that the ferry is canceled or that it's several hours until the next ferry. They'll offer the services of a private *lancha* (small boat) for about $40 (£20)—and it's nothing but a scam. Small boats are available and, on a co-op basis, charge $15 to $25 (£18–£13) one-way, based on the number of passengers. They take about 50 minutes and are not recommended on days with rough seas. Check with the ticket office—the only accurate source for information.

Taxi fares are posted by the street where the taxis park, so be sure to check the rate before agreeing to a taxi for the ride back to Cancún. Rates generally run $12 to $15 (£6–£7.50), depending upon your destination. Moped and bicycle rentals are also readily available as you depart the ferry. This small complex also has public bathrooms, luggage storage, a snack bar, and souvenir shops.

Isla Mujeres is so small that a vehicle isn't necessary, but if you're taking one, you'll use the **Punta Sam** port a little beyond Puerto Juárez. The 40-minute car ferry (© 998/877-0065) runs five or six times daily between 8am and 8pm, year-round except in bad weather. Times are generally as follows: Cancún to Isla 8 and 11am and 2:45, 5:30, and 8:15pm; Isla to Cancún 6:30 and 9:30am and 12:45, 4:15, and 7:15pm. Always check with the tourist office in Cancún to verify this schedule. Cars should arrive an hour before the ferry departure to register for a place in line and pay the posted fee, which varies depending on the weight and type of vehicle. A gas pump is at Avenida Rueda Medina and Calle Abasolo, northwest of the ferry docks.

Ferries to Isla Mujeres also depart from **Playa Linda,** known as the Embarcadero pier in Cancún, but they're less frequent and more expensive than those from Puerto Juárez. There are 4 to 6 scheduled departures per day to Isla Mujeres, depending upon the season. Adult fares are $15 (£7.50) round trip; kids ages 3 to 12 pay $7.50 (£3.75); children younger than 3 ride free. A **Water Taxi** (© 998/886-4270 or -4847; asterix@cablered.net.mx) to Isla Mujeres operates from **Playa Caracol,** between the Fiesta Americana Coral Beach Hotel and the Xcaret terminal on the island; prices are about the same as those from Playa Linda.

To get to Puerto Juárez or Punta Sam from **Cancún,** take any Ruta 8 city bus from Avenida Tulum. From the Cancún airport, take the shuttle bus to the pier ($16/£8).

Arriving   Passenger ferries arrive at the docks in the center of town. The main road that passes in front is Avenida Rueda Medina. Most hotels are close by. Tricycle taxis are the least expensive and most fun way to get to your hotel; you and your luggage pile in the open carriage compartment, and the driver pedals through the streets. Regular taxis are always lined up in a parking lot to the right of the pier, with their rates posted. If someone on the ferry offers to arrange a taxi for you, politely decline, unless you'd like some help with your luggage down the short pier—it just means an extra, unnecessary tip for your helper.

VISITOR INFORMATION   The **City Tourist Office** (©/fax **998/877-0767** or -0307) is at Av. Rueda Medina 130, just across the street from the pier. It's open Monday through Friday from 9am to 4pm, closed on Saturdays and Sundays. *Islander* is a free publication with local information, advertisements, and event listings.

ISLAND LAYOUT   Isla Mujeres is about 8km (5 miles) long and 4km (2½ miles) wide, with the town at the northern tip. "Downtown" is a compact 4 blocks by 6 blocks, so it's very easy to get around. The **passenger ferry docks** are at the center of town, within walking distance of most hotels, restaurants, and shops. The street running along the waterfront is **Avenida Rueda Medina,** commonly called the *malecón* **(boardwalk).** The **Mercado Municipal (town market)** is by the post office on **Calle Guerrero,** an inland street at the north edge of town, which, like most streets in the town, is unmarked.

GETTING AROUND   A popular form of transportation on Isla Mujeres is the electric **golf cart,** available for rent at many hotels or rental shops for $15 (£7.50) per hour or $45 (£23) per day. Prices are set the same at all rental locations. **El Sol Golf Cart Rental,** Av. Benito Juárez Mza 3 #20 (corner of Matamoros; © **998/877-0791**) is one good option in the town center. The golf carts don't go more than 30kmph (20 mph), but they're fun. Anyway, you aren't on Isla Mujeres to hurry. Many people enjoy touring the island by *moto* **(motorized bike or scooter).** Fully automatic versions are available for around $35 (£18) per day or $8 (£4) per hour. They come with helmets and seats for two people. There's only one main road with a couple of offshoots, so you won't get lost. Be aware that the rental price does not include insurance, and any injury to yourself or the vehicle will come out of your pocket. **Bicycles** are also available for rent at some hotels for $4 (£2) per hour or $10 (£5) per day, usually including a basket and a lock.

If you prefer to use a taxi, rates are about $2.50 (£1.25) for trips within the downtown area, or $5 (£2.50) for a trip to the southern end of Isla. You can also hire them for about $10 (£5) per hour. The number to call for taxis is ✆ **998/877-0066.**

FAST FACTS: Isla Mujeres

Area Code The telephone area code is **998.**

Consumer Protection You can reach the local branch of **Profeco** consumer protection agency at ✆ **998/887-3960.**

Currency Exchange Isla Mujeres has numerous *casas de cambio,* or currency exchanges, along the main streets. Most of the hotels listed here change money for their guests, although often at less favorable rates than the commercial enterprises. There is only one bank in Isla, **HSBC Bank** (✆ **998/877-0005**), across from the ferry docks. It's open Monday through Friday from 8:30am to 6pm, and Saturdays from 9am to 2pm. It has ATM machines.

Drugstore **Isla Mujeres Farmacía** (✆ **998/877-0178**) has the best selection of prescription and over-the-counter medicines.

Emergencies To report an emergency, dial ✆ **065** anywhere in Mexico.

Hospital The **Hospital de la Armada** is on Avenida Rueda Medina at Ojón P. Blanco (✆ **998/877-0001**). It's less than a kilometer (a half mile) south of the town center. It will only treat you in an emergency. Otherwise, you're referred to the **Centro de Salud** on Avenida Guerrero, a block before the beginning of the *malecón* (✆ **998/877-0117**).

Internet Access Owned by a lifelong resident of Isla, **Cyber Isla Mujeres.com,** Av. Francisco y Madero 17, between Hidalgo and Juárez streets (✆ **998/877-0272**), offers Internet access for $1.50 (75p) per hour, daily 7am to 10pm, and serves complimentary Veracruzano coffee all day.

Post Office The *correo* is at Calle Guerrero 12 (✆ **998/877-0085**), at the corner of López Mateos, near the market. It's open Monday through Friday from 9am to 4pm.

Taxis To call for a taxi, dial ✆ **998/877-0066.**

Telephone Ladatel phones accepting coins and prepaid phone cards are at the plaza and throughout town.

Tourist Seasons Isla Mujeres's tourist season (when hotel rates are higher) is a bit different from that of other places in Mexico. High season runs December through May, a month longer than in Cancún. Some hotels raise their rates in August, and some raise their rates beginning in mid-November. Low season is from June to mid-November.

BEACHES & OUTDOOR ACTIVITIES

THE BEACHES   The most popular beach in town is **Playa Norte** ⚓. The long stretch of beach extends around the northern tip of the island. This is perhaps the world's best municipal beach—a wide swath of fine white sand and calm, translucent, turquoise-blue water. The beach is easily reached on foot from the ferry and from all downtown hotels. Watersports equipment, beach umbrellas, and lounge chairs are available for rent. Areas in front of restaurants usually cost nothing if you use the restaurant as your headquarters for drinks and food, and the best of them have hammocks and swings from which to sip your piña coladas.

Garrafón Natural Reef Park ⚓⚓ (see p. 124) is best known as a snorkeling area, but there is a nice stretch of beach on either side of the park. **Playa Lancheros** is on the Caribbean side of Laguna Makax. Local buses go to Lancheros, and then turn inland and return downtown. The beach at Playa Lancheros is nice, with a variety of casual restaurants.

SWIMMING   Playa Norte is the best swimming beach, with Playa Lancheros second. There are no lifeguards on duty on Isla Mujeres, which does not use the system of water-safety flags employed in Cancún and Cozumel. The bay between Cancún and Isla Mujeres is calm, with warm, transparent waters ideal for swimming, snorkeling, and diving. The east side of the island facing the open Caribbean Sea is typically rougher with much stronger currents.

SNORKELING   One of the most popular places to snorkel is **Garrafón Natural Reef Park** ⚓⚓ (see p. 124). **Manchones Reef,** off the southeastern coast, is also good. It's just offshore and accessible by boat. You can snorkel around *el faro* (the lighthouse) in the **Bahía de Mujeres** at the southern tip of the island. The water is about 2m (6½ ft.) deep. Boatmen will take you for around $25 (£13) per person if you have your own snorkeling equipment or $30 (£15) if you use theirs.

DIVING   Most of the dive shops on the island offer the same trips for the same prices: one-tank dives cost about $50 (£25), two-tank dives about $70 (£35). **Bahía Dive Shop,** Rueda Medina 166, across from the car-ferry dock (☎ **998/877-0340**), is a full-service shop that offers dive equipment for sale or rent. The shop is open daily from 10am to 7pm, and accepts MasterCard and Visa. Another respected dive shop is **Coral Scuba Center,** at Matamoros 13A and Rueda Medina (☎ **998/877-0061** or -0763). It's open daily from 8am to 12:30pm and 4 to 10pm. Both offer 2-hour snorkeling trips for about $20 (£11).

Cuevas de los Tiburones (Caves of the Sleeping Sharks) is Isla's most renowned dive site—but the name is slightly misleading, as shark sightings are rare these days. Two sites where you could traditionally see the sleeping shark are the Cuevas de Tiburones and **La Punta,** but the sharks have mostly been driven off, and a storm collapsed the arch featured in a Jacques Cousteau film showing them, but the caves survive. Other dive sites include a **wreck** 15km (9⅓ miles) offshore; **Banderas** reef, between Isla Mujeres and Cancún, where there's always a strong current; **Tabos** reef on the eastern shore; and **Manchones** reef, 1km (a half mile) off the southeastern tip of the island, where the water is 4.5 to 11m (15–36 ft.) deep. **The Cross of the Bay** is close to Manchones reef. A bronze cross, weighing 1 ton and standing 12m (40 ft.) high, was placed in the water between Manchones and Isla in 1994, as a memorial to those who have lost their lives at sea.

FISHING   To arrange a day of fishing, ask at the **Sociedad Cooperativa Turística** (the boatmen's cooperative), on Avenida Rueda Medina (© **998/877-1363**), next to Mexico Divers and Las Brisas restaurant, or the travel agency mentioned in "A Visit to Isla Contoy," p. 126. Four to six others can share the cost, which includes lunch and drinks. Captain Tony Martínez (© **998/877-0274**) also arranges fishing trips aboard the *Marinonis,* with advanced reservations recommended. Year-round you'll find bonito, mackerel, kingfish, and amberjack. Sailfish and sharks (hammerhead, bull, nurse, lemon, and tiger) are in good supply in April and May. In winter, larger grouper and jewfish are prevalent. Four hours of fishing close to shore costs around $120 (£60); 8 hours farther out goes for $250 (£125). The cooperative is open Monday through Saturday from 8am to 1pm and 5 to 8pm, and Sunday from 7:30 to 10am and 6 to 8pm.

YOGA   Increasingly, Isla is becoming popular among yoga enthusiasts. The trend began at **Hotel Na Balam** ⟨⟨ (p. 127 © **998/877-0279** or -0058; www. nabalam.com), which offers yoga classes under its large poolside *palapa,* complete with yoga mats and props. The hotel also offers yoga instruction vacations featuring respected teachers and a more extensive practice schedule; the current schedule of yoga retreats is posted on their website. Another yoga center that has sprung up and is drawing together a community is **Elements of the Island** (www.elementsofthe island.com). It's located at Juárez 64, between López Mateos and Matamoros. And there's **Casa de los Sueños Resort and Zenter** (© **998/877-0651;** www.casadelos suenosresort.com), which regularly holds yoga classes, as well as chi gong and Pilates.

MORE ATTRACTIONS

DOLPHIN DISCOVERY ⟨⟨   You can swim with dolphins (© **998/849-4748** or 849-4757; fax 998/849-4751; www.dolphindiscovery.com) in an enclosure at Treasure Island, on the side of Isla Mujeres that faces Cancún. Groups of eight people swim with two dolphins and one trainer. Swimmers view an educational video and spend time in the water with the trainer and the dolphins before enjoying 15 minutes of free swimming time with them. Reservations are necessary, and you must arrive an hour before your assigned swimming time, at 10:30am, noon, 2 or 3:30pm. The cost is $139 (£70) per person for the Dolphin Royal Swim. There are less expensive programs that allow you to learn about, touch, and hold the dolphins (but not swim with them) starting at $79 (£40).

TURTLE SANCTUARY ⟨⟨   Years ago, fishermen converged on the island nightly from May to September to capture turtles when they would come ashore to lay eggs. Then a concerned fisherman, Gonzalo Chale Maldonado, began convincing others to spare at least the eggs, which he protected. It was a start. Following his lead, the fishing ministry founded the **Centro de Investigaciones Pesqueras** to find ways to protect the species and increase the turtle populations. Although the local government provides some assistance, most of the funding comes from private-sector donations. Since the center opened, tens of thousands of young turtles have been released, and local schoolchildren have participated, helping to educate a new generation of islanders for the cause. Releases are scheduled from May to October, and visitors are invited to take part. Inquire at the center.

Three species of sea turtles nest on Isla Mujeres. An adult green turtle, the most abundant species, is 1 to 1.5m (3¼–5 ft.) long and can weigh 204kg (450 lb.). At the center, visitors walk through the indoor and outdoor turtle pool areas, where the creatures paddle around. Turtles are separated by age, from newly hatched up to 1 year. People who come here usually end up staying at least an hour, especially if they opt for the guided tour, which I recommend. They also have a small gift shop and snack bar. The sanctuary is on a spit of land jutting out from the island's west coast. The address is Carr. Sac Bajo #5; you'll need a taxi to get there. Admission is $2 (£1.50); the shelter is open daily from 9am to 5pm. For more information, call ✆ **998/877-0595.**

GARRAFON NATIONAL PARK AND PUNTA SUR ⭐⭐   El Garrafón (✆ **998/ 849-4748;** www.garrafon.com) is at the southern end of the island. The pricy but well-equipped park has two restaurant/bars, beach chairs, a swimming pool, kayaks, changing rooms, rental lockers, showers, a gift shop, and snack bars. Once a public national underwater park, Garrafón is now operated by Dolphin Discovery. Public facilities have vastly improved, with the addition of new attractions and facilities each year. Activities include snorkeling and Snuba (a tankless version of scuba diving, when you descend while breathing through a long air tube); "Sea Trek," which allows you to explore the Caribbean seabed wearing a helmet with compressed air; crystal-clear canoes for viewing underwater life; and a zip-line that takes you over the water. On land are tanning decks, shaded hammocks, a 12m (40-ft.) climbing tower, and—of course—a souvenir superstore. A new panoramic tower had yet to open as of my last trip. At 50m (164-ft.) high, it will afford visitors a bird's-eye view of the entire island. Several restaurants and snack bars are available. Basic admission is $36 (£18); the all-inclusive package is $50 (£25; American Express, MasterCard, and Visa are accepted). More expensive packages include transportation and/or swims with dolphins at Dolphin Discovery (see above). The park is open daily in high season from 9am to 5pm. In low season it closes for 2 or 3 days per week.

Next to the panoramic tower you'll find **Sculptured Spaces,** an impressive and extensive garden of large sculptures donated to Isla Mujeres by internationally renowned sculptors as part of the 2001 First International Sculpture Exhibition. Among Mexican sculptors represented by works are José Luis Cuevas and Vladimir Cora.

Nearby is the **Caribbean Village,** with narrow lanes of colorful clapboard buildings that house cafes and shops displaying folkloric art. Plan to have lunch or a snack here at the kiosk and stroll around, before heading on to the lighthouse and Maya ruins.

Also at this southern point of the island, and part of the ruins, is **Cliff of the Dawn,** the southeasternmost point of Mexico. Services are available from 9am to 5pm, but you can enter at any time; if you make it there early enough to see the sunrise, you can claim you were the first person in Mexico that day to be touched by the sun!

A MAYA RUIN ⭐⭐   Just beyond the lighthouse, at the southern end of the island, are the remains of a small Maya temple. Archaeologists believe it was dedicated to the moon and fertility goddess Ixchel. The location, on a lofty bluff overlooking the sea, is worth seeing and makes a great place for photos. It is believed that Maya women traveled here on annual pilgrimages to seek Ixchel's blessings of fertility.

A PIRATE'S FORTRESS   Almost in the middle of the island is large building purported to have been a pirate fortress. A slave trader who arrived here in the early 19th century, claimed to have been the pirate Mundaca Marecheaga. He set up a business selling slaves to Cuba and Belize and prospered here. According to island lore, a charming local girl captivated him, only to spurn him in favor of a local. Admission is $2 (£1); the fortress is open daily from 10am to 6pm.

A VISIT TO ISLA CONTOY ⚓ Try to visit this pristine uninhabited island, 30km (20 miles) by boat from Isla Mujeres. It became a national wildlife reserve in 1981. Lush vegetation covers the oddly shaped island, which is 6km (3¾ miles) long and harbors 70 species of birds as well as a host of marine and animal life. Bird species that nest on the island include pelicans, brown boobies, frigates, egrets, terns, and cormorants. Flocks of flamingos arrive in April. Most excursions troll for fish (which will be your lunch), anchor en route for a snorkeling expedition, skirt the island at a leisurely pace for close viewing of the birds without disturbing the habitat, and then pull ashore. While the captain prepares lunch, visitors can swim, sun, follow the nature trails, and visit the fine nature museum, which has bathroom facilities. The trip from Isla Mujeres takes about 45 minutes each way and can be longer if the waves are choppy. Because of the tight-knit boatmen's cooperative, prices for this excursion are the same everywhere: $40 (£22). You can buy a ticket at the **Sociedad Cooperativa** on Avenida Rueda Medina, next to Mexico Divers and Las Brisas restaurant (© **998/877-1363**). Isla Contoy trips leave at 9am and return around 4:30pm. The price (cash only) is $55 (£28) for adults, $28 (£14) for children. Boat captains should respect the cooperative's regulations regarding ecological sensitivity and boat safety, including the availability of life jackets for everyone on board. If you're not given a life jacket, ask for one. Snorkeling equipment is usually included in the price, but double-check before heading out.

SHOPPING

Shopping is a casual activity here. Several shops, especially concentrated on Avenida Hidalgo, sell Saltillo rugs, onyx, silver, Guatemalan clothing, blown glassware, masks, folk art, beach paraphernalia, and T-shirts in abundance. Prices are lower than in Cancún or Cozumel.

WHERE TO STAY

You'll find plenty of hotels in all price ranges on Isla Mujeres. Rates peak during high season, which is the most expensive and most crowded time to go. Elizabeth Wenger of **Yucatan Peninsula Travel** in Montello, Wisconsin (© **800/552-4550** in the U.S.), specializes in Mexico travel and books a lot of hotels in Isla Mujeres. Her service is invaluable in the high season. Those interested in private home rentals or longer-term stays can contact **Mundaca Travel and Real Estate** in Isla Mujeres (© **998/877-0025;** fax 998/877-0076; www.mundaca.com.mx), or book online with **Isla Beckons** property rental service (www.islabeckons.com).

VERY EXPENSIVE

Casa de los Sueños Resort & Spa Zenter ⚓⚓⚓ Originally built as a private residence and later converted into an adults-only boutique hotel in 1998, this property has nine guest rooms loaded with plush amenities and thoughtful comforts, and each comes with a balcony or terrace overlooking the water. There's an open breezeway, tropical gardens, a sunken living area (with Wi-Fi access), and an infinity pool that melts into the cool Caribbean waters. One master suite has an extra-large bathroom area with whirlpool and steam room/shower. The Zenter has an extensive menu of massages and holistic spa treatments, and yoga classes, held either outdoors or in a serene indoor space. The property is on the west side of the southern end of the island.

Carretera Garrafón Lote 9, Fracc. Mar Turquesa, 77400 Isla Mujeres, Q. Roo. © **998/877-0651** or -0369. Fax 998/877-0708. www.casadelossuenosresort.com. 9 units. High season $386–$496 (£193–£248) double; low season $330–$440 (£165–£220) double. Rates include continental breakfast and taxes. AE, MC, V. No one younger than 21.

Amenities: Restaurant; bar; infinity pool; tour desk; watersports equipment; spa; open-air massage area; room service; yoga center; nonsmoking rooms. *In room:* A/C, minibar, hair dryer, safe.

Hotel Villa Rolandi Gourmet & Beach Club ★★★ (Moments)   Villa Rolandi is a

romantic escape on a little sheltered cove with a pristine white-sand beach. Each of the luxurious suites holds a separate sitting area and large terrace or balcony with private whirlpool overlooking the sea. All rooms feature in-room sound systems, subtle lighting, and marble surfaces. The bathrooms have Bulgari products and enticing showers with multiple showerheads that convert into steam baths. In-room breakfast is delivered through a small portal. The hotel spa also offers an outdoor Thalasso therapy whirlpool and beachside massages. The owner is a Swiss-born restaurateur who made a name for himself with his restaurants on Isla Mujeres and in Cancún. This intimate hideaway is ideal for honeymooners.

Fracc. Lagunamar, SM 7, Mza. 75, Locs. 15 and 16, 77400 Isla Mujeres, Q. Roo. ⓒ 998/877-0700. Fax 998/877-0100. www.villarolandi.com. 28 units. High season $504 (£252) double, $560 (£280) junior suite; low season $358–$426 (£179–£213) double, $426–$492 (£213–£246) junior suite. Rates include continental breakfast, and a la carte lunch or dinner in the on-site restaurant. AE, MC, V. **Amenities:** Restaurant (see "Where to Dine," below); infinity pool w/waterfall; small fitness room; spa; airport transfer via van and catamaran; concierge; tour desk; room service; nonsmoking rooms. *In room:* TV, minibar, hair dryer, safe.

EXPENSIVE

Hotel Na Balam ★★ (Finds)   This popular, two-story hotel on Playa Norte has sim-

ple, comfortable rooms and well-tended beach grounds. Rooms are in three sections; some face the beach, and others are across the street in a garden setting with a swimming pool. The large rooms contain a king-size or two double beds, a seating area, folk-art decorations, and a terrace or balcony with hammocks. Master suites have additional amenities, including small pools with hydromassage. The older section is well kept and surrounds a peaceful, palm-filled, sandy inner yard and Playa Norte. The hotel gets a lot of yoga practitioners and offers classes on a regular basis. The restaurant, **Zazil Ha,** is one of the island's most popular (see "Where to Dine," below). A beachside bar serves a selection of natural juices and is one of the most popular spots for sunset watching.

Zazil Ha 118, 77400 Isla Mujeres, Q. Roo. ⓒ **998/877-0279.** Fax 998/877-0446. www.nabalam.com. 33 units. High season $264–$496 (£132–£248) suite; low season $198–$416 (£99–£213) suite. Ask about weekly and monthly rates. AE, MC, V. **Amenities:** Restaurant; snack bar; bar; outdoor swimming pool; yoga classes; spa; mopeds, golf carts for rent; game room w/TV; diving and snorkeling trips available; salon; in-room massage; babysitting; laundry service; Wi-Fi. *In room:* A/C, minibar, hair dryer, safe, no phone.

Secreto ★★ (Finds)   This boutique hotel has a chic Mediterranean feel. It has nine

suites that overlook an infinity-edge pool and the open sea beyond. Located on the northern end of the island, Secreto lies within walking distance of town, yet feels removed enough to make for an idyllic retreat. Tropical gardens surround the pool area, and an outdoor living area offers comfy couches and places to dine. Guest rooms are contemporary, featuring clean, white spaces and several extras. Each includes a veranda with private cabaña ideal for ocean-gazing beyond Halfmoon Beach. Three suites include king-size beds draped in mosquito netting, while the remaining six have two double beds. Secreto is distinguished by its style and service.

Sección Rocas, Lote 1, 77400 Isla Mujeres, Q. Roo. ⓒ **998/877-1039.** Fax 998/877-1048. www.hotelsecreto.com. 9 units. $252–$280 (£126–£140) double. Extra person $25 (£13). 1 child younger than 5 stays free in parent's room. Rates include continental breakfast. AE, MC, V. **Amenities:** Bar; coffee service; outdoor pool; tours, diving, and snorkeling available; dinner delivery from Rolandi's restaurant available; nonsmoking rooms. *In room:* A/C, TV/DVD, CD player, minibar, fridge, hairdryer, iron, safe.

MODERATE

Hotel Cabañas María del Mar ⚜   A good choice for simple beach accommodations, the Cabañas María del Mar is on the popular Playa Norte. The older two-story section behind the reception area and beyond the garden offers nicely outfitted rooms facing the beach. All have two single or double beds, refrigerators, and oceanview balconies strung with hammocks. Eleven single-story cabañas closer to the reception area are decorated in a rustic Mexican style. The third section, **El Castillo,** is located across the street, over and beside Buho's restaurant. All rooms are "deluxe," though some are larger than others. The five rooms on the ground floor have large patios. Upstairs rooms have small balconies. Most have ocean views. The central courtyard contains a small pool.

Av. Arq. Carlos Lazo 1 (on Playa Norte, one-half block from the Hotel Na Balam), 77400 Isla Mujeres, Q. Roo. ⓒ 800/223-5695 in the U.S. and Canada, or 998/877-0179. Fax 998/877-0213. www.cabanasdelmar.com. 73 units. High season $134–$146 (£67–£73) double; low season $82–$108 (£41–£54) double. MC, V. **Amenities:** Pool; golf cart and *moto* rentals; nonsmoking rooms. *In room:* A/C, fridge in some, safe.

INEXPENSIVE

Hotel Belmar ⚜⚜   In the center of Isla's entertainment district, this charming three-story hotel (no elevator) sits above Rolandi's restaurant. The simple, attractive rooms come with tile floors, nicely finished bathrooms, and either a king bed or two twins or two doubles. The rooms are well maintained and have good, quiet air conditioning. It's one of the few island hotels that offer televisions with U.S. channels. One large suite with a sitting area, large patio, and whirlpool goes for close to $100 (£50). The rooms have double-glazed windows. Though I had no trouble with noise from the restaurant in my third-floor room, light sleepers might want to look elsewhere.

Av. Hidalgo 110 (between Madero and Abasolo, 3½ blocks from the passenger-ferry pier), 77400 Isla Mujeres, Q. Roo. ⓒ 998/877-0430. Fax 998/877-0429. www.rolandi.com. 11 units. High season $56 (£28) double; low season $35–$45 (£18–£23) double. AE, MC, V. **Amenities:** Restaurant/bar (see "Where to Dine," below); room service; laundry service. *In room:* A/C, TV, fan.

Hotel D'Gomar *Value*   This hotel is at the bottom of the inexpensive range while still being comfortable. The basic accommodations are regularly updated. Rooms have two double beds and a wall of windows affording breezes and views. The higher prices are for air-conditioned rooms. The hotel is four stories with no elevator, but it's conveniently located cater-cornered from the ferry pier (look right). The name of the hotel is the most visible sign on the "skyline."

Rueda Medina 150, 77400 Isla Mujeres, Q. Roo. ⓒ/fax **998/877-0541.** www.hoteldgomar.com. 20 units. High season $60–$66 (£30–£33) double; low season $40–$56 (£20–£28) double. MC, V. *In room:* A/C (in some), fan, no phone.

Hotel Francis Arlene ⚜   The Magaña family operates this neat little two-story inn built around a shady courtyard. It's bright, cheerful, well-managed, and has attractive common spaces. For these reasons, it gets a lot of return guests; it's especially popular with families and seniors. Some rooms have ocean views, and all are remodeled or updated each year. They are comfortable, with tile floors, tiled bathrooms, and a very homey feel. Each downstairs room has a coffeemaker, refrigerator, and stove; each upstairs room comes with a refrigerator and toaster. Some have either a balcony or a patio. Higher prices are for the 14 rooms with air-conditioning; other units have fans. Rates are substantially better if quoted in pesos.

Guerrero 7 (5½ blocks inland from the ferry pier, between Abasolo and Matamoros), 77400 Isla Mujeres, Q. Roo. ⓒ/fax **998/877-0310** or -0861. www.francisarlene.com. 24 units. High season $60–$90 (£30–£45) double; low season $45–$70 (£23–£35) double. MC, V. **Amenities:** Safe; currency exchange. *In room:* A/C (in some), kitchenettes (in some), fridge, no phone.

Hotel Posada del Mar (Kids)   Simply furnished, quiet, and comfortable, this long-established hotel faces the water 3 blocks north of the ferry pier. This is probably the best choice in Isla for families. For the spaciousness of the rooms (half of which have ocean views) and the location, it's also among the island's best values. A wide, appealing but seldom-used stretch of Playa Norte lies across the street, where watersports equipment is available for rent. A casual *palapa* bar and a lovely pool are on the back lawn along with hammocks, and the restaurant **Pinguinos** (see "Where to Dine," below) is by the sidewalk at the front of the property, and also provides room service to hotel guests.

Av. Rueda Medina 15 A, 77400 Isla Mujeres, Q. Roo. ✆ 800/544-3005 in the U.S. and Canada, or 998/877-0044. Fax 998/877-0266. www.posadadelmar.com. 52 units. High season $110 (£55) double; low season $66 (£33) double. Children younger than 12 stay free in parent's room. AE, MC, V. **Amenities:** Restaurant/bar; outdoor pool. *In room:* A/C, TV, fan.

WHERE TO DINE

At the **Municipal Market,** next to the telegraph office and post office on Avenida Guerrero, obliging, hardworking women operate several little food stands. At the **Panadería La Reyna** (no phone), at Madero and Juárez, you can pick up inexpensive sweet bread, muffins, cookies, and yogurt. It's open Monday through Saturday from 7am to 9:30pm. For a frozen treat, check out **Cool** ice cream store (✆ 998/167-6351), on Av. Madero between Hidalgo and Juárez. It serves some wonderful flavors. The German and Peruvian owners might be opening another store on north Juárez.

EXPENSIVE

Casa Rolandi (👍👍) ITALIAN/SEAFOOD   A gourmet restaurant that's outside town in the Villa Rolandi hotel, this place offers a beautiful setting with windows facing out over the western shore of the island and an open-air terrace. The menu here is more sophisticated than Rolandi's downtown, including some original creations not offered by the other locale. But there are several dishes common to both, including one of the signature dishes, *pescado a la sal* (fish baked in a cocoon of salt and egg whites). Both restaurants make good use of wood-burning stoves to produce some great baked fish dishes. And take care with the wood-oven-baked bread; it arrives looking like a puffer fish, and it's so divine you're apt to fill up on it. This is a great place to enjoy the sunset. They stock a selection of fine international wines and more than 80 premium tequilas. Service is personalized and attentive.

On the pier of Villa Rolandi, Lagunamar SM 7. ✆ 998/877-0700. Reservations necessary. Main courses $8–$35 (£4–£18). AE, MC, V. Daily 7–10:30pm.

Sunset Grill (👍👍) SEAFOOD/STEAKS   This outdoor venue approaches the ideal for a beach restaurant, with its comfortable tables and chairs by the water, under a shady *palapa*. When the sun goes down, the restaurant sets up tables on the beach, and, weather permitting, there's no better ambience. The breakfasts are good, lunch includes a variety of sandwiches and burgers, and for dinner they serve such specialties as fish seared in a light *achiote* sauce, fish and chips, and a variety of steaks. To get to this restaurant, you have to walk through the parking lot of the Nautibeach Condominiums, which you access via a sand road that is the continuation of Rueda Medina.

Nautibeach Condominiums, North Beach. ✆ 998/877-0785. Reservations recommended. Main courses $14–$24 (£7–£12); sandwiches and breakfasts $6–$9 (£3–£4.50). AE, MC, V. Daily 8am–9pm.

MODERATE

Angelo (👍) ITALIAN   An Italian restaurant in the town center, Angelo offers an enticing selection of antipasti, pasta, grilled seafood, and wood oven-baked pizzas. The

Sardinian-born owner instills his menu with the flavors of his homeland, including a rich tomato sauce. Consider starting with a bowl of seafood soup or black mussels au gratin and continuing with the grilled shrimp kabobs or seafood pasta in an olive oil and white-wine sauce. The open-air restaurant includes an inviting sidewalk terrace and lies across the street from a casual Cuban restaurant also owned by Angelo.

Av. Hidalgo 14 (between Lopez Mateos and Matamoros). $\mathcal{C}$ **998/877-1273.** Main courses $8–$12 (£4–£6). MC, V. Daily 4pm–midnight.

Pinguinos MEXICAN/SEAFOOD   Seafood grilled Mexican style is the specialty of this open-air restaurant and bar facing the ocean. Late in the evening, it's sometimes a place to party. Dishes include fresh lobster—you'll get a large, beautifully presented lobster tail with a choice of butter, garlic, and secret sauces. The grilled seafood platter, seafood casserole, and fajitas are also standouts. Breakfasts include fresh fruit, yogurt, and granola, or sizable platters of eggs, served with homemade wheat bread.

In front of the Hotel Posada del Mar (3 blocks west of the ferry pier), Av. Rueda Medina 15-A. $\mathcal{C}$ **998/877-0044,** ext. 157. Breakfast $4–$8 (£2–£4); main courses $5–$12 (£2.50–£6); lobster $15–$40 (£7.50–£20). AE, MC, V. Daily 7am–11pm; bar closes at midnight.

Rolandi's $\hat{\mathcal{R}}$ ITALIAN/SEAFOOD   This restaurant is an Isla institution. The plate-size pizzas and calzones feature exotic ingredients—including lobster, black mushrooms, pineapple, and Roquefort cheese—as well as more traditional tomatoes, olives, basil, and salami. A wood-burning oven imparts the signature flavor of the pizzas, as well as baked chicken, roast beef, and mixed seafood casserole with lobster. The extensive menu offers a selection of salads and appetizers, plus an ample array of homemade pasta dishes, steaks, fish, and desserts. The setting is the open courtyard of the Hotel Belmar, with a porch overlooking the action on Avenida Hidalgo.

Av. Hidalgo 10 (3½ blocks inland from the pier, between Madero and Abasolo). $\mathcal{C}$ **998/877-0430,** ext. 18. Main courses $8–$16 (£4–£8). AE, MC, V. Daily 11am–11pm.

Zazil Ha $\hat{\mathcal{R}}\hat{\mathcal{R}}$ CARIBBEAN/INTERNATIONAL   Here you can enjoy some of the island's best food while sitting at tables on the sand among palms and gardens. Come night, candlelit tables sparkle underneath the open-air *palapa*. Specialties include Maya chicken stuffed with corn mushroom and goat cheese, black pasta with calamari and pesto sauce, and fish of the day with *achiote* sauce draped in a banana leaf. A selection of fresh juices complements the vegetarian options, and there's even a special menu for those participating in yoga retreats. The delicious breads are baked in house. Between the set meal times, you can order all sorts of enticing food, such as tacos and sandwiches, ceviche, terrific nachos, and vegetable and fruit drinks.

At the Hotel Na Balam (at the end of Playa Norte, almost at the end of Calle Zazil Ha). $\mathcal{C}$ **998/877-0279.** Fax 998/877-0446. Breakfast $4–$10 (£2–£5); main courses $8–$22 (£4–£11). AE, MC, V. Daily 7:30am–10:30pm.

INEXPENSIVE
Café Cito CAFE   Brisa and Luis Rivera own this adorable, Caribbean-blue corner restaurant where you can begin the day with flavorful coffee and a croissant and cream cheese (this is the only place in town where you can have breakfast until 2pm). Terrific crepes come with yogurt, ice cream, fresh fruit, or *dulce de leche* (caramel sauce made from goat's milk), as well as ham and cheese.

Calle Matamoros 42, at Juárez. $\mathcal{C}$ **998/877-1470.** Crepes $3–$6 (£1.50–£3); breakfast $4–$6 (£1.95–£3); sandwiches $3.50–$4.50 (£1.95–£2.50). No credit cards. Daily 7am–2pm.

ISLA MUJERES AFTER DARK

Those in a party mood by day's end may want to start out at the beach bar of the **Na Balam** hotel on Playa Norte, which usually hosts a crowd until around midnight. On Saturday and Sunday, live music plays between 4 and 7pm. **Jax Bar & Grill** on Avenida Rueda Medina, close to Hotel Posada del Mar, is a Texas-style sports bar offering live music nightly. **Las Palapas Chimbo's** restaurant on the beach becomes a jammin' dance joint with a live band from 9pm until whenever. Farther along the same stretch of beach, **Buho's,** the restaurant/beach bar of the Cabañas María del Mar, has its moments as a popular, low-key hangout, complete with swinging seats over the sand. **Pinguinos** (p. 130) in the Hotel Posada del Mar offers a convivial late-night hangout, where a band plays nightly during high season from 9pm to midnight. If you want to sample one of nearly 100 tequila brands on a relaxing sidewalk terrace, stop by **La Adelita,** located at Av. Hidalgo 12 and open nightly from 5:30pm to 2:30am. Near Matamoros and Hidalgo, **KoKo Nuts** caters to a younger crowd, with international music for late-night dancing. **Om Bar and Chill Lounge,** on Calle Matamoros, serves cocktails in an atmosphere that includes jazzy Latino music, open from 6pm to 2am. For a late night dance club, **Club Nitrox,** on Avenida Guerrero, is open Wednesday to Sunday from 9pm to 3am. In general, the crowds hitting these bars are in their 20s.

2 Cozumel ★★★

70km (43 miles) S of Cancún; 19km (12 miles) SE of Playa del Carmen

Cozumel has ranked for years among the top five dive destinations in the world. Tall reefs line the southwest coast, creating towering walls that offer divers a fairy-tale landscape to explore. For nondivers, it has the beautiful water of the Caribbean with all the accompanying watersports and seaside activities. The island gets a lot more visitors from North America than Europe for reasons that probably have to do with the limited flights. It is in many ways more cozy and mellow than the mainland—no big highways, no big construction projects. It's dependable. And one of my favorite things about this island is that the water on the protected side (western shore) is as calm as an aquarium, unless a front is blowing through. The island is 45km (28 miles) long and 18km (11 miles) wide, and lies 19km (12 miles) from the mainland. Most of the terrain is flat and clothed in a low tropical forest.

The only town on the island is San Miguel, which, despite the growth of the last 20 years, can't be called anything more than a small town. It's not a stunningly beautiful town, but it and its inhabitants are agreeable—life moves along at a slow pace, and every Sunday evening, residents congregate around the plaza to enjoy live music and see their friends. Staying in town can be fun and convenient. You get a choice of a number of restaurants and nightspots.

Because Cozumel enjoys such popularity with the cruise ships, the waterfront section of town holds wall-to-wall jewelry stores, duty-free, and souvenir shops. This and the area around the town's main square are about as far as most cruise-ship passengers venture into town.

Should you come down with a case of island fever, **Playa del Carmen** and the mainland are a 40-minute ferry ride away. Some travel agencies on the island can set you up with a tour of the major ruins on the mainland, such as **Tulum** or **Chichén Itzá,** or a visit to a nature park such as **Xel-Ha** or **Xcaret** (see "Trips to the Mainland," later in this chapter).

The island has its own ruins, but they cannot compare with the major sites of the mainland. During pre-Hispanic times, Maya women would cross over to the island to make offerings to the goddess of fertility, Ixchel. More than 40 sites containing shrines remain around the island, and archaeologists still uncover the small dolls that were customarily part of those offerings.

ESSENTIALS
GETTING THERE & DEPARTING
BY PLANE   During high season, several more international commercial flights fly in and out of Cozumel's airport (CZM) than in low season, including a few flights from northern U.S. cities. You might also inquire about buying a ticket on one of the charter flights. Some packagers, such as **Fun Jet** (www.funjet.com), will sell you just a ticket. But look into packages, too. Several of the island's independent hotels work with packagers.

BY FERRY   Passenger ferries run to and from Playa del Carmen. **Barcos México** (© 987/872-1508 or -1588) and **Ultramar** (© 987/869-2775) offer departures almost every hour in the morning and about every 2 hours in the afternoon. The schedules change according to seasons. The trip takes 30 to 45 minutes, depending on conditions, and costs $11 (£5.50) one-way. The boats are air-conditioned. In Playa del Carmen, the ferry dock is 1½ blocks from the main square. In Cozumel, the ferries use Muelle Fiscal, the town pier, a block from the main square. Luggage storage at the Cozumel dock costs $2 (£1) per day.

The car ferry that used to operate from Puerto Morelos now uses the Calica pier just south of Playa del Carmen. The fare for a standard car is $80 (£40). **Marítima Chancanaab** (© 987/872-7671 or -7504) has four departures daily from Calica at 4am, 8am, 1:30pm, and 6pm. Arrive 1 hour before departure. The schedule is subject to change, so double-check it. The ferry docks in Cozumel at the **Muelle Internacional** (the **International Pier,** which is south of town near La Ceiba Hotel).

BY BUS   If you plan to travel on the mainland by bus, there is a ticket office for **ADO buses** called **Ticket Bus** where you can purchase tickets in advance. One is located on the municipal pier and is open while the ferries are running. Another is on Calle 2 Norte and Avenida 10 (© 987/872-1706). Hours are from 8am to 9pm daily.

ORIENTATION
ARRIVING   Cozumel's **airport** is inland from downtown. **Transportes Terrestres** provides hotel transportation in air-conditioned Suburbans. Buy your ticket as you exit the terminal. To hotels downtown, the fare is $7 (£3.50) per person; to hotels along the north shore, $10 (£5), and to hotels along the south shore, $11 to $15 (£5.50–£7.50). Passenger ferries arrive at the Muelle Fiscal, the municipal pier, by the town's main square. Cruise ships dock at the **Punta Langosta** pier, several blocks south of the Muelle Fiscal, and at the **International Pier,** which is at Km 4 of the southern coastal road. A third cruise ship pier, the **Puerta Maya,** suffered the most damage from Hurricane Wilma and will be nonoperational for at least another year.

Tips **Be Streetwise**

North-south streets—the *avenidas*—have the right of way, and traffic doesn't slow down or stop.

Cozumel

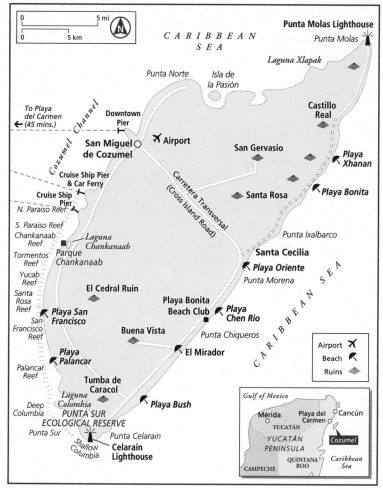

The International Pier was also damaged, but one side was working when I was last on the island, and the other side was scheduled to open sometime in 2008. On days when several cruise ships arrive, some of the boats will anchor offshore, and tender boats will ferry passengers and crew to land. It seems to be working smoothly—I heard no complaints from passengers.

VISITOR INFORMATION   The **Municipal Tourism Office** (©/fax **987/ 869-0212**) has an information booth at the municipal ferry pier, on the main square. It's open 8am to 8pm Monday to Saturday. There are other information booths at each of the ferry piers and at the airport.

CITY LAYOUT   San Miguel's main waterfront street is **Avenida Rafael Melgar.** Running parallel to Rafael Melgar are other *avenidas* numbered in multiples of five— 5, 10, 15. **Avenida Juárez** runs perpendicular to these, heading inland from the ferry

An All-Inclusive Vacation in Cozumel

Booking a room at an all-inclusive should be done through a vacation packager. Booking lodging directly through the hotel usually doesn't make sense, even with frequent-flier mileage to burn, because the discounts offered by most packagers are so deep. I include websites for you to find out more info about the properties, but don't expect to find clear info on rates. The game of setting rates with these hotels is complicated and always in flux. All these beach properties made significant upgrades to the rooms when they made repairs after the hurricane, so expect such things as new mattresses and extra amenities.

Two all-inclusives are north of town: **El Cozumeleño** (www.elcozumeleno. com) and the **Meliá Cozumel** (www.meliacozumel.com). Both occupy multistory modern buildings. Both have attractive rooms. El Cozumeleño is the larger of the two resorts and has the nicest hotel pool on the island. It's best suited for active types. The Meliá is quieter and offers golf discounts for the nearby golf course. Though the Cozumeleño's small beach was lost with Wilma, the hotel brought in replacement sand and is now back to normal. The Meliá's beach is long and narrow and pretty, but occasionally seaweed washes up, which doesn't happen on the rest of the island's coast. The advantages of staying in these two are the proximity to town, with its restaurants, clubs, movie theaters, and so on, and the fact that most rooms at these hotels come with views of the ocean.

A recent addition to the all-inclusives is the **Cozumel Palace** (www.palace resorts.com). It's right on the water on the southern fringes of town, occupying the property that used to be Plaza las Glorias. Despite the location, it

dock. Avenida Juárez divides the town into northern and southern halves. The *calles* (streets) that parallel Juárez to the north have even numbers. The ones to the south have odd numbers, except for Calle Rosado Salas, which runs between calles 1 and 3.

ISLAND LAYOUT   One road runs along the western coast of the island, which faces the Yucatán mainland. It has different names. North of town it's **Santa Pilar** or **San Juan;** in the city it is **Avenida Rafael Melgar;** south of town it's **Costera Sur.** Hotels stretch along this road north and south of town. The road runs to the southern tip of the island (Punta Sur), passing **Chankanaab National Park. Avenida Juárez** (and its extension, the **Carretera Transversal**) runs east from the town across the island. It passes the airport and the turnoff to the ruins of San Gervasio before reaching the undeveloped ocean side of the island. It then turns south and follows the coast to the southern tip, where it meets the Costera Sur.

GETTING AROUND   You can walk to most destinations in town. Getting to outlying hotels and beaches requires a taxi, rental car, or moped.

Car rentals are roughly the same price as on the mainland, depending on demand. **Avis** (© 987/872-0099) and **Executive** (© 987/872-1308) have counters in the airport.

doesn't have a beach. But that's not so bad. The water is usually so calm on Cozumel's west shore that swimming here is like swimming in the pool, and you can snorkel right out of the hotel.

Of the all-inclusives to the south, my favorites are the two **Occidental** properties (**Allegro Cozumel** and **Grand Cozumel;** www.occidentalhotels.com) and the **Iberostar Cozumel** (www.iberostar.com). These are "village" style resorts with two- and three-story buildings, often with thatched roofs, spread over a large area at the center of which is the pool and activities area. The Allegro is older than the other two and has the plainest rooms, but these were completely remodeled after the hurricane. The Grand Cozumel, next door to the Allegro, is the newest property. Its rooms are larger and more attractive than the Allegro, and staying here gives you access to both Occidental resorts. Like the Occidental chain, Iberostar has several properties in the Mexican Caribbean. This one is the smallest. I like its food and service and the beauty of the grounds. The rooms are attractive and well maintained. The added sand from Wilma improved the resort a lot. The advantage to staying in these places is that you're close to a lot of dive sites; the disadvantage is that you're somewhat isolated from town, and you don't have the views that the taller buildings in the north give you.

Of the other all-inclusives, I've heard several complaints about the service at the **Reef Club** (unless you stay in the VIP section), and I think the rooms are too closely set together. The **Costa Club** is on the inland side of the road in a crowded section of the island.

Other major rental companies have offices in town. Rentals are easy to arrange through your hotel or at any of the many local rental offices.

Moped rentals are readily available and cost $20 to $40 (£15–£20) for 24 hours, depending upon the season. If you rent a moped, be careful. Riding a moped made a lot more sense when Cozumel had less traffic; now it involves a certain amount of risk as taxi drivers and other motorists have become more numerous and pushier. Moped accidents easily rank as the greatest cause of injury in Cozumel. Before renting one, inspect it carefully to see that all the gizmos—horn, light, starter, seat, mirror—are in good shape. I've been offered mopeds with unbalanced wheels, which made them unsteady at higher speeds, but the renter quickly exchanged them upon my request. You are required to stay on paved roads. It's illegal to ride a moped without a helmet outside of town (subject to a $25/£13 fine).

Cozumel has lots of **taxis** and a strong drivers' union. Fares have been standardized—there's no bargaining. Here are a few sample fares for two people (there is an additional charge for extra passengers to most destinations): island tour, $50 (£25); town to southern hotel zone, $6 to $18 (£3–£9); town to northern hotels, $5 to $7 (£2.50–£3.50); town to Chankanaab, $10 (£5) for up to four people; in and around town, $3 to $4 (£1.50–£2).

FAST FACTS: Cozumel

Area Code The telephone area code is **987**.

Climate From October to December there can be strong winds all over the Yucatán, as well as some rain. June through October is the rainy season.

Clinics **Médica San Miguel** (© **987/872-0103**) works for most things and includes intensive-care facilities. It's on Calle 6 Norte between Av. 5 and 10. **Centro Médico Cozumel** (© **987/872-3545**) is an alternative. It's at the intersection of Calle 1 Sur and Av. 50.

Currency Exchange The island has several banks and *casas de cambio,* as well as ATMs. Most places accept dollars, but you usually get a better deal paying in pesos.

Diving Bring proof of your diver's certification and your log. Underwater currents can be strong, and many of the reef drops are quite steep, so dive operators want to make sure divers are experienced.

Emergencies To report an emergency, dial © **065,** which is similar to 911 emergency service in the United States.

Internet Access Several cybercafes are in and about the main square. If you go just a bit off Avenida Rafael Melgar and the main square, prices drop. **Modutel,** Av. Juárez 15 (at Av. 10), offers good rates. Hours are Monday through Saturday from 10am to 8pm.

Post Office The *correo* is on Avenida Rafael Melgar at Calle 7 Sur (© **987/ 872-0106**), at the southern edge of town. It's open Monday through Friday from 9am to 3pm, Saturday from 9am to noon.

Recompression Chamber There are four *cámaras de recompresión.* The best are **Buceo Médico Mexicano,** staffed 24 hours, at Calle 5 Sur 21-B, between Avenida Rafael Melgar and Avenida 5 Sur (© **987/872-2387** or -1430); and the **Hyperbaric Center of Cozumel** (© **987/872-3070**) at Calle 6 Norte, between avenidas 5 and 10.

Seasons High season is August and from Christmas to Easter.

EXPLORING THE ISLAND

For **diving** and **snorkeling,** there are plenty of dive shops to choose from, including those recommended below. For **island tours, ruins tours** on and off the island, **evening cruises,** and other activities, go to a travel agency, such as **InterMar Cozumel Viajes,** Calle 2 Norte 101-B, between avenidas 5 and 10 (© **987/872-1535** or -2022; fax 987/872-0895; cozumel@travel2mexico.com). Office hours are Monday through Saturday from 8am to 8pm, Sunday from 9am to 5pm.

WATERSPORTS

SCUBA DIVING   Cozumel is the number-one dive destination in the Western Hemisphere. Don't forget your dive card and dive log. Dive shops will rent you scuba gear, but won't take you out on a boat until you show some documentation. If you have a medical condition, bring a letter signed by a doctor stating that you've been

San Miguel de Cozumel

Information ⓘ
Pedestrians only
Post office ✉

Bulevar Aeropuerto Internacional
To Airport
Calle 14 Norte

0   200 yds
0   200 m

To
Hotels North

Calle 12 Norte
Calle 10 Norte
Calle 8 Norte
Calle 6 Norte
Calle 4 Norte
Calle 2 Norte

Museo de Cozumel

Avenida Benito Juárez
Carretera Transversal
Calle 1 Sur

To Playa
del Carmen

Plaza ⓘ

■ Market
Calle Dr. Adolfo Rosado Salas

Calle 3 Sur

Calles Morelos

Recompression Chamber

To Hotels South
& Cruise/Car Pier

Calle Hidalgo

Channel
Cozumel
Avenida Rafael Melgar

5 Avenida Norte
10 Avenida Norte
15 Avenida Norte
20 Avenida Norte
25 Avenida Norte
30 Avenida Norte
35 Avenida Norte
40 Avenida Norte

15 Avenida Sur
20 Avenida Sur
25 Avenida Sur
30 Avenida Sur
35 Avenida Sur
40 Avenida Sur

5 Av. Sur
10 Av. Sur
Calle 5 Sur
Calle 7 Sur

ACCOMMODATIONS ■

Hacienda de
  San Miguel **1**
La Casona Real **17**
Suites Colonial **9**
Suites Vima **6**
Vista del Mar **15**

DINING ◆

Capicúa **2**
Cocos Cozumel **8**
Comida Casera Toñita **11**
El Amigo Mario **16**
French Quarter **12**
Guido's **4**

La Choza **13**
La Cocay **3**
Le Chef **14**
Prima **10**
Restaurant
  del Museo **5**
Zermatt **7**

San Miguel
de Cozumel

**COZUMEL
ISLAND**

cleared to dive. A two-tank morning dive costs from $60 to $85 (£30–£43); some shops offer an additional afternoon one-tank dive for $30 (£15) for those who took the morning dives. A lot of divers save some money by buying a dive package with a hotel. These usually include two dives a day.

Diving in Cozumel is drift diving, which can be a little disconcerting for novices. The current that sweeps along Cozumel's reefs, pulling nutrients into them and making them as large as they are, also dictates how you dive here. The problem is that it pulls at different speeds at different depths and in different places. When it's pulling strong, it can quickly scatter a dive group. The role of the dive master becomes more important, especially with choosing the dive location. Cozumel has a lot of dive locations. To mention but a few: the famous **Palancar Reef,** with its caves and canyons, plentiful fish, and sea coral; the monstrous **Santa Rosa Wall,** famous for its depth, sea life, coral, and sponges; the **San Francisco Reef,** with a shallower drop-off wall and fascinating sea life; and the **Yucab Reef,** with its beautiful coral.

I've seen a number of news reports about reef damage caused by hurricane Wilma. Almost all of it occurred in the shallower parts, above 15m (50 ft.). In deeper areas, the currents produced by Wilma actually improved matters by clearing sand away from parts of the reef, and in some cases exposing new caverns. Wildlife is plentiful. In the shallow parts fan coral and such are gradually growing back.

Finding a dive shop in town is even easier than finding a jewelry store. Cozumel has more than 50 dive operators. I know and can recommend Bill Horn's **Aqua Safari,** which has a location on Avenida Rafael Melgar at Calle 5 (© 987/872-0101; fax 987/872-0661; www.aquasafari.com). I also know Roberto Castillo at **Liquid Blue Divers** (© 987/869-2812; www.liquidbluedivers.com), on Avenida 5 between Rosado Salas and Calle 3 Sur. He does a good tour, has a fast boat, and keeps the number of divers to 12 or fewer. His wife, Michelle, handles the Internet inquiries and reservations and is quick to respond to questions.

A popular activity in the Yucatán is cenote diving. The peninsula's underground **cenotes** (seh-*noh*-tehs)—sinkholes or wellsprings—lead to a vast system of underground caverns. The gently flowing water is so clear that divers seem to float on air through caves complete with stalactites and stalagmites. If you want to try this but didn't plan a trip to the mainland, contact **Yucatech Expeditions,** Avenida 5, on the corner of Calle 3 Sur (©/fax **987/872-5659;** www.yucatech.net), which offers a trip five times a week. Cenotes are 30 to 45 minutes from Playa del Carmen, and a dive in each cenote lasts around 45 minutes. Dives are within the daylight zone, about 40m (131 ft.) into the caverns, and no more than 18m (59 ft.) deep. Company owner Germán Yañez Mendoza inspects diving credentials carefully, and divers must meet his list of requirements before cave diving is permitted. For information and prices, call or drop by the office.

SNORKELING Anyone who can swim can snorkel. When contracting for a snorkel tour, stay away from the companies that cater to the cruise ships. Those tours

---

Moments **Carnaval**

Carnaval (similar to Mardi Gras) is Cozumel's most colorful fiesta. It begins the Thursday before Ash Wednesday, with daytime street dancing and nighttime parades on Thursday, Saturday, and Monday (the best).

are crowded and not very fun. For a good snorkeling tour, contact **Victor Casanova** (© 987/872-1028; wildcatcozumel@hotmail.com). He speaks English, owns a couple of boats, and does a good 5-hour tour. He takes his time and doesn't rush through the trip. You can also try the **Kuzamil Snorkeling Center,** 50 Av. bis 565 Int. 1, between 5 Sur and Hidalgo, Colonia Adolfo López Mateos (© 987/872-4637 or -0539). Even though you won't see a lot of the more delicate structures, such as fan coral, you will still see plenty of sea creatures and enjoy the clear, calm water of Cozumel's protected west side.

BOAT TRIPS   Travel agencies and hotels can arrange boat trips, a popular pastime on Cozumel. Choose from evening cruises, cocktail cruises, glass-bottom boat cruises, and other options. One novel boat ride is offered by **Atlantis Submarines** (© 987/ 872-5671). The sub can hold 48 people. It operates almost 3km (2 miles) south of town in front of the Casa del Mar hotel and costs $81 (£41) per adult, $46 (£23) for kids ages 4 to 12. This is a superior experience to the **Sub See Explorer** offered by **Aqua World,** which is really just a glorified glass-bottom boat.

FISHING   The best months for fishing are March through June, when the catch includes blue and white marlin, sailfish, tarpon, and swordfish. The least expensive option would be to contact a boat owner directly. Try Victor Casanova, listed above under "Snorkeling." Or try an agency such as **Aquarius Travel Fishing,** Calle 3 Sur 2 between Avenida Rafael Melgar and Avenida 5 (© 987/872-1092; gabdiaz@yahoo.com).

CHANKANAAB NATIONAL PARK & PUNTA SUR ECOLOGICAL RESERVE

Chankanaab National Park ⚓ is the pride of many islanders. In Mayan, Chankanaab means "little sea," which refers to a beautiful land-locked pool connected to the sea through an underwater tunnel—a sort of miniature ocean. Snorkeling in this natural aquarium is not permitted, but the park itself has a beach for sunbathing and snorkeling. Arrive before 9am to stake out a chair and *palapa* before the cruise-ship crowd arrives. The snorkeling is also best before noon. There are bathrooms, lockers, a gift shop, several snack huts, a restaurant, and a *palapa* for renting snorkeling gear.

You can also swim with dolphins. **Dolphin Discovery** (© 800/293-9698; www.dolphindiscovery.com) has several programs for experiencing these sea creatures. These are popular, so plan ahead—you should make reservations well in advance. The surest way is through the website—make sure to pick the Cozumel location, as there are a couple of others on this coast. There are three different programs for swimming with dolphins. The one of longest duration costs $139 (£70) and features close interaction with the beautiful swimmers. There are also swim and snorkel programs for $75 and $100 (£38–£50) that get you in the water with these creatures.

Surrounding the land-locked dolphin pool is a botanical garden that suffered greatly from the hurricane and will take some time to come back. Admission to the park is expensive, costing $17 (£8.50) for adults, $8 (£4) for children 9 to 12. I think the authorities are trying to recoup some of the money spent restoring the park, and it is being marketed to the cruise ship crowd. The park is open daily from 8am to 5pm. It's south of town, just past the Fiesta Americana Hotel. Taxis run constantly between the park, the hotels, and town ($10/£5 from town for up to four people).

Punta Sur Ecological Reserve (admission $10/£5) is a large area that encompasses the southern tip of the island, including the Columbia Lagoon. The only practical way of going there is to rent a car or scooter; there is no taxi stand, and, usually, few people. This is an ecological reserve, not a park, so don't expect much infrastructure. The reserve has an information center, several observation towers, and a snack bar. The observation towers were destroyed in the hurricane and were still not reconstructed on my last visit. The information center was struck hard, too. And many of the trees on this side of the island came down, while others completely lost their leaves. These will make a comeback, but before you go all the way out to the park and pay admission, ask around about the condition of the vegetation—it adds a good bit to a visit here. Punta Sur has some interesting snorkeling (bring your own gear), and lovely beaches that are kept as natural as possible. Regular hours are daily 9am to 5pm.

THE BEACHES

Along both the west and east sides of the island you'll see signs advertising beach clubs. A "beach club" in Cozumel can mean just a *palapa* hut that's open to the public and serves soft drinks, beer, and fried fish. It can also mean a recreational beach with the full gamut of offerings from banana boats to parasailing. They also usually have locker rooms, a pool, and food. The two biggest of these are **Mr. Sancho's** (© 987/879-0021; www.mrsanchos.com) and **Playa Mía** (© 987/872-9030; www.playamia.com). They get a lot of business from the cruise ships. Mr. Sancho's is free, while Playa Mía charges between $12 (£6) for simple admission to $42 (£21) for the full all-inclusive package. Quieter versions of beach clubs are **Playa San Francisco** (no phone), **Paradise Beach** (no phone, next to Playa San Francisco), and **Playa Palancar** (no phone). All of these beaches are south of Chankanaab Park and easily visible from the road. Several have swimming pools with beach furniture, a restaurant, and snorkel rental. Most of these beaches cost around $5 (£2.50).

Once you get to the end of the island, the beach clubs become simple places where you can eat, drink, and lay out on the beach for free. **Paradise Cafe** is on the southern tip of the island across from Punta Sur Nature Park, and as you go up the eastern side of the island you pass **Playa Bonita, Chen Río,** and **Punta Morena** (not yet back in business on my last visit). Except on Sunday, when the locals head for the beaches, these places are practically deserted. Most of the east coast is unsafe for swimming because of the surf. The beaches tend to be small and occupy gaps in the rocky coast.

TOURS OF THE ISLAND

Travel agencies can arrange a variety of tours, including horseback, Jeep, and ATV tours. Taxi drivers charge $50 (£25) for a 4-hour tour of the island, which most people would consider only mildly amusing, depending on the driver's personality. The best horseback tours are offered at **Rancho Palmitas** (no phone) on the Costera Sur highway, across from the Occidental Cozumel resort. Unless you're staying in a resort on the south end, talk to the owners of **Cocos Cozumel** restaurant to arrange a tour (see the listing later in this chapter, making sure to note the limited hours). Rides can be from 1 to 2½ hours long and cost $20 to $30 (£10–£15).

OTHER ATTRACTIONS

MAYA RUINS   One of the most popular island excursions is to **San Gervasio** (100 B.C.–A.D. 1600). Follow the paved transversal road. You'll see the well-marked turnoff about halfway between town and the eastern coast. About 3km (2 miles) farther, pay the $6 (£3) fee to enter; still and video camera permits cost $5 (£2.50) each. A small tourist center at the entrance sells cold drinks and snacks. The ruins are open from 7am to 4pm.

When it comes to Cozumel's Maya ruins, getting there is most of the fun—do it for the mystique and for the trip, not for the size or scale of the ruins. The buildings, though preserved, are crudely made and would not be much of a tourist attraction if they were not the island's principal ruins. More significant than beautiful, this site was once an important ceremonial center where the Maya gathered, coming even from the mainland. The important deity was Ixchel, the goddess of weaving, women, child-birth, pilgrims, the moon, and medicine. Although you won't see any representations of Ixchel at San Gervasio today, Bruce Hunter, in his *Guide to Ancient Maya Ruins,* writes that priests hid behind a large pottery statue of her and became the voice of the goddess, speaking to pilgrims and answering their petitions. Ixchel was the wife of Itzamná, the sun god.

Guides charge $20 (£10) for a tour for one to six people. A better option is to find a copy of the green booklet *San Gervasio,* sold at local checkout counters and book-stores, and tour the site on your own. Seeing it takes 30 minutes. Taxi drivers offer a tour for about $30 (£15); the driver will wait for you outside the ruins.

A HISTORY MUSEUM   The **Museo de la Isla de Cozumel** ⌖, Avenida Rafael Melgar between calles 4 and 6 Norte (© **987/872-1475**), is more than just a nice place to spend a rainy hour. On the first floor an exhibit illustrates endangered species, the origin of the island, and its present-day topography and plant and animal life, including an explanation of coral formation. The second-floor galleries feature the his-tory of the town, artifacts from the island's pre-Hispanic sites, and Colonial-Era can-nons, swords, and ship paraphernalia. It's open daily from 9am to 5pm (but closes at 4pm on Sundays). Admission is $3 (£1.50). A rooftop restaurant serves breakfast and lunch (and you don't need to pay admission to eat there; p. 147).

GOLF   Cozumel has a new 18-hole course designed by Jack Nicklaus. It's at the **Cozumel Country Club** (© **987/872-9570**), north of San Miguel. Greens fees are $169 (£85) for a morning tee time, including cart rental and tax. Afternoon tee times cost $105 (£53). Tee times can be reserved 3 days in advance. A few hotels have spe-cial memberships with discounts for guests and advance tee times; guests at Playa Azul Golf and Beach Club pay no greens fees, but the cart costs $25 (£13).

TRIPS TO THE MAINLAND

PLAYA DEL CARMEN & XCARET   Going on your own to the nearby seaside vil-lage of **Playa del Carmen** and the **Xcaret** nature park is as easy as a quick ferry ride from Cozumel (for ferry information, see "Getting There & Departing," earlier in this chapter). For information on Playa and Xcaret, see chapter 7. Cozumel travel agencies offer an Xcaret tour that includes the ferry ride, transportation to the park, and the admission fee. The price is $100 (£55) for adults, $55 (£30) for kids. The tour is avail-able Monday through Saturday.

CHICHEN ITZA, TULUM & COBA   Travel agencies can arrange day trips to the ruins of **Chichén Itzá** ⌖⌖⌖ by air or bus. The ruins of **Tulum** ⌖, overlooking the Caribbean, and **Cobá** ⌖, in a dense jungle setting, are closer and cost less to visit. These latter two cities are quite a contrast to Chichén Itzá. Cobá is a large, mostly unrestored city beside a lake in a remote jungle setting, while Tulum is smaller, more compact, and right on the beach. It's more intact than Cobá. A trip to both Cobá and Tulum begins at 8am and returns around 6pm. A shorter, more relaxing excursion goes to Tulum and the nearby nature park of Xel-Ha.

SHOPPING

If you're looking for silver jewelry or souvenirs, go no farther than the town's coastal avenue, Rafael Melgar. Along this road you find one store after another—jewelry, souvenirs, and duty-free merchandise. But, if you're looking for something original, seek out a gallery and store called **Inspiración** (© 987/869-8293) on Avenida 5 between Rosado Salas and Calle 3. Owner Dianne Hartwig displays the creations of some of the best-known folk artists in the Yucatán—objects that are very hard to come by if you don't actually go the villages where many of these artists live. She also represents some talented contemporary local artists. Stores carrying Mexican handicrafts include **Los Cinco Soles** (© 987/872-2040), **Indigo** (© 987/872-1076), and **Viva México** (© 987/872-5466). All of these are on Avenida Rafael Melgar. There are also some import/export stores in the Punta Langosta Shopping Center in the southern part of town in front of the cruise ship pier. Prices for serapes, T-shirts, and the like are lower on the side streets off Avenida Melgar.

WHERE TO STAY

I've grouped Cozumel's hotels by location—**north** of town, **in town,** and **south** of town—and I describe them in that order. The prices I've quoted are rack rates and include the 12% tax. High season is from December to Easter. Expect rates from Christmas to New Year's to be still higher than the regular high-season rates quoted here. Low season is the rest of the year, though a few hotels raise their rates in August when Mexican families go on vacations.

All of the beach hotels in Cozumel, even the small ones, have deals with vacation packagers. Keep in mind that some packagers will offer last-minute deals to Cozumel with hefty discounts; if you're the flexible sort, keep an eye open for these.

Most hotels have an arrangement with a dive shop and offer dive packages. These can be good deals, but if you don't buy a dive package, it's quite okay to stay at one hotel and dive with a third-party operator—any dive boat can pull up to any hotel pier to pick up customers. Most dive shops won't pick up from the hotels north of town.

All the beach hotels suffered damage from the two hurricanes that passed through here. All were closed. Most took advantage of the closure to make upgrades to amenities and rooms. This is good news for those who come now. Some of the hotels in town are also remodeling, but nothing major.

As an alternative to a hotel, you can try **Cozumel Vacation Villas and Condos,** Av. Rafael Melgar 685 (between calles 3 and 5 Sur; © 800/224-5551 in the U.S., or 987/872-0729; www.cvvmexico.com), which offers accommodations by the week.

NORTH OF TOWN

Carretera Santa Pilar, or San Juan, is the name of Avenida Rafael Melgar's northern extension. All the hotels lie close to each other on the beach side of the road a short distance from town and the airport.

Very Expensive

Playa Azul Golf-Scuba-Spa ✦✦✦   This quiet hotel is perhaps the most relaxing of the island's properties. It's smaller than the others, and service is personal. It's an excellent choice for golfers; guests pay no greens fees, only cart rental. The hotel's small, sandy beach with shade *palapas* has a quiet little beach bar. Almost all the rooms have balconies and ocean views. The units in the original section are all suites—very large, with oversize bathrooms with showers. The new wing has mostly standard rooms that are comfortable and large. The corner rooms are master suites and have large balconies with Jacuzzis overlooking the sea. If you prefer lots of space over having a Jacuzzi, opt for a suite in the original building. Rooms contain a king-size bed or two double beds; some suites offer two convertible single sofas in the separate living room. The hotel also offers deep-sea- and fly-fishing trips.

Carretera San Juan Km 4, 77600 Cozumel, Q. Roo. ℂ 987/869-5160 or -5165. Fax 987/869-5173. www.playa-azul.com. 50 units. High season $263 (£132) double, $314–$364 (£157–£182) suite; low season $196–$202 (£98–£101) double, $246–$342 (£123–£171) suite. Rates include unlimited golf and full breakfast. Internet specials available. AE, MC, V. Free guarded parking. **Amenities:** Restaurant; 2 bars; medium-size outdoor pool; unlimited golf privileges at Cozumel Country Club; spa; dive shop; watersports gear rental; game room; tour info; room service; in-room massage; babysitting; laundry service, nonsmoking rooms. *In room:* A/C, TV, fridge, coffeemaker, hair dryer, safe.

Expensive

Condumel Condobeach Apartments
If you want some distance from the crowds, consider lodging here. It's not a full-service hotel, but in some ways it's more convenient. The one-bedroom apartments are designed and furnished in practical fashion—airy, with sliding glass doors that face the sea and allow for good cross-ventilation (especially in the upper units). They also have ceiling fans, air-conditioning, and two twin beds or one king-size. Each apartment has a separate living room and a full kitchen with a partially stocked fridge, so you don't have to run to the store on the first day. There's a small, well-tended beach area (with shade *palapas* and a grill for guests' use) that leads to a low, rocky fall-off into the sea.

Carretera Hotelera Norte s/n, 77600 Cozumel, Q. Roo. ℂ **987/872-0892.** Fax 987/872-0661. www.condumel.com. 10 units. High season $160 (£80) double; low season $134 (£67) double. No credit cards. *In room:* A/C, kitchen, no phone.

IN TOWN

Staying in town is not like staying in Playa del Carmen, where you can walk to the beach. The oceanfront in town is too busy for swimming, and there's no beach, only the *malecón*. Prices are considerably lower, but you'll have to drive or take a cab to the beach; it's pretty easy. English is spoken in almost all of the hotels.

Moderate

Hacienda San Miguel ⋆ 𝘝𝘢𝘭𝘶𝘦
This is a peaceful hotel built in Mexican colonial style around a large garden courtyard. The property is well maintained and the service is good. It's located a half block from the shoreline on the town's north side. Rooms are large and attractive and come with equipped kitchens, including full-size refrigerators. Most of the studios have a queen-size bed or two doubles. The junior suites have more living area and come with a queen-size and a twin bed. The two-bedroom suite comes with four double beds.

Calle 10 Norte 500 (between Rafael Melgar and Av. 5), 77600 Cozumel, Q. Roo. ℂ **866/712-6387** in the U.S., or 987/872-1986. Fax 987/872-7036. www.haciendasanmiguel.com. 11 units. High season $105 (£53) studio, $120 (£60) junior suite, $165 (£83) 2-bedroom suite; low season $90 (£45) studio, $105 (£53) junior suite, $136 (£68) 2-bedroom suite. Rates include continental breakfast and free entrance to Mr. Sancho's beach club. MC, V. Guarded parking on street. **Amenities:** Tour info; car rental. *In room:* A/C, TV, kitchen, hair dryer, safe, no phone.

Vista del Mar ⋆
This hotel is located on the town's shoreline boulevard. All the rooms in front have ocean views. The balconies are large enough to be enjoyable and are furnished with a couple of chairs. Rooms are a little larger than your standard room, with better lighting than you find in most of the hotels in town. They are simply furnished and decorated, but come with several amenities. Bathrooms are medium-size or

a little smaller and have showers. The rooms in back go for $10 (£5.50) less than the oceanview rooms and look out over a small pool and large Jacuzzi.

Av. Rafael Melgar 45 (between Calles 5 and 7 Sur), 77600 Cozumel, Q. Roo. © **888/309-9988** in the U.S., or 987/872-0545. Fax 987/872-7036. www.hotelvistadelmar.com. 20 units. High season $90–$100 (£45–£50) double; low season $80–$90 (£40–£45). Discounts sometimes available. AE, MC, V. Limited street parking. **Amenities:** Bar; outdoor pool; Jacuzzi; tour info; car rental; in-room massage; laundry service. *In room:* A/C, TV, fridge, hair dryer, safe.

Inexpensive
La Casona Real *Value*   Five blocks from the waterfront, this two-story hotel is a bargain for those wanting a hotel with a pool. The rooms are small to medium in size but modern and attractive and come with good air conditioning. The hotel underwent a complete remodeling after the hurricanes. Management changed, too. Rooms are attractive and come with two double beds or one king-size (costing $10/£5 less). The beds are comfortable. Bathrooms are medium in size. A courtyard with an oval pool is on the west side of the building. This is not the quietest of properties. Next door is a club that opens on weekends with drag queen shows from Acapulco (p. 148). On the other side of the hotel is a fairly busy street.

Av. Juárez 501, 77600 Cozumel, Q. Roo. © **987/872-5471.** 14 units. $45–$55 (£23–£28) double. Discounts sometimes available in low season. No credit cards. Limited street parking. **Amenities:** Medium-size outdoor pool. *In room:* A/C, TV, no phone.

Suites Vima *Value*   This three-story hotel is 4 blocks from the main square. It offers large, plainly furnished rooms for a good price. The lighting is okay, the showers are good, and every room comes with its own fridge, which for island visitors can be a handy feature. The rooms are fairly quiet. Choose between two doubles or one king bed. There is no restaurant, but there is a pool and lounge area. As is the case with other small hotels on the island, the staff at the front desk doesn't speak English. Reservations through e-mail can be made in English. This is one of the few hotels in town that doesn't use high season/low season rates.

Av. 10 Norte between Calles 4 and 6, 77600 Cozumel, Q. Roo. © **987/872-5118.** suitesvima@hotmail.com. 12 units. $55 (£28) double. No credit cards. Limited street parking. **Amenities:** Pool. *In room:* A/C, fridge.

SOUTH OF TOWN
The hotels in this area tend to be more spread out and farther from town than hotels to the north. Some are on the inland side of the road; some are on the beach side, which means a difference in price. Those farthest from town are all-inclusive properties. The beaches tend to be slightly better than those to the north, but all the hotels have swimming pools and piers from which you can snorkel, and all of them accommodate divers. Head south on Avenida Rafael Melgar, which becomes the coastal road **Costera Sur** (also called Carretera a Chankanaab).

Very Expensive
Presidente InterContinental Cozumel *ƒƒƒ*   Palatial in scale and modern in style, the Presidente spreads out across a long stretch of coast with only distant hotels for neighbors. The rooms have all been redesigned top to bottom, and the smallest rooms were eliminated. Another pool has been added with a larger pool area. Rooms come in three categories depending mostly on location—pool view, ocean view, and beach front. All come with such offerings as a pillow menu. A terrace or a balcony offers the indoor/outdoor mix that's so enjoyable in a beach hotel. Downstairs rooms are beachfront, ocean suites, and reef rooms (larger and practically right up to the water), upstairs are ocean view. Rooms are oversize and have large, beautifully finished

bathrooms. A long stretch of sandy beach, dotted with *palapas* and palm trees, fronts the entire hotel. This property is now a member of Leading Hotels of the World.

Costera Sur Km 6.5, 77600 Cozumel, Q. Roo. © 800/327-0200 in the U.S., or 987/872-9500. Fax 987/872-9528. www.intercontinentalcozumel.com. 220 units. High season $318 (£159) pool view, $382 (£191) ocean view, $503 (£252) and up for beach fronts and suites; low season $254–$301 (£127–£156) pool view, $299–$346 (£150–£173) ocean view, $322–$466 (£161–£233) and up for beach fronts and suites. Internet specials sometimes available. AE, MC, V. Free valet parking. **Amenities:** 3 restaurants; 4 bars; 2 outdoor pools; wading pool; access to golf club; 2 lighted tennis courts; fully equipped fitness center; spa; dive shop; watersports equipment rental; children's club; concierge; tour desk; car rental; business center; shopping arcade; room service; 24-hr. butler service in reef section; in-room massage; babysitting; laundry service; dry cleaning; nonsmoking rooms. *In room:* A/C, TV w/pay movies, Wi-Fi, minibar, coffeemaker, hair dryer, safe.

Expensive

El Cantil Condominiums 🖈🖈 A condo property on the south side of town that rents out 30 (of the 45 total) units by the night or the week. This place is worth consideration because it's an attractive property with large rooms and convenient location. The shore here is rocky, but there's a sandy area for guests and a beautiful seaside pool and Jacuzzi, as well as a boat dock and easy entry into the sea. Extras include free long-distance calls to the U.S.

Av. Rafael Melgar, between calles 13 and 15. 77600 Cozumel, Q. Roo. © 954/323-8491 in the U.S., or 987/869-1517. Fax 987/869-2053. www.elcantilcondos.com. 30 units. $170–$200 (£85–£100) studio, $260–$310 (£130–£155) 1-bedroom, $320–$370 (£160–£185) 2-bedroom. AE, DISC, MC, V. Free sheltered parking. **Amenities:** Restaurant (see "Where to Dine," below); bar; heated outdoor pool; saltwater Jacuzzi; watersports equipment rental; concierge; tour desk; car rental, business center; room service; laundry service and coin-op laundry; nonsmoking rooms. *In room:* A/C, TV, Wi-Fi or high-speed Internet, kitchens in all but studio units, hair dryer, safe.

WHERE TO DINE

The island offers a number of good restaurants. Taxi drivers will often steer you toward restaurants that pay them commissions; don't heed their advice.

Zermatt (© 987/872-1384), a nice little bakery, is on Avenida 5 at Calle 4 Norte. **Le Chef** (© 987/876-3437), at Avenida 5 and Calle 5 Sur, is a deli/gourmet food store. It has a daily menu of salads, pizzas, and prepared foods, as well as cold meats, cheeses, baguettes, and other makings for a picnic. For inexpensive local fare during the day, I like **Comida Casera Toñita** (© 987/872-0401), at Calle Rosado Salas 265 between avenidas 10 and 15. It closes at 6pm. For morning tacos of *cochinita pibil* (traditionally a breakfast item), go to **El Amigo Mario** (© 987/872-0742) on Calle 5 Sur, between Francisco Mújica and Avenida 35. The doors close at half-past noon.

Finally, there's a new restaurant in town called **The Wynston** (© 987/869-1517). It's on the top floor of El Cantil condos and has great views of the ocean. The owner also owns Prima. It had opened when I was last in Cozumel, but I didn't get a chance to try it. The menu is mostly steaks and seafood; main courses run from $18 to $40 (£9–£20). Definitely make reservations in high season.

VERY EXPENSIVE

Cabaña del Pescador (Lobster House) 🖈🖈 LOBSTER Lobster is the main attraction here. You select a lobster tail, and brothers Fernando or Enrique will weigh it, boil it with a hint of spices, and serve it with melted butter, accompanied by sides of rice, vegetables, and bread. Does lobster require anything more? This is the only thing on the menu on Fernando's side of the restaurant, but Enrique will cook up steaks, shrimp, or fish if you don't feel like lobster. The setting is quite tropical—a pair of thatched bungalows bordering a pond with lily pads and reeds, traversed by a small footbridge. The rooms are softly lit with the glow of candles and furnished with rustic tables and chairs. A year later, you could still see some of the marks left by Hurricane Wilma, but the Cabaña del Pescador has lost none of its charm. The restaurant rambles around quite a bit, so explore until you find the spot most to your taste.

Carretera Santa Pilar Km 4 (across from Playa Azul Hotel). No phone. Reservations not accepted. Lobster (by weight) $25–$40 (£13–£20). No credit cards. Daily 6–10:30pm.

EXPENSIVE

French Quarter ✿✿ SOUTHERN   You can dine very well here in a comfortable upstairs open-air setting. The owners are from Louisiana and care a great deal about food. You can order Southern and Creole classics, such as jambalaya and étouffée, or you can order the daily catch stuffed or blackened, or choose a steak of imported Black Angus beef. I tried a filet mignon with red-onion marmalade, which was delicious. The downstairs bar is a popular hangout for many locals.

Av. 5 Sur 18. ✆ 987/872-6321. Reservations recommended during Carnaval. Main courses $10–$30 (£5–£15). AE, MC, V. Wed–Mon 5–11pm.

Guido's ✿✿ MEDITERRANEAN   The inviting interior, with director's chairs and rustic wood tables, makes this a restful place in daytime and a romantic spot at night. The specialty is oven-baked pizzas. Also keep an eye out for the daily specials, which may include an appetizer of sea bass carpaccio, a couple of meat dishes, and usually a fish dish, depending on what the daily catch is. The other thing that people love here is the *pan de ajo*—a house creation of bread made with olive oil, garlic, and rosemary. There's a good wine list.

Av. Rafael Melgar, between calles 6 and 8 Norte. ✆ 987/872-0946. Reservations accepted. Main courses $13–$21 (£7.15–£12); pizzas $12–$13 (£6.60–£7.15). AE, MC, V. Mon–Sat 11am–11pm.

La Cocay ✿✿✿ SEAFOOD/MEDITERRANEAN   This kitchen serves the most original cooking on the island. The dining room and outdoor courtyard, modern in style and softly lit, make for a comfortable ambience. I tried a few *tapas* for appetizers, and they were beautifully seasoned concoctions of garbanzos, chorizo, bell peppers, panela cheese, and sun-dried tomatoes on small slices of bread. For a main course, try the subtle and tender grilled fish in lavender sauce. The choice of meat dishes is usually good. And give special consideration to the daily specials and the wonderful chocolate torte. It takes a little extra time to prepare, so order it early.

Calle 8 Norte 208 (between avs. 10 and 15). ✆ 987/872-5533. Reservations recommended. Main courses $9–$30 (£4.50–£15). AE, MC, V. Mon–Sat 1:30–11pm.

Prima ✿✿✿ ITALIAN   Everything at this ever-popular hangout is fresh—pastas, vegetables, and seafood. The menu changes daily and concentrates on seafood. It might include shrimp scampi, fettuccine with pesto, and lobster and crab ravioli with cream sauce. The fettuccine Alfredo is wonderful, the salads crisp, and the steaks are Black Angus beef. Pizzas are cooked in a wood-burning oven. Desserts include Key lime pie and tiramisu. The food and the service are consistently good here. Dining is upstairs on an open-air terrace.

Calle Rosado Salas 109A (corner of Av. 5) ✆ 987/872-4242. Reservations recommended during high season. Pizzas and pastas $6–$14 (£3–£7); seafood $12–$20 (£6–£10); steaks $15–$20 (£7.50–£10). AE, MC, V. Daily 4:30–10pm.

MODERATE

Capicúa TAPAS/SEAFOOD   A new restaurant for the island, Capicúa looks to attract customers bored with the usual run of the island's restaurants with some original cooking. The selection of *tapas* varies, but usually includes such things as smoked duck or abalone. And for those wanting something closer to comfort food there are barbecued chicken wings or shrimp *al ajillo* (with garlic and strips of toasted *guajillo* chile). I enjoyed the mahimahi encrusted with white and black sesame seeds, which was cooked just right. Salads can be had, too. There is an okay selection of wines and a full bar. The house in which the restaurant is located is decorated with a sense of humor; choose between a dining room with one of those beautiful, old tile floors and an old patio sheltered by a large tamarind tree.

Calle 10 Norte 299 (corner of Av. 15). *C* **987/869-8265**. Reservations accepted. Tapas $4–$10 (£2–£5); main courses $10–$15 (£5–£7.50). MC, V. Tues–Sun 5pm–midnight.

El Moro ⭐ *Value* REGIONAL   El Moro is an out-of-the-way place that has been around for a long time and has always been popular with the locals, who come for the food, the service, and the prices—but not the decor, which is orange, orange, orange, and Formica. Get there by taxi, which will cost a couple of bucks. Portions are generous. Any of the shrimp dishes use the real jumbo variety when available. For something different, try the *pollo Ticuleño,* a specialty from the town of Ticul, a layered dish of tomato sauce, mashed potatoes, crispy baked corn tortillas, and fried chicken breast, topped with shredded cheese and green peas. Other specialties include enchiladas and seafood prepared many ways, plus grilled steaks and sandwiches.

75 bis Norte 124 (between calles 2 and 4 Norte). *C* **987/872-3029**. Reservations not accepted. Main courses $5–$15 (£2.50–£7.50). MC, V. Fri–Wed 1–11pm.

La Choza ⭐ YUCATECAN/MEXICAN   For Mexican food, I like this place, and so do a lot of locals. Platters of poblano chiles stuffed with shrimp, grilled *brochetas* (kebobs), and *pollo en relleno negro* (chicken in a sauce of blackened chiles) are among the specialties. The table sauces and guacamole are great, and the daily specials can be good, too. This is an open-air restaurant with well-spaced tables under a tall thatched roof. Breakfasts are good as well.

Rosado Salas 198 (at Av. 10 Sur). *C* **987/872-0958**. Reservations accepted for groups of 6 or more. Breakfast $4 (£2.20); main courses $10–$16 (£5–£8). AE, MC, V. Daily 7am–10pm.

INEXPENSIVE

Cocos Cozumel MEXICAN/AMERICAN   Cocos offers the largest breakfast menu on the island, including all the American and Mexican classics, from *huevos divorciados* (fried eggs on corn tortillas) to ham and eggs. Indulge in such stateside favorites as hash browns, corn flakes and bananas, gigantic blueberry muffins, cinnamon rolls, and bagels, or go for something with tropical ingredients, such as a blended fruit drink. The service and the food are excellent. The American and Mexican owners, Terri and Daniel Ocejo, are good folk and can set you up with a horseback ride or a fishing or snorkeling trip.

Av. 5 Sur 180 (1 block south of the main plaza). *C* **987/872-0241**. Breakfast $4–$6 (£2–£3). No credit cards. Tues–Sun 6am–noon. Closed Sept–Oct.

Restaurant del Museo BREAKFAST/MEXICAN   The most pleasant place in San Miguel for breakfast or lunch (weather permitting) is at this rooftop cafe above the island's museum. It offers a serene view of the water, removed from the traffic noise below and sheltered from the sun above. Choices are limited to American and Mexican breakfast staples, and lunch dishes such as sandwiches and enchiladas.

Av. Rafael Melgar (corner of Calle 6 Norte). *C* **987/872-0838**. Reservations not accepted. Breakfast $4–$5 (£2–£2.50); lunch main courses $5–$10 (£2.50–£5). No credit cards. Daily 7am–2pm.

COZUMEL AFTER DARK

Most of the music and dance venues are along Avenida Rafael Melgar. **Carlos 'n' Charlie's** (© **987/869-1648** or -1646), which is in the Punta Langosta shopping center, practically next to **Señor Frog's** (© **987/869-1650**). Punta Langosta is just south of Calle 7 Sur. The **Hard Rock Cafe** (© **987/872-5271**) is also on Avenida Rafael Melgar, at #2, just north of the municipal pier.

In town, there are a few Latin music clubs. These open and close with every high season. They do well when people have cash in their pockets, but then they have to close down when the flow of tourism stops bringing in money. There's a sports bar at the corner of Avenida 5 and Calle 2 Norte called **All Sports Bar** (© **987/869-2246**), which operates as a salsa club Thursday to Saturday from 10pm to 3am. So go for sports, stay for salsa. Also, there's a working-class night club on Avenida Juárez, between avenidas 25 and 30, called **Los Delfines** (no phone), which puts on drag shows from Thursday to Sunday. These start around 11pm.

On Sunday evenings, the place to be is the main square, which usually has a free concert and lots of people strolling about and visiting with friends.

The town of San Miguel has three **movie theaters.** Your best option is **Cinépolis,** the modern multicinema in the Chedraui Plaza Shopping Center at the south end of town. It mainly shows Hollywood movies. Most of these are in English with Spanish subtitles *(película subtitulada);* before buying your tickets, make sure the movie hasn't been dubbed *(doblada).*

7

The Caribbean Coast: The Riviera Maya, Including Playa del Carmen & the Costa Maya

by David Baird

Famously distinguished by its soft white sand and turquoise water, the Yucatán's Caribbean coast stretches 380km (236 miles) from Cancún all the way to Chetumal, at the border with Belize.

The world's second-longest reef system protects most of the shoreline. Where the reef breaks, you find good beaches in the gaps, such as Playa del Carmen, Xpu-Ha, and Tulum. Surf action cleans away silt and sea grass and erodes rocks here, leaving the bottom sandy.

Where the reef is prominent, you get good snorkeling and diving, with lots of fish and other sea creatures. Here mangrove often lines the shore, and beaches are usually sandy up to the water's edge but shallow, with a silty or rocky floor.

The northern half of the coast is now known as the "Riviera Maya"; the southern half, the "Costa Maya." In between is the large Sian Ka'an Biosphere Reserve. Inland you'll find jungle, caverns, cenotes (limestone wells that lead to an underwater river), and the better known ruins of the Maya.

Activities abound, as do lodging options. On this coast you can stay in a variety of communities or distance yourself from all of them. Just about every type of accommodations you can think of is a possibility: rustic cabins, secluded spa resorts, boutique hotels, B&Bs, or all-inclusive megaresorts. With so many options, you'll need to make some tough calls. I hope that what follows will help you decide.

EXPLORING MEXICO'S CARIBBEAN COAST

A single road, Highway 307, runs down the coast from Cancún to Chetumal. The section between Cancún's airport and Playa del Carmen (51km/32 miles) is a four-lane divided highway with speed limits up to 110kmph (68 mph). There are a couple of traffic lights and several reduced-speed zones around the major turnoffs. From Playa to Tulum (80km/50 miles) expect road construction, as the government is widening the highway to four lanes. The project is complete as far south as Paamul, and as of the time of this writing, construction is ongoing around Akumal. It still takes about 1½ hours to drive from the Cancún airport to Tulum.

From Tulum, the highway turns inland to skirt the edges of Sian Ka'an. The roadway is narrower, without shoulders, and in some areas the forest crowds in on both sides. The speed limit is mostly 80kmph (50 mph), but you'll need to slow down where the road passes through villages, and keep an eye out for *topes* (speed bumps). After the town of Limones, new road construction has widened and smoothed the highway. To drive from Tulum to Chetumal takes 3 hours.

COASTAL STOPS NORTH TO SOUTH

PUERTO MORELOS   This town between Cancún and Playa remains a little village affectionately known by the locals as "Muerto Morelos" (*muerto* means "dead"), for its phenomenally quiet low season. It has a few small hotels and rental houses, and nearby are a few secluded spa resorts. The coast is sandy and well protected by an off-shore reef, which means good snorkeling and diving nearby, but the lack of surf means sea grass and shallow water. If you're looking for good swimming, head farther down the coast. If you're looking for a relaxing seaside retreat with a clean beach in an easy-going community, this will work for you.

PLAYA DEL CARMEN   Playa, as it is called, is the most happening place on the coast—a delightful beach (especially when the wind and currents are flowing in the right direction), hotels for every budget, a good choice of restaurants, and an active nightlife, most of which is on or around Quinta Avenida (Fifth Avenue), Playa's well-known promenade. In the last few years, the town has grown quickly, and local residents and the tourism board are working to keep it from becoming a smaller version of Cancún.

PUERTO AVENTURAS   The first major town south of Playa is a modern condo-marina development with a 9-hole golf course, several restaurants, and a few hotels. I don't think it's a fun place to stay, but you might come here to go deep-sea fishing or swim with dolphins.

AKUMAL   A bit farther south are Akumal and Half Moon Bay. The community is relatively old for this shore, which means that it's already built up and doesn't have the boomtown feel of Playa and Tulum. Akumal has a strong ecological orientation and is a prominent scuba and snorkeling center. The locals are a mix of Americans and Mexicans who enjoy the unhurried lifestyle of the tropics, making this a good place to relax and work on your hammock technique. There are a few hotels; most of the lodging is rental houses and condos. Consequently, the town is a favorite with families who enjoy the calmness of the place and can save money by buying groceries and cooking for themselves.

TULUM   The town of Tulum (near the ruins of the same name) has a hotel district of about 30 *palapa* (palm-leaf roofed) hotels, which stretch down the coast of the Punta Allen peninsula. A few years ago, it was mainly a destination for backpacker types, but with some of the most beautiful beaches on this coast and many improvements in hotel amenities, it now attracts people with big budgets. Here you can enjoy the beach in relative solitude and quiet (unless your hotel is busy building additional rooms). The downside of this is that Tulum doesn't have the variety of restaurants that Playa and Cancún do, but you can still eat well.

COSTA MAYA   South of Tulum lies the large Sian Ka'an Biosphere Reserve and, beyond that, what is known as the Costa Maya, which designates the rest of the coast all the way down to Belize. The Costa Maya is a relaxing getaway. Most of the coast is along the Majahual Peninsula, which has a lot of sandy beaches with silt bottoms. It's attractive to scuba divers, snorkelers, fly fishermen, and people who want to get away from the crowds. Farther south is Lake Bacalar, a large, clear freshwater lake. Inland from here are the impressive Maya ruins of the Río Bec area.

The Yucatán's Upper Caribbean Coast

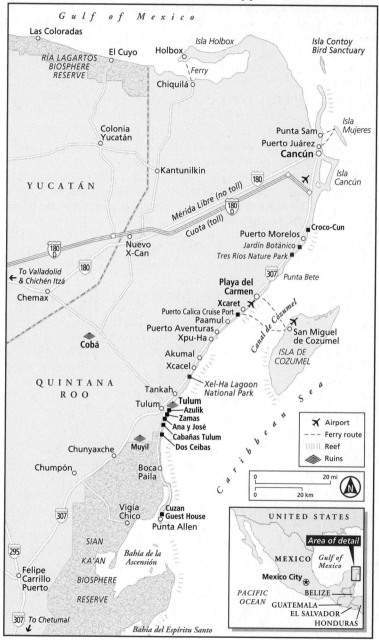

Gulf of Mexico

Las Coloradas

RÍA LAGARTOS BIOSPHERE RESERVE

El Cuyo

Holbox

Isla Holbox

Ferry

Chiquilá

Isla Contoy Bird Sanctuary

Colonia Yucatán

Punta Sam

Isla Mujeres

Puerto Juárez

Cancún

Kantunilkin

YUCATÁN

Isla Cancún

Mérida Libre (no toll)

Cuota (toll)

Nuevo X-Can

Croco-Cun

Puerto Morelos

Jardín Botánico

Tres Ríos Nature Park

To Valladolid & Chichén Itzá

Chemax

Punta Bete

Playa del Carmen

Xcaret

Puerto Calica Cruise Port

Paamul

Puerto Aventuras

Xpu-Ha

Cobá

San Miguel de Cozumel

Canal de Cozumel

ISLA DE COZUMEL

Akumal

Xcacel

QUINTANA ROO

Tankah

Xel-Ha Lagoon National Park

Tulum

Tulum

Azulik

Zamas

Ana y José

Cabañas Tulum

Dos Ceibas

Chunyaxche

Muyil

Chumpón

Boca Paila

Caribbean Sea

✈ Airport
--- Ferry route
||||| Reef
🔺 Ruins

0   20 mi
0   20 km

N

SIAN

Vigía Chico

Cuzan Guest House

Punta Allen

KA'AN

Bahía de la Ascensión

BIOSPHERE

Felipe Carrillo Puerto

RESERVE

To Chetumal

Bahía del Espíritu Santo

UNITED STATES

Area of detail

MEXICO

Gulf of Mexico

Mexico City

BELIZE

PACIFIC OCEAN

GUATEMALA
EL SALVADOR
HONDURAS

THINGS TO DO ALONG THE RIVIERA MAYA

If you need a break from lounging on the beach, you can find plenty of activities up and down this coast. The following is a brief list to help you consider your options.

DAY SPA To relax after all that exertion, try **Spa Itzá**. It's in downtown Playa between calles 12 and 14 in a retail area called Calle Corazón. The phone number is © **984/803-2588.**

DEEP-SEA FISHING The largest marina on the coast is at **Puerto Aventuras,** not far south of Playa. Here's where you'll find most of your options for boating and fishing. See p. 168.

FLY FISHING The **Boca Paila Fishing Lodge** (www.bocapaila.com) specializes in fly-fishing, with weeklong all-inclusive fishing packages.

GOLF & TENNIS The Playacar Golf Club (© **984/873-4990;** www.palace-resorts.com/playacar-golf-club) has an 18-hole **golf course** designed by Robert von Hagge. It's run by the Palace Resorts hotel chain, which offers golf packages. Greens fees are $180 (£90) in the morning (including tax and cart) and $120 (£60) after 2pm; club rental costs $30 (£15). The club also has two **tennis** courts, which cost $10 (£5) per hour. If you stay at one of the Mayakoba resort hotels, you'll have access to a course designed by Greg Norman, which hosts a PGA tour event. See www.mayakoba.com.

HORSEBACK RIDING A few places along the highway offer horseback rides. The best of these, **Rancho Punta Venado,** is just south of Playa, past the Calica Pier. This ranch is less touristy than the others, and the owner takes good care of his horses. It has a nice stretch of coast with a sheltered bay and offers kayaking and snorkeling outings. It's best to make arrangements in advance and tell them you're a Frommer's reader, so that they can schedule you on a day when they have fewer customers. E-mail (ptavenado@yahoo.com) is the best way to reach them; sometimes they don't answer their office number © **984/803-5224.** Another option is to call the ranch's cellphone from Mexico (© **044-984/116-3213**); there is a charge for the call. Talk to Gabriela or Francisco; both speak English. Or try dropping by. The turn-off for the ranch is 2km (1¼ miles) south of the Calica overpass near Km 279.

SCUBA & SNORKELING In Playa, **Tank-Ha Dive Center** (© **984/873-0302;** www.tankha.com) arranges reef and cavern diving. Snorkeling trips cost around $40 (£20) per person. Two-tank dive trips are $70 (£35); resort courses with SSI and PADI instructors cost $110 (£55). The area around Akumal has a number of underwater caverns and cenotes that are popular scuba and snorkeling destinations. The **Akumal Dive Shop** specializes in cavern diving and offers a variety of dives. But the easiest way to try cavern diving or snorkeling is through **Hidden Worlds Cenotes,** which is right on the highway, 15km (9 miles) south of Akumal. They provide everything, including wet suit. See "South of Playa del Carmen," later in this chapter.

SWIMMING WITH DOLPHINS In the two nature parks south of Playa, Xcaret and Xel-Ha, you can interact with these intelligent creatures. Also, there's an outfit in Puerto Aventuras called **Dolphin Discovery** that is quite good. See "South of Playa del Carmen," later in this chapter, and "Swimming with Dolphins," p. 167.

TOURS From Playa and the rest of the coast there are tours to all of the ruins mentioned below. The tour buses usually stop at a few places along the way for refreshments and souvenirs, which is why I prefer the small tours. Some combine the ruins of Tulum with a visit to a nature park. A tour agency in Playa called **Alltournative** (© **800/507-1902** in the U.S. and Canada or 984/803-9999; www. alltournative.com) offers small tours that combine a little of everything: culture (visit a contemporary Maya village), adventure (kayaking, rappelling, snorkeling, cenote diving), natural history, and ruins. It offers these tours daily using vans for transportation. The tours are fun. You can call the agency directly or arrange a tour through your hotel; they pick up at most of the large resorts along the coast. **Selvática** (© **866/552-8825** in the U.S. or 998/898-4312; www.selvatica.com.mx), operating out of offices in Cancún, offers guests a little adventure tourism in the jungle, with 2.5km (1½ miles) of zip lines strung up in the forest canopy. The tour also includes biking and swimming in cenotes. In high season you should make your reservation a month before your trip. The $70–$80 (£35–£40) cost includes transportation, activities, a light lunch, locker, and all equipment. Another interesting option is an ecological tour of the **Sian Ka'an Biosphere Reserve.** To do this, however, you have to get to Tulum. See the Tulum section, later in this chapter.

VISITING THE RUINED CITIES OF THE MAYA   Four cities are within easy reach of Playa and most of the coast. The easiest to access is **Tulum** (see Tulum, Punta Allen & Sian Ka'an, below). A half-hour inland from Tulum on a pock-marked road is **Cobá** (see Cobá below), rising up from a jungle setting. This city has not been reconstructed to the same degree as the other three and doesn't have the rich imagery or clearly delineated architecture. The other two cites, **Chichén Itzá** and **Ek Balam,** are 2½ hours distant in the interior of the peninsula. My favorite way to see them is to rent a car and drive to Chichén in the afternoon, check into a hotel (perhaps one with a pool), see the sound-and-light show that evening, and then tour the ruins in the cool of the morning before the big bus tours arrive. Then drive back via Valladolid and Ek Balam. See chapter 8 for a description of these places.

XCARET & XEL-HA NATURE PARKS   These parks make full-day excursions, offering opportunities for swimming, snorkeling, and other seaside activities, and educational tours about the region's natural history and local Maya culture and entertainment. They are completely self-contained and offer food, drink, watersports equipment, and various kinds of merchandise. Xcaret is just south of Playa, while Xel-Ha is farther south, almost to Tulum. (See section 3, later in this chapter.)

Cozumel is a half-hour away by ferry from Playa, but it makes for a poor day trip unless you simply want to shop. You'll see exactly what the cruise-ship passengers see—lots of duty-free, souvenir, and jewelry stores. To enjoy Cozumel best, you have to spend at least a couple of nights there to explore the island. See chapter 6.

1 Puerto Morelos & Vicinity

BETWEEN CANCUN & PLAYA DEL CARMEN

The coast directly south of the Cancún airport has several roadside attractions, all-inclusive hotels, small cabaña hotels, and some spa resorts. Much of the latest development is targeting the well-heeled traveler—small luxury hotels with or without a marina and with or without a golf course. This stretch of coast between the airport and Playa del Carmen is only 51km (32 miles) long. Midway is Puerto Morelos.

ROADSIDE ATTRACTIONS   Near the Puerto Morelos turnoff is **Rancho Loma Bonita,** which has all the markings of a tourist trap and offers horseback riding and ATV tours. For this sort of activity, I prefer Rancho Punta Venado, just south of Playa (see "Things to Do Along the Riviera Maya" earlier in this chapter). You'll also come across **Jardín Botánico Dr. Alfredo Barrera** (no phone). Opened in 1990 and named after a biologist who studied tropical forests, the botanical garden is open Monday to Saturday from 9am to 5pm. Admission is $7 (£3.50). This place is disappointing because it's not maintained well. It will be of most interest to gardeners and plant enthusiasts, but it will probably bore children. They are much more likely to enjoy the interactive zoo, **CrocoCun** (© **998/850-3719**), a zoological park a mile north of Puerto Morelos. It raises crocodiles from eggs and keeps several species of animals native to the Yucatán Peninsula. A visit to the reptile house is fascinating, though it may make you wary of venturing into the jungle. The rattlesnakes and boa constrictors are particularly intimidating, and the tarantulas are downright enormous. The guided tour lasts 1½ hours. The guides have great enthusiasm, and the spider monkeys and wild pigs entrance kids. Wear plenty of bug repellent. The onsite restaurant, CrocoCun, is open daily from 8:30am to 5:30pm. Entrance fees are high: $18 (£9) adults, $12 (£6) children 6 to 12, free for children younger than 6.

NEW GOLF RESORT

Competition for the luxury tourism market has heated up with the arrival of **Mayakoba.** They started with a golf course designed by Greg Norman. Then they organized a PGA tour event here in 2007—the first PGA tournament ever in Mexico. And they've lined up a dazzling collection of resort properties: Fairmount, Viceroy, Rosewood, and Banyan Tree. When I visited, only the Fairmount was open, but the rest were going to be in operation by 2008. The resorts are designed to be a kind of connected endeavor—guests of one resort can sample the amenities of the other three, including restaurants and spas. For more information, check out www.mayakoba.com.

SPA RESORTS 🏵🏵🏵

In the area around Puerto Morelos, four spa resorts provide variations on the hedonistic resort experience. Only 20 to 30 minutes from the Cancún airport, they are well situated for a quick weekend escape from the daily grind. You can jet down to Cancún, get whisked away by the hotel car, and be on the beach with a cocktail in hand before you can figure out whether you crossed a time zone. All four resorts pride themselves on their service, amenities, and spa and salon treatments. Being in the Yucatán, they add the healing practices of the Maya, especially the use of *temazcal,* the native steam bath. Rates quoted below include taxes but not the 5% to 10% service charge.

Ceiba del Mar   This resort consists of seven three-story buildings set on a landscape of ponds and pools. Two years ago, the rooftop sections were converted to penthouses, and the other rooms were remodeled. Rooms are large with a terrace or balcony. Bathrooms are large, with a shower and tub and stone counters. Service remains the same—attentive and unobtrusive—exemplified by the morning coffee and juice delivery, accomplished without disturbing the guests through the use of a blind pass-through. The spa area is ample, quite attractive, and well designed.

Av. Niños Héroes s/n, 77580 Puerto Morelos, Q. Roo. © 877/545-6221 in the U.S., or 998/872-8060. Fax 998/872-8061. www.ceibadelmar.com. 88 units. High season $460–$515 (£230–£258) deluxe and junior suite, from $884 (£442) suite; low season $436–$492 (£218–£246) deluxe and junior suite, from $822 (£411) suite. Rates include continental breakfast. Spa packages available. AE, MC, V. Free parking. **Amenities:** 2 restaurants; 2 bars; 2 outdoor pools (1 heated); lighted tennis court; complete state-of-the-art gym w/sauna, steam room, whirlpool, and Swiss showers; spa offering a wide variety of treatments; dive shop w/watersports equipment; bikes; concierge; tour info; car rental; salon; room service; babysitting, laundry service; nonsmoking rooms. *In room:* A/C, TV/VCR, Wi-Fi, CD player, minibar, hair dryer, safe.

Maroma This resort has been around the longest, owns a large parcel of land inland that it protects from development, and has a gorgeous beach and beautifully manicured grounds. Two- and three-story buildings house the large guest rooms; most have king-size beds. The grounds are lovely, and the beach is fine white sand. The hotel has also spent a lot of effort and money on upgrades to the rooms. Nine new suites are outrageous examples of extravagance. There is a new beach bar that makes for an enjoyable place to pass the evening hours; it's a little more glitzy than the old one but still comfy. As at Tides Riviera Maya (see below), but to a lesser degree, the smaller size makes for more personal service and a deeper sense of escape.

Carretera 307 Km 51, 77710 Q. Roo. © 866/454-9351 in the U.S., or 998/872-8200. Fax 998/872-8220. www.maromahotel.com. 65 units. $570 (£285) garden-view double; $684 (£342) premium double; $930 (£465) oceanfront double; from $1,276 (£638) suite. Rates include ground transfer, full breakfast, and snorkeling tour. AE, MC, V. Free valet parking. No children younger than 16 allowed. **Amenities:** Restaurant; 3 bars; 3 outdoor spring-fed pools; fitness center; spa; Jacuzzi; steam bath; watersports equipment rental; game room; concierge; tours; car rental; salon; room service; in-room massage; laundry service; dry cleaning. In room: A/C, hair dryer.

Paraíso de la Bonita This resort has the most elaborate spa of all. I'm not a spa-goer and cannot discuss the relative merits of different treatments, but my work takes me to plenty of spas, and this one, which operates under the French system of thalassotherapy, is beyond anything I've seen. It uses seawater, sea salts, and sea algae in its treatments. The beach is open. The pool area and the common areas of the spa are uncommonly attractive. The rooms occupy some unremarkable three-story buildings. They are, in decor and furnishings, more impressive than the rooms of the three other resorts reviewed in this section. The ground-floor rooms have a plunge pool; upstairs rooms come with a balcony.

Carretera Cancún–Chetumal Km 328, Bahía Petempich, 77710 Q. Roo. © 866/751-9175 in the U.S., or 998/872-8300. Fax 998/872-8301. www.paraisodelabonita.com. 90 units. High season from $1,008 (£504) suite; low season from $800 (£400) suite. Rates include ground transfer. AE, MC, V. Free valet parking. No children younger than 12 allowed. **Amenities:** 2 restaurants; 2 bars; 4 outdoor pools; lighted tennis court; spa; 2 Jacuzzis; watersports equipment rental; concierge; tour info; rental cars; salon; room service; in-room massage; laundry service; dry cleaning; nonsmoking rooms. In room: A/C, TV/DVD, minibar, hair dryer, safe.

The Tides Riviera Maya (formerly Ikal del Mar) The smallest of the four resorts in this section, this property is all about privacy and tranquillity. Thirty well-separated bungalows—each with its own piece of jungle, a little pool, and an outdoor shower—are connected by lit pathways through the vegetation. The bungalows are large, filled with amenities, and decorated in a modern, spare style. The bathrooms have only a shower. Service here is the most personal of the four—you never have to leave your bungalow. The bar and restaurant, overlooking an inviting pool, make for an attractive common area. And of course, there's the spa. The beach was narrow and rocky, but the hurricane widened it considerably. The new owners have made numerous improvements in the rooms and the spa as run by Ikal del Mar.

Playa Xcalacoco, Carretera Cancún–Tulum, 77710 Q. Roo. © 800/578-0281 in the U.S. and Canada, or 984/877-3000. Fax 713/528-3697. www.tidesrivieramaya.com. 30 units. High season from $784 (£392) villa; low season from $655 (£328) double. Rates include full breakfast. AE, MC, V. Free secure parking. Children younger than 18 not accepted. **Amenities:** Restaurant; 2 bars; large outdoor pool; spa; 2 Jacuzzis; steam bath; watersports equipment; concierge; tour info; car rental; courtesy shuttle to Playa; salon; room service; in-room massage; laundry service. In room: A/C, TV/DVD, fridge, hair dryer, safe.

PUERTO MORELOS

Puerto Morelos remains a quiet place—perfect for lying on the white-sand beach and reading, with the occasional foray into watersports, especially snorkeling, diving, kitesurfing, windsurfing, and kayaking. A prominent reef offshore was declared a national park for its protection. It's shallow and easy to snorkel, and it protects the coast from storm surges. The beaches are great, maintained by the local government. The water is shallow, calm, and clear, with sea grass growing on the bottom. The town is small, and the inhabitants are laid-back. There is a large English-language bookstore that sells new and used titles. The car ferry that used to depart from here for Cozumel has moved down the coast to the Calica pier just south of Playa del Carmen.

ESSENTIALS
GETTING THERE   **By Car**   At Km 31 there's a traffic light at the intersection, and a large sign pointing to Puerto Morelos.

By Bus   Buses from Cancún to Tulum and Playa del Carmen usually stop here, but be sure to ask in Cancún if your bus makes the Puerto Morelos stop.

EXPLORING IN & AROUND PUERTO MORELOS
Puerto Morelos attracts visitors who seek seaside relaxation without crowds and high prices. The town has a few hotels and a few restaurants. For outdoor recreation, there are two dive shops and plenty of recreational boats for fishing or snorkeling. Try **Dive In Puerto Morelos** (www.diveinpuertomorelos.com) at Av. Rojo Gómez 14. On the main square, **Alma Libre** (© 998/871-0713; www.almalibrebooks.com) sells more English-language books than any other in the Yucatán. The owners, a couple of Canadians named Joanne and Rob Birce, stock everything from volumes on Maya culture to English classics to maps of the region. The store is open October through the first week in June, Tuesday to Sunday from 10am to 3pm and 6 to 9pm.

The reef directly offshore is very shallow and protected by law. Snorkelers are required to wear life vests to prevent them from diving down to the reef. I'm unaccustomed to snorkeling in a vest and found it bothersome, but it didn't prevent me from getting a close look at the reef, which is quite shallow—3m (10 ft.) at its deepest, rising to within a foot of the surface. In a short time, I spotted four different eels and sea snakes, lots of fish, and a ray.

WHERE TO STAY
Rates include the 12% hotel tax. For condo rentals check out the website of Alma Libre books (see above).

Amar Inn   Simple rooms on the beach, in a home-style setting, make this small inn a good place for those wanting a quiet seaside retreat. The cordial hostess, Ana Luisa Aguilar, is the daughter of Luis Aguilar, a Mexican singer and movie star of the 1940s and 1950s. She keeps busy promoting environmental and equitable-development causes. She can line up snorkeling and fishing trips and jungle tours for guests with local operators. There are three cabañas in back, opposite the main house, and six upstairs rooms with views of the beach. The most expensive rooms are the third-story "penthouse" rooms with a great view of the ocean. The cabañas get less of a cross-breeze than the rooms in the main house. Bedding choices include one or two doubles, one king-size, or five twin beds. A full Mexican breakfast is served in the garden.

Av. Javier Rojo Gómez (at Lázaro Cárdenas), 77580 Puerto Morelos, Q. Roo. © 998/871-0026. amar_inn@hotmail.com. 10 units. High season $55–$85 (£28–£43) double; low season $40–$75 (£20–£38) double. Rates include full breakfast. No credit cards. Limited free parking. **Amenities:** Tour and rental info. *In room:* Fan, fridge, no phone.

Hacienda Morelos   This hotel on the water has pleasant rooms and good prices. The simple rooms are spacious and comfortable and all have ocean views. Most come

Beach Cabañas

Five kilometers (3 miles) north of Playa are some economical lodgings on a mostly rocky beach. A sign that says PUNTA BETE marks the access road to Xcalacoco; in a short time you reach the water. Before you do, the road forks off in a few places, and you'll see signs for different cabañas. The word may conjure up visions of idyllic dwellings with thatched roofs, but on the Yucatecan coast, it usually means simple lodging. This is mostly the case here; rates run $70 to $85 (£35–£43) a night for two people. Of the four groupings of cabañas in Xcalacoco, the best is **Coco's Cabañas** (www.travel-center.com). It's a handful of rooms with electricity and ceiling fans; a good little budget restaurant; and a small pool. Two of the rooms have air-conditioning. Next door is the spa resort Tides Riviera Maya (see "Spa Resorts," above).

with two double beds, and some have a king-size bed. There's a small pool and a restaurant on the premises. It's close to the main square, so you don't need a car.

Av. Rafael Melgar 2 Lote 5, 77580 Puerto Morelos, Q. Roo. © 998/871-0448. www.haciendamorelos.com. 31 units. $89 (£45) double. Promotional rates sometimes available. MC, V. Limited free parking. **Amenities:** Restaurant; bar; outdoor pool. *In room:* A/C, TV, safe, no phone.

WHERE TO DINE

Most of Puerto Morelos's restaurants are on or around the main square. These include **Los Pelícanos** for seafood, **Bodo's** (in the hotel Hacienda Morelos) for good lunch specials and a few German dishes, **David Lau's** for Asian food, **El Pirata** if you have kids (for its large menu), and **Le Café d'Amancia** for coffee and pastries. The most expensive is **John Grey's**, a couple blocks north of the plaza and 3 blocks inland. It's open for dinner except on Sundays. The owner is a former chef for the Ritz-Carlton.

SOUTH OF PUERTO MORELOS

Petit Lafitte Hotel 🖈🖈 One kilometer (a half-mile) south of the original Posada Lafitte, this new property has the same easy-going attitude that characterized the old property. In relative isolation, you still get all the amenities of a relaxing vacation. The three-story building has 30 units, and plans are in place to build a dozen or more free-standing bungalows. Rooms are comfortable and contemporary. The staff is the same from the old property, so service is still personal and attentive.

Carretera Cancún–Tulum Km 63 (Xcalacoco), 77710 Playa del Carmen, Q. Roo. © 800/538-6802 in the U.S. and Canada. www.mexicoholiday.com. 30 units. High season $250–$275 (£125–£138) double, $270–$350 (£135–£175) bungalow; low season $180–$200 (£90–£100) double, $200–$270 (£100–£135) double. Minimum 2–4 nights. Rates include breakfast and dinner. MC, V. Free guarded parking. **Amenities:** Restaurant; bar; outdoor pool; ground transfer; activities desk; laundry service. *In room:* A/C (in some), Wi-Fi, minibar, safe.

2 Playa del Carmen 🖈🖈🖈

32km (20 miles) S of Puerto Morelos; 70km (43 miles) S of Cancún; 10km (6½ miles) N of Xcaret; 13km (8 miles) N of Puerto Calica

Though it no longer has the feel of a village, Playa still provides that rare combination of simplicity (at its core, still primarily a beach town) and variety (many unique hotels, restaurants, and stores). There is a comfortable feel to the town. The local architecture has adopted elements of native building—rustic clapboard walls; stucco; thatched

Tips Driving the Riviera Maya

Driving along this coast isn't difficult. There's only one highway, so you can't get lost. Speed limits are clearly posted, but lots of cars ignore them, *except around Playa,* where police are known to ticket drivers. Watch your speed when you're passing through town. Maximum speed for the center lanes is 60kmph (40 mph) and, for the outside lanes, it's 40kmph (25 mph).

South of Playa, the highway is four lanes as far as Akumal. South of there it's still undivided. You're not allowed to stop on the highway to make a left turn. You're supposed to pull over to the right and wait for traffic in both directions to clear before crossing the road. Another tip: Drivers here customarily pretend that there's a center passing lane. Oncoming traffic moves to the right to make room for the passing vehicle. You should do the same, but look out for cyclists and cars on the shoulder. This is why I recommend not driving at night. There are several more gas stations in the Riviera Maya now, so you shouldn't have a problem getting gas. But make sure the attendant gives you back the right amount of money—I've had people try to short-change me.

---

roofs; rough-hewn wood; and a ramshackle, unplanned look to many structures. Cheap-looking commercial architecture has intruded, with chain restaurants and stores, detracting from Playa's individuality, but Playa still retains the feel of a cosmopolitan getaway with a counterculture ethos.

A strong European influence has made topless sunbathing (nominally against the law in Mexico) a nonchalantly accepted practice anywhere there's a beach. The beach grows and shrinks, from broad and sandy to narrower with rocks, depending on the currents and wind. When this happens, head to the beaches in north Playa.

From Playa, it's easy to shoot out to Cozumel on the ferry, drive south to the nature parks and the ruins at Tulum and Cobá, or drive north to Cancún. Directly south of town is the Playacar development, which has a golf course, several large all-inclusive resorts, and a residential development.

ESSENTIALS
GETTING THERE & DEPARTING

BY AIR   You can fly into Cancún and take a bus directly from the airport (see "By Bus," below), or fly into Cozumel and take the passenger ferry.

BY CAR   Highway 307 is the only highway that passes through Playa. As you approach Playa from Cancún, the highway divides. Keep to the inside lanes to permit turning left at any of the traffic lights. The two main arteries into Playa are Avenida Constituyentes, which works well for destinations in northern Playa, and Avenida Juárez, which leads to the town's main square. If you stay in the outside lanes, you will need to continue past Playa until you get to the turnaround, then double back, staying to your right.

BY FERRY   Air-conditioned passenger ferries to Cozumel leave from the town's pier 1 block from the main square. There is also a car ferry to Cozumel from the Calica pier just south of the Playacar development. The schedule for the passenger ferries has been in flux. Lately, ferries have been departing every hour in the mornings, and every

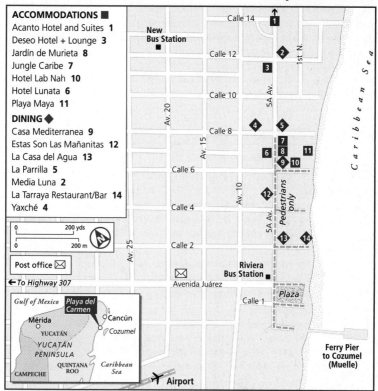

Playa del Carmen

ACCOMMODATIONS ■
Acanto Hotel and Suites **1**
Deseo Hotel + Lounge **3**
Jardín de Murieta **8**
Jungle Caribe **7**
Hotel Lab Nah **10**
Hotel Lunata **6**
Playa Maya **11**

DINING ◆
Casa Mediterranea **9**
Estas Son Las Mañanitas **12**
La Casa del Agua **13**
La Parrilla **5**
Media Luna **2**
La Tarraya Restaurant/Bar **14**
Yaxché **4**

Post office ✉
← To Highway 307

Calle 14
New Bus Station ■
Calle 12
Calle 10
Calle 8
Calle 6
Calle 4
Calle 2
Riviera Bus Station ■
Avenida Juárez
Calle 1
Plaza

Av. 20
Av. 15
Av. 25
Av. 10
5A Av.
1st. N.
Pedestrians only
Caribbean Sea

Ferry Pier to Cozumel (Muelle)

Gulf of Mexico
Playa del Carmen
Mérida
YUCATÁN
YUCATÁN PENINSULA
Cancún
Cozumel
QUINTANA ROO
CAMPECHE
Caribbean Sea
✈ Airport

---

2 hours in the afternoons. For more information about both ferries, see "Getting There & Departing" in the Cozumel section of chapter 6.

BY TAXI   Taxi fares from the Cancún airport are about $60 to $70 (£30–£35) one-way.

BY BUS   **Autobuses Riviera** offers service from the Cancún airport about 12 times a day. Cost is $8 (£4) one-way. You'll see a ticket counter in the corridor leading out of the airport. From the Cancún bus station there are frequent departures—almost every 30 minutes.

ORIENTATION

ARRIVING   Playa has two **bus** stations. Buses coming from Cancún and places along the coast, such as Tulum, arrive at the Riviera bus station, at the corner of Juárez and Quinta Avenida, by the town square. Buses coming from destinations in the interior of the peninsula arrive at the new ADO station, on Avenida 20 between calles 12 and 14.

  A word of caution: Approach any timeshare salesperson as you would a wounded rhino. And remember that whatever free trinket is offered for simply viewing apartments, it either won't materialize or won't be worth the time you invest in your dealings with these people. You have been warned.

CITY LAYOUT   The main street, **Avenida Juárez,** leads to the town square from Highway 307. As it does so, it crosses several numbered avenues that run parallel to the beach, all of which are multiples of 5. **Quinta Avenida (Fifth Avenue)** is closest to the beach; it's closed to traffic from the *zócalo* to Calle 6 (and some blocks beyond, in the evening). On this avenue are many hotels, restaurants, and shops. Almost the entire town is north and west of the square. To the south is "Playacar" a golf-course development of private residences and a dozen resort hotels.

FAST FACTS: Playa del Carmen

Area Code The telephone area code is **984.**

Currency Exchange Playa has several banks and ATMs. Many currency-exchange houses are close to the pier or along Quinta Avenida at Calle 8.

Doctor For serious medical attention, go to **Hospitén** in Cancún (© 998/881-3700). In Playa, **Dr. G. Ambriz** speaks English and was trained in the U.S. and Europe. His office is at the corner of Avenida 30 and Calle 14 (© 984/109-1245).

Drugstore The **Farmacía del Carmen,** Avenida Juárez between avenidas 5 and 10 (© 984/873-2330), is open 24 hours.

Internet Access Internet cafes are all over town; most have fast connections.

Parking Most parking in Playa is on the street. Spots can be hard to come by. The most accessible parking lot is the Estacionamiento México, at avenidas Juárez and 10 (where the entrance is located). It's open daily 24 hours and charges $1.25 (65p) per hour, $10 (£5.50) per day. There's also a 24-hour lot a block from the pier, where you can leave your car while you visit Cozumel.

Post Office The *correo,* on Avenida Juárez, 3 blocks from the plaza, is on the right past the Hotel Playa del Carmen and the launderette.

Seasons The main high season is from mid-December to Easter. There is a mini high season in August. Low season is all other months.

WHERE TO STAY

Playa has a lot of small hotels with affordable prices that give you a better feel for the town than staying in one of the resorts in Playacar. Don't hesitate to book a place that's not on the beach. Town life here is much of the fun, and staying on the beach in Playa has its disadvantages—in particular, the noise from a couple of beach bars. Beaches are public property in Mexico, and you can lay out your towel anywhere you like. There are some beach clubs in north Playa where, for a small sum, you can have the use of lounge chairs, towels, and food and drink.

High season is mid-December to Easter. August is also high season for some hotels but not others. At other times of the year, you can come to Playa and score walk-in offers. The rates listed below include the 12% hotel tax. I don't include the rates for Christmas to New Year's, which are still higher than the standard high-season rates.

VERY EXPENSIVE

Acanto Hotel & Suites 🏨🏨 *Finds*   In my view, this property is (dare I say it) the most romantic in Playa. There is intimacy and drama and an even a sense of isolation.

Seven stylish suites endowed with color and texture encircle a pool and softly lit court-yard. Figures of Buddha and Asian decoration add an exotic feel and draw a division between this small enclave and the larger world outside the hotel's door. The suites come with kitchens so you can, should you choose, limit your comings and goings. The rooms are large and comfortable and come with a queen bed and small sitting area. The location is great, just around the corner from Quinta Avenida, on a secluded street. There are plans to build more units next door with the same concept.

Calle 16 Bis (between avs. 5th and 1st) 77710 Playa del Carmen, Q. Roo. © **631/882-1986** in the U.S. or 984/873-1252. www.acantohotels.com. 7 units. $170–$215 (£85–£158) suite. 3-night minimum stay for holidays. AE, MC, V. Street parking. **Amenities:** Small outdoor pool; tour info; in-room massage; laundry service; nonsmoking rooms. *In room:* A/C, TV, CD player, coffeemaker, hair dryer, safe, no phone.

Deseo Hotel + Lounge ⨍⨍⨍   This hotel is designed to foster social interaction. The lounge plays the central role, appropriating the functions of lobby, restaurant, bar, and pool area at once. It's a raised open-air platform with bar, pool, self-serve kitchen, and daybeds for sunning or sipping an evening drink when the bar is in full swing. The clientele is predominantly 25- to 45-year-olds.

The guest rooms are comfortable, original, and striking but don't tempt one to stay indoors—no TV, no cushy armchair. Their simplicity gives them an almost Asian feel, heightened by nice touches such as sliding doors of wood and frosted glass. All rooms have king-size beds with deep mattresses. From the bottom of each bed, a little drawer slides out with a night kit containing incense, earplugs, and condoms.

And in case Deseo doesn't work for you, the owners have opened another archly styled hotel 2 blocks down called **Hotel Básico** (© **984/879-4448;** www.hotelbasico. com). It's a fun mix of industrial and '50s styles, built with materials that have found a lot of favor with architects these days: concrete, plywood, and plastics. Along with all this you get a cushy bed and a forceful shower. As with Deseo, the common areas are not wasted space.

Av. 5 (at Calle 12), 77710 Playa del Carmen, Q. Roo. © **984/879-3620.** Fax 984/879-3621. www.hoteldeseo.com. 15 units. $199 (£100) lounge view; $222 (£111) balcony; $274 (£137) suite. Rates include continental breakfast. AE, MC, V. No parking. Children younger than 18 not accepted. **Amenities:** Bar; small rooftop pool; Jacuzzi; tour info; room service; in-room massage; laundry service. *In room:* A/C, minibar, hair dryer (on request), safe.

EXPENSIVE

Hotel Lunata ⨍⨍   In the middle of Playa, there isn't a more comfortable or more attractive place to stay than this small hotel on Quinta Avenida. The rooms offer char-acter, good looks, and polish. There are a few standard rooms, which are midsize and come with a queen-size or a double bed. Deluxe rooms are large and come with a king-size bed and small fridge. Junior suites come with two doubles. Bathrooms are well designed and have good showers. Light sleepers should opt for a room facing the gar-den. On my last stay, I took a room facing the street with double-glazed glass doors that opened to a balcony. I enjoyed looking out over Quinta Avenida, and, with the doors shut, the noise was not bothersome.

Av. 5 (between calles 6 and 8), 77710 Playa del Carmen, Q. Roo. © **984/873-0884.** Fax 984/873-1240. www.lunata.com. 10 units. High season $129 (£65) standard, $169–$179 (£85–£90) deluxe and junior suite; low sea-son $115 (£58) standard, $135–$159 (£68–£80) deluxe and junior suite. Rates include continental breakfast. Promo-tional rates available. AE, MC, V. Secure parking $5 (£2.50). No children younger than 13 allowed. **Amenities:** Free use of bike and watersports equipment; tour desk; in-room massage; laundry service; nonsmoking rooms. *In room:* A/C, TV, fridge (in some), hair dryer (on request), safe, no phone.

Los Itzaes ⓕ This small hotel in the middle of Playa accommodates business people, making it something of a refuge from tourists. The rooms are attractive and comfortable, with good A/C and double glazed windows. The mattresses are comfortable.
Rates include membership at one of the local beach clubs. Rooms with a king bed cost
a little less than rooms with two doubles. Junior suites have two doubles and a sofa
bed. There is no pool, but there is an enjoyable rooftop whirlpool tub.

Av. 10 between calles 6 and 8, 77710 Playa del Carmen, Q. Roo. ⓒ **984/873-2397** or -2398. www.itzaes.com. 16
units. $150–$175 (£75–£88) standard; $220–$250 (£110–£125) suites. Rates include full breakfast and beach club
membership. 5-night minimum stay during holidays. AE, MC, V. Secured parking $13. Small pets accepted. **Ameni-
ties:** Restaurant; bar; small outdoor Jacuzzi; tour info; ground transfer; in-room massage; laundry service, nonsmoking rooms. *In room:* A/C, TV, Wi-Fi, minibar, hair dryer, safe.

Playa Maya ⓕ ⓥⁿ⁽ᵉ This is the best beach hotels in downtown Playa. There are
many reasons to like it (good location, good price, comfortable rooms, and helpful
management), but one thing that strikes my fancy is that you enter the hotel from the
beach. This little detail isn't good reason to choose a hotel, but it establishes the mood
of the overall place and gives it a remove from the busy street scene. What's more, the
design and location make it a quiet hotel; it's a couple of blocks from the nearest live-
music venue and sheltered by the neighboring hotels. The pool and sunning terrace
are attractive and nicely set apart. Rooms are large with midsize bathrooms; a couple
of them have private garden terraces with Jacuzzis, while others have balconies that
face the beach.

Zona FMT (between calles 6 and 8 Norte), 77710 Playa del Carmen, Q. Roo. ⓒ **984/803-2022.** www.playa
maya.com. 20 units. High season $150–$196 (£75–£98) double; low season $112–$168 (£56–£84) double. Rates
include continental breakfast. MC, V. Limited street parking. **Amenities:** Restaurant; bar; outdoor pool; Jacuzzi; tour
info; room service; massage; laundry service. *In room:* A/C, TV, Wi-Fi, fridge, hair dryer, safe.

INEXPENSIVE

Hotel Lab Nah ⓥⁿ⁽ᵉ Good rooms in a central location for a good price are the
main attraction at this economy hotel in the heart of Playa. The cheapest rooms have
windows facing Quinta Avenida. There was some noise—mostly late-night bar hop-
pers. It didn't bother me too much. Nevertheless, I think it's worth the money to get
one of the partial oceanview standards with balcony on the third floor because they
are quieter and larger. The gardenview rooms are directly below the oceanview, are just
as large and quiet, but not quite as fixed up. And the difference in price is little. A
rooftop *palapa* is the largest room available, good for more than a couple.

Calle 6 (and Av. 5), 77710 Playa del Carmen, Q. Roo. ⓒ 984/873-2099 www.labnah.com. 33 units. High season
$50–$80 (£25–£40) double, $105 (£53) rooftop *palapa;* low season $45–$60 (£23–£30) double, $80 (£40) rooftop
palapa. Rates include continental breakfast. MC, V. Limited street parking. **Amenities:** Small outdoor pool; tour info;
laundry service. *In room:* A/C, hair dryers in some, no phone.

Jardín de Murieta ⓥⁿ⁽ᵉ ⓕⁱⁿᵈˢ Besides the economical rates, I like this place for its
central, yet half-hidden location in a small interior property without any street
frontage on la Quinta. Rooms vary a good bit, but most are large, bright, and cheerful. And the location is quiet. Four rooms have kitchenettes, which can work for some
simple meals. Most of the rooms encircle a tree-shaded patio with a few shops and a
restaurant. The place has a pleasant, quirky feel.

Av. 5 Norte 173 (between calles 6 and 8), 77710 Playa del Carmen, Q. Roo. ⓒ **984/873-0224.** www.jardindemurieta.
com. 10 units. High season $56–$96 (£28–£48) double; low season $46–$72 (£23–£36) double. No credit cards. Limited street parking. **Amenities:** Restaurant; tour info. *In room:* A/C, TV, Wi-Fi, kitchenette (in 4), fridge, no phone.

WHERE TO DINE

Aside from the restaurants listed below, I would point you in the direction of a few that don't need a full review. For a delicious Veracruz-style breakfast in pleasant, breezy surroundings, try the upstairs terrace restaurant of the **Hotel Básico**, at Quinta Avenida and Calle 10 Norte. For fish tacos and inexpensive seafood, try **El Oasis**, on Calle 12, between avenidas 5 and 10 (no phone). For *arrachera* (fajita) tacos, the place to go is **Super Carnes H C de Monterrey** (© **984/803-0488**) on Calle 1 Sur between avenidas 20 and 25.

EXPENSIVE

La Casa del Agua *ୱ* EUROPEAN/MEXICAN   Excellent food in inviting sur-roundings. Instead of obtrusive background music, you hear the sound of falling water. The German owners work at presenting what they like best about the Old and New worlds. They do a good job with seafood—try the grilled seafood for two. For a mild dish, try chicken in a scented sauce of fine herbs accompanied by fettuccine; for something heartier, there's the tortilla soup listed as "Mexican soup." The restaurant offers a number of cool and light dishes that would be appetizing for lunch or an after-noon meal, for example, an avocado stuffed with shrimp and flavored with a subtle horseradish sauce on a bed of alfalfa sprouts and julienne carrots—a good mix of tastes and textures. For dessert, try the chocolate mousse. This is an upstairs restaurant under a large and airy *palapa* roof.

Av. 5 (at Calle 2). © 984/803-0232. Reservations recommended in high season. Main courses $16–$26 (£8–£13). MC, V. Daily 10am–midnight.

La Parrilla MEXICAN/GRILL   Still a fun place, but it's having problems handling its success. Prices have gone up, and service is slower. But the fajitas remain good as well as many of the Mexican standards such as tortilla soup, enchiladas, and quesadil-las. Mariachis show up around 8pm; plan accordingly.

Av. 5 (at Calle 8). © 984/873-0687. Reservations recommended in high season. Main courses $10–$25 (£5–£13). AE, MC, V. Daily noon–1am.

Yaxché *ୱୱ* YUCATECAN   The menu here makes use of many native foods and spices to present a more elaborate regional cooking than the usual offerings at Yucate-can restaurants—and it was about time for someone to show a little creativity with such an interesting palette of tastes. Excellent examples are a cream of *chaya* (a native leafy vegetable), and an *xcatic* chili stuffed with *cochinita pibil*. I also like the classic Mexican-style fruit salad with lime juice and dried powdered chili. There are several seafood dishes; the ones I had were fresh and well prepared.

Calle 8 (between aves. 5 and 10). © 984/873-2502. Reservations recommended in high season. Main courses $10–$26 (£5–£13). AE, MC, V. Daily noon–midnight.

MODERATE

Casa Mediterránea *ୱୱ* ITALIAN   Tucked away on a quiet little patio off Quinta Avenida, this small, homey restaurant serves excellent food. Maurizio Gabrielli and Mary Michelon are usually there to greet customers and make recommendations. Maurizio came to Mexico to enjoy the simple life, and this inclination shows in the restaurant's welcoming, unhurried atmosphere. The menu is mostly northern Italian, with several dishes from other parts of Italy. There are daily specials, too. Pastas (except penne and spaghetti) are made in-house, and none are precooked. Try fish and shrimp ravioli or penne alla Veneta. The lobster is prepared beautifully. There are several

Choosing an All-Inclusive in the Riviera Maya

More than 40 all-inclusive resorts line this coast. Most people are familiar with the concept—large hotels that work with economies of scale to offer lodging, food, and drink all for a single, low rate. All-inclusives offer convenience and economy, especially for families with many mouths to feed. Because they are enclosed areas, they make it easy for parents to watch their children.

A certain sameness pervades these hotels so that a lot can be said that applies to all. They're usually built around a large pool with activities and an activities organizer. There is often a quiet pool, too. One large buffet restaurant and a snack bar serve the needs of most guests, but there will be a couple of specialty restaurants at no extra charge but that require reservations. Colored bracelets serve to identify guests. In the evenings a show is presented at the hotel's theater.

These resorts work best for those who are looking for a relaxing beach vacation and to get away from the cold weather. They don't work for those who aim to get away from crowds—these hotels are large and operate with a high occupancy rate. Yes, staying at these all-inclusives is convenient and hassle-free. They make everything easy, including taking tours and day trips—all the organizing is done for you. On the downside, you don't often get the spontaneity or the sense of adventure that comes with other styles of travel. The question you have to ask yourself is "what kind of vacation am I looking for?"

The best way to get a room at an all-inclusive is through a vacation packager or one of its travel agents. You get a better deal than by contacting the

wines, mostly Italian, to choose from. The salads are good and carefully prepared—dig in without hesitation.

Av. 5 (between calles 6 and 8; look for a sign for Hotel Marieta). ⓒ **984/876-3926.** Reservations recommended in high season. Main courses $12–$22 (£6–£11). No credit cards. Wed–Mon 2–11pm.

El Asador de Manolo ⓕⓕ STEAKS/ARGENTINE   If I want a steak in Playa, this is where I go. (Well, actually, I would try the address listed below in hopes that the restaurant pulled off the move as planned, but this being Mexico, I would be prepared to find it back at its old location on Avenida 10 between 24 and 26.) The owner is an Argentine who has been living in Mexico so long, he's gone Mexican. But the food is faithful to his native land: steaks, good *empanadas,* and southern-style pastas, and you can't go wrong with any of the soups. When ordering a steak, see p. 297, Appendix B, for the proper terminology. For dessert there are crepes and flan.

Calle 28 (at Av. 10). ⓒ **984/803-0632.** Reservations recommended in high season. Main courses $7–$20 (£3.50–£10); steaks $14–$30 (£7–£15). MC, V. Mon–Fri 1–11pm; Sat–Sun 4pm–midnight.

La Cueva del Chango ⓕ MEXICAN   Good food in original surroundings with a relaxed "mañana" attitude. True to its name ("The Monkey's Cave"), the place suggests a cave and has little waterways meandering through it, and there are two spider hotel directly. Even if you have frequent-flier miles to burn, you will still find it difficult to match the rates of a full package offered by one of the biggies like Funjet.

Of the many all-inclusives in the Riviera Maya, there are a few that are my favorites and might bear looking into.

Of the several all-inclusives that are in Playa del Carmen/Playacar, I like **Iberostar Quetzal** or **Tucán** (two names for different halves of the same hotel; www.iberostar.com). The food is better than at most, and the central part of the hotel is made of raised walkways and terraces over the natural mangrove habitat. Other resorts in Playacar that bear investigation are the **Sandos Playacar** and any of the hotels in the southern half. Those in the northern half are losing beach.

The **Hotel Copacabana** in Xpu-Ha (www.hotelcopacabana.com) has raised walkways, preserving much of the flora and making it visually interesting. And Xpu-Ha is blessed with a stunning beach.

Aventura Spa Palace (www.palaceresorts.com) is another hotel in the Palace chain—this one is just for grownups. It has a large spa and gym and attractive common areas and guest rooms. There is a large pool but no beach; guests can take a shuttle to the Xpu-Ha property if they want.

Freedom Paradise (www.freedomparadise.com) is billed as the first size-friendly vacation resort. The management has worked hard to create an environment that large people will find comfortable. I like it because it doesn't have all the froufrou of so many other resorts—it's friendly and unpretentious.

monkeys that hang about in the back of the place. But take away the water and the monkeys, and, oddly enough, it brings to mind the Flintstones. You'll enjoy great juices, blended fruit drinks, salads, soups, Mexican specialties with a natural twist, and handmade tortillas. The fish is fresh and delicious. Mosquitoes can sometimes be a problem at night, but the management has bug spray for the guests.

Calle 38 (between Av. 5 and the beach, near the Shangri-la Caribe). © **984/116-3179**. Main courses $8–$14 (£4–£7). No credit cards. Mon–Sat 8am–11pm; Sun 8am–2pm.

La Vagabunda ITALIAN/MEXICAN   This place is old-style Playa in its simple charm. A large *palapa* shelters several simple wood tables sitting on a gravel floor. It's low-key and quiet—a good place for breakfast, with many options, including delicious blended fruit drinks, waffles, and omelets. The specials are a good value. In the afternoon and evening they serve light fare such as panini, pastas, and ceviche.

Av. 5 (between calles 24 and 26). © **984/873-3753**. Breakfast $4–$6 (£2–£3); main courses $7–$12 (£3.50–£6). MC, V. High season daily 7am–11:30pm; low season daily 7am–3:30pm.

Media Luna ✸✸ FUSION   This restaurant has an inventive menu that favors grilled seafood, sautés, and pasta dishes. Everything is fresh and prepared beautifully. Try the very tasty pan-fried fish cakes with mango and honeyed hoisin sauce. Another choice is the black pepper–crusted fish. Be sure to eye the daily specials. For lunch you can get sandwiches and salads, as well as black-bean quesadillas and crepes. The decor is primitive-tropical chic.

Av. 5 (between calles 12 and 14). ⓒ 984/873-0526. Breakfast $4–$6 (£2–£3); sandwich with salad $5–$7 (£2.50–£3.50); main courses $8–$15 (£4–£7.50). No credit cards. Daily 8am–11:30pm.

INEXPENSIVE

La Tarraya Restaurant/Bar ⟨Value⟩ SEAFOOD/YUCATECAN   THE RESTAURANT THAT WAS BORN WITH THE TOWN, proclaims the sign. It's right on the beach, where the water practically laps at the foundation. Because the owners are fishermen, the fish is so fresh it's still practically wiggling. The wood hut doesn't look like much, but they also have tables right on the beach. You can have your fish prepared in several ways. If you haven't tried the Yucatecan specialty *tik-n-xic*—fish with *achiote* and bitter-orange sauce, cooked in a banana leaf—this is a good place to do so. I can also recommend the ceviche and the beer.

Calle 2 Norte. ⓒ 984/873-2040. Main courses $5–$10 (£2.50–£5); whole fish $9 (£4.50) per kilo (2.2 lbs.). No credit cards. Daily noon–9pm.

PLAYA DEL CARMEN AFTER DARK

It seems as if everyone in town is out strolling along "la Quinta" until midnight; there's pleasant browsing, dining, and drinking available at the many establishments on the street. Here's a quick rundown of the bars that you won't find on Quinta Avenida. The beach bar that is an institution in Playa is the **Blue Parrot** (ⓒ 984/873-0083). It gets live acts, mostly rock, and attracts a mixed crowd. It's between calles 12 and 14. Just to the south is **Om** (no phone), which gets a younger crowd with louder musical acts.

Alux (ⓒ 984/110-5050) is a one-of-a-kind club occupying a large cave with two dramatically lit chambers and several nooks and sitting areas. It's worth going to, if only for the novelty. The local conservancy group approved all the work, and great care was taken not to contaminate the water, which is part of a larger underground river system. The club books a variety of music acts, usually with no cover. Often there's belly dancing, which is quite in keeping with the surroundings, and I couldn't help but think that I had stepped into a scene from a James Bond film. The bar is cash only and is open Tuesday to Sunday from 7pm to 2am. Take Avenida Juárez across to the other side of the highway—2 blocks down on your left.

For movie going, **Cine Hollywood,** Avenida 10 and Calle 8, in the Plaza Pelícanos shopping center, shows a lot of films in English with Spanish subtitles. Before you buy your ticket, make sure the film is subtitled *(subtitulada)* and not dubbed *(doblada).*

3 South of Playa del Carmen

South of Playa del Carmen you'll find a succession of small communities and resorts and two nature parks. From north to south, this section covers them in the following order: Xcaret, Paamul, Puerto Aventuras, Xpu-Ha, Akumal, Xel-Ha, Punta Solimán, and Tankah. This section spans about 56km (35 miles).

HEADING SOUTH FROM PLAYA DEL CARMEN   Renting a car is the best way to move around down here. Southbound buses depart regularly from Playa, but the best they might do is get you close to your destination. And from the highway it can be a hot walk to the coast. Another option is to hire a car and driver.

Beyond Paamul, you'll see signs for this or that cenote or cave. There are thousands of cenotes in the Yucatán, and each is slightly different. These turnoffs are less visited than the major attractions and can make for a pleasant visit. Two major attractions bear specific mention: **Hidden Worlds,** offering remarkable snorkeling and diving tours of a couple of cenotes, and **Aktun Chen** cavern with a small nature park. Both are south of Akumal and described later in this chapter.

XCARET: A PARK CELEBRATING THE YUCATAN

A billboard in the airport of faraway Guadalajara reads in Spanish "And when visiting Xcaret, don't forget to enjoy the pleasures of the Riviera Maya, too." An exaggeration, but its point is well taken: Xcaret (pronounced "eesh-ca-*ret*") is the biggest attraction in these parts and is practically a destination unto itself. It even has its own resort. If you're coming to these shores to avoid crowds, avoid this place. If you're here for entertainment and activities, you should consider visiting Xcaret. What Xcaret does, it does very well, and that is to present in one package a little bit of everything that the Yucatán (and the rest of Mexico for that matter) has to offer.

Think of the activities that people come to the Yucatán for: hanging out on the beach, scuba and snorkeling, cavern diving, visiting ruins, taking a siesta in a hammock under a grove of palm trees, hiking through tropical forest, meeting native Maya peoples—Xcaret has all that plus handicraft exhibitions; a bat cave; a butterfly pavilion; mushroom and orchid nurseries; and lots of wildlife on display, including native jaguars, manatees, sea turtles, monkeys, macaws, flamingos, and a petting aquarium. Children love it. What probably receives most of the comments is the underground river (a natural feature of the park and common in much of the Yucatán) that's been opened in places to allow snorkelers to paddle along with the current. What else? A number of tours and shows, including *charros* (Mexican cowboys) from the state of Jalisco, and the Totonac Indian *voladores* ("flyers" who do a daring pole dance high above the ground) from the state of Veracruz.

The park is famous for its evening spectacle that is a celebration of the Mexican nation. I've seen it and have to say that it is some show, with a large cast and lots of props. It starts with the Maya and an interpretation of how they may have played the pre-Hispanic ball game/ritual known as *pok-ta-pok*, and then to another version of a ball game still practiced in the western state of Michoacán. From there it moves on to the arrival of the Spanish and eventually to the forging of the new nation, its customs, its dress, and its music and dance.

Xcaret is 10km (6½ miles) south of Playa del Carmen (you'll know when you get to the turnoff). It's open daily from 8:30am to 9pm. Admission prices are $59 (£30) for adults, $41 (£21) for children 5 to 12. Some activities cost extra: horseback ride $30 (£15), Snuba/sea trek/snorkel tour $45 (£23), scuba $50 to $75 (£25–£38), swimming with dolphins $115 (£108). Other costs: lockers $2 (£1) per day, snorkel equipment $10 (£5) per day, food and drink variable. The park is an all-day affair; it's best to arrive early and register for tours and activities right away. For more info, call ✆ **998/883-3143** or visit www.xcaret.net.

⌐Tips Avoiding the Cruise Ship Crowds

Fewer ships arrive on weekends than on weekdays, which makes the weekend a good time for visiting the major attractions on this coast.

Four kilometers (2½ miles) south of the entrance to Xcaret is the turnoff for **Puerto Calica,** the cruise-ship pier. Passengers disembark here for tours of Playa, Xcaret, the ruins, and other attractions on the coast.

PAAMUL: SEASIDE GETAWAY

About 15km (10 miles) beyond Xcaret and 25km (15 miles) from Playa del Carmen is Paamul, which in Mayan means "a destroyed ruin." The exit is clearly marked. At Paamul (also written Pamul), you can enjoy the Caribbean with relative quiet; the water at the out-of-the-way beach is wonderful, but the shoreline is rocky. There are four rooms for rent, a restaurant, and many trailer and RV lots with hookups.

There's also a dive shop. **Scuba-Mex** (✆ 984/875-1066; fax 984/874-1729; www.scubamex.com) is a fully equipped PADI- and SSI-certified dive shop next to the cabañas. Using two boats, the staff takes guests on dives 8km (5 miles) in either direction. If it's too choppy, the reefs in front of the hotel are also good. The cost for a two-tank dive is $50 (£25), plus $25 (£13) to rent gear. Snorkeling is also excellent in this protected bay and the one next to it. The shop offers a great 3-hour snorkeling trip ($25/£13).

WHERE TO STAY & DINE

Cabañas Paamul ⚲   Mostly Paamul works with the trailer crowd renting spaces by the day or month. But there are also 12 modern units called "junior suites" on or near the water's edge that are comfortable and spacious. These units are large and come with a kitchenette and two queen beds. Slightly cheaper, but more limited in size and amenities are the "eco-cabañas." Trailer guests have access to 12 showers and separate bathrooms for men and women. Laundry service is available nearby. The large, breezy *palapa* restaurant is a Brazilian-style grill under the management of Kalú da Silva, a retired Brazilian soccer player, who closed his restaurant in León, Guanajuato, to live on the coast. Restaurant customers are welcome to use the beach, which is rocky along this stretch of the coast. Prices vary according to season.

Carretera Cancún–Tulum Km 85. ✆ **984/875-1053.** paamulmx@yahoo.com. 22 units; 190 trailer spaces (all with full hookups). $100–$150 (£50–£75) junior suite; $80–$120 (£40–£60) cabaña. RV space with hookups $30 (£15) per day, $600 (£300) per month. No credit cards. Ask about discounts for stays longer than 1 week. Free parking. **Amenities:** Restaurant; bar; dive shop. *In room:* A/C, TV, kitchenette.

PUERTO AVENTURAS: A RESORT COMMUNITY

Five kilometers (3 miles) south of Paamul and 104km (65 miles) from Cancún is the glitzy development of Puerto Aventuras, on Chakalal Bay. It's a condo/marina community with a 9-hole golf course. At the center of the development is a collection of restaurants bordering a dolphin pool. They offer a variety of food—Mexican, Italian, steaks, even a popular pub. The major attraction is the dolphins. To swim with them in a highly interactive program, you must make reservations by contacting **Dolphin Discovery** (✆ **998/849-4757;** www.dolphindiscovery.com). Make reservations well in advance—the surest way is through the website. A 1-hour session costs $125 (£63). There are shorter programs that cost less.

This is also the place to come for boating and deep-sea fishing. I recommend **Capt. Rick's Sportfishing Center** (✆ **984/873-5195** or -5387; www.fishyucatan.com). The best fishing on this coast is from March to August. The captain will be happy to combine a fishing trip with some snorkeling, which makes for a leisurely day.

I don't find Puerto Aventuras to be an interesting place for lodging and prefer to stay elsewhere on the coast. It's like a mini Cancún, but lacking Cancún's vibrancy.

Tips **In Case of Emergency**

The Riviera Maya, south of Puerto Aventuras, is susceptible to power failures that can last for hours. Gas pumps and cash machines shut down when this happens, and once the power returns, they attract long lines. It's a good idea to keep a reserve of gas and cash.

There are a couple of fancy hotels. The main one is the **Omni Puerto Aventuras** (© **800/843-6664** in the U.S., or 984/873-5101). It looks larger than its 30 rooms would indicate and was probably intended to be bigger but didn't get the expected traffic.

XPU-HA: BEAUTIFUL BEACH

Three kilometers (2 miles) beyond Puerto Aventuras is **Xpu-Ha** (eesh-poo-*hah*) *ჩ*ჩ*ჩ*, a wide bay lined by a broad, beautiful sandy beach. Much of the bay is taken up by private houses and condos. There are a few all-inclusive resorts. One is **Xpu-Ha Palace** and another is the **Copacabana.** These suffered a lot of damage with Hurricane Emily but are open and back in business. Only a part of Xpu-Ha Palace is open as the other half awaits repair. The beach is big enough to accommodate the hotel guests, residents, and day-trippers without feeling crowded.

Besides the establishments reviewed here, a few hotels offer basic lodging—a couple of beds, cement floors, small private bathroom, and minimal decoration. These rent on a first-come, first-served basis. Rates vary from $50 to $80 (£25–£40) a night, depending upon how busy they are. Lodging options are better in nearby Akumal, and, if you're renting a car, you can come for the day to enjoy the beach.

Al Cielo *ჩ* *Moments*   This is a good choice if you want a small hotel on the beach where you can go native. The four rooms (two upstairs, two down) occupy a large thatched building right on the beach. The restaurant is very popular, but the rooms are rustic and simple, which sometimes works to draw guests into the beach experience as an escape from the modern world. If you're looking for more amenities, this won't be for you.

Carretera Cancún-Tulum Km. 118, 77710 Xpu-Ha, Q. Roo. No phone. www.alcielohotel.com. 4 units. $212–$258 (£106–£129) double. MC, V. No children accepted. Rates include full breakfast. Free secure parking. **Amenities:** Restaurant; bar; Hobie cat; tour info; room service. *In room:* Fan, Wi-Fi, hair dryer, safe, no phone.

Esencia *ჩ*ჩ*ჩ*   There's not a property on this entire coast that epitomizes leisure and escape more than this one. Lots of space, lots of beauty, lots of privacy, and an air of serenity pervades the entire complex. And, of course, the beach is magnificent. Service is personal and understated (a service fee is added to the room rate). If the spa were any more relaxing, it would lead to an out-of-body experience.

Predio Rústico Xpu-Ha, Fracc. 16 y 18, L. 18, 19 (exit Xpu-Ha-2), 77710 Xpu-Ha, Q. Roo. © **877/528-3490** in the U.S. or Canada or 984/873-4830. www.hotelesencia.com. 29 units. High season $582 (£291) and up for room or suite; low season $494 (£247) and up for room or suite. AE, MC, V. Free valet parking. **Amenities:** Restaurant; 2 bars; 2 pools; spa; Jacuzzi; concierge; tour desk; room service; in-room massage; babysitting; laundry; nonsmoking rooms. *In room:* A/C, TV/DVD, high-speed Internet access, minibar, hair dryer, safe.

AKUMAL: BEAUTIFUL BAYS & CAVERN DIVING

Continuing south on Highway 307 for 2km (1¼ miles), you'll come to the turnoff for Akumal, marked by a traffic light. This is a small, ecologically oriented community built on the shores of two beautiful bays. Akumal has been around long enough that it feels more relaxed than booming places such as Playa and Tulum, and hotel rooms tend to go for less here. Akumal draws a lot of families, who can save money by renting a condo with a kitchen to fix meals. Less than 1km (a half-mile) down the road is a white arch. Just before it are a couple of grocery stores (the one named Super Chomak has an ATM) and a laundry service. Just after it (to the right) is the Hotel Akumal Caribe. If you follow the road to the left and keep to the left, you'll reach Half Moon Bay, lined with two- and three-story condos, and eventually Yal-ku Lagoon, which is a snorkeling park. For renting a condo, contact **Info-Akumal** (© 800/381-7048 in the U.S.; www.info-akumal.com), **Akumal Vacations** (© 800/448-7137 in the U.S.; www.akumalvacations.com), or **Loco Gringo** (www.locogringo.com).

Both bays have sandy beaches with rocky or silt bottoms. This is a popular diving spot. There are three dive shops in town and at least 30 dive sites offshore. The **Akumal Dive Shop** (© 984/875-9032; www.akumal.com), one of the oldest and best dive shops on the coast, offers courses in technical diving and cavern diving trips. It and **Akumal Dive Adventures** (© 984/875-9157), at the Vista del Mar hotel on Half Moon Bay, offer resort courses as well as complete certification.

Yal-ku Lagoon snorkeling park is like a miniature and more primitive Xel-Ha. It's open daily from 8am to 5:30pm. Admission is $7 (£3.50) for adults, $4 (£2) for children 3 to 14. The lagoon is about 700m (2,296 ft.) long and about 200m (656 ft.) at its widest. You can paddle around comfortably in sheltered water with little current and see fish and a few other creatures. It makes for a relaxing outing, but for sheer variety, I prefer snorkeling along the reefs.

WHERE TO STAY

Rates below are for two people and include taxes. Most hotels and condo rentals charge higher rates than those listed here for the holidays.

Hotel Akumal Caribe *Kids*   The hotel rooms and garden bungalows of this hotel sit along Akumal Bay. Both are large and comfortable, with tile floors and good-size bathrooms. The 40 bungalows are simply and comfortably furnished, with kitchenettes. The 21 rooms in the three-story beachside hotel are more elaborately furnished, with refrigerators. They have a king-size bed or two queen-size beds, tile floors, and Mexican accents. There is a large pool on the grounds. Other rooms belonging to the hotel are condos and the lovely **Villas Flamingo** on Half Moon Bay. The villas have two or three bedrooms and large living, dining, and kitchen areas, as well as lovely furnished patios just steps from the beach. The four villas share a pool.

Carretera Cancún–Tulum (Hwy. 307) Km 104. © 984/206-3500. www.hotelakumalcaribe.com. (Reservations: P.O. Box 13326, El Paso, TX 79913; © 800/351-1622 in the U.S., 800/343-1440 in Canada, or 915/584-3552.) 70 units. High season $123 (£62) bungalow, $156 (£78) hotel room, $190–$360 (£95–£180) villa or condo; low season $100 (£50) bungalow, $122 (£61) hotel room, $130–$212 (£65–£106) villa or condo. Reservations with prepayment by check only. AE, MC, V. Free parking. Low-season packages available. **Amenities:** 2 restaurants; bar; large outdoor pool; dive shop; tour desk; children's activities (seasonal); in-room massage; babysitting. *In room:* A/C, kitchenette (in some), fridge, coffeemaker, no phone.

Vista del Mar Hotel and Condos *Value*   This beachside property is a great place to stay for several reasons. It offers hotel rooms at good prices, and large, fully equipped condos that you don't have to rent by the week. The lovely, well-tended beach in front of the hotel has chairs and umbrellas. There's an on-site dive shop, which eliminates the hassle of organizing dive trips. Hotel rooms are small and contain either a queen-size bed or a double and a twin bed. They consist of a well-equipped kitchen, a living area, two or three bedrooms, and one to three bathrooms. All have balconies or terraces facing the sea and are furnished with hammocks. Several rooms come with whirlpool tubs.

Half Moon Bay, 77760 Akumal, Q Roo. © 877/425-8625 in the U.S. Fax 505/988-3882. www.akumalinfo.com. 27 units. High season $102 (£51) double, $207–$325 (£104–£163) condo; low season $84 (£42) double, $124–$196 (£62–£98) condo. MC, V. Limited free parking. **Amenities:** Restaurant; bar; small outdoor pool; watersports equipment rental; dive shop. *In room:* A/C, TV, CD player, kitchenette, fridge, coffeemaker, no phone.

WHERE TO DINE

There are about 10 places to eat in Akumal, and there's a convenient grocery store, **Super Chomak,** by the archway. The **Turtle Bay Café and Bakery** is good (not open for supper in low season), as is **La Buena Vida,** on Half Moon Bay.

XEL-HA: SNORKELING & SWIMMING ⋒⋒

Before you get to Xel-Ha (shell-*hah*) nature park, you'll pass the turnoff for **Aktun Chen** ⋒ cavern (a bit beyond Akumal). Of the several caverns that I've toured in the Yucatán, this is one of the best—it has lots of geological features, good lighting, several underground pools, and large chambers, all carefully preserved. The tour takes about an hour and requires a good amount of walking, but the footing is good. You exit not far from where you enter. There is also a zoo with specimens of the local fauna. Some of the critters are allowed to run about freely. In my opinion, the cost of admission is high—$17 (£8.50) for adults, $9 (£4.50) for children—but this is true of several attractions on this coast. The cavern is open 9am to 5pm daily. The turnoff is to the right, and the cave is about 4km (2½ miles) from the road.

Thirteen kilometers (8 miles) south of Akumal is **Xel-Ha** (© 998/884-9422 in Cancún, 984/873-3588 in Playa, or 984/875-6000 at the park; www.xelha.com.mx). The centerpiece of Xel-Ha is a large, beautiful lagoon where freshwater and saltwater meet. You can swim, float, and snorkel in beautifully clear water surrounded by jungle. A small train takes guests upriver to a drop-off point. There, you can store all your clothes and gear in a locked sack that is taken down to the locker rooms in the main part of the building. The water moves calmly toward the sea, and you can float along with it. Snorkeling here is more comfortable than on the open sea—there are no waves and currents to pull you about, but there are several species of fish, including rays.

Inside the park, you can rent snorkeling equipment and an underwater camera. Platforms allow nonsnorkelers to view the fish. Another way to view fish is to use the park's Snuba gear—a contraption that allows you to breathe air through 6-m (20-ft.) tubes connected to scuba tanks floating on the surface. It frees you of the cumbersome tank while allowing you to stay down without having to hold your breath. Rental costs $50 (£25) for about an hour. Like Snuba but more involved is sea-trek, a device consisting of an elaborate plastic helmet with air hoses. It allows you to walk around on the bottom breathing normally and perhaps participate in feeding the stingrays.

The park has completely remodeled and enlarged the dolphin area. This has improved the experience of swimming with these intelligent, powerful creatures. A 1-hour swim costs $125 (£63) plus park admission. You can also participate in a program that includes transportation from most hotels in the Riviera Maya and takes you to the dolphin area. It includes locker and equipment, too, all for $139 (£76). Make reservations (© 998/887-6840) at least 24 hours in advance.

Other attractions include a plant nursery; an apiary for the local, stingerless Maya bees; and a lovely path through the tropical forest bordering the lagoon. Xel-Ha is open daily from 8:30am to 5pm. Parking is free. Admission is $40 (£20) adults, and

$30 (£15) children ages 5 to 11; children younger than 5 enter free. Admission includes use of inner tubes, life vest, and shuttle train to the river, and the use of changing rooms and showers. (Though not listed on the website, the park often has discount admission during the weekend.) An all-inclusive option includes snorkeling equipment rental, locker rental, towels, food, and beverages: Adults for $75 (£38), and children for $50 (£25). These prices are not discounted on the weekend. The park has five restaurants, two ice-cream shops, and a store. It accepts American Express, MasterCard, and Visa, and it has an ATM.

Signs clearly mark the turnoff to Xel-Ha, close to the ruins of Tulum. A popular day tour from Cancún or Playa combines the two. If you're traveling on your own, the best time to enjoy Xel-Ha without the crowds is during the weekend from 9am to 2pm.

About 2km (1 mile) south of Xel-Ha are the **Hidden Worlds Cenotes** ★★★ (© **984/877-8535;** www.hiddenworlds.com.mx), which offers an excellent opportunity to snorkel or dive in a couple of nearby caverns. The caverns are part of a vast network that makes up a single underground river system. The water is crystalline (and cold), and the rock formations impressive. These caverns were filmed for the IMAX production *Journey into Amazing Caves.* The people running the show are resourceful. The snorkel tour costs $40 (£20) and takes you to two different caverns (a half tour costs $25/£13). The main form of transportation is "jungle mobile," with a guide who throws in information and lore about the jungle plant life that you see. You'll be walking some, so take shoes or sandals. I've toured several caverns, but floating through one gave me an entirely different perspective. For divers, a one-tank dive is $50 (£25), a two-tank experience is $90 (£45). The owners have also installed a 180m (590-ft.) zip line on the property. I haven't tried it, but it looks fast.

PUNTA SOLIMAN & TANKAH BAYS

The next couple of turnoffs lead to Punta Solimán and Tankah bays. On Punta Solimán Bay is a beach restaurant called **Oscar y Lalo's.** Here you can rent kayaks and snorkel equipment and paddle out to the reefs for some snorkeling. Three kilometers (2 miles) farther is the turnoff for Tankah Bay, which has a handful of lodgings and some rental houses. The most interesting hotel is **Casa Cenote** (© **998/874-5170;** www.casacenote.com). It has an underground river that surfaces at a cenote in the back of the property then goes underground and bubbles up into the sea just a few feet offshore. Casa Cenote has seven rooms, all on the beach. The double rate runs from $150 to $200 (£75–£100) depending upon the season, including breakfast. The American owner provides kayaks and snorkeling gear and can arrange dives, fishing trips, and sailing charters.

A beach road connects the two bays. I found the snorkeling in Tankah better than in Punta Solimán. Snorkeling in the latter was both interesting and frustrating. I've never before experienced so many thermoclines, which are produced by freshwater seeping from the floors of the bay and coming in contact with the warmer saltwater. Light passing through the water is refracted in funny ways. At first I found the effect interesting—it lent an ethereal shininess to everything I was seeing—but then it just got annoying as it cut down sharply on visibility. At one point I was floating through some of the worst of it, trying not to stir up the water, when a giant silvery barracuda came ghostlike through the shimmering water and crossed my field of vision about 2m (6 ft.) away. As he passed slowly by me, I was astonished at how beautiful and luminescent he looked. Still, I will take clear water over shimmering water every time.

4 Tulum ★★★, Punta Allen & Sian Ka'an

Tulum *pueblo* (130km/80 miles from Cancún) is a small town on Highway 307 where it intersects the road to Cobá. Nearby is an incredible beach, which has become the Tulum hotel zone—a collection of about 30 *palapa* hotels stretching from the Tulum ruins southward, along the Punta Allen Peninsula, all the way to the entrance to the Sian Ka'an Biosphere Reserve. The Tulum ruins are a walled Maya city of the post-Classic age perched on a rocky cliff overlooking the Caribbean. Tulum beach used to be a destination for backpackers, but the *palapa* hotels have gone upscale, and the beach now attracts a well-heeled crowd that seeks to get away from the bustle of the big hotels and resorts. The town of Tulum has several modest hotels, more than a dozen restaurants, several stores and pharmacies, three cybercafes, a few dive shops, a bank, two ATMs, and a new bus station.

For those who really want to leave the modern world behind, there's the Punta Allen Peninsula. Getting to the end of the peninsula from Tulum can take 1½ to 3 hours, depending on the condition of the road, which can be downright ugly. It's a quiet, out-of-the-way place; the generator (if there is one) shuts down at 10pm. For most people, Tulum will be far enough away from the crowds. But in Punta Allen, you'll find great fishing and snorkeling, the natural riches of the Sian Ka'an Biosphere Reserve, and a chance to rest up at what truly feels like the end of the road. A few beach cabañas offer reliable power, telephones, and hot showers.

ORIENTATION To visit the Tulum area, get a rental car; it will make everything much easier. From the north you'll pass the entrance to the ruins before the town. After the ruins, you'll come to a highway intersection with a traffic light. To the right is the highway leading to the ruins of Cobá (see "Cobá Ruins," later in this chapter); to the left is the Tulum hotel zone, which begins about 2km (1½ miles) away. The road sign reads BOCA PAILA, which is a place halfway down the **Punta Allen Peninsula.** This road eventually goes all the way to the tip of the peninsula and the town of Punta Allen, a lobstering and fishing village. It is a rough road that is slow going for most of the way. A few kilometers down the road is the entrance to the **Biosphere Reserve.**

The town of Tulum is growing quickly. It now extends for 3 or 4 blocks in either direction from the highway. The highway widens here and is called Avenida Tulum. It is lined with stores, restaurants, and what seems like a drug store on every corner. One place that I find handy is a travel agency/communications/package center called **Savana** (*©* 984/871-2081) on the east side of Avenida Tulum between calles Orion and Beta. Most of the staff speaks English and can answer questions about tours and

---

Tips Getting to the Beach

If you're staying elsewhere but want some beach time in Tulum, the easiest thing to do is drive to El Paraíso Beach Club. It's about 1km (a half mile) south of the ruins (take a left at the "T" junction). This is a great place—there's a long, broad beach that is pure sand, and access is free. The owners make money by selling food and drink, so they ask you not to bring your own. If you want isolation, drive down the dirt road towards Punta Allen. After you pass the last of the beach hotels there are a couple of places where the beach comes into view. You can pull over and spread out your beach towel.

calling home. There's also a good bicycle rental store: **Iguana Bike** (© 984/871-2357; hugo_bike@hotmail.com) on Calle Satélite Sur near the corner of Calle Andrómeda. The owner, Hugo Herrera, maintains his bikes well and organizes tours.

EXPLORING THE TULUM ARCHEOLOGICAL SITE

Thirteen kilometers (8 miles) south of Xel-Ha are the ruins of Tulum, a Maya fortress-city on a cliff above the sea. The ruins are open to visitors daily from 7am to 5pm in the winter, 8am to 6pm in the summer. It's always best to go early, before the crowds start showing up (around 9:30am). The entrance to the ruins is about a 5-minute walk from the archaeological site. There are artisans' stands, a bookstore, a museum, a restaurant, several large bathrooms, and a ticket booth. Admission fee to the ruins is $5 (£2.50). If you want to ride the shuttle from the visitor center to the ruins, it's another $1.50 (75p). Parking is $3 (£1.50). A video camera permit costs $4 (£2). Licensed guides have a stand next to the path to the ruins and charge $20 (£10) for a 45-minute tour in English, French, or Spanish for up to four persons. In some ways, they are like performers and will tailor their presentation to the responses they receive from you. Some will try to draw connections between the Maya and Western theology, and they will point out architectural details that you might otherwise miss.

By A.D. 900, the end of the Classic period, Maya civilization had begun its decline, and the large cities to the south were abandoned. Tulum is one of the small city-states that rose to fill the void. It came to prominence in the 13th century as a seaport, controlling maritime commerce along this section of the coast, and remained inhabited well after the arrival of the Spanish. The primary god here was the diving god, depicted on several buildings as an upside-down figure above doorways. Seen at the Palace at Sayil and Cobá, this curious, almost comical figure is also known as the bee god.

The most imposing building in Tulum is a large stone structure above the cliff called the **Castillo** (castle). Actually a temple as well as a fortress, it was once covered with stucco and painted. In front of the Castillo are several unrestored palacelike buildings partially covered with stucco. On the **beach** below, where the Maya once came ashore, tourists swim and sunbathe, combining a visit to the ruins with a dip in the Caribbean.

The **Temple of the Frescoes,** directly in front of the Castillo, contains interesting 13th-century wall paintings, though entrance is no longer permitted. Distinctly Maya, they represent the rain god Chaac and Ixchel, the goddess of weaving, women, the moon, and medicine. On the cornice of this temple is a relief of the head of the rain god. If you pause a slight distance from the building, you'll see the eyes, nose, mouth, and chin. Notice the remains of the red-painted stucco—at one time all the buildings at Tulum were painted bright red.

Much of what we know of Tulum at the time of the Spanish Conquest comes from the writings of Diego de Landa, third bishop of the Yucatán. He wrote that Tulum was a small city inhabited by about 600 people who lived in platform dwellings along a street and supervised the trade traffic from Honduras to the Yucatán. Though it was a walled city, most of the inhabitants probably lived outside the walls, leaving the interior for the residences of governors and priests and ceremonial structures. Tulum survived about 70 years after the conquest, when it was finally abandoned. Because of the great number of visitors this site receives, it is no longer possible to climb all of the ruins. In many cases, visitors are asked to remain behind roped-off areas to view them.

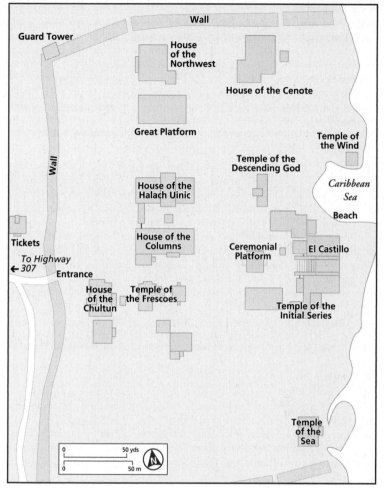

Wall

Guard Tower

House of the Northwest

House of the Cenote

Great Platform

Temple of the Wind

Wall

Temple of the Descending God

Caribbean Sea

Beach

House of the Halach Uinic

House of the Columns

Ceremonial Platform

El Castillo

Tickets

To Highway
← 307

Entrance

House of the Chultun

Temple of the Frescoes

Temple of the Initial Series

Temple of the Sea

0   50 yds
0   50 m

WHERE TO STAY

If you can afford staying at one of the small beach hotels in Tulum, do so. The experience is enjoyable and relaxing. But most are on the expensive side. Demand is high, supply is limited, and the hotels have to generate their own electricity (bring a flashlight). Most of the inexpensive hotels are not that comfortable. If you're on a budget, you will be more comfortable staying in Akumal or in one of the modest hotels in town and be a day-tripper to the beach.

Take the Boca Paila road from Highway 307. Three kilometers (2 miles) ahead, you come to a T-junction. To the south are most of the *palapa* hotels; to the north are several, too. The rates listed below don't include the week of Christmas and New Year, when prices go above regular high-season rates.

Very Expensive

Ana y José ⭐⭐ This *palapa* hotel has gone "boutique" with a spa, suites, and serious remodeling of rooms. It's a far cry now from what it used to be—a simple collection of cabins and a restaurant on the beach. Now there are marble countertops and marble tile floors. Rooms are large and comfortable. There's A/C in all the lower rooms that don't catch the sea breeze. The beach here is excellent. Ana y José is 6.5km (4 miles) south of the Tulum ruins.

Carretera Punta Allen Km 7 (Apdo. Postal 15), 77780 Tulum, Q. Roo. ⓒ **998/880-5629**. Fax 998/880-6021. www.anayjose.com. 22 units. $232–$256 (£116–£128) garden and pool view; $304–$370 (£152–£185) beachfront and ocean view. AE, MC, V. Free parking. **Amenities:** Restaurant; outdoor pool; spa; tour info; car rental. *In room:* A/C in some rooms, safe, no phone.

Azulik ⭐⭐ Azulik is all about slowing down, leaving civilization behind (except for such niceties as indoor plumbing and room service), and enjoying the simple life (with or without clothes). I enjoyed the simple life during a brief stay here, and appreciated the design and positioning of the individual cabañas. Most sit on a stone ledge above the sea. The ledge is just high enough to provide privacy while you sit out on the semi-shaded wood deck in front of your cabaña enjoying either the sun or the stars. For that purpose, they come with chairs, hammocks, and a wooden tub for soaking. (There is a larger wooden tub indoors for bathing.) Each cabaña is constructed entirely of wood and glass and thatch. There is no electricity, only candles. Each has a king-size bed with mosquito netting and a queen-size bed, suspended on ropes, for lounging during the day.

Carretera Boca Paila Km 5.5, 77780 Tulum, Q. Roo. ⓒ **877/532-6737** in the U.S. and Canada. www.azulik.com. 15 units. High season $325–$350 (£163–£175) double; low season $255–$285 (£128–£143) double. MC, V. Limited free parking. Children younger than 18 not accepted. **Amenities:** Restaurant; bar; spa; room service. *In room:* Safe, no phone.

Moderate

Posada Dos Ceibas ⭐ Of all the places along this coast, this one reminds me the most of the way hotels in Tulum used to be: simple, quiet, and ecological without being pretentious. This is a good choice for a no-fuss beach vacation. The one- and two-story cottages are spread out through the vegetation. Rooms are simply furnished and come with ceiling fans, and almost all have private patios or porches. Price varies according to the size of the rooms. The grounds are well tended. The electricity is solar generated and comes on at 6pm. There is a pure sand beach.

Carretera Tulum-Boca Paila Km 10, 77780 Tulum, Q. Roo. ⓒ **984/877-6024**. www.dosceibas.com. 8 units. High season $130–$250 (£65–£125) double; low season $90–$160 (£45–£80). MC, V. **Amenities:** Restaurant; massage; yoga classes. *In room:* No phone.

Zamas ⭐⭐ A couple from San Francisco has made this rustic getaway most enjoyable by concentrating on the essentials: comfort, privacy, and good food. The cabañas are simple, attractive, well situated for catching the breeze. Most rooms are in individual structures; the suites and oversize rooms are in modest two-story buildings. For the money, I like the garden *palapas,* which are attractive, spacious, and comfortable, and come with a queen-size bed and a twin or a king- and queen-size bed. Two small beachfront cabañas with one queen-size bed go for a little less. The most expensive rooms are the upstairs oceanview units, which enjoy a large terrace and lots of sea breezes. They come with a king-size and a queen-size bed or 2 queen-size beds. The

The Sian Ka'an Biosphere Reserve

Down the peninsula a few miles south of the Tulum ruins, you'll pass the guardhouse of the Sian Ka'an Biosphere Reserve. The reserve is a tract of 500,000 hectares (1.3 million acres) set aside in 1986 to preserve tropical forests, savannas, mangroves, coastal and marine habitats, and 110km (70 miles) of coastal reefs. The area is home to jaguars; pumas; ocelots; margays; jaguarundis; spider and howler monkeys; tapirs; white-lipped and collared peccaries; manatees; brocket and white-tailed deer; crocodiles; and green, loggerhead, hawksbill, and leatherback sea turtles. It also protects 366 species of birds—you might glimpse of an ocellated turkey, a great curassow, a brilliantly colored parrot, a toucan or trogon, a white ibis, a roseate spoonbill, a jabiru (or wood stork), a flamingo, or one of 15 species of herons, egrets, and bitterns.

The park has three parts: a "core zone" restricted to research; a "buffer zone," to which visitors and families already living there have restricted use; and a "cooperation zone," which is outside the reserve but vital to its preservation. There are two principal entrances to the biosphere reserve: one is from the community of Muyil, which is off Highway 307, south of Tulum (you take a boat down canals built by the Maya that connect to the Boca Paila lagoon); the other is from the community of Punta Allen (by Jeep down the peninsula, which separates the Boca Paila Lagoon from the sea).

Visitors can arrange day trips in Tulum from **Centro Ecológico de Sian Ka'an** (© 984/871-2499; www.cesiak.org). It's office is at Av. Tulum 68. This is a nonprofit for the support of Sian Ka'an.

restaurant serves the freshest seafood—I've seen the owner flag down passing fishermen to buy their catch. A white-sand beach stretches between rocky areas.

Carretera Punta Allen Km 5, 77780 Tulum, Q. Roo. © 415/387-9806 in the U.S. www.zamas.com. 20 units. High season $120–$160 (£60–£80) beachfront double, $130–$160 (£65–£80) garden double, $200 (£100) oceanview double; low season $90–$125 (£45–£63) beachfront double, $95–$125 (£48–£63) garden double, $145 (£73) oceanview double. No credit cards. Limited free parking. **Amenities:** Restaurant. *In room:* No phone.

Inexpensive

Cabañas Tulum   Next to Ana y José is a row of cinderblock bungalows facing the same beautiful ocean and beach. Rooms are simple and poorly lit, with basic bathrooms. All rooms have two double beds (most with new mattresses), screens on the windows, a table, one electric light, and a porch facing the beach. Electricity is available from 7 to 11am and 5 to 11pm.

Carretera Punta Allen Km 7 (Apdo. Postal 63), 77780 Tulum, Q. Roo. © 984/115-9912. Fax 984/802-5326. www.hotelstulum.com. 32 units. $70–$100 (£35–£50) double. No credit cards. Limited free parking. **Amenities:** Restaurant; game room. *In room:* No phone.

WHERE TO DINE

There are several restaurants in the town of Tulum. They are reasonably priced and do an okay job. On the main street are **Charlie's** (© 984/871-2136), my favorite for

Mexican food, and **Don Cafeto's** (© 984/871-2207). **La Nave** (© 984/871-2592) is a good Italian restaurant. At **Azafrán** (© 984/129-6130) you can get surprisingly sophisticated cooking served in a small, rustic dining room. Also in town are a couple of roadside places that grill chicken and serve it with rice and beans. And there's a local people's restaurant at the southern end of town called **Doña Tina.** Meals on the coast are going to be more expensive but more varied. Many of the hotels have restaurants—I've eaten well at **Copal**, north of the T-junction, and **Zamas**, which is south.

EXPLORING THE PUNTA ALLEN PENINSULA

If you've been captured by an adventurous spirit and have an excessively sanguine opinion of your rental car's off-road capabilities, you might want to take a trip down the Punta Allen Peninsula, especially if your interests lie in fly-fishing, birding, or simply exploring new country. The far end of the peninsula is only 50km (30 miles) away, but it can be a very slow and bouncy trip (up to 3 hr., depending on the condition of the road). Not far from the last cabaña hotel is the entrance to the 500,000-hectare (1.3-million-acre) **Sian Ka'an Biosphere Reserve** (see below).

Halfway down the peninsula, at a small bridge, is the **Boca Paila Fishing Lodge** (www.bocapaila.com). Not for the general traveler, it specializes in hosting fly-fishers, with weeklong all-inclusive fishing packages. At this point, the peninsula is quite narrow. You can see the Boca Paila lagoon on one side and the sea on the other. Another 25km (15 miles) gets you to the village of Punta Allen. Before the town is a little hotel called **Rancho Sol Caribe.** It has only four rooms and a lovely beach all to itself. Punta Allen is a lobstering and fishing village on a palm-studded beach. Isolated and rustic, it's very much the laid-back end of the line. It has a lobster cooperative, a few streets with modest homes, and a lighthouse. The **Cuzan Guesthouse** (www.fly fishmx.com) is a collection of 12 cabins and one restaurant on a nice sandy beach. Its main clientele is fly-fishers, and it offers all-inclusive fishing packages. But co-owner Sonia Litvak, a Californian, will rent to anyone curious enough to want to go down there. She also offers snorkeling trips and boat tours.

5 Cobá Ruins

168km (104 miles) SW of Cancún

Older than most of Chichén Itzá and much larger than Tulum, Cobá was the dominant city of the eastern Yucatán before A.D. 1000. The site is large and spread out, with thick forest growing between the temple groups. Rising high above the forest canopy are tall and steep pyramids of the Classic Maya style. Of the major sites, this one is the least reconstructed and so disappoints those who expect another Chichén Itzá. The stone sculpture here has worn off and has become impossible to make out. But the structures themselves and the surrounding jungle and twin lakes make the experience enjoyable. This is not a cenote area, and the water has nowhere to go but stay on the surface. The forest canopy is also higher than in the northern part of the peninsula.

ESSENTIALS

GETTING THERE & DEPARTING   By Car   The road to Cobá begins in Tulum and continues for 65km (40 miles). Watch out for both *topes* (speed bumps) and potholes. The road is going to be repaved and widened this year. Close to the village of Cobá you will come to a triangle offering you three choices: Nuevo Xcan, Valladolid, and Cobá. Make sure not to get on the other two roads. The entrance to the ruins is a short distance down the road past some small restaurants and the large lake.

By Bus   Several buses a day leave Tulum and Playa del Carmen for Cobá. Several companies offer bus tours.

EXPLORING THE COBA RUINS

The Maya built many intriguing cities in the Yucatán, but few grander than Cobá ("water stirred by wind"). Much of the 67-sq.-km (26-sq.-mile) site remains unexcavated. A 100km (62-mile) *sacbé* (a pre-Hispanic raised road) through the jungle linked Cobá to Yaxuná, once an important Maya center 50km (30 miles) south of Chichén Itzá. It's the Maya's longest known *sacbé*, and at least 50 shorter ones lead from here. An important city-state, Cobá flourished from A.D. 632 (the oldest carved date found here) until after the rise of Chichén Itzá, around 800. Then Cobá faded in importance and population until it was finally abandoned. Scholars believe Cobá was an important trade link between the Yucatán Caribbean coast and inland cities.

Once at the site, keep your bearings—you can get turned around in the maze of dirt roads in the jungle. And bring bug spray. As spread out as this city is, renting a bike (which you can do at the entrance for $3/£1.50) is a good option. Branching off from every labeled path, you'll notice unofficial narrow paths into the jungle, used by locals as shortcuts through the ruins. These are good for birding, but be careful to remember the way back. Turn to the color section of this book for a map of the ruins.

The **Grupo Cobá** holds an impressive pyramid, **La Iglesia (the Temple of the Church).** Take the path bearing right after the entrance. The urge to climb the temple is great, but the view is better from El Castillo in the Nohoch Mul group farther back.

From here, return to the main path and turn right. You'll pass a sign pointing right to the ruined *juego de pelota* (**ball court),** but the path is obscure.

Continuing straight ahead on this path for 5 to 10 minutes, you'll come to a fork in the road. To the left and right you'll notice jungle-covered, unexcavated pyramids, and at one point, you'll see a raised portion crossing the pathway—this is the visible remains of the *sacbé* to Yaxuná. Throughout the area, carved stelae stand by pathways or lie forlornly in the jungle underbrush. Although protected by crude thatched roofs, most are weatherworn enough that they're indiscernible.

The left fork leads to the **Nohoch Mul Group,** which contains **El Castillo.** With the exception of Structure 2 in Calakmul, this is the tallest pyramid in the Yucatán (even higher than El Castillo at Chichén Itzá and the Pyramid of the Magician at Uxmal). Visitors can climb to the top. From this lofty perch, you can see unexcavated jungle-covered pyramidal structures poking up through the forest canopy all around.

The right fork (more or less straight on) goes to the **Conjunto Las Pinturas.** Here, the main attraction is the **Pyramid of the Painted Lintel,** a small structure with traces of its original bright colors above the door. You can climb up for a close look. Though maps of Cobá show ruins around two lakes, there are really only two excavated groups.

Admission is $4 (£2), free for children younger than age 12. Parking is $1 (50p). A video camera permit costs $4 (£2). The site is open daily from 8am to 5pm, sometimes longer. **Note:** Visit Cobá in the morning or after the heat of the day has passed. Mosquito repellent, drinking water, and comfortable shoes are imperative.

WHERE TO STAY & DINE

If nightfall catches you in Cobá, you have limited lodging choices. There is one tourist hotel called **Villas Arqueológicas Cobá,** which fronts the lake. Though smaller than its sister hotels in Uxmal and Chichén Itzá, it's the same in style—modern rooms that are attractive and functional, so long as you're not too tall. It has a restaurant that serves all three meals and a swimming pool. The hotel could be empty or full given that most of its business comes from bus tours. This hotel and the other Villas Arqueológicas were sold in late 2007 by Club Med to the Islander Collection, a Mexican hotel group. To make reservations, call ✆ **987/872-9300,** ext. 8101. There's also a cheap hotel in town called **El Bocadito** (no phone), with simple rooms for $25 (£13) per night. It has a small restaurant; there are a couple more eateries in the town as well.

EN ROUTE TO THE LOWER CARIBBEAN COAST: FELIPE CARRILLO PUERTO

Mexico's lower Caribbean coast is officially called the Costa Maya. This area attracts fishermen, divers, archeology enthusiasts, birders, and travelers looking to get away from the crowds. For divers there is some great diving along the coastal reefs and at the Chinchorro Reef, which lies about 30km (20 miles) offshore (see below). You'll find sandy beaches good for sunbathing, but not for swimming because of the prominent coastal reef. But if you want to snorkel or dive among less-visited reefs, kayak in calm turquoise water, or perhaps do some fly-fishing away from the crowds, this area is a great option. And there's fine swimming in Lake Bacalar.

You also might enjoy the astounding Maya ruins in the Río Bec area, west of Bacalar. Here, too, you'll find a richer ecosystem than the northern part of the peninsula. The forest canopy is higher, and the wildlife is more abundant. If you're interested in exploring this territory, see "Side Trips to Maya Ruins from Chetumal," later in this chapter.

Continue south on Highway 307 from Tulum. The road narrows, the speed limit drops, and you begin to see *topes.* Down the road some 25km (15 miles), a sign points to the small but interesting ruins of **Muyil.** Take bug spray. The principal ruins are a small group of buildings and a plaza dominated by the Castillo, a pyramid of medium height but unusual construction. From here, a canal dug by the Maya enters what is now the Sian Ka'an Biosphere Reserve and empties into a lake, with other canals going from there to the saltwater estuary of Boca Paila. The local community offers a boat ride through these canals and lakes. The 3½-hour tour includes snorkeling the canal and letting the current carry you along. Soft drinks are also included. This is much the same Sian Ka'an tour offered by travel agencies in Tulum, but without some of the infrastructure. The agencies charge more but provide transportation, better interpretation, and lunches.

Felipe Carrillo Puerto (pop. 60,000) is the first large town you pass on the road to Ciudad Chetumal. It has two gas stations, a market, a bus terminal, and a few modest hotels and restaurants. Next to the gas station in the center of town is a bank with an ATM. Highway 184 goes from here into the interior of the peninsula, leading eventually to Mérida, which makes Carrillo Puerto a turning point for those making the "short circuit" of the Yucatán Peninsula.

The town is of interest for having been a rebel stronghold during the War of the Castes and the center of the intriguing millenarian cult of the "Talking Cross." The town is still home to a strong community of believers in the cult who practice their own brand of religion and are respected by the entire town. Every month, a synod of sorts is held here for the church leaders of 12 neighboring towns.

6 Majahual, Xcalak & the Chinchorro Reef

South of Felipe Carrillo Puerto, the speed bumps begin in earnest. In 45 minutes you reach the turnoff for Majahual and Xcalak, which is after the town of Limones. From here, the highway has been widened and repaved. The roadwork was done to facilitate bus tours from the cruise-ship pier in **Majahual** (mah-hah-*wahl*) to some of the Maya ruins close by. Many passengers elect to enjoy some beach time in Majahual instead. The best option is to keep your distance from the pier and stay either in the lower Majahual area or at the bottom of the peninsula near Xcalak. You'll come to the turnoff for Xcalak before you get to Majahual. Xcalak has a decent dive shop. From Majahual to Xcalak takes a little less than an hour.

Xcalak (eesh-kah-*lahk*) is a depopulated, weather-beaten fishing village with a few comfortable places to stay and a couple of restaurants. It once had a population as large as 1,200 before the 1958 hurricane washed most of the town away; now it has only 300 permanent residents. It's charming in a run-down way, and you'll certainly feel miles away from the crush of the crowds. From here you work your way back up the coast to get to one of the several small inns just beyond the town.

ORIENTATION

ARRIVING   By Car   Driving south from Felipe Carrillo Puerto, you'll come to the clearly marked turnoff onto Highway 10, 2.5km (1½ miles) after Limones, at a place called Cafetal (before the turnoff, there's a gas station). From there it's a 50km (30-mile) drive to the coast, and Majahual. The pier is north of the road; Hotel Balamkú, which I like, is to the south. If you're going to Xcalak, the turn-off will be 2km (1¼ miles) before Majahual, at a military checkpoint. The road is paved, but usually with some potholes. It's 55km (34 miles) long.

DIVING THE CHINCHORRO REEF

The **Chinchorro Reef Underwater National Park** is 38km (24 miles) long and 13km (8 miles) wide. The oval reef is as shallow as 1m (3¼ ft.) on its interior and as deep as 900m (2,952 ft.) on its exterior. It lies some 30km (19 miles) offshore. Locals claim it's the last virgin reef system in the Caribbean. It's invisible from the ocean side; hence, one of its diving attractions is the **shipwrecks**—at least 30—that decorate the underwater landscape. One is on top of the reef. Divers have counted 40 cannons at one wreck site. On the west side are walls and coral gardens.

Aventuras XTC (© **983/839-8865;** www.xtcdivecenter.com) is a fully equipped dive shop in Xcalak (technical diving, Nitrox, snorkel and fishing trips). You can arrange dives to the local reefs, San Pedro in Belize, and to the Chinchorro Reef.

WHERE TO STAY & DINE

Balamkú Inn on the Beach ⭐⭐   This is a comfortable and friendly place to stay in south Majahual. Rooms are in one- and two-story thatched bungalows distributed across 110m (360 ft.) of beautiful white beach. They are large and breezy with large attractive bathrooms and comfortable mattresses. All have terraces facing the beach. This hotel is very ecological. All the energy is produced by wind and sun. To run this kind of operation takes a rare combination of skill and talent, which these owners have in ample supply.

Carretera Costera Km 5.7, Majahual, Q. Roo. © 983/839-5332. www.balamku.com. 10 units. $75–$85 (£38–£43) double. Rates include full breakfast. AE, MC, V for deposits only; no credit cards at hotel. Free guarded parking. **Amenities:** Watersports equipment; activities arranged; airport transportation arranged; in-room massage; non-smoking rooms. *In room:* Wi-Fi, no phone.

Costa de Cocos Dive & Fly-Fishing Resort 𝒢𝒢   Several freestanding cabañas sit around a large, attractive sandy beach graced with coconut palms. The cabañas are comfortable and have a lot of cross-ventilation, ceiling fans, hot water, and comfortable beds. They also come with 24-hour electricity using wind and solar power and purified tap water. One is a two-bedroom unit with two bathrooms. Activities include kayaking, snorkeling, scuba diving, and fly-fishing. The resort has experienced English-speaking fishing guides and a dive instructor. It has a large dive boat capable of taking divers to the Chinchorro Reef. The casual restaurant/bar offers good home-style cooking.

Carretera Majahual–Xcalak Km 52, Q. Roo. No phone. www.costadecocos.com. 16 cabañas. High season $85 (£43) double; low season $79 (£40) double. Dive and fly-fishing packages available by e-mail request. Rates include breakfast buffet. AE, MC, V. Free parking. **Amenities:** Restaurant; bar; watersports equipment; dive shop. *In room:* No phone.

Hotel Tierra Maya 𝒢   This is a comfortable, modern-style hotel on the beach. Rooms in the two-story building are spacious and designed to have good cross ventilation. They come with ceiling fans. Each has a private balcony or terrace that looks out to the sea, hammocks, and bottled purified water. Solar generators provide electricity. Bathrooms are large, and beds are either twins or queen-size. The owners arrange diving, fishing, and snorkeling trips for guests. Guests have Internet access and the use of kayaks and bikes.

Carretera Majahual–Xcalak Km 54, Q. Roo. No phone. www.tierramaya.net. 7 units. High season $90–$110 (£50–£61) double; low season $70–$90 (£39–£50) double. Rates include continental breakfast. MC, V for advance payments. Limited free parking. **Amenities:** Restaurant; bar; kayaks; bikes; Internet access. *In room:* No phone.

7 Lago Bacalar 𝒢𝒢𝒢

104km (65 miles) SW of Felipe Carrillo Puerto; 37km (23 miles) NW of Chetumal

Bacalar Lake is an elaborate trick played upon the senses. I remember once standing on a pier on the lake and gazing down into perfectly clear water. As I lifted my eyes I could see the blue tint of the Caribbean. Beyond lay a dense tropical forest. A breeze blowing in from the sea smelled of the salt air, and though I knew it to be untrue, I couldn't help but believe that the water I was gazing on was, in fact, an inlet of the sea and not a lake at all—perhaps a well-sheltered lagoon like Xel-Ha. Lakes in tropical lowlands, especially those surrounded by tropical jungle, are turbid and muddy. How could this one be so clear? It's because Bacalar is not fed by surface runoff, but by several cenotes that lie beneath its surface. Only in the Yucatán is such a thing possible.

This is the perfect spot for being bone idle. But there's plenty to do, too. You can explore the jungle, visit some particularly elegant Maya ruins in the nearby Río Bec area, or take in a wonderful museum about the Maya in Chetumal. The town of Bacalar is quiet and quaint. There are a few stores and a couple of restaurants. An 18th-century fort with a moat and stout bastions is by the lake. Inside the fort is a small museum (admission is 50¢/25p) that has several artifacts on display. All text is in Spanish.

ORIENTATION   Driving south on Highway 307, the town of Bacalar is 1½ hours beyond Felipe Carrillo Puerto, clearly marked by signs. If you're driving north from Chetumal, it takes about a half-hour. Buses going south from Cancún and Playa del Carmen stop here, and there are frequent buses from Chetumal. There are now a couple of gas stations on the highway here.

The Yucatán's Lower Caribbean Coast

WHERE TO STAY

Hotel Laguna   The Laguna overlooks the lake from a lovely vantage point. All the rooms share the view and have little terraces that make enjoyable sitting areas. The midsize rooms have ceiling fans, and most come with two double beds. The mattresses in the bungalows aren't good. The bathrooms are simple but have no problem delivering hot water. A restaurant that shares the same view is open from 7am to 9pm. The bar makes a credible margarita. The highest occupancy rates are from July to August and December to January, when you should make a reservation. The hotel is hard to spot from the road; look for the sign about 1km (half a mile) after you pass through the town of Bacalar.

Bulevar Costera de Bacalar 479, 77010 Lago Bacalar, Q. Roo. ✆ **983/834-2206.** Fax 983/834-2205. 34 units. $55 (£28) double; $93–$116 (£48–£58) bungalow for 5–8 persons. MC, V. Free parking. **Amenities:** Restaurant; bar; small outdoor pool, boat rides on the lake. *In room:* No phone.

Rancho Encantado Cottage Resort 🐾🐾   This serene lakeside retreat consists of 13 white-stucco cottages scattered over a shady lawn beside the smooth Lago Bacalar. Each is large and has louvered windows, a red-tile floor, a dining table and chairs, a living room or sitting area, a porch with chairs, and hammocks strung between trees. Some rooms have cedar ceilings and red-tiled roofs, and others have thatched roofs.

Four cottages are waterfront (nos. 9–12). Beds come in different combinations of doubles and twins. The "laguna suite" is a one-bedroom townhouse with study, air-conditioning, and private dock; it rents by the week. Orange, lime, mango, sapote, Ceiba, banana, palm, and oak trees; wild orchids; and bromeliads on the grounds make great bird shelters, attracting flocks of chattering parrots, turquoise-browed motmots, toucans, and many more species. The hotel offers almost a dozen excursions.

Carretera Bacalar–Felipe Carrillo Puerto Km 3, 77930 Chetumal, Q. Roo. ℂ/fax **983/101-3358.** www.encantado.com. (Reservations: P.O. Box 1256, Taos, NM 87571. ℂ **800/505-6292** in the U.S., or ℂ/fax 505/894-7074.) 13 units. High season $160–$190 (£80–£95) double; low season $110–$150 (£55–£75) double. Rates include continental breakfast and dinner. MC, V. Free parking. **Amenities:** Restaurant; bar; large outdoor whirlpool; spa; watersports equipment; tour desk; massage. *In room:* Fridge, coffeemaker.

WHERE TO DINE

Besides the restaurants at the hotels discussed above, you may enjoy the **Restaurante Cenote Azul** (ℂ **983/834-2460;** www.cenoteazul.com.mx), a comfortable open-air thatched-roof restaurant on the edge of the beautiful Cenote Azul. Main courses cost $5 to $16 (£2.50–£8). To get to Restaurant Cenote Azul, follow the highway to the south edge of town and turn left at the restaurant's sign; follow the road around to the restaurant. At the restaurant, you can take a dip in placid Cenote Azul as long as you don't have creams or lotions on your skin.

8 Chetumal

251km (156 miles) S of Tulum; 37km (23 miles) S of Lago Bacalar

Capital of the state, and the second-largest city (after Cancún), Chetumal (pop. 210,000) is not a tourist destination. The old part of town, down by the river (Río Hondo), has a Caribbean feel, but the rest is unremarkable. Chetumal is the gateway to Belize, Tikal, and the Río Bec ruins. If you're going to spend the night here, visit the **Museo de la Cultura Maya** (ℂ **983/832-6838**), especially if you plan to follow the Río Bec ruin route (see "Side Trips to Maya Ruins from Chetumal," below).

ESSENTIALS
GETTING THERE & DEPARTING
BY PLANE **Aviacsa** (ℂ **983/872-7698**) and **Click** (ℂ **983]832-6675**) have a direct flight to and from Mexico City. The airport is west of town, just north of the entrance from the highway.

BY CAR It's a little more than 3 hours from Tulum. If you're heading to Belize, you won't be able to take your rental car because the rental companies won't allow it. To get to the ruins of Tikal in Guatemala, you must go through Belize to the border crossing at Ciudad Melchor de Mencos. To drive into Chetumal, there's a flyover now where the road splits off for Belize.

BY BUS The main bus station (ℂ **983/832-5110**) is 20 blocks from the town center on Insurgentes at Niños Héroes. Buses go to Cancún, Tulum, Playa del Carmen, Puerto Morelos, Mérida, Campeche, Villahermosa, and Tikal, Guatemala.

   To Belize: Buses depart from the Lázaro Cárdenas market (most often called *el mercado nuevo*). Ask for **Autobuses Novelo.** The company has local service every 45 minutes ($12/£6) and four express buses per day ($16/£8).

VISITOR INFORMATION
The **State Tourism Office** (© **983/835-0860,** ext. 1811) is at Calzada del Centenario 622, between Comonfort and Ciricote. It's open Monday to Friday from 9am to 6pm.

ORIENTATION
The telephone **area code** is **983.**

Traffic enters the city from the west and feeds onto Avenida Obregón into town. Stay on Obregón and don't take the exit for Av. Insurgentes. Eventually you'll cross Avenida Héroes, which is the main north-south street.

A MUSEUM NOT TO MISS
Museo de la Cultura Maya ★★★ This modern museum unlocks the complex world of the Maya through interactive exhibits and genuine artifacts. Push a button, and an illustrated description appears, explaining the medicinal and domestic uses of plants with their Mayan and scientific names; another exhibit describes the social classes of the Maya by their manners of dress. One of the most fascinating exhibits describes the Maya's ideal of personal beauty and the subsequent need to deform craniums, scar the face and body, and induce cross-eyed vision. An enormous screen flashes images taken from an airplane flying over more than a dozen Maya sites from Mexico to Honduras. Another large television shows the architectural variety of Maya pyramids and how they were probably built. Then a walk on a glass floor takes you over representative ruins in the Maya world. In the center of the museum is the three-story, stylized, sacred Ceiba tree, which the Maya believed connected Xibalba (the underworld), Earth, and the heavens. If you can arrange it, see the museum before you tour the Río Bec ruins.

Av. Héroes s/n. © 983/832-6838. Admission $6 (£3.30). Tues–Thurs 9am–7pm; Fri–Sat 9am–8pm. Between Colón and Gandhi, 8 blocks from Av. Obregón, just past the Holiday Inn.

WHERE TO STAY
Hotel Holiday Inn Puerta Maya This modern hotel (formerly the Hotel Continental) has the best air-conditioning in town and is only a block from the Museo de la Cultura Maya. Most rooms are midsize and come with two double beds or one king-size bed. Bathrooms are roomy and well lit.

Av. Héroes 171, 77000 Chetumal, Q. Roo. © 800/465-4329 in the U.S., or 983/835-0400. Fax 983/832-1676. 85 units. $125 (£69) double. AE, MC, V. Free secure parking. From Av. Obregón, turn left on Av. Héroes, go 6 blocks, and look for the hotel on the right. **Amenities:** Restaurant; bar; midsize outdoor pool; fitness room; room service; laundry service. *In room:* A/C, TV, Wi-Fi.

Hotel Nachancán One block from *el mercado nuevo* (the new market), this hotel offers plain rooms, with one or two double beds. Bathrooms are small, with no counter space, but they offer plenty of hot water.

Calzada Veracruz 379, 77000 Chetumal, Q. Roo. © 983/832-3232. 20 units. $31 (£16) double; $50 (£25) suite. No credit cards. Drive the length of Av. Obregón to where it stops at Calzada Veracruz, turn left, and drive 2km (1¼ miles); the hotel will be on the right. Off-street parking. **Amenities:** Restaurant; bar. *In room:* A/C, TV, no phone.

WHERE TO DINE
For an economical meal with some local atmosphere, try **Restaurante Pantoja,** on the corner of calles Ghandi and 16 de Septiembre (© **983/832-3957**), 2 blocks east of the Museum of Maya Culture. It offers a cheap daily special, good green enchiladas,

and such local specialties as *poc chuc* (grilled marinated pork). It's open Monday to Saturday from 7am to 7pm. To sample excellent *antojitos,* the local supper food, go to **El Buen Gusto,** on Calzada Veracruz across from the market (no phone). A Chetumal institution, it serves excellent *salbutes* and *panuchos* (both dishes are similar to *gorditas*), tacos, and sandwiches. It's open in the morning until 2pm and then opens again around 7pm and closes at midnight. If for some reason it's closed, go next door **La Ideal,** which many locals hold to be the better of the two supper joints. It has delicious *tacos de pierna* (soft tacos with thinly sliced pork shoulder) and *agua de horchata* (water flavored with rice, vanilla, and toasted pumpkin seed).

ONWARD FROM CHETUMAL

From Chetumal you have several choices. The Maya ruins of Lamanai, in Belize, are an easy day trip if you have transportation (not a rental car). You can explore the Río Bec ruin route directly west of the city (see below) by taking Highway 186. If you want a guided tour of any of the ruins, contact Luis Téllez (© 983/832-3496; www.mayaruinsandbirds.com). He lives in Chetumal, knows the region, its wildlife, and stays up to date with the archeological excavations. He speaks English and is a good driver.

9 Side Trips to Maya Ruins from Chetumal

A few miles west of Bacalar and Chetumal begins an area of Maya settlement known to archaeologists as the Río Bec region. A number of ruins stretch from close to Bacalar well into the state of Campeche. These ruins are numerous, intriguing, and dramatic. Their architecture is heavily stylized, with lots of decoration. In recent years, excavation has led to many discoveries. With excavation has come restoration, but the ruins here have not been rebuilt to the same degree as those at Uxmal and Chichén Itzá. Often, though, buildings were in such great shape that reconstruction was unnecessary.

Nor have these sites been cleared of jungle growth in the same manner as the marquee ruins mentioned above. Trees and vines grow in profusion around the buildings, giving the sites the feel of lost cities. In visiting them, you can imagine what John Lloyd Stephens and Frederick Catherwood must have felt when they traipsed through the Yucatán in the 19th century. And watch for wildlife; on my last visit I saw several denizens of the tropical forest. The fauna along the entire route is especially rich. You might see a toucan, a grand curassow, or a macaw hanging about the ruins, and orioles, egrets, and several birds of prey are extremely common. Gray fox, wild turkey, *tesquintle* (a bushy-tailed, plant-eating rodent), the raccoon relative coatimundi (with its long tapered snout and tail), and armadillos inhabit the area in abundance. At Calakmul, and in the surrounding jungle, circulate two groups of spider monkeys and four groups of howler monkeys.

> **Opening Hours**
> The archaeological sites along the Río Bec are open daily, 8am to 5pm.

THE ROUTE'S STARTING POINT Halfway between Bacalar and Chetumal is the turnoff for Highway 186 to Escárcega (about 20km/12 miles from either town). A major highway, it's well marked. This is the same road that leads to Campeche, Palenque, and Villahermosa. A couple of gas stations are en route; one is at the town of Xpujil. Keep plenty of cash with you, as credit cards are little used in the area. The Río Bec sites are at varying distances off this highway. You pass through a guard station at the border with Campeche State. The guards might ask you to present your travel papers, or they might just wave you on. You can divide your sightseeing into several day trips from Bacalar or Chetumal, or you can spend the night in this area and see more the next day. If you get an early start, you can easily visit a few of the sites mentioned here in a day.

Evidence shows that these ruins, especially Becán, were part of the **trade route** linking the Caribbean coast at Cobá to Edzná and the Gulf coast, and to Lamanai in Belize and beyond. At one time, a great number of cities thrived in this region, and much of the land was dedicated to the intensive cultivation of maize. Today everything lies hidden under a dense jungle, which blankets the land from horizon to horizon.

I've listed the following sites in east-to-west order, the way you would see them driving from the Caribbean coast. If you decide to tour these ruins, take the time to visit the Museo de la Cultura Maya (p. 185) in Chetumal first. It will lend context to what you see. If you want a guide to show you the area, contact **Luis Téllez** (© 983/ 832-3496; www.mayaruinsandbirds.com), who lives in Chetumal. The best way to reach him is through the e-mail link on his website. Luis is the best guide for this region; he's knowledgeable, speaks English, and drives safely and well. He's acquainted with most of the archaeologists excavating these ruins and stays current with their discoveries. He also knows and can identify the local wildlife and guides many tours for birders. Entry to each site is $2 to $4 (£1–£2). Informational signs at each building are in Mayan, Spanish, and English. Few if any refreshments are available at the ruins, so bring your own water and food. All the principal sites have toilets.

Food & Lodging   Your lodging choices are growing. On the upscale side are the Explorean hotel (see below) near Kohunlich and the eco-village in Chicanná. Food and lodging of the no-frills sort can be found in the town of Xpujil and near Calakmul.

The **Explorean** (© 888/679-3748 in the U.S.; www.theexplorean.com) is an eco-lodge for adventure travelers who like their comfort. It sits all alone on the crest of a small hill not far from the ruins of Kohunlich. It has a small pool and spa and lovely rooms, and offers guide services and adventure tours (mountain biking, rappelling, kayaking) as part of an all-inclusive package. The cost is over $500 (£250) for two people and, in addition to the tours, includes food and drink. The hotel is a member of the Fiesta Americana chain.

The **Chicanná Eco Village,** Carretera Escárcega Km 296 (© 981/811-9191 for reservations; www.hoteldelmar.com.mx), is just beyond the town of Xpujil. It offers 42 nicely furnished rooms distributed among several two-story thatched bungalows. The comfortable rooms have two doubles or a king-size bed, ceiling fans, a large bathroom, and screened windows. The manicured lawns and flower beds are lovely, with pathways linking the bungalows to each other and to the restaurant and swimming pool. Double rooms go for $116 (£58).

In the village of Xpujil (just before the ruins of Xpujil) are three modest hotels and a couple of restaurants. The best food and lodging are at **Restaurant y Hotel Calakmul** (© 983/871-6029), run by Doña María Cabrera. The hotel has 27 rooms that go for $48 (£24). They have tile floors, private bathrooms with hot water, and good beds. The restaurant is open daily from 6am to midnight. Main courses cost $4 to $12 (£2–£6). The chicken cooked in herbs is worth ordering. Between Xpujil and Calakmul are three hotels. Two are simple, comfortable, and attractive; one is large and was made with bus tours in mind.

Tips Recommended Reading

For a bit of background reading to help you make the most of your visit, I recommend *A Forest of Kings: The Untold Story of the Ancient Maya,* by Linda Schele and David Freidel (William Morrow, 1990); *The Blood of Kings: Dynasty and Ritual in Maya Art,* by Linda Schele and Mary Ellen Miller (George Braziller, 1968); and *The Maya Cosmos,* by David Freidel and Linda Schele (William Morrow, 1993). *Arqueología Mexicana* magazine devoted its July/August 1995 issue to the Quintana Roo portion of the Río Bec ruin route. The best companion book to have is Joyce Kelly's *An Archaeological Guide to Mexico's Yucatán Peninsula* (University of Oklahoma, 1993), despite the fact that it lacks historical and cultural information, and many sites have expanded since it was written.

Rio Bec Dreams (© 983/871-6057; www.riobecdreams.com) is a good choice because the owners live on the premises and keep maintenance and service sharp. It's 11km (7 miles) west of Xpujil. You can choose between a private or shared bathroom. The rooms are attractive and well spaced across a nice tract of tropical forest. Each has a little terrace, plenty of screened windows, and lots of cross-ventilation. The hotel restaurant is better than anything else in the area. Another choice is **Puerta Calakmul** (www.puertacalakmul.com.mx), at the turnoff for the ruins of Calakmul.

DZIBANCHE & KINICHNA

The turnoff for this site is 37km (23 miles) from the highway intersection and is well marked. From the turnoff, it's another 23km (14 miles) to the ruins. You should ask about the condition of the road before going. These unpaved roads can go from good to bad pretty quickly, but this is such an important site that road repair is generally kept up. Dzibanché (or Tzibanché) means "place where they write on wood"—obviously not the original name, which remains unknown. Exploration began here in 1993, and the site opened to the public in late 1994. Scattered over 42 sq. km (16 sq. miles) are several groupings of buildings and plazas; only a small portion is excavated. It dates from the Classic period (A.D. 300–900) and was occupied for around 700 years.

TEMPLES & PLAZAS   Two large adjoining plazas have been cleared. The most important structure yet excavated is called the Temple of the Owl, which is in the main plaza, Plaza Xibalba. Archaeologists found a stairway that descends from the top of the structure deep into the pyramid, ending in a burial chamber. It's closed to visitors. But there they uncovered a number of beautiful polychromatic lidded vessels, one of which has an owl painted on the top handle with its wings spreading onto the lid. White owls were messengers of the gods of the underworld in the Maya religion. Also found here were the remains of a sacrificial victim and what appear to be the remains of a Maya queen, which is unique in the archaeology of the Maya.

Opposite the Temple of the Owl is the **Temple of the Cormorant,** named after a polychromed drinking vessel found here depicting the bird. Here, too, archaeologists have found evidence of an interior tomb similar to the one in the Temple of the Owl, but excavations of it have not yet begun. Other magnificently preserved pottery pieces found during excavations include an incense burner with an almost three-dimensional figure of the diving god attached to the outside, and another incense burner with an elaborately dressed representation of the god Itzamná attached.

Situated all by itself is **Structure 6,** a miniature rendition of Teotihuacán's style of *tablero* and *talud* architecture. Each step of the pyramid is made of a *talud* (sloping surface) crowned by a *tablero* (vertical stone facing). Teotihuacán was near present-day Mexico City, but its influence stretched as far as Guatemala. At the top of the pyramid is a doorway with a wooden lintel still intact after centuries of weathering. This detail gave the site its name. Carved into the wood are date glyphs for the year A.D. 733.

Near the site is another city, **Kinichná** (Kee-neech-*nah*). About 2.5km (1½ miles) north, it is reachable by a road that becomes questionable during the rainy season. An Olmec-style jade figure was found there. It has a large acropolis with five buildings on three levels, which have been restored and are in good condition, with fragments of the remaining stucco still visible.

KOHUNLICH 𝆕

Kohunlich (Koh-*hoon*-leech), 42km (26 miles) from the turnoff for Highway 186, dates from around A.D. 100 to 900. Turn left off the road, and the entrance is 9km (5½ miles) ahead. From the parking area, you enter the grand, parklike site, crossing a large and shady ceremonial area flanked by four large, conserved pyramidal edifices. Continue walking, and just beyond this grouping you'll come to Kohunlich's famous **Pyramid of the Masks** under a thatched covering. The masks, actually enormous plaster faces from around A.D. 500, are on the facade. Each mask has an elongated face and wears a headdress with a mask on its crest and a mask on the chin piece, essentially masks within masks. The top one is thought to represent the astral world, while the lower one represents the underworld, suggesting that the wearer of this headdress is among the living and not in either of the other worlds. Note the carving on the pupils, which suggests a solar connection, possibly with the night sun that illuminated the underworld. This may mean that the person had shamanic vision.

It's speculated that masks covered much of the facade of this building, built in the Río Bec style, with rounded corners, a false stairway, and a false temple on the top. At least one theory holds that the masks are a composite of several rulers at Kohunlich. In the buildings immediately to the left after you enter, recent excavations uncovered two intact pre-Hispanic skeletons and five decapitated heads that were probably used in a ceremonial ritual. To the right after you enter (follow a shady path through the jungle) is another recently excavated plaza. It's thought to have housed priests or rulers, due to the high quality of pottery found there and the fine architecture of the rooms. Scholars believe that overpopulation led to the decline of Kohunlich.

XPUJIL

Xpujil (Eesh-poo-*heel*; also spelled Xpuhil), meaning either "cattail" or "forest of kapok trees," flourished between A.D. 400 and 900. This is a small site that's easy to get to. Look for a blue sign on the highway pointing to the right. The entrance is just off the highway. After buying a ticket ($3/£1.50), you have to walk 180m (590 ft.) to the main structure. Along the path are some *chechén* trees. Don't touch; they are poisonous and a stick from one will provoke blisters. You can recognize them by their blotchy bark. On the right, you'll see a platform supporting a restored two-story building with a central staircase on the eastern side. Decorating the first floor are the remnants of a decorative molding and two galleries connected by a doorway. About 90m (295 ft.) farther you come to the site's main structure—a rectangular ceremonial platform 2m (6½ ft.) high and 50m (164 ft.) long supporting the palace, decorated with three tall towers shaped like miniature versions of the pyramids in Tikal,

Guatemala. These towers are purely decorative, with false stairways and temples that are too small to serve as such. The effect is beautiful. The main body of the building holds 12 rooms, which are now in ruins.

BECAN 🏛🏛🏛

Becán (Beh-*kahn*) is about 7km (4½ miles) beyond Xpujil and is visible on the right side of the highway. Becán means "moat filled by water," and, in fact, it was protected by a moat spanned by seven bridges. The extensive site dates from the early Classic to the late post-Classic (600 B.C.–A.D. 1200) period. Although it was abandoned by A.D. 850, ceramic remains indicate that there may have been a population resurgence between 900 and 1000, and it was still used as a ceremonial site as late as 1200. Becán was an administrative and ceremonial center with political sway over at least seven other cities in the area, including Chicanná, Hormiguero, and Payán.

The first plaza group you see after you enter was the center for grand ceremonies. From the highway, you can see the back of a pyramid (Structure 1) with two temples on top. Beyond and in between the two temples you can see the Temple atop Structure 4, which is opposite Temple 1. When the high priest appeared exiting the mouth of the earth monster in the center of this temple (which he reached by way of a hidden side stairway that's now partially exposed), he would have been visible from well beyond the immediate plaza. It's thought that commoners had to watch ceremonies from outside the plaza—thus the site's position was for good viewing purposes. The back of Structure 4 is believed to have been a civic plaza where rulers sat on stone benches while pronouncing judgments. The second plaza group dates from around A.D. 850 and has perfect twin towers on top, where there's a big platform. Under the platform are 10 rooms that are thought to be related to Xibalba (Shee-*bahl*-bah), the underworld. Hurricane Isidore damaged them, and they are still closed. Earth monster faces probably covered this building (and appeared on other buildings as well). Remains of at least one ball court have been unearthed. Next to the ball court is a well-preserved figure in an elaborate headdress behind glass. He was excavated not far from where he is now displayed. The markings are well defined, displaying a host of details.

CHICANNA

Slightly over 1.5km (1 mile) beyond Becán, on the left side of the highway, is Chicanná, which means "house of the mouth of snakes." Trees loaded with bromeliads shade the central square surrounded by five buildings. The most outstanding edifice features a monster-mouth doorway and an ornate stone facade with more superimposed masks. As you enter the mouth of the earth monster, note that you are walking on a platform configured as the open jaw of the monster with stone teeth on both sides. Again you find a lovely example of an elongated building with ornamental miniature pyramids on each end.

CALAKMUL 🏛🏛🏛

This area is both a massive Maya archaeological zone, with at least 60 sites, and as a 70,000-hectare (172,900-acre) rainforest designated in 1989 as the Calakmul Biosphere Reserve, including territory in both Mexico and Guatemala. The best way to see Calakmul is to spend the night at Xpujil or Chicanná and leave early in the morning for Calakmul. If you're the first one to drive down the narrow access road to the ruins (1½ hr. from the highway), you'll probably see plenty of wildlife. On my last trip to the ruins, I saw two groups of spider monkeys swinging through the trees on the outskirts of the city and a group of howler monkeys sleeping in the trees in front of Structure 2. I also saw a couple of animals that I couldn't identify, and heard the growl of a jungle cat that I wasn't able to see.

THE ARCHAEOLOGICAL ZONE   Since 1982, archaeologists have been excavating the ruins of Calakmul, which dates from 100 B.C. to A.D. 900. It's the largest of the area's 60 known sites. Nearly 7,000 buildings have been discovered and mapped. At its zenith, at least 60,000 people may have lived around the site, but by the time of the Spanish Conquest in 1519, there were fewer than 1,000 inhabitants. Visitors arrive at a large plaza filled with a forest of trees. You immediately see several stelae; Calakmul contains more of these than any other site, but they are much more weathered and indistinguishable than the stelae of Palenque or Copán in Honduras. On one of them you can see the work of looters who carefully used some sort of stone-cutting saw to slice off the face of the monument. By Structure 13 is a stele of a woman that dates from A.D. 652. She is thought to have been a ruler.

Several structures here are worth checking out; some are built in the Petén style, some in the Río Bec style. Structure 3 must have been the residence of a noble family. Its design is unique and quite lovely; it managed to retain its original form and was never remodeled. Offerings of shells, beads, and polychromed tripod pottery were found inside. Structure 2 is the tallest pyramid in the Yucatán, at 54m (177 ft.). From the top of it you can see the outline of the ruins of El Mirador, 50km (31 miles) across the forest in Guatemala. Notice the two stairways that ascend along the sides of the principal face of the pyramid in the upper levels, and how the masks break up the space of the front face.

Temple 4 charts the line of the sun from June 21, when it falls on the left (north) corner; to September 21 and March 21, when it lines up in the east behind the middle temple on the top of the building; to December 21, when it falls on the right (south) corner. Numerous jade pieces, including spectacular masks, were uncovered here, most of which are on display in the Museo Regional in Campeche. Temple 7 is largely unexcavated except for the top, where, in 1984, the most outstanding jade mask yet to be found at Calakmul was uncovered. In their book *A Forest of Kings,* Linda Schele and David Freidel tell of wars between the Calakmul, Tikal, and Naranjo (the latter two in Guatemala), and how Ah-Cacaw, king of Tikal (120km/74 miles south of Calakmul), captured King Jaguar-Paw in A.D. 695 and later Lord Ox-Ha-Te Ixil Ahau, both of Calakmul. The site is open Tuesday to Sunday from 7am to 5pm, but it gets so wet during the rainy season from June to October that it's best not to go during that time.

CALAKMUL BIOSPHERE RESERVE   Set aside in 1989, this is the peninsula's only high forest, a rainforest that annually records as much as 5m (16 ft.) of rain. Notice that the canopy of the trees is higher here than in the forest of Quintana Roo. It lies very close to the border with Guatemala, but, of course, there is no way to get there. Among the plants are cactus, epiphytes, and orchids. Endangered animals include the white-lipped peccary, jaguar, and puma. So far, more than 250 species of birds have been recorded. At present, no overnight stay or camping is permitted. If you want a tour of a small part of the forest and you speak Spanish, you can inquire for a guide at one of the two

A Driving Caution

Numerous curves in the road obscure oncoming traffic (what little there is).

nearby *ejidos* (cooperatives). Some old local *chicleros* (the men who tap sapodilla trees for their gum) have expert knowledge of flora and fauna and can take you on a couple of trails.

The turnoff on the left for Calakmul is located 53km (33 miles) from Xpujil, just before the village of Conhuas. There's a guard station there where you pay $4 (£2) per car and a $2 (£1) per person toll. From the turnoff, it's an hour drive on a paved one-lane-road. Admission to the site is $3.50 (£1.75).

It's advisable to take with you some food and drink and, of course, bug spray.

BALAMKU 🐾🐾

Balamkú (Bah-lahm-*koo*) is easy to reach and worth the visit. A couple of buildings in the complex were so well preserved that they required almost no reconstruction. Inside one you will find three impressive figures of men sitting in the gaping maws of crocodiles and toads as they descend into the underworld. The concept behind this building, with its molded stucco facade, is life and death. On the head of each stucco figure are the eyes, nose, and mouth of a jaguar figure, followed by the full face of the human figure, then a neck formed by the eyes and nose of another jaguar, and an Olmec-like face on the stomach, with its neck ringed by a necklace. These figures were saved from looters who managed to get away with a fourth one. Now they're under the protection of a caretaker, who keeps the room under lock and key. If you speak Spanish, you can get the caretaker to explain something of the figures and their complex symbolism. A beautiful courtyard and another set of buildings are adjacent to the main group.

8

Mérida, Chichén Itzá & the Maya Interior

by David Baird

Ask most people about the Yucatán, and they think of Cancún, the Caribbean coast, and Chichén Itzá. With a little exploring, though, you'll find a world beyond the region's tourist magnets. You might spend a morning scrambling over Maya ruins and in the afternoon take a dip in the cool, clear water of a cenote (a limestone well that leads to an underground river). The next day may find you strolling along a lonely beach or riding in a skiff through mangroves to visit a colony of pink flamingos. By the evening, you might be dancing in the central plaza of the Yucatán capital, **Mérida.** This chapter covers the interior of the Yucatán peninsula, including the famous Maya ruins at **Chichén Itzá** and **Uxmal,** the flamingo sanctuaries at **Celestún** and **Río Lagartos,** as well as many other spots that might find special favor with you.

EXPLORING THE YUCATAN'S MAYA HEARTLAND

The best way to see the Yucatán is by car. The terrain is flat, there is little traffic once you get away from the cities, and the main highways are in good shape. If you drive at all around this area, you will add at least one new word to your Spanish vocabulary—*topes* (*toh*-pehs), meaning speed bumps. And along with *topes* you might learn a few new curse words. *Topes* come in varying shapes and sizes and with varying degrees of warning. Don't let them surprise you.

Off the main highways, the roads are narrow and rough, but hey—you'll be driving a rental car. Rentals are, in fact, a little pricey compared with those in the U.S. (due perhaps to wear and tear?), but some promotional deals are available, especially in low season. For more on renting a car, see "By Car," in "Mérida: Gateway to the Maya Heartland," below.

Plenty of buses ply the roads between the major towns and ruins. And plenty of tour buses circulate, too. But buses to the smaller towns and ruins and the haciendas are infrequent. One bus company, Autobuses del Oriente (ADO), controls most of the first-class bus service and does a good job with the major destinations. Second-class buses go to some out-of-the-way places, but they can be slow, stop a lot, and usually aren't air-conditioned. I will take them to cover short distances. If you don't want to rent a car, a few tour operators transport small groups to more remote attractions such as ruins, cenotes, and villages.

The Yucatán is *tierra caliente* (the hot lands). Don't travel in this region without a hat, sun block, mosquito repellent, and water. The coolest weather is from November to February; the hottest is from April to June. From July to October, thundershowers

> **Tips**   **The Best Websites for Mérida, Chichén Itzá &**
> **the Maya Interior**
>
> ● **Maya: Portraits of a People: www.nationalgeographic.com/explorer/**
>   **maya/more.html**   A fascinating collection of articles from *National Geo-*
>   *graphic* and other sources.
> ● **Yucatán Travel Guide: www.mayayucatan.com**   Yucatán's Ministry of
>   Tourism maintains this site. It has an update section and good general
>   info on different destinations in the state.
> ● **Mexico's Yucatán Directory: www.mexonline.com/yucatan.htm**   A nice
>   roundup of vacation rentals, tour operators, and information on the
>   Maya sites. For more information on Mexico's indigenous history, see the
>   links on the pre-Columbian page (www.mexonline.com/precolum.htm).

moderate temperatures. More tourists come to the interior during the winter months, but not to the same extent as on the Caribbean coast. The high-season/low-season distinction is less pronounced here.

Should you decide to travel into this part of the world, don't miss **Mérida.** It is, and has been for centuries, the cultural and commercial center of the Yucatán. You won't find a more vibrant tropical city anywhere. Every time I visit, there is some festival or celebration to attend, on top of the nightly performances that the city offers its citizens and visitors. It's also the Yucatán's shopping center, where you can buy the area's specialty items, such as hammocks, Panama hats, and the embroidered native blouses known as *huipiles.* Aside from Mérida, here are some other places to consider.

CHICHEN ITZA & VALLADOLID   These destinations are almost midway between Mérida and Cancún. From Mérida, it's 2½ hours by car to Chichén on the new *autopista* (toll road). You can spend a day at the ruins and then stay at one of the nearby hotels—or drive 40km (25 miles) to Valladolid, a quiet, charming colonial town with a pleasant central square. Valladolid features two eerie cenotes. The spectacular ruins at Ek Balam are only 40km (25 miles) to the north. Also in the area is the Río Lagartos Nature Reserve, teeming with flamingos and other native birds.

CELESTUN NATIONAL WILDLIFE REFUGE   These flamingo-sanctuary wetlands along the Gulf coast contain a unique shallow-water estuary where freshwater from cenotes mixes with saltwater, creating the perfect feeding ground for flamingos. Touring this area by launch is relaxing and rewarding. Only 1½ hours from Mérida, Celestún makes for an easy day trip.

DZIBILCHALTUN   This Maya site, now a national park, is 14km (8⅔ miles) north of Mérida along the road to Progreso. Here you'll find pre-Hispanic ruins, nature trails, a cenote, and the Museum of the Maya. You can make this the first stop in a day trip to Progreso and other attractions north of Mérida.

PROGRESO   A modern city and Gulf Coast beach escape 34km (21 miles) north of Mérida, Progreso has a wide beach and oceanfront drive that's popular on the weekends and during the summer. The recent arrival of cruise ships might make Progreso even more popular, but with so much beach, you'll easily have a place to yourself.

From Progreso, you can drive down the coast to **Uaymitún** to see some flamingos and visit the recently excavated ruins of **Xcambó.**

UXMAL   Smaller than Chichén, but architecturally more striking and mysterious, Uxmal is about 80km (50 miles) south of Mérida. You can see it in a day, though it's a good idea to extend that somewhat to see the sound-and-light show and spend the night at one of the hotels by the ruins. Several other nearby sites make up the Puuc route and can be explored the following day. It's also possible, though a bit rushed, to see Uxmal and the other ruins on a 1-day trip by special excursion bus from Mérida.

CAMPECHE   This beautiful, walled colonial city has been so meticulously restored that it's a delight just to stroll down the streets. Campeche is about 3 hours southwest of Mérida in the direction of Palenque. A full day should give you enough time to see its highlights and museums, but there is something about Campeche that makes you want to linger.

1 Mérida: Gateway to the Maya Heartland 👁👁

1,440km (893 miles) E of Mexico City; 320km (198 miles) W of Cancún

Mérida is the capital of the state of Yucatán and has been the dominant city in the region since the Spanish Conquest. It is a busy city and suffers from the same problems that plague other colonial cities in Mexico—traffic and noise. Still, it is a fun city and has many admirers. I get comments from people all the time about how much they enjoyed Mérida. People there know how to have a good time, and they seem driven to organize concerts, theater productions, art exhibitions, and such. In recent years the city has been in the midst of a cultural explosion.

ESSENTIALS
GETTING THERE & DEPARTING
BY PLANE   AeroMéxico (© **01-800/021-4000** in Mexico, or 999/927-9277; www. aeromexico.com) flies nonstop to/from Miami and Mexico City. **Mexicana** (© **01-800/502-2000** in Mexico, or 999/924-6633; www.mexicana.com.mx) has nonstop service to and from Mexico City. **Continental** (© **999/946-1888** or -1900; www. continental.com) has nonstop service to and from Houston. **Click** (© **01-800/122-5425** in Mexico), a Mexican budget airline, provides nonstop service to and from Mexico City and Veracruz. **Aviacsa** (© **01-800/006-2000** in Mexico) provides nonstop service to and from Villahermosa and Mexico City.

BY CAR   **Highway 180** is the old *carretera federal* (federal highway) between Mérida and Cancún. The trip takes 6 hours, and the road is in good shape; you will pass through many Maya villages. A four-lane divided *cuota,* or *autopista* (toll road) parallels Highway 180 and begins at the town of Kantunil, 56km (35 miles) east of Mérida. By avoiding the tiny villages and their not-so-tiny speed bumps, the *autopista* cuts 2 hours from the journey between Mérida and Cancún; one-way tolls cost $32 (£16). Coming from the direction of Cancún, Highway 180 enters Mérida by feeding into Calle 65, which passes 1 block south of the main square.

Coming from the south (Campeche or Uxmal), you will enter the city on Avenida Itzáes. To get to the town center, turn right on Calle 59 (the first street after the zoo).

A *periférico* (loop road) encircles Mérida, making it possible to skirt the city. Directional signs into the city are generally good, but going around the city on the loop requires vigilance.

BY BUS   There are five bus stations in Mérida, two of which offer first-class buses; the other three provide local service to nearby destinations. The larger of the first-class stations, **CAME,** is on Calle 70, between calles 69 and 71 (see "City Layout," below). The ADO bus line and its affiliates operate the station. When you get there, you'll see a row of ticket windows; all but the last couple to the right sell first-class tickets. The last two windows sell tickets for ADO's deluxe services, ADO-GL and UNO. The former is only slightly better than first class; the latter has super-wide roomy seats. Unless it's a long trip, I generally choose the bus that has the most convenient departure time. Tickets can be purchased in advance; just ask the ticket agent for the different options and departure times for the route you need.

The other first-class station is the small **Maya K'iin** used by the bus company **Elite.** It's at Calle 65 no. 548, between calles 68 and 70.

To and from Cancún: You can pick up a bus at the CAME (almost every hour) or through Elite (five per day). Both bus lines also pick up passengers at the Fiesta Americana Hotel, across from the Hyatt (12 per day). You can buy a ticket in the hotel's shopping arcade at the **Ticket Bus** agency or at the Elite ticket agency. Cancún is 4 hours away; a few buses stop in **Valladolid.** If you're downtown, you can purchase tickets from the agency in Pasaje Picheta, on the main square a couple of doors down from the Palacio de Gobierno.

To and from Chichén Itzá: Three buses per day (2½-hr. trip) depart from the CAME. Also, check out tours operating from the hotels in Mérida if you want to visit for the day.

To and from Playa del Carmen, Tulum, and Chetumal: From the CAME, there are 10 departures per day for Playa del Carmen (5-hr. trip), six for Tulum (6-hr. trip), and eight for Chetumal (7-hr. trip). From Maya K'iin there are three per day to Playa, which stop at the Fiesta Americana.

To and from Campeche: From the CAME station, there are 36 departures per day. Elite has four departures per day. It's a 2½-hour trip.

To and from Palenque and San Cristóbal de las Casas: There is service to San Cristóbal twice daily from the CAME, and once daily on Elite. To Palenque there are three and one, respectively. There have been reports of minor theft on buses to Palenque. You should do three things: Don't take second-class buses to this destination; check your luggage so that it's stowed in the cargo bay; and put your carry-on in the overhead rack, not on the floor.

The main **second-class bus station** is around the corner from the CAME on Calle 69, between calles 68 and 70.

To and from Uxmal: There are four buses per day. (You can also hook up with a tour to Uxmal through most hotels or any travel agent or tour operator in town.) One bus per day combines Uxmal with the other sites to the south (Kabah, Sayil, Labná, and Xlapak—known as the Puuc route) and does the whole round-trip in a day. It stops for 2 hours at Uxmal and 30 minutes at each of the other sites.

To and from Progreso and Dzibilchaltún: Transportes AutoProgreso offers service to/from its station at Calle 62 no. 524, between calles 65 and 67. The trip to Progreso takes an hour by second-class bus.

To and from Celestún: The Celestún station is at Calle 50 between calles 65 and 67. The trip takes 1½ to 2 hours, depending on how often the bus stops. There are 10 buses per day.

To and from Izamal: The bus station is at the corner of Calle 65 and Calle 48. Departures are every half-hour. The trip takes 1½ hours.

ORIENTATION

ARRIVING BY PLANE   Mérida's airport is 13km (8 miles) from the city center on the southwestern outskirts of town, near the entrance to Highway 180. The airport has desks for rental cars, hotel reservations, and tourist information. Taxi tickets to town ($16/£8) are sold outside the airport doors, under the covered walkway.

VISITOR INFORMATION   There are city tourism offices and state tourism offices, which have different resources; if you can't get the information you're looking for at one, go to the other. I have better luck with the city's **visitor information office** (© 999/942-0000, ext. 80119), which is on the ground floor of the Ayuntamiento building facing the main square on Calle 62. Look for a glass door under the arcade. Hours are Monday to Saturday from 8am to 8pm and Sunday from 8am to 2pm. Monday through Saturday, at 9:30am, the staff offers visitors a free tour of the area around the main square. The state operates two downtown tourism offices: One is in the **Teatro Peón Contreras,** facing Parque de la Madre (© 999/924-9290); and the other is on the main plaza, in the **Palacio de Gobierno,** immediately to the left as you enter. These offices are open daily from 8am to 9pm. There are also information booths at the airport and the CAME bus station.

Also keep your eye out for the free monthly magazine *Yucatán Today;* it's a good source of information for Mérida and the rest of the region.

CITY LAYOUT   Downtown Mérida has the standard layout of towns in the Yucatán: Streets running north-south are even numbers; those running east-west are odd numbers. The numbering begins on the north and the east sides of town, so if you're walking on an odd-numbered street and the even numbers of the cross streets are increasing, then you are heading west; likewise, if you are on an even-numbered street and the odd numbers of the cross streets are increasing, you are going south.

Address numbers don't tell you anything about what cross street to look for. This is why addresses almost always list cross streets, usually like this: "Calle 60 no. 549 × 71 y 73." The "×" is a multiplication sign—shorthand for the word *por* (meaning "by")—and *y* means "and." So this place would be on Calle 60 between calles 71 and 73. Outside of the downtown area, the numbering of streets gets a little crazy, so it's important to know the name of the neighborhood *(colonia)* where you're going. This is the first thing taxi drivers will ask you.

The town's main square is the busy **Plaza Mayor,** known as **El Centro.** It's bordered by calles 60, 62, 61, and 63. Calle 60, which runs in front of the cathedral, is an important street to remember; it connects the main square with several smaller plazas, some theaters and churches, and the University of Yucatán, just to the north. Here you'll find a concentration of handicraft shops, restaurants, and hotels. Around Plaza Mayor are the cathedral, the Palacio de Gobierno (state government building), the Ayuntamiento (town hall), and the Palacio Montejo. The plaza always has a crowd, and it's full on Sunday, when it holds a large street fair. (See "Festivals & Special Events in Mérida," below.) Within a few blocks are several smaller plazas and the bustling market district.

Mérida's most fashionable district is the broad, tree-lined boulevard **Paseo de Montejo** and its surrounding neighborhood. The Paseo de Montejo parallels Calle 60 and begins 7 blocks north and a little east of the main square. There are a number of

Moments   Daily Festivals & Special Events in Mérida

Many Mexican cities offer weekend concerts in the park and such, but Mérida surpasses them all by offering performances every day of the week. Unless otherwise indicated, admission to the following is free.

Sunday   Each Sunday from 9am to 9pm, there's a fair called *Mérida en Domingo* (Mérida on Sunday). The main plaza and a section of Calle 60 from El Centro to Parque Santa Lucía close to traffic. Parents come with their children to stroll around and take in the scene. There are booths selling food and drink, along with a lively little flea market and used-book fair, children's art classes, and educational booths. At 11am in front of the Palacio del Gobierno, musicians play everything from jazz to classical and folk music. Also at 11am, the police orchestra performs Yucatecan tunes at the Santa Lucía park. At 11:30am, you'll find bawdy comedy acts at the Parque Hidalgo, on Calle 60 at Calle 59. There's a lull in the midafternoon, and then the plaza fills up again as people walk around and visit with friends. Around 7pm in front of the Ayuntamiento, a large band starts playing mambos, rumbas, and cha-chas with great enthusiasm; you may see 1,000 people dancing in the street. Afterward, folk ballet dancers reenact a typical Yucatecan wedding inside.

Monday   Every Monday at 9pm in front of the *Palacio Municipal* performers play *Vaquería regional,* traditional music and dancing to celebrate the Vaquerías feast, which was associated originally with the branding of cattle on Yucatecan haciendas. Among the featured performers are dancers with trays of bottles or filled glasses balanced on their heads—a sight to see.

Tuesday   At 9pm in Parque Santiago, Calle 59 at Calle 72, the Municipal Orchestra plays Latin and American big-band music from the 1940s.

Wednesday   At 9pm in the Teatro Peón Contreras, Calle 60 at Calle 57, the University of Yucatán Ballet Folklórico presents "Yucatán and Its Roots." Admission is $5 (£2.75).

Thursday   Yucatecan *trova* music (boleros, baladas) and dance are presented at the Serenata in Parque Santa Lucía at 9pm.

Friday   At 9pm in the courtyard of the University of Yucatán, Calle 60 at Calle 57, the University of Yucatán Ballet Folklórico performs typical regional dances from the Yucatán.

Saturday   Noche Mexicana at the park at the beginning of Paseo de Montejo begins at 9pm. It features several performances of traditional Mexican music and dance. Some of the performers are amateurs who acquit themselves reasonably well; others are professional musicians and dancers who thoroughly know their craft. Food stands sell very good *antojitos* (finger foods), as well as drinks and ice cream.

trendy restaurants, modern hotels, offices of various banks and airlines, and a few clubs here, but the boulevard is mostly known for its stately mansions built during the boom times of the *henequén* industry. Near where the Paseo intersects Avenida Colón, you'll find the two fanciest hotels in town: the Hyatt and the Fiesta Americana.

GETTING AROUND   By Car   In general, reserve your car in advance from the U.S. to get the best weekly rates during high season (Nov–Feb); in low season, I usually do better renting a car once I get to Mérida. The local rental companies are competitive and have promotional deals that you can get only if you are there. When comparing, make sure that it's apples to apples; ask if the price quote includes the IVA tax and insurance coverage. Practically everybody offers free mileage. For tips on saving money on car rentals, see "Getting Around," in chapter 3. Rental cars are generally a little more expensive (unless you find a promotional rate) than in the U.S. By renting for only a day or two, you can avoid the high cost of parking lots in Mérida. These *estacionamentos* charge one price for the night and double that if you leave your car for the following day. Many hotels offer free parking, but make sure they include daytime parking in the price.

By Taxi   Taxis are easy to come by and much cheaper than in Cancún.

By Bus   City buses are a little tricky to figure out but aren't needed very often because almost everything of interest is within walking distance of the main plaza. Still, it's a bit of a walk from the plaza to the Paseo de Montejo, and you can save yourself some work by taking a bus, minibus, or *colectivo* (Volkswagen minivan) that is heading north on Calle 60. Most of these will take you within a couple of blocks of the Paseo de Montejo. The *colectivos* or *combis* (usually painted white) run out in several directions from the main plaza along simple routes. They usually line up along the side streets next to the plaza.

FAST FACTS: Mérida

American Express   The office is at Paseo de Montejo 492 (© 999/942-8200). It's open for travelers' services weekdays from 9am to 2pm and 4 to 6pm.

Area Code   The telephone area code is **999**.

Bookstore   The English-language bookstore **Amate Books** (© 999/924-2222) is at Calle 60 453-A, by Calle 51. It stocks a large selection of books on many subjects and is open Tuesday through Sunday from 10:30am to 8:30pm. **The Librería Dante,** Calle 59 between calles 60 and 62 (© 999/928-3674), has a small selection of English-language cultural-history books on Mexico.

Business Hours   Generally, businesses are open Monday to Saturday from 10am to 2pm and 4 to 8pm.

Climate   From November to February, the weather can be pleasantly cool and windy. In other months, it's just hot, especially during the day. Rain can occur any time of year, especially during the rainy season (July–Oct), and usually comes in the form of afternoon tropical showers.

Consulates   The **American Consulate** has moved. It's now at Calle 60 no. 338-K, 1 block north of the Hyatt hotel (Col. Alcalá Martín). The phone number is © 999/942-5700. Office hours are Monday to Friday from 9am to 1pm.

Currency Exchange I prefer *casas de cambio* (currency exchange offices) over banks. There are many of these; one called **Cambios Portales,** Calle 61 no. 500 (© **999/923-8709**), is on the north side of the main plaza in the middle of the block. It's open daily from 8:30am to 8:30pm. There are also many ATMs; one is on the south side of the same plaza.

Drugstore **Farmacía Yza,** Calle 63 no. 502, between calles 60 and 62 (© **999/924-9510**), on the south side of the plaza, is open 24 hours.

Hospitals The best hospital is **Centro Médico de las Américas,** Calle 54 no. 365 between 33-A and Avenida Pérez Ponce. The main phone number is © **999/926-2619**; for emergencies, call © **999/927-3199.** You can also call the **Cruz Roja (Red Cross)** at © **999/924-9813.**

Internet Access There are so many Internet access providers in town that you hardly have to walk more than a couple of blocks to find one.

Police Mérida has a special body of police to assist tourists. They patrol the downtown area and the Paseo de Montejo. They wear white shirts bearing the words POLICIA TURISTICA. Their phone number is © **999/925-2555.**

Post Office The *correo* moved recently. It's now on calle 53 between calles 52 and 54. It's open Monday to Friday from 8am to 4:30pm, Saturday from 9am to 1pm.

Seasons There are two high seasons for tourism, but they aren't as pronounced as on the coast. One is in July and August, when Mexicans take their vacations, and the other is between November 15 and Easter Sunday, when Canadians and Americans flock to the Yucatán to escape winter weather.

Spanish Classes Maya scholars, Spanish teachers, and archaeologists from the United States are among the students at the **Centro de Idiomas del Sureste,** Calle 14 no. 106 at Calle 25, Col. México, 97000 Mérida, Yuc. (© **999/926-1155;** fax 999/926-9020). The school has two locations: in the Colonia México, a northern residential district, and on Calle 66 at Calle 57, downtown. Students live with local families or in hotels; sessions running 2 weeks or longer are available for all levels of proficiency and areas of interest. For brochures and applications, contact the director, Chloe Conaway de Pacheco.

Telephones There are long-distance phone service centers at the airport and the bus station. In the downtown area is **TelWorld,** Calle 59 no. 495-4 between calles 56 and 58. To use the public phones, buy a **Ladatel** card from just about any newsstand or store. The cards come in a variety of denominations and work for long distance within Mexico and even abroad.

EXPLORING MERIDA

Most of Mérida's attractions are within walking distance from the downtown area. To see a larger area of the city, take a popular **bus tour** by **Transportadora Carnaval.** The owner bought a few buses, painted them bright colors, pulled out the windows, raised the roof several inches, and installed wooden benches; the overall effect will remind you of the folksy buses of coastal Latin America, known as *chivas* in Colombia and Venezuela or as *guaguas* in other places. You can find these buses on the corner of calles 60 and 55 (next to the church of Santa Lucía) at 10am and 1, 4, and 7pm. The tour costs $7 (£3.50) per person and lasts 2 hours. A national company, called Turibus,

What to See & Do in Mérida

Casa del Alguacil **7**
Cathedral **2**
El Nuevo Olimpo **6**
Iglesia de Jesús **10**
Iglesia de Santa Lucía **13**
Museo de Arte Contemporáneo **3**
Museo de la Ciudad **9**
Palacio Cantón/Museo Regional
  de Antropología **14**

Palacio de Gobierno **8**
Palacio Montejo **4**
Palacio Municipal **5**
Plaza Mayor **1**
Teatro Ayala **8**
Teatro Peón Contreras **11**
Universidad de Yucatán **12**

operates another city tour in large, modern, bright-red, double-decker buses. You can pick them up in front of the cathedral every half hour. The tour costs $8 (£4.40). Another option for seeing the city is a **horse-drawn carriage.** A 45-minute ride around central Mérida costs $25 (£13). You can usually find the carriages beside the cathedral on Calle 61.

EXPLORING PLAZA MAYOR Downtown Mérida is a great example of a lowland colonial city. The town has a casual, relaxed feel. Buildings lack the severe baroque and neoclassical features that characterize central Mexico; most are finished in stucco and painted light colors. Mérida's gardens add to this relaxed, tropical atmosphere. Gardeners don't strive for control over nature. Here, natural exuberance is the ideal; plants grow in a wild profusion that disguises human intervention. Mérida's plazas are a slightly different version of this aesthetic: Unlike the highland plazas, with their carefully sculpted trees, Mérida's squares are typically built around large trees that are left to grow as tall as possible. Hurricane Isidore blew down several of these in 2002, and has changed the appearance of these plazas as well as the Paseo de Montejo.

Plaza Mayor has been relandscaped after the hurricane and is now the exception to the rule. It still remains a comfortable and informal place to meet up with friends. Even when there's no orchestrated event in progress, the park is full of people sitting on the benches, talking, or taking a casual stroll. A plaza like this is a great advantage for a big city such as Mérida, giving it a personal feel and a sense of community. Notice the beautiful scale and composition of the major buildings surrounding it. The most prominent of these is the cathedral.

The oldest **cathedral** on the continent, it was built between 1561 and 1598. Much of the stone in the cathedral's walls came from the ruined buildings of Tihó, the former Maya city. The original finish was stucco, and you can see some remnants still clinging to the bare rock. However, people like the way the unfinished walls show the cathedral's age. Notice how the two top levels of the bell towers are built off-center from their bases, marking them as later additions. Inside, decoration is sparse, with altars draped in fabric colorfully embroidered like a Maya woman's shift. The most notable item is a picture of Ah Kukum Tutul Xiú, chief of the Xiú people, visiting the Montejo camp to make peace; it's hanging over the side door on the right.

To the left of the main altar is a small shrine with a curious figure of Christ that is a replica of one recovered from a burned-out church in the town of Ichmul. In the 1500s a local artist carved the original figure from a miraculous tree that was hit by lightning and burst into flames—but did not char. The statue later became blistered in the church fire at Ichmul, but it survived. In 1645 it was moved to the cathedral in Mérida, where the locals attached great powers to the figure, naming it *Cristo de las Ampollas* (Christ of the Blisters). It did not, however, survive the sacking of the cathedral in 1915 by revolutionary forces, so another figure, modeled after the original, was made. Take a look in the side chapel (daily 8–11am and 4:30–7pm), which contains a life-size diorama of the Last Supper. The Mexican Jesus is covered with prayer crosses brought by supplicants asking for intercession.

Next door to the cathedral is the old bishop's palace, now converted into the city's contemporary art museum, **Museo de Arte Contemporáneo Ateneo de Yucatán** (© **999/928-3236**). The palace was confiscated and rebuilt during the Mexican Revolution in 1915. The museum's entrance faces the cathedral from the recently constructed walkway between the two buildings called the Pasaje de la Revolución. The 17 exhibition rooms display work by contemporary artists, mostly from the Yucatán.

(The best known are Fernando García Ponce and Fernando Castro Pacheco, whose works also hang in the government palace described below.) Nine of the rooms hold the museum's permanent collection; the rest are for temporary exhibits. It's open Wednesday to Monday from 10am to 6pm. Admission is free.

As you move clockwise around the plaza, the **Palacio Montejo** is on the south side. Its facade, with heavy decoration around the doorway and windows, is a good example of the Spanish architectural style known as plateresque. But the content of the decoration is very much a New World creation. Conquering the Yucatán was the Montejo family business, begun by the original Francisco Montejo and continued by his son and nephew, both named Francisco Montejo. Construction of the house started in 1542 under the son, Francisco Montejo El Mozo ("The Younger"). Bordering the entrance are politically incorrect figures of conquistadors standing on the heads of vanquished Indians—borrowed, perhaps, from the pre-Hispanic custom of portraying victorious Maya kings treading on their defeated foes. The posture of the conquistadors and their facial expression of wide-eyed dismay make them less imposing than the Montejos might have wished. A bank now occupies the building, but you can enter the courtyard, view the garden, and see for yourself what a charming residence it must have been for the descendants of the Montejos, who lived here as recently as the 1970s. (Curiously enough, Mérida society keeps track of who is descended from the Montejos, as well as who is descended from the last Maya king, Tutul Xiú.)

In stark contrast to the severity of the cathedral and Casa Montejo is the light, unimposing **Ayuntamiento** or **Palacio Municipal (town hall).** The exterior dates from the mid–19th century, an era when a tropical aesthetic tinged with romanticism began asserting itself across coastal Latin America. On the second floor, you can see the meeting hall of the city council and enjoy a view of the plaza from the balcony. Next door to the Ayuntamiento is a recently completed building called **El Nuevo Olimpo (The New Olympus).** It took the place of the old Olimpo, which a misguided town council demolished in the 1970s, to the regret of many older Meridanos. The new building tries to incorporate elements of the original while presenting something new. It holds concert and gallery space, a bookstore, and a lovely courtyard. There is a comfortable cafe under the arches, and a bulletin board at the entrance to the courtyard with postings of upcoming performances.

Cater-cornered from the Nuevo Olimpo is the old **Casa del Alguacil (Magistrate's House).** Under its arcades is something of an institution in Mérida: the **Dulcería y Sorbetería Colón,** an ice-cream and sweet shop that will appeal to those who prefer less-rich ice creams. A spectacular side doorway on Calle 62 bears viewing, and across the street is the **Cine Mérida,** with two movie screens showing art films and one stage for live performances. Returning to the main plaza, down a bit from the ice-cream store, is a **shopping center** of boutiques and convenience food vendors called **Pasaje Picheta.** At the end of the arcade is the **Palacio de Gobierno (state government building),** dating from 1892. Large murals by the Yucatecan artist Fernando Castro Pacheco, completed between 1971 and 1973, decorate the walls of the courtyard. Scenes from Maya and Mexican history abound, and the painting over the stairway depicts the Maya spirit with ears of sacred corn, the "sunbeams of the gods." Nearby is a painting of mustachioed Lázaro Cárdenas, who as president, in 1938, expropriated 17 foreign oil companies and was hailed as a Mexican liberator. Upstairs is a long, wide gallery with more of Pacheco's paintings, which achieve their effect by localizing color and imitating the photographic technique of double exposure. The palace is open Monday to Saturday from 8am to 8pm, Sunday from 9am to 5pm. There is a small tourism office to the left as you enter.

A few blocks from Plaza Mayor is the **Museo de la Ciudad (City Museum)** on Calle 56 between 65 and 65A. It now occupies the former Post Office building. An exhibit outlining the history of Mérida will be of interest to those curious about the city; there is explanatory text in English. Hours are Tuesday to Friday from 9am to 8pm, Saturday and Sunday from 9am to 2pm. Admission is free.

EXPLORING CALLE 60   Heading north from Plaza Mayor up Calle 60, you'll see many of Mérida's old churches and squares. Several stores along Calle 60 sell gold-filigree jewelry, pottery, clothing, and folk art. A stroll along this street leads to the Parque Santa Ana and continues to the fashionable boulevard Paseo de Montejo and its **Museo Regional de Antropología (Anthropology Museum).**

The first place of interest is the **Teatro Daniel de Ayala,** only because it sometimes schedules interesting performances. On the right side of Calle 60 will be a small park called **Parque Cepeda Peraza** (or Parque Hidalgo). Named for 19th-century General Manuel Cepeda Peraza, the *parque* was part of Montejo's original city plan. Small outdoor restaurants front hotels on the park, making it a popular stopping place at any time of day. Across Calle 59 is the **Iglesia de Jesús,** or El Tercer Orden (the Third Order). Built by the Jesuit order in 1618, it has the richest interior of any church in Mérida, making it a favorite spot for weddings. The entire block on which the church stands belonged to the Jesuits, who are known as great educators. The school they left behind after their expulsion became the Universidad de Yucatán.

On the other side of the church is the **Parque de la Madre.** The park contains a modern statue of the Madonna and Child, a copy of the work by Renoir. Beyond the Parque de la Madre and across the pedestrian-only street is the **Teatro Peón Contreras,** an opulent theater designed by Italian architect Enrico Deserti a century ago. The theater is noted for its Carrara marble staircase and frescoed dome. Try to peek inside, and check the schedule to see if any performances will take place during your stay. National and international performers appear here often. In the southwest corner of the theater, facing the Parque de la Madre, is a **tourist information office.** Across Calle 60 is the main building of the **Universidad de Yucatán.** Inside is a flagstone courtyard where the *ballet folklórico* performs on Friday nights.

A block farther north is **Parque Santa Lucía.** Bordered by an arcade on the north and west sides, this park was where visitors first alighted from the stagecoach. On Sunday, Parque Santa Lucía holds a used-book market, and several evenings a week it hosts popular entertainment. On Thursday nights, performers present Yucatecan songs and poems. Facing the park is the **Iglesia de Santa Lucía** (1575).

Four blocks farther up Calle 60 is **Parque Santa Ana;** if you turn right, you'll come to the beginning of the Paseo de Montejo in 2 blocks.

EXPLORING THE PASEO DE MONTEJO   The Paseo de Montejo is a broad, tree-lined boulevard that runs north-south starting at Calle 47, 7 blocks north and 2 blocks east of the main square. In the late 19th century, stalwarts of Mérida's upper crust (mostly plantation owners) decided that the city needed something grander than its traditional narrow streets lined by wall-to-wall town houses. They built this monumentally proportioned boulevard and lined it with mansions. Things went sour when the *henequén* industry went bust, but several mansions survive—some in private hands, others as offices, restaurants, or consulates. Today, this is the fashionable part of town, with many restaurants, trendy dance clubs, and expensive hotels.

Of the mansions that survived, the most notable is the Palacio Cantón, which houses the **Museo Regional de Antropología (Anthropology Museum)** ✷✷ (© 999/ 923-0557). Designed and built by Enrico Deserti, the architect of the Teatro Peón Contreras, it was constructed between 1909 and 1911, during the last years of the Porfiriato. It was the residence of General Francisco Cantón Rosado, who enjoyed his palace for only 6 years before dying in 1917. For a time the mansion served as the official residence of the state's governor. Viewing the museum affords you an opportunity to see some of the surviving interior architecture.

The museum's main focus is the pre-Columbian cultures of the peninsula, especially the Maya. Topics include cosmology, history, and culture. Starting with fossil mastodon teeth, the exhibits take you through the Yucatán's history, paying special attention to the daily life of its inhabitants.

Exhibits illustrate such strange Maya customs as tying boards to babies' heads to create the oblong shape that they considered beautiful, and filing teeth or perforating them to inset jewels. Enlarged photos of several archaeological sites and drawings illustrate the various styles of Maya dwellings. Captions for the permanent displays are mostly in Spanish, but even if you barely know Spanish, this is a worthwhile stop, providing background for explorations of Maya sites. The museum is open Tuesday to Saturday from 8am to 8pm, Sunday from 8am to 2pm. Admission is $4 (£2).

SHOPPING

Mérida is known for hammocks, *guayaberas* (lightweight men's shirts worn untucked), and Panama hats. Baskets and pottery made in the Yucatán are for sale in the **central market.** Mérida is also the place to pick up prepared *adobo,* a pastelike mixture of ground *achiote* seeds (annatto), oregano, garlic, and other spices used as a marinade for making dishes such as *cochinita pibil* (pit-baked pork). Simply mix the paste with sour orange to a soupy consistency before applying to the meat. Try it on chicken for *pollo pibil.* It can be purchased in a bottle, too.

EXPLORING THE MARKET   Mérida's bustling **market district** is a few blocks southeast of the Plaza Mayor. The market and surrounding few blocks make up the commercial center of the city. Hordes of people come here to shop and work. It is by far the most crowded part of town, and the city government is refurbishing the whole area to relieve the traffic congestion. Behind the post office (at calles 65 and 56) is the oldest part of the market, the **Portal de Granos (Grains Arcade),** a row of maroon arches where the grain merchants used to sell their goods. Just east, between calles 56 and 54, is the market building, Mercado Lucas de Gálvez. The city has built a new municipal market building on the south side of this building, but it was having difficulty persuading the market venders to move. When this happens the city's plan is to tear down the Lucas de Gálvez and replace it with a plaza. Inside, chaos seems to reign, but after a short while a certain order emerges. Here you can find anything from fresh fish to flowers to leather goods. In and around the market, you can find more locally manufactured goods; a secondary market is on Calle 56, labeled **Bazaar de Artesanías (crafts market)** in big letters. Another crafts market, **Bazaar García Rejón,** lies a block west of the market on Calle 65 between calles 58 and 60.

CRAFTS

Casa de las Artesanías ✷   This store occupies the front rooms of a restored monastery. Here you can find a wide selection of crafts, 90% of which come from the Yucatán. For the most part, the quality of work is higher than elsewhere, but so are the prices. The monastery's back courtyard is used as a gallery, with rotating exhibits on folk and fine arts. It's open Monday to Saturday from 9am to 8pm, Sunday from 9am to 1pm. Calle 63 no. 513 (between calles 64 and 66). ✆ 999/928-6676.

Miniaturas   This fun little store is packed to the rafters with miniatures, a traditional Mexican folk art form that has been evolving in a number of directions, including social and political satire, pop art, and bawdy humor. Alicia Rivero, the owner, collects them from several parts of Mexico and offers plenty of variety, from traditional miniatures, such as dollhouse furniture, to popular cartoon characters and celebrities. The store also sells other forms of folk art such as masks, games, and traditional crafts. Hours are Monday to Saturday from 10am to 8pm. Calle 59 no. 507A-4 (between calles 60 and 62). ✆ 999/928-6503.

GUAYABERAS

Business suits are hot and uncomfortable in Mérida's tropical climate, so businessmen, bankers, and bus drivers alike wear the *guayabera,* a loose-fitting shirt decorated with narrow tucks, pockets, and sometimes embroidery, worn over the pants rather than tucked in. Mérida is famous as the best place to buy *guayaberas,* which can go for less than $15 (£7.50) at the market or for more than $50 (£25) custom-made. A *guayabera* made of linen can cost about $80 (£40). Most are made of cotton, although other materials are available. The traditional color is white.

Most shops display ready-to-wear shirts in several price ranges. *Guayabera* makers pride themselves on being innovators. I have yet to enter a shirt-maker's shop in Mérida that did not present its own version of the *guayabera.* When looking at *guayaberas,* here are a few things to keep in mind: When Yucatecans say *seda,* they mean polyester; *lino* is linen or a linen/polyester combination. Take a close look at the stitching and such details as the way the tucks line up over the pockets; with *guayaberas,* the details are everything.

Guayaberas Jack   The craftsmanship here is good, the place has a reputation to maintain, and some of the salespeople speak English. Prices are as marked. This will give you a good basis of comparison if you want to hunt for a bargain elsewhere. If the staff does not have the style and color of shirt you want, they will make it for you in about 3 hours. This shop also sells regular shirts and women's blouses. Hours are Monday to Saturday from 10am to 8pm, Sunday from 10am to 2pm. Calle 59 no. 507A (between calles 60 and 62). ✆ 999/928-6002.

HAMMOCKS

Natives across tropical America used hammocks long before the Europeans arrived in the New World. The word comes from the Spanish *hamaca,* which is a borrowing from Taino, a Caribbean Indian language. Hammocks are still in use throughout Latin America and come in a wide variety of forms, but none is so comfortable as the Yucatecan hammock, which is woven with cotton string in a fine mesh. For most of us, of course, the hammock is lawn furniture, something to relax in for an hour or so on a lazy afternoon. But for the vast majority of Yucatecans, hammocks are the equivalent of beds, and they greatly prefer hammocks to mattresses. I know a hotel owner who has 150 beds in his establishment but won't sleep on any of them. When he does, he complains of waking up unrested and sore. Many well-to-do Meridanos keep a bed just for show. In hotels that cater to Yucatecans, you will always find hammock hooks in the walls because many Yucatecans travel with their own hammock.

My advice to the hammock buyer: The woven part should be cotton, it should be made with fine string, and the strings should be so numerous that when you get in it and stretch out diagonally (the way you're supposed to sleep in these hammocks), the gaps between the strings remain small. Don't pay attention to the words used to describe the size of a hammock; they have become practically meaningless. Good hammocks don't cost a lot of money ($20–$35/£10–£18). If you want a superior hammock, ask for one made with fine crochet thread, *hilo de crochet* (the word *crochet* is also over used, but you can readily see the difference). This could run as high as $120 (£60).

Nothing beats a tryout; the shops mentioned here will gladly hang a hammock for you to test-drive. When it's up, look to see that there are no untied strings. You can also see what street vendors are offering, but you have to know what to look for, or they are likely to take advantage of you.

Hamacas El Aguacate   El Aguacate sells hammocks wholesale and retail. It has the greatest variety and is the place to go for a really fancy or extra-large hammock. A good hammock is the no. 6 in cotton; it runs around $32 (£16). The store is open Monday to Friday from 8:30am to 7:30pm, Saturday from 8am to 5pm. It's 6 blocks south of the main square. Calle 58 no. 604 (at Calle 73). ✆ 999/928-6429.

Tejidos y Cordeles Nacionales   This place near the municipal market sells only cotton hammocks, priced by weight—a pretty good practice because hammock lengths are fairly standardized. The prices are better than at El Aguacate, but quality control isn't as good. My idea of a good hammock is one that weighs about 1½ kg (3½ lb.) and runs about $25 (£13). Calle 56 no. 516-B (between calles 63 and 65). ✆ 999/928-5561.

PANAMA HATS

Another useful and popular item is this soft, pliable hat made from the fibers of the jipijapa palm in several towns south of Mérida along Highway 180, especially Becal, in the neighboring state of Campeche. The hat makers in these towns work inside caves so that the moist air keeps the palm fibers pliant.

Jipi hats come in various grades determined by the quality (pliability, softness, and fineness) of the fibers and closeness of the weave. The difference in weave is easy to see, as a fine weave improves the shape of a hat. It has more body and retains its shape better. You'll find Panama hats for sale in several places, but often without much selection. One of the market buildings has a hat store: Walk south down Calle 56 past the post office; right before the street ends in the market place, turn left into a passage with hardware stores at the entrance. The fourth or fifth shop is **Casa de los Jipis.**

WHERE TO STAY

Mérida is easier on the budget than the resort cities. The stream of visitors is steadier than on the coast, so most hotels no longer use a high-season/low-season rate structure. Still, you are more likely to find promotional rates during low season. Mérida has a convention center, which attracts large trade shows that can fill the city's hotels, so it's a good idea to make reservations. The rates quoted here include the 17% tax. When inquiring about prices, always ask if the price quoted includes tax. Most hotels in Mérida offer at least a few air-conditioned rooms, and some also have pools. But many inexpensive hotels haven't figured out how to provide a comfortable bed. Either the mattresses are poor quality, or the bottom sheet is too small to tuck in properly. Some hotels here would offer a really good deal if only they would improve their beds. One last thing to note: Without exception, every hotel in Mérida that doesn't have its own parking has an arrangement with a nearby parking garage, where you can park your car for a fee. Or you can park on the street, where for the most part cars are safe from vandalism. In Mérida, free parking is a relative concept—for many hotels, free parking means only at night; during the day there may be a charge.

VERY EXPENSIVE

Fiesta Americana Mérida ✿✿   This six-story hotel on the Paseo de Montejo is built in the grand *fin-de-siècle* style of the old mansions along the Paseo. Guest rooms are off the cavernous lobby, so all face outward and have views of one or another of the avenues. The rooms are comfortable and large, with furnishings and decorations striving for, and achieving, innocuousness in light, tropical colors. The floors are tile and the bathrooms large and well equipped. Service is very attentive, better than at the Hyatt. There is a shopping center on the ground floor, below the lobby.

Av. Colón 451, corner of Paseo Montejo, 92127 Mérida, Yuc. ✆ 800/343-7821 in the U.S. and Canada, or 999/942-1111. Fax 999/942-1112. www.fiestaamericana.com.mx. 350 units. $220 (£110) double; $260 (£130) executive level; $280 (£140) junior suite. AE, DC, MC, V. Free secure parking. **Amenities:** 2 restaurants; bar; midsize outdoor pool; tennis court; health club w/saunas, men's steam room, unisex whirlpool; children's programs; concierge; tour desk; small business center; shopping arcade; room service; massage; babysitting; laundry service; dry cleaning; executive-level rooms. *In room:* A/C, TV w/pay movies, high-speed Internet, minibar, coffeemaker, hair dryer, safe.

Hyatt Regency Mérida ✿✿   This Hyatt is much like Hyatts elsewhere, wherein lies this hotel's chief asset. The rooms are dependably comfortable and quiet, the quietest in a noisy city. They're carpeted and well furnished, with great bathrooms. In decoration and comfort, I find them superior to those of the Fiesta Americana, but they certainly don't have any local flavor. The Hyatt's facilities, especially its tennis courts and health club, also rank above the Fiesta Americana's. The pool is more attractive and larger, but its location keeps it in the shade for most of the day, and the water never gets a chance to heat up. Rising 17 stories, the Hyatt is not hard to find in Mérida's skyline; it's near the Paseo de Montejo and across Avenida Colón from the Fiesta Americana.

Calle 60 no. 344 (at Av. Colón), 97000 Mérida, Yuc. ✆ 800/223-1234 in the U.S. and Canada, or 999/942-1234. Fax 999/925-7002. www.merida.regency.hyatt.com. 299 units. $200 (£100) standard double; $220 (£110) Regency Club double. Ask about promotional rates. AE, DC, MC, V. Free guarded parking. **Amenities:** 2 restaurants; 2 bars (1 swim-up, open seasonally); large outdoor pool; 2 lighted tennis courts; state-of-the-art health club w/men's and women's whirlpool, sauna, and steam rooms; children's activities (seasonal); concierge; tour desk; car rental; business center; shopping arcade; room service; massage; babysitting; laundry service; dry cleaning; nonsmoking rooms; executive-level rooms. *In room:* A/C, TV, minibar, hair dryer.

MODERATE

Casa Mexilio Guest House ✿ (Moments)   This bed-and-breakfast is unlike any other I know. The owners are geniuses at playing with space in an unexpected and delightful manner. Rooms are at different levels, creating private spaces joined to each other and to rooftop terraces by stairs and catwalks. Most are spacious and airy, furnished and decorated in an engaging mix of new and old, polished and primitive. Five come with air-conditioning. A small pool with a whirlpool and profuse tropical vegetation take up most of the central patio. Breakfasts are great. It's 4 blocks west of the plaza. A small bar serves drinks during happy hour, and, weather permitting, you can have your cocktail on one of the rooftop terraces.

Calle 68 no. 495 (between calles 57 and 59), 97000 Mérida, Yuc. ✆ 877/639-4546 in the U.S. and Canada, or 999/928-2505. www.casamexilio.com. 9 units. $50–$85 (£25–£43) double; $120 (£60) penthouse. Rates include full breakfast. MC, V. Limited street parking. **Amenities:** Bar; small outdoor pool; whirlpool; nonsmoking rooms. *In room:* A/C (in some), no phone.

Where to Stay & Dine in Mérida

ACCOMMODATIONS ■
Casa Mexilio Guest House **6**
Casa San Juan **20**
Fiesta Americana Mérida **1**
Hotel Caribe **18**
Hotel Dolores Alba **19**
Hotel Maison Lafitte **12**
Hotel Marionetas **4**

Hotel MedioMundo **5**
Hotel Mucuy **14**
Hyatt Regency Mérida **2**

DINING ◆
Alberto's Continental **9**
Amaro **11**
Café Alameda **13**

Casa de Frida **8**
Eladio's **16**
El Templo **17**
La Flor de Santiago **7**
Restaurante Kantún **3**
Restaurant Los Almendros **15**
Vito Corleone **10**

Haciendas & Hotels

Haciendas in the Yucatán have had a bumpy history. During the colonial period they were isolated, self-sufficient fiefdoms—not terribly efficient, but they didn't have to be. Mostly they produced foodstuffs—enough for the needs of the owners and peasants plus a little extra that the owners could sell for a small sum in the city. The owners, though politically powerful, especially within the confines of their large estates, were never rich.

This changed in the 19th century, when the expanding world market created high demand for *henequén*, the natural fiber of the sisal plant, which was used to bale hay. In a few years, all of the haciendas shifted to mass production of this commodity. Prices and profits kept climbing through the end of the century and into the 20th. Hacienda owners now had lots of cash to spend on their estates and on heavy machinery to process the *henequén* fiber more efficiently. Then came the bust. Throughout the 1920s, prices and demand fell, and no other commodity could replace sisal. The haciendas entered a long decline, but by then, the cultivation and processing of sisal had become part of local culture.

To see and understand what things were like during the golden age, you can visit a couple of haciendas. One, by the name of **Sotuta de Peón,** has recently been refurbished and runs much like in the old days—a living museum involving an entire community (see "Side Trips from Mérida," later in this chapter). At the other one, **Yaxcopoil** (see "En Route to Uxmal," later in this chapter), you can wander the shell of a once-bustling estate and look for remnants of splendor.

Now another boom of sorts has brought haciendas back; this time as retreats, country residences, and hotels. The hotels convey an air of the past—elegant gateways, thick walls, open arches, and high ceilings—you get the feel of an era gone by. Indeed, there are a few features that make a guest feel like lord and master, especially the extravagant suites and personal service. But what strikes me the most when I visit these haciendas is the contrast between them and the world outside. They are like little islands of order and tranquillity in the sea of chaos that is the Yucatán.

There are five luxury hacienda hotels. The most opulent of these is **La Hacienda Xcanatún** (© 888/883-3633 in the U.S.; www.xcanatun.com). It's on

Hotel Caribe   This three-story colonial-style hotel (no elevator) is great for a couple of reasons: Its location at the back of Plaza Hidalgo is both central and quiet, and it has a nice little pool and sun deck on the rooftop with a view of the cathedral. The rooms are moderately comfortable, though they aren't well lit, and have only small windows facing the central courtyard. Thirteen *clase económica* rooms don't have air-conditioning, but standard rooms do; and superior rooms (on the top floor) have been remodeled and have safes, hair dryers, larger windows, and quieter air-conditioning. Avoid the rooms on the ground floor. The hotel offers a lot of variety in bedding arrangements, mostly combinations of twins and doubles. Mattresses are often softer the outskirts of Mérida, off the highway to Progreso. The suites are large and have extravagant bathrooms. The decor is in muted colors with rich materials and modern pieces that evoke the simplicity of an earlier age. It has the best restaurant in the Mérida area and a complete spa. The owners personally manage their hotel and keep the service sharp.

The other four luxury hotels are all owned by Roberto Hernández, one of the richest men in Mexico. The hospitality and reservation system are handled by **Starwood Hotels** (© 800/325-3589 in the U.S. and Canada; www.luxurycollection.com). The owner has taken great pains to restore all four haciendas to original condition, and all are beautiful. **Temozón,** off the highway to Uxmal, is the most magnificent. **Uayamón,** located between the ruins of Edzná and the colonial city of Campeche, is perhaps the most romantic. **Hacienda San José Cholul,** located east of Mérida towards Izamal, is my personal favorite, and picturesque **Santa Rosa** lies southwest of Mérida, near the town of Maxcanú. Packages are available for staying at two or more of these haciendas. All offer personal service, activities, and spas.

Two haciendas offer economical lodging. On the western outskirts of Mérida by the highway to Chichén Itzá and Cancún is **Hacienda San Pedro Nohpat** (© 999/988-0542; www.haciendaholidays.com). It retains only the land that immediately surrounds the residence, but it offers a great bargain in lodging—large, comfortable rooms and an attractive garden area and pool. The other is **Hacienda Blanca Flor** (© 999/925-8042; www.mexonline.com/blancaflor.htm), which lies between Mérida and Campeche just off the highway. It's the only hacienda hotel that actually operates like one, producing most of the food served there. The owners work with bus tours but also welcome couples and individuals. Rooms are in a modern building and are large and simply furnished.

Two other haciendas can be leased by small groups for retreats and group vacations: **Hacienda Petac** (© 800/225-4255 in the U.S.; www.haciendapetac.com) and **Hacienda San Antonio** (© 999/910-6144; www.haciendasanantonio.com.mx). Both have beautiful rooms, common areas, and grounds.

than standard. Nearby parking is free at night but costs extra during the day beginning at 7am. The restaurant serves good Mexican food.

Calle 59 no. 500 (at Calle 60), 97000 Mérida, Yuc. © 888/822-6431 in the U.S. and Canada, or 999/924-9022. Fax 999/924-8733. www.hotelcaribe.com.mx. 53 units. $50 (£25) *clase económica* double; $66–$78 (£33–£39) standard or superior double. AE, MC, V. Free nearby night parking. **Amenities:** Restaurant; bar; small outdoor pool; tour desk; room service; laundry service. *In room:* A/C (in some), TV, hair dryer (in some), safe (in some).

Hotel Maison Lafitte ⭐   This three-story hotel has modern, attractive rooms with good air-conditioning, and tropical touches such as wooden louvers over the windows and light furniture with caned backs and seats. Rooms are medium to large, with midsize bathrooms that have great showers and good lighting. Most rooms come with either two doubles or a king-size bed. Rooms are quiet and overlook a pretty little garden with a fountain. A few rooms don't have windows. The location is excellent.

Calle 60 no. 472 (between calles 53 and 55), 97000 Mérida, Yuc. ℂ 800/538-6802 in the U.S. and Canada, or 999/928-1243. Fax 999/923-9159. www.maisonlafitte.com.mx. 30 units. $82 (£41) double. Rates include full breakfast. AE, MC, V. Free limited secure parking for compact cars. **Amenities:** Restaurant; bar; small outdoor pool; tour desk; car rental; room service; in-room massage; laundry service; dry cleaning. *In room:* A/C, TV, Wi-Fi, minibar, hair dryer, safe.

Hotel Marionetas ✿ This quiet and attractive B&B, 6 blocks north of the main square, has a comforting feel to it. Even though I've heard the story, I'm still not clear on how the hosts, Sofi (Macedonian) and Daniel (Argentinean), ended up in Mérida. But they are engaging, interesting people and attentive innkeepers. They have created a lovely space with common areas in front, rooms in back and a lush garden/pool area in between. It's the kind of place that tempts you to lounge about.

Calle 49 no. 516 (between calles 62 and 64), 97000 Mérida, Yuc. ℂ 999/928-3377. www.hotelmarionetas.com. 8 units. $80–$95 (£40–£48) double. Rates include full breakfast. 2-night minimum stay. MC, V. Free secure parking for compact cars. Children under 12 not accepted. **Amenities:** Small outdoor pool; tour desk; in-room massage; laundry service; nonsmoking rooms. *In room:* A/C, Wi-Fi, fridge, hair dryer, safe.

Hotel MedioMundo ✿ *Finds* This is a quiet courtyard hotel with beautiful rooms and a good location 3 blocks north of the main plaza. The English-speaking owners, Nicole and Nelson, have been in the hotel business for years and have invested their money in the right places, going for high-quality mattresses, good lighting, quiet air-conditioning, lots of space, and good bathrooms with strong showers. What they didn't invest in were TVs, which adds to the serenity. Higher prices are for the eight rooms with air-conditioning, but all units have windows with good screens and get ample ventilation. Breakfast is served in one of the two attractive courtyards.

Calle 55 no. 533 (between calles 64 and 66), 97000 Mérida, Yuc. ℂ/fax 999/924-5472. www.hotelmediomundo. com. 12 units. $60–$90 (£30–£45) double. MC, V. Limited street parking. **Amenities:** Small outdoor pool; tour info; in-room massage; laundry service; nonsmoking rooms. *In room:* A/C (in some), no phone.

INEXPENSIVE

Casa San Juan ✿ *Value* This B&B, in a colonial house, is loaded with character and provides a good glimpse of the old Mérida that lies behind the colonial facades in the historic district. Guest rooms are beautifully decorated, large, and comfortable. Those in the original house have been modernized but maintain a colonial feel, with 7m (23-ft.) ceilings and 45cm-thick (18-inch) walls. The modern rooms in back look out over the rear patio. The lower rate is for the rooms without air-conditioning (they have ceiling and floor fans). Choice of beds includes one queen-size, one double, or two twins, all with good mattresses and sheets. Breakfast includes fruit or juice, coffee, bread, and homemade preserves. Casa San Juan is 4 blocks south of the main square.

Calle 62 no. 545a (between calles 69 and 71), 97000 Mérida, Yuc. ℂ/fax 999/986-2937. www.casasanjuan.com. 8 units (7 with private bathroom). $30–$60 (£15–£30) double. Rates include continental breakfast. No credit cards. Parking nearby $2 (£1). *In room:* A/C (in some), no phone.

Hotel Dolores Alba *Value* The Dolores Alba offers attractive, comfortable rooms, an inviting swimming pool, good A/C, and free parking, all for a great price. The three-story section (with elevator) surrounding the back courtyard offers large rooms with good-size bathrooms. Beds (either two doubles or one double and one twin) have supportive foam-core mattresses, usually in a combination of one medium-firm and one medium-soft. All rooms have windows or balconies looking out over the pool. An old mango tree shades the front courtyard. The older rooms in this section are decorated with local crafts and have small bathrooms. The family that owns the Hotel Dolores Alba outside Chichén Itzá manages this hotel; you can make reservations at one hotel for the other. This hotel is 3½ blocks from the main square.

Calle 63 no. 464 (between calles 52 and 54), 97000 Mérida, Yuc. © **999/928-5650.** Fax 999/928-3163. www.dolores alba.com. 100 units. $45 (£23) double. MC, V (with 8% surcharge). Internet specials available. Free guarded parking. **Amenities:** Restaurant; outdoor pool; tour desk; room service; laundry service; laundromat. *In room:* A/C, TV, safe.

Hotel Mucuy *(Value*   The Mucuy is a simple, quiet, pleasant hotel in a great location. The gracious owners strive to make guests feel welcome, with conveniences such as a communal refrigerator in the lobby and, for a small extra charge, the use of a washer and dryer. Guest rooms are basic; most contain two twin beds or a queen (with comfortable mattresses) and some simple furniture. A neat garden patio with comfortable chairs is the perfect place for sitting and reading. The Mucuy is named for a small dove said to bring good luck to places where it alights. The hotel has a few rooms with A/C, which cost $5 (£2.50) more. English is spoken.

Calle 57 no. 481 (between calles 56 and 58), 97000 Mérida, Yuc. © **999/928-5193.** Fax 999/923-7801. www.mucuy. com or cofelia@yahoo.com.mx. 21 units. $22 (£11) double. No credit cards. Limited street parking. **Amenities:** Small outdoor pool; tour info; self-serve laundry. *In room:* A/C (in some), no phone.

WHERE TO DINE

The people of Mérida have strong ideas and traditions about food. Certain dishes are always associated with a particular day of the week. In households across the city, Sunday would feel incomplete without *puchero* (a kind of stew). On Monday, at any restaurant that caters to locals, you are sure to find *frijol con puerco* (pork and beans). Likewise, you'll find *potaje* (potage) on Thursday; fish, of course, on Friday; and *chocolomo* (a beef dish) on Saturday. These dishes are heavy and slow to digest; they are for the midday meal, and not suitable for supper. What's more, Meridanos don't believe that seafood is a healthy supper food. All seafood restaurants in Mérida close by 6pm unless they cater to tourists. The preferred supper food is turkey (which, by the way, is said to be high in tryptophan, a soporific), and it's best served in the traditional *antojitos*—*salbutes* (small thin rounds of *masa* fried and topped with turkey, pork, or chicken, and onions, tomatoes, and lettuce) and *panuchos* (sliced open and lightly stuffed with bean paste, before having toppings added)—and turkey soup.

Another thing you may notice about Mérida is the surprising number of Middle Eastern restaurants. The city received a large influx of Lebanese immigrants around 1900. This population has had a strong influence on local society, to the point where Meridanos think of kibbe the way Americans think of pizza. Speaking of pizza, if you want to get some to take back to your hotel room, try **Vito Corleone,** on Calle 59 between calles 60 and 62. Its pizzas have a thin crust with a slightly smoky taste from the wood-burning oven.

It's becoming more difficult to recommend good restaurants for fine dining in the downtown area. Most of the best places are in the outlying districts, near the upper-class neighborhoods and shopping plazas. They are a little difficult to get to. If you want something special, I would recommend dining at the Hacienda Xcanatún on the outskirts of town, off the Progreso road. (See "Of Haciendas & Hotels," above.)

EXPENSIVE

Alberto's Continental LEBANESE/YUCATECAN   There's nothing quite like dining here at night in a softly lit room or on the wonderful old patio framed in

Moorish arches. Nothing glitzy—just elegant *mudejar*-patterned tile floors, simple furniture, decoration that's just so, and the gurgling of a fountain creating a romantic mood. I find the prices on the expensive side. For supper, you can choose a sampler plate of four Lebanese favorites, or traditional Yucatecan specialties, such as *pollo pibil* or fish Celestún (bass stuffed with shrimp). You can finish with Turkish coffee.

Calle 64 no. 482 (at Calle 57). ✆ 999/928-5367. Reservations recommended. Main courses $8–$22 (£4–£11). AE, MC, V. Daily 1–11pm.

Casa de Frida 🐗🐗 MEXICAN   If you're longing for some classic Mexican food from the central highlands, try this place. It serves some of the dishes Mexico is best known for, such as *mole poblano* and *sopa azteca*. The *mole* was good when I was last there, as was an interesting *flan de berenjena* (a kind of eggplant timbale). This is a comfortable no-nonsense sort of place decorated a la Mexicana. The menu has enough breadth to satisfy any appetite.

Calle 61 no. 526 (at Calle 66). ✆ 999/928-2311. Reservations recommended. Main courses $10–$13 (£5–£6.50). No credit cards. Mon–Sat 6–10pm.

MODERATE

Amaro REGIONAL/VEGETARIAN   The menu at this courtyard restaurant lists some interesting vegetarian dishes, such as *crema de calabacitas* (cream of squash soup), apple salad, and avocado pizza. There is also a limited menu of fish and chicken dishes; you might want to try the Yucatecan chicken. The *agua de chaya* (chaya is a leafy vegetable prominent in the Maya diet) is refreshing on a hot afternoon. All desserts are made in-house. The restaurant is a little north of Plaza Mayor.

Calle 59 no. 507 Interior 6 (between calles 60 and 62). ✆ 999/928-2451. Main courses $5–$9 (£2.50–£4.50). MC, V. Mon–Sat 11am–2am.

El Príncipe Tutul Xiú 🐗🐗 (Finds) REGIONAL   Yucatecan specialties from a limited menu. The original is in the town of Maní—the owner opened this restaurant because he got tired of hearing Meridanos asking him why he didn't open one in the capital. It's a short taxi ride from downtown, and to return you can pick up a local bus that passes by the restaurant. This is a great place to try the famous *sopa de lima,* and one of the six typical main courses, served with great handmade tortillas. And you can order, with confidence, one of the flavored waters such as *horchata* or *tamarindo.*

Calle 123 no. 216 (between calles 46 and 46b), Colonia Serapio Rendón. ✆ 999/929-7721. Reservations not accepted. Main courses $6 (£3). MC, V. Daily 11am–6pm.

El Templo 🐗 MEXICAN NUEVA COCINA   The odd layout of the place and the decor, which plays loosely with Mexican popular culture and iconography, are amusing. And the triptych menu, divided into Yucatecan, Mexican, and original, holds a lot of uncommon choices, plus a couple of daily specials. Sample dishes include the Cornish game hen in a guava-lime glaze and a salmon in a tamarind and black sesame sauce. I get the feeling that chef hasn't settled down into a groove yet, but there is no denying his enthusiasm. I just hope the locals enjoy this place as much as I did.

Calle 59 no. 438 (between calles 50 and 52). ✆ 999/930-9303. Reservations accepted. Main courses $7–$10 (£3.50–£5). MC, V. Mon–Sat 6–1pm.

Restaurante Kantún 🐗🐗 (Value) SEAFOOD   This modest restaurant serves up the freshest seafood for incredibly low prices. The owner-chef is always on the premises taking care of details. The menu includes excellent ceviche and seafood cocktails and fish cooked in a number of ways. I had the *especial Kantún,* which was lightly battered and stuffed with lobster, crab, and shrimp. The dining room is air-conditioned, the furniture comfortable, and the service attentive.

Calle 45 no. 525-G (between calles 64 and 66). ✆ **999/923-4493.** Reservations recommended. Main courses $6–$12 (£3–£6). MC, V. Daily noon–8pm (occasionally closes Mon).

Restaurant Los Almendros *(Overrated* YUCATECAN   Ask where to eat Yucatecan food, and locals will inevitably suggest this place, mostly because it was the first place to offer tourists such Yucatecan specialties as *salbutes, panuchos* and *papadzules, cochinita pibil,* and *poc chuc.* The menu even comes with color photographs to facilitate acquaintance with these strange-sounding dishes. The food is okay and not much of a risk, but you can find better elsewhere. The service is slow. Still, it's a safe place to try Yucatecan food for the first time, and it's such a fixture that the idea of a guidebook that doesn't mention this restaurant is unthinkable. It's 5 blocks east of Calle 60, facing the Parque de la Mejorada.

Calle 50A no. 493. ✆ **999/928-5459.** Main courses $6–$10 (£3–£5). AE, MC, V. Daily 10am–11pm.

INEXPENSIVE

Café Alameda MIDDLE EASTERN/VEGETARIAN   The trappings here are simple and informal (metal tables, plastic chairs), and it's a good place for catching a light meal. The trick is figuring out the Spanish names for popular Middle Eastern dishes. Kibbe is *quebbe bola* (not *quebbe cruda*), hummus is *garbanza,* and shish kabob is *alambre.* I leave it to you to figure out what a spinach pie is called (and it's excellent). Café Alameda is a treat for vegetarians, and the umbrella-shaded tables on the patio are perfect for morning coffee and *mamules* (walnut-filled pastries).

Calle 58 no. 474 (between calles 55 and 57). ✆ **999/928-3635.** Main courses $2–$5 (£1–£2.50). No credit cards. Daily 8am–5pm.

Eladio's ✪ YUCATECAN   This is where locals come to relax in their off hours, drink very cold beer, and snack on Yucatecan specialties. There are 4 or 5 of these restaurants scattered about the city; this is the closest to the center of downtown. You have two choices: order a beer and enjoy *una botana* (a small portion that accompanies a drink, in this case usually a Yucatecan dish), or order from the menu. *Cochinita, poc chuc,* and *relleno negro* (turkey flavored with burnt chiles) are all good. Or try the *panuchos* or *salbutes.* Often there is live music in this open-air restaurant, which is 3 blocks east of Parque de la Mejorada.

Calle 59 (at Calle 44). ✆ **999/923-1087.** Main courses $4–$8 (£2–£4). AE, MC, V. Daily noon–9pm.

La Flor de Santiago REGIONAL   This is a curious place with classic ambience and classically slow service. I like it best in the morning for breakfast. The dining area is very typical of Mérida, with its high ceiling, plain furniture, and local clientele. A wood-fired stove produces baked goods, and there's a sampling of Yucatecan specialties on the menu. Often it can be annoying because the cooks run out of food.

Calle 70 no. 478 (between calles 57 and 59). ✆ **999/928-5591.** *Comida corrida* $4 (£2); main courses $5–$6 (£2.50–£3). No credit cards. Daily 7am–11pm.

MERIDA AFTER DARK

For nighttime entertainment, see the box, "Festivals & Special Events in Mérida," earlier in this chapter, or check out the theaters noted here.

   Teatro Peón Contreras, Calle 60 at Calle 57, and **Teatro Ayala,** Calle 60 at Calle 61, feature a wide range of performing artists from Mexico and around the world. **El**

Nuevo Olimpo, on the main square, schedules frequent concerts; and **Cine Mérida,** a half-block north of the Nuevo Olimpo, has two screens for showing classic and art films, and one live stage.

Mérida's club scene offers everything from ubiquitous rock/dance to some one-of-a-kind spots that are nothing like what you find back home. Most of the dance clubs are in the big hotels or on Paseo de Montejo. For dancing, a small cluster of clubs on Calle 60, around the corner from Santa Lucía, offer live rock and Latin music. For salsa, go to **Mambo Café** in the Plaza las Américas shopping center.

ECOTOURS & ADVENTURE TRIPS

The Yucatán Peninsula has seen a recent explosion of companies that organize nature and adventure tours. One well-established outfit with a great track record is **Ecoturismo Yucatán,** Calle 3 no. 235, Col. Pensiones, 97219 Mérida (© **999/920-2772;** fax 999/925-9047; www.ecoyuc.com). Alfonso and Roberta Escobedo create itineraries to meet just about any special or general interest you may have for going to the Yucatán or southern Mexico. Alfonso has been creating adventure and nature tours for more than a dozen years. Specialties include archaeology, birding, natural history, and kayaking. The company also offers day trips that explore contemporary Maya culture and life in villages in the Yucatán. Package and customized tours are available.

SIDE TRIPS FROM MERIDA
SOTUTA DE PEON

What started out as one man's hobby—to restore an old hacienda for a weekend getaway and perhaps see what it takes to plant a couple of acres of *henequén*—spiraled out of control until it grew into one of the best living-museums you'll see anywhere; it has engrossed the imagination of an entire rural community. Presto! You have a completely functional *hacienda henequenera.*

You can arrange transportation from any of Mérida's hotels by calling **Hacienda Sotuta de Peón** at © **999/941-8639.** Call to make a reservation even if you have your own car, and be sure to bring your bathing suit; there's a cenote on the property. The best days to visit are when the giant fiber-extracting machine is in operation—Tuesday, Thursday, or Saturday. The tour starts with a visit to the *henequén* fields via mule-drawn carts, the same as are used to transport the leaves of the plant to the hacienda's headquarters. You get to see it being harvested, and later, processed at the *casa de máquinas,* and even used in the manufacturing of twine and such. Along the way you get a glimpse into the local culture surrounding *henequén* production. You visit a house of one of the workers, as well as the house of the *hacendado* (the owner). You can also try some of the regional cooking—a restaurant on the premises turns out some good food. Admission costs $25 (£13) per adult, $15 (£7.50) per child. Transportation is extra. For more information see **www.haciendatour.com**.

IZAMAL

Izamal is a sleepy town some 80km (50 miles) east of Mérida, an easy day trip by car. You can visit the famous Franciscan convent of San Antonio de Padua and the ruins of four large pyramids that overlook the center of town. One pyramid is partially reconstructed. Life in Izamal is easygoing in the extreme, as evidenced by the *victorias,* the horse-drawn buggies that serve as taxis here. Even if you come by car, you should make a point of touring the town in one of these. There is also a sound and light show in the old convent. The half-hour show costs $4.50 (£2.25) and is held on Tuesday,

Thursday, Friday, and Saturday at 8:30pm. It's in Spanish, but you can rent headphones in other languages for $2.50 (£1.25).

CELESTUN NATIONAL WILDLIFE REFUGE: FLAMINGOS & OTHER WATERFOWL

On the coast, west of Mérida, is a large wetlands area that has been declared a biopreserve. It is a long, shallow estuary where freshwater mixes with Gulf saltwater, creating a habitat perfect for flamingos and many other species of waterfowl. This *ría* (estuary), unlike others that are fed by rivers or streams, receives fresh water through about 80 cenotes, most of which are underwater. It is very shallow (.3–1m/1–4 ft. deep) and thickly grown with mangrove, with an open channel .5km (a quarter mile) wide and 50km (31 miles) long, sheltered from the open sea by a narrow strip of land. Along this corridor, you can take a launch to see flamingos as they dredge the bottom of the shallows for a species of small crustacean and a particular insect that make up the bulk of their diet.

You can get here by car or bus; it's an easy 90-minute drive. (For information on buses, see "Getting There & Departing: By Bus," earlier in this chapter.) To drive, leave downtown Mérida on Calle 57. Shortly after Santiago Church, Calle 57 ends and there's a dogleg onto Calle 59-A. This crosses Avenida Itzáes, and its name changes to Jacinto Canek; continue until you see signs for Celestún Highway 178. This will take you through Hunucmá, where the road joins Highway 281, which takes you to Celestún. You'll know you have arrived when you get to the bridge.

In the last few years, the state agency CULTUR has come into Celestún and established order where once there was chaos. Immediately to your left after the bridge, you'll find modern facilities with a snack bar, clean bathrooms, and a ticket window. Prices for tours are fixed. A 75-minute tour costs about $50 (£25) and can accommodate up to six people. You can join others or hire a boat by yourself. On the tour you'll definitely see some flamingos; you'll also get to see some mangrove close up, and one of the many underwater springs. Please do not urge the boatmen to get any closer to the flamingos than they are allowed to; if pestered too much, the birds will abandon the area for another, less fitting habitat. The ride is quite pleasant—the water is calm, and CULTUR has supplied the boatmen with wide, flat-bottom skiffs that have canopies for shade.

In addition to flamingos, you will see frigate birds, pelicans, spoonbills, egrets, sandpipers, and other waterfowl feeding on shallow sandbars at any time of year. At least 15 duck species have been counted, and there are several species of birds of prey. Of the 175 bird species that are here, some 99 are permanent residents. Nonbreeding flamingos remain here year-round; the larger group of breeding flamingos takes off around April to nest on the upper Yucatán Peninsula east of Río Lagartos, returning to Celestún in October.

Hotel Eco Paraíso Xixim 🐟🐟   Eco Paraíso is meant to be a refuge from the modern world. It sits on a deserted 4km (2½-mile) stretch of beach that was once part of a coconut plantation. It attracts much the same clientele as the former-haciendas-turned-luxury-hotels, but in some ways it has more going for it (like the beach). Some guests come here for a week of idleness; others use this as a base of operations for visiting the biopreserve and making trips to the Maya ruins in the interior. The hotel offers its own tours to various places. Rooms are quite private; each is a separate bungalow with *palapa* roof. Each comes with two comfortable queen-size beds, a sitting area, ceiling fans, and a private porch with hammocks. On my last visit, the food was very good, and the service was great. The hotel composts waste, and treats and uses wastewater.

Antigua Carretera a Sisal Km 10, 97367 Celestún, Yuc. © **988/916-2100.** Fax 988/916-2111. www.ecoparaiso.com. 15 units. High season $220 (£110) double; low season $184 (£92) double. Rates include 2 meals per person. AE, MC, V. Free parking. **Amenities:** Restaurant; bar; midsize outdoor pool; tour desk. *In room:* Coffeemaker, hair dryer, safe.

DZIBILCHALTUN: MAYA RUINS & MUSEUM

This destination makes for a quick morning trip that will get you back to Mérida in time for a siesta, or it could be part of a longer trip to Progreso, Uaymitún, and Xcambó. It's located 14km (8⅔ miles) north of Mérida along the Progreso road and 4km (2½ miles) east of the highway. To get there, take Calle 60 all the way out of town and follow signs for Progreso and Highway 261. Look for the sign for Dzibilchaltún, which also reads UNIVERSIDAD DEL MAYAB; it will point you right. After a few miles, you'll see a sign for the entrance to the ruins and the museum. If you don't want to drive, take one of the *colectivos* that line up along Parque San Juan.

Dzibilchaltún was founded about 500 B.C., flourished around A.D. 750, and was in decline long before the coming of the conquistadors. Since the ruins were discovered in 1941, more than 8,000 buildings have been mapped. The site covers an area of almost 15 sq. km (6 sq. miles) with a central core of almost 25 hectares (62 acres), but the area of prime interest is limited to the buildings surrounding two plazas next to the cenote, and another building, the Temple of the Seven Dolls, connected to these by a *sacbé* (causeway). Dzibilchaltún means "place of the stone writing," and at least 25 stelae have been found.

Start at the **Museo del Pueblo Maya,** which is worth seeing. It's open Tuesday to Sunday from 8am to 4pm. Admission is $6 (£3). The museum's collection includes artifacts from various sites in the Yucatán. Explanations are printed in bilingual format and are fairly thorough. Objects include a beautiful example of a plumed serpent from Chichén Itzá and a finely designed incense vessel from Palenque. From this general view of the Maya civilization, the museum moves on to exhibit specific artifacts found at the site of Dzibilchaltún, including the rather curious dolls that have given one structure its name. Then there's an exhibit on Maya culture in historical and present times, including a collection of *huipiles,* the woven blouses that Indian women wear. From here a door leads out to the site.

The first thing you come to is the *sacbé* that connects the two areas of interest. To the left is the **Temple of the Seven Dolls.** The temple's doorways and the *sacbé* line up with the rising sun at the spring and autumnal equinoxes. To the right are the buildings grouped around the Cenote Xlacah, the sacred well, and a complex of buildings around **Structure 38,** the **Central Group** of temples. The Yucatán State Department of Ecology has added nature trails and published a booklet (in Spanish) of birds and plants seen along the mapped trail.

PROGRESO, UAYMITUN & XCAMBO: GULF COAST CITY, FLAMINGO LOOKOUT & MORE MAYA RUINS

For a beach escape, go to the port of Progreso, Mérida's weekend beach resort. This is where Meridanos have their vacation houses and where they come in large numbers in July and August. It is also the part-time home of some Americans and Canadians escaping northern winters. Except for July and August, it is a quiet place where you can enjoy the Gulf waters in peace. Along the *malecón,* the wide oceanfront drive that extends the length of a sandy beach, you can pull over and enjoy a swim anywhere you like. The water here isn't the blue of the Caribbean, but it's clean. A long pier extends several kilometers into the gulf to load and unload large ships. Cruise ships dock here twice a week. Along or near the *malecón* are several hotels and a number of restaurants where you can get good fresh seafood.

From Mérida, buses to **Progreso** leave from the bus station at Calle 62 no. 524, between calles 65 and 67, every 15 minutes, starting at 5am. The trip takes almost an hour and costs $3 (£1.50).

If you have a car, you might want to drive down the coastal road east toward Telchac Puerto. After about 20 minutes, on the right you'll see a large, solid-looking wooden observation tower for viewing flamingos. A sign reads UAYMITUN. The state agency CULTUR constructed the tower, operates it, and provides binoculars free of charge. A few years ago, flamingos from Celestún migrated here and established a colony. Your chances of spotting them are good, and you don't have to pay for a boat.

Twenty minutes farther down this road, there's a turnoff for the road to Dzemul. On my last trip I didn't see any flamingos at Uaymitún, but just after turning here, I found a flock of 500, only 30m (98 ft.) from the highway. After a few minutes, you'll see a sign for **Xcambó** that points to the right. This Maya city is thought to have prospered as a production center for salt. Archaeologists have reconstructed the small ceremonial center, which has several platforms and temples. Admission is free. After viewing these ruins, you can continue on the same road through the small towns of Dzemul and Baca. At Baca, take Highway 176 back to Mérida.

EN ROUTE TO UXMAL

Two routes go to Uxmal, about 80km (50 miles) south of Mérida. The most direct is Highway 261 via Umán and Muna. On the way, you can stop to see Hacienda Yaxcopoil, which is 30km (20 miles) from Mérida. If you have the time and want a more scenic route, try the meandering State Highway 18. It's sometimes called the Convent Route, but all tourism hype aside, it makes for a pleasant drive with several interesting stops. One thing you might do is make your trip to Uxmal into a loop by going one way and coming back the other with an overnight stay at Uxmal. You could plan on arriving in Uxmal in the late afternoon, attend the sound-and-light show in the evening, and see the ruins the next morning while it is cool and uncrowded.

While traveling in this area you'll pass through small villages without directional signs, so get used to poking your head out the window and saying *"Buenos días. ¿Dónde está el camino para . . . ?"* which translates as "Good day. Where is the road to . . . ?" I end up asking more than one person. The streets in these villages are full of children, bicycles, and livestock, so drive carefully and, as always, keep an eye out for unmarked *topes*. The attractions on these routes all have the same hours: Churches are open daily from 10am to 1pm and 4 to 6pm; ruins are open daily from 8am to 5pm.

HIGHWAY 261: YAXCOPOIL & MUNA   From downtown, take Calle 65 or 69 to Avenida Itzáes and turn left; this feeds onto the highway. You can save some time by looping around the busy market town of Umán. To do so, take the exit for Highway 180 Cancún and Campeche, and then follow signs towards Campeche. You'll be on 180 headed south; take it for a few miles to where it intersects with Highway 261; take the exit labeled UXMAL. Very shortly you'll come to the town and **Hacienda Yaxcopoil** (yash-koh-*poyl;* © **999/900-1193;** www.yaxcopoil.com), a ruined hacienda in plain sight on the right side of the road. In the front courtyard—now a parking lot—is a giant Indian laurel tree. You can take a half-hour tour of the place, including the manor, and the *henequén* factory. It's open from Monday to Saturday from 8am to

5pm and Sunday 9am to 1pm. Admission is $5 (£2.50). It's a little overpriced because the owners have not put much effort into making it a special attraction, but the grounds are attractive, and there are some things of interest.

After Yaxcopoil comes the little market town of **Muna** (65km/40 miles from Mérida). Here you can find excellent **reproductions of Maya ceramics.** An artisan named Rodrigo Martín Morales has worked 25 years perfecting the style and methods of the ancient Maya. He and his family have two workshops in town. They do painstaking work and sell a lot of their production to archeologists and museum stores. The first store is on the right at the junction of a bypass for Muna. Look for a typical Maya dwelling and a small store. The main store is 3km (2 miles) farther on, just as you enter Muna. Keep an eye out for two large Ceiba trees growing on the right-hand side of the road. Under the trees a small plaza with stalls sell handcrafts or food. Make a right turn and go down 45m (150 ft.). On your left will be a store. It's not well marked, but it will be obvious. The name of the place is **Taller de Artesanía Los Ceibos** (© **997/971-0036**). The family will be working in the back. Only Spanish is spoken. The store is open from 9am to 6pm daily. In addition to ceramics, Rodrigo works in stone, wood, and jade. Uxmal is 15km (9⅓ miles) beyond Muna.

HIGHWAY 18 (THE CONVENT ROUTE): KANASIN, ACANCEH, MAYAPAN & TICUL   From downtown take Calle 63 east to Circuito Colonias and turn right; look for a traffic circle with a small fountain and turn left. This feeds onto Highway 18 to Kanasín (kah-nah-*seen*) and then Acanceh (ah-kahn-*keh*). In **Kanasín,** the highway divides into two roads, and a sign will tell you that you can't go straight; instead, you go to the right, which will curve around and flow into the next parallel street. Go past the market, church, and the main square on your left, and then stay to the right when you get to a fork.

Shortly after Kanasín, the highway has been upgraded and now bypasses a lot of villages. After a few of these turnoffs you'll see a sign pointing left to Acanceh. Across the street from and overlooking Acanceh's church is a restored pyramid. On top of this pyramid, under a makeshift roof, are some large stucco figures of Maya deities. The caretaker, Mario Uicab, will guide you up to see the figures and give you a little explanation (in Spanish). Admission is $2.50 (£1.25). There are some other ruins a couple of blocks away called **El Palacio de los Estucos.** In 1908, a stucco mural was found here in mint condition. It was left exposed and has deteriorated somewhat. Now it is sheltered, and you can still easily distinguish the painted figures in their original colors. To leave Acanceh, head back to the highway on the street that passes between the church and the plaza.

The next turnoff will be for **Tecoh** on the right side. Tecoh's parish church sits on a massive pre-Columbian raised platform—the remains of a ceremonial complex that was sacrificed to build the church. With its rough stone and simple twin towers that are crumbling around the edges, the church looks ancient. Inside are three carved *retablos* (altarpieces) covered in gold leaf and unmistakably Indian in style. In 1998, they were refurbished and are well worth seeing.

Also in Tecoh are some caverns, shown by a local. The bad news is that the owner doesn't have a very good flashlight, and I found myself groping around in the dark. You'll find them as you leave town heading back to the highway. Then it's on to the ruins of Mayapán.

MAYAPAN &

Founded, according to Maya lore, by the man-god Kukulkán (Quetzalcoatl in central Mexico) in about A.D. 1007, Mayapán quickly established itself as the most important city in northern Yucatán. For almost 2 centuries, it was the capital of a Maya confederation of city-states that included Chichén Itzá and Uxmal. But before 1200, the rulers of Mayapán ended the confederation by attacking and subjugating the other two cities. Eventually, a successful revolt by the other cities brought down Mayapán, which was abandoned during the mid-1400s.

The city extended out at least 4 sq. km (1½ sq. miles), but the ceremonial center is quite compact. In the last few years, archaeologists have been busy excavating and rebuilding it, and work continues. Several buildings bordering the principal plaza have been reconstructed, including one that is similar to El Castillo in Chichén Itzá. The excavations have uncovered murals and stucco figures that provide more grist for the mill of conjecture: atlantes (columns in the form of a human figure supporting something heavy, in the way Atlas supported the sky in Greek myth), skeletal soldiers, macaws, entwined snakes, and a stucco jaguar. This place is definitely worth a stop.

The site is open daily from 8am to 5pm. Admission is $3.50 (£1.75). Use of a personal video camera is $4 (£2).

FROM MAYAPAN TO TICUL   About 20km (12 miles) after Mayapán, you'll see the highway for **Mama** on your right. This will put you on a narrow road that quickly enters the town. For some reason I really like this village; some parts of it are quite pretty. It's often called Mamita by the locals, using the affectionate diminutive suffix. The main attraction is the church and former convent. Inside are several fascinating *retablos* sculpted in a native form of baroque. During the restoration of these buildings, colonial-age murals and designs were uncovered and restored. Be sure to get a peek at them in the sacristy. From Mama, continue on for about 20km (12 miles) to Ticul, a large (for this area) market town with a couple of simple hotels.

TICUL

Best known for the cottage industry of *huipil* (native blouse) embroidery and for the manufacture of women's dress shoes, Ticul isn't the most exciting stop on the Puuc route, but it's a convenient place to wash up and spend the night. It's also a center for large commercially produced pottery; most of the widely sold sienna-colored pottery painted with Maya designs comes from here. If it's a cloudy, humid day, the potters may not be working (part of the process requires sun drying), but they still welcome visitors to purchase finished pieces.

Ticul is only 20km (12 miles) northeast of Uxmal, so thrifty tourists stay either here or in Santa Elena instead of the more expensive hotels at the ruins. On the main square is the **Hotel Plaza,** Calle 23 no. 202, near the intersection with Calle 26 (© **997/972-0484**). It's a modest but comfortable hotel. A double room with air-conditioning costs $35 (£18); without air-conditioning, $25 (£13). In both cases, there's a 5% charge if you want to pay with a credit card (MasterCard and Visa accepted). Get an interior room if you're looking for quiet, because Ticul has quite a lively plaza. From Ticul, you can do one of two things: head straight for Uxmal via Santa Elena, or loop around the Puuc Route, the long way to Santa Elena. For information on the Puuc route, see "The Puuc Maya Route & Village of Oxkutzcab," below.

FROM TICUL TO UXMAL   Follow the main street (Calle 23) west through town. Turn left on Calle 34. It's 15km (9⅓ miles) to Santa Elena; and from there another

15km (9⅓ miles) to Uxmal. In Santa Elena, by the side of Highway 261, is a clean restaurant with good food, **El Chaac Mool,** and on the opposite side of the road is the **Flycatcher Inn B&B** (see listing, below).

2 The Ruins of Uxmal ⟨★⟨★⟨★

80km (50 miles) SW of Mérida; 19km (12 miles) W of Ticul; 19km (12 miles) S of Muna

The ceremonial complex of Uxmal (pronounced "oosh-*mahl*") is one of the master-works of Maya civilization. It is strikingly different from all other cities of the Maya for its expansive and intricate facades of carved stone. Unlike other sites in northern Yucatán, such as Chichén Itzá and Mayapán, Uxmal isn't built on a flat plane. The builders worked into the composition of the ceremonial center an interplay of eleva-tions that adds complexity. And then, there is the strange and beautiful oval-shaped Pyramid of the Magician, which is unique among the Maya. The great building period took place between A.D. 700 and 1000, when the population probably reached 25,000. After 1000, Uxmal fell under the sway of the Xiú princes (who may have come from central Mexico). In the 1440s, the Xiú conquered Mayapán, and not long afterward the age of the Maya ended with the arrival of the Spanish conquistadors.

Close to Uxmal, four smaller sites—**Sayil, Kabah, Xlapak,** and **Labná**—can be visited in quick succession. With Uxmal, these ruins are collectively known as the **Puuc route.** See "Seeing Puuc Maya Sites," below, if you want to explore these sites.

ESSENTIALS

GETTING THERE & DEPARTING   By Car   Two routes to Uxmal from Mérida, Highway 261 and State Highway 18, are described in "En Route to Uxmal," above. *Note:* There's no gasoline at Uxmal.

By Bus   See "Getting There & Departing" in "Mérida: Gateway to the Maya Heart-land," earlier in this chapter, for information about bus service between Mérida and Uxmal. To return, wait for the bus on the highway at the entrance to the ruins. To see the sound-and-light show, don't bother with regular buses; sign up with a tour opera-tor in Mérida.

ORIENTATION   Entrance to the ruins is through the visitor center where you buy your tickets (two per person, hold on to both). It has a restaurant; toilets; a first-aid station; shops selling soft drinks, ice cream, film, batteries, and books; a state-run Casa de Artesanía (crafts house); and a small museum, which isn't very informative. The site is open daily from 8am to 5pm. Admission to the archaeological site is around $11 (£5.50), which includes admission to the nightly sound-and-light show. Bringing in a video camera costs $4 (£2). Parking costs $1 (50p). If you're staying the night in Uxmal, it is possible (and I think preferable) to get to the site late in the day and buy a ticket that allows you to see the sound-and-light show that evening and lets you enter the ruins the next morning to explore them before it gets hot. Just make sure that the ticket vendor knows what you intend to do and keep the ticket. Turn to the color section of this book for a map of the ruins.

Guides at the entrance of Uxmal give tours in a variety of languages and charge $40 (£20) for a single person or a group. The guides frown on unrelated individuals join-ing a group. They'd rather charge you as a solo visitor, but you can ask other English speakers if they'd like to join you in a tour and split the cost. As at other sites, the guides vary in quality but will point out areas and architectural details that you might otherwise miss. You should think of these guided tours as performances—the guides try to be as entertaining as possible and adjust their presentations according to the interests of the visitors.

Included in the price of admission is a 45-minute **sound-and-light show,** each evening at 7pm. It's in Spanish, but headsets are available for rent ($2.50/£1.25) for listening to the program in several languages. The narrative is part Hollywood, part high school, but the lighting of the buildings is worth making the effort to see it. After the show, the chant *"Chaaac, Chaaac"* will echo in your mind for weeks.

A TOUR OF THE RUINS

THE PYRAMID OF THE MAGICIAN   As you enter the ruins, note a *chultún,* or cistern, where Uxmal stored its water. Unlike most of the major Maya sites, Uxmal has no cenote to supply fresh water. The city's inhabitants were much more dependent on rainwater, and consequently venerated the rain god Chaac with unusual devotion.

Rising in front of you is the Pirámide del Adivino. The name comes from a myth told to John Lloyd Stephens on his visit in the 19th century. It tells the story of a magician-dwarf who reached adulthood in a single day after being hatched from an egg and built this pyramid in one night. Beneath it are five earlier structures. The pyramid has an oval base and rounded sides. You are looking at the east side. The main face is on the west side. Walk around the left or south side to see the front. The pyramid was designed so that the east side rises less steeply than the west side, which shifts the crowning temples to the west of the central axis of the building, causing them to loom above the plaza below. The temple doorway is heavily ornamented, characteristic of the Chenes style, with 12 stylized masks representing Chaac.

THE NUNNERY QUADRANGLE   From the plaza you're standing in, you want to go to the large Nunnery Quadrangle. Walk out the way you walked into the plaza, turn right, and follow the wall of this long stone building until you get to the building's main door—a corbelled arch that leads into the quadrangle. You'll find yourself in a plaza bordered on each side by stone buildings with elaborate facades. The 16th-century Spanish historian Fray Diego López de Cogullado gave the quadrangle its name when he decided that its layout resembled a Spanish convent.

The quadrangle does have a lot of small rooms, about the size of a nun's cell. You might poke your head into one to see the shape and size of it, but don't bother trying to explore them all. These rooms were long ago abandoned to the swallows that fly above the city. No interior murals or stucco work have been found here—at least, not yet. No, the richness of Uxmal lies in the stonework on its exterior walls.

The Nunnery is a great example of this. The first building your eye latches onto when you enter the plaza is the north building in front of you. It is the tallest, and the view from the top includes all the major buildings of the city, making it useful for the sound-and-light show. The central stairway is bordered by a common element in Puuc architecture, doorways supported by rounded columns. The remnants of the facade on the second level show elements used in the other three buildings and elsewhere throughout the city. There's a crosshatch pattern and a pattern of square curlicues, called a step-and-fret design, and the long-nosed god mask repeated vertically, used often to decorate the corners of buildings—what I call a Chaac stack. Though the facades of these buildings share these common elements and others, their composition varies. On the west building you'll see long feathered serpents intertwined at head and tail. A human head stares out from a serpent's open mouth. I've heard and read a number of interpretations of this motif, repeated elsewhere in Maya art, but they all leave me somewhat in doubt. And that's the trouble with symbols: They are usually the condensed expression of multiple meanings, so any one interpretation could be true, but only partially true.

THE BALL COURT   Leaving the Nunnery by the same way you entered, you will see a ball court straight ahead. What would a Maya city be without a ball court? And this one is a particularly good representative of the hundreds found elsewhere in the Maya world. Someone has even installed a replica of one of the stone rings that were the targets for the players, who would make use of their knees, hips, and maybe their arms to strike a solid rubber ball (yes, the Maya knew about natural rubber and extracted latex from a couple of species of rubber trees). The inclined planes on both sides of the court were in play and obviously not an area for spectators, who are thought to have observed the game from atop the two structures.

THE GOVERNOR'S PALACE   Continuing in the same direction (south), you come to the large raised plaza on top of which sits the Governor's Palace, running in a north-south direction. The surface area of the raised plaza measures 140m×170m (459 ft.×558 ft.), and it is raised about 10m (33 ft.) above the ground—quite a bit of earth-moving. Most of this surface is used as a ceremonial space facing the front (east side) of the palace. In the center is a double-headed jaguar throne, which is seen elsewhere in the Maya world. From here, you get the best view of the building's remarkable facade. Like the rest of the palaces here, the first level is smooth, and the second is ornate. Moving diagonally across a crosshatch pattern is a series of Chaac masks. Crowning the building is an elegant cornice projecting slightly outward from above a double border, which could be an architectural reference to the original crested thatched roofs of the Maya. Human figures adorned the main doors, though only the headdress survives of the central figure.

THE GREAT PYRAMID   Behind the palace, the platform descends in terraces to another plaza with a large pyramid on its south side. This is known as the Great Pyramid. On top is the Temple of the Macaws, for the repeated representation of macaws on the face of the temple, and the ruins of three other temples. The view from the top is wonderful.

THE DOVECOTE   This building is remarkable in that roof combs weren't a common feature of temples in the Puuc hills, although you'll see one (of a very different style) on El Mirador at Sayil.

WHERE TO STAY

Flycatcher Inn B&B _Value_   This pleasant little bed-and-breakfast is in the village of Santa Elena, just off Highway 261. The rooms are quiet, attractive, and spacious, and come with comfortable beds and decorative ironwork made by one of the owners, Santiago Domínguez. The other owner is Kristine Ellingson, an American from the Northwest who has lived in Santa Elena for years and is happy to aid her guests in their travels. Last year they replaced the mattresses in all the rooms, added a cottage, and made various improvements to the hotel's large grounds.

Carretera Uxmal–Kabah, 97840 Santa Elena, Yuc. No phone. www.flycatcherinn.com. 7 units. $45–$65 (£23–£33) double ($10/£5 extra for A/C). Rates include breakfast. No credit cards. Free secure parking. *In room:* A/C in 6 units.

Hacienda Uxmal and The Lodge at Uxmal _★★★_   The Hacienda is the oldest hotel in Uxmal. Located just up the road from the ruins, it was built for the archaeology staff. Rooms are large and airy, exuding a feel of days gone by, with patterned tile floors, heavy furniture, and louvered windows. Room nos. 202 through 214 and 302 through 305 are the nicest of the superiors. Corner rooms are labeled A through F and are even larger and come with Jacuzzi tubs. A handsome garden courtyard with towering royal palms, a bar, and a pool adds to the air of tranquillity. A guitar trio usually plays on the open patio in the evenings.

The Lodge is right at the entrance to the ruins. It's made up of several two-story thatched buildings ("bungalows") situated around two pools and surrounded by landscaped grounds. Each building has a large, open breezeway with ceiling fans and rocking chairs. Rooms are extra large and attractively finished with details such as carved headboards. Bathrooms are large and come with stone countertops and either a bathtub or a Jacuzzi tub. Upstairs rooms have thatched roofs.

High season is from November through April; low season May to October.

Carretera Mérida–Uxmal Km 80, 97844 Uxmal, Yuc. ℂ 997/976-2011. www.mayaland.com. (Reservations: Mayaland Resorts, Robalo 30 SM3, 77500 Cancún, Q. Roo; ℂ 800/235-4079 in the U.S., or 998/887-2450; fax 998/887-4510.) 113 units. Hacienda: High season rooms from $172 (£86), suites from $404 (£202); low season rooms from $103 (£52), suites from $298 (£149). Lodge: High season bungalows from $266 (£133); low season bungalows from $184 (£92). AE, MC, V. Free guarded parking. **Amenities:** 2 restaurants; bar; 4 outdoor pools; tour info; laundry service; nonsmoking rooms. In room: A/C, TV, minibar, coffeemaker, hair dryer (upon request).

Villas Arqueológicas Uxmal 🌾   This hotel and its sister properties were recently sold to a Mexican resort group called Islander Collection, but it's still business as usual, much as it was when the place was part of Club Med. A two-story layout surrounds a garden patio and a pool. At guests' disposal are a tennis court, a library, and an audiovisual show on the ruins in English, French, and Spanish. Each of the modern, medium-size rooms has a double and a twin bed that fit into spaces that are walled on three sides. Very tall people should stay elsewhere. You can also ask for rates that include half- or full board.

Ruinas Uxmal, 97844 Uxmal, Yuc. ℂ 987/872-9300, ext. 8101. www.islandercollection.com. 48 units. $130 (£65) double. Rates include continental breakfast. Half-board (breakfast plus lunch or dinner) $20 (£10) per person; full board (3 meals) $40 (£20) per person. AE, MC, V. Free guarded parking. **Amenities:** Restaurant; bar; outdoor pool; tennis court, laundry service. In room: A/C, hair dryer.

WHERE TO DINE

I've eaten well at the hotel restaurant of the Lodge at Uxmal, ordering the Yucatecan specialties, which were fresh and well prepared. I've also eaten well at the hotel restaurant at the Villas Arqueológicas, but again, keeping it simple. There are some *palapa* restaurants by the highway as you approach the ruins from Mérida. I've had good and bad experiences at these. They do a lot of business with bus tours, so the best time to try them is early afternoon.

THE PUUC MAYA ROUTE & VILLAGE OF OXKUTZCAB

South and east of Uxmal are several other Maya cities worth visiting. Though smaller in scale than Uxmal or Chichén Itzá, each contains gems of Maya architecture. The Palace of Masks at **Kabah,** the palace at **Sayil,** and the fantastic caverns of **Loltún** are well worth viewing.

Kabah is 28km (17 miles) southeast of Uxmal via Highway 261 through Santa Elena. From there it's only a couple kilometers to Sayil. Xlapak is almost walking distance (through the jungle) from Sayil, and Labná is just a bit farther east. A short drive beyond Labná brings you to the caves of Loltún. Oxkutzcab is at the road's intersection with Highway 184, which you can follow west to Ticul or east all the way to

---

Tips Seeing Puuc Maya Sites

All of these sites are currently undergoing excavation and reconstruction, and some buildings may be roped off when you visit. The sites are open daily from 8am to 5pm. Admission is $2 to $3 (£1–£1.50) for each site, and $5 (£2.50) for Loltún. Loltún has specific hours for tours—9:30 and 11am, and 12:30, 2, 3, and 4pm. Even if you're the only person at the cave at one of these times, the guide must give you a tour, and he can't try to charge you more money as if you were contracting his services for an individual tour. Sometimes the guides try to do this. Use of a video camera at any time costs $4 (£2); if you're visiting Uxmal in the same day, you pay only once for video permission and present your receipt as proof at each ruin.

Felipe Carrillo Puerto. If you aren't driving, a daily bus from Mérida goes to all these sites, with the exception of Loltún. (See "By Bus" in "Getting There & Departing," earlier in this chapter.)

PUUC MAYA SITES

KABAH ✪   To reach Kabah from Uxmal, head southwest on Highway 261 to Santa Elena (1km/½ mile), then south to Kabah (13km/8 miles). The ancient city lies along both sides of the highway. Turn right into the parking lot.

The most outstanding building at Kabah is the **Palace of Masks,** or Codz Poop ("rolled-up mat"), named for its decorative motif. You'll notice it to the right as you enter. Its outstanding feature is the Chenes-style facade, completely covered in a repeated pattern of 250 masks of Chaac, each one with curling remnants of Chaac's elephant-trunk-like nose. There's nothing else like this facade in all of Maya architecture. For years, parts of this building lay lined up in the weeds like pieces of a puzzle awaiting the master puzzle-solver to put them into place. Sculptures from this building are in the anthropology museums in Mérida and Mexico City.

Just behind and to the left of the Codz Poop is the **Palace Group** (also called the East Group), with a fine Puuc-style colonnaded facade. Originally it had 32 rooms. On the front are seven doors, two divided by columns, a common feature of Puuc architecture. Across the highway is what was once the **Great Temple.** Past it is a **great arch,** which was much wider at one time and may have been a monumental gate into the city. A *sacbé* linked this arch to a point at Uxmal. Compare this corbelled arch to the one at Labná (see below), which is in much better shape.

SAYIL   About 4km (2½ miles) south of Kabah is the turnoff (left, or east) to Sayil, Xlapak, Labná, Loltún, and Oxkutzcab. The ruins of **Sayil** ("place of the ants") are 4km (2½ miles) along this road.

Sayil is famous for **El Palacio** ✪✪. This palace of more than 90 rooms is impressive for its size alone. At present it is roped off. Climbing is not permitted. But this is unimportant because what makes it a masterpiece of Maya architecture is the facade, which is best appreciated from the ground. It stretches across three terraced levels, and its rows of columns give it a Minoan appearance. On the second level, notice the upside-down stone figure known to archaeologists as the Diving God, or Descending God, over the doorway; the same motif was used at Tulum a couple of centuries later.

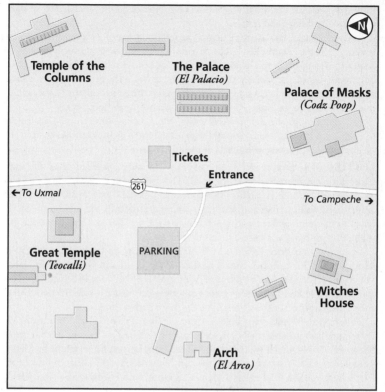

The large circular basin on the ground below the palace is an artificial catch basin for a *chultún* (cistern); this region has no natural cenotes (wells) to use to irrigate crops.

In the jungle beyond El Palacio is **El Mirador,** a small temple with an oddly slotted roof comb. Beyond El Mirador, a crude stele (tall, carved stone) has a phallic idol carved on it in exaggerated proportions. Another building group, the Southern Group, is a short distance down a trail that branches off from the one heading to El Mirador.

XLAPAK Xlapak (*shla*-pahk) is a small site with one building; it's 5.5 km (3½ miles) down the road from Sayil. The Palace at Xlapak bears the masks of the rain god Chaac. You won't miss much if you skip this place.

LABNA Labná, which dates from between A.D. 600 and 900, is 30km (19 miles) from Uxmal and only 3km (2 miles) past Xlapak. Descriptive placards fronting the main buildings are in Spanish, English, and German. The first thing you see on the left as you enter is **El Palacio,** a magnificent Puuc-style building much like the one at Sayil, but in poorer condition. Over a doorway is a large, well-conserved mask of Chaac with eyes, a huge snout nose, and jagged teeth around a small mouth that seems on the verge of speaking. Jutting out on one corner is a highly stylized serpent's mouth from which pops a human head with an unexpectedly serene expression. From the front, you can gaze out to the enormous grassy interior grounds flanked by vestiges of unrestored buildings and jungle.

From El Palacio, you can walk across the interior grounds on a reconstructed *sacbé* leading to Labná's **corbelled arch.** At one time, there were probably several such arches spread through the region. This one has been extensively restored, although only remnants of the roof comb can be seen. It was once part of a more elaborate structure that is completely gone. Chaac's face is on the corners of one facade, and stylized Maya huts are fashioned in stone above the two small doorways.

You pass through the arch to **El Mirador,** or El Castillo. Towering above a large pile of rubble is a singular room crowned with a roof comb etched against the sky.

There's a snack stand with toilets at the entrance.

LOLTUN   The caverns of Loltún are 31km (19 miles) past Labná on the way to Oxkutzcab, on the left side of the road. These fascinating caves, home of ancient Maya, were also used as a refuge during the War of the Castes (1847–1901). Inside are statuary, wall carvings and paintings, *chultunes* (cisterns), and other signs of Maya habitation. Guides will explain much of what you see. When I was there, the guide spoke English but was a little difficult to understand.

The admission price includes a 90-minute **tour;** tours begin daily at 9:30 and 11am, and 12:30, 2, 3, and 4pm. The floor of the cavern can be slippery in places; if you have a flashlight, take it with you. Admission is $5 (£2.50). What you see is quite interesting. I've heard reports of guides canceling the regularly scheduled tour so that they can charge for a private tour. Don't agree to such a thing.

To return to Mérida from Loltún, drive the 7km (4½ miles) to Oxkutzcab. From there, you have a couple of options for returning to Mérida: The slow route is through Maní and Teabo, which will allow you to see some convents and return by Highway 18, known as the "Convent Route" (see "En Route to Uxmal," earlier in this chapter). Alternately, you can head towards Muna to hook up with Highway 261 (also described earlier).

OXKUTZCAB
Oxkutzcab (ohsh-kootz-*kahb*), 11km (7 miles) from Loltún, is the center of the Yucatán's fruit-growing region. Oranges abound. The tidy village of 21,000 centers on a beautiful 16th-century church and the market. **Su Cabaña Suiza** (no phone) is a dependable restaurant in town. The last week of October and first week of November is the **Orange Festival,** when the village turns exuberant, with a carnival and orange displays in and around the central plaza.

EN ROUTE TO CAMPECHE
From Oxkutzcab, head back 43km (27 miles) to Sayil, and then drive south on Highway 261 to Campeche (126km/78 miles). After crossing the state line, you'll pass through the towns of Bolonchén and Hopelchén. The drive is pleasant, and there's little traffic. Both towns have gas stations. When going through the towns, watch carefully for directional traffic signs so that you stay on the highway. From Hopelchén, Highway 261 heads west. After 42km (26 miles), you'll find yourself at Cayal and the well-marked turnoff for the ruins of the city of Edzná, 18km (11 miles) farther south.

EDZNA ⊛   This city is interesting for several reasons. The area was populated as early as 600 B.C., with urban formation by 300 B.C. From that point on, Edzná grew impressively in a way that evinces considerable urban-planning skills. An ambitious and elaborate canal system was dug, which must have taken decades to complete, but

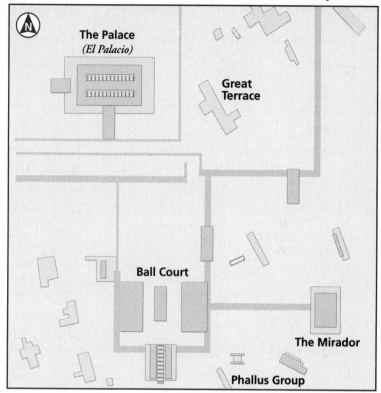

The Palace
(El Palacio)

Great
Terrace

Ball Court

The Mirador

Phallus Group

would have allowed for a great expansion in agricultural production and, hence, concentration of population. This made Edzná the preeminent city for a wide territory.

Another boom in construction began around A.D. 500, amid the Classic period. This was when the city's most prominent feature, the **Great Acropolis,** was started.

Sitting on top of this raised platform are five main pyramids, the largest being the much-photographed **Pyramid of Five Stories.** It combines the features of temple platform and palace. In Maya architecture, you have palace buildings with many vaulted chambers and you have solid pyramidal platforms with a couple of interior temples or burial passages. These are two mutually exclusive categories—but not here. Such a mix is found only in the Puuc and Río Bec areas and only in a few examples, and none similar to this, which makes this pyramid a bold architectural statement. The four lesser pyramids on the Acropolis are each constructed in a different style, and each is a pure example of that style. It's as if the rulers of this city were flaunting their cosmopolitanism, showing that they could build in any style they chose but preferred creating their own, superior architecture.

West of the Acropolis, across a large open plaza, is a long, raised building whose purpose isn't quite clear. But its size, as well as that of the plaza, makes you wonder just how many people this city actually held to necessitate such a large public space.

Labná Ruins

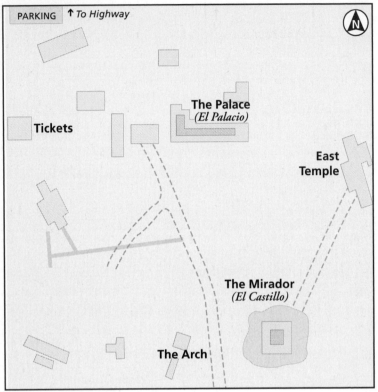

The site takes an hour to see, and is open daily from 8am to 5pm. Admission is $4 (£2), plus it's around $4 (£2) to use your video camera.

3 Campeche ★★

251km (156 miles) SW of Mérida; 376km (233 miles) NE of Villahermosa

Campeche, the capital of the state of the same name, is a beautifully restored colonial city. The facades of all the houses in the historic center of town have been repaired and painted, all electrical and telephone cables have been routed underground, and the streets have been paved to look cobbled. Several Mexican movie companies have taken advantage of the restoration to shoot period films here.

Despite its beauty, not many tourists come to Campeche. Those who do, tend to be either on their way to the ruins at Palenque (see chapter 9) or the Río Bec region (see chapter 7) or the kind of travelers who are accidental wanderers. A couple of things do need to be said: Campeche is not geared to foreign tourism the way Mérida is, so expect less in the way of English translations and such at museums and other sights. Also, expect less in the way of nightlife, except on weekend nights when they block off the main square for a street party.

Campeche

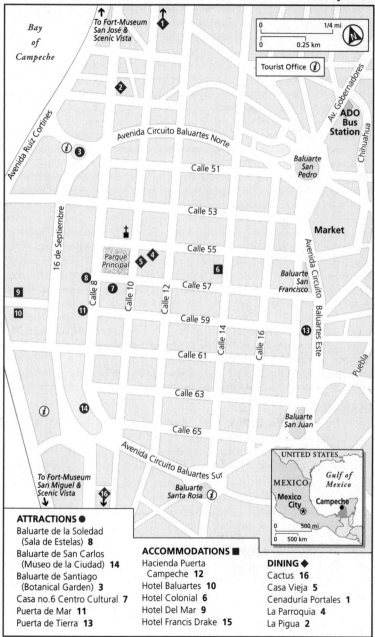

Bay
of
Campeche

To Fort-Museum
San José &
Scenic Vista

Tourist Office (i)

Avenida Ruíz Cortines

Avenida Circuito Baluartes Norte

Calle 51

Calle 53

Calle 55

Calle 57

Calle 59

Calle 61

Calle 63

Calle 65

16 de Septiembre

Parque
Principal

Calle 8

Calle 10

Calle 12

Calle 14

Calle 16

Av. Gobernadores

ADO
Bus
Station

Chihuahua

Baluarte
San
Pedro

Market

Avenida Circuito Baluartes Este

Baluarte
San
Francisco

Puebla

Baluarte
San Juan

Avenida Circuito Baluartes Sur

To Fort-Museum
San Miguel &
Scenic Vista

Baluarte
Santa Rosa (i)

UNITED STATES

MEXICO

MEXICO
City

Gulf of
Mexico

Campeche

0   500 mi
0   500 km

ATTRACTIONS ●
Baluarte de la Soledad
  (Sala de Estelas) **8**
Baluarte de San Carlos
  (Museo de la Ciudad) **14**
Baluarte de Santiago
  (Botanical Garden) **3**
Casa no.6 Centro Cultural **7**
Puerta de Mar **11**
Puerta de Tierra **13**

ACCOMMODATIONS ■
Hacienda Puerta
  Campeche **12**
Hotel Baluartes **10**
Hotel Colonial **6**
Hotel Del Mar **9**
Hotel Francis Drake **15**

DINING ◆
Cactus **16**
Casa Vieja **5**
Cenaduría Portales **1**
La Parroquia **4**
La Pigua **2**

If you're interested in seeing the ruins along the Río Bec route, see the section "Side Trips to Maya Ruins from Chetumal," in chapter 7. **Calakmul** ✦✦✦ is a large and important site, with the tallest pyramid in the Yucatán peninsula, and if you're going that far, you should stop at Balamkú and perhaps a few other ruins in the area. From the Campeche side you can get information and contract a tour with one of several tour operators. You can also rent a car. Calakmul is too far away for a day trip. There are a few small hotels in the area. Hotel Del Mar in Campeche has two: **Chicanná Eco-village** and **Puerta Calakmul.**

From the Calakmul area, it's easy to cross over the peninsula to Yucatán's southern Caribbean coast. Then you can head up the coast and complete a loop of the peninsula.

Campeche has an interesting history. The conquistadors arrived in 1517, when Francisco de Córdoba landed here while exploring the coast and stayed just long enough to celebrate Mass. Attempts to settle here were unsuccessful because of native resistance until Montejo The Younger was able to secure a settlement in 1540.

In the 17th and 18th centuries, pirates repeatedly harassed the city. The list of Campeche's attackers reads like a who's who of pirating. On one occasion, several outfits banded together under the famous Dutch pirate Peg Leg (who most likely was the inspiration for the many fictional one-legged sailors) and managed to capture the city. The Campechanos grew tired of hosting pirate parties and erected walls around the city, showing as much industry then as they now show in renovating their historic district. The walls had a number of *baluartes* (bastions) at critical locations. For added security, they constructed two forts, complete with moats and drawbridges, on the hills flanking the city. There were four gates to the city, and the two main ones are still intact: the Puerta de Mar (Sea Gate) and the Puerta de Tierra (Land Gate). The pirates never cared to return, but, in Mexico's stormy political history, the city did withstand a couple of sieges by different armies. Eventually, in the early 1900s, the wall around the city was razed, but the bastions and main gates were left intact, as were the two hilltop fortresses. Most of the bastions and both forts now house museums.

ESSENTIALS

GETTING THERE & DEPARTING   By Plane   AeroMéxico (© 981/816-6656; www.aeromexico.com.mx) flies once daily to and from Mexico City. The **airport** is several kilometers northeast of the town center, and you'll have to take a taxi into town (about $5/£2.50).

By Car   Highway 180 goes south from Mérida, passing near the basket-making village of Halacho and near Becal, known for its Panama-hat weavers. The trip takes 2½ hours. At Tenabo, take the shortcut (right, Highway 24) to Campeche rather than going farther to the crossroads near Chencoyí. The longer way from Mérida is along Highway 261 past Uxmal.

When returning to Mérida via Highway 180, go north on Avenida Ruiz Cortines, bearing left to follow the water (this becomes Avenida Pedro Sainz de Baranda, but there's no sign). Follow the road as it turns inland to Highway 180, where you turn left (there's a gas station at the intersection).

If you're leaving Campeche for Edzná and Uxmal, go north on either Ruiz Cortines or Gobernadores and turn right on Madero, which feeds onto **Highway 281.** To go south to Villahermosa, take Ruiz Cortines south.

By Bus   ADO (© 981/816-2802) offers a first-class *de paso* (passing through) bus to Palenque (6 hr.; $16/£8) four times a day and buses to Mérida (2½ hr.; $8/£4) every hour from 5:30am to midnight. The ADO **bus station** is on Avenida Patricio Trueba, a kilometer (a half-mile) from the Puerta de Tierra.

INFORMATION   The **State of Campeche Office of Tourism** (©/fax **981/816-6767;** www.campechetravel.com) is in Plaza Moch-Couoh, Avenida Ruiz Cortines s/n, 24000 Campeche. This is in one of the state buildings between the historic center and the shore. There are also information offices in the bastions of Santa Rosa, San Carlos, and Santiago. It's open Monday to Friday from 9am to 2pm and 4 to 7pm.

CITY LAYOUT   The most interesting part of the city is the restored old part, most of which once lay within the walls. Originally, the seaward wall was at the water's edge, but now land has been gained from the sea between the old walls and the coastline. This is where you'll find most of the state government buildings, which were built in a glaringly modernist style around **Plaza Moch-Couoh:** buildings such as the office tower **Edificio de los Poderes (Judicial Building)** or **Palacio de Gobierno (headquarters for the state of Campeche),** and the futuristic **Cámara de Diputados (Chamber of Deputies),** which looks like a cubist clam.

Campeche's system of street numbering is much like that of other cities in the Yucatán, except that the numbers of the north-south streets increase as you go east instead of the reverse. (See "City Layout" in "Mérida: Gateway to the Maya Heartland," earlier in this chapter.)

GETTING AROUND   Most of the recommended sights, restaurants, and hotels are within walking distance of the old city, except for the two fort-museums. Campeche isn't easy to negotiate by bus, so take taxis for anything beyond walking distance—they are inexpensive.

FAST FACTS: Campeche

American Express Local offices are at Calle 59 no. 4 and 5 (© **981/811-1010**), in the Edificio Del Mar, a half-block toward town from the Hotel Del Mar. Open Monday to Friday from 9am to 2pm and 5 to 7pm, and Saturday from 9am to 1pm. This office does not cash traveler's checks.

Area Code The telephone area code is **981.**

ATMs There are more than 10 cash machines around the downtown area.

Emergencies To report an emergency, dial © **060,** which is supposed to be similar to 911 emergency service in the United States.

Internet Access There are plenty of places to check e-mail—just look for signs with the words INTERNET or CYBERCAFE.

Post Office The correo is in the Edificio Federal, at Avenida 16 de Septiembre and Calle 53 (© **981/816-2134**), near the Baluarte de Santiago; it's open Monday to Saturday from 7:30am to 8pm. The telegraph office is also here.

EXPLORING CAMPECHE

With beautiful surroundings, friendly people, and an easy pace of life, Campeche is worthy of at least a day on your itinerary. It has some interesting museums, one outstanding restaurant, and plenty to do.

INSIDE THE CITY WALLS

A good place to begin is the pretty *zócalo,* or **Parque Principal,** bounded by calles 55 and 57 running east and west and calles 8 and 10 running north and south. On Saturday nights and Sundays, the city closes the main square to traffic and contracts bands to play. People set up tables in the streets and the entire scene becomes a fun kind of block party. Construction of the church on the north side of the square began in 1650 and was finally completed 150 years later. A pleasant way to see the city is to take the *tranvía* (trolley) tour that leaves three or four times a day from the main plaza; check with one of the tourist information offices for the schedule. The cost is $7 (£3.50) for a 45-minute tour.

Baluarte de la Soledad   This bastion next to the sea gate houses Maya stelae recovered from around the state. Many are badly worn, but the line drawings beside the stones allow you to appreciate their former design.

Calle 57 and Calle 8, opposite Plaza Principal. No phone. Admission $2.50 (£1.25). Tues–Sat 9am–8pm; Sun 9am–1pm.

Baluarte de San Carlos/Museo de la Ciudad   The city museum deals primarily with the design and construction of the fortifications. A model of the city shows how it looked in its glory days and provides a good overview for touring within the city walls. There are several excellent ship models as well. All text is in Spanish.

Circuito Baluartes and Av. Justo Sierra. No phone. Admission $2.50 (£1.25). Tues–Sat 9am–8pm; Sun 9am–1pm.

Baluarte de Santiago   The Jardín Botánico Xmuch'haltun is a jumble of exotic and common plants within the stone walls of this bastion. More than 250 species of plants and trees share a small courtyard.

Av. 16 de Septiembre and Calle 49. No phone. Free admission. Mon–Fri 9am–8pm; Sat–Sun 9am–1pm.

Casa no. 6 Centro Cultural   In this remodeled colonial house, you'll see some rooms decorated with period furniture and accessories. The patio of mixtilinear arches supported by simple Doric columns is striking. Exhibited in the patio are photos of the city's fine colonial architecture. Several of the photographed buildings have recently been renovated. There is also a small bookstore in back, as well as temporary exhibition space.

Calle 57 no. 6. No phone. Free admission. Daily 9am–9pm.

Puerta de Tierra   At the Land Gate is a small museum displaying portraits of pirates and the city founders. The 1732 French 5-ton cannon in the entryway was found in 1990. On Tuesday, Friday, and Saturday at 8pm, there's a light-and-sound show, as long as 15 or more people have bought tickets. Some shows are in English and some are in Spanish; it depends on the audience. The show is amusing.

Calle 59 at Circuito Baluartes/Av. Gobernadores. No phone. Free admission to museum; show $3 (£1.50) adults, $1 (50p) children younger than 11. Daily 9am–9pm.

OUTSIDE THE WALLS: SCENIC VISTAS

Fuerte–Museo San José el Alto   This fort is higher and has a more sweeping view of Campeche and the coast than Fuerte San Miguel, but it houses only a small exhibit of 16th- and 17th-century weapons and scale miniatures of sailing vessels. It's a nice place for a picnic. Take a cab. En route, you will pass an impressive statue of Juárez.

Av. Morazán s/n. No phone. Admission $2.50 (£1.25). Tues–Sun 8am–8pm.

Fuerte–Museo San Miguel ☎☎   For a good view of the city and a great little museum, take a cab up to Fuerte–Museo San Miguel. San Miguel is a small fort with a moat and a drawbridge. Built in 1771, it was the most important of the city's defenses. General Santa Anna captured it when he attacked the city in 1842. The museum of the Maya world was renovated in 2000 and is well worth seeing. It groups the artifacts around central issues in Maya culture. In a room devoted to Maya concepts of the afterlife, there's a great burial scene with jade masks and jewelry from Maya tombs at Calakmul. Another room explains Maya cosmology, another depicts war, and another explains the gods. There are also exhibits on the history of the fort.

Ruta Escénica s/n. No phone. Admission $2.50 (£1.25). Tues–Sat 9am–8pm; Sun 8am–noon.

SHOPPING

Casa de Artesanías Tukulná   This store, run by DIF (a government family-assistance agency), occupies a restored mansion. There is an elaborate display of regional arts and crafts in the back. The wares in the showrooms represent everything that is produced in the state. There are quality textiles, clothing, and locally made furniture. Open Monday to Saturday from 9am to 8pm. Calle 10 no. 333 (between calles 59 and 61). ☎ 981/816-9088.

WHERE TO STAY

Rates quoted include the 17% tax.

VERY EXPENSIVE

Hacienda Puerta Campeche ☎☎☎   This hotel was created from several adjoining colonial houses. It's a beautiful and original property just inside the Puerta de Tierra in Campeche's colonial center. There is a tropical garden in the center and a pool that runs through the ruined walls of one of the houses. It's quite picturesque. Rooms are colonial with flare—large with old tile floors, distinctive colors, and beamed ceilings. "Hacienda" is in the name to make it apparent that this is one of the properties connected to the four haciendas managed by Starwood hotels. (See "Of Haciendas & Hotels" in the Mérida section, earlier in this chapter).

Calle 59 71, 24000 Campeche, Camp. ☎ 800/325-3589 in the U.S. or Canada, or 981/816-7508. www.luxurycollection. com. 15 units. $400 (£200) superior; $500 (£250) and up for suite. AE, MC, V. Free guarded parking. **Amenities:** Restaurants; 2 bars; outdoor pool; spa services; concierge; tours; car-rental desk; airport transportation; room service; babysitting; laundry service. *In room:* A/C, TV, high-speed Internet, minibar, fridge, coffeemaker, hair dryer, iron.

EXPENSIVE

Hotel Del Mar ☎   Rooms in this four-story hotel are large, bright, and comfortably furnished. All have balconies that face the Gulf of Mexico. The beds (two doubles or one king-size) are comfortable. The Del Mar is on the main oceanfront boulevard, between the coast and the city walls. It offers more services than the Baluartes and is a little more expensive. You can make a reservation here to stay in the Río Bec area, or you can buy a package that includes guide and transportation. The hotel also offers a tour to Edzná.

Av. Ruiz Cortines 51, 24000 Campeche, Camp. ☎ 981/811-9192 or -9193. Fax 981/811-1618. www.delmarhotel. com.mx. 146 units. $126 (£63) double; $140 (£70) executive-level double. AE, MC, V. Free parking. **Amenities:** 2 restaurants; bar; large outdoor pool; gym w/sauna; travel agency; car-rental desk; business center; room service; babysitting; laundry service; nonsmoking rooms; executive level. *In room:* A/C, TV, safe.

MODERATE

Hotel Baluartes ☎   Between the Sea Gate and the Gulf of Mexico, this was the city's original luxury hotel. All the rooms have been completely refurbished with new tile floors, new furniture, and new mattresses—one king-size bed or two doubles. They are cheerful and have good lighting, but the bathrooms are small.

Av. 16 de Septiembre no. 128, 24000 Campeche, Camp. ✆ **981/816-3911.** Fax 981/816-2410. www.baluartes.com.mx. 128 units. $108 (£54) double; $158 (£79) suite. Rates include breakfast buffet. AE, MC, V. Free guarded parking. **Amenities:** 2 restaurants; bar; large outdoor pool; travel agency; car rental; room service; laundry service; nonsmoking rooms. *In room:* A/C, TV, hair dryer, safe.

Hotel Francis Drake ✿ *(Value* A three-story hotel in the *centro histórico* (historical district) with comfortable, attractive rooms at good prices. Rooms are midsize and come with tile floors and one king-size bed, two doubles, or two twins. The bathrooms are modern with large showers. Suites are larger and better furnished. The location is excellent.

Calle 12 no. 207 (between calles 63 and 65), 24000 Campeche, Camp. ✆ **981/811-5626** or -5627. www.hotelfrancis drake.com. 24 units. $76 (£38) double; $86 (£43) junior suite; $99 (£50) suite. AE, MC, V. Limited free parking. **Amenities:** Restaurant; tour info; car-rental desk; room service; laundry service. *In room:* A/C, TV, minibar, hair dryer.

INEXPENSIVE

Hotel Colonial *(Moments* What, you ask, in a cheap hotel could possibly qualify for a Frommer's Mexican Moment? Well, first of all, the hotel hasn't changed in 50 years; it exudes an air of the past long since disappeared with the coming of globalization. The rooms have the original tiles—once made in Mérida, but alas, no longer—beautiful things with lovely colors in swirls and geometrics; each room has a different pattern. And then there's the plumbing, which, in my room was so bodacious in design and execution that to hide it within the walls would have been pure Philistinism. Remarkable, too, are the bathroom fixtures, the four-color paint job, and the '40s-style furniture. Sure, you have to make sacrifices for such character—the rooms and bathrooms are small, and the mattresses aren't the best—but even character aside, this hotel is cleaner and more cheerful than any in its class.

Calle 14 no. 122, 24000 Campeche, Camp. ✆ **981/816-2222.** 30 units. $24 (£12) double; $34 (£17) double with A/C. No credit cards. *In room:* A/C (some units), no phone.

WHERE TO EAT

Campeche is a fishing town, so seafood predominates. The outstanding restaurant is **La Pigua.** For breakfast, you have your hotel restaurant or one of the traditional eateries such as **La Parroquia.** For a light supper, either get some *antojitos* (small dishes) in the old *barrio* of San Francisco, or have supper above the main plaza at **La Casa Vieja.** If you want a steak, your best bet is **Cactus.**

MODERATE

Cactus STEAKS/MEXICAN If seafood isn't to your taste, try this steakhouse; it's a favorite with the locals. The rib-eyes are good, as is everything but the *arrachera,* which is the same cut of meat used for fajitas and is very tough.

Av. Malecón Justo Sierra. ✆ **981/811-1453.** Main courses $10–$20 (£5–£10). No credit cards. Daily 7am–2am.

Casa Vieja MEXICAN/INTERNATIONAL I'm afraid that Casa Vieja has gotten a little old. There's been a drop in effort here, but it still has the prettiest dining space in the city—an upstairs arcade overlooking the main square. Your best option is to order something simple. If you're lucky, they'll be on the upswing in that mysterious cycle of quality through which so many restaurants operate.

Calle 10 no. 319. ✆ **981/811-1311.** Reservations not accepted. Main courses $6–$16 (£3–£8). No credit cards. Tues–Sun 9am–2am; Mon 5:30pm–2am.

La Pigua ĢĢĢ SEAFOOD   The dining area is an air-conditioned version of a traditional Yucatecan cabin, but with walls of glass looking out on green vegetation. The owner has recently remodeled and enlarged his restaurant so that there's less trouble getting a table these days. He also is now opening in the evenings to accommodate tourists. Spanish nautical terms pepper the large menu as the headings for different courses. Sure to be on the menu is fish stuffed with shellfish, which I wholeheartedly recommend. If you're lucky, you might find pompano in a green-herb sauce seasoned with a peppery herb known as *hierba santa*. Other dishes that are sure to please are coconut-battered shrimp with applesauce and *chiles rellenos* with shark. Service is excellent, and the accommodating owner can have your favorite seafood prepared in any style you want.

Av. Miguel Alemán no. 179A. © 981/811-3365. Reservations recommended. Main courses $10–$20 (£5–£10). AE, MC, V. Daily noon–8pm. From Plaza Principal, walk north on Calle 8 for 3 blocks; cross Av. Circuito by the botanical garden where Calle 8 becomes Miguel Alemán; the restaurant is 1½ blocks farther up, on the right side of the street.

INEXPENSIVE

Cenaduría Portales Ģ ANTOJITOS   This is the most traditional of supper places for Campechanos. It's a small restaurant under the stone arches that face the Plaza San Francisco in the *barrio* (neighborhood) of San Francisco. This is the oldest part of town, but it lies outside the walls just to the north. Don't leave without ordering the *horchata* (a sweet milky-white drink made of a variety of things, in this case coconut). For food, try the turkey soup, which is wonderful, and the *sincronizadas* (tostadas) and *panuchos*.

Calle 10 no. 86, Portales San Francisco. © 981/811-1491. *Antojitos* 40¢–$1.50 (22p–75p). No credit cards. Daily 6pm–midnight.

La Parroquia MEXICAN   This local hangout offers good, inexpensive fare. It's best for breakfasts and the afternoon *comida corrida*. Selections on the *comida corrida* might include pot roast, meatballs, pork, or fish, with rice or squash, beans, tortillas, and fresh-fruit-flavored water.

Calle 55 no. 9. © 981/816-8086. Breakfast $4 (£2); main courses $4–$12 (£2–£6); *comida corrida* (served noon–3pm) $4–$5 (£2–£2.50). MC, V. Daily 24 hr.

4 The Ruins of Chichén Itzá ĢĢĢ

179km (111 miles) W of Cancún; 120km (74 miles) E of Mérida; 138km (86 miles) NW of Tulum

The fabled ruins of Chichén Itzá (no, it doesn't rhyme with "chicken pizza"; the accents are on the last syllables: chee-*chen* eet-*zah*) are the Yucatán's best-known ancient monuments. They are plenty hyped, but the ruins live up to it. Walking among these stone platforms, pyramids, and ball courts gives you an appreciation for this ancient civilization that books cannot convey. The city is built on a scale that evokes a sense of wonder: To fill the plazas during one of the mass rituals that occurred here a millennium ago would have required an enormous number of celebrants. Even today, with the massive flow of tourists through these plazas, the ruins feel empty.

When visiting the ruins, keep in mind that much of what is said about the Maya (especially by tour guides, who speak in tones of utter certainty) is merely educated guessing. This much we do know: The area was settled by farmers as far back as the 4th century A.D. The first signs of an urban society appear in the 7th century in the construction of stone temples and palaces in the traditional Puuc Maya style. These buildings can be found in the "Old Chichén" section of the city. Construction continued for a couple hundred years. In the 10th century (the post-Classic Era), the city came under the rule of the Itzáes, who arrived from central Mexico by way of the Gulf Coast. They may have been a mix of highland Toltec Indians (the people who built the city of Tula in central Mexico) and lowland Putún Maya, who were a commercial people thriving on trade between the different regions of the area. In the following centuries, the city saw its greatest growth. Most of the grand architecture was built during this age in a style that is clearly Toltec influenced. The new rulers may have been refugees from Tula. There is a myth told in pre-Columbian central Mexico about a fight that occurred between the gods Quetzalcoatl and Tezcatlipoca, which resulted in Quetzalcoatl being forced to leave his homeland and venture east. This may be a shorthand account of a civil war in Tula, different religious factions, with the losers fleeing to the Yucatán, where they were welcomed by the local Maya. Over time, the Itzáes adopted more and more the ways of the Maya. Sometime at the end of the 12th century, the city was captured by its rival, Mayapán.

Though it's possible to make a day trip from Cancún or Mérida, it's preferable to overnight here or in nearby Valladolid. It makes for a more relaxing trip. You can see the light show in the evening and return to see the ruins early the next morning when it is cool and before the tour buses arrive.

ESSENTIALS

GETTING THERE & DEPARTING   By Plane   Travel agents in the United States, Cancún, and Cozumel can arrange day trips from Cancún and Cozumel.

By Car   Chichén Itzá is on old Highway 180 between Mérida and Cancún. The fastest way to get there from either city is to take the *autopista* (or *cuota*). The toll is $8 (£4) from Mérida, $22 (£11) from Cancún. Once you have exited the *autopista,* you will turn onto the road leading to the village of Pisté. Once in the village, you'll reach a T junction at Highway 180 and turn left to get to the ruins. The entrance to the ruins is well marked. If you stay on the highway for a few kilometers more you'll come to the exit for the hotel zone at Km 121 (before you reach the turn-off, you'll pass the eastern entrance to the ruins, which is usually closed). Chichén is 1½ hours from Mérida and 2½ hours from Cancún. From Tulum, take the highway that leads to Cobá and Chemax. It connects to Hwy. 180 a bit east of Valladolid.

By Bus   From Mérida, there are three first-class ADO buses per day. There are also a couple of first-class buses to Cancún and Playa. Otherwise, you can buy a second-class bus ticket to Valladolid and a first-class from there. If you want to take a day trip from Mérida or Cancún, go with a tour company.

AREA LAYOUT   The village of **Pisté,** where most of the economical hotels and restaurants are located, is about 2.5km (1½ miles) to the west of the ruins. Public buses can drop you off here. And located on the old highway 2.5km (1½ miles) east from the ruins is another economical hotel, the Hotel Dolores Alba (see "Where to Stay," below). Situated at the ruins of Chichén Itzá are three luxury hotels.

EXPLORING THE RUINS

The site occupies 6.5 sq. km (2½ sq. miles), and it takes most of a day to see all the ruins, which are open daily from 8am to 5pm. Service areas are open from 8am to 10pm. Admission is $10 (£5), free for children younger than age 12. A video camera permit costs $4 (£2). Parking is extra. *You can use your ticket to re-enter on the same day.* The cost of admission includes the **sound-and-light show,** which is worth seeing since you're being charged for it anyway. The show, held at 7 or 8pm depending on

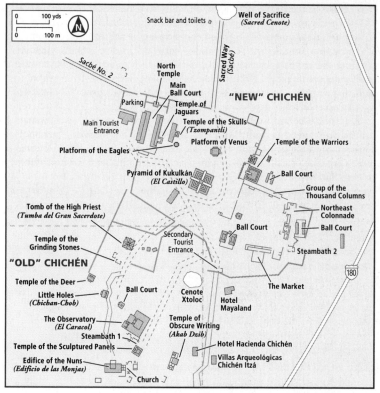

the season, is in Spanish, but headsets are available for rent in several languages. The narrative is okay, but the real reason for seeing the show is the lights, which show off the beautiful geometry of the city.

The large, modern visitor center, at the main entrance where you pay admission, is beside the parking lot. It consists of a museum, an auditorium, a restaurant, a bookstore, and bathrooms. You can see the site on your own or with a licensed guide who speaks English or Spanish. Guides usually wait at the entrance and charge around $45 (£23) for one to six people. Although the guides frown on it, there's nothing wrong with approaching a group of people who speak the same language and asking if they want to share a guide. These guides can point out architectural details you might miss on your own. Chichén Itzá has two parts: the central (new) zone, which shows distinct Toltec influence, and the southern (old) zone, with mostly Puuc architecture.

EL CASTILLO   As you enter from the tourist center, the magnificent 25m (82-ft.) El Castillo pyramid (also called the Pyramid of Kukulkán) will be straight ahead across a large open area. It was built with the Maya calendar in mind. The four stairways leading up to the central platform each have 91 steps, making a total of 364, which when you add the central platform equals the 365 days of the solar year. On either side of each stairway are nine terraces, which makes 18 on each face of the pyramid, equaling the number of months in the Maya religious calendar. On the facing of these terraces are 52 panels (we don't know how they were decorated), which represent the 52-year cycle when both the solar and religious calendars would become realigned. The pyramid's alignment is such that on the **spring** or **fall equinox** (Mar 21 or Sept 21) a curious event occurs. The setting sun casts the shadow of the terraces onto the ramp of the northern stairway. A diamond pattern is formed, suggestive of the geometric designs on snakes. Slowly it descends into the earth. The effect is more conceptual than visual, and to view it requires being with a large crowd. It's much better to see the ruins on other days when it's less crowded.

El Castillo was built over an earlier structure. A narrow stairway at the western edge of the north staircase leads inside that structure, where there is a sacrificial altar-throne—a red jaguar encrusted with jade. The stairway is open from 11am to 3pm and is cramped, usually crowded, humid, and uncomfortable. A visit early in the day is best. Photos of the jaguar figure are not allowed.

JUEGO DE PELOTA (MAIN BALL COURT)   Northwest of El Castillo is Chichén's main ball court, the largest and best preserved anywhere, and only one of nine ball courts built in this city. Carved on both walls of the ball court are scenes showing Maya figures dressed as ball players and decked out in heavy protective padding. The carved scene also shows a headless player kneeling with blood shooting from his neck; another player holding the head looks on.

Players on two teams tried to knock a hard rubber ball through one of the two stone rings placed high on either wall, using only their elbows, knees, and hips. According to legend, the losing players paid for defeat with their lives. However, some experts say the victors were the only appropriate sacrifices for the gods. One can only guess what the incentive for winning might be in that case. Either way, the game must have been riveting, heightened by the wonderful acoustics of the ball court.

THE NORTH TEMPLE   Temples are at both ends of the ball court. The North Temple has sculptured pillars and more sculptures inside, as well as badly ruined murals. The acoustics of the ball court are so good that from the North Temple, a person speaking can be heard clearly at the opposite end, about 135m (443 ft.) away.

TEMPLE OF JAGUARS   Near the southeastern corner of the main ball court is a small temple with serpent columns and carved panels showing warriors and jaguars. Up the steps and inside the temple, a mural chronicles a battle in a Maya village.

TZOMPANTLI (TEMPLE OF THE SKULLS)   To the right of the ball court is the Temple of the Skulls, an obvious borrowing from the post-Classic cities of central Mexico. Notice the rows of skulls carved into the stone platform. When a sacrificial victim's head was cut off, it was impaled on a pole and displayed in a tidy row with others. Also carved into the stone are pictures of eagles tearing hearts from human victims. The word *Tzompantli* is not Mayan but comes from central Mexico. Reconstruction using scattered fragments may add a level to this platform and change the look of this structure by the time you visit.

PLATFORM OF THE EAGLES   Next to the Tzompantli, this small platform has reliefs showing eagles and jaguars clutching human hearts in their talons and claws, as well as a human head emerging from the mouth of a serpent.

PLATFORM OF VENUS   East of the Tzompantli and north of El Castillo, near the road to the Sacred Cenote, is the Platform of Venus. In Maya and Toltec lore, a feathered monster or a feathered serpent with a human head in its mouth represented

Venus. This is also called the tomb of Chaac-Mool because a Chaac-Mool figure was discovered "buried" within the structure.

SACRED CENOTE   Follow the dirt road (actually an ancient *sacbé,* or causeway) that heads north from the Platform of Venus; after 5 minutes you'll come to the great natural well that may have given Chichén Itzá (the Well of the Itzáes) its name. This well was used for ceremonial purposes. Sacrificial victims were thrown in. Anatomical research done early in the 20th century by Ernest A. Hooten showed that bones of both children and adults were found in the well.

Edward Thompson, who was the American consul in Mérida and a Harvard professor, purchased the ruins of Chichén early in the 20th century and explored the cenote with dredges and divers. His explorations exposed a fortune in gold and jade. Most of the riches wound up in Harvard's Peabody Museum of Archaeology and Ethnology—a matter that continues to disconcert Mexican classicists today. Excavations in the 1960s unearthed more treasure, and studies of the recovered objects detail offerings from throughout the Yucatán and even farther away.

TEMPLO DE LOS GUERREROS (TEMPLE OF THE WARRIORS)   Due east of El Castillo is one of the most impressive structures at Chichén: the Temple of the Warriors, named for the carvings of warriors marching along its walls. It's also called the Group of the Thousand Columns for the rows of broken pillars that flank it. During the recent restoration, hundreds more of the columns were rescued from the rubble and put in place, setting off the temple more magnificently than ever. A figure of Chaac-Mool sits at the top of the temple, surrounded by impressive columns carved in relief to look like enormous feathered serpents. South of the temple was a square building that archaeologists call **El Mercado (The Market);** a colonnade surrounds its central court. Beyond the temple and the market in the jungle are mounds of rubble, parts of which are being reconstructed.

The main Mérida-Cancún highway once ran straight through the ruins of Chichén, and though it has been diverted, you can still see the great swath it cut. South and west of the old highway's path are more impressive ruined buildings.

TUMBA DEL GRAN SACERDOTE (TOMB OF THE HIGH PRIEST)   Past the refreshment stand to the right of the path is the Tomb of the High Priest, which stood atop a natural limestone cave in which skeletons and offerings were found, giving the temple its name.

CASA DE LOS METATES (TEMPLE OF THE GRINDING STONES)   This building, the next one on your right, is named after the concave corn-grinding stones the Maya used.

TEMPLO DEL VENADO (TEMPLE OF THE DEER)   Past Casa de los Metates is this fairly tall though ruined building. The relief of a stag that gave the temple its name is long gone.

CHICHANCHOB (LITTLE HOLES)   This next temple has a roof comb with little holes, three masks of the rain god Chaac, three rooms, and a good view of the surrounding structures. It's one of the oldest buildings at Chichén, built in the Puuc style during the late Classic period.

EL CARACOL (OBSERVATORY)   Construction of the Observatory, a complex building with a circular tower, was carried out over centuries; the additions and modifications reflected the Maya's careful observation of celestial movements and their need for increasingly exact measurements. Through slits in the tower's walls, astronomers could observe the cardinal directions and the approach of the all-important spring and autumn equinoxes, as well as the summer solstice. The temple's name, which means "snail," comes from a spiral staircase within the structure.

On the east side of El Caracol, a path leads north into the bush to the **Cenote Xtoloc,** a natural limestone well that provided the city's daily water supply. If you see lizards sunning there, they may well be *xtoloc,* the species for which this cenote is named.

TEMPLO DE LOS TABLEROS (TEMPLE OF PANELS)   Just south of El Caracol are the ruins of a *temazcalli* (a steam bath) and the Temple of Panels, named for the carved panels on top. This temple was once covered by a much larger structure, only traces of which remain.

EDIFICIO DE LAS MONJAS (EDIFICE OF THE NUNS)   If you've visited the Puuc sites of Kabah, Sayil, Labná, or Xlapak, the enormous nunnery here will remind you of the palaces at those sites. Built in the late Classic period, the new edifice was constructed over an older one. Suspecting that this was so, Le Plongeon, an archaeologist working early in the 20th century, put dynamite between the two and blew away part of the exterior, revealing the older structures within. You can still see the results of Le Plongeon's indelicate exploratory methods.

On the east side of the Edifice of the Nuns is **Anexo Este (annex)** constructed in highly ornate Chenes style with Chaac masks and serpents.

LA IGLESIA (THE CHURCH)   Next to the annex is one of the oldest buildings at Chichén, the Church. Masks of Chaac decorate two upper stories. Look closely, and you'll see other pagan symbols among the crowd of Chaacs: an armadillo, a crab, a snail, and a tortoise. These represent the Maya gods, called *bacah,* whose job it was to hold up the sky.

AKAB DZIB (TEMPLE OF OBSCURE WRITING)   Beloved of travel writers, this temple lies east of the Edifice of the Nuns. Above a door in one of the rooms are some Mayan glyphs, which gave the temple its name because the writings are hard to make out. In other rooms, traces of red handprints are still visible. Reconstructed and expanded over the centuries, Akab Dzib may be the oldest building at Chichén.

CHICHEN VIEJO (OLD CHICHEN)   For a look at more of Chichén's oldest buildings, constructed well before the time of Toltec influence, follow signs from the Edifice of the Nuns southwest into the bush to Old Chichén, about 1km (a half-mile) away. Be prepared for this trek with long trousers, insect repellent, and a local guide. The attractions here are the **Templo de los Inscripciones Iniciales (Temple of the First Inscriptions),** with the oldest inscriptions discovered at Chichén, and the restored **Templo de los Dinteles (Temple of the Lintels),** a fine Puuc building. Some of these buildings have recently undergone restoration.

WHERE TO STAY

The expensive hotels in Chichén all occupy beautiful grounds, are close to the ruins, and serve decent food. All have toll-free reservations numbers. These hotels do a lot of business with tour operators—they can be empty one day and full the next. From these hotels you can easily walk to the back entrance of the ruins, next to the Hotel Mayaland. There are several inexpensive hotels in the village of Pisté, just to the west of the ruins. There is no advantage to staying in Pisté other than the proximity to

Chichén Itzá. It is an unattractive village with little to recommend it. Another option is to stay in the colonial town of Valladolid, 40 minutes away.

EXPENSIVE

Hacienda Chichén Resort &&   This is the smallest and most private of the hotels at the ruins, also the quietest. This former hacienda served as the headquarters for the Carnegie Institute's excavations in 1923. Several bungalows scattered about the property were built to house the institute's staff. Each one houses one or two units. Rooms come with a dehumidifier, a ceiling fan, and good air-conditioning. The floors are ceramic tile, the ceilings are stucco with wood beams, and the walls are decorated with carved stone trim. Trees and tropical plants fill the manicured gardens. You can enjoy these from your room's porch or from the terrace restaurant, which occupies part of the original main house. Standard rooms come with a queen-size, two twin, or two double beds. Suites come with king-size beds.

Zona Arqueológica, 97751 Chichén Itzá, Yuc. ©/fax 985/851-0045. www.haciendachichen.com. (Reservations office in Mérida: 877/631-4005 in the U.S., or 999/920-8407.) 28 units. High season $188 (£94) double, $199–$264 (£100–£132) suite; low season $140 (£70) double, $152–$193 (£76–£97) suite. AE, MC, V. Free guarded parking. **Amenities:** Restaurant; 2 bars; large outdoor pool; spa; nonsmoking rooms. *In room:* A/C, minibar, hair dryer, no phone.

Hotel & Bungalows Mayaland, The Lodge at Chichén Itzá &&&   The main doorway frames El Caracol (the Observatory) in a stunning view—that's how close these hotels are to the ruins. There is an entrance right by the hotel. The long main building is three stories high. The rooms are large, with comfortable beds and large tiled bathrooms. Bungalows, scattered about the rest of the grounds, are built native style, with thatched roofs and stucco walls; they're a good deal larger than the rooms. The grounds are gorgeous, with huge trees and lush foliage—the hotel has had 75 years to get them in shape. The suites are on the top floor of the main building and come with terraces and two-person Jacuzzis. The Lodge consists of two groupings of larger bungalows in the back of the property surrounded by a lovely garden and pool area. High season is November through April (higher still for the March equinox); low season is May through October.

Zona Arqueológica, 97751 Chichén Itzá, Yuc. © 985/851-0100. www.mayaland.com. (Reservations: Mayaland Resorts, Robalo 30 SM3, 77500 Cancún, Q. Roo; © 800/235-4079 in the U.S., or 998/887-2495; fax 998/887-4510.) 97 units. Hotel: High season rooms from $172 (£86), suites and bungalows from $254 (£127); low season rooms from $103 (£52), suites and bungalows from $168 (£84). Lodge: High season bungalows from $285 (£143); low season bungalows from $192 (£96). AE, MC, V. Free guarded parking. **Amenities:** 2 restaurants; bar; 3 outdoor pools; tour desk; room service; babysitting; laundry service. *In room:* A/C, TV, minibar, coffeemaker.

MODERATE

Villas Arqueológicas Chichén Itzá &   This hotel is built around a courtyard and pool. Two massive royal Poinciana trees tower above the grounds, and bougainvillea drapes the walls. This chain has similar hotels at Cobá and Uxmal, and is no longer part of Club Med. The rooms are modern and comfortable, unless you're 1.9m (6 ft., 2 in.) or taller—each bed is in a niche, with walls at the head and foot. Most rooms have one double bed and a twin bed. You can book a half- or full-board plan or just the room.

Zona Arqueológica, 97751 Chichén Itzá, Yuc. © 987/872-9300, ext. 8101 or 985/851-0034 or 985/856-2830. www. islandercollection.com. 40 units. $120 (£60) double. Rates include continental breakfast. Half-board (breakfast plus lunch or dinner) $20 (£10) per person; full board (3 meals) $38 (£19) per person. AE, MC, V. Free parking. **Amenities:** Restaurant; bar; large outdoor pool; tennis court; tour desk. *In room:* A/C, hair dryer.

INEXPENSIVE

Hotel Dolores Alba *(Value)*   This place is of the motel variety, perfect if you come by car. It is a bargain for what you get: two pools (one really special), *palapas* and hammocks around the place, and large, comfortable rooms. The restaurant serves good meals at moderate prices. There is free transportation to the ruins and the Caves of Balankanché during visiting hours, though you will have to take a taxi back. The hotel is on the highway 2.5km (1½ miles) east of the ruins (toward Valladolid). Rooms come with two double beds.

Carretera Mérida–Valladolid Km 122, Yuc. ⓒ 985/858-1555. www.doloresalba.com. (Reservations: Hotel Dolores Alba, Calle 63 no. 464, 97000 Mérida, Yuc.; ⓒ 999/928-5650; fax 999/928-3163.) 40 units. $45 (£23) double. MC, V (8% service charge). Free parking. **Amenities:** Restaurant; bar; 2 outdoor pools; room service. *In room:* A/C, TV, no phone.

WHERE TO DINE

Although there's no great food in this area, there is plenty of decent food. The best idea is to stick to simple choices. The restaurant at the visitor center at the ruins serves decent snack food. The hotel restaurants mostly do a fair job, and, if you're in the village of Pisté, you can try one of the restaurants along the highway there that cater to the bus tours, such as **Fiesta** (ⓒ **985/851-0111**). The best time to go is early lunch or regular supper hours, when the buses are gone.

OTHER ATTRACTIONS IN THE AREA

Ik-Kil is a large cenote on the highway just across from the Hotel Dolores Alba, 2.5km (1½ miles) east of the main entrance to the ruins. And it's deep, with lots of steps leading down to the water's edge. Unlike Dzitnup, these steps are easy to manage. The view from both the top and the bottom is dramatic, with lots of tropical vegetation and curtains of hanging tree roots stretching all the way to the water's surface. Take your swimsuit and enjoy the cold water. The best swimming is before 11:30am, at which time bus tours start arriving from the coast. These bus tours are the main business of Ik-Kil, which also has a restaurant and souvenir shops. Ik-Kil is open from 8am to 5pm daily. Admission is $6 (£3) per adult, $3 (£1.50) per child 7 to 12 years old.

The **Cave of Balankanché** is 5.5km (3½ miles) from Chichén Itzá on the road to Valladolid and Cancún. Taxis will make the trip and wait. The entire excursion takes about a half-hour, but the walk inside is hot and humid. Of the cave tours in the Yucatán, this is the tamest; it has good footing and requires the least amount of walking and climbing. It includes a cheesy and uninformative recorded tour. The highlight is a round chamber with a central column that gives the impression of being a large tree. You exit the same way you enter. The cave became a hideout during the War of the Castes. You can still see traces of carving and incense burning, as well as an underground stream that supplied water to the refugees. Outside, take time to meander through the botanical gardens, where most of the plants and trees are labeled with their common and botanical names.

Admission is $5 (£2.50), free for children 6 to 12. Children younger than age 6 are not admitted. Use of a video camera costs $4 (£2) or it's free if you've already bought a video permit in Chichén the same day. Tours in English are at 11am and 1 and 3pm, and, in Spanish, at 9am, noon, and 2 and 4pm. Double-check these hours at the main entrance to the Chichén ruins.

5 Valladolid

40km (25 miles) E of Chichén Itzá; 160km (100 miles) SW of Cancún; 98km (61 miles) NW of Tulum

Valladolid (pronounced "bah-yah-doh-*leed*")is a small, pleasant colonial city halfway between Mérida and Cancún. The people are friendly and informal, and, except for the heat, life is easy. The city's economy is based on commerce and small-scale manufacturing. There is a large cenote in the center of town and a couple more 4km (2½ miles) down the road to Chichén. Not far away are the intriguing ruins of Ek Balam, the flamingo-infested waters of Río Lagartos, and the sandy beaches of Holbox (see "Side Trips from Valladolid," below).

ESSENTIALS

GETTING THERE & DEPARTING   By Car   From Mérida or Cancún, you have two choices: the *cuota* (toll road) or Highway 180. The toll from Cancún is $20 (£10), from Mérida $10 (£5). The *cuota* passes 2km (1¼ miles) north of the city; the exit is at the crossing of Highway 295 to Tizimín. **Highway 180** takes significantly longer because it passes through a number of villages (with their requisite speed bumps). Both 180 and 295 lead directly to downtown. Leaving is just as easy: From the main square, Calle 41 turns into 180 East to Cancún; Calle 39 heads to 180 West to Chichén Itzá and Mérida. To take the *cuota* to Mérida or Cancún, take Calle 40 (see "City Layout," below).

By Bus   There are several direct buses to Mérida (13 per day) or Cancún (five per day). Each runs $11 (£5.50). You can also get direct buses for Playa (five per day) and Tulum (four per day). Buses to Playa take the toll road and cost $14 (£7); buses to Tulum take the shortcut via Chemax and cost $6 (£3). To get to Chichén Itzá, take a second-class bus, which leaves every hour and sometimes on the half-hour. The recently remodeled bus station is at the corner of calles 39 and 46.

VISITOR INFORMATION   The small **tourism office** is in the Palacio Municipal. It's open Monday to Friday from 8am to 9pm, Saturday and Sunday from 9am to 9pm.

CITY LAYOUT   Valladolid has the standard layout for towns in the Yucatán: Streets running north-south are even numbers; those running east-west are odd numbers. The main plaza is bordered by Calle 39 on the north, 41 on the south, 40 on the east, and 42 on the west. The plaza is named Parque Francisco Cantón Rosado, but everyone calls it **El Centro.** Taxis are easy to come by.

EXPLORING VALLADOLID

Before it became Valladolid, the city was a Maya settlement called Zací (zah-*kee*), which means "white hawk." There is one cenote in town: **Cenote Zací,** at the intersection of calles 39 and 36, in a small park. A trail leads down close to the water. Caves, stalactites, and hanging vines contribute to a wild, prehistoric feel. The park has a large *palapa* restaurant. Admission is $1.50 (75p).

Ten blocks to the southwest of the main square is the Franciscan monastery of **San Bernardino de Siena** (1552). Most of the compound was built in the early 1600s; a large underground river is believed to pass under the convent and surrounding neighborhood, which is called Barrio Sisal. "Sisal," in this case, is a corruption of the Mayan phrase *sis-ha,* meaning "cold water." The *barrio* underwent extensive restoration and is a delight to behold.

Valladolid's main square is the social center of town and a thriving market for Yucatecan dresses. On its south side is the principal church, **La Parroquia de San Servacio.** Vallesoletanos, as the locals are known, believe that almost all cathedrals in Mexico point east, and they cherish a local legend to explain why theirs points north—but don't believe a word of it. On the east side of the plaza is the municipal building, **El Ayuntamiento.** Get a look at the dramatic paintings outlining the peninsula's history. My favorite depicts a horrified Maya priest foreseeing the arrival of Spanish galleons. On Sunday nights, beneath the stone arches of the Ayuntamiento, the municipal band plays *jaranas* and other traditional music of the region.

SHOPPING

The **Mercado de Artesanías de Valladolid (crafts market),** at the corner of calles 39 and 44, gives you a good idea of the local merchandise. Perhaps the main handicraft of the town is embroidered Maya dresses, which can be purchased here or from women around the main square. The area around Valladolid is cattle country; locally made leather goods such as *huaraches* (sandals) and bags are inexpensive and plentiful. On the main plaza is a small shop above the municipal bazaar. A good sandal maker has a shop called **Elios,** Calle 37 no. 202, between calles 42 and 44 (no phone). An Indian named **Juan Mac** makes *alpargatas,* the traditional sandals of the Maya, in his shop on Calle 39, near the intersection with Calle 38, 1 block from the main plaza. It's almost on the corner, across from the Bar La Joya. There's no sign, but the door jamb is painted yellow. Juan Mac can be found there most mornings. Most of his output is for locals, but he's happy to knock out a pair for visitors. He also makes a dress *alpargata,* but I like the standard ones better.

WHERE TO STAY

Aside from the hotels listed below, you can stay in town at **Hotel Zací,** Calle 44 between calles 37 and 39 (© **985/856-2167**), for about $40/night. Or María de la Luz on the main square for about $45. The Zací has nicer beds.

For something a bit different, you can stay in a small ecohotel in the nearby village of Ek Balam, close to the ruins: **Genesis Retreat Ek Balam** (© **985/858-9375;** www.genesisretreat.com). It is owned and operated by a Canadian woman, Lee Christie. She takes guests on tours of the village showing what daily life is like among the contemporary Maya. There are other activities, too. She rents some simple cabañas (with shared or private bathrooms) that surround a lovely pool and a restaurant.

Casa Quetzal ⊕ The landlady, Judith Fernández, is a gracious Mexican woman who moved to Valladolid to slow down. She has created an airy and attractive lodging space in the refurbished Barrio Sisal, which is within easy walking distance of the main square. Emphasis is on comfort and service—good linens and mattresses, quiet A/C, and a large and inviting central courtyard. There is a full line of spa treatments and therapies. English is spoken, and Sra. Fernández has lined up a good guide you can contract to take you to outlying areas.

Calle 51 no. 218, Barrio Sisal, 97780 Valladolid, Yuc. ©/fax **985/856-4796.** www.casa-quetzal.com. 7 units. $70 (£35) double. Rates include full breakfast. 2-night minimum stay. No credit cards. Free secure parking. **Amenities:** Small outdoor pool; spa; tour info; room service; babysitting; laundry. *In room:* A/C, TV, Wi-Fi, no phone.

El Mesón del Marqués ⊕ This was originally a small colonial hotel that has grown large and modern. The first courtyard surrounds a fountain and abounds with hanging plants and bougainvillea. This was the original house, now occupied mostly by the restaurant (see "Where to Dine," below). In back are the new construction and the pool. Rooms are medium to large and are attractive. Most come with two double beds. The hotel is on the north side of El Centro, opposite the church.

Calle 39 no. 203, 97780 Valladolid, Yuc. (© 985/856-3042 or -2073. Fax 985/856-2280. www.mesondelmarques.com. 90 units. $58 (£29) double; $72 (£36) superior; $110 (£55) junior suite. AE. Free secure parking. **Amenities:** Restaurant; bar; outdoor pool; room service; laundry service. *In room:* A/C, TV.

WHERE TO DINE

Valladolid is not a center for haute cuisine, but you can try some of the regional specialties. Some of the best food I had was at **El Mesón del Marqués** right on the main square. There is another restaurant on the main square called **Las Campanas,** which is okay. Locals like to eat at one of the stalls in the **Bazar Municipal,** next door to the Mesón del Marqués. They also frequent the **taco stands** that set up around the square. I did a quick sampling of *cochinita pibil, bistec,* and *lechón asado* at the three most popular stands. I enjoyed it all and wasn't the worse for it. These stands serve customers only until around noon.

SIDE TRIPS FROM VALLADOLID
CENOTES DZITNUP & SAMMULA

The **Cenote Dzitnup** ✿ (also known as Cenote Xkekén) is 4km (2½ miles) west of Valladolid off Highway 180 in the direction of Chichén Itzá. It is worth a side trip, especially if you have time for a dip. You can take the bike trail there. Antonio Aguilar, who owns a sporting goods store at Calle 41 no. 225, between calles 48 and 50, rents bikes. Once you get there, you descend a short flight of rather perilous stone steps, and at the bottom, inside a beautiful cavern, is a natural pool of water so clear and blue that it seems plucked from a dream. If you decide to swim, be sure that you don't have creams or other chemicals on your skin—they damage the habitat of the small fish and other organisms living there. Also, no alcohol, food, or smoking is allowed in the cavern. Admission is $2.50 (£1.25). The cenote is open daily from 7am to 7pm. If it's crowded, about 90m (295 ft.) down the road on the opposite side is another recently discovered cenote, **Sammulá,** where you can swim.

EK BALAM: DARK JAGUAR ✿✿✿

About 18km (11 miles) north of Valladolid, off the highway to Río Lagartos, are the spectacular ruins of **Ek Balam,** which, owing to a certain ambiguity in Mayan, means either "dark jaguar" or "star jaguar." Relatively unvisited by tourists, the Ek Balam ruins are about to hit it big. A new road now runs from the highway to the ruins.

Take Calle 40 north out of Valladolid to Highway 295; go 20km (12 miles) to a large marked turnoff. Ek Balam is 13km (8 miles) from the highway; admission is $3 (£1.50); $4 (£2) for each video camera. The site is open daily from 8am to 5pm.

In the last few years, a team of archeologists have been doing extensive excavation and renovation. What they have found has the world of Mayan scholars all aquiver. Built between 100 B.C. and A.D. 1200, the smaller buildings are architecturally unique—especially the large, perfectly restored **Caracol.** Flanked by two smaller pyramids, the imposing central pyramid is about 160m (525 ft.) long and 60m (197 ft.) wide. At more than 30m (100 ft.) high, it is easily taller than the highest pyramid in Chichén Itzá. On the left side of the main stairway, archaeologists have uncovered a large ceremonial doorway of perfectly preserved stucco work. It is an astonishingly elaborate representation of the gaping mouth of the underworld god. Around it are several beautifully detailed human figures. Excavation inside revealed a long chamber filled with Mayan hieroglyphic writing. From the style, it appears that the scribes probably came from Guatemala. So far this chamber is closed to the public. From this script, an epigrapher, Alfonso Lacadena, has found the name of one of the principal kings of the city—Ukit Kan Le'k Tok'. If you climb to the top of the pyramid, in the middle distance you can see untouched ruins looming to the north. To the southeast, you can spot the tallest structures at **Cobá,** 50km (31 miles) away.

Also visible are the **raised causeways** of the Maya—the *sacbé* appear as raised lines in the forest. More than any of the better-known sites, Ek Balam inspires a sense of mystery and awe at the scale of Maya civilization and the utter ruin to which it fell.

RIO LAGARTOS NATURE RESERVE ✦

Some 80km (50 miles) north of Valladolid (40km/25 miles north of Tizimín) on Highway 295 is Río Lagartos, a 50,000-hectare (123,500-acre) refuge established in 1979 to protect the largest nesting population of flamingos in North America. The nesting area is off limits, but you can see plenty of flamingos as well as many other species of fowl and take an enjoyable boat ride around the estuary here.

To get to Río Lagartos, you pass through Tizimín, which is about 30 minutes away. If you need to spend the night there, try **Hotel 49,** Calle 49 373-A (ⓒ **986/863-2136**), by the main square. There is not much to do in Tizimín unless you are there during the first 2 weeks of January, when it holds the largest fair in the Yucatán. The prime fiesta day is January 6.

SEEING THE RIO LAGARTOS REFUGE Río Lagartos is a small fishing village of around 3,000 people who make their living from the sea and from the occasional tourist who shows up to see the flamingos. Colorfully painted houses face the *malecón* (the oceanfront street), and brightly painted boats dock here and there.

When you drive into town, keep going straight until you get to the shore. Look for where Calle 10 intersects with the *malecón;* it's near a modern church. There, in a little kiosk, is where the guides can be found (no phone). The sign reads PARADOR TURISTICO NAHOCHIN. There you can make arrangements for a 2-hour tour, which will cost $50 to $60 (£25–£30) for two to three people. The best time to go is in the early morning, so it's best to overnight here at one of the cheap hotels along the *malecón.* I looked at a few and liked **Posada Lucy** (no phone; $25/£13 for two).

I had a pleasant ride the next morning, and saw several species of ducks, hawks, cranes, cormorants, an osprey, and lots of flamingos. The guide also wanted to show me how easy it was to float in some evaporation pools used by the local salt producer at Las Coloradas (a good source of employment for the locals until it was mechanized) and a place where fresh water bubbles out from below the saltwater estuary.

ISLA HOLBOX ✦

A sandy strip of an island off the northeastern corner of the Yucatán Peninsula, Holbox (pronounced "hohl-*bosh*") was a remote corner of the world with only a half-deserted fishing village, until tourists started showing up for the beach. Now it's a semiprosperous little community that gets its livelihood from tourist services, employment at the beach hotels, and tours. It's most popular with visitors from May to September, when over a hundred **whale sharks** congregate in nearby waters (why precisely they come here is not known). These gentle giants swim slowly along the surface of the water and don't seem to mind the boat tours and snorkelers that come to experience what it's like to be in the wild with these creatures. Whale sharks don't fit

ⓘ Tips Visiting the Whale Sharks of Isla Holbox

In 2002, Mexico's whale sharks were designated an endangered species. As a result, the government, along with environmental groups, closely monitors their activity and the tours that visit them off Isla Holbox. Several restrictions apply to how tours are run and all tour operators must abide by them. To learn more about the whale sharks, and the measures being taken to protect them, go to www.domino.conanp.gob.mx/rules.htm.

Tours to visit the sharks are kept small, since only two people at a time are allowed to snorkel with the sharks. Tours typically cost around $90 (£45) per person, and last between 4 to 6 hours. Many of the hotels or outfitters on the island can arrange a tour for you.

the common picture of a shark; they are much larger, attaining a length of up to 18m (59 ft.), and they are filter feeders for the most part, dining on plankton and other small organisms. That said, they can do some mischief if you annoy them.

The beach here is broad and sandy (with fine-textured sand). It is also shallow. Instead of the amazing blue color of the Caribbean, it's more of a dull green. There are several beach hotels just beyond town. These experienced lots of damage from Hurricane Emily in the summer of 2005, but they've since come back: **Villas Flamingos** (ⓒ 800/538-6802 in the U.S. and Canada) and **Villas Delfines,** which has an office in Cancún (ⓒ **998/884-8606** or 984/875-2197; www.holbox.com). The latter is a personal favorite. Rates run between $100 and $150 (£55–£83) for a large free-standing beach bungalow with a large porch, a thatched roof, mosquito netting, and plenty of cross-ventilation. This is very much an ecohotel, with composting toilets and solar water heaters. There is a pool, a good restaurant, and lovely grounds. If you want A/C, try **Casa Sandra** (ⓒ **984/875-2171**).

From Valladolid, take Highway 180 east for about 90km (56 miles) toward Cancún; turn north after Nuevo Xcan at the tiny crossroads of El Ideal. Drive nearly 100km (62 miles) north on a state highway to the tiny port of Chiquilá, where you can park your car in a secure parking lot; walk 180m (590 ft.) to the pier, and catch the ferry to the island. It runs 10 times per day. When you get off in the village, you can contract with one of the golf cart taxis for a ride to your hotel.

9

Tabasco & Chiapas

by David Baird

Even though these two states aren't part of the Yucatán, we've included them so that we can present Mexico's entire **Maya region.** Many travelers who go to the Yucatán to see Chichén Itzá and Uxmal also take a side trip to Chiapas to see the famous ruins of Palenque. Some go even farther, all the way to San Cristóbal, to visit the highland Maya.

If you have the time, you might even want to make this part of Mexico the object of a separate trip. First, there's a lot to see and do; second, much of it is best appreciated at a leisurely pace; and third, transportation in, out, and through the area is a bit problematic—not the kind of challenge you want to take on with a tight schedule.

The terrain and climate of Chiapas and Tabasco differ from that of the Yucatán. The lowland jungle is denser and taller than all but the most southern part of the peninsula. The central highlands of Chiapas are cool and wet, and the mountain air feels refreshing after you've experienced the heat and humidity of the lowlands. The area has striking mountain vistas, deep canyons, and isolated cloud forests.

Tabasco is a small, oil-rich state along the Gulf coast. The capital, **Villahermosa,** has a distinct boomtown feel. It was in this coastal region that the Olmec, the mother-culture of Mesoamerica, rose to prominence. At the Parque–Museo La Venta, you can see some artifacts this culture left to posterity, including its famous megalithic heads.

Chiapas has much that is interesting, but perhaps the most important areas to visit are the eastern lowland jungles and the central highlands. In the former lie the famous ruins of **Palenque,** a city that dates from the Classic age of Maya civilization. The ruins look unspeakably old, and the surrounding jungle seems poised to reclaim them, should their caretakers ever falter in their duties. Deeper into the interior are the sites of **Yaxchilán** and **Bonampak.** The central highlands are just as dramatic but easier to enjoy. Of particular interest are the colonial city of **San Cristóbal de las Casas** and its surrounding Indian villages. The Indians here cling so tenaciously to their beliefs and traditions that at one time this area was more popular with anthropologists than tourists.

Fifteen years ago, Chiapas made international news when the Zapatista Liberation Army launched an armed rebellion and captured San Cristóbal. This forced the Mexican government to recognize the existence of social and economic disparities in Chiapas. Negotiations achieved minor results, and then stalled. Political violence erupted again in the winter of 1997 and 1998. But no foreigners were attacked, and no restrictions were ever placed on travel to Palenque or the San Cristóbal region. Since then, especially in the last couple of years, the Zapatista movement has dropped the talk about armed insurrection in an effort to broaden its base as a political movement.

1 Villahermosa

142km (88 miles) NW of Palenque; 469km (291 miles) SW of Campeche; 160km (99 miles) N of San Cristóbal de las Casas

Villahermosa (pop. 550,000) is the capital of and the largest city in the state of Tabasco. It lies in a shallow depression about an hour's drive from the Gulf coast, at the confluence of two rivers: the Grijalva and the Carrizal. The land is marshy, with shallow lakes scattered here and there. For most of the year it's hot and humid.

Recent Flooding: In October and November of 2007 tremendous flooding in the area forced many thousands from their homes in Tabasco and lowland Chiapas, but particularly in Villahermosa, making for a humanitarian disaster on par with New Orleans. It will be some time before life returns to normal for the city. At press time, several hotels and a few of the museums were still closed. Transportation infrastructure, however, is quickly returning to normal.

Oil has brought money to this town and raised prices. Villahermosa is one of the most expensive cities in the country and contrasts sharply with inexpensive Chiapas. Though there's a lot of money, it's all being pulled to the modern western sections surrounding a development called Tabasco 2000. This area, especially the neighborhoods around the **Parque–Museo La Venta,** is the most attractive part of town, surrounded by small lakes. The historic center has been left to decay. It's gritty, crowded, and unpleasant. The main reason to be downtown is for the cheap hotels.

Two names that you will likely see and hear are Carlos Pellicer Cámara and Tomás Garrido Canabal; both were interesting people. The first was a mid-20th-century Tabascan poet and intellectual. The best known of Mexico's *modernista* poets, he was a fiercely independent thinker. Garrido Canabal, socialist governor of Tabasco in the 1920s and 1930s, tried to turn the conservative, backwater state of Tabasco into a model of socialism. He fought for many socialist causes, but his enmity for Mexico's Catholic church is what he is most remembered for today. He went so far as to name his son Lucifer and his farm animals Jesus and the Virgin Mary.

ESSENTIALS
GETTING THERE & DEPARTING
BY PLANE **Continental ExpressJet** (© 800/525-0280 in the U.S., or 01-800/900-5000 in Mexico; www.continental.com) has direct service to/from Houston on a regional jet. **Mexicana** (© 800/531-7921 in the U.S., 01-800/502-2000; www.mexicana.com) and **AeroMéxico** (© 800/237-6639 in the U.S., or 01-800/021-4000; www.aeromexico.com) both have flights to and from Mexico City. **Aviación de Chiapas (Aviacsa;** © 993/316-5700 or 01-800/006-2200; www.aviacsa.com) flies to and from Mexico City and Mérida. The regional airline **Aerolitoral,** a subsidiary of AeroMéxico (© 800/237-6639 in the U.S., or 993/312-6991), goes through Mexico City with a connection to Veracruz, Tampico, Monterrey, and Houston. **Click** (© 01-800/122-5425 in Mexico; www.clickmx.com), a Mexican budget airline, provides nonstop service to and from Mexico City.

BY CAR Highway 180 connects Villahermosa to Campeche (6 hr.). Highway 186, which passes by the airport, joins Highway 199 to Palenque and San Cristóbal de las Casas. The road to Palenque is a good one, and the drive takes 2 hours. Between Palenque and San Cristóbal, the road enters the mountains and takes 4 to 5 hours. On any of the mountain roads, conditions are apt to get worse during the rainy season from May to October.

BY BUS   The **bus station** is at Mina and Merino (☎ **993/312-8900;** www.ticket bus.com.mx), 3 blocks off Highway 180. There are eight nonstop buses per day to/ from Palenque (2½ hr.). There are seven nonstop buses per day to Mexico City (10 hr.), six deluxe service on **ADO-GL,** and two superdeluxe on **UNO.** To Campeche, there are eight buses nonstop per day (7 hr.); some of these go on to Mérida.

ORIENTATION

ARRIVING   Villahermosa's **airport** is 10km (6¼ miles) east of town. Driving in, you'll cross a bridge over the Río Grijalva, and then turn left to reach downtown. Taxis to the downtown area cost $15 (£7.50).

Parking downtown can be difficult; it's best to find a parking lot. Use one that's guarded round-the-clock.

VISITOR INFORMATION   The **State Tourism Office** (☎ **993/316-5122,** ext. 229) has two information booths: The one at the **airport** is staffed daily from 10am to 5pm; the one at **Parque–Museo La Venta** (next to the ticket counter for the park) is staffed Tuesday to Sunday from 10am to 5pm.

CITY LAYOUT   The downtown area, including the pedestrian-only **Zona Luz,** is on the west bank of the Grijalva River. About 1.5km (1 mile) upstream (south) is **CICOM,** an academic organization with the large archaeology museum named for the poet Carlos Pellicer Cámara. The **airport** is on the east side of the river. Highway 180 passes the airport and crosses the river just north of downtown, becoming **Bulevar Ruiz Cortines.** To get to the downtown area, turn left onto **Madero** or **Pino Suárez.** By staying on Ruiz Cortines you can reach the city's biggest attraction, the Parque–Museo la Venta. It's well marked. Just beyond that is the intersection with **Paseo Tabasco,** the heart of the modern hotel and shopping district.

GETTING AROUND   Taxis are your best way to get around town. Villahermosa is rare for being a Mexican city without meaningful public transportation.

FAST FACTS   American Express is represented by Turismo Creativo, Av. Paseo Tabasco 1404, Col. Tabasco 2000 (☎ **993/310-9900**). The telephone **area code** is **993.** There aren't a lot of *casas de cambio,* but you can exchange money at the airport, the hotels, and downtown banks on calles Juárez and Madero. ATMs are plentiful.

EXPLORING VILLAHERMOSA

Major sights include the **Parque–Museo La Venta** and the **Museo Regional de Antropología Carlos Pellicer Cámara.** You can hit them both in a day. There is also an ecological park called **Yumká** (see below), which is 16km (10 miles) out of town in the direction of the airport.

Stroll about the pedestrian-only Zona Luz, and you'll see signs that investment might be returning to the old downtown area. Outside the Zona Luz, things get more unpleasant, with lots of traffic and crowds of pedestrians. But, as unpleasant as it is, there are things of interest for those who like to explore Mexican society and culture. You can walk south along the banks of the Grijalva until you come to a pedestrian bridge with an observation tower. That's the highlight. You won't miss much by keeping away.

Museo Regional de Antropología Carlos Pellicer Cámara 𝒦𝒦   This museum on the west bank of the river about 1.5km (1 mile) south of the town center will probably remain closed until early 2009 due to the 2007 floods. It normally has a well-organized collection of pre-Hispanic artifacts, not only from the local region

Villahermosa

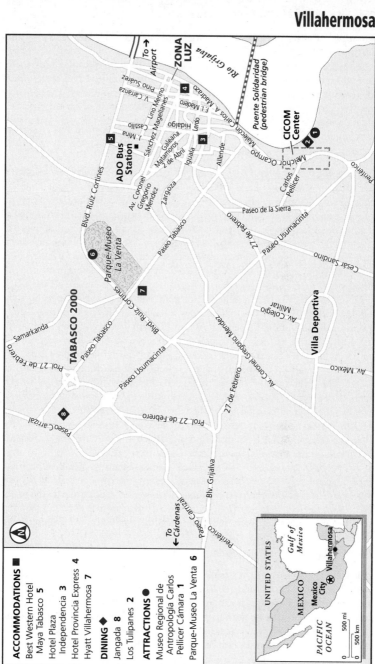

To → Airport

ZONA LUZ

Rio Grijalva

Puente Solidaridad
(pedestrian bridge)

CICOM Center

Melchor Ocampo

Malecón Carlos A. Madrazo

V. Carranza

Pino Suárez

Lino Merino

F.T. Madero

Sánchez Magellanes

Hidalgo

Lerdo

Castillo

J. Mina

Galeana

Matamoros

Iguala

Z. de Abril

Allende

Carlos Pellicer

ADO Bus Station ■

Av Coronel Gregorio Méndez

Zaragoza

Blvd. Ruiz Cortines

Paseo de la Sierra

Peribérico

Paseo Tabasco

27 de febrero

Paseo Usumacinta

César Sandino

Parque-Museo La Venta

TABASCO 2000

Blvd. Ruiz Cortines

Samarkanda

Prol. 27 de Febrero

Paseo Tabasco

Paseo Usumacinta

Av. Colegio Militar

Villa Deportiva

Av. México

Av Coronel Gregorio Méndez

27 de Febrero

Prol. 27 de Febrero

27 de Febrero

Paseo Carrizal

Blv. Grijalva

Paseo Canizal

Peribérico

To ← Cárdenas

N

UNITED STATES

Gulf of Mexico

PACIFIC OCEAN

MEXICO

Mexico City ✪

Villahermosa ●

0   500 mi
0   500 km

(Totonac, Zapotec, and Olmec), but from other parts of Mexico and Central America, as well.

The second floor is devoted to the Olmec. The third floor features artifacts from central Mexico, including the Tlatilco and Teotihuacán cultures; the Huasteca culture of Veracruz, San Luis Potosí, and Tampico states; and the cultures of Nayarit State, on the west coast. Photographs and diagrams provide vivid images, but the explanatory signs are mostly in Spanish. Look especially for the figurines that were found in this area and for the colorful Codex (an early book of pictographs). Allow 1 to 2 hours.

CICOM Center, Av. Carlos Pellicer Cámara 511. ✆ 993/312-6344. Admission $3 (£1.50). Tues–Sun 9am–5pm.

Parque–Museo La Venta 🐾🐾   The Olmec created the first civilization in Mexico and developed several cultural traits that later spread to all subsequent civilizations throughout Mesoamerica. In addition to their monumental works, they carved small exquisite figurines in jade and serpentine, which can be seen in the Museo Regional de Antropología (see above). The park and museum occupy a portion of a larger park named after Tomás Garrido Canabal, which includes a serene lake, a zoo, a natural history museum, and a lot of green space with several walkways frequented by joggers. Once inside the park and museum, a trail leads you from one sculpture to the next. Most of the pieces are massive heads or altars. These can be as tall as 2m (6½ ft.) and weigh as much as 40 tons. The faces seem to be half adult, half infant. They have highly stylized mouths with thick fleshy lips that turn down (known as the "jaguar mouth," this is a principal characteristic of Olmec art). At least 17 heads have been found: 4 at La Venta, 10 at San Lorenzo, and 3 at Tres Zapotes—all Olmec cities on Mexico's east coast. The pieces in this park were taken from La Venta, a major city during the pre-Classic period (2000 B.C.–A.D. 300). Most were sculpted around 1000 B.C. without the use of metal chisels. The basalt rock used for these heads and altars was transported to La Venta from more than 113km (70 miles) away. It is thought that the rock was brought most of the way by raft. Most of these pieces were first discovered in 1938. Now all that remains at La Venta are some grass-covered mounds that were once earthen pyramids. An exhibition area at the entrance to the park does a good job of illustrating how La Venta was laid out and what archaeologists think the Olmec were like.

As you stroll along, you will see labels identifying many species of local trees, including a grand ceiba tree of special significance to the Olmec and, later, the Maya. A few varieties of local critters scurry about, seemingly unconcerned with the presence of humans or with escaping from the park. Allow at least 2 hours for wandering through the jungly sanctuary and examining the 3,000-year-old sculpture. *Note:* Don't forget the mosquito repellent.

Bulevar Ruiz Cortines s/n. ✆ 993/314-1652. Admission $4 (£2). Tues–Sun 8am–4pm.

Yumká   Half safari park, half ecological reserve, Yumká contains native and not-so-native wildlife. A good choice for kids, the park offers visitors a guided tour of the indigenous tropical forest, a boat tour of the wetlands ($1/50p extra for the ride), and a small train ride through grasslands populated with various species of African wildlife. This is a large park; allow at least 2 hours. There's a restaurant on the premises. Yumká is 16km (10 miles) from downtown, toward the airport. A minibus provides transportation (ask at your hotel or at a travel agency), or you can take a cab ($16/£8).

Camino Yumká s/n, 86200 Ejido Dos Montes, Tab. ✆ 993/356-0107. Admission $8 (£4) adults, $5 (£2.50) children younger than 13. Daily 9am–5pm.

WHERE TO STAY

You can expect to pay a little extra for rooms in Villahermosa. Rates here include the 17% tax. Several of the inexpensive downtown hotels have figured out that to survive they must offer nightly entertainment to their mostly businessmen clientele. It's unfortunate that they aren't really set up to do this and provide quiet guest rooms at the same time. The only inexpensive hotel I could find that didn't have a bar is listed below, as well as some nicer, albeit more expensive, accommodations.

VERY EXPENSIVE

Hyatt Villahermosa ★★   A simple hotel for a Hyatt, the Villahermosa still has the services and amenities you'd expect. I like it better than the Camino Real (which is the other top hotel in the city), for its great location and service. A short walk away is the Parque–Museo La Venta. The rooms are large, quiet, and comfortable. A thorough remodeling, all the way down to the plumbing and wiring, was completed in 2004. The majority of clients are business travelers.

Av. Juárez 106, 86000 Villahermosa, Tab. ℂ **800/233-1234** in the U.S., or 993/310-1234. Fax 993/315-1963. www.villahermosa.regency.hyatt.com. 206 units. $260 (£130) double; $300 (£150) Regency Club room; $340 (£170) junior suite. AE, DC, MC, V. Free guarded parking. **Amenities:** 2 restaurants; 3 bars (1 w/live music; 1 sports bar); large pool, wading pool; 2 lighted tennis courts; small exercise room; concierge; tour desk; car rental; business center; room service until 11:30pm; laundry service; dry cleaning; nonsmoking floor; concierge level. *In room:* A/C, TV, high-speed Internet, minibar, coffeemaker, hair dryer, iron, safe.

EXPENSIVE

Best Western Hotel Maya Tabasco   This hotel is centrally located between the downtown area and the modern western section. It's close to the Parque–Museo La Venta, the bus station, and the city's principal restaurant district. The rooms are large, and most are carpeted and have midsize bathrooms. They don't offer any surprises. An attractive pool area separates the hotel from the hotel's bar, which gets fairly good live talent—Latin music and comedy acts. A quiet bar inside has soft piano or guitar music.

Bulevar Ruiz Cortines 907, 86000 Villahermosa, Tab. ℂ **800/528-1234** in the U.S. and Canada, or 993/358-1111, ext. 822. Fax 993/312-1097. www.bestwestern.com. 151 units. $170 (£85) double; $198 (£99) junior suite. AE, MC, V. Rates include full breakfast. Free guarded parking. **Amenities:** Restaurant; 2 bars; large pool; tour desk; free shuttle service to airport and downtown; business center, room service until 10pm; laundry service; dry cleaning; nonsmoking rooms. *In room:* A/C, TV, dataport, minibar, coffeemaker, hair dryer, safe.

MODERATE

Hotel Plaza Independencia *Value*   The Plaza Independencia is the only hotel in this area charging less than $80 (£40) with a pool and enclosed parking. Get a room on one of the first three floors, which have been remodeled. End rooms, which end in 01, 02, 14, and 15, have balconies and are generally preferable. It's 2 blocks south of the Plaza de Armas.

Independencia 123, 86000 Villahermosa, Tab. ℂ **993/312-1299** or -7541. Fax 993/314-4724. www.hotelesplaza.com.mx. 90 units. $78 (£39) double. AE, MC, V. Free secure parking. **Amenities:** Restaurant; bar; small pool; tour desk; business center; room service until 11pm; laundry service. *In room:* A/C, TV, minibar, dataport, hair dryer, safe.

INEXPENSIVE

Hotel Provincia Express *Value*   For $50 (£25), this place is your best option. Located downtown in the Zona Luz pedestrian-only section of town, rooms are simple, quiet, and medium-size, with good air-conditioning. Management is capable and doesn't complicate things by offering services and options that its clientele doesn't want.

Lerdo de Tejada 303, 86000 Villahermosa, Tab. ⓒ 993/314-5376, or 01-800/715-3968 in Mexico. Fax 993/314-5442. willaop@prodigy.net.mx. 25 units. $50 (£25) double. MC, V. **Amenities:** Restaurant. *In room:* A/C, TV.

WHERE TO DINE

Like other Mexican cities, Villahermosa has seen the arrival of U.S. franchise restaurants, but as these things go, I prefer the Mexican variety: **Sanborn's,** Av. Ruiz Cortines 1310, near Parque–Museo La Venta (ⓒ **993/316-8722**), and **VIPS,** Av. Fco. I. Madero 402, downtown (ⓒ **993/312-3237**). Both usually do a good job with traditional dishes such as enchiladas or *antojitos* (supper dishes).

Jangada 𝒢𝒢 SEAFOOD   My favorite restaurant in the city is an all-you-can-eat seafood buffet. Before you get to the line, you are served a small glass of delicious seafood broth and an appetizing empanada of *pejelagarto* (a freshwater fish for which Tabasco is famous—it is also, in fact, the political moniker of Andrés Manuel López Obrador, the former mayor of Mexico City and former presidential candidate, who hails from Tabasco). From here, move on to the salad and cold seafood bar, which offers a seafood salad made with freshwater lobster, different kinds of ceviche, and an area where you can get a seafood cocktail made to order. There's a variety of seafood soups—don't leave without trying the shrimp-and-*yuca* chowder, a dish I remember fondly. And then, of course, there are the main dishes, including a well-made paella, charcoal-grilled *pejelagarto* (mild taste—light and almost nutty), and fish kabobs. Jangada is in the fancy western part of town in La Choca neighborhood. It closes early, but next door is a good Brazilian-style steakhouse (Rodizio) that stays open until 9pm.

Paseo de la Choca 126, Fracc. La Choca. ⓒ 993/317-6050. Reservations not accepted. $28 (£14) per person, excluding drinks and dessert. AE, DC, MC, V. Daily 12:30–7pm.

Los Tulipanes SEAFOOD/STEAKS/REGIONAL   Los Tulipanes offers good food and has excellent service. The staff tends to a full house with ease, and, on busy days, a guitar trio strolls and serenades. Because the restaurant is on the Río Grijalva near the Pellicer Museum of Anthropology, you can combine a visit to the museum with lunch here. The staff may bring you a plate of *tostones de plátano*—mashed banana chips. In addition to seafood and steaks, Los Tulipanes serves such Mexican specialties as chiles rellenos, tacos, and enchiladas. It has a popular buffet on Sunday.

CICOM Center, Periférico Carlos Pellicer Cámara 511. ⓒ 993/312-9209 or -9217. Main courses $8–$18 (£4–£9); Sun buffet $16 (£8). AE, MC, V. Daily 1–9pm.

A SIDE TRIP TO CHOCOLATE PLANTATIONS & THE RUINS OF COMALCALCO

Eighty kilometers (50 miles) from Villahermosa is **Comalcalco,** the only pyramid site in Mexico made of kilned brick. This site will be of interest to the hard-core Maya freaks, but it isn't as stunning as Palenque or the picturesque ruins of the Río Bec region. If you have a car, you can get there in an hour, but be prepared for a lack of good directional signs. You'll have to ask directions when you get to the town of Comalcalco. If you don't have a car, you can take a taxi, which will run $50 to $60 (£25–£30) to get you there and back with time to see the place. Or you can take a bus to the town of Comalcalco, and a taxi from there. ADO runs first-class buses twice daily. From the town of Comalcalco, the ruins are 3km (2 miles) away. This part of Tabasco is cacao-growing country, where you can visit plantations and factories to see the cacao from the pod on the tree to the finished chocolate bars.

The fastest route from Villahermosa is Highway 180 west to a new (and, as far as I could tell, unnumbered) highway that leads to Cunduacán. The turnoff is clearly marked, but if you miss it, you can continue to Cárdenas and take Highway 187 north.

Comalcalco is a busy agricultural center and market town. The **ruins of Comalcalco** are about 3km (2 miles) on the same highway past the town; watch for signs to the turnoff on the right. Park in the lot and pay admission at the visitor center by the museum. The museum, with many pre-Hispanic artifacts, is small but interesting and worth the 20 minutes or so it takes to see it. Unfortunately, all the descriptions are in Spanish. It presents a history of the people who lived here, the Putún/Chontal Maya. They were traders, spoke Mayan dialect, and were believed to have founded, or at least greatly influenced, Chichén Itzá.

This city had an extension of 7 sq. km (2¾ sq. miles), but the site contains only the ceremonial center, comprising an expansive plaza bordered by pyramidal structures and an acropolis with the remains of a palace and some ceremonial structures, probably funerary temples. This city reached its height during the Classic period, A.D. 300 to 900. Of the pyramids around the plaza, one has been fully excavated. A carpet of grass grows over others, with partial excavation here and there. These pyramids were made of compacted earth with brick facing, in some places covered in stucco. To the south of the plaza and above it is the acropolis, a complex of temples and palace rooms that sits well above the plaza. There you will find a couple of structures with carvings and molded stucco with scenes of Maya royalty. There are only a few. Workers had cordoned off a couple of the structures in this complex when I was last there, and I'm not sure whether they will be open soon. Because of the fragile nature of these ruins, there are many NO SUBIR ("no climbing") signs warning visitors against scaling particular structures. But there is one path with arrows that leads you up to the **palace** where you have a good view of the whole site. You can make out the remains of a double vault and a colonnaded chamber that were the principal chambers of this palace. Seeing the ruins takes an hour or so. Admission is $3.50 (£1.75), and the site is open daily from 8am to 5pm.

2 Palenque ★★

142km (88 miles) SE of Villahermosa; 229km (142 miles) NE of San Cristóbal de las Casas

The ruins of Palenque look out over the jungle from a tall ridge that juts out from the base of steep, thickly forested mountains. It is a dramatic sight colored by the mysterious feel of the ruins themselves. The temples here are in the Classic style, with high-pitched roofs crowned with elaborate combs. Inside many are representations in stone and plaster of the rulers and their gods, which give evidence of a cosmology that is—and perhaps will remain—impenetrable to our understanding. This is one of the grand archaeological sites of Mexico.

Eight kilometers (5 miles) from the ruins is the town of Palenque. There you can find lodging and food, as well as make travel arrangements. Transportation between the town and ruins is cheap and convenient.

ESSENTIALS
GETTING THERE & DEPARTING
BY PLANE There is no regular commercial air service to Palenque.

BY CAR The 230km (143-mile) trip from San Cristóbal to Palenque takes 5 hours and passes through lush jungle and mountain scenery. Take it easy, though, and watch out for potholes and other hindrances. **Highway 186** from Villahermosa should take about 2 hours. You may encounter military roadblocks that involve a cursory inspection of your travel credentials and perhaps your vehicle.

BY BUS   The two first-class bus stations are 2 blocks apart. Both are on Palenque's main street between the main square and the turnoff for the ruins. The smaller company, **Transportes Rodolfo Figueroa** (© **916/345-1322**), offers first-class service four times a day to and from San Cristóbal (5 hr.) and Tuxtla (6½ hr.). **ADO/Cristóbal Colón** (© **916/345-1344**) runs to those destinations and Campeche (six per day, 5 hr.), Villahermosa (nine per day, 2 hr.), and Mérida (two per day, 9 hr.).

ORIENTATION

VISITOR INFORMATION   The downtown tourism office is a block from the main square at the corner of Avenida Juárez and Abasolo. It's open Monday to Saturday from 9am to 9pm, Sunday from 9am to 1pm. There's no phone at the downtown office. To get info over the phone, call the tourism office's business office (© **916/ 345-0356**).

CITY LAYOUT   **Avenida Juárez** is Palenque's main street. At one end is the **main plaza;** at the other is the oversized sculpture of the famous Maya head that was discovered here. To the right of the statue is the entrance to the Cañada; to the left is the road to the ruins, and straight ahead past the statue are the airport and the highway to Villahermosa. The distance between the town's main square and the monument is about 1.5km (1 mile).

La Cañada is a restaurant and hotel zone tucked away in the forest. Aside from the main plaza area, this is the best location for travelers without cars, because the town is within a few blocks, and the buses that run to the ruins pass right by.

GETTING AROUND   The cheapest way to get back and forth from the ruins is on the white **VW buses** *(colectivos)* that run down Juárez every 10 minutes from 6am to 6pm. The buses pass La Cañada and hotels along the road to the ruins and can be flagged down at any point, but they may not stop if they're full. The cost is $1 (50p) per person.

FAST FACTS   The telephone **area code** is **916.** As for the **climate,** Palenque's high humidity is downright oppressive in the summer, especially after rain showers. During the winter, the damp air can occasionally be chilly in the evening. Rain gear is handy at any time of year. **Internet service** and **ATMs** are easily available.

EXPLORING PALENQUE

The reason to come here is the ruins; although you can tour them in a morning, many people savor Palenque for days. There are no must-see sights in town.

PARQUE NACIONAL PALENQUE ✸✸✸

A **museum and visitor center** sits not far from the entrance to the ruins. Though it's not large, the museum is worth the time it takes to see; it's open Tuesday to Sunday from 10am to 5pm and is included in the price of admission. It contains well-chosen and artistically displayed exhibits, including jade from recently excavated tombs. Explanatory text in Spanish and English explains the life and times of this magnificent city. New pieces are sometimes added as they are uncovered in ongoing excavations.

The **main entrance,** about 1km (½ mile) beyond the museum, is at the end of the paved highway. There you'll find a large parking lot, a refreshment stand, a ticket booth, and several shops. Among the vendors selling souvenirs are often some Lacandón Indians wearing white tunics and hawking bows and arrows.

Admission to the ruins is $7 (£3.50). The fee for using a video camera is $5 (£2.50). Parking at the main entrance and at the visitor center is free. The site and visitor center shops are open daily from 8am to 4:45pm. Turn to the color section of this book for a map of the ruins.

TOURING THE RUINS   Pottery shards found during the excavations show that people lived in this area as early as 300 B.C. By the Classic period (A.D. 300–900), Palenque was an important ceremonial center. It peaked around A.D. 600 to 700.

When John Stephens visited the site in the 1840s, the ruins that you see today were buried under centuries of accumulated earth and a thick canopy of jungle. The dense jungle surrounding the cleared portion still covers unexcavated temples, which are easily discernible in the forest even to the untrained eye. But be careful not to drift too far from the main path—there have been a few incidents where tourists venturing alone into the rainforest were assaulted.

Of all Mexico's ruins, this is the most haunting, because of its majesty; its history, recovered by epigraphers; and its mysterious setting. Scholars have identified the rulers and constructed their family histories, putting visitors on a first-name basis with these ancient people etched in stone. You can read about it in *A Forest of Kings,* by Linda Schele and David Freidel.

As you enter the ruins, the building on your right is the **Temple of the Inscriptions,** named for the great stone hieroglyphic panels found inside. (Most of the panels, which portray the family tree of King Pacal, are in the National Anthropological Museum in Mexico City.) This temple is famous for the crypt of King Pacal deep inside the pyramid, but the crypt is closed to the public. The archaeologist Alberto Ruz Lhuillier discovered the tomb in the depths of the temple in 1952—an accomplishment many scholars consider one of the great discoveries of the Maya world. In exploratory excavations, Ruz Lhuillier found a stairway leading from the temple floor deep into the base of the pyramid. The original builders had carefully concealed the entrance by filling the stairway with stone. After several months of excavation, Ruz Lhuillier finally reached King Pacal's crypt, which contained several fascinating objects, including a magnificent carved stone sarcophagus. Ruz Lhuillier's own gravesite is opposite the Temple of the Inscriptions, on the left as you enter the park.

Just to your right as you face the Temple of the Inscriptions is **Temple 13,** which is receiving considerable attention from archaeologists. They recently discovered the burial of another richly adorned personage, accompanied in death by an adult female and an adolescent. Some of the artifacts found there are on display in the museum.

Back on the main pathway, the building directly in front of you is the **Palace,** with its unique tower. The explorer John Stephens camped in the Palace when it was completely covered in vegetation, spending sleepless nights fighting off mosquitoes. A pathway between the Palace and the Temple of the Inscriptions leads to the **Temple of the Sun,** the **Temple of the Foliated Cross,** the **Temple of the Cross,** and **Temple 14.** This group of temples, now cleared and in various stages of reconstruction, was built by Pacal's son, Chan-Bahlum, who is usually shown on inscriptions with six toes. Chan-Bahlum's plaster mask was found in Temple 14 next to the Temple of the Sun. Archaeologists have begun probing the Temple of the Sun for Chan-Bahlum's tomb. Little remains of this temple's exterior carving. Inside, however, behind a fence, a carving of Chan-Bahlum shows him ascending the throne in A.D. 690. The panels depict Chan-Bahlum's version of his historic link to the throne.

To the left of the Palace is the North Group, also undergoing restoration. Included in this area are the **Ball Court** and the **Temple of the Count.** At least three tombs, complete with offerings for the underworld journey, have been found here, and the lineage of at least 12 kings has been deciphered from inscriptions left at this site.

Just past the North Group is a small building (once a museum) now used for storing the artifacts found during restorations. It is closed to the public. To the right of the building, a stone bridge crosses the river, leading to a pathway down the hillside to the new museum. The rock-lined path descends along a cascading stream on the banks of which grow giant ceiba trees. Benches are placed along the way as rest areas, and some small temples have been reconstructed near the base of the trail. In the early morning and evening, you may hear monkeys crashing through the thick foliage by the path; if you keep noise to a minimum, you may spot wild parrots as well. Walking downhill (by far the best way to go), it will take you about 20 minutes to reach the main highway. The path ends at the paved road across from the museum. The *colectivos* (minibuses) going back to the village will stop here if you wave them down.

WHERE TO STAY

English is spoken in all the more expensive hotels and about half of the inexpensive ones. The quoted rates include the 17% tax. High season in Palenque is Easter week, July to August, and December.

EXPENSIVE

Chan-Kah Resort Village ⋒   This hotel is a grouping of comfortable, roomy bungalows that offer privacy and quiet in the surroundings of a tropical forest. The hotel is on the road between the ruins and the town, but because the town of Palenque isn't particularly worth exploring, you won't miss much by staying here. The grounds are beautifully tended, and there is an inviting pool that resembles a lagoon. A broad stream runs through the property. Some of the bungalows can have a musty smell. Christmas prices will be higher than those quoted here, and you may be quoted a higher price if you reserve a room in advance from outside the country. The outdoor restaurant and bar serves only passable Mexican food. Room service is pricey.

Carretera Las Ruinas Km 3, 29960 Palenque, Chi. ☏ **916/345-1100.** Fax 916/345-0820. www.chan-kah.com.mx. 73 units. $150 (£75) double. MC, V. Free guarded parking. **Amenities:** Restaurant; bar; 3 outdoor pools (1 large w/natural spring); game room; room service; laundry service. *In room:* A/C, hair dryer.

Misión Palenque ⋒⋒   This hotel has returned to being among the most comfortable in the city after a total remodeling that includes new air-conditioning and other amenities. Rooms are medium-size and attractively furnished with light, modern furniture. Bathrooms are spacious with ample counters. The hotel has extensive grounds, and is very quiet. In one corner of the property, a natural spring flows through an attractive bit of jungle, where the hotel has installed the spa. Part of the spa is a *temazcal,* or Native American steam bath. There's also a mud bath along with the more common elements. The hotel is a few blocks east of the town's main square.

Periférico Oriente d/c, 29960 Palenque, Chi. ☏ **916/345-0241,** or 01/800-900-3800 in Mexico. Fax 916/345-0300. www.hotelesmision.com.mx. 156 units. $140 (£70) double. AE, MC, V. Free guarded parking that includes vehicle checkup. **Amenities:** Restaurant; bar; 2 outdoor pools; 2 tennis courts; fitness room; spa; Jacuzzi; tour service; car-rental desk; courtesy trips to ruins; room service; in-room massage; babysitting; laundry service. *In room:* A/C, TV, hair dryer (on request), safe.

Where to Stay & Dine in Palenque

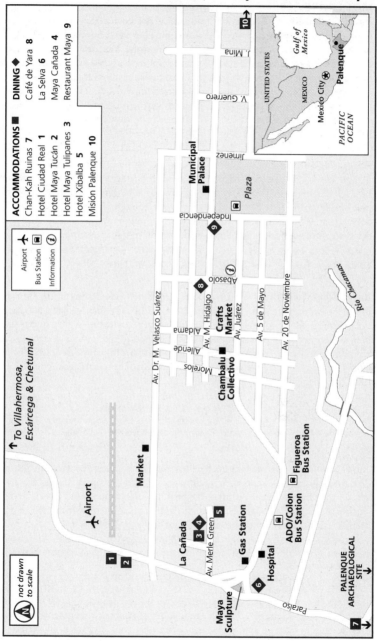

ACCOMMODATIONS ■
Chan-Kah Ruinas **7**
Hotel Ciudad Real **1**
Hotel Maya Tucán **2**
Hotel Maya Tulipanes **3**
Hotel Xibalba **5**
Misión Palenque **10**

DINING ◆
Café de Yara **8**
La Selva **6**
Maya Cañada **4**
Restaurant Maya **9**

Airport ✈
Bus Station ▣
Information ⓘ

not drawn to scale

← To Villahermosa, Escárcega & Chetumal

Airport

Market

La Cañada
Av. Merle Green

Gas Station

Maya Sculpture

Hospital

ADO/Colon Bus Station

Figueroa Bus Station

Chambalu Collectivo

Crafts Market

Morelos
Allende
Av. M. Hidalgo
Aldama
Av. Dr. M. Velasco Suárez

Av. Juárez
Av. 5 de Mayo
Av. 20 de Noviembre

Abasolo

Independencia

Municipal Palace

Plaza

Jimenez

V. Guerrero

J. Mina

Paraíso

PALENQUE ARCHAEOLOGICAL SITE →

Río Chacamax

UNITED STATES
Gulf of Mexico
MEXICO
Palenque
Mexico City ★
PACIFIC OCEAN

MODERATE

Hotel Ciudad Real   Though not really fancy, this hotel does the important things right—the rooms are ample, quiet, and well lit. They are comfortably, if plainly, furnished. Suites have a sitting room with sleeping sofa. Most units hold two double beds; some king-size beds are available. All rooms have a small balcony, which in the best case overlooks an attractive garden. When making a reservation, specify the hotel in Palenque. It's at the edge of town in the direction of the airport.

Carretera a Pakal-Na Km 1.5, 29960 Palenque, Chi. ✆ **916/345-1343** (reservations: ✆ 967/678-4400). www.ciudad real.com.mx. 72 units. High season $110 (£55) double, $130 (£65) suite; low season $100 (£50) double, $120 (£60) suite. AE, MC, V. Free secured parking. **Amenities:** Restaurant; bar; outdoor pool; baby pool; game room; travel agency; car-rental desk; room service; laundry service; nonsmoking rooms. *In room:* A/C, TV, hair dryer.

Hotel Maya Tucán   Book a room in back, and you will have a view of the hotel's natural pond. The cheerfully decorated rooms are adequate in size; they have double beds and large bathrooms. Suites are larger and have king-size beds. The grounds are well tended and lush; scarlet macaws kept by the hotel fly about the parking lot. The Maya Tucán is on the highway to the airport. Bathrooms are larger and better lit but done with less polish than at Ciudad Real. Beds have rubber mattress covers.

Carretera-Palenque Km 0.5, 29960 Palenque, Chi. ✆ **916/345-0443.** Fax 916/345-0337. mayatucan@palenque. com.mx. 56 units. $110 (£55) double, $140 (£70) suit. MC, V. Free secured parking. **Amenities:** Restaurant; bar; outdoor pool; room service; laundry service. *In room:* A/C, TV, hair dryer, no phone.

Hotel Maya Tulipanes   This is an attractive hotel tucked away in the Cañada. I like it for its location, and the close attention paid by the management. Service and upkeep are both good. Rooms are medium to large and come with a queen-size, a king-size, or two double beds. Tropical vegetation adorns the grounds along with some reproductions of famous Mayan architecture. The Maya Tulipanes has an arrangement with a sister hotel at the ruins of Tikal, in Guatemala. The travel agency operates daily tours to Bonampak and other attractions.

Calle Cañada 6, 29960 Palenque, Chi. ✆ **916/345-0201** or -0258. Fax 916/345-1004. www.mayatulipanes.com.mx. 73 units. High season $120 (£60) standard; low season $70 (£35) standard. Internet packages available. AE, MC, V. Free secured parking. **Amenities:** Restaurant; bar; outdoor pool; travel agency; ground transportation to/from Villahermosa airport; room service; laundry service; nonsmoking rooms. *In room:* A/C, TV, Wi-Fi, hair dryer, no phone.

INEXPENSIVE

Hotel Xibalba   This modern small two-story hotel is inspired by Maya architecture. The medium-to-small rooms are clean and cheerful. The upstairs units are a little smaller than the downstairs. Most of the beds have firm mattresses. You can arrange a trip to Bonampak or Misol Ha with the hotel management, which owns a travel agency, Viajes Shivalva (pronounced like Xibalba: "shee-*bahl*-bah").

Calle Merle Green 9, Col. La Cañada, 29960 Palenque, Chi. ✆ **916/345-0392.** Fax 916/345-0411. www.palenquemx. com/shivalva. 15 units. $50–$60 (£25–£30) double. MC, V. No parking. **Amenities:** Restaurant; bar; laundry service; travel agency. *In room:* A/C, TV, no phone.

WHERE TO DINE

Palenque and, for that matter, the rest of backwater Chiapas, is not for gourmets. Who'd a thunk? I had an easy time eliminating a number of restaurants that didn't even seem to be keeping up the appearance of serving food. But the situation has been improving, and you can at least get some decent Mexican food.

MODERATE

La Selva ⓕ MEXICAN/INTERNATIONAL   At La Selva (the jungle), you dine under a large, attractive thatched roof beside well-tended gardens. The menu includes seafood, freshwater fish, steaks, and Mexican specialties. The most expensive thing on the menu is *pigua,* freshwater lobster caught in the large rivers of southeast Mexico. These can get quite large—the size of small saltwater lobsters. This and the finer cuts of meat have been frozen, but you wouldn't want otherwise in Palenque. I liked the fish stuffed with shrimp, and the *mole* enchiladas. La Selva is on the highway to the ruins, near the statue of the Maya head.

Carretera Palenque Ruinas Km 0.5. ⓒ **916/345-0363.** Main courses $8–$17 (£4–£8.50). MC, V. Daily 11:30am–11:30pm.

INEXPENSIVE

Café de Yara MEXICAN   A small, modern cafe and restaurant with a comforting, not overly ambitious menu. The cafe's strong suit is healthy salads (with disinfected greens), and home-style Mexican entrees, such as the beef or chicken *milanesa* or chicken cooked in a *chile pasilla* sauce.

Av. Hidalgo 66 (at Abasolo). ⓒ **916/345-0269.** Main courses $4–$7 (£2–£3.50). MC, V. Daily 7am–11pm.

Restaurant Maya and Maya Cañada ⓕ MEXICAN   These two are the most consistently good restaurants in Palenque. One faces the main plaza from the corner of Independencia and Hidalgo, the other is in the Cañada (ⓒ **916/345-0216**). Menus are somewhat different, but much is the same. Both do a good job with the basics—good strong, locally grown coffee and soft, pliant tortillas. The menu offers a nice combination of Mexican standards and regional specialties. If you're in an exploratory mood, try one of the regional specialties such as the *mole chiapaneco* (dark red, like *mole poblano,* but less sweet) or any of the dishes based on *chaya* or *chipilin* (mild-flavored local greens), such as the soup with *chipilin* and *bolitas de masa* (corn dumplings). If you want something more comforting, go for the chicken and rice vegetable soup, or the *sopa azteca.* The plantains stuffed with cheese and fried Mexican-style are wonderful. Waiters sometimes offer specials not on the menu, and these are often the thing to get. You can also try *tascalate,* a pre-Hispanic drink made of water, *masa,* chocolate, and *achiote,* and served room temperature or cold.

Av. Independencia s/n. ⓒ **916/345-0042.** Breakfast $4–$5 (£2–£2.50); main courses $6–$12 (£3–£6). AE, MC, V. Daily 7am–11pm.

ROAD TRIPS FROM PALENQUE
BONAMPAK & YAXCHILAN: MURALS IN THE JUNGLE

Intrepid travelers may want to consider the day trip to the Maya ruins of Bonampak and Yaxchilán. The **ruins of Bonampak,** southeast of Palenque on the Guatemalan border, were discovered in 1946. The site is important for the vivid **murals** of the Maya on the interior walls of one temple. Particularly striking is an impressive battle scene, perhaps the most important painting of pre-Hispanic Mexico. Reproductions of these murals are on view in the Regional Archaeology Museum in Villahermosa.

Several tour companies offer a day trip. The drive to Bonampak is 3 hours. From there you continue by boat to the **ruins of Yaxchilán,** famous for its highly ornamented buildings. Bring rain gear, boots, a flashlight, and bug repellent. All tours include meals and cost about $60 (£30). No matter what agency you sign up with, the hours of departure and return are the same because the vans of the different agencies caravan down and back for safety. You leave at 6am and return at 7pm.

Try **Viajes Na Chan Kan** (© 916/345-2154), at the corner of avenidas Hidalgo and Jiménez, across from the main square, or **Viajes Shivalva,** Calle Merle Green 1 (© **916/345-0411; fax 916/345-0392**). A branch of Viajes Shivalva (© **916/345-0822**) is a block from the *zócalo* (main plaza) at the corner of Juárez and Abasolo, across the hall from the State Tourism Office. It's open Monday to Saturday from 9am to 9pm.

WATERFALLS AT MISOL HA & AGUA AZUL

A popular excursion from Palenque is a day trip to the Misol Ha waterfall and Agua Azul. **Misol Ha** is 20km (12 miles) from Palenque, in the direction of Ocosingo. It takes about 30 minutes to get there, depending on the traffic. The turn-off is clearly marked; you'll turn right and drive another 1½ km (1 mile). The place is absolutely beautiful. Water pours from a rocky cliff into a broad pool of green water bordered by thick tropical vegetation. There's a small restaurant and some rustic cabins for rent for $30 to $40 (£15–£20) per night, depending on the size of the cabin. The place is run by the *ejido* cooperative that owns the site, and it does a good job of maintaining the place. To inquire about the cabins, call © **916/345-1506.** Admission for the day is $1 (50p).

Approximately 44km (27 miles) beyond Misol Ha are the **Agua Azul waterfalls**—270m (886 ft.) of tumbling falls with lots of water. There are cabins for rent here, too, but I would rather stay at Misol Ha. You can swim either above or below the falls, but make sure you don't get pulled by the current. You can see both places in the same day or stop to see them on your way to Ocosingo and San Cristóbal. Agua Azul is prettiest after 3 or 4 consecutive dry days; heavy rains can make the water murky. Check with guides or other travelers about the water quality before you decide to go. The cost to enter is $2 (£1) per person. Trips to both of these places can be arranged through just about any hotel.

OCOSINGO & THE RUINS OF TONINA

By the time you get to Agua Azul, you're half way to Ocosingo, which lies halfway between Palenque and San Cristóbal. So, instead of returning for the night to Palenque, you can go on to Ocosingo. It's higher up and more comfortable than Palenque. It's a nice little town, not touristy, not a lot to do other than see the ruins of Toniná. But it is a nice place to spend the night so that you can see the ruins early before moving on to San Cristóbal. There are about a half dozen small hotels in town; the largest is not the most desirable. I would stay at the **Hospedaje Esmeralda** (© **919/673-0014**) or the **Hotel Central** (© **919/673-0024**) on the main square. Both of these are small and simple, but welcoming.

Ruins of Tonina ⊛

The ruins of Toniná (the name translates as "house of rocks") are 14km (9 miles) east of Ocosingo. You can take a cab there and catch a *colectivo* to return. The city dates from the Classic period and covered a large area, but the excavated and restored part is all on one hillside that faces out towards a broad valley. This site is not really set up for lots of tourists. There's a lot of up and down, and some of it is a little precarious. It's not a good place to take kids. Admission is $3.50 (£1.75).

This complex of courtyards, rooms, and stairways is built on multiple levels that are irregular and asymmetrical. The overall effect is that of a ceremonial area with multiple foci instead of a clearly discernable center.

As early as A.D. 350, Toniná emerged as a dynastic center. In the 7th and 8th centuries it was locked in a struggle with rival Palenque and, to a lesser degree, with far-away Calakmul. This has led some scholars to see Toniná as more militaristic than its neighbors—a sort of Sparta of the classic Maya. Toniná's greatest victory came in 711, when, under the rule of Kan B'alam, it attacked Palenque and captured its king, K'an Joy Chitam, depicted on a stone frieze twisted, his arms bound with rope.

But the single most important artifact yet found at Toniná, is up around the fifth level of the acropolis—a large stucco frieze divided into panels by a feathered framework adorned with the heads of sacrificial victims (displayed upside down) and some rather horrid creatures. The largest figure is a skeletal image holding a decapitated head—very vivid and very puzzling. There is actually a stylistic parallel with some murals of the Teotihuacán culture of central Mexico. The other special thing about Toniná is that it holds the distinction of having the last ever date recorded in the long count (A.D. 909), which marks the end of the Classic period.

3 San Cristóbal de las Casas ⟨★⟨★⟨★

229km (142 miles) SW of Palenque; 80km (50 miles) E of Tuxtla Gutiérrez; 74km (46 miles) NW of Comitán; 166km (103 miles) NW of Cuauhtémoc; 451km (280 miles) E of Oaxaca

San Cristóbal is a colonial town of white stucco walls and red-tile roofs, of cobblestone streets and narrow sidewalks, of graceful arcades and open plazas. It lies in a green valley 2,120m (6,954 ft.) high. The city owes part of its name to the 16th-century cleric Fray Bartolomé de las Casas, who was the town's first bishop and spent the rest of his life waging a political campaign to protect the indigenous peoples of the Americas.

Surrounding the city are many villages of Mayan-speaking Indians who display great variety in their language, dress, and customs, making this area one of the most fascinating in Mexico. San Cristóbal is the principal market town for these Indians, and their point of contact with the outside world. Most of them trek down from the surrounding mountains to sell goods and run errands

Several Indian villages lie within reach of San Cristóbal by road: **Chamula,** with its weavers and unorthodox church; **Zinacantán,** whose residents practice their own syncretic religion; **Tenejapa, San Andrés,** and **Magdalena,** known for brocaded textiles; **Amatenango del Valle,** a town of potters; and **Aguacatenango,** known for embroidery. Most of these "villages" consist of little more than a church and the municipal government building, with homes scattered for miles around and a general gathering only for church and market days (usually Sun).

Many Indians now live on the outskirts of town because they've been expelled from their villages over religious differences. They are known as *los expulsados.* No longer involved in farming, they make their living in commerce and handicrafts. Most still wear traditional dress, but they've adopted Protestant religious beliefs that prevent them from partaking in many of their community's civic and religious celebrations.

The influx of outsiders hasn't created in most Indians a desire to adopt mainstream customs and dress. It's interesting to note that the communities closest to San Cristóbal are the most resistant to change. The greatest threat to the cultures in this area comes not from tourism but from the action of large market forces, population pressures, environmental damage, and poverty. The Indians aren't interested in acting or looking like the foreigners they see. They may steal glances or even stare at tourists, but mainly they pay little attention to outsiders, except as potential buyers for handicrafts.

You may see or hear the word *Jovel,* San Cristóbal's Indian name, incorporated often in the names of businesses. You'll hear the word *coleto,* used in reference to someone or something from San Cristóbal. You'll see signs for *tamales coletos, pan coleto,* and *desayuno coleto* (Cristóbal breakfast).

The Zapatista Movement & Chiapas

In January 1994, Indians from this area rebelled against the Mexican government over health care, education, land distribution, and representative government. Their organization, the **Zapatista Liberation Army,** known as EZLN (Ejército Zapatista de Liberación Nacional), and its leader, Subcomandante Marcos, have become emblematic of the problems Mexico has with social justice. In the last couple of years, the rhetoric of armed revolt has ended, and the Zapatistas are talking about building a broad leftist coalition—but not a political party. What this means for Mexican politics is not clear, but for travelers it means not having to worry about political unrest.

ESSENTIALS
GETTING THERE & DEPARTING
BY PLANE   Flights from Mexico City have been canceled. The closest airport is in Tuxtla Gutiérrez.

BY CAR   From Tuxtla Gutiérrez, the 1½-hour trip winds through beautiful mountain country. From Palenque, the road is just as beautiful (if longer—5 hr.), and it provides jungle scenery, but portions of it may be heavily potholed or obstructed during rainy season. Check with the local state tourism office before driving.

BY TAXI   Taxis from Tuxtla Gutiérrez to San Cristóbal cost around $50 (£25). Another way to travel to and from Tuxtla is by *combi.* The Volkswagen vans, which can get extremely crowded, make the run every 15 to 30 minutes. They can be found just off the highway by the bus station. You'll have to ask someone to point them out to you because there isn't a sign.

BY BUS   The two bus stations in town are directly across the Pan American Highway from each other. The smaller one belongs to **Transportes Rodolfo Figueroa,** which provides first-class service to and from Tuxtla (every 40 min.) and Palenque (four buses per day, with a stop in Ocosingo—cheaper than the competition). For other destinations, go to the large station run by **ADO** and its affiliates, Altos, Cristóbal Colón, and Maya de Oro. This company offers service to and from Tuxtla (12 buses per day), Palenque (almost every hour), and several other destinations: Mérida (two buses per day), Villahermosa (two buses per day), Oaxaca (two buses per day), and Puerto Escondido (two buses per day). To buy a bus ticket without going down to the station, go to the **Ticket Bus** agency, Real de Guadalupe 5 (© **967/678-8503**). Hours are Monday to Saturday from 7am to 11pm, Sunday from 9am to 5pm.

ORIENTATION
ARRIVING   To get to the main plaza from the highway, turn on to **Avenida Insurgentes** (at the traffic light). From the bus station, the main plaza is 9 blocks north up Avenida Insurgentes (a 10-min. walk, slightly uphill). Cabs are cheap and plentiful.

VISITOR INFORMATION   The **State Tourism Office** is better than the municipal office. It's just half a block south of the main plaza, at Av. Hidalgo 1-B (© **967/678-6570**); it's open Monday to Friday from 8am to 8pm, Saturday from 9am to 8pm, and Sunday from 9am to 2pm. The **Municipal Tourism Office** (©/fax **967/678-0665**)

San Cristóbal de las Casas

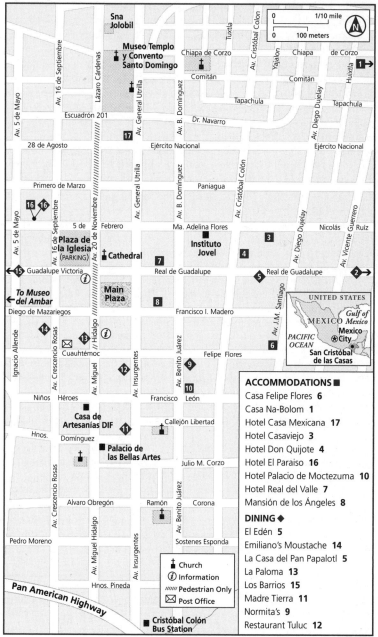

is in the town hall, west of the main square. Hours are Monday to Saturday from 9am to 8pm. Check the bulletin board here for apartments, shared rides, cultural events, and local tours. Both offices are helpful, but the state office is open an hour later and is better staffed.

CITY LAYOUT San Cristóbal is laid out on a grid; the main north-south axis is **Insurgentes/Utrilla,** and the east-west axis is **Mazariegos/Madero.** All streets change names when they cross either of these streets. The *zócalo* (main plaza) lies where they intersect. An important street to know is **Real de Guadalupe,** which runs from the plaza eastward to the church of Guadalupe; located on it are many hotels and restaurants. The market is 7 blocks north of the *zócalo* along Utrilla.

Take note that this town has at least three streets named Domínguez and two streets named Flores. There are Hermanos Domínguez, Belisario Domínguez, and Pantaleón Domínguez; and María Adelina Flores and Dr. Felipe Flores.

GETTING AROUND Most of the sights and shopping in San Cristóbal are within walking distance of the plaza.

Urbano **buses** (minibuses) take passengers between town and the residential neighborhoods. All buses pass by the market and central plaza on their way through town. Utrilla and Avenida 16 de Septiembre are the two main arteries; all buses use the market area as the last stop. Any bus on Utrilla will take you to the market.

Colectivos to outlying villages depart from the public market at Avenida Utrilla. Buses late in the day are usually very crowded. Always check to see when the last or next-to-last bus returns from wherever you're going, and then take the one before that—those last buses sometimes don't materialize, and you might be stranded. I speak from experience!

Rental cars come in handy for trips to the outlying villages and may be worth the expense when shared by a group, but keep in mind that insurance is invalid on unpaved roads. Try **Optima Car Rental,** Av. Mazariegos 39 (© **967/674-5409**). Office hours are daily from 9am to 1pm and 5 to 8pm. You'll save money by arranging the rental from your home country; otherwise, a day's rental with insurance will cost around $60 (£30) for a VW Beetle with manual transmission, the cheapest car available.

Scooters can be rented from Darren and Natasha, two easygoing Australians who tell me that they've found the best way to enjoy the city and surrounding countryside. Look for **Croozy Scooters** (© **967/631-4329**) at Belisario Domínguez 7-A.

Bikes are another option for getting around the city; a day's rental is about $10 (£5). **Los Pingüinos,** Av. Ecuador 4-B (© **967/678-0202;** pinguinosmex@yahoo. com), offers bike tours to a few out-of-town locations. Tours in the valley around San Cristóbal last 4 to 6 hours and cost $25 to $30 (£13–£15). It's open daily from 10am to 2:30pm and 4 to 7pm.

FAST FACTS: San Cristóbal de las Casas

Area Code The telephone area code is 967.

Books The People of the Bat: Mayan Tales and Dreams from Zinacantán, by Robert M. Laughlin, is a priceless collection of beliefs from that village near San Cristóbal. Another good book with a completely different view of today's Maya is *The Heart of the Sky,* by Peter Canby, who traveled among the Maya to chronicle their struggles (and wrote his book before the Zapatista uprising).

Bookstore For the best selection of new and used books and reading material in English, go to **La Pared,** Av. Hidalgo 2 (© **967/678-6367**). The owner, Dana Gay Burton, keeps a great collection of books on the Maya, and Mexico in general, both fiction and nonfiction.

Bulletin Boards San Cristóbal is a cultural crossroads for travelers, and several places maintain bulletin boards with information on Spanish classes, local specialty tours, rooms or houses to rent, rides needed, and so on. These include boards at the **Tourism Office, Café El Puente, Madre Tierra,** and **Casa Na-Bolom.**

Climate San Cristóbal can be chilly when the sun isn't out, especially during the winter. It's 2,120m (6,954 ft.) above sea level. Most hotels are not heated, although some have fireplaces. There is always a possibility of rain, but I would avoid going to San Cristóbal from late August to late October, during the height of the rainy season.

Currency Exchange There are at least five *casas de cambio* on Real de Guadalupe, near the main square, and a couple under the colonnade facing the square. Most are open until 8pm, and some are open Sunday. There are also a number of ATMs.

Doctor Try **Dr. Roberto Lobato,** Av. Belisario Domínguez 17, at Calle Flavio A. Paniagua (© **967/678-7777**). Don't be unsettled by the fact that his office is next door to Funerales Canober.

Internet Access There are Internet cafes everywhere.

Parking If your hotel does not have parking, use the *estacionamiento* (underground public lot) in front of the cathedral, just off the main square on 16 de Septiembre. Entry is from Calle 5 de Febrero.

Post Office The *correo* is at Crescencio Rosas and Cuauhtémoc, a block south and west of the main square. It's open Monday to Friday from 8am to 7pm, Saturday from 9am to 1pm.

Spanish Classes The **Instituto Jovel,** María Adelina Flores 21 (Apdo. Postal 62), 29250 San Cristóbal de las Casas, Chi. (©/fax **967/678-4069**), gets higher marks for its Spanish courses than the competition. It also offers classes in weaving and cooking. The **Centro Bilingüe,** at the Centro Cultural El Puente, Real de Guadalupe 55, 29250 San Cristóbal de las Casas, Chi. (© **800/303-4983** in the U.S., or ©/fax 967/678-3723), offers classes in Spanish. Both schools can arrange home stays for their students.

Telephone The best price for long-distance telephone calls and faxing is at **La Pared** bookstore (see "Bookstore," above) at Av. Hidalgo 2, across the street from the State Tourism Office.

EXPLORING SAN CRISTOBAL

San Cristóbal is a lovely town in a lovely region. A lot of people come for the beauty, but the main thing that draws most visitors here is the highland Maya. They can be seen anywhere in San Cristóbal, but most travelers take at least one trip to the outlying villages to get a close-up of Maya life.

ATTRACTIONS IN TOWN

Casa Na-Bolom 𝕬𝕬   If you're interested in the anthropology of the region, you'll want to visit this house museum. Stay here, if you can. The house, built as a seminary in 1891, became the headquarters of anthropologists Frans and Trudy Blom in 1951, and the gathering place of outsiders interested in studying the region. Frans Blom led many early archaeological studies in Mexico, and Trudy was noted for her photographs of the Lacandón Indians and her efforts to save them and their forest homeland. A room at Na-Bolom contains a selection of her Lacandón photographs, and postcards of the photographs are on sale in the gift shop (daily 9am–2pm and 4–7pm). A tour of the home covers the displays of pre-Hispanic artifacts collected by Frans Blom; the cozy library, with its numerous volumes about the region and the Maya (weekdays 10am–2pm); and the gardens Trudy Blom started for the ongoing reforestation of the Lacandón jungle. The tour ends with a showing of *La Reina de la Selva*, an excellent 50-minute film on the Bloms, the Lacandón, and Na-Bolom. Trudy Blom died in 1993, but Na-Bolom continues to operate as a nonprofit public trust.

The 12 guest rooms, named for surrounding villages, are decorated with local objects and textiles. All rooms have fireplaces and private bathrooms. Prices (including breakfast and admission to the museum) are $70 (£35) single, $90 (£45) double.

Even if you're not a guest here, you can come for a meal, usually an assortment of vegetarian and other dishes. Just be sure to make a reservation at least 2½ hours in advance, and be on time. The colorful dining room has one large table, and the eclectic mix of travelers sometimes makes for interesting conversation. Breakfast costs $5 to $7 (£2.50–£3.50); lunch and dinner cost $15 (£7.50) each. Dinner is served at 7pm. Following breakfast (8–10am), a guide not affiliated with the house offers tours to San Juan Chamula and Zinacantán (see "The Nearby Maya Villages & Countryside," below).

Av. Vicente Guerrero 3, 29200 San Cristóbal de las Casas, Chi. ✆ **967/678-1418**. Fax 967/678-5586. Group tour and film $5 (£2.50). Tours daily 11:30am (Spanish only) and 4:30pm. Leave the square on Real de Guadalupe, walk 4 blocks to Av. Vicente Guerrero, and turn left; Na-Bolom is 5½ blocks up Guerrero.

Catedral   San Cristóbal's main cathedral was built in the 1500s. It has little of interest inside besides a lovely, uncommon beam ceiling and a carved wooden pulpit.

Calle 20 de Noviembre at Guadalupe Victoria. No phone. Free admission. Daily 7am–6pm.

El Mercado   Once you've visited Santo Domingo (see listing below), meander through the San Cristóbal town market and the surrounding area. Every time I do, I see something different to elicit my curiosity.

By Santo Domingo church. No phone. Mon–Sat 8am–7pm.

Museo del Ambar 𝕬   If you've been in this town any time at all, you know what a big deal amber is here. Chiapas is the third-largest producer of amber in the world, and many experts prefer its amber for its colors and clarity. A couple of stores tried calling themselves museums, but they didn't fool anybody. Now a real museum moves methodically through all the issues surrounding amber—mining, shaping, and identifying it, as well as the different varieties found in other parts of the world. It's interesting, it's cheap, and you get to see the restored area of the old convent it occupies. There are a couple of beautiful pieces of worked amber that are on permanent loan—make sure you see them. In mid-August, the museum holds a contest for local artisans who work amber. Check it out.

Exconvento de la Merced, Diego de Mazariegos s/n. ℂ **967/678-9716**. Admission $2 (£1). Tues–Sun 10am–2pm and 4–7pm.

Museo Templo y Convento Santo Domingo   Inside the front door of the carved-stone plateresque facade, there's a beautiful gilded wooden altarpiece built in 1560, walls with saints, and gilt-framed paintings. Attached to the church is the former Convent of Santo Domingo, which houses a small museum about San Cristóbal and Chiapas. The museum has changing exhibits and often shows cultural films. It's 5 blocks north of the *zócalo,* in the market area.

Av. 20 de Noviembre. ℂ **967/678-1609**. Free admission to church; museum $2 (£1). Museum Tues–Sun 10am–5pm; church daily 10am–2pm and 5–8pm.

Palacio de las Bellas Artes   Don't miss this building if you are interested in the arts. It periodically hosts dance events, art shows, and other performances. The schedule of events is usually posted on the door if the Bellas Artes is not open. There's a public library next door. Around the corner, the Centro Cultural holds concerts and other performances; check the posters on the door to see what's scheduled.

Av. Hidalgo, 4 blocks south of the plaza. No phone.

Templo de San Cristóbal   For the best view of San Cristóbal, climb the seemingly endless steps to this church and *mirador* (lookout point). A visit here requires stamina. There are 22 more churches in town, some of which also demand strenuous climbs.

At the very end of Calle Hermanos Domínguez.

HORSEBACK RIDING

The **Casa de Huéspedes Margarita,** Real de Guadalupe 34, and **Hotel Real del Valle** (see "Where to Stay," below) can arrange horseback rides for around $15 (£7.50) for a day, including a guide. Reserve your steed at least a day in advance. A horseback-riding excursion might go to San Juan Chamula, to nearby caves, or up into the hills.

THE NEARBY MAYA VILLAGES & COUNTRYSIDE

The Indian communities around San Cristóbal are fascinating worlds unto themselves. If you are unfamiliar with these indigenous cultures, you will understand and appreciate more of what you see by visiting them with a guide, at least for your first foray out into the villages. Guides are acquainted with members of the communities and are viewed with less suspicion than newcomers. These communities have their own laws and customs—and visitors' ignorance is no excuse. Entering these communities is tantamount to leaving Mexico, and if something happens, the state and federal authorities will not intervene except in case of a serious crime.

The best guided trips are the locally grown ones. Three operators go to the neighboring villages in small groups. They all charge the same price ($12/£6 per person), use minivans for transportation, and speak English. They do, however, have their own interpretations and focus.

Pepe leaves from **Casa Na-Bolom** (see "Attractions in Town," above) for daily trips to San Juan Chamula and Zinacantán at 10am, returning to San Cristóbal between 2 and 3pm. Pepe looks at cultural continuities, community relationships, and religion.

Alex and Raúl can be found in front of the cathedral between 9:15 and 9:30am. They are quite personable and get along well with the Indians in the communities. They focus on cultural values and their expression in social behavior, which provides a glimpse of the details and the texture of life in these communities (and, of course, they talk about religion). Their tour is very good. They can be reached at © **967/678-3741** or chamul@hotmail.com.

For excursions farther afield, see "Road Trips from San Cristóbal," later in this chapter. Also, Alex and Raúl can be contracted for trips to other communities besides Chamula and Zinacantán; talk to them.

CHAMULA & ZINACANTAN   A side trip to the village of San Juan Chamula will get you into the spirit of life around San Cristóbal. Sunday, when the market is in full swing, is the best day to go for shopping; other days, when you'll be less impeded by eager children selling their crafts, are better for seeing the village and church.

The village, 8km (5 miles) northeast of San Cristóbal, has a large church, a plaza, and a municipal building. Each year, a new group of citizens is chosen to live in the municipal center as caretakers of the saints, settlers of disputes, and enforcers of village rules. As in other nearby villages, on Sunday local leaders wear their leadership costumes, including beautifully woven straw hats loaded with colorful ribbons befitting their high position. They solemnly sit together in a long line somewhere around the central square. Chamula is typical of other villages in that men are often away working in the "hot lands," harvesting coffee or cacao, while women stay home to tend the sheep, the children, the cornfields, and the fires.

Don't leave Chamula without seeing the **church interior.** As you step from bright sunlight into the candlelit interior, you feel as if you've been transported to another country. Pine needles scattered amid a sea of lighted candles cover the tile floor. Saints line the walls, and before them people are often kneeling and praying aloud while passing around bottles of Pepsi-Cola. Shamans are often on hand, passing eggs over sick people or using live or dead chickens in a curing ritual. The statues of saints are similar to those you might see in any Mexican Catholic church, but beyond sharing the same name, they mean something completely different to the Chamulas. Visitors can walk carefully through the church to see the saints or stand quietly in the background.

In Zinacantán, a wealthier village than Chamula, you must sign a strict form promising *not to take any photographs* before you see the two side-by-side **sanctuaries.** Once permission is granted and you have paid a small fee, an escort will usually show you the church, or you may be allowed to see it on your own. Floors may be covered in pine needles here, too, and the rooms are brightly sunlit. The experience is an altogether different one from that of Chamula.

AMATENANGO DEL VALLE   About an hour's ride south of San Cristóbal is Amatenango, a town known mostly for its **women potters.** You'll see their work in San Cristóbal—small animals, jars, and large water jugs—but in the village, you can visit the potters in their homes. Just walk down the dirt streets. Villagers will lean over the walls of family compounds and invite you in to select from their inventory. You may even see them firing the pieces under piles of wood in the open courtyard or painting them with color derived from rusty iron water. The women wear beautiful red-and-yellow *huipiles,* but if you want to take a photograph, you'll have to pay. To get here, take a *colectivo* from the market in San Cristóbal. Before it lets you off, be sure to ask about the return-trip schedule.

AGUACATENANGO   This village, 16km (10 miles) south of Amatenango is known for its **embroidery.** If you've visited San Cristóbal's shops, you'll recognize the white-on-white and black-on-black floral patterns on dresses and blouses for sale. The locals' own regional blouses, however, are quite different.

TENEJAPA   The **weavers** of Tenejapa, 28km (17 miles) from San Cristóbal, make some of the most beautiful and expensive work you'll see in the region. The best time to visit is on market day (Sun and Thurs, though Sun is better). The weavers of Tenejapa taught the weavers of San Andrés and Magdalena—which accounts for the similarity in their designs and colors. To get to Tenejapa, try to find a *colectivo* in the very last row by the market, or hire a taxi. On Tenejapa's main street, several stores sell locally woven regional clothing, and you can bargain for the price.

THE HUITEPEC CLOUD FOREST   **Pronatura,** Av. Benito Juárez 11-B (© **967/ 678-5000**), a private, nonprofit, ecological organization, offers environmentally sensitive tours of the cloud forest. The forest is a haven for **migratory birds,** and more than 100 bird species and 600 plant species have been discovered here. Guided tours run from 9am to noon Tuesday to Sunday. They cost $25 (£13) per group of up to eight people. Make reservations a day in advance. To reach the reserve on your own, drive on the road to Chamula; the turnoff is at Km 3.5. The reserve is open Tuesday to Sunday from 9am to 4pm.

SHOPPING

Many Indian villages near San Cristóbal are noted for **weaving, embroidery, brocade work, leather,** and **pottery,** making the area one of the best in the country for shopping. You'll see beautiful woolen shawls, indigo-dyed skirts, colorful native shirts, and magnificently woven *huipiles,* all of which often come in vivid geometric patterns. A good place to find textiles as well as other handicrafts, besides what's mentioned below, is in and around Santo Domingo and the market. There are a lot of stalls and small shops in that neighborhood that make for interesting shopping. Working in leather, the craftspeople are artisans of the highest caliber. Tie-dyed *jaspe* from Guatemala comes in bolts and is made into clothing. The town is also known for **amber,** sold in several shops, one of the best of which is mentioned below.

CRAFTS

Casa de Artesanías Amanecer   The showroom has examples of every craft practiced in the state. It is run by the government in support of Indian crafts. You should take a look, if only to survey what crafts the region practices. It's open Monday to Friday from 9am to 9pm, Saturday 10am to 9pm, and Sunday 10am to 3pm. Niños Héroes at Hidalgo. © 967/678-1180.

El Encuentro   Noted for having reasonable prices, this shop carries many ritual items, such as new and used men's ceremonial hats, false saints, and iron rooftop adornments, plus many *huipiles* and other textiles. It's open Monday to Saturday from 9am to 8pm. Calle Real de Guadalupe 63-A (between Diego Dujelay and Vicente Guerrero). © 967/ 678-3698.

La Galería   This art gallery beneath a cafe shows the work of well-known national and international painters. Also for sale are paintings and greeting cards by Kiki, the owner, a German artist who has found her niche in San Cristóbal. There are some Oaxacan rugs and pottery, plus unusual silver jewelry. It's open daily from 10am to 9pm. Hidalgo 3. © 967/678-1547.

Lágrimas de la Selva   "Tears of the Jungle" deals in amber and jewelry, and no other amber shop in town that I know of has the variety, quality, or artistic flair of this one. It's not a bargain hunter's turf, but a great place for the curious to go. Often you can watch the jewelers in action. Open daily from 10am to 8pm. Hidalgo 1-C (half block south of the main square). (967/674-6348.

TEXTILES

Plaza de Santo Domingo   The plazas around this church and the nearby Templo de Caridad fill with women in native garb selling their wares. Here you'll find women from Chamula weaving belts or embroidering, surrounded by piles of loomed woolen textiles from their village. Their inventory includes Guatemalan shawls, belts, and bags. There are also some excellent buys on Chiapanecan-made wool vests, jackets, rugs, and shawls, similar to those at Sna Jolobil (described below), if you take the time to look and bargain. Vendors arrive between 9 and 10am and begin to leave around 3pm. Av. Utrilla. No phone.

Sna Jolobil   Meaning "weaver's house" in Mayan, this place is in the former convent (monastery) of Santo Domingo, next to the Templo de Santo Domingo. Groups of Tzotzil and Tzeltal craftspeople operate the cooperative store, which has about 3,000 members who contribute products, help run the store, and share in the moderate profits. Their works are simply beautiful; prices are high, as is the quality. It's open Monday to Saturday from 9am to 2pm and 4 to 6pm; credit cards are accepted. Calzada Lázaro Cárdenas 42 (Plaza Santo Domingo, between Navarro and Nicaragua). (967/678-2646.

Unión Regional de Artesanías de los Altos   Also known as J'pas Joloviletic, this cooperative of weavers is smaller than Sna Jolobil (described above) and not as sophisticated in its approach to potential shoppers. It sells blouses, textiles, pillow covers, vests, sashes, napkins, baskets, and purses. It's near the market and worth looking around. Open Monday to Saturday from 9am to 2pm and 4 to 7pm, Sunday from 9am to 1pm. Av. Utrilla 43. (967/678-2848.

WHERE TO STAY

Among the most interesting places to stay in town is the seminary-turned-hotel-museum **Casa Na-Bolom;** see "Attractions in Town," earlier in this chapter.

Hotels in San Cristóbal are inexpensive. You can do pretty well for $40 to $60 (£20–£30) per night per double. Rates listed here include taxes. High season is Easter week, July, August, and December.

MODERATE

Casa Felipe Flores ✿✿   This beautifully restored colonial house is the perfect setting for getting a feel for San Cristóbal. The patios and common rooms are relaxing and comfortable, and their architectural details are so very *coleto*. The guest rooms are nicely furnished and full of character. And they are warm in winter. The owners, Nancy and David Orr, are gracious people who enjoy sharing their appreciation and knowledge of Chiapas and the Maya. Their cook serves up righteous breakfasts.

Calle Dr. Felipe Flores 36, 29230 San Cristóbal de las Casas, Chi. (/fax 967/678-3996. www.felipeflores.com. 5 units. $90–$110 (£45–£50) double. Rates include full breakfast. 10% service charge. No credit cards. Limited street parking. **Amenities:** Tour info; laundry service; library. *In room:* No phone.

Hotel Casa Mexicana ✿✿   Created from a large mansion, this beautiful hotel with a colonial-style courtyard offers comfortable lodging. Rooms, courtyards, the restaurant, and the lobby are decorated in modern-traditional Mexican style, with warm tones of yellow and red. The rooms are carpeted and come with two double beds or one king-size. They have good lighting, electric heaters, and spacious bathrooms. Guests are welcome to use the sauna, and inexpensive massages can be arranged. The hotel handles a lot of large tour groups; it can be quiet and peaceful one day, full and bustling the next. There is a new addition to the hotel across the street, but I like the doubles in the original section better. This hotel is 3 blocks north of the main plaza.

28 de Agosto 1 (at Utrilla), 29200 San Cristóbal de las Casas, Chi. ℂ **967/678-1348** or -0698. Fax 967/678-2627. www.hotelcasamexicana.com. 55 units. High season $100 (£50) double, $160 (£80) junior suite, $180 (£90) suite; low season $85 (£43) double, $140 (£70) junior suite, $170 (£85) suite. AE, MC, V. Free secure parking 1½ blocks away. **Amenities:** Restaurant; bar; sauna; tour info; room service; massage; babysitting; laundry service. *In room:* TV, hair dryer (on request).

Hotel Casavieja
The Casavieja is aptly named: It has a charming old feel that is San Cristóbal to a tee. Originally built in 1740, it has undergone restoration and new construction faithful to the original design in essentials such as wood-beam ceilings. One nod toward modernity is carpeted floors, a welcome feature on cold mornings. The rooms also come with electric heaters. Bathrooms vary, depending on what section of the hotel you're in, but all are adequate. The hotel's restaurant, Doña Rita, faces the interior courtyard, with tables on the patio and inside, and offers good food at reasonable prices. The hotel is 3½ blocks northeast of the plaza.

María Adelina Flores 27 (between Cristóbal Colón and Diego Dujelay), 29200 San Cristóbal de las Casas, Chi. ℂ/fax **967/678-6868** or -0385. www.casavieja.com.mx. 39 units. $66–$82 (£33–£41) double. AE, MC, V. Free parking. **Amenities:** Restaurant; bar; room service; laundry service. *In room:* TV.

Hotel El Paraíso
For the independent traveler, this is a safe haven from the busloads of tour groups that can disrupt the atmosphere and service at other hotels. Rooms are small but beautifully decorated. They have comfortable beds and good reading lights; some even have a ladder to a loft holding a second bed. Bathrooms are small, too, but the plumbing is good. The entire hotel is decorated in terra cotta and blue, with beautiful wooden columns and beams supporting the roof. The hotel's restaurant, El Edén (see "Where to Dine," below) may be the best in town.

Av. 5 de Febrero 19, 29200 San Cristóbal de las Casas, Chi. ℂ **967/678-0085** or -5382. Fax 967/678-5168. www. hotelposadaparaiso.com. 14 units. $60–$72 (£30–£36) double. AE, MC, V. No parking. **Amenities:** Restaurant; bar; tour info; room service; laundry service. *In room:* TV.

Mansión de los Angeles
This hotel with a good location offers good service and tidy rooms and public areas. Guest rooms are medium size and come with either a single and a double bed or two double beds. The rooms are warmer and better lit than at most hotels in this town. They are also quiet. Some of the bathrooms are a little small. Most rooms have windows that open onto a pretty courtyard with a fountain. The rooftop sun deck is a great siesta spot.

Calle Francisco Madero 17, 29200 San Cristóbal de las Casas, Chi. ℂ **967/678-1173** or -4371. hotelangeles@ prodigy.com.mx. 20 units. $60–$72 (£30–£36) double. MC, V. Limited street parking. *In room:* TV.

INEXPENSIVE
Hotel Don Quijote
Rooms in this three-story hotel (no elevator) are small but quiet, carpeted, and well lit, but a little worn. All have two double beds with reading lamps over them, tiled bathrooms, and plenty of hot water. There's complimentary coffee in the mornings. It's 2½ blocks east of the plaza.

Cristóbal Colón 7 (near Real de Guadalupe), 29200 San Cristóbal de las Casas, Chi. ℂ **967/678-0920.** Fax 967/678-0346. 24 units. $28–$40 (£14–£20) double. MC, V. Limited street parking. *In room:* TV.

Hotel Palacio de Moctezuma
This three-story hotel has open courtyards and more greenery than others in this price range. Fresh-cut flowers tucked around tile

fountains are its hallmark. The rooms have carpeting and tiled bathrooms with showers; many are quite large but, alas, can be cold in winter. The restaurant looks out on the interior courtyard. On the third floor is a solarium with comfortable tables and chairs and great city views. The hotel is 3½ blocks southeast of the main plaza.

Juárez 16 (at León), 29200 San Cristóbal de las Casas, Chi. ✆ **967/678-0352** or -1142. Fax 967/678-1536. 42 units. $38–$44 (£19–£22) double. MC, V. Free limited parking. **Amenities:** Restaurant. *In room:* TV, no phone.

Hotel Real del Valle *(Value)*   This hotel has great location just off the main plaza. The rooms in the back three-story section have new bathrooms, big closets, and tile floors. The beds are comfortable, and the water is hot—all for a good price. In winter the rooms are a little cold. Amenities include a rooftop solarium.

Real de Guadalupe 14, 29200 San Cristóbal de las Casas, Chi. ✆ **967/678-0680**. Fax 967/678-3955. hrvalle@mundo maya.com.mx. 36 units. $28–$38 (£14–£19) double. No credit cards. Free parking. **Amenities:** Solarium; laundry service. *In room:* TV, no phone.

WHERE TO DINE

San Cristóbal is not known for its cuisine, but you can eat well at several restaurants. For baked goods, try the **Panadería La Hojaldra,** Insurgentes 14 (✆ **967/678-4286**). It's open daily from 8am to 9:30pm. In addition to the restaurants listed below, consider making reservations for dinner at **Casa Na-Bolom** (see "Attractions in Town," earlier in this chapter).

MODERATE

El Edén *(★★)* INTERNATIONAL   This is a small, quiet restaurant where it is obvious that somebody who enjoys the taste of good food prepares the meals; just about anything except Swiss rarebit is good. The meats are especially tender, and the margaritas are especially dangerous (one is all it takes). Specialties include Swiss cheese fondue for two, Edén salad, and brochette. This is where locals go for a splurge. It's 2 blocks from the main plaza.

In the Hotel El Paraíso, Av. 5 de Febrero 19. ✆ **967/678-5382**. Breakfast $5 (£2.50); main courses $6–$12 (£3–£6). AE, MC, V. Daily 8am–9pm.

La Paloma INTERNATIONAL/MEXICAN   La Paloma I particularly like in the evening because the lighting is so well done. Both the Mexican and the other dishes are much more mainstream than what you get at Los Barrios—fewer surprises. For starters, I enjoyed the *quesadillas* cooked Mexico City style (small fried packets of *masa* stuffed with a variety of fillings). Don't make my mistake of trying to share them with your dinner companion; it will only lead to trouble. Mexican classics include *albóndigas en chipotle* (meatballs in a thick chipotle sauce), Oaxacan black *mole,* and a variety of *chiles rellenos.* Avoid the *profiteroles.*

Hidalgo 3. ✆ **967/678-1547**. Main courses $7–$15 (£3.50–£7.50). MC, V. Daily 9am–midnight.

Los Barrios CONTEMPORARY MEXICAN   For Mexican food in San Cristóbal, I can't think of a better place than this. The tortilla soup was the best I've had here (called *sopa de la abuela*). For something different, there's a mushroom–and–cactus paddle soup. The main courses, while kept to a manageable number, offer enough variety to please several tastes. There are a couple of novel *chile relleno* combinations and a chicken breast *adobado* with plantain stuffing. The restaurant is in a patio with an interesting rough-wood enclosure. It's quiet and inviting.

Guadalupe Victoria 25 (between 3 de Mayo and Matamoros). ✆ **967/678-1910**. Main courses $6–$10 (£3–£5). MC, V. Mon–Sat 1–10pm; Sun buffet 1:30–6pm.

Pierre *(★* FRENCH   Who would have thought that you could get good French food in San Cristóbal? And yet, Frenchman Pierre Niviere offers an appealing selection of traditional French dishes, simplified and tweaked for the tropical surroundings. I showed up on a Sunday, enjoyed the fixed menu, and left well satisfied.

Real de Guadalupe 73. *(© 967/678-7211.* Main courses $6–$16 (£3–£8); Sunday fixed menu $10 (£5). No credit cards. Daily 1:30–11pm.

INEXPENSIVE

Emiliano's Moustache *(Finds* MEXICAN/TACOS   Like any right-thinking traveler, I initially avoided this place on account of its unpromising name and some cartoonlike figures by the door. But a conversation with some local folk overcame my prejudice and tickled my sense of irony. Sure enough, the place was crowded with *coletos* enjoying the restaurant's highly popular *comida corrida* and delicious tacos, and there wasn't a foreigner in sight. The daily menu is posted by the door; if that doesn't appeal, you can choose from a menu of taco plates (a mixture of fillings cooked together and served with tortillas and a variety of hot sauces).

Crescencio Rosas 7. *(© 967/678-7246.* Main courses $4–$8 (£2–£4); *comida corrida* $4 (£2). No credit cards. Daily 8am–midnight.

La Casa del Pan Papalotl VEGETARIAN   This place is best known for its vegetarian lunch buffet with salad bar. The vegetables and most of the grains are organic. Kippy, the owner, has a home garden and a field near town where she grows vegetables. She buys high-altitude, locally grown, organic red wheat with which she bakes her breads. These are all sourdough breads, which she likes because she feels they are easily digested and have good texture and taste. The pizzas are a popular item. The restaurant shares space with other activities in the cultural center El Puente, which has gallery space, a language school, and cinema.

Real de Guadalupe 55 (between Diego Dujelay and Cristóbal Colón). *(© 967/678-7215.* Main courses $5–$10 (£2.50–£5); lunch buffet $5–$6 (£2.50–£3). No credit cards. Mon–Sat 9am–10pm, lunch buffet 2–4pm.

Madre Tierra INTERNATIONAL/VEGETARIAN   A lot of vegetarians live in this town, and they have many options. This one is almost an institution in San Cristóbal. The restaurant is known for its baked goods, pastas, pizza, and quiche. They also offer fresh salads and international main courses that are safe and dependable. Good for breakfast, too. Madre Tierra is 3½ blocks south of the plaza.

Av. Insurgentes 19. *(© 967/678-4297.* Main courses $4–$8 (£2–£4); *comida corrida* (served after noon) $6 (£3). No credit cards. Restaurant daily 8am–9:45pm. Bakery Mon–Sat 9am–8pm; Sun 9am–2pm.

Normita's MEXICAN   Normita's is famous for its *pozole,* a hearty chicken and hominy soup to which you add a variety of things. It also offers cheap, dependable, short-order Mexican mainstays. Normita's is an informal "people's" restaurant; the open kitchen takes up one corner of the room, and tables sit in front of a large mural of a fall forest scene from some faraway place. It's 2 blocks southeast of the plaza.

Av. Juárez 6 (at Dr. José Flores). No phone. Breakfast $2–$3 (£1–£1.50); *pozole* $3 (£1.50); tacos $2.50 (£1.25). No credit cards. Daily 7am–11pm.

Restaurant Tuluc *(Value* MEXICAN/INTERNATIONAL   A real bargain here is the popular *comida corrida*—it's delicious and filling. Other favorites are sandwiches and enchiladas. The house specialty is *filete Tuluc,* a beef filet wrapped around spinach and cheese served with fried potatoes and green beans; while not the best cut of meat, it's certainly priced right. The Chiapaneco breakfast is a filling quartet of juice, toast, two Chiapanecan tamales, and coffee. Tuluc also has that rarest of rarities in Mexico, a nonsmoking section. The restaurant is 1½ blocks south of the plaza.

Av. Insurgentes 5 (between Cuauhtémoc and Francisco León). © 967/678-2090. Breakfast $2–$3 (£1–£1.50); main courses $4–$5 (£2–£2.50); *comida corrida* (served 2–4pm) $4 (£2). No credit cards. Daily 7am–10pm.

COFFEEHOUSES

Because Chiapas-grown coffee is highly regarded, it's not surprising that coffeehouses proliferate here. Most are concealed in the nooks and crannies of San Cristóbal's side streets. Try **Café La Selva,** Crescencio Rosas 9 (© **967/678-7244**), for coffee served in all its varieties and brewed from organic beans; it is open daily from 9am to 11pm. A more traditional-style cafe, where locals meet to talk over the day's news, is **Café San Cristóbal,** Cuauhtémoc 1 (© **967/678-3861**). It's open Monday to Saturday from 9am to 10pm, Sunday from 9am to 9pm. There is also a coffee museum with a cafe inside with the confusing name **Café Museo Café.** It's at María Adelina Flores 10 (© **967/678-7876**)

SAN CRISTOBAL AFTER DARK

San Cristóbal is blessed with a variety of nightlife, both resident and migratory. There is a lot of live music, surprisingly good and varied. The bars and restaurants are cheap. And they are easy to get to: You can hit all the places mentioned here without setting foot in a cab. Weekends are best, but on any night you'll find something going on.

Almost all the clubs in San Cristóbal host Latin music of one genre or another. **El Cocodrilo** (© **967/678-1140**), on the main plaza in the Hotel Santa Clara, has acoustic performers playing Latin folk music *(trova, andina)*. Relax at a table in what usually is a not-too-crowded environment. After that your choices are varied. For Latin dance music there's a place just a block away on the corner of Madero and Juárez called **Latino's** (© **967/678-9972**)—good bands playing a mix of salsa, merengue, and cumbia. On weekends it gets crowded, but it has a good-size dance floor. Another club, **Blue** (© **967/678-2000**), is in the opposite direction on the other side of the main square. It has live music on weekends playing salsa, reggae, and some electronic music. The place is dark and has just a bit of the urban edge to it. From there you can walk down the pedestrian-only 20 de Noviembre to visit a couple of popular bars—**Revolución** and **El Circo.**

ROAD TRIPS FROM SAN CRISTOBAL

For excursions to nearby villages, see "The Nearby Maya Villages & Countryside," earlier in this chapter; for destinations farther away, there are several local travel agencies. But first you should try **Alex and Raúl** (p. 271). You can also try **ATC Travel and Tours,** Calle 5 de Febrero 15, at the corner of 16 de Septiembre (© **967/678-2550;** fax 967/678-3145), across from El Fogón restaurant. The agency has bilingual guides and reliable vehicles. ATC regional tours focus on birds and orchids, textiles, hiking, and camping.

Strangely, the cost of the trips includes a driver but not necessarily a bilingual guide or guided information of any kind. You pay extra for those services, so when checking prices, be sure to flesh out the details.

PALENQUE, BONAMPAK & YAXCHILAN

For information on these destinations, see the section on Palenque, earlier in this chapter.

CHINCULTIC RUINS, COMITAN & MONTEBELLO NATIONAL PARK

Almost 160km (100 miles) southeast of San Cristóbal, near the border with Guatemala, is the **Chincultic** archaeological site and Montebello National Park, with **16 multicolored lakes** and exuberant pine-forest vegetation. Seventy-four kilometers (46 miles) from San Cristóbal is **Comitán,** a pretty hillside town of 40,000 inhabitants known for its flower cultivation and a sugar cane–based liquor called *comitecho.* It's also the last big town along the Pan-American Highway before the Guatemalan border.

The Chincultic ruins, a late Classic site, have barely been excavated, but the main **acropolis,** high up against a cliff, is magnificent to see from below and is worth the walk up for the view. After passing through the gate, you'll see the trail ahead; it passes ruins on both sides. More unexcavated tree-covered ruins flank steep stairs leading up the mountain to the acropolis. From there, you can gaze upon distant Montebello lakes and miles of cornfields and forest. The paved road to the lakes passes six lakes, all different colors and sizes, ringed by cool pine forests; most have parking lots and lookouts. The paved road ends at a small restaurant. The lakes are best seen on a sunny day, when their famous brilliant colors are optimal.

Most travel agencies in San Cristóbal offer a daylong trip that includes the lakes, the ruins, lunch in Comitán, and a stop in the pottery-making village of Amatenango del Valle. If you're driving, follow Highway 190 south from San Cristóbal through the pretty village of Teopisca and then through Comitán; turn left at La Trinitaria, where there's a sign to the lakes. After the Trinitaria turnoff and before you reach the lakes, there's a sign pointing left down a narrow dirt road to the Chincultic ruins.

4 Tuxtla Gutiérrez

82km (51 miles) W of San Cristóbal; 277km (172 miles) S of Villahermosa; 242km (150 miles) NW of Ciudad Cuauhtémoc on the Guatemalan border

Tuxtla Gutiérrez (altitude 557m/1,827 ft.) is the commercial center of Chiapas. Coffee is the basis of the region's economy, along with recent oil discoveries. Tuxtla (pop. 350,000) is a business town, and not a particularly attractive one. For travelers, it's mainly a way station en route to San Cristóbal or the Sumidero Canyon.

ESSENTIALS
GETTING THERE & DEPARTING

BY PLANE Aviacsa (© **961/612-6880** or -8081; www.aviacsa.com) can get you to several cities in Mexico, but all flights go through Mexico City—even flights to Cancún, Chetumal, Mérida, Guatemala City, Villahermosa, and Oaxaca. **Click,** a subsidiary of Mexicana (© **01-800/122-5425** or 961/612-5402; www.clickmx.com), has nonstop flights to and from Mexico City.

Tuxtla has two airports: **Terán** and **Llano San Juan.** The airlines go back and forth with them depending on the season. Be sure to double-check which airport you're departing from, and allow enough time to get there. The Terán airport is 8km (5 miles) from town; the Llano San Juan airport is 18km (11 miles). There is taxi and minivan service from both airports.

BY CAR From Oaxaca, you'll enter Tuxtla by Highway 190. From Villahermosa, or Palenque and San Cristóbal, you'll enter at the opposite end of town on the same highway from the east. In both cases, you'll arrive at the large main square at the center of town, La Plaza Cívica (see "City Layout," below).

From Tuxtla to Villahermosa, take Highway 190 east past the town of Chiapa de Corzo; soon you'll see a sign for Highway 195 north to Villahermosa. To San Cristóbal and Palenque, take Highway 190 east. The road is beautiful but tortuous. It's in good repair to San Cristóbal, but there may be bad spots between San Cristóbal and Palenque. The trip from Tuxtla to Villahermosa takes 8 hours by car; the scenery is beautiful.

BY BUS   The first-class **bus station** (© 961/612-2624) is at the corner of calles 2 Norte and 2 Poniente (see "City Layout," below). All bus lines serving this station and the deluxe section across the street (Uno, Maya de Oro, Cristóbal Colón, Servicios Altos) belong to the same parent company, ADO. The main station sells tickets for all buses. All buses are air-conditioned and have bathrooms. There are two levels of first class; the first-class *económico* has less legroom. Then there's deluxe, which features a few extras: slightly better seats, better movies, and free coffee and soda. There are buses every half-hour to San Cristóbal, eight buses a day to Villahermosa, three or four buses a day to Oaxaca, and five to Palenque. There's usually no need to buy a ticket ahead of time, except during holidays.

ORIENTATION

ARRIVING   The Llano San Juan airport is off Highway 190 west of town, about 40 minutes away; the Terán airport is off the same highway going east of town, about 15 minutes away. A *colectivo* (minivan) is much cheaper than a taxi if you can find one; they leave as soon as they are full. The ADO/Cristóbal Colón bus terminal is downtown.

VISITOR INFORMATION   The **Tourist Office** (© 01-800/280-3500 in Mexico, or 961/613-4499) is in the Secretaría de Fomento Económico building, formerly the Plaza de las Instituciones, on Avenida Central/Bulevar Domínguez, near the Hotel Bonampak Tuxtla. It's on the first floor of the plaza and is open Monday to Friday from 8am to 9pm. The staff at the information booth in front of the office can answer most questions. There are also information booths at the **international airport** (staffed when flights are due) and at the **zoo** (p. 282; Tues–Sun 9am–3pm and 6–9pm).

CITY LAYOUT   Tuxtla is laid out on a grid. The main street, **Avenida Central,** is the east-west axis and is the artery through town for Highway 190. West of the central district it's called **Bulevar Belisario Domínguez,** and in the east it's **Bulevar Angel Albino Corzo.** **Calle Central** is the north-south axis. The rest of the streets have names that include one number and two directions. This tells you how to get to the street. For example, to find the street 5 Norte Poniente (5 North West), you walk 5 blocks north from the center of town and turn west (which is left). To find 3 Oriente Sur, you walk 3 blocks east from the main square and turn south. When people indicate intersections, they can shorten the names because it's redundant. The bus station is at the corner of 2 Norte and 2 Poniente.

GETTING AROUND   **Buses** to all parts of the city converge upon the Plaza Cívica along Calle Central. **Taxi** fares are higher here than in other regions.

FAST FACTS   The local **American Express** representative is Viajes Marabasco, Plaza Bonampak, Loc. 4, Col. Moctezuma, near the tourist office (© **961/612-6998;** fax 961/612-4053). Office hours are Monday to Friday from 9am to 1:30pm and 3:30 to

The Chiapas Highlands

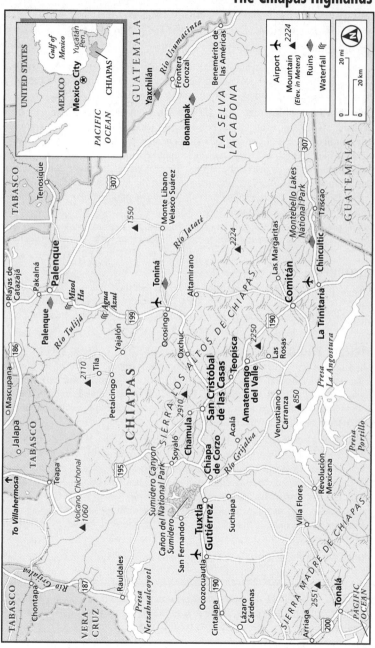

6:30pm. The telephone **area code** is **961.** If you need medical help, the best **clinic** in town is Sanatorio Rojas, Calle 2 Sur Poniente 1847 (© **961/611-2079** or 612-5414).

EXPLORING TUXTLA

Most travelers simply pass through Tuxtla on their way to San Cristóbal or Oaxaca. The excellent zoo and the Sumidero Canyon are the top sights, and you might also visit the Parque Madero and its anthropology museum.

Miguel Alvarez del Toro Zoo (ZOOMAT) 🎯   Located in the forest called El Zapotal, ZOOMAT is one of the best zoos in Mexico. The collection of animals and birds indigenous to this area gives the visitor a tangible sense of what the wilds of Chiapas are like. The zoo keeps jaguars, howler monkeys, owls, and many more exotic animals in roomy cages that replicate their home terrain; the whole zoo is so deeply buried in vegetation that you can almost pretend you're in a natural habitat. Unlike at other zoos I've visited, the animals are almost always on view; many will come to the fence if you make a kissing noise.

Bulevar Samuel León Brinois, southeast of downtown. No phone. Free admission; donations solicited. Tues–Sun 9am–5:30pm. The zoo is about 8km (5 miles) southeast of downtown; catch a bus along Av. Central and at the Calzada.

SHOPPING

The government-operated **Instituto de las Artesanías,** Bulevar Domínguez 2035 (© **961/612-2275**), is a shop and gallery. The two stories of rooms feature an extensive collection of crafts grouped by region and type from throughout the state of Chiapas. It's open Monday to Saturday from 10am to 8pm.

WHERE TO STAY

As Tuxtla booms, the center of the hotel industry has moved out of town, west to Highway 190. As you come in from the airport, you'll notice the new motel-style hotels, such as the **Hotel Flamboyán, Palace Inn, Hotel Laganja,** and **La Hacienda.** All of these are more expensive than those listed here, which are within walking distance of all the downtown attractions.

Hotel Bonampak Tuxtla   This hotel is almost a mile from the town's main square. It's one of those hotels in Mexico to which change comes slowly. This gives it character, and the place is well maintained. The furniture is an old heavy-style, but the mattresses are new and comfortable. The rooms could use a bit more light but they are of good size, with ample bathrooms and closet space.

Bulevar Domínguez 180, 29030 Tuxtla Gutiérrez, Chi. © **961/613-2050.** 70 units. $90 (£45) double. AE, MC, V. Free secured parking. **Amenities:** Restaurant; bar; pool; travel agency; boutique; room service until midnight; laundry service. *In room:* A/C, TV.

Hotel María Eugenia   This five-story hotel on Avenida Central in the middle of town is well maintained. Rooms are medium-size with bathrooms to match. Most of the mattresses are firm.

Av. Central 507, 29030 Tuxtla Gutiérrez, Chi. © **961/613-3767** or 01-800/716-0149 in Mexico. 83 units. $80 (£40) double. AE, MC, V. Free guarded parking. **Amenities:** Restaurant; bar; pool; travel agency; room service until 11pm; laundry service; dry cleaning; nonsmoking rooms. *In room:* A/C, TV, Wi-Fi.

Hotel Regional San Marcos   For a discount hotel, this was by far the best I could find in this town. It's in the downtown zone and very close to the *colectivos* that go to Chiapa de Corzo. Rooms are distributed on four floors (no elevator). They are medium in size, but cheerful. The air-conditioning window units are a bit noisy, but at this rate, it's a minor inconvenience.

1 Sur Oriente 176, 29030 Tuxtla Gutiérrez, Chi. ✆ **961/613-1948** or -1887. hotelsanmarcos@prodigy.net.mx. 40 units. $40 (£20) double. Anyone showing a Frommer's book receives a 10% discount. MC, V. Free parking. **Amenities:** Restaurant; bar; tour info; room service until 11pm. *In room:* A/C, TV.

WHERE TO DINE

For a full sit-down meal, you can try local Chiapan food at **Las Pichanchas,** Av. Central Oriente 837 (✆ **961/612-5351**). It's festively decorated and pretty to look at. The emphasis is on meat, with several heavy dishes on the menu. I would recommend the *filete simojovel* (a thin steak in a not-spicy chile sauce) or the *comida grande,* which is beef in a pumpkin-seed sauce. Eating here is a cultural experience, but I usually head over to the **Flamingo,** 1 Poniente 168, just off Avenida Central (✆ **961/612-0922**), which serves standard Mexican dishes: enchiladas, mole, roast chicken. The restaurant is owned by a Spaniard, who also owns a decent steakhouse called El Asador Castellano, which is on the west side of town. Take a taxi.

If all you want is tacos, there are several good places around the plaza called **El Parque de la Marimba.** This plaza has free *marimba* music nightly and is enjoyable. There you'll find a couple of local taco restaurants bordering the plaza, **Parrilla Suiza** and **El Fogón Norteño.** Both have good grilled tacos. The Parque de la Marimba is on Avenida Central Poniente, 8 blocks west of the main square.

ROAD TRIPS FROM TUXTLA GUTIERREZ: CHIAPA DE CORZO & THE SUMIDERO CANYON

The real reason to stay in Tuxtla is to take a boat trip through the **Canyon of El Sumidero** 𝆑𝆑. The canyon is spectacular, and the boat ride is fun. Boats leave from the docks in **Chiapa de Corzo,** a colonial town of about 50,000 inhabitants that bumps up to Tuxtla. To get there take a taxi or hop on the *colectivo* operated by Transportes Chiapa-Tuxtla (2nd Oriente at 2nd Sur; ✆ 961/616-1339). Buses leave every half-hour from 5:30am to 9:30pm. Cost is $1 (50p). The ride takes a half-hour. Ask to get off at the main square *(parada del parque).* Chiapa de Corzo has a large main square. The two main boat cooperatives have ticket booths under the archways bordering the square. But you don't have to look for these; just go straight to the boats at the embarcadero 1½ blocks below the square.

As you pass the church of Santo Domingo, you'll see a large **ceiba** tree shading the churchyard. In better circumstances these trees get even larger than this, but this one has taken up an interesting position in front of the church. The Maya felt that these trees embodied the connection between the heavens, the world of men, and the underworld because they extend into all three realms.

The **two cooperatives** (the reds and the greens identified by the color of their boats) offer the same service. They work together sharing passengers and such. Boats leave as soon as a minimum of 12 people show up. The interval can be up to an hour or as short as 10 minutes, depending on the season. The cost is $12 (£6). The ride takes 2 hours. Besides the canyon vistas, you're likely to see some crocodiles and other things of interest. The boat's pilot will explain a few things in Spanish, but much of what he says adds little to the tour. At the deepest point in the canyon, our pilot said the walls stretch up vertically 1,000m (3,280 ft.) above the water, which in turn is about 100m (328 ft.) deep at that point. I wasn't about to double-check this statement—all I know is that the view was really something. There are some interesting things happening on the walls; water seeps out in places creating little micro-environments of moss, grass, and mineral deposits. One of these places is called the Christmas Tree, for its form. Our boat glided slowly by as a fine mist fell on us from the plants.

The boats operate from 8am to 4pm. They are fast, and the water is smooth. The best times to see the canyon are early or late in the day when the sun is at an angle and shines on one or the other of the canyon walls. The boats are necessarily open, so you should take an adjustable cap or a hat with a draw string or some sunscreen. A pair of earplugs would probably be nice to have, too, especially if they are connected to an iPod playing some kind of dramatic music to complement the rugged vistas. This river is the Grijalva, which flows to the Gulf of Mexico from Guatemala and is one of Mexico's largest.

If you'd rather stay in Chiapa de Corzo than Tuxtla, check out the simple but nice hotel off the main square: **Hotel Los Angeles** at Av. Julián Grajales 2 (© **916/616-0048**). It offers rooms with or without air-conditioning for $20 to $30 (£10–£15) per night.

Appendix A: Fast Facts, Toll-Free Numbers & Websites

1 Fast Facts: The Yucatán Peninsula, Tabasco & Chiapas

Business Hours   In general, businesses in larger cities are open between 9am and 7pm; in smaller towns many close between 2 and 4pm. Most close on Sunday. In resort areas it's common to find stores open at least in the mornings on Sunday, and for shops to stay open late, often until 8 or even 10pm. Bank hours are Monday through Friday from 9 or 9:30am to anywhere between 3 and 7pm. Increasingly, banks open on Saturday for at least a half-day.

Car Rentals   See "Toll-Free Numbers & Websites," p. 290.

Drinking Laws   The legal drinking age in Mexico is 18; however, asking for ID or denying purchase is extremely rare. Grocery stores sell everything from beer and wine to national and imported liquors. You can buy liquor 24 hours a day, but during major elections, dry laws often are enacted by as much as 72 hours in advance of the election—and they apply to tourists as well as local residents. Mexico does not have laws that apply to transporting liquor in cars, but authorities are beginning to target drunk drivers more aggressively. It's a good idea to drive defensively.

It is not legal to drink in the street; however, many tourists do so. If you are getting drunk, you shouldn't drink in the street, because you are more likely to get stopped by the police.

Driving Rules   See "Getting Around by Car," p. 54.

Electricity   The electrical system in Mexico is 110 volts AC (60 cycles), as in the United States and Canada. In reality, however, it may cycle more slowly and overheat your appliances. To compensate, select a medium or low speed on hair dryers. Many older hotels still have electrical outlets for flat two-prong plugs; you'll need an adapter for any plug with an enlarged end on one prong or with three prongs. Many better hotels have three-hole outlets (*trifásicos* in Spanish). Those that don't may have loan adapters, but to be sure, it's always better to carry your own.

Embassies & Consulates   They provide valuable lists of doctors and lawyers, as well as regulations concerning marriages in Mexico. Contrary to popular belief, your embassy cannot get you out of jail, provide postal or banking services, or fly you home when you run out of money. Consular officers can provide advice on most matters and problems, however. Most countries have an embassy in Mexico City, and many have consular offices or representatives in the provinces.

The Embassy of the **United States** in Mexico City is at Paseo de la Reforma 305, next to the Hotel María Isabel Sheraton at the corner of Río Danubio (© **55/ 5080-2000**); hours are Monday through Friday from 8:30am to 5:30pm. Visit http://mexico.usembassy.gov for information related to U.S. Embassy services. There are U.S. Consulates at López Mateos

924-N, Ciudad Juárez (© 656/611-3000); Progreso 175, Guadalajara (© 333/268-2100); Av. Constitución 411 Pte., Monterrey (© 818/345-2120); Tapachula 96, Tijuana (© 664/622-7400); Monterrey 141, Hermosillo (© 662/289-3500); Primera 2002, Matamoros (© 868/812-4402); Calle 60 No. 338 K, Mérida (© 999/942-5700); Calle San Jose, Nogales, Sonora (© 631/311-8150); and Allende 3330, Col. Jardín, Nuevo Laredo (© 867/714-0512). In addition, there are consular agencies in Acapulco (© 744/469-0556); Cabo San Lucas (© 624/143-3566); Cancún (© 998/883-0272); Cozumel (© 987/872-4574); Ixtapa/Zihuatanejo (© 755/553-2100); Mazatlán (© 669/916-5889); Oaxaca (© 951/516-2853); Puerto Vallarta (© 322/222-0069); San Luis Potosí (© 444/811-7802); and San Miguel de Allende (© 415/152-2357).

The Embassy of **Australia** in Mexico City is at Rubén Darío 55, Col. Polanco (© 55/1101-2200; www.mexico.embassy.gov.au). It's open Monday through Thursday from 8:30am to 5:15pm.

The Embassy of **Canada** in Mexico City is at Schiller 529, Col. Polanco (© 55/5724-7900 or for emergencies 01-800-706-2900); it's open Monday through Friday from 9am to 1pm and 2 to 5pm. Visit www.dfait-maeci.gc.ca or www.canada.org.mx for addresses of consular agencies in Mexico. There are Canadian consulates in Acapulco (© 744/484-1305); Cancún (© 998/883-3360); Guadalajara (© 333/671-4740); Mazatlán (© 669/913-7320); Monterrey (© 818/344-2753); Oaxaca (© 951/513-3777); Puerto Vallarta (© 322/293-0098); San José del Cabo (© 624/142-4333); and Tijuana (© 664/684-0461).

The Embassy of **New Zealand** in Mexico City is at Jaime Balmes 8, 4th floor, Col. Los Morales, Polanco (© 55/5283-9460). It's open Monday through Thursday from 8:30am to 2pm and 3 to 5:30pm, and Friday from 8:30am to 2pm.

The Embassy of the **United Kingdom** in Mexico City is at Río Lerma 71, Col. Cuauhtémoc (© 55/5207-2089 or 5242-8500; www.embajadabritanica.com.mx). It's open Monday through Thursday from 8am to 4pm and Friday from 8am to 1:30pm.

The Embassy of **Ireland** in Mexico City is at Cda. Boulevard Manuel Avila Camacho 76, 3rd floor, Col. Lomas de Chapultepec (© 55/5520-5803). It's open Monday through Friday from 9am to 5pm.

The **South African** Embassy in Mexico City is at Andrés Bello 10, Edificio Fórum, 9th floor, Col. Polanco (© 55/5282-9260). It's open Monday through Friday from 8am to 4pm.

Emergencies   In case of emergency, dial © 065 from any phone within Mexico. For police emergency numbers, turn to the "Fast Facts" section in each chapter and for each major city. The operators don't always speak English, but they are always willing to help.

Hotlines   There are several helpful numbers to know: **Tourist Help Line,** available 24 hours (© 01-800/987-8224 toll-free inside Mexico; or dial 078); **Mexico Hot Line** (© 800/446-3942); **U.S. Department of State Travel Advisory,** staffed 24 hours (© 202/647-5225); **U.S. National Passport Center** (© 877/487-2778); and the **U.S. Centers for Disease Control and Prevention International Traveler's Hot Line** (© 877/394-8747).

Insurance   Medical Insurance   For travel to Mexico, most U.S. health plans (including Medicare and Medicaid) do not provide coverage, and the ones that do often require you to pay for services upfront and reimburse you only after you return home.

As a safety net, you may want to buy travel medical insurance, particularly if you're traveling to a remote or high-risk area where emergency evacuation might be necessary. If you require additional medical insurance, try **MEDEX Assistance** (📞 410/453-6300; www.medex assist.com) or **Travel Assistance International** (📞 800/821-2828; www.travel assistance.com; for general information on services, call the company's **Worldwide Assistance Services, Inc.,** at 📞 800/ 777-8710).

Canadians should check with their provincial health plan offices or call **Health Canada** (📞 866/225-0709; www. hc-sc.gc.ca) to find out the extent of their coverage and what documentation and receipts they must take home in case they are treated overseas.

Travelers from the U.K. should carry their European Health Insurance Card (EHIC), which replaced the E111 form as proof of entitlement to free/reduced cost medical treatment abroad (📞 0845/ 606-2030; www.ehic.org.uk). Note, however, that the EHIC only covers "necessary medical treatment," and for repatriation costs, lost money, baggage, or cancellation, travel insurance from a reputable company should always be sought (www.travelinsuranceweb.com).

Travel Insurance The cost of travel insurance varies widely, depending on the destination, the cost and length of your trip, your age and health, and the type of trip you're taking, but expect to pay between 5% and 8% of the vacation itself. You can get estimates from various providers through **InsureMyTrip.com.** Enter your trip cost and dates, your age, and other information, for prices from more than a dozen companies.

U.K. citizens and their families who make more than one trip abroad per year may find an annual travel insurance policy works out cheaper. Check **www.money supermarket.com**, which compares prices across a wide range of providers for single- and multi-trip policies.

Most big travel agents offer their own insurance and will probably try to sell you their package when you book a holiday. Think before you sign. **Britain's Consumers' Association** recommends that you insist on seeing the policy and reading the fine print before buying travel insurance. **The Association of British Insurers** (📞 020/7600-3333; www.abi. org.uk) gives advice by phone and publishes Holiday Insurance, a free guide to policy provisions and prices. You might also shop around for better deals: Try **Columbus Direct** (📞 0870/033-9988; www.columbusdirect.net).

Trip Cancellation Insurance Trip-cancellation insurance will help retrieve your money if you have to back out of a trip or depart early, or if your travel supplier goes bankrupt. Trip cancellation traditionally covers such events as sickness, natural disasters, and State Department advisories. The latest news in trip-cancellation insurance is the availability of **expanded hurricane coverage** and the **"any-reason"** cancellation coverage— which costs more but covers cancellations made for any reason. You won't get back 100% of your prepaid trip cost, but you'll be refunded a substantial portion. **TravelSafe** (📞 888/885-7233; www.travelsafe. com) offers both types of coverage. Expedia also offers any-reason cancellation coverage for its air-hotel packages. For details, contact one of the following recommended insurers: **Access America** (📞 866/807-3982; www.accessamerica. com); **Travel Guard International** (📞 800/826-4919; www.travelguard.com); **Travel Insured International** (📞 800/ 243-3174; www.travelinsured.com); and **Travelex Insurance Services** (📞 888/ 457-4602; www.travelex-insurance.com).

Language   Spanish is the official language in Mexico. English is spoken and understood to some degree in most tourist areas. Mexicans are very accommodating with foreigners who try to speak Spanish, even in broken sentences. See "Appendix B," for a glossary of simple phrases for expressing basic needs.

Legal Aid   International Legal Defense Counsel, 405 Lexington Ave., 26th floor, New York, NY 10174 (© 212/ 907-6442), is a law firm specializing in legal difficulties of Americans abroad. See also "Embassies & Consulates" and "Emergencies," above.

Lost & Found   Be sure to tell all of your credit card companies the minute you discover your wallet has been lost or stolen and file a report at the nearest police precinct. Your credit card company or insurer may require a police report number or record of the loss. Most credit card companies have an emergency toll-free number to call if your card is lost or stolen; they may be able to wire you a cash advance immediately or deliver an emergency credit card in a day or two. **Visa**'s Mexico emergency number is © **001-800/847-2911.** American Express cardholders and traveler's check holders should call © **001-800/001-3600.** MasterCard holders should call © **001/ 800-307-7309.**

If you need emergency cash over the weekend when all banks and American Express offices are closed, you can have money wired to you via **Western Union** (© **800/325-6000;** www.westernunion. com).

Mail   Postage for a postcard or letter is 11 pesos ($1/50p); it may arrive anywhere from 1 to 6 weeks later. The price for registered letters and packages depends on the weight, and unreliable delivery time can take 2 to 6 weeks. The recommended way to send a package or important mail is through FedEx, DHL, UPS, or another reputable international mail service.

Measurements   See the chart on the inside back cover of this book for details on converting metric measurements to nonmetric equivalents.

Newspapers & Magazines   The English language newspaper is the *Miami Herald* published in conjunction with *El Universal.* You can find it at most newsstands. Newspaper kiosks in larger cities also carry a selection of English-language magazines.

Passports   The websites listed provide downloadable passport applications as well as the current fees for processing applications. For an up-to-date, country-by-country listing of passport requirements around the world, go to the "International Travel" tab of the U.S. State Department at **http://travel.state.gov**.

For Residents of Australia   You can pick up an application from your local post office or any branch of Passports Australia, but you must schedule an interview at the passport office to present your application materials. Call the **Australian Passport Information Service** at © **131-232,** or visit the government website at www.passports.gov.au.

For Residents of Canada   Passport applications are available at travel agencies throughout Canada or from the central **Passport Office,** Department of Foreign Affairs and International Trade, Ottawa, ON K1A 0G3 (© **800/567-6868;** www.ppt.gc.ca). *Note:* Canadian children who travel must have their own passport. However, if you hold a valid Canadian passport issued before December 11, 2001, that bears the name of your child, the passport remains valid for you and your child until it expires.

For Residents of Ireland   You can apply for a 10-year passport at the **Passport Office,** Setanta Centre, Molesworth

Street, Dublin 2 (© **01/671-1633;** www. irlgov.ie/iveagh). Those under age 18 and over 65 must apply for a 3-year passport. You can also apply at 1A South Mall, Cork (© **21/494-4700**) or at most main post offices.

For Residents of New Zealand   You can pick up a passport application at any New Zealand Passports Office or download it from their website. Contact the **Passports Office** at © **0800/225-050** in New Zealand or 04/474-8100, or log on to www.passports.govt.nz.

For Residents of the United Kingdom To pick up an application for a standard 10-year passport (5-year passport for children under 16), visit your nearest passport office, major post office, or travel agency or contact the **United Kingdom Passport Service** at © **0870/521-0410** or search its website at www.ukpa.gov.uk.

For Residents of the United States: Whether you're applying in person or by mail, you can download passport applications from the U.S. State Department website at **http://travel.state.gov**. To find your regional passport office, either check the U.S. State Department website or call the **National Passport Information Center** toll-free number (© **877/ 487-2778**) for automated information

Police   In Mexico City, police are to be suspected as frequently as they are to be trusted; however, you'll find many who are quite honest and helpful. In the rest of the country, especially in the tourist areas, most are very protective of international visitors. Several cities, including Cancún, have a special corps of English-speaking Tourist Police to assist with directions, guidance, and more. In case of emergency, dial © **065** from any phone within Mexico. For police emergency numbers, turn to the "Fast Facts" sections in the individual chapters.

Taxes   The 15% IVA (value-added) tax applies on goods and services in most of Mexico, and it's supposed to be included in the posted price. This tax is 10% in Cancún, Cozumel, and Los Cabos. There is a 5% tax on food and drinks consumed in restaurants that sell alcoholic beverages with an alcohol content of more than 10%; this tax applies whether you drink alcohol or not. Tequila is subject to a 25% tax. Mexico imposes an exit tax of around $24 (£12) on every foreigner leaving the country by plane.

International tourists to Mexico can now make tax-free purchases while vacationing, thanks to a law passed by Mexico's Congress. The law grants international visitors a full refund of the tax added to purchases if the buyer adheres to certain criteria. The merchandise must be purchased in Mexico and verified by airport or seaport Customs, and be verified with a receipt presented at time of departure to be worth at least 1,200 Mexican pesos (approximately $110/£61 at current exchange rates). Reimbursement to tourists will be contingent upon any added costs that a possible return may generate.

Time   Central Time prevails throughout most of Mexico. The states of Sonora, Sinaloa, and parts of Nayarit are on Mountain Time. The state of Baja California Norte is on Pacific Time, but Baja California Sur is on Mountain Time. All of Mexico observes **daylight saving time.**

Tipping   Most service employees in Mexico count on tips for the majority of their income, and this is especially true for bellboys and waiters. Bellboys should receive the equivalent of 50¢ to $1 (25p–50p) per bag; waiters generally receive 10% to 15%, depending on the level of service. It is not customary to tip taxi drivers, unless they are hired by the hour or provide touring or other special services.

Toilets   Public toilets are not common in Mexico, but an increasing number are available, especially at fast-food restaurants and Pemex gas stations. These facilities, and restaurant and club restrooms, commonly have attendants, who expect a small tip (about 50¢/25p).

Water Tap water in Mexico in generally not potable and it is safest to drink purified bottled water. Some hotels and restaurants purify their water, but you should ask rather than assume this is the case. Ice may also come from tap water and should be used with caution.

2 Toll-Free Numbers & Websites

MAJOR U.S. AIRLINES
(* with service to Mexico)

Alaska Airlines/Horizon Air*
℃ 800/252/7522
www.alaskaair.com

American Airlines*
℃ 800/433-7300 (in U.S. or Canada)
℃ 020/7365-0777 (in U.K.)
www.aa.com

Continental Airlines*
℃ 800/523-3273 (in U.S. or Canada)
℃ 084/5607-6760 (in U.K.)
www.continental.com

Delta Air Lines
℃ 800/221-1212 (in U.S. or Canada)
℃ 084/5600-0950 (in U.K.)
www.delta.com

Frontier Airlines*
℃ 800/432-1359
www.frontierairlines.com

JetBlue Airways*
℃ 800/538-2583 (in U.S.)
℃ 080/1365-2525 (in U.K. or Canada)
www.jetblue.com

Midwest Airlines
℃ 800/452-2022
www.midwestairlines.com

North American Airlines
℃ 800/371-6297
www.flynaa.com

Northwest Airlines/KLM*
℃ 800/225-2525 (in U.S.)
℃ 870/0507-4074 (in U.K.)
www.flynaa.com

Southwest Airlines (serving the U.S. border)
℃ 800/435-9792 (in U.S., U.K., and Canada)
www.southwest.com

United Airlines*
℃ 800/864-8331 (in U.S. and Canada)
℃ 084/5844-4777 in U.K.
www.united.com

US Airways*
℃ 800/428-4322 (in U.S. and Canada)
℃ 084/5600-3300 (in U.K.)
www.usairways.com

Virgin America
℃ 877/359-8474
www.virginamerica.com

MAJOR INTERNATIONAL AIRLINES

AeroMéxico
℃ 800/237-6639 (in U.S.)
℃ 020/7801-6234 (in U.K., information only)
www.aeromexico.com

Air France
℃ 800/237-2747 (in U.S.)
℃ 800/375-8723 (U.S. and Canada)
℃ 087/0142-4343 (in U.K.)
www.airfrance.com

Mexicana
© 800/531-7921 (in U.S. or Canada)
© 800/801-2010 (in Mexico)
www.mexicana.com

TACA
© 800/535-8780 (in U.S.)
© 800/722-TACA (8222; in Canada)

BUDGET AIRLINES

Aviacsa
© 800/284-2272 (in U.S. and Mexico)
www.aviacsa.com

Aero California
© 800/237-6225 (in U.S. and Mexico)
www.aerocalifornia.com.mx

AeroMéxico Connect
© 800/800-2376 (in U.S. and Mexico)
www.amconnect.com

Avolar
© 888/3-AVOLAR (800/326-8527; in U.S.)
© 800/21-AVOLAR (800/326-8527; in Mexico)
© 086/6370-4065 (in U.K.)
www.avolar.com.mx

CAR RENTAL AGENCIES

Advantage
© 800/777-5500 (in U.S.)
© 021/0344-4712 (outside of U.S.)
www.advantagerentacar.com

Auto Europe
© 888/223-5555 (in U.S. and Canada)
© 0800/2235-5555 (in U.K.)
www.autoeurope.com

Avis
© 800/331-1212 (in U.S. and Canada)
© 084/4581-8181 (in U.K.)
www.avis.com

Budget
© 800/527-0700 (in U.S.)
© 087/0156-5656 (in U.K.)
© 800/268-8900 (in Canada)
www.budget.com

© 087/0241-0340 (in U.K.)
© 503/2267-8222 (in El Salvador)

Cubana
© 888/667-1222 (in Canada)
© 020/7538-5933 (in UK)
www.cubana.cu

Click Mexicana
© 800/11-click (800/112-5425; international)
© 800/112-5425 (in Mexico)
www.clickmx.com

Interjet
© 800/101-2345
www.interjet.com.mx

Volaris
© 866/988-3527
© 800/7-VOLARIS (800/786-5274; in Mexico)
www.volaris.com.mx

WestJet
© 800/538-5696 (in U.S. and Canada)
www.westjet.com

Hertz
© 800/645-3131
© 800/654-3001 (for international reservations)
www.hertz.com

Kemwel (KHA)
© 877/820-0668
www.kemwel.com

National
© 800/CAR-RENT (800/227-7368)
www.nationalcar.com

Thrifty
© 800/367-2277
© 918/669-2168 (international)
www.thrifty.com

MAJOR HOTEL & MOTEL CHAINS

Comfort Inns
℡ 800/228-5150
℡ 0800/444-444 (in U.K.)
www.comfortinn.com

Courtyard by Marriott
℡ 888/236-2427 (in U.S.)
℡ 0800/221-222 (in U.K.)
www.marriott.com/courtyard

Crowne Plaza Hotels
℡ 888/303-1746
www.ichotelsgroup.com/crowneplaza

Embassy Suites
℡ 800/EMBASSY (800/362-2779)
www.embassysuites.hilton.com

Four Seasons
℡ 800/819-5053 (in U.S. and Canada)
℡ 0800/6488-6488 (in U.K.)
www.fourseasons.com

Hampton Inn
℡ 800/HAMPTON (800/426-4766)
www.hamptoninn.hilton.com

Hilton Hotels
℡ 800/HILTONS (800/445-8667; in
    U.S. and Canada)
℡ 087/0590-9090 (in U.K.)
www.hilton.com

Holiday Inn
℡ 800/315-2621 (in U.S. and Canada)
℡ 0800/405-060 (in U.K.)
www.holidayinn.com

Howard Johnson
℡ 800/446-4656 (in U.S. and Canada)
www.hojo.com

Hyatt
℡ 888/591-1234 (in U.S. and Canada)
℡ 084/5888-1234 (in U.K.)
www.hyatt.com

InterContinental Hotels & Resorts
℡ 800/424-6835 (in U.S. and Canada)
℡ 0800/1800-1800 (in U.K.)
www.ichotelsgroup.com

La Quinta Inns and Suites
℡ 800/642-4271 (in U.S. and Canada)
www.lq.com

Marriott
℡ 877/236-2427 (in U.S. and Canada)
℡ 0800/221-222 (in U.K.)
www.marriott.com

Omni Hotels
℡ 888/444-OMNI (888/444-6664)
www.omnihotels.com

Quality
℡ 877/424-6423 (in U.S. and Canada)
℡ 0800/444-444 (in U.K.)
www.qualityinn.com

Radisson Hotels & Resorts
℡ 888/201-1718 (in U.S. and Canada)
℡ 0800/374-411 (in U.K.)
www.radisson.com

Ramada Worldwide
℡ 888/2-RAMADA (888/272-6232; in
    U.S. and Canada)
℡ 080/8100-0783 (in U.K.)
www.ramada.com

Sheraton Hotels & Resorts
℡ 800/325-3535 (in U.S.)
℡ 800/543-4300 (in Canada)
℡ 0800/3253-5353 (in U.K.)
www.starwoodhotels.com/sheraton

Westin Hotels & Resorts
℡ 800-937-8461 (in U.S. and Canada)
℡ 0800/3259-5959 (in U.K.)
www.starwoodhotels.com/westin

Wyndham Hotels & Resorts
℡ 877/999-3223 (in U.S. and Canada)
℡ 050/6638-4899 (in U.K.)
www.wyndham.com

Appendix B:
Survival Spanish

Most Mexicans are very patient with foreigners who try to speak their language; it helps a lot to know a few basic phrases. I've included simple phrases for expressing basic needs, followed by some common menu items.

ENGLISH-SPANISH PHRASES

English	Spanish	Pronunciation
Good day	**Buen día**	Bwehn *dee*-ah
Good morning	**Buenos días**	*Bweh*-nohs *dee*-ahs
How are you?	**¿Cómo está?**	*Koh*-moh eh-*stah*
Very well	**Muy bien**	Mwee byehn
Thank you	**Gracias**	*Grah*-syahs
You're welcome	**De nada**	Deh *nah*-dah
Goodbye	**Adiós**	Ah-*dyohs*
Please	**Por favor**	Pohr fah-*bohr*
Yes	**Sí**	See
No	**No**	Noh
Excuse me	**Perdóneme**	Pehr-*doh*-neh-meh
Give me	**Déme**	*Deh*-meh
Where is . . . ?	**¿Dónde está . . . ?**	*Dohn*-deh eh-*stah*
the station	**la estación**	lah eh-stah-*syohn*
a hotel	**un hotel**	oon oh-*tehl*
a gas station	**una gasolinera**	*oo*-nah gah-soh-lee-*neh*-rah
a restaurant	**un restaurante**	oon res-tow-*rahn*-teh
the toilet	**el baño**	el *bah*-nyoh
a good doctor	**un buen médico**	oon bwehn *meh*-dee-coh
the road to . . .	**el camino a/hacia**	el cah-*mee*-noh ah/*ah*-syah
To the right	**A la derecha**	Ah lah deh-*reh*-chah
To the left	**A la izquierda**	Ah lah ees-*kyehr*-dah
Straight ahead	**Derecho**	Deh-*reh*-choh
I would like	**Quisiera**	Key-*syeh*-rah
I want	**Quiero**	*Kyeh*-roh
to eat	**comer**	koh-*mehr*
a room	**una habitación**	*oo*-nah ah-bee-tah-*syohn*

English	Spanish	Pronunciation
Do you have . . . ?	¿Tiene usted . . . ?	Tyeh-neh oo-*sted*
a book	**un libro**	oon *lee*-broh
a dictionary	**un diccionario**	oon deek-syoh-*nah*-ryoh
How much is it?	¿Cuánto cuesta?	*Kwahn*-toh *kweh*-stah
When?	¿Cuándo?	*Kwahn*-doh
What?	¿Qué?	Keh
There is (Is there . . . ?)	(¿)Hay (. . . ?)	Eye
What is there?	¿Qué hay?	Keh eye
Yesterday	**Ayer**	Ah-*yer*
Today	**Hoy**	Oy
Tomorrow	**Mañana**	Mah-*nyah*-nah
Good	**Bueno**	*Bweh*-noh
Bad	**Malo**	*Mah*-loh
Better (best)	**(Lo) Mejor**	(Loh) Meh-*hohr*
More	**Más**	Mahs
Less	**Menos**	*Meh*-nohs
No smoking	**Se prohibe fumar**	Seh proh-*ee*-beh foo-*mahr*
Postcard	**Tarjeta postal**	Tar-*heh*-tah poh-*stahl*
Insect repellent	**Repelente contra insectos**	Reh-peh-*lehn*-teh *cohn*-trah een-*sehk*-tohs

MORE USEFUL PHRASES

English	Spanish	Pronunciation
Do you speak English?	¿Habla usted inglés?	*Ah*-blah oo-*sted* een-*glehs*
Is there anyone here who speaks English?	¿Hay alguien aquí que hable inglés?	Eye *ahl*-gyehn ah-*kee* keh *ah*-bleh een-*glehs*
I speak a little Spanish.	Hablo un poco de español.	*Ah*-bloh oon *poh*-koh deh eh-spah-*nyohl*
I don't understand Spanish very well.	No (lo) entiendo muy bien el español.	Noh (loh) ehn-*tyehn*-doh mwee byehn el eh-spah-*nyohl*
The meal is good.	Me gusta la comida.	Meh *goo*-stah lah koh-*mee*-dah
What time is it?	¿Qué hora es?	Keh *oh*-rah ehs
May I see your menu?	¿Puedo ver el menú (la carta)?	*Pweh*-doh vehr el meh-*noo* (lah *car*-tah)
The check, please.	La cuenta, por favor.	Lah *kwehn*-tah pohr fa-*borh*
What do I owe you?	¿Cuánto le debo?	*Kwahn*-toh leh *deh*-boh
What did you say?	¿Mande? (formal)	*Mahn*-deh
	¿Cómo? (informal)	*Koh*-moh

English	Spanish	Pronunciation
I want (to see) . . .	**Quiero (ver)** . . .	*kyeh*-roh (vehr)
a room	**un cuarto** or **una habitación**	oon *kwar*-toh, *oo*-nah ah-bee-tah-*syohn*
for two persons	**para dos personas**	*pah*-rah dohs pehr-*soh*-nahs
with (without) bathroom	**con (sin) baño**	kohn (seen) *bah*-nyoh
We are staying here only . . .	**Nos quedamos aquí solamente** . . .	Nohs keh-*dah*-mohs ah-*kee* soh-lah-*mehn*-teh
one night.	**una noche.**	*oo*-nah *noh*-cheh
one week.	**una semana.**	*oo*-nah seh-*mah*-nah
We are leaving . . . tomorrow.	**Partimos (Salimos)** . . . **mañana.**	Pahr-*tee*-mohs (sah-*lee*-mohs) mah-*nya*-nah
Do you accept . . . ?	**¿Acepta usted . . . ?**	Ah-*sehp*-tah oo-*sted*
traveler's checks?	**cheques de viajero?**	*cheh*-kehs deh byah-*heh*-roh

NUMBERS

1	uno (ooh-noh)		17	diecisiete (dyeh-see-syeh-teh)
2	dos (dohs)		18	dieciocho (dyeh-syoh-choh)
3	tres (trehs)		19	diecinueve (dyeh-see-nweh-beh)
4	cuatro (kwah-troh)		20	veinte (bayn-teh)
5	cinco (seen-koh)		30	treinta (trayn-tah)
6	seis (sayes)		40	cuarenta (kwah-ren-tah)
7	siete (syeh-teh)		50	cincuenta (seen-kwen-tah)
8	ocho (oh-choh)		60	sesenta (seh-sehn-tah)
9	nueve (nweh-beh)		70	setenta (seh-tehn-tah)
10	diez (dyehs)		80	ochenta (oh-chehn-tah)
11	once (ohn-seh)		90	noventa (noh-behn-tah)
12	doce (doh-seh)		100	cien (syehn)
13	trece (treh-seh)		200	doscientos (do-syehn-tohs)
14	catorce (kah-tohr-seh)		500	quinientos (kee-nyehn-tohs)
15	quince (keen-seh)		1,000	mil (meel)
16	dieciséis (dyeh-see-sayes)			

TRANSPORTATION TERMS

English	Spanish	Pronunciation
airport	**Aeropuerto**	Ah-eh-roh-*pwehr*-toh
flight	**Vuelo**	*Bweh*-loh
rental car	**Arrendadora de autos**	Ah-*rehn*-da-doh-rah deh *ow*-tohs
bus	**Autobús**	Ow-toh-*boos*

English	Spanish	Pronunciation
bus or truck	**Camión**	Ka-*myohn*
lane	**Carril**	Kah-*reel*
nonstop (bus)	**Directo**	Dee-*rehk*-toh
baggage (claim area)	**Equipajes**	Eh-kee-*pah*-hehss
intercity	**Foraneo**	Foh-rah-*neh*-oh
luggage storage area	**Guarda equipaje**	*Gwar*-dah eh-kee-*pah*-heh
arrival gates	**Llegadas**	Yeh-*gah*-dahss
originates at this station	**Local**	Loh-*kahl*
originates elsewhere	**De paso**	Deh *pah*-soh
Are seats available?	**Hay lugares disponibles?**	Eye loo-*gah*-rehs dis-pohn-*ee*-blehss
first class	**Primera**	Pree-*meh*-rah
second class	**Segunda**	Seh-*goon*-dah
nonstop (flight)	**Sin escala**	Seen ess-*kah*-lah
baggage claim area	**Recibo de equipajes**	Reh-*see*-boh deh eh-kee-*pah*-hehss
waiting room	**Sala de espera**	*Sah*-lah deh ehss-*peh*-rah
toilets	**Sanitarios**	Sah-nee-*tah*-ryohss
ticket window	**Taquilla**	Tah-*kee*-yah

DINING TERMINOLOGY
Meals
desayuno   Breakfast

comida   Main meal of the day, taken in the afternoon.

cena   Supper

Courses
botana   A small serving of food that accompanies a beer or drink, and usually served free of charge.

entrada   Appetizer

sopa   Soup course. (Not necessarily a soup—it can be a dish of rice or noodles, called *sopa seca* [dry soup].)

ensalada   Salad.

plato fuerte   Main course.

postre   Dessert.

comida corrida   Inexpensive daily special usually consisting of three courses.

menú del día   Same as *comida corrida.*

Degree of Doneness
término un cuarto   Rare, literally means one fourth.

término medio   Medium rare, one half.

término tres cuartos   Medium, three fourths.

bien cocido   Well-done.

Note: Keep in mind, when ordering a steak, that *medio* does not mean medium.

Miscellaneous Restaurant Terminology

cucharra   Spoon.

cuchillo   Knife.

la cuenta   The bill.

plato   Plate.

plato hondo   Bowl.

propina   Tip.

servilleta   Napkin.

tenedor   Fork.

vaso   Glass.

IVA   Value-added tax.

POPULAR MEXICAN & YUCATECAN DISHES

a la tampiqueña   (Usually *bistec a la t.* or *arrachera a la t.*) A steak served with several sides, including but not limited to an enchilada, guacamole, rice, and beans.

achiote   Small red seed of the *annatto* tree with mild flavor, used both for taste and color.

adobo   Marinade made with chiles and tomatoes, often seen in adjectival form "adobado"/"adobada"

agua fresca   Any sweetened fruit-flavored water, including limonada (limeade), *horchata* (see below), *tamarindo* (see below), *sandía* (watermelon), and *melón* (cantaloupe).

alambre   Brochette.

albóndigas   Meat balls, usually cooked in a *chile chipotle* sauce.

antojito   Literally means "small temptation." It's a general term for tacos, *tostadas, quesadillas,* and the like, which are usually eaten for supper or as a snack.

arrachera   Skirt steak, fajitas.

arroz   Rice.

atole   A thick, hot drink made with finely ground corn and flavored with fruit usually, but also can be flavored with chile chocolate, or spices.

bistec   Steak.

bolillo   Small bread with a crust much like baguette.

café con leche   Hot coffee with milk. In cheap restaurants often made with powdered instant coffee.

calabaza   Zucchini squash.

caldo tlalpeño   Chicken and vegetable soup, with rice, *chile chipotle, avocado,* and garbanzos. Its name comes from a suburban community of Mexico City, Tlalpan.

caldo xochitl   Mild chicken and rice soup served with a small plate of chopped onion, chile serrano, avocado, and limes, to be added according to individual taste.

camarones   Shrimp. For common cooking methods, see **pescado.**

carne   Meat.

carnitas   Slow cooked pork dish from Michoacán and parts of central Mexico, served with tortillas, guacamole, and salsa or pickled jalapeños.

cecina   Thinly sliced pork or beef, dried or marinated, depending on the region.

cebolla   Onion.

ceviche   Fresh raw seafood marinated in fresh lime juice and garnished with chopped tomatoes, onions, chiles, and sometimes cilantro.

chayote   A type of spiny squash boiled and served as an accompaniment to meat dishes.

chilaquiles   Fried tortilla quarters softened in either a red or green sauce and served with Mexican sour cream, onion, and sometimes chicken *(con pollo)*.

chile   Any of the many hot peppers used in Mexican cooking in fresh, dried, or smoked forms.

chile ancho   A dried *chile poblano,* which serves as the base for many varieties of sauces and *moles.*

chile chilpotle (or **chipotle**)   A smoked jalapeño sold dried or canned in an *adobo* sauce.

chile poblano   Fresh pepper that is usually dark green in color, large and not usually spicy. Often stuffed with a variety of fillings *(chile relleno).*

chile en nogada   *Chile poblano* stuffed with a complex filling of shredded meat, nuts, and dried, candied, and fresh fruit, topped with walnut cream sauce and a sprinkling of pomegranate seeds.

chile relleno   Stuffed pepper.

chivo   Kid or goat.

churro   Fried pastry dusted with sugar and served plain or filled. The Spanish equivalent of a donut.

cochinita pibil   Yucatecan dish of pork, pit-baked in a *pibil* sauce of *achiote,* sour orange, and spices.

col   Cabbage. Also called *repollo.*

cortes   Another way of saying steaks; in full it would be *cortes finas de carne* (fine cuts of meat).

cuitlacoche   Variant of **huitlacoche.**

elote   Fresh corn.

empanada   For most of Mexico a turnover with a savory or sweet filling. In Oaxaca and southern Mexico it is corn masa or a tortilla folded around a savory filling and roasted or fried.

empanizado   Breaded.

enchilada   A lightly fried tortilla, dipped in sauce, and folded or rolled around a filling. It has many variations, such as *enchiladas suizas* (made with a cream sauce), enchiladas del portal or enchiladas placeras (made with a predominantly *chile ancho* sauce), and enchiladas verdes (in a green sauce of tomatillos, cilantro, and chiles).

enfrijoladas   Like an enchilada, but made with a bean sauce flavored with toasted avocado leaves.

enmoladas   Enchiladas made with a *mole* sauce.

entomatadas   Enchiladas made with a tomato sauce.

ensalada   Salad.

escabeche   Vegetables pickled in a vinegary liquid.

flan   Custard.

flautas   Tortillas that are rolled up around a filling (usually chicken or shredded beef) and deep fried; often listed on a menu as *taquitos* or *tacos fritos.*

frijoles refritos   Beans mashed and cooked with lard.

gorditas   Thick, fried corn tortillas, slit open and stuffed with meat or cheese filling.

horchata   Drink made of ground rice, melon seeds, ground almonds, or coconut and cinnamon.

huazontle   A vegetable vaguely comparable to broccoli, but milder in taste.

huevos mexicanos   Scrambled eggs with chopped onions, *chiles serranos,* and tomatoes.

huevos rancheros   Fried eggs, usually placed on tortillas, and bathed in a light tomato sauce.

huitlacoche   Salty and mild-tasting corn fungus that is considered a delicacy in Mexico.

jitomate   Tomato.

limón   A small lime. Mexicans squeeze these limes on everything from soups to tacos.

lechuga   Lettuce.

lomo adobado   Pork loin cooked in an ***adobo.***

masa   Soft dough made of corn that is the basis for making tortillas and tamales.

menudo   Soup made with beef tripe and hominy.

milanesa   Beef cutlet breaded and fried.

molcajete   A three-legged mortar made of volcanic stone and used for grinding. Often used now as a cooking dish that is brought to the table steaming hot and filled with meat, chiles, onions, and cheese.

mole   Any variety of thick sauce made with dried chiles, nuts, fruits or vegetables, and spices. Variations include *m. poblano* (Puebla style, with chocolate and sesame), *m. negro* (black mole from Oaxaca, also with chocolate), m. verde (made with herbs and/or pumpkin seeds, depending on the region).

pan   Bread. A few of the varieties include *p. dulce* (general term for a variety of sweet breads), *p. de muerto* (bread made for the Day of the Dead holidays), and p. Bimbo (packaged sliced white bread).

panuchos   A Yucatecan dish of *masa* cakes stuffed with refried black beans and topped with shredded turkey or chicken, lettuce, and onion.

papas   Potatoes.

papadzules   A Yucatecan dish of tortillas stuffed with hard-boiled eggs and topped with a sauce made of pumpkin seeds.

parrillada   A sampler platter of grilled meats or seafood.

pescado   Fish. Common ways of cooking fish include *al mojo de ajo* (pan seared with oil and garlic), *a la veracruzana* (with tomatoes, olives, and capers), *al ajillo* (seared with garlic and fine strips or rings of *chile guajillo*).

pibil   See **cochinita pibil.** When made with chicken it is called *pollo pibil.*

picadillo   Any of several recipes using shredded beef, pork, or chicken and onions, chiles, and spices. Can also contain fruits and nuts.

pipián   A thick sauce made with ground pumpkin seeds, nuts, herbs, and chiles. Can be red or green.

poc chuc   Pork with onion marinated in sour orange and then grilled; a Yucatecan dish.

pollo   Chicken.

pozole   Soup with chicken or pork, hominy, lettuce, and radishes, served with a small plate of other ingredients to be added according to taste (onion, pepper, lime juice, oregano). In Jalisco it's red *(p. rojo),* in Michoacán it's clear *(p. blanco),* and in Guerrero it's green *(p. verde).* In the rest of Mexico it can be any one of these.

puerco   Pork.

pulque   A drink made of fermented juice of the maguey plant; most common in the states of Hidalgo, Tlaxcala, Puebla, and Mexico.

quesadilla   Corn or flour tortillas stuffed with white cheese and cooked on hot griddle. In Mexico City it made with raw masa folded around any of a variety of fillings (often containing no cheese) and deep fried.

queso   Cheese.

res   Beef.

rompope   Mexican liqueur, made with eggs, vanilla, sugar, and alcohol.

salbute   A Yucatecan dish much like a *panucho,* but without bean paste in the middle.

solomillo   Filet mignon.

sopa azteca   Tortilla soup.

sopa tarasca   A blended soup from Michoacán made with beans and tomatoes.

sope   Small fried masa cake topped with savory meats and greens.

tacos al pastor   Small tacos made with thinly sliced pork marinated in an *adobo* and served with pineapple, onion, and cilantro.

tamal   (Not tamale.) Masa mixed with lard and beaten until light and folded around a savory or sweet filling and encased in a cornhusk or a plant leaf (usually corn or banana), then steamed. *Tamales* is the plural form.

taquitos   See flautas.

tinga   Shredded meat stewed in a *chile chipotle* sauce.

torta   A sandwich made with a bolillo.

Index

See also Accommodations and Restaurant indexes, below.

ACCOMMODATIONS